MAPPAE MUNDI

Mappae Mundi

Humans and their Habitats in a Long-Term
Socio-Ecological Perspective

Myths, Maps and Models

Bert de Vries and Johan Goudsblom
(eds.)

Rijksinstituut
voor **Volksgezondheid**
en Milieu

AMSTERDAM UNIVERSITY PRESS

Cover design: Magenta Ontwerpers, Amsterdam
Lay-out: Magenta Ontwerpers, Amsterdam

ISBN 90 5356 535 3
NUGI 661

Contents

Preface

This book is published on the occasion of the celebration of the 250th anniversary of the Holland Society of Arts and Sciences. The founders of our Institution were – as could be expected in the middle of the 18th century – deeply convinced that science, and perhaps also to some extent the arts, should play a significant role in the prosperous development of the town of Haarlem and its surroundings in Holland. Several comparable 'Learned Societies' already existed in Europe and America, but our Society was the first to be established in the Netherlands.

Since the foundation of the Holland Society the enlightened optimism about the impact of scientific work has changed to a more prudent vision. Nevertheless, we undertook this project following the traditional aim of our Institution to advance science for the benefit of society, by selecting as its subject the interaction between humanity and the biosphere. This subject is of course not new. Through the last decades many different and richly faceted studies have been undertaken and articles and books that shed new light on this interaction are published almost daily. However, many questions remain unanswered and it seems that the number of issues and questions increases rather than diminishes.

It is obviously beyond the scope of one limited project – limited in time, manpower and budget – to give satisfactory answers to many of these questions. But we think that this book will give a new and deeper understanding by means of the approach taken and the inclusion of recent and innovative points of view. As the title of the book suggests, the authors have made extensive use of maps, both historical and contemporary, while exploring less known or unknown territory. These maps and many local and regional narratives do not only illustrate this study, they also facilitate our view of the complex interaction between humans and the environment.

In this book sustainable development is not dealt with as a rather static desirable track between the present and the future, but as part of a long-term, dynamic and evolutionary process of the co-existence of humanity and its environment that started many millennia ago. A fundamental opinion of the authors is that we need a thorough understanding of the past in order to be able to say something sensible about the future. And even then we will have to be prepared to encounter surprises and disappointments, as we did in the past. Another important element of the book is that we have tried, contrary to most studies on humans and the biosphere, to approach the subject not only from a natural science angle, but also integrate views from the historical and social sciences. The attempt to present a truly interdisciplinary synthesis of many different points of view was a major motivation to embark on this project.

We hope to have delivered a contribution to constructive thinking about the future challenges that mankind is facing in its quest for sustainable development. We should learn from the mistakes we have made, which often stem from our tendency to think in terms of simple relationships of cause and effect and to rely too much on implicitly deterministic models. We should recognize that we probably have less coherent knowledge than we thought. We hope that this study will stimulate further research into the *terra incognita* that we have entered and we are convinced that a better understanding of these complex issues is the best guarantee against future errors.

We would like to thank the authors for their important contributions and in particular Dr Bert de Vries and Professor Johan Goudsblom for their highly valuable work in editing and for writing a large part of this book. We thank Professor Frans Saris for his help in finding and keeping this work on the right track. We acknowledge with gratitude the substantial support and scientific input from the Dutch National Institute of Public Health and the Environment (RIVM). Finally, we gratefully acknowledge the support of the Energy Centre Netherlands (ECN) and the substantial financial contribution from the Jan Brouwer Foundation.

Ir Maarten van Veen
Chairman Holland Society of Arts and Sciences

Editors' Acknowledgements

We wish to thank first of all the Hollandsche Maatschappij der Wetenschappen for its initiative to launch this project and for its invitation to us to carry it out. We have received valuable suggestions and comments in meetings with directors and members of the Maatschappij. We are particularly grateful to Maarten van Veen and Frans Saris who have shown a strong personal interest in our work throughout its progress. Evidently, this interdisciplinary attempt at synthesis would not have reached its present stage without important contributions from other people, foremost our co-authors who have accepted the challenge to contribute to such an ambitious and multi-faceted adventure.

One of us (BdV) wishes to thank the members of the Balaton Group which in diverse ways contributed to the initial idea and who were instrumental in getting the much appreciated contribution from Emma Romanova of the Department of the Physical Geography of the World, Lomonosov Moscow State University. We also wish to thank participants of two workshops, in Santa Fe and Abisko, on complexity in socio-natural systems who were a great source of inspiration and information. In particular, the contributions on multi-agent simulations from Tim Kohler of the Department of Anthropology of Washington State University, from Dwight Read of the Department of Anthropology and the Department of Statistics of the University of California Los Angeles and from Lena Sanders of the team Géographie-cités of CNRS-Université Paris 1 are appreciated.

We are grateful to David Henley of the KITLV (Royal Institute of Linguistics and Anthropology) in Leiden for sharing his insights on the environmental history of Indonesia and to the scholars who contributed textboxes on some themes – Jan Boersema, Pieter Bol, Paul Erdkamp and Frans Wiggermann. We also wish to thank Hugo Burger of ECN, David Christian, Stephen Mennell and Jan Luiten van Zanden for their inquisitive, helpful and encouraging comments. Last but not least, invaluable assistance in making the maps has been given by Kees Klein Goldewijk of the the Dutch National Institute of Public Health and the Environment (RIVM) – his expertise and patient persistence made it possible to communicate not only by words but also by maps and graphs.

.

1

Introduction: Towards a Historical View of Humanity and the Biosphere

GOUDSBLOM AND DE VRIES

1.1.　A new sense of change

We live in a world that is changing, and we know we do. When we compare the conditions in which we find ourselves today with those prevailing around 1750, a mere ten generations ago, we can draw up an almost endless list of differences. There are, to mention just one of the most striking facts, far more of us. In 1750 humankind numbered around 771 million people; that is about 25% less than the population of India today (see Table 1.1). Most people were younger, with an average life expectancy of 27 years across the world, about half of today's global average. Mass-produced consumer goods did not exist at all; most of the technical and hygienic amenities that we tend to take for granted today were either unknown or available only to small privileged groups.

TABLE 1.1　WORLD POPULATION AND LIFE EXPECTANCY, 10,000 BC - 1990

	10,000 BC	0	1750	1970	1990
Population (millions)	6	252	771	2530	5292
Annual growth (%)	0.008	0.037	0.064	0.596	1.8452q
Doubling time in years	8369	1854	1083	116	38
Life expectancy at birth	20	22	27	35	55

Source: Livi-Bacci 1992: 31

At the time, the conditions of a basically rural world dominated by scarcity must have seemed timeless to most people. And yet, on closer inspection, the world of 1750 was changing, as indeed the world had been doing since time immemorial. Moreover, as we now know, around 1750 humanity was approaching a cascade of radical and rapidly accelerating transformations. Among some people of that era, an awareness of ubiquitous and pervasive change was already dawning.

This sense of change was brilliantly expressed and elaborated in two lectures delivered in the summer of the year 1750 at the Sorbonne by the then 23-year-old future statesman Turgot. He pointed out the contrast between physical nature, which he saw as subject to constant laws, and the human world, which is continuously changing. In nature, he said, the same cycles repeat themselves endlessly: day and night, full moon and new moon, summer and winter. There is, however, one exception to all these patterns of never ending recurrence, and that is human society. While the rest of the universe keeps going through the same motions eternally, human beings are able to conceive new ideas, put these ideas into practice and transmit their innovations to the generations that come after them (see Manuel 1962: 11-52).

Turgot's view itself was something new, confirming his own thesis. Perhaps that thesis was not entirely original, and he gave voice only to certain ideas that were already circulating in intellectual circles. But he did so with great sagacity, and he is still remembered as one of the first to see that human societies are involved in long-term processes of change. He tried to bring home to his audience that humankind had come a long way before arriving at the conditions with which the people of his day and age were familiar.

The picture of nature as fundamentally unchanging – used by Turgot partly as a rhetorical contrast to his own dynamic view of human society – corresponded with the theories of physics of Newton and, later, Laplace, as well as Linnaeus' botanical and anatomical theories. These theories seemed to imply that all changes were essentially ephemeral – variations on a basic pattern which remained constant. In a rural society attuned to the regular cycles of the always recurring seasons such an idea of natural stasis was highly plausible.

France around 1750 was an agrarian society. The ancient mode of subsistence by means of foraging had long become economically insignificant, and industrialization had not yet fully begun. In agrarian societies all over the world there has always been a strong tendency to see the past, the present and the future as essentially similar. Of course, stories were told about great and cataclysmic events that occurred in a distant past: acts of creation; struggles between gods, between gods and men, between men; disasters such as earthquakes and floods. All those stories suggested, however, that the events had taken place against a background that did not change. The books of the Old Testament offer a good example: they are full of drama and disaster. But while men come and go, while terrible battles are waged and cities are destroyed to the last stone, the setting in which the events occur remains in essence unchanged. Landscape and climate appear as a fixed décor; it seems that ever since Adam and Eve were driven out of paradise, humanity has lived in the same natural environment of hills and valleys, covered with similar fields and pastures. When, in the European Middle Ages, painters made pictures of biblical stories, they used as a background the sort of scenery with which they themselves were familiar, as if the landscape had never changed.

The biblical accounts certainly contain several references to environmental up-heavals; the great flood is the best known and most dramatic. All these events are described as unique, as singular acts of God to punish men. They are not treated as episodes in what we today might regard as a long-term transformation of the relation-ships between human groups and their habitats.

1.2. The static character of ancient world views

In trying to understand the present and anticipate the future, people have always con-structed images of the past. For a long time, their accounts were, by our current stan-dards, imprecise, vague, and hampered by an inevitably narrow view of the world. No one could help being ethnocentric: their range of action and information was necessari-ly limited, and they lacked the means to extend their vision in a realistic manner beyond the region with which they were familiar. For explanations reaching further than their own experience, their best bet was often to rely on generally accepted lore about super-natural forces, to which they ascribed similar motives and powers as they were wont to observe in human beings and animals.

In Turgot's time, intellectuals considered such lore with contempt. They were in the vanguard of a change in mentality which the sociologist Max Weber called a 'disenchant-ment of the world'. Enlightened citizens increasingly came to entertain a world view in which spirits and gods no longer played a prominent part. Deliberate attempts were made to diminish the element of fantasy and to broaden the range and scope of reliable observations on which the world view was founded. With the decreasing interest in gods, the question of origins also receded and was replaced by a search for the fundamental mechanisms operating in the universe – a long-term change in mental orientation that has been described by the Dutch historian of science, E.J. Dijksterhuis (1969), as the 'mechanization' of the worldview.

The 'mechanization' of the world view did not really disturb the essentially static image of nature. Its effect was rather to render that image even more solidly static than it had been before. Newtonian physics could be interpreted as being in perfect harmony with the biblical version of cosmology: the divine act of creation of the world included the creation of the eternal laws that governed all motion in the universe. In the well-known epigram of the poet Alexander Pope:

Nature and Nature's laws lay hid in night:
God said: let Newton be! and all was light.[1]

At the same time in 18th century Europe that the 'mechanization' of the world view was reaching its apex, a more dynamic, historical orientation was also emerging. Turgot's idea of the cumulative progression of human society is an example. Turgot failed to acknowledge, however, that a similar reorientation in the direction of 'historicalization' was also occurring in some of the natural sciences, notably in geology and biology. Buffon's concept of 'natural history' for the study of life bears witness to this reorientation. Geologists in particular produced a lot of empirical evidence – and speculation – supporting the idea of irreversible secular change. In the 19th century, biology followed suit with Darwin's theory of evolution. With that theory, biology provided the missing link between geology and sociology in the construction of an encompassing dynamic world-view. The process of 'historicalization' gained still more momentum when, in the second half of the 20th century, the time dimension and the concept of 'deep time' became incorporated in the theories of astronomy and physics.[2]

The general shift toward a dynamic world view has also led to new ways of conceiving the relationship between human beings and their habitats. That relationship is no longer seen as inherently stable, but rather as marked by tendencies toward change on both sides. On the one hand, there are continuous processes of 'spontaneous' natural change in landscape and climate, sometimes bursting forth dramatically in such events as hurricanes, earthquakes, and volcanic eruptions which interfere relentlessly with human affairs. On the other hand, human society generates processes of change which, in turn, affect landscape and climate. An increasing portion of the land surface of our planet has been transformed for agrarian and industrial production, for urban living, and for traffic and trade by rail, by road, on water, and through the air. In a process extending over countless generations, the anthroposphere has been expanding within the planetary biosphere. The dynamic two-way interaction between these two spheres is the subject of this book.

1.3.   Myths, maps, and models

It has often been observed that humanity is a unique species – just like every other species. In this book we are mainly concerned with the most recent stages in human development, after humanity had established a position that made it 'uniquely unique' in the animal kingdom: a position of dominance in which the balance of power between human groups and all other large animals is tilted strongly in favour of humans. This position of dominance has obviously not put an end to human dependence on the forces of nature, but it has certainly increased the possibilities for the growth of human societies. It has led, particularly in our own time, to an enormous increase in sheer human numbers ('extensive growth') as well as a staggering rise in the standard of living ('intensive growth') among the rich part of humanity.

In the inquiries that follow we hope to make the general trend of the expansion of the anthroposphere more visible, more understandable and, ideally, more explainable. We shall do this by looking at human history not as a continuous success story, but rather as a bundle of divergent, and often discontinuous, episodes, many of which have ended in inconspicuous transitions, and quite a few in downright disaster. In our view, the trend toward increasing dominance has been matched by a trend toward greater complexity of human societies; we shall argue that, in spite of discontinuities, the latter trend has until now proved irresistible. The greater complexity of the relationships between humans and the biosphere has made these relationships in many ways less transparent and more threatening. That very same process has also entailed greater concern for and scientific interest in those relationships.

Clearly, the subject of our book is vast. It can be approached from a variety of angles: from the humanities, the social sciences and the natural sciences. Many impressive contributions have been made in all of these fields, and we have consulted them eagerly – not in order to give an encyclopaedic survey but in search of some provisional common ground. We present our results under three alliterating headings: myths, maps and models.

The word myth is the least satisfactory of these, and the most likely to cause confusion since it carries a strong association of fiction and falsehood. This negative association prevailed for the sociologist Norbert Elias (1978: 50-70) when he declared that a primary task of sociologists, and scientists in general, is to destroy myths. The world historian William McNeill (1986: 1-22) has taken a more lenient attitude toward the term in his advocacy of 'mythistory'. Underlying McNeill's argument is the idea of myth as a narrative account intended to make sense of the present by explaining it in terms of events and developments in the past. After some hesitation, we have decided to follow McNeill's interpretation. It has the advantage of not drawing a sharp dividing line between 'true' and 'untrue' images of the past. Rather, it leaves open the possibility that many meaningful images are composed of a mixture of hard evidence and imaginative reasoning, of fact and fantasy. The standards by which we measure the validity of our myths evolve; but this applies to our maps and models as well.

Maps are a pictorial means of orientation and communication. They are primarily designed to represent relations in physical space: proximity and distance in the first place, but numerous other dimensions as well, ranging from altitude or soil condition to property rights and political authority. The standards by which the quality of maps is measured obviously depend on the purpose for which we wish to use the maps. Over the past few centuries, those standards have become progressively stricter with regard to empirical precision, while aesthetically they tend to have become less demanding.

The sequence of the terms myths, maps and models suggests an ascending order of scientific rigour. Loosely speaking, any scheme representing associations between events may be called a model. Such schemes can be formalized into mathematical models. In the process, the complex forces actually at work are interpreted and simplified. Even rudimentary and relatively simple models can serve important heuristic purposes by pointing to significant problems for further research. Formalization of models helps to make observations more systematic, and to apply strict rules of inference in formulating and testing hypotheses.

A good rhetorical effect might perhaps be achieved by speaking of the integration of myths, maps, and models; at the present level of knowledge, however, complete integration or synthesis is an illusion. Myths, maps and models represent three modes of discourse, that is, of thinking and communicating, which are, respectively, mainly narrative, descriptive or explanatory. These modes of discourse are distributed unevenly over the scientific and scholarly communities. Some disciplines exhibit a clear preference for the narrative mode, others for the descriptive or the explanatory mode.

In this study we have tried if not to integrate, at least to incorporate each of these modes. This is reflected in the typography. The main body of the book consists of plain text, supplemented with tables, graphs, and diagrams. The text is also interspersed with 'boxes', some of which contain brief summaries of historical processes or theoretical expositions, while others are intended to enliven the main argument with an illustrative story. Finally, a large and important section of the book consists of maps.

The authors of this volume come from different disciplines. This is reflected in the style and format of their contributions. They all share a commitment to the scientific study of the co-evolution of socio-natural systems; but different theoretical orientations and different vocabularies are strongly built into each discipline's traditions, attitudes and conceptual frameworks. We found that, in trying to overcome the differences and to weave the various threads into a common fabric, we had to engage in long discussions and in serious attempts to understand and respect one another's points of view. Even when we were able to find common ground, it often still proved difficult to arrive at a formulation that would meet the requirements of each perspective. What constitutes a 'sociological generalization' to one author may be regarded by the other as a 'social science narrative' or a 'good homology of certain system dynamics representations'. In discussing such issues, we found ourselves confronted with the stubborn fact that scientific research is a social process in which the history of each discipline and the influence of current peer groups make themselves felt constantly. Apart from our substantive findings we also consider this experience, with its frustrations and moments of relief, to be interesting and enlightening. We hope that others may also benefit from it.

2

Introductory Overview: the Expanding Anthroposphere

GOUDSBLOM

2.1. Life before humans

Human life, like all life, consists of matter and energy structured and directed by information. All life is part of an ecosystem; all ecosystems together constitute the biosphere – the total configuration of living things interacting with each other and with non-living things. Every form of life continuously affects, and is affected by, its ecosystem.

2.1.1. The first environmental crisis in the biosphere[1]

The origins of life remain a mystery, but it seems safe to assume that interactions between living and non-living matter are as old as life itself. According to current insights, life probably began around 3.8 billion years ago, deep beneath the earth's surface near volcanic vents, feeding on chemicals such as sulphur. These earliest forms of life consisted solely of bacteria – unicellular organisms, some of which gradually 'migrated' and reached the surface of the seas where they made contact with air and sunlight, and where they acquired the ability to absorb solar energy by means of photosynthesis.

Originally all microbes were anaerobic, that is, unable to digest oxygen. Any oxygen contained in the compounds they used as nutrients was rejected by their metabolism and released into the atmosphere. Eventually this made the atmosphere so rich in oxygen as to be lethal to the anaerobic bacteria. By that time, however, some varieties had evolved a metabolism capable of coping with such high levels of oxygen. While the older varieties could survive only in anaerobic niches, these new varieties were able to thrive and reproduce in an atmosphere that had been filled with free oxygen by anaerobic life itself.

The dynamics of the biosphere thus brought about a drastic transformation of the non-living planetary atmosphere. From their earliest beginnings, organisms did not merely adapt to the environment in which they lived: by the very act of living they also modified their environment. The impact exerted by each single organism during its lifetime could only be minute; but the cumulative effect of countless generations has been enormous. The early environmental crisis also shows that in the long run a species may destroy the very conditions for its survival. However, while the majority of the anaerobic organisms perished in their own emissions, their very destruction created space for new forms of life. As the biogeologist Peter Westbroek observes:

> This event must have been the greatest environmental disaster ever. Oxygen, a calamitous pollutant, made the atmosphere reactive to organic matter and poisonous to most life then in existence. Virtually all the existing biota were forced into sediments, stagnant waters, and other environments where this poisonous gas had no access. Some organisms, however, managed to survive the reactivity of oxygen, and others even 'learned' to exploit it for energy. They transformed the peril of oxygen into a driving force of life on earth (Westbroek 1991: 202).

The crucial factor in the further evolution of life was the potential for individual cells to combine and to enter into increasingly more complex forms of specialization and collaboration such as fungi, plants, and animals. The great bulk of living biomass is still made up of bacteria, even today (see Gould 1996). All the bacteria that live within the intestines of humans and other large animals are still anaerobic.

We may well find the tenacity of the most ancient unicellar life forms, which have persisted over billions of years, spectacular. No less spectacular has been the capacity of certain cells to combine, to form larger structures, and to continue life collectively, in the form of 'higher' organisms – organized in particular individual physical structures such as trees or bodies, as well as in swarms, flocks or societies comprising many distinct physical structures.

All such swarms, flocks, and societies consist of separate organisms in which myriad cells are competing and collaborating. Each organism is a distinct structure of matter and energy, feeding on its environment, and engaged in a continuous exchange of information with other members of the flock. Humans, latecomers in the evolutionary process, are no exception.

2.1.2.   *Continental drift*

Globes often contain a small lamp, enabling us to see two very different aspects of the earth's surface. As long as the light is switched off, the globe shows the political division of the world, with for example China and India as clearly distinct big countries. When the light is switched on, the political boundaries become invisible and the natural differences in altitude are displayed. Instead of China and India we now see the Himalayas.

While it is generally known that political boundaries are subject to change, the natural contours of the earth's surface appear to be fixed. But that is, of course, a misleading impression: the natural condition of the soil, including the partition of water and land, is also subject to continuous changes. From a geological perspective, the very soil on which we live is a transient cover to the planetary surface, half way between the stages of solid mountain rock and submerged ocean mineral.

At one time India and China were separated by an ocean. As a result of convection streams in the mantle of the earth, the subcontinent which we know as India broke loose from the southern supercontinent in which it had been locked together with South America, Africa, Antarctica and Australia, and started moving in a northerly direction until, about fifty million years ago, it hit the Asian continent; in that collision, the Himalayas arose – and they have not yet ceased to rise.

The continents continue to move. South America and Africa, connected with each other until fifty million years ago, are drifting apart at an average speed of 10 centimetres a year. The plate tectonics causing this drift are geological processes which have until now gone on independently of any human interference.

About fifteen million years ago similar processes caused a rupture from south to north in East Africa, splitting the continent from Mozambique to the Red Sea into two parts divided by a deep canyon and a mountain ridge. According to a theory first proposed by the Dutch ethologist, Adriaan Kortlandt (1972), the first hominids evolved out of primates that found themselves isolated on the eastern side of this grand divide, in a region where progressive desiccation gradually turned the forests, their original habitat, into savannah.

2.2. Early humans and their first big impact: fire

2.2.1. *Human origins and extensive growth*

The first stage in human evolution is still in many respects shrouded in uncertainties (see Lewin 1999). Most experts agree, however, that climate changes most likely gave strong impulses to the process of hominization – in line with the current view that changes in temperature and precipitation have generally played a major part in the formation of new species ('speciation') as well as in their extinction (see Vrba 1995). New evidence for Kortlandt's original idea about the connection between geological events and the origins of the human species, has been put forward by the Belgian palaeontologist Yves Coppens (1994) under the heading 'East Side Story' – a felicitous allusion to humanity's supposed East African roots.

After they made their first appearance, humans gradually strengthened their position in the biosphere – at first slowly and almost imperceptibly, later at an increasingly more

> **'Man' or 'people'?** It is customary to use the word 'man' when discussing the relationships between humans and the biosphere. There are several reasons for not following this custom. First of all we have to acknowledge that humankind consists of men and women; the male form 'man', which is matched by the personal pronoun 'he', actually leaves out half of all human beings – even more, if we take into account that it also does not immediately evoke an image of children. The grammatically singular form of the word 'man' also obscures the fact that humans are social beings, who live and develop in interdependence with other humans. So, rather than resorting to the familiar image of 'man' as a single, male, and adult individual we prefer to speak of humans or people, in the plural, in order to bring out the inherent diversity and the thoroughly social nature of human beings.

rapid pace with ever more striking consequences.[2] In the process, they expanded their domain extensively as well as intensively. They appropriated increasingly more terrain and incorporated more and more non-human resources into their groups: first fire, then, much later, certain selected plants and animals and, later again, fossil fuels. As they incorporated more energy and matter into their societies, these societies grew in size, strength and productivity, while at the same time becoming more complex, more vulnerable and more destructive. Throughout this entire process of transformation, humans shared the same natural environment with other species, including microbes, plants and animals; this fundamental fact continues to be part of the human condition.

The first stage in human history and 'prehistory' is known in archaeology as the Palaeolithic or Old Stone Age. During this stage, which lasted for thousands of millennia, the overall pace of social and cultural development was slow in comparison with later stages. Yet some momentous changes took place, with great consequences for the relationships between humans and the natural environment. Humans began not only to use but also to make tools of their own, and they learned to control fire. The combination of tools and fire enabled groups of humans to leave their original habitat, the savannah of East Africa, and to migrate into other parts of the world, penetrating first into remote corners of Eurasia and then also into Australia and the Americas. The Palaeolithic can thus be seen as a long run up, which was later followed by an enormously accelerating sprint of which our present age is the latest episode. It was the scene of incipient 'extensive' and 'intensive' growth of the anthroposphere.

Extensive growth in the Palaeolithic had two related aspects: humans increased in numbers, and came to occupy more and more territorial space. According to the hypothesis that is currently considered most plausible, there were at least two big movements 'out of Africa': first, groups belonging to the species *Homo erectus* migrated into Asia Minor, from where they dispersed over large sections of the Eurasian continent; much

The concepts of extensive and intensive growth The concepts of 'extensive' and 'intensive' growth are derived from economic history (see Jones 2000), and are intended to serve 'sensitizing' or 'heuristic' purposes. The distinction allows us to perceive different dimensions and thus broaden and enrich the idea of growth.

Analytically, the concepts of extensive and intensive growth have distinct meanings. Empirically, however, the processes thus designated need not exclude each other. They may sometimes counteract, and sometimes support each other. Their actual interaction is a matter for empirical investigation.

In economic history, extensive growth refers to the extension of human numbers first of all in a demographic then also in a geographic sense. Intensive growth refers to a general rise in the standard of living: increase per capita in income.

The distinction may be applied to various other fields as well. In military-political development, extensive growth may refer to the extension of military-political units (regimes) first of all in a territorial, then also in a demographic sense: more land, more people. Intensive growth may then refer to a general rise in political commitment and participation and an increasing complexity of political institutions.

We may also conceive of a similar use of the two concepts in human ecology. Land that has been cultivated intensively (in which a great deal of human labour has been invested) represents a high degree of interdependence between humans and the vegetation. Even a monoculture of sugar cane or soya beans which looks like a homogeneous extension of one single crop can be shown in a more comprehensive perspective to reflect a high degree of ecological complexity.

later (between 250,000 and 150,000 years ago) members of the *Homo sapiens* species followed similar routes. Australia was reached around 60,000 years ago (although some Australian archaeologists now claim a much earlier arrival of the first human inhabitants), the Americas not later than 12,000 years ago (and probably a great deal earlier).

The great waves of migration have never come to a halt, and continue to this very day. The Pacific islands were among the last regions to be reached; human settlement there was completed by circa 500 CE.[3] Only for the migrations of the past few centuries do we have sufficient evidence to establish their size and trajectories. Because of the general growth of human numbers and big advances in the means of transportation, these most recent migrations were probably the largest of all time both in terms of human numbers and the distances covered. In addition, more and more animals and plant seeds travelled along with these movements of humankind, causing major changes in the earth's flora and fauna (see Crosby 1986).

For humanity's early demographic development we have to rely on informed guesses. As for any other species, the total number of humans at any given moment is a function of two variables: birth and death, fertility and mortality. The available evidence suggests that, during the Palaeolithic, both were relatively high (although not as high as in the following agrarian phase), with a slight excess of births over deaths. The nomadic way of life tended to act as a constraint limiting the number of children; it may also have made exposure to lethal microparasites less frequent among foragers than among sedentary farmers (Harris and Ross 1987: 21-36). The net result of these factors was a slow overall rate of extensive growth, as explained at greater length in Chapter 4.

According to the Italian demographer Massimo Livi-Bacci (1992: 2), the total human population must have reached one million at some time in the Palaeolithic, ten million at the beginning of the Neolithic, a hundred million during the Bronze Age and a thousand million at the beginning of the Industrial Revolution; the next tenfold increase, to ten billion, may be expected to be completed in the near future. On the basis of the same material Livi-Bacci (1992: 33) estimates that the total lifespan of all members of the world population today amounts to no less than a seventh of the total life span of all human beings who have ever lived. Along similar lines, the Russian physicist and demographer Sergey Kapitza (2000: 40) concludes that the human species now numbers at least one hundred thousand times more members than any other mammal of similar size and with a similar position in the food chain. There is only one exception: animals domesti-

FIGURE 2.1

World population 2000 BCE - 2000 CE

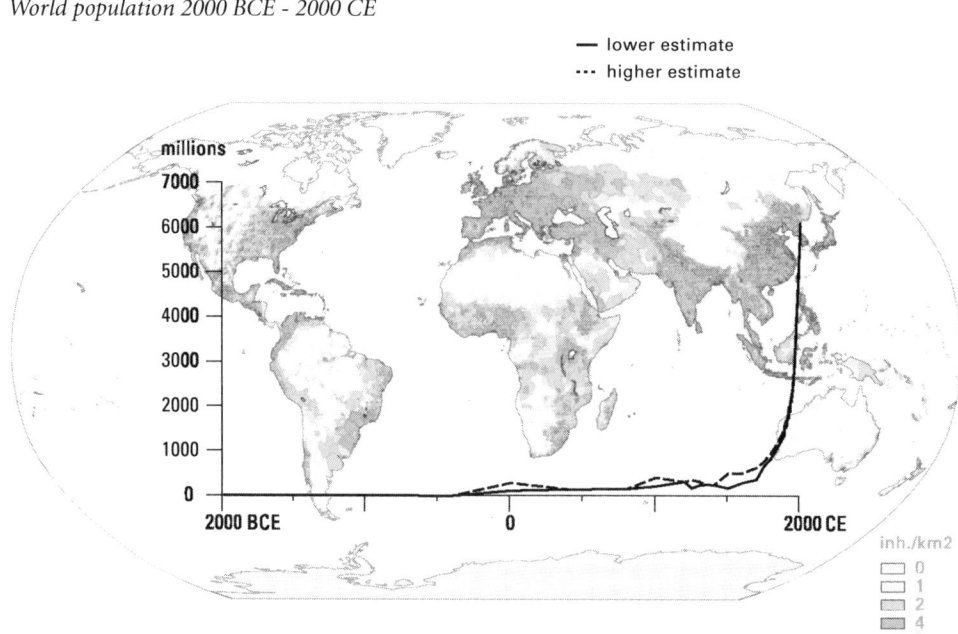

Source: RIVM-Hyde.

cated by humans. Their numbers include more than two billion cattle and sheep which consume more food than all humans together (see also Grübler 1998: 133-4; McNeill 2000: 264).

2.2.2.   *Intensive growth: technology, organization and civilization*

Intensive growth is harder to define and measure than extensive growth, but its impact on the biosphere is at least as important. In the process of intensive growth, things and forces which were previously completely beyond human control have been brought within the human domain and subjected to a certain measure of human control. Intensive growth always implies innovations in behaviour, which usually lead to a shift (however slight) in existing balances of power as well as to changes (again, however slight) in mentality or habitus. Extensive and intensive growth are not mutually exclusive. They can either support and reinforce or obstruct each other.

A basic trend in all human history, and certainly during its earliest phases (often designated 'prehistory'), has been the increasing differentiation between humans and all closely related animals in terms of their behaviour, their power, and their general disposition or attitude – their habitus. Thanks to the flexibility acquired in the course of evolution, humans were able to learn a large repertory of new forms of behaviour. Those innovations in behaviour that added to human power *vis-à-vis* other large animals, both predators and competitors, were particularly successful. Transmitted by learning from generation to generation, these innovations entered into the human habitus and became 'second nature'.

The primary condition for the process of differentiation in behaviour, power and habitus has been, and continues to be, the innate human capacity for culture as manifested in technology, organization and civilization – each of which represents the results of social learning. Social learning is the crux of culture: gathering information and passing it on to others – at first in direct interaction, at a later stage in history through written texts and today also by other audio-visual means. The stores of cumulated information (or 'cultural capital') have enabled people to tap increasingly larger and more varied flows of matter and energy and to integrate those flows into their societies.

The term 'technology' primarily refers to the means of harnessing various forms of matter and energy for human purposes. With the aid of technology, extra-somatic forces are used to supplement human strength and compensate for human weakness and slowness.

Technology could not have developed without 'social organization': the various means by which people are able to exchange information, co-ordinate their activities and take into consideration the intentions and interests of others. Less obvious perhaps, but equally important, is the part played by 'civilization': the social process in the course of which individuals learn to handle their own drives and emotions. Simple though this definition may sound, it refers to an area of human life that is still relatively unexplored, especially if we consider the historical dimension to the way human personalities are shaped in social processes (see Elias 2000: 363-447). The controversies that continue to rage about such issues as 'nature and nurture' reveal the wide margin of uncertainty and the lack of clarity in this area (see Rose and Rose 2000; Segerstråle 2000). Still, the theme is highly relevant to this book, since it touches on the problem of how individuals learn to cope with the outside world in both its social and its natural aspects and to what extent they are prepared to take into consideration the effects that their own actions may have on other people and on the natural environment. Both technology and social organization require civilization; neither can function without it.

Technology, social organization and civilization are closely interwoven. They correspond to what the sociologist Norbert Elias (1978: 156-7) calls the 'triad of controls' over extra-human, inter-human, and intra-human processes, respectively. Each of the three forms of control can only exist and evolve in connection with the other two. It is of course possible to describe the history of technology as a mere succession of new tools and appliances; while this might look like a very 'concrete' description, it would actually represent a great abstraction from reality. Even the seemingly simplest objects from the Palaeolithic could only be manufactured by virtue of socially transmitted knowledge and motivation.

With the expansion of the anthroposphere, increasingly more natural forces that were originally beyond human control came to be incorporated in the human domain. New ecological regimes were formed in which humans participated, along with the forces they tried to control. This is clearly illustrated by the domestication of fire. We discuss its early history at some length because, as the first manifestation of human mastery over a strong and potentially destructive force of nature, control over fire was a basic condition for the subsequent emergence of agriculture and industry that are highlighted in the chapters that follow.

2.2.3. *The original domestication of fire*

The domestication of fire was the first great act of human interference with natural processes. It had numerous far-reaching implications, stretching from the first hesitant beginnings to our contemporary fuel-driven economy. It therefore demands our attention, even though it took place long before the period in human history with which this book is mainly concerned.

In more than one way, the original fire regime may be seen as a paradigm for the socio-ecological regimes that were developed later. It presents a paradigm in two senses. First of all, in practice, the regime by which humans learned to extend their care for and control over fire could serve as a model for subsequent forms of care for and control over other forces in non-human nature such as plants and animals. Secondly, we may regard the domestication of fire as a model case in a more theoretical fashion, since it brings out the strong link between such apparently contradictory tendencies as increases in control and dependency, in robustness and vulnerability, in the potential for production and for destruction.

Fire, like all natural forces, has a history. Chemically fire is a process of highly accelerated oxidation of matter (fuel) induced by heat (ignition). Three conditions are therefore necessary for it to occur: oxygen, fuel and heat. During the earliest history of the earth, at least two of these – oxygen and fuel – were absent. Oxygen did not become available until life emerged after at least a billion years. And it was only less than half a billion years ago, during the Devonian geological age, that life assumed the form of plants, providing matter suitable for burning. From then on, most places on earth with seasonally dry vegetation were regularly visited by fire, ignited on rare occasions by falling rocks, volcanic discharges or extraterrestrial impacts, but most often by lightning (cf. Pyne 2001: 3-23).

Its domestication by humans opened an entirely new episode in the history of fire. Humans altered the frequency and intensity of fires. They brought fire to regions of the planet where it seldom or never burned spontaneously. And they tried to banish it from places where without human interference it would have burned repeatedly. As a result, 'natural' fire receded increasingly and made way for 'human' or, more precisely, anthropogenic fire.

Wherever humans migrated, they took their fire along. Areas such as rain forests, deserts, and the polar regions, which were not receptive to fire proved to be hard to penetrate for humans too. Everywhere else, the presence of humans-with-fire deeply altered the landscape, including flora and fauna. The human impact is amply documented (though still controversial) for a continent that was colonized by humans rather late: Australia (see Pyne 1991; Flannery 1995).

Humans are the only species that have learned to manipulate fire. Control over fire has become a 'species monopoly', with an enormous impact on other species, both animals and plants. It provides us with an excellent example of how new forms of behaviour may change the balance of power – in this case between humans and all other animals, ranging from primates to insects – and how shifts in the balance of power could engender changes in habitus, both among the humans who gained greater self-confidence from the presence of fire in their groups and among animals that might be bigger and stronger than humans but had learned to respect and fear their agility with fire.

Control over fire, in addition to having become exclusively human, has also become universally human. We know of no human society of the past 100,000 years that has lacked the skills needed to control fire.

The original domestication of fire was a dramatic transition. Palaeo-anthropologists are still debating when exactly it took place. The estimates range from as much as 1.5 million to a mere 150,000 years ago. Whether the first steps to control over fire coincided with other changes in early human development is still an open and fascinating question.

In retrospect, the initial domestication of fire was an event of momentous import. A wild force of nature – blind, capricious, hazardous – was now tended, cared for, protected from rain and supplied with fuel. Our early ancestors went to all this trouble, not out of 'altruism' but because it served them well. They put the potentially destructive and essentially purposeless force of fire to work for their own productive purposes. They managed to make fire regularly available. They no longer had to 'hunt' for it, hoping to find the smouldering remains of a natural blaze somewhere; they made it part (and even the centre) of their own group and they revered it as a symbol of eternal life.

The domestication of fire made humans less directly dependent on natural forces that continued to be beyond their control such as the alternation of day and night or the cycle of the seasons. It made the contrast between dark and light, between warm and cold or between wet and dry more amenable to manipulation, and thus gave humans a greater margin of freedom from the grip of nature. It increased their power – defined as the capacity to influence the outcome of an interaction. Armed with fire, humans were able to open up impenetrable tracts of bush, and to drive away animals much fiercer and stronger than themselves. The gain in power made their lives more comfortable and secure. The possibilities of heating, lighting and cooking all contributed to what we would now call a higher standard of living.

2.2.4. *Long-term consequences*

'Wherever primitive man had the opportunity to turn fire loose on a land, he seems to have done so from time immemorial.' This statement by the American geographer Carl Sauer (1981: 340) may sound like an exaggeration; but it still fails to convey the full impact that the domestication of fire has had, both on the larger biosphere and, within the biosphere, on human society itself.

The most immediate effect of the domestication of fire on the biosphere in general was an increase in the frequency with which fires occurred. Prior to its human mastery, fire had mostly been ignited by lightning. From now on another source was added: even before they learnt to make fire themselves humans were able to preserve it in their hearths and to use it wherever they saw fit. Consequently, as the number of anthropogenic fires increased, the proportion of natural fires diminished. It has been suggested, admittedly in a speculative manner, that the earliest human fire use may have affected the planetary atmosphere and caused some of the major climate changes in the Pleistocene (Westbroek *et al.* 1993). More substantive evidence indicating modification of the landscape by human foragers equipped with fire has been put forward for Australia, where most of the indigenous forests were burnt down in the millennia following the arrival of the first Aborigines (Flannery 1995; Pyne 2001).

From the very beginning humans used fire in two basic forms: the hearth and the torch. The hearth was the original site at which a fire was kept, usually a cave entrance where it could be protected against the rain and still receive some air circulation. Since it had to be tended and fuel had to be brought to it, it served almost naturally as a centre for group life, providing heat, light and a common focus. From the hearth developed, with time, a variety of fire containers such as crucibles, stoves, kilns and furnaces and, in our day, the mobile engines of motorcars and aeroplanes.

The hearth-like uses of fire have always had two kinds of environmental side effects. First of all, fuel had to be supplied. As long as human communities were small and living

---

The human impact on the environment raises problems similar to those in a thriller. When a murder has been committed, the coroner establishes the effects of the interaction and the detective examines the causes: the motives and the means of the perpetrator. What made him do it, how was he able to do it?

When we consider the issue of anthropogenic fire (and most fire on our planet today is anthropogenic), the natural sciences deal with the consequences or the effects; the social sciences deal with the conditions, the causes, the motives and the means of the perpetrators.

This is, of course, only an analogy. Instead of a single suspect, an individualized, masculine 'he', we have to look at 'we', humans, in the plural: including men, women and children, and including our earliest ancestors as well as those of us alive today. (We are links in a chain of generations. Our current interactions with fire should be seen in that context.)

In dealing with the distant human past, it may be more appropriate not to speak of 'we' but 'they'. Our early ancestors who were the first to domesticate fire were akin to us, but they must also in many ways have been very different. In fact, in learning to control fire, they became more like us and less like our closest relatives among the mammals.

If indeed the basic long-term trend in human history (underlying most other developments and events) has been the very process of increasing differentiation in behaviour, power and habitus between humans and all related species, the domestication of fire was an important step in this trend – not the single cause but an integral part of it. Since control of fire became a species monopoly, exclusively human and shared equally by all human societies, it made humans everywhere more alike among themselves and more different from all other creatures.

---

in areas with abundant wood, this did not cause much of a problem. When greater numbers of people started living in large urban concentrations, however, the need for fuel became a strong contributing factor to deforestation over large areas and, in our own age, to the depletion of fossil resources. The second side-effect of hearth-like fire consists of its waste products: ashes and smoke. Although smoke might be useful for driving away insects and other insidious creatures, it has generally been considered to be a nuisance to be got rid of. As long as people lived in isolated caves or huts, this was relatively easy. Urbanization and industrialization have seriously aggravated the problem.

While the original functions of the hearth were primarily turned inwards ('centripetal'), the torch was a more outwardly directed ('centrifugal') implement. It was used not only to provide light at night, but also to set fire to shrubs and grasses by day – an effective way to destroy obstacles for foraging and to rout animals, both predators and prey. The torch undoubtedly contributed to deforestation: wood was burned wholesale, regardless of its possible value as timber or fuel. In the age of agriculture, the torch was used for slash-and-burn and other land-clearing techniques and it served as the model for a whole array of fire weapons culminating in our own time in rocket-propelled missiles.

Surveying the entire trajectory of the human use of fire from its earliest beginnings, we can distinguish three stages. During the first stage, there were no groups possessing fire; there were only groups *without* fire. There must then have been a second stage when there were both groups *with* fire and groups *without* fire. We do not know how long that stage lasted – nor how often it may have recurred. All we know is that it came to an end. It was a transitional stage, leading up to the stage in which humankind has now lived for thousands of generations: the stage when there are no longer any groups without fire. All human groups are groups *with* fire.

Although we lack empirical evidence for the first two stages, this very lack leaves us no choice but to accept an unavoidable conclusion: societies *with* fire were in the long run obviously more 'fit to survive' than societies *without* fire. If we then ask why it was that societies without fire disappeared, there seems to be only one plausible answer: because they had to co-exist with societies *with* fire – and apparently in the long run such co-existence proved impossible.

This may sound like a dismal conclusion suggesting fierce contests ending in the elimination of the losers. If such contests did indeed take place, they have left no trace of empirical evidence; we only have the highly imaginative evocations of what might have happened in books and films such as *The Quest for Fire*, directed by Jean-Jacques Annaud. However, we can also view the fact that possession of fire has become a universal attribute of all human societies as an important example of the general rule that changes in one human group lead to changes in related other groups. If group A had fire and neighbouring group B did not, group B 'had a problem'. It could either try to minimize contact with group A and perhaps move away or do as group A had done and adopt a regime with fire – this should not pose insurmountable problems given a sufficient capacity to learn from the others. In the latter case, instead of a 'zero-sum' elimination struggle there would have been what the American freelance author and scientist Robert Wright (2000) calls a 'nonzero' situation, with an outcome in which neither party was the loser.

The rule that changes in one human group lead to changes in other related groups may sound like a rather tautological explanation for social change, but it is not. It is a highly generalized empirical observation, similar to an observation we can make about fire: fire generates fire – in a similar, more general, fashion change generates change and social change generates social change.

Such is the nature of the dynamics of human society and culture. After the original domestication of fire, it was never humans alone who interacted with other human groups and with non-human nature. It was always humans-with-fire, equipped with fire and with the products of pyrotechnology: cooked food, pointed spears and arrows, earthenware and metal objects. Their presence put an end to humans-without-fire.

Another general conclusion to be drawn from these observations is the following: changes in climate and precipitation have never ceased to be important reasons for humans to change their way of life. Humans are no different from other species in that they will always have to accommodate the basic conditions of earthly nature, such as the alteration of day and night or of monsoons and seasons. In the course of human history, however, in addition to these overriding extra-human conditions, conditions brought about by humans themselves have become increasingly more important – to the extent that, in our contemporary world, humanity has become a major agent of ecological change.

2.2.5.   Regimes

The domestication of fire meant that people tamed a strong and potentially destructive natural force, and made it into a regularly available source of energy. In so doing they initiated changes in the natural environment, in their social arrangements, and in their personal lives. These three aspects (ecological, sociological, psychological) are all part of the changing human relationships with fire.

In its ecological aspects, the domestication of fire affected the relationships between humans and the non-human world so deeply that we can call it the first great ecological transformation brought about by humans, which was followed much later by the second and third of such transformations – generally known as the agricultural and industrial revolutions, and better characterized in terms of the long term processes of agrarianization and industrialization.

Each of the three transformations spelled the formation of a new socio-ecological regime: the fire regime, the agrarian regime and the industrial regime, marked by the utilization of fire and elementary tools, the rise and spread of agriculture and animal husbandry and the rise and spread of large-scale modern industry, respectively. The later regimes have not made the earlier regimes obsolete; rather, they have absorbed them and, in the process, transformed them. Each new regime brought an expansion of the anthroposphere within the biosphere.

Defining the three regimes jointly in similar terms is helpful in order to better understand each of them separately as well as in their interrelations. A common conceptual model invites and facilitates comparison. The comparison allows us to explain the sequence in the emergence of the regimes, and to perceive not only their similarities and differences but also their interlocking.

2.3. Intensified human impact: agrarianization

The history of the past ten thousand years can be read as a series of events accompanying the process of the agrarianization of humankind – a process in the course of which humanity has extended the domain of agriculture and animal husbandry all over the world, and in so doing made itself increasingly more dependent upon this very mode of production.

In terms of geology, the era of agrarianization coincides with the Holocene – the relatively brief and climatologically relatively stable era following the much longer and, in its overall effects, much more turbulent era of the Pleistocene.[4] The Pleistocene period lasted approximately 0.8 million years and saw at least nine oscillations between extremely cold and somewhat milder global climates known as the glacial and interglacial periods. The last of these ice ages, between 130,000 and 10,000 BP, reached a peak between 22,000 and 16,000 BP and was succeeded by the Holocene period, our contemporary epoch, which may well turn out to be one more interglacial age (cf. Chapter 3).

The transition from Pleistocene to Holocene was marked by great environmental changes. As the ice melted and the glaciers receded, the sea level rose world-wide by at least 100 metres, terminating the land bridge between Siberia and Alaska and turning large sections of the Eurasian continent into islands, including the British Isles and Indonesia. As the temperature rose, the tree line shifted away from the equator, turning tundra and savannah into woodland and forest.

During the Holocene period, the climate continued to change, but in a less drastic fashion. The most extreme fluctuation was a prolonged increase in precipitation in northern Africa, which allowed savannah vegetation to flourish in the Sahara area for several millennia (9000-5000 yr BP). This period is discussed more fully in Chapter 3.

2.3.1.   *Emergence*

As the reference to the Sahara implies, once we have reached the era of agriculture and animal husbandry, we find ourselves on firmer empirical ground than in discussing the earliest domestication of fire. For this stage in socio-ecological development there is far more archaeological evidence to rely on when probing into such problems as when it began, where it began and how and why it began. Nevertheless, we should not pitch our expectations too high. The problem of tracing and explaining first origins in socio-cultural development remains tricky. Even if it were possible to determine the time and the place of the first occurrence of particular agricultural practices, the question of why those innovations first began then and there would be far more difficult to answer than the question of why some innovations, once they had been accomplished, became successful and spread far beyond their original location.

As a result, we have to accept the fact that some of the most intriguing problems regarding the emergence of agriculture and animal husbandry remain unsolved, at least for the time being. According to current insights, there appear to have been several origins: the transition to agrarian production probably took place independently in different periods in different parts of the world, including Mesopotamia, the East Asian mainland, New Guinea, Meso-America, and the Andes region. The reasons why the transition occurred are most likely to be found in a combination of necessity and opportunity or, in other words, motives and means (cf. Chapter 4).

Fortunately some important points regarding the transition and its consequences are beyond dispute. Until recently, established scholarly opinion held that the 'agricultural revolution' meant the first big human impact on the biosphere. As shown in the preceding section, humans had already initiated far-reaching changes in the biosphere at a much earlier stage with the domestication of fire.

Contrary to common usage, we have decided to avoid the term 'agricultural revolution' altogether, and to speak consistently of 'agrarianization'. An obvious advantage of the latter concept is that it draws attention to the close parallel with the subsequent process of industrialization. It also conveys clearly that, like industrialization, agrarianization is not to be seen as a one-time event but as an ongoing process. Having started on a relatively small scale, the agrarian mode of production and way of life have never ceased expanding. Nor did agrarianization stop at the advent of industrialization; on the contrary, the rise of modern industry has given it strong new impetus towards further development.

So far the era of agrarianization has been marked by a steadily increasing rate of change. Between the original domestication of fire and the first appearance of agriculture came a period of at least 100,000 years. In contrast, only 10,000 years passed between the rise of agriculture and the rise of modern industry. And while industrialization began to gain momentum no more than 250 years ago, we may well currently be witnessing the onset of another great socio-ecological transformation.

The most plausible explanation for this acceleration is probably implied by the principle expounded above to the effect that once social and cultural development get started, they have a tendency to become self-propelling and self-accelerating. For a very long period in early human history (comprising the era known as 'prehistory'), changes in the non-human environment posed the greatest challenge to human adaptability. As will be discussed in Chapter 4, it was perhaps still this kind of 'external' change, and especially the great rise in temperature at the end of the last Ice Age, which triggered the first emergence of agriculture in Mesopotamia and possibly also in other areas.

The argument is indeed persuasive. As the sea flooded fertile coastal land and the advancing forest encroached upon more and more savannah, there were many areas where both humans and the large herbivores upon which they hunted found their natural habitats under severe stress. It hardly seems to be a coincidence that precisely during this period at the end of the Pleistocene many large mammals became extinct, including herbivores such as the woolly mammoth as well as their predators such as the sabre-tooth tiger (see Livingston 1994: 49-51). As living conditions for the freely roaming herbivores deteriorated, and the competition for the resources of food and fresh water grew more intense, humans may have used their technical and organizational superiority to destroy a number of their rivals forever, thereby depriving themselves of the chance of any future benefit from those species. The areas that were most vulnerable to the rising water levels were coastal zones where humans had been able to prosper on plentiful supplies of food both from the land and in the sea. It stands to reason that especially in those regions which were hardest hit, with relatively great numbers of people being confronted with gravely deteriorating environmental conditions, more active cultivation of edible plants was adopted as a substitute for the diminishing chance of obtaining food by fishing, gathering and hunting. Again, Chapter 4 reports some impressive recent evidence on these issues.

2.3.2.   *Continuities*

The initial transition from gathering and hunting to agriculture and animal husbandry was not necessarily abrupt. A group that started to cultivate a few crops would not have to give up its older ways altogether. There would have been very few, if any, agrarian societies from which gathering and hunting disappeared completely at once. However, the proportion of products acquired in the older way inevitably diminished as agriculture and animal husbandry advanced.

From the very beginning, the process of agrarianization was linked closely to the domestication of fire. It is hard to imagine how people could have begun to cultivate plants and to domesticate animals had the art of handling fire not already been familiar to them. If nothing else, they needed a hearth fire to cook on. The first crops cultivated on any large scale were cereal grains such as wheat, rice and maize which, owing to their high nutritional value and their capacity to withstand storage for long periods, formed a highly appropriate staple food for a human community; to serve this purpose, however, they had to be made more easily digestible with the help of fire.

A second and very different reason why the control of fire formed a precondition for agrarianization was the human predominance over all other mammals, which was grounded partly in the use of fire. The human species' monopoly over fire was so solidly established by the time agriculture began, and is today so easily taken for granted, that it is seldom given separate attention in this context. Yet it deserves mention. Their hegemony in the animal kingdom enabled people not only to bring certain species, such as goats and sheep, under direct control, but also – at least as important – to keep most of the remaining 'wild' animals at a distance from their crops and herds.

Thirdly, experience in controlling fire may have furthered plant and animal domestication in another, even more intangible way, which our distance in time makes it difficult to assess precisely but which we are also, for that very reason, likely to underestimate. The time-honoured practice of handling fire could not have failed to prepare humans for the many tasks involved in agriculture and animal husbandry. It taught them that expending care upon something non-human could be well worth the trouble and thus made it more acceptable to them to accommodate the strains of an agrarian life, full of self-imposed renunciation for the sake of a possible future yield.

The most immediately visible link between early agriculture and the ancient use of fire lay in the custom of burning off land with an eye to food production. Of old, foraging peoples were wont to apply their torches in order to keep the land open for gathering and hunting. Even in recent times those firing practices were continued in some parts of the world, as in Australia where the Aborigines' judicious use of fire in keeping their land open for kangaroos and humans has become known as 'firestick farming' (cf. Flannery 1995; Pyne 2001) – a term suggesting a form of 'proto-agrarianization'.

2.3.3.   Sequences

The rise of agriculture was in many respects remarkably similar to the domestication of fire. Again, humans added new sources of energy to their own, this time by adopting certain plants and animals and integrating them into their societies. Plants that were formerly 'wild' now began to be cultivated, 'wild' animals were tamed and used for food or other purposes such as traction, and all these species were made part of the human domain – of the anthroposphere which correspondingly increased in size and complexity.

The transition from foraging to agriculture did not automatically make people hap-

pier and healthier. Agrarian life brought new hardships. Diets became more monotonous. Sedentary life in villages, in close company with domesticated animals, increased
the susceptibility to disease. It allowed for a rise in fertility but also caused higher
mortality. The result was large numbers of children, many of whom did not reach adult-
hood. Not surprisingly, research on skeletons reveals that, after agrarianization, human
lives tended to become briefer and bodies shorter. It is equally understandable that the
texts of the great religions of Eurasia all exhibit nostalgia for the lost paradise of a pre-
agrarian era.

The nature of agrarian life prevented a return to foraging, however. There are a few
known cases of such a return, but these are exceptions (see Diamond 1997: 55, 109). Almost everywhere, with so many people, and so little land, the only option for the survival
of an agrarian population was cultivation. 'Work' was writ large over the agrarian world.

If, at a very early stage, the domestication of fire had made human groups more productive but also more vulnerable (as from now on they had to rely on fire), the rise of
agriculture had the same twofold effect. Being able to grow more food, human groups
grew more populous and became more dependent on their crops, and thus more vulnerable to the failure or loss of their harvests. As the expansion of agriculture and pastoralism left increasingly less land available for foraging, the opportunity to escape from this
vicious circle dwindled.

The first stage in the process of agrarianization necessarily involved clearing the land
and removing any existing vegetation that would compete with the planted crops. In
many cases, the most efficient way to accomplish this was by means of fire. As long as
land remained plentiful, continued recourse was often taken to fire in a system practised
throughout the world, and known under various regional names that are usually sub-
sumed in the standard literature under the label 'shifting cultivation'. Shifting cultivation
implies that an area of primary forest is first cleared by slash-and-burn and is then used
for one or more harvests of crops. When, after a while, crop nutrients in the soil become
exhausted and undesirable plants ('weeds') begin to dominate, the farmers temporarily
abandon the land, turn to an adjacent lot, burn the vegetation down and bring it under
cultivation until they again find harvesting unrewarding. Eventually they return to their
first plot, which by then has become 'secondary forest' or 'secondary bush', and resume
their activities of burning, planting and harvesting there. The duration of the entire cycle
may vary as to time and place, but the principle remains the same. This is discussed in
more detail in Section 9.3 on population dynamics in Indonesia.

In many parts of the world, over time, burning the land and letting it lie fallow for a
number of years or seasons ceased to be a regular practice and was replaced by more
intensive methods of working the soil, requiring greater investments of labour but yielding a larger output per acre and thus making it possible to feed more mouths. The most
common means of accomplishing higher yields by harder work were irrigation and
ploughing.

The actual practices of agriculture varied greatly according to differences in climate and soil. Yet wherever cultivation was intensified this led to structurally similar results. There was a recurrent sequence which almost reads like a series of simple equations: more food meant more people, living in increasingly large concentrations in permanent settlements, with the possibility for some of the people to specialize in pursuits other than tilling the land. The process of specialization was in turn accompanied by the increasing organization of people in larger economic, religious and political units (such as markets, churches, and states), and by increasing social stratification or the division of people into upper and lower tiers with greater or lesser access to power, property and prestige. This complex of interrelated processes unfolded in different epochs in different parts of the world. Because of the distances in place and time, these trends led to the development of apparently highly divergent cultures, marked by very specific traditions in such aspects of life as preparing food, religious worship and the building of houses and palaces. The remarkable results of cultural divergence in those fields can easily blind us to the convergence of some underlying social trends, notably the process of social stratification.

2.3.4. *Hypertrophy and atrophy*

Social stratification as a long-term process led to the formation of tiered agrarian societies in which some groups managed to attain a 'higher' position with great power and privilege, while others (the 'lower' majority, consisting mostly of peasants) were deprived of such power and privilege. This process occurred in every part of the world, from the British Isles to Japan and from Peru to Mexico. Wherever more intensive forms of work made land more productive, new social regimes developed – often in a sequence of religious-agrarian regimes, dominated by priestly elite groups, followed by military-agrarian regimes, in which warrior elite groups attained equally or even more powerful positions than the priestly.

Religious-agrarian regimes have played an important part in shaping the relations between humans and the biosphere in agrarian societies. Humans are not equipped by birth with a natural aptitude for agrarian life. They have no innate calendar telling them when the time has come for preparing the soil, for planting the seeds, for removing weeds, for harvesting. The only calendar available to them is a socio-cultural one, roughly geared to the alteration of the seasons but regulated with greater precision by human convention, as a part of an agrarian regime.

Agrarian regimes provide people with the competence and the motivation needed to live in an agrarian community so that they are capable and willing to work hard in order to produce food crops, prepared to store stocks of those crops as food and seed for future use, and respectful of ownership rights to the land and its produce.

A typical set of such instructions can be found in the teachings of the Old Testament. An important function of the priests who propagated those teachings consisted of upholding the agrarian regime. Recognizing this function may give us a clue to a better understanding of the prominent position of priests, not only in ancient Israel but also in many other agrarian societies. Priestly authority helped to stabilize relations both between the people themselves and towards the non-human elements they had integrated into their societies. Arguably, at a particular stage of social development, societies with priests were better equipped for survival than societies without priests.[5]

Wherever religious-agrarian regimes were established, they found themselves in the course of time in competition with, and having to make room for, military-agrarian regimes, led by warriors. Originally, in tribal agrarian societies, the warriors would include virtually all adult men, who would assemble for war on special occasions. They might go on a raid after an unsuccessful harvest, or defend their own community against invaders. In the wake of extensive and intensive growth, warring activities became more specialized – a process with an inextricable momentum that is well characterized by the term 'arms race' (cf. Wright 2000: 270). The result was that most agrarian societies eventually found themselves ruled by warriors whose primary function was to fight – against other warriors (cf. Section 4.6).

While this may sound like a tautology, it actually refers to a situation in which many agrarian societies were trapped. The majority of the people lived a farming life that was productive but also left them extremely vulnerable. The warriors formed a robust minority specializing in destructive violence. This simple formulation captures the basic mechanism of military-agrarian society. The peasants' productivity and vulnerability and the warriors' powers of destruction were drawn together like the opposite poles of a magnet. Once a warrior class was formed, the warriors needed the peasants to supply food, and the peasants needed the warriors for protection. This unplanned – and in a profound sense fatal – combination formed the backdrop for a great variety of mixtures of military protection and economic exploitation that generally mark the history of advanced agrarian societies.

New inventions added to the force of warriors and helped to widen the gap between them and the rest of the population. In this way, the development of metallurgy did not only create, during the Bronze and Iron Ages, 'a whole range of valuable objects worth hoarding in quantity' (Renfrew 1972: 339) but it also supplied the weapons with which these objects might be appropriated. It reinforced the trend, present in most settled agrarian societies, toward accumulation of property, and it also turned this trend in the direction of a highly uneven distribution of the accumulated property. The possession of weapons, which had tended for a long time already to be the monopoly of adult and fully initiated men, to the exclusion of women and children, now came to be monopolized by the warriors as a specific class of 'noblemen' or 'aristocrats'. Increasingly, as the American sociologist Gerhard Lenski notes, 'the energies of this powerful and influential class were

... turned from the conquest of nature to the conquest of people' (Lenski 1987: 174).

The trend indicated by Lenski had antecedents stretching a long way back. As human dominance over many other species increased, relations between and within human groups became increasingly important in the dynamics between humans and the biosphere. Challenges posed by other people often took precedence over challenges posed by nature.

With the intensification of agriculture, more and more land was transformed into fields, terraces, and meadows, yielding an increasing amount of food and other products upon which society at large grew increasingly dependent. Those who owned the land were inclined to regard it mainly as an economic and political asset – a source of revenue and prestige. Since they managed to appropriate a sizeable portion of the total wealth produced and accumulated in their societies, increases in wealth did not result in either clear-cut extensive or intensive growth, but in a lopsided increment of luxury possessions that may be typified as *hypertrophy*. The material remains from episodes of such hypertrophy in the past are numerous; they range from the Egyptian pyramids to the Taj Mahal, from the triumphal arches of Rome to the Aztec solar temples.

Hypertrophy had a reverse side: increasing poverty on the part of the peasants and the landless poor, resulting as already noted in briefer lives and shorter bodies (cf. Harris and Ross 1987: 76; Tilly 1998: 1-4). Using the same metaphor we may call this a tendency toward atrophy. Similar insights have been formulated by archaeologists (cf. Section 8.4).

The combined trends toward hypertrophy and atrophy led to a social degradation of ecological regimes. Members of the ruling elite tended to take a greater interest in the vicissitudes of military and political affairs than in the day-to-day management of their rural estates. The peasants and slaves, for their part, lived in destitute circumstances that were only likely to add to their masters' contempt for such matters.

Altogether the process of stratification in advanced agrarian societies amounted to a form of differentiation, resembling the primal differentiation in behaviour, power and habitus between humans and related species in the animal world. The crucial difference was that differentiation now took place between and within human groups themselves.

One result of social stratification was the relative decline in the esteem of ecological regimes. As elite groups became further divorced from the work of tilling the land, the aspects of social life directly related to the control of the natural environment were relegated to peasants and slaves and their overseers – in other words, to the lower orders. Working the land tended to be regarded as dirty and degrading to a person of rank.

The degree to which the leading elite became divorced from direct ecological pressures made itself felt in the way the relationships between humans and the biosphere developed in various societies. In general, Lenski's rule, that control over people prevailed over control over nature, applied if only because the latter was exercised by means of the former. As the American sociologist Randall Collins (1984: 107) observes, the most ancient monuments of advanced agrarian societies, the megaliths, testify to the ability of those societies to employ 'massed human energy'. Constructions such as the Egyptian pyramids embodied a combination of technology and social organization, as did the irrigation works in 'hydraulic societies' in river deltas from China and Mesopotamia to Mexico (see Wittfogel 1957).

In many cases, hypertrophy ended in catastrophe, in the collapse of established hierarchies and their cultural trappings. However, the long-term trend toward extensive growth persisted, in time leading to continuing pressures toward ever more intensive use of the available land. More and more people came to live in villages and towns, and in the cities that emerged as the centres of accumulated power and wealth. Those who flocked to the towns and cities needed large supplies of food and fuel, while at the same time creating great problems of waste disposal and pollution. Among them were specialists such as tanners and dyers whose work produced noxious side-effects. Altogether a number of environmental impacts were so obtrusive that the ruling urban groups considered them hardly bearable and had statutes drawn up to eliminate the worst excesses of pollution of water and air.

Outside the urban centres, elite groups do not seem to have shared such great concern for environmental issues. In advanced agrarian societies such as medieval Europe or late imperial China various dominant groups competed and contended for power and privilege: priests, warriors, courtiers, entrepreneurs and bureaucrats. With a variation on Max Weber's concept of the 'economic ethos', we can investigate the 'ecological ethos' of these groups and examine how it changed over time. Empirical findings and theoretical ideas combine to suggest that the ecological ethos of the elite groups has been waning for a long time. This became even more manifest during the early stages of industrialization.

2.4. Industrialization: the rise of the third regime

Historians nowadays tend to avoid the once popular term 'Industrial Revolution'. Most of them do so not because they wish to diminish the importance of industrialization, but in order to stress that industrialization is a long-term process that was not confined to a relatively brief 'revolutionary' period in one particular country but is still continuing, and making its impact felt all over the world.

In our view, industrialization means the rise and spread of a third socio-ecological regime – the industrial regime, following the fire regime and the agrarian regime. It did not put an end to the older regimes. On the contrary, new applications of fire lay at the very heart of industrialization: using fossil fuel to generate steam power and to smelt and refine iron. The smokestacks of the coal and iron industries became the icons of early industrialization.

There were also close connections with agriculture. Agrarian production had to provide a subsistence base for all workers employed in the mines and factories. Moreover, as soon as industrialization came to include the production of textiles and foodstuffs, the raw materials had to be supplied by agriculture. And before long, factories started generating means of production for agriculture: first simple iron tools, then more complex new mechanized implements, and then, in the 20th century, various types of combustion-driven machines, fertilizers and pesticides. By the end of that century, agriculture and industry in many parts of the world had become inseparable and often even barely distinguishable.

Since the beginnings of industrialization are so much closer to us in time than the beginnings of agrarianization, they are much better documented. There is a fairly general consensus about the question where and when the transition first occurred: in Britain, in the eighteenth century. On the other hand, the question of why this was so is still much disputed. A number of conditions and causes have been listed; we return to this controversy in Chapter 10 (see also Goldstone 2000; O'Brien 2001).

Industrialization ultimately constitutes a unique historical process, which is part of the even more widely encompassing and equally unique process of the expansion of the anthroposphere. It will never be possible to repeat the beginnings of industrialization under experimental conditions. Attempts at 'modelling' the incipient stages under artificial circumstances can be no more than approximations, at best helping to sharpen our imagination. As with biological evolution, it is far more difficult to explain why a successful mutation or innovation arose at all than why, once it existed, it survived and became successful.

This pertains equally to the staying power of the control of fire, of agriculture and of fossil-fuel-based industry. The words that the sociologist David Riesman (1961: xxix) used for modernization apply to industrialization as well: it 'appears to proceed with an almost irreversible impact, and no tribe or nation has found a place to hide'. Like the earlier socio-economic regimes, the industrial regime has kept expanding; the explanation for this fact must be sought in some of its effects – its functions.[6]

This is not to say that all effects of industrialization were beneficial in every respect. Far from it; but the point is that industrialization maintained its momentum because it apparently had certain effects or 'functions' which were valued positively by sufficient numbers of people with sufficient means to keep the process going. It is the task of the human sciences (anthropology, sociology, psychology, economics and history) to trace those functions and understand the valuations.

The primary effect of industrialization was that immense supplies of fossil fuel energy were made available which had lain virtually unused by any living species. In the 18th century, a series of inventions made it possible for humans to start tapping these supplies and to use them to generate heat and mechanical motion. No longer were people completely dependent on the flows of energy which reach the earth from the sun and which are partly converted into vegetation by means of photosynthesis. Just as at one time humans had been able to strengthen their position in the biosphere by learning to control fire, they now learned the art of using fire to exploit the energy contained in coal, oil and gas. With this extra energy they also developed means of technology and organization that enabled them to make much more extensive and intensive use of materials such as tin and copper and, subsequently, to develop a range of new 'synthetic' chemical substances.

Seen from a wide perspective, all of these developments concerned humanity at large. At closer quarters, however, it was only a tiny section of humanity that took the lead and was the first to profit. A small entrepreneurial class in Britain had the advantage of being the pioneers of industrialization.

While industrialization began on a modestly local scale, it was enveloped in a context of much wider range. Industrialization was preceded by European expansion, and that gave strong impetus to it from the very start. British society in the 18th century was connected in many ways to a larger world: not just to the European continent but also to other continents. It had a strong navy and a large commercial fleet; trade with other continents (including the slave trade) brought in substantial wealth; emigration across the Atlantic helped to relieve population pressures. The ensemble of these military, political, and economic relationships provided a robust infrastructure for the burgeoning industries, guaranteeing protected access to a worldwide array of resources and markets (cf. Section 9.2 for a South-Asian perspective).

The combined thrust of industrialization and globalization has produced an enormously accelerating rate of intensive and extensive growth all over the world. Growth did not continue evenly. There were 'peak' periods of economic development such as 1870-1913 and 1950-73 which were later dubbed 'golden ages', whereas the world economy grew much more slowly in other periods such as 1913-50 (Maddison 2001: 22). Nor did growth affect the entire world in the same way. On the contrary, up to now it has proceeded in a very uneven fashion, leading to such extremes that the per capita income in the United States of America today exceeds that in Ethiopia by a factor 70 (Maddison 2001: 224, 276; Figures 9.1 and 9.2).

However, while economic growth has hardly raised the living standards of billions of people, it has affected the economy and the forms of land use in practically every country on earth. It has also resulted in an enormous increase in population. In the 18th and 19th centuries, most nations in Western Europe went through the first phase of the so-called demographic transition, marked by a combination of rapidly declining death rates and continuing high birth rates. The resulting population pressure was considerably relieved by massive emigration overseas, especially to North America, while millions of Russians migrated eastwards into Siberia (cf. Section 9.4). In the 20th century, the annual surplus of births over deaths came to an end in Europe, but by that time the conditions prevailing in the first phase of the demographic transition were becoming characteristic of the poorer parts of the world where the majority of humans live.

The reduction of the death rates in the industrializing world was clearly connected with advances in public hygiene. These, in turn, were predicated to a general rise in societal affluence allowing the construction of public waterworks and sewers, as well as con-comitant developments in technology and science and in standards of individual behav-iour. The same set of factors conditioned the next phase in the demographic transition, the decrease in fertility: new techniques of birth control, based on scientific research, and new attitudes towards family size.

The demographic structure of contemporary societies has thus become clearly influ-enced by a steadily developing corpus of information by which individuals let them-selves be directed in their behaviour. The information as such is a form of cultural capi-tal: the collective result of the efforts of a great many researchers. How it is applied at the level of personal conduct depends on the way the individuals perceive their own situa-tion and prospects – which is yet another kind of information.

The entire state of affairs is in many ways paradigmatic for contemporary society. Flows of highly complex information are widely available in a standardized and easily understandable form. Many of them are hardly recognized as information because they come to people in the shape of material objects, delivered with a manual. Owners are apt to forget that the instructions are an integral part of the appliance. If a machine is aban-doned in the absence of anyone prepared to carry out the instructions, the dead and rusting object is testimony to the vital importance of information in an age of advanced technology.

Information is the decisive principle in the organization of matter and energy. It holds global society together: the networks of long-distance transportation and commu-nication, the worldwide division of labour and land use. Its exponential growth in the era of industrialization has enabled people to mobilize energy and matter in unprece-dented quantities and over distances spanning the entire globe, often with consequences that turned out to be detrimental to the biosphere.

Assessing the physical consequences, and establishing human responsibilities is also a matter of information. In this context people sometimes speak of a paradox because one and the same factor appears as both cause and remedy (see Grübler 1998: 341). As so often, underlying the apparent paradox is a real tension, inherent in all evolutionary processes: every successful strategy of growth is bound to reach limits where further growth becomes too costly. Here the primeval 'oxygen crisis' mentioned at the beginning of this chapter can serve as a parable.

The parable fails in one respect: although there must have been some exchange of information, there is no trace of consciousness in the bacteria of two billion years ago. This is in stark contrast to the anthroposphere today in which continuous efforts are being made to collect information and use it intelligently. Science and technology have not only been instrumental in designing machinery that has inadvertently contributed to the depletion of natural resources and the pollution of air, water and soil – they also provide the means for monitoring and, possibly, solving environmental problems caused by human action.

Public alarm over those problems reached a first climax around 1970. The report to the Club of Rome and similar publications aroused the concern of large audiences and prompted politicians and businessmen to action. An awareness dawned that humanity might be squandering natural energy and matter in an ill-informed and irresponsible manner, creating unmanageable quantities of waste and thus jeopardizing its own future.

The same concern is directly reflected in one of the central issues addressed in this book – in what sense are today's environmental problems really new, and to what extent? Is it mainly a matter of quantity or scale? Or do recent developments also have distinct qualitative features that make them fundamentally different from anything that has happened before?

3

The Holocene: Global Change and Local Response

MARCHANT AND DE VRIES

> Climatic and environmental catastrophes are only catastrophes because human beings and activities are involved. For nature alone, climate changes, floods, earthquakes, volcanic eruptions, etc. are a self-evident part of its dynamic processes.
>
> *Messerli, 2000: 477*

3.1.   Introduction

Nature is change. Geological forces of change are a mixture of slow, constant processes and sudden pulsed events such as earthquakes; such forces have been in operation ever since planet Earth came into being. Their domain, the lithosphere, interacts with the hydrosphere and the atmosphere, each having its own suite of processes. How these processes interact, particularly with human populations, is the focus of this chapter. Let us start at the beginning. As life evolved over the course of time, large parts of the earth's crust became covered with vegetation. The biosphere was born. Animals appeared, which in turn modified the vegetation cover. Natural landscapes developed from the interplay of geological, physico-chemical and biological processes. Then, only recently on the geological clock, the genus *Homo* entered the scene – another step in the unfolding complexity of the earth. With the emergence of cognition, language and culture, the notion of an environment-for-humans got its meaning. The anthroposphere had come into existence. The 'natural' landscape became, as an environment-for-humans, dotted with 'human' imprints, the material remains of which now help us to construct the puzzle of past changes. In addition to these artefacts, numerous symbolic and religious structures were built, some of which are present, others are lost but all are harder to reconstruct than material remains.

There is little doubt that the physical, biological and climatic environment has influenced human populations as civilizations emerged, rose and declined. Transformation processes, increasingly leading to completely human-dominated landscapes, can be collectively referred to as 'environmental change'.[1] This is the subject of recent scientific disciplines such as historical ecology, environmental history or human ecology. This chapter then is about nature and the environment as experienced, and possibly acted upon by human groups during the last 10,000 years. This length of time, forming the most recent geological period of the Holocene, follows the Last Glacial period and encompasses the development of hunter-gatherers, early agriculturists and increasingly sedentary life. These topics can be investigated from many different stances that have developed into rather specialized disciplines with their own empirical concepts, facts, hypotheses and theories. Each of these disciplines – anthropology, archaeology, biology, climatology, ecology, geology, medical and social sciences – contribute pieces to the puzzle of humanity's past and its dynamic interaction with the environment.

Historical analyses have often omitted or played down the role of the variability of the natural environmental, focusing on 'Great Men' and 'Great Events'. This may partly stem from authors being confronted with a lack of data on environmental change. The opposite extreme has invoked 'Great Catastrophes', among them climate change, to explain the discrepancy between the present and an often romanticized glorious past. Such a view of environmental determinism cannot be maintained.

In this book we will be cautious with regard to the early – and some modern – 'cause-and-effect' linkages in whatever guise. They are usually rather an oversimplification.

Fashion in science Digging into the history of science reveals how prevailing worldviews and biased valuations led to 'fashions' in facts, theories and explanations dominating the discourse. 'While today [in the 1970s] it is considered that no lasting climatic changes of any importance have taken place since the last sub-Pluvial (2000–3000 BC), earlier this century it was a common axiom that the Graeco-Roman-Byzantine period, characterized by agricultural expansion into marginal lands and by great economic prosperity, was 'blessed' by bountiful rainfall, a copious water supply and oases in what is now a desert... This hypothesis was chiefly advanced by historians and archaeologists... [many scholars] advancing the view that the desiccation of Eurasia and the decline of civilization were the result of climatic change independent of human agency, and Arab scholars were later to hold the same belief. In fact, these ideas were not new. Classical man had himself looked back to a more humid and floristically richer heroic age... Writings that are more recent adopt the view that aridity has been caused by man. Present-day Mediterranean land managers believe that the landscape decay and general desiccation of the Mediterranean region is not the consequence of adverse climatic changes but a result of man's misuse of the land.' (Thirgood 1981: 21-25)

Apart from the palaeo-environmental evidence of change, the way in which individuals and cultures have perceived and interpreted people's behaviour and environmental change is an essential component of their response and its interpretation (Hassan 2000). As long-term climatic changes are likely to be beyond the reach of social memories, short-term cycles of humidity/aridity – especially dry episodes that lead to food short-ages – are more likely to influence societal perception and hence be impressed upon the memories of several generations (Togola 2000). Furthermore, cultural response may be immediate or delayed depending on the technology, the social organization, the ideology and the nature of the link between those likely to detect environmental change and those likely to take action (Hassan 2000).

Correlating environment and culture by invoking adaptation does not tell us how or why a particular cultural manifestation took place. The argument for environmental causation of cultural changes runs roughly as follows: vegetation changes indicated by climatic changes led to a reduction in the abundance or availability of the resource. This in turn resulted in a shifting attention to other resources, or migration, changes in tech-nology, subsistence strategy, settlement pattern and social and political structural change. Reversing this argument leads us to think that for any adaptive shift there must have been an environmental change to precipitate it – this verges on environmental determinism and fails to take into account other non-environmental variables.

Notwithstanding well-founded doubts over unidirectional 'cause-and-effect' relation-ships between a dynamic environment and human population, in many examples, some presented within this chapter, there is strong synchronicity between archaeo-historical and palaeo-environmental data. In fact, some cultural and socio-economic changes may have been motivated by environmental changes that impacted in a very realistic manner, such as climatic variations leading to shortages, or changes in natural resources. In the search for explanations, one should accept the full complexity of the constraints and opportunities of the physical environment in shaping people's activities, the resulting changes in the physical environment and the subsequent sequences of interactions. Social purpose and cultural concerns may steer a cultural system along a particular path among the many paths which environmental, ecological, demographic, historical and other variables might make available. We will come back to this in subsequent chapters.

In the past few decades, an enormous amount of new data about how the environ-ment and associated phenomena such as vegetation have changed over the Holocene period. These recent findings are based on a combination of established, new and still expanding methods (cf. Chapter 5) applied to locations throughout the world, although with a bias towards Europe and North America. Much of these data now available that have been obtained from sites are summarized as maps of past environments and lost worlds (www.pages-igbp.org).[2] Given this present wealth of data it may be time to take a fresh, new look at our planet's environment, and how this has evolved over the Holocene period.

Volcano eruptions and the course of history   An interesting – and not necessarily false – example of environmental determinism, or rather environmental triggering, is the theory of a huge volcanic eruption in 535 AD that separated Java from Sumatra according to old Javanese scriptures. It is evocatively advocated by Keys in his recent book *Catastrophe* (Keys 1999). Tree rings across the American and Eurasian landmass testify to severe climate change. The eruption caused one or two years of reduced sunlight, leading to a drop in temperature in large parts of the Northern Hemisphere. In its aftermath, history may have experienced crucial political effects. The Eastern Roman Empire and its capital Constantinople suffered from a severe pest epidemic, possibly brought in with the ivory trade from the East African highlands – where a temperature drop could have increased the survival chances of the pest *Bacillus*. The Avars, invincible warriors on horseback in the Mongolian plains, were rather enigmatically beaten by the Turks – was it due to the different responses of horses and cows to severe drought? Those who fled westwards reached the Caucasian and Hungarian steppes where they inflicted great havoc on the Eastern Roman Empire, extracting more than one billion (present-day) dollars equivalent in gold – a second blow to the crumbling empire. The population of the largest city in the Mexican plain, Teotihuacan, with over 125,000 inhabitants, shows a severe decline in health after 540 AD – and recent dating has shifted its decline from the 8th century AD to the second half of the 6th century. A long period of drought in this water-poor region caused famine with subsequent political turmoil. Another lasting effect may have been the breakdown of the large Marib dam in the then mighty state of Jemen. As the productive agriculture declined, the population may have been forced to move northwards – as the plague killed many here, too – which in turn enhanced the importance of Medina and Mecca. Here, Mohammed's family took care of the hungry, which made his message easier to spread – the prelude to the Arab/Islamic outburst? Similarly, could it be that the Celts in western Britain, who still traded with the Romans, were decimated by the plague, which in turn allowed the Anglo-Saxon and Scandinavian peoples to move in? Of course, with so much going on culturally and politically, it is difficult to indicate the role of climate change.

3.2. Holocene climate and climate change

There is growing awareness, in both the scientific and public domain, of the processes of environmental change and their impact on our planet and its human population. Within the all-encompassing environmental change, climate is possibly the dominant factor. Climate is a word used to describe the longer-term characteristics (averages and extremes) of variables such as temperature and precipitation. Until recently, the climate over the Holocene period was considered to have been relatively stable. When compared to those of glacial and interglacial cycles of the Quaternary period, Holocene fluctuations are of relatively low amplitude and 'complicated' by human impacts. Yet the environment was nevertheless variable (*Figure 3.1*). A comprehensive review of global Holocene climate variability is beyond the scope of this chapter. Furthermore, an in-depth explanation of climate variability during the Holocene period is difficult as the causes of climate change are not completely understood despite recent good progress (Perry 2000). We will therefore provide a general overview and focus in more detail on a series of case studies where estimates of important environmental parameters, such as temperature, precipitation, seasonal variation etc., are available over a range of time-scales. One particularly good archive that has become available recently comes from ice cores; these can be used to reconstruct past climate/environment variations in excess of 400,000 years (Petit 1999). By accessing these ice cores, and analysing the composition of the ice and of air bubbles that form a time capsule of the atmospheric composition at the time of deposition, an excellent record of environmental change over long periods of time can be produced (*Figure 3.1*).

Reconstructions of climate and environmental change are based on indirect or 'proxy' records that have several methodological and interpretative limitations, these being best explored within the scientific literature. Although some fragmentary direct records, such as from the Nilometer[3] at Roda, and ancient texts, often associated with monuments, date back several thousands of years, continuous, reliable climate measurements have only recently become available. Over the past century, a host of techniques has been developed to estimate climate variability beyond the reach of these direct measurements. One important suite of commonly applied techniques concentrates on sediments accumulating within ocean, lake, swamp and ice basins (cf. Chapter 5).

However, before we can hope to understand past climate variability we first need to understand the present climate system and some of the spatial variability in this. Climate systems are ultimately driven by the sun's energy, with this being principally redistributed by ocean currents (*Figure 3.2*; see p. 161) that convey weather to the land. The important forces behind climate change are: inherent and forced variability in oceanic processes; solar output and character; volcanic aerosol loading; variations in the earth's orbit; and changes in atmospheric trace gas concentrations, including greenhouse gases. One of the surprising outcomes of the earth's past environmental history has been the growing band of evidence to indicate that the climate changes quickly (Adams 1999): a series of pulses from one steady state to another. This can be exemplified by *Figure 3.1*, the periods of change being shorter than the periods of relatively stability. One of the largest shifts in climate is described by the twenty or so glacial interglacial cycles that characterize the Quaternary period[4] (*Figure 3.1A*). These major pulses of climate change are ultimately driven by the orbital relationship between the earth and the sun that

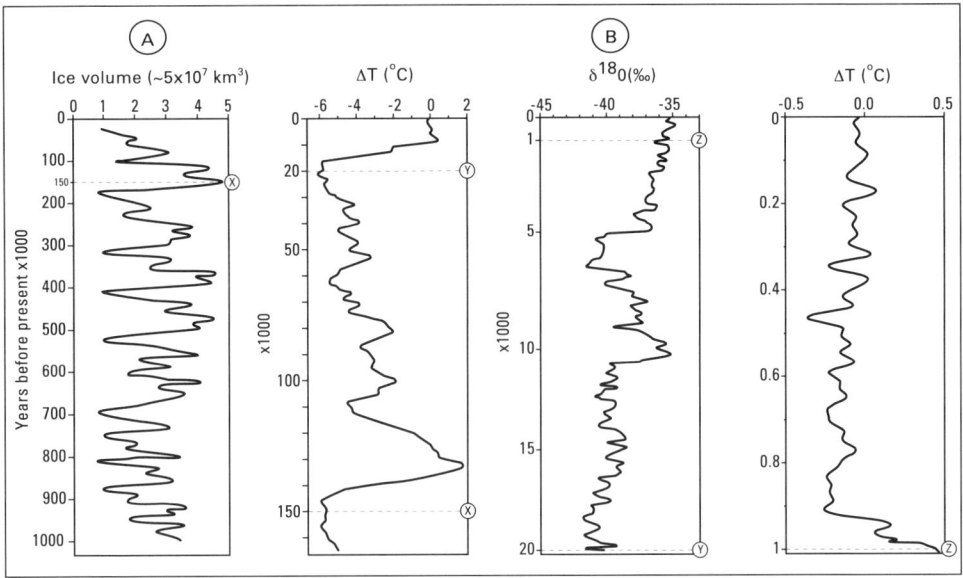

FIGURE 3.1

Climate changes over a variety of time scales during the past million years. The composite figure involves different proxies of environmental change. On curve 'A' a shift to the left equates to a temperature increase, on all other curves a shift to the right equates to a temperature increase.

change on a regular basis. The so-called Milankovitch cycles contain three components: eccentricity, occurring at a 100,000-year periodicity (variations in the earth's orbit that varies from the elliptical to the almost circular), obliquity (variation in the tilt of the earth's axis) operating at a periodicity of 42,000 years, and precession which is the timing of the seasons relative to the earth's elliptical track (near or far from the sun) with a periodicity of between 19,000 and 23,000 years. Although the time scales inherent in these cycles is quite coarse, these do provide a framework to correlate records. The disparity between records from different places indicates less synchronicity in climate change than expected. For example, a change in the El Niño/Southern Oscillation (ENSO) that originates in the Pacific is known to influence a wide belt thorough the tropics but has little influence at temperate latitudes.

The Holocene period is characterized by a global temperature increase following the transition from the last glacial period (*Figure 3.1B*). For much of the earth's surface, early Holocene temperatures were still 2.5-1.5°C lower than at present with relatively high rainfall resulting from increased evaporation over the world's oceans due to rising temperatures and reduced ice cover. There is a growing body of evidence demonstrating major phases of rapid climate change during the early Holocene period. For example, across the Atlantic Ocean, in terms of global landmass and climate the most influential of the world's oceans (Menocal 2000), the terminal collapse of the main northern ice mass (Laurentide ice sheet) near Hudson Bay led to a rapid release of cool, fresh water to the Atlantic and a corresponding sea surface temperature cooling. The maximum rate of cooling occurred about 8000 yr BP[5], in what is termed the 8200-year event. This cool water influx influenced circulation of the Atlantic Ocean and therefore the climate systems that arise from this ocean (*Figure 3.2*). The North Atlantic thermohaline circulation[6] may be from a cycle paced according to a 1500±500-year rhythm with a temperature variation for each oscillation (Broecker 2000). A change in this thermohaline circulation around 8200 yr BP due to freshwater input from the melting Laurentide ice sheet may have been an important trigger for climate, leading to some parts of the African climate to switch abruptly between wet and dry conditions.

These climate changes would, with time delays and spatial differentiation, manifest themselves in changes in vegetation, geomorphological processes, soil formation and all the associated biogeochemical cycles that constitute world ecosystems, i.e. an environmental response. Of all these dynamics, changes in vegetation are possibly the best understood – and one of the most relevant from the point of view of human habitats. The BIOME 6000 initiative has been a recent research project that has produced global biome reconstructions, biomes being large vegetation units such as tropical rainforest, temperate deciduous forest, and tundra, etc. They are based on in excess of 1500 individual sites where radiocarbon-dated pollen data are available (Prentice 1998).

Another way to produce maps of vegetation that reflect past environments is based on vegetation modelling, a procedure in which the potential vegetation in a given area is inferred from climate (notably temperature, precipitation and seasonality), soils and atmospheric data (cf. Chapter 4). These environmental parameters are combined by equations that constrain plant growth. The vegetation reconstructions produced by this modelling approach can be confronted with the vegetation maps produced from pollen data. The combination of these two approaches is an important input for the calibration, verification and improvement of global climate models that can be used to penetrate the future. The resulting discrepancies are often found to arise from local conditions of soil, rainfall patterns and how these are parameterized within the model for plant growth.

These investigations of past biomes show dramatic changes in the composition and distribution of the vegetation. The melting of large ice sheets in Europe made the large Eurasian steppes and the northern lands of Europe and Canada available for habitation. For example, it is thought that migration into North America, from Siberia, was not possible until the Bering land bridge was free of ice. This climatic amelioration allowed the development of vegetation in eastern North America vegetation belts spreading north-

Biomization of pollen: the BIOME 6000 project   A good example for pollen data investigation has developed as part of the Global Palaeo-vegetation Mapping Project (BIOME 6000) (Prentice 1998). This aims to understand changes in the distribution of biomes over recent geological time, and how these changes reflect global climate change. A community-wide collaboration started in 1994 as part of the International Geosphere-Biosphere Program (IGBP). The aims of BIOME 6000 are to create pollen and plant macrofossil data sets for 6000 and 18,000 years ago and construct global maps of biomes for these periods. The technique is based on the sequential calculation of data contained within three matrices that are assigned a priori. These could be used to evaluate climate models and quantify the importance of changes in global plant distribution on the climate system.

The biomization of pollen data has greater utility than just providing a benchmark to validate [climate] model output. Of particular interest, from a vegetation dynamics perspective, is how climate system-biosphere interactions have developed under the rapidly changing environment characteristics of the earth since the last glacial maximum. Biomized pollen data can be used to investigate vegetation dynamics in a range of spatial and temporal scales and to investigate the feedback loops between atmosphere, biosphere and oceanic systems under different conditions of solar activity, human activity, etc.

A good example comes from Colombia. Pollen data were analysed at ten 'time windows' from the present day to 6000 yr BP. At 6000 yr BP the biomes were mainly characteristic of warmer environmental conditions relative to those of the present day. This trend continued until between 4000 and 3000 yr BP when there was a shift to more mesic vegetation that is thought to equate to an increase in precipitation levels. The period between 2500 and 1000 yr BP represents little or no change in biome assignment and is interpreted as a period of environmental stability. The influence attributed to human-induced impact on the vegetation is recorded from 5000 yr BP, but is particularly important from 2000 yr BP. The extent of this impact increases over the late Holocene period and is recorded at increasingly high altitudes.

wards as boreal forests were able to colonize areas previously covered in tundra (see e.g. www.nceas.vcsb.edu and www.soton.ac.uk). In Europe, following the maximum period of temperature reduction of the last glacial period, forests were able to migrate northwards, coniferous forest replacing tundra, broadleaf forest replacing coniferous forest. Broadleaf woodlands were present in the Mediterranean during the last glacial period and, as the climate warmed, these penetrated northwards as the Mediterranean flora that is present today became established (*Figure 3.3*; see p. 162).

The last glacial period, from 22,000 to 13,000 yr BP, was very cold and dry throughout Europe. In addition to the Arctic ice sheet, large ice caps covered the Alps and the Pyrenees. Forest and woodland would have been almost non-existent, except for isolated pockets of woody vegetation in locally damp locations, such as along watercourses and close to the mountain ranges of southern Europe. The majority of the area was characterized by a sparse grassland or semi-desert coverage. Following initial warming, as the ice mass started to melt, some open woodland cover appeared quite rapidly. Within a few hundred years, the steppe vegetation of the area around the Levant Valley was replaced by woodlands, with relatively 'boreal' species such as birch and willow. Typical 'Mediterranean' tree species such as evergreen oaks and pistachio were not common until approximately 8000 yr BP. Following a transition period of gradual tree recolonization, the most heavily wooded conditions of the Holocene occurred between 9000 and 6000 yr BP when the Levant had open woodlands rich in pistachio. These changes in climate and vegetation also provided important opportunities for human settlements. One area where there is a particularly long history of human development is in the Levant Valley where there is considerable evidence for the onset of farming and domestication of early wheat varieties. (*Figure 3.4*; see p. 163). Given the long history of these records, extending beyond 10,000 yr BP, it is almost certain that the environmental response to a warmer and wetter climate would have impacted on the development of plant domestication. In most parts of Europe, however, agriculture was probably still not significant as a modifier of landscape other than on a local scale.

It should be stressed that the beautiful maps shown should be viewed with a sceptical eye and not blind us to the fact that large uncertainties still remain regarding past climate change and the environmental responses. For example, vegetation change was most likely influenced by climate change but increased levels of atmospheric CO_2 are also shown to have been important (Marchant 2002).

The causes and consequences of climate changes are also linked to the local or regional geography, tectonic shifts, rises in sea level and volcanic eruptions. For example, the northward movement of the Indian subcontinent has greatly influenced the dynamics of large rivers over the past 10,000 years in northern India and Pakistan. Although usually more local in origin, these may spread their influence and in this case possibly cause further aridization of north-western China. Another example comes from the alluvial plain of the Euphrates and Tigris river basins (Pollock 2001). This was formed by sediments while the Arabian shield slowly pushed against the Asiatic landmass. The sediments laid down in the plains made the Gulf shoreline shift south-eastwards, possibly some 150–200 kilometres since 6000 yr BP – so the ancient city of Uruk might have been a port. However, it has been argued that the sedimentation process was balanced by the simultaneous subsidence of the Mesopotamian trough and change in sea level. At around 18,000 yr BP the level of the Gulf Sea was approximately 100 metres below the present-day level and 20 metres below this at 8000 yr BP – but about 2 metres *above* at

The earliest settlements New measurements and interpretations indicate that the Holocene period has experienced climatic instabilities, the effects of which were locally specific and sufficiently abrupt, severe and unanticipated to seriously disrupt early human societies. One of the earliest documented examples of societal collapse and adaptation is that of the Natufian communities in southwest Asia about 12,000 yr BP (Weiss 2001). In the process, these populations abandoned low labour–intensive hunting and gathering activities for more labour-intensive plant cultivation and animal husbandry strategies. Recent palaeo-climatic data show that this transition coincided with changes in climate and vegetation from open woodlands and wild cereals to cooler and dryer conditions. As the harvests of wild resources dwindled, the human populations were probably forced to migrate and start intentional cultivation. Population and social complexity may have induced another migration and settlement in the Tigris-Euphrates alluvial plain and delta up to a pulsed climate change.

A similar story can be told for the region west of the Nile valley (Sandweiss 1999). In this area, now desert, cattle herders occupied villages as early as 9000 yr BP when stronger monsoons resulted in relatively wet conditions. These villages were abandoned as aridity increased around 6300 yr BP. At the same time peoples in the Nile valley began to worship cattle and create monuments. Cause or coincidence? Megaliths (2–3 m) forming stone circles and aligned to the sun are found embedded in sedimentary deposits from a former lake in western Central Sahara. The location of the megaliths suggests a spatial awareness and symbolic geometry that integrated death, water and the sun that predates most of the megalithic features of Europe (Malville 1998).

6000 yr BP. Thus, the environmental history of one of these cradles of civilization is still unresolved.

Increasing human impact on the environment during the Holocene period is another complication in palaeo-environmental reconstructions. Signals originating from human- and climate-induced change on the environment can be difficult to separate out from poorly resolved proxy records. As with the synthesis of the information derived from the accumulated sediments, a range of techniques combine to construct a picture of how cultures have changed in their composition and distribution over the Holocene period. In addition, standard archaeological investigations of past occupation layers and the associated artefacts, such as pottery, and recent innovations provide information on past cultures and their relationship with the environment. For instance, starch grains identifiable as manioc (*Manihot esculentia*), yams (*Dioscorea* sp.) and arrowroot (*Maranta arundinacea*) found on milling stones date between 7000 and 5000 yr BP from Panama, indicating ancient and independent emergence of plant domestication in the lowland Neotropical forest (Piperno 2000). Other information on past human activity comes from a range of fingerprints on the present-day ecological composition of vegetation communities. For example, the present vegetation of north-eastern Guatemala is predominantly tropical semi-evergreen forest interspersed with patches of savannah; some researchers believe this patchwork is a relic of past land-use practices by the Maya (Leyden 1987). As with the palaeo-environmental data, evidence for cultural change is riddled with numerous gaps between the living world and the proxy traces.

In spite of all of these shortcomings in methods, portrayal and interpretations, the emerging picture is becoming clearer for more places and periods. As more data become available the mists clear. However, although we have demonstrated the complexity of how the climate system changes in response to external forces and internal dynamics, with added complexity resulting from tectonics, we are beyond the point of discovering our previous ignorance: more scientific enquiry starts to reduce not increase uncertainty. Obviously, there is no easy way of establishing how human groups were influenced by environmental change and, in particular, climate change. In some situations it has been a serious threat, in others it offered new opportunities – and in many situations possibly both, via the processes of adaptation. Let us first look at scientific tales from some regions.

3.3.   Climate change and human populations: Equatorial Africa

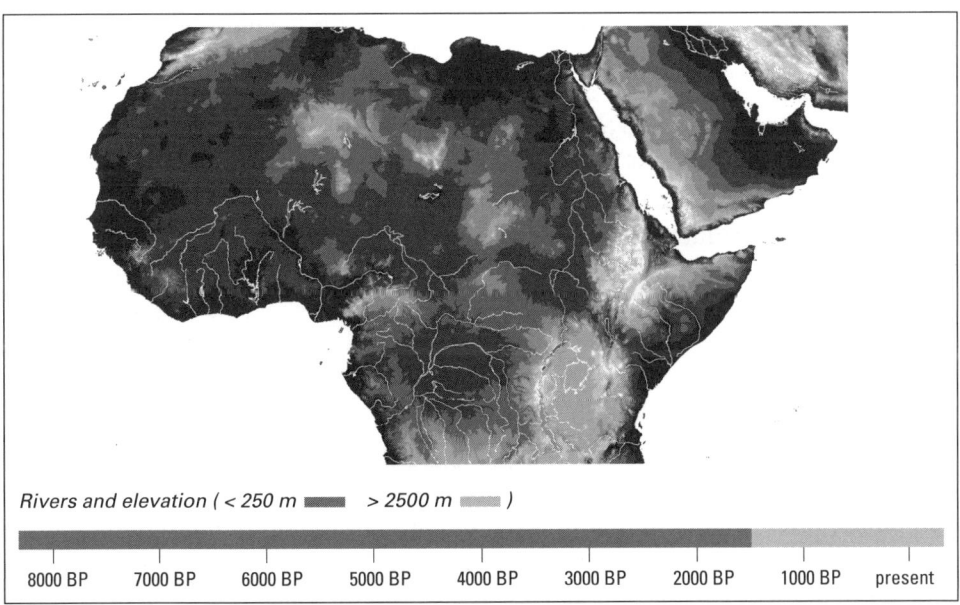

Rivers and elevation (< 250 m ▬▬   > 2500 m ▭▭)

| 8000 BP | 7000 BP | 6000 BP | 5000 BP | 4000 BP | 3000 BP | 2000 BP | 1000 BP | present |

Most paragraphs show a map of the region being discussed, with an indication of the elevation, the major rivers and the period under discussion starting 8500 yr BP.

Africa, the birthplace of humankind, is slowly revealing its cultural and environmental prehistory. A number of archaeological investigations indicate a transgressive development from nomadic, hunter-gatherer populations to food-producing societies that are settled and socially structured. This picture of cultural change is complimented by growing insights in past environmental changes. As such, it is an ideal place to investigate environmental-cultural dynamics over the Holocene period. This section will focus on environmental change for a large area of equatorial and northern Africa (*Figure 3.5;* see p. 164). For this investigation, the Holocene is divided into two main periods: the transition from the Late Glacial towards the middle-Holocene climate 'optimum' of 6000 yr BP; and the transition to a particularly dry period around 4000 yr BP, followed by a number of environmental oscillations combined with increasing vegetation degradation.

3.3.1.   *From the Late Glacial towards the middle-Holocene climatic 'optimum'*

The period around 6000 yr BP is regarded as the mid-Holocene climatic 'optimum'. At this time, the northern boundary of the savannah was shifted some 700 kilometres northwards and in north-eastern Africa closed lakes extended tens to hundreds of metres above their present levels (Gasse 2000). These higher lake levels continued until shortly after 6000 yr BP, although this very broad pattern is quite complex with numerous local exceptions (Street-Perrot 1988). For example, some sites, particularly in the Sahelian area, started to desiccate as early as 8000 yr BP, the main period of aridity being recorded from 7000 yr BP. The composition and distribution of the vegetation at this time reflected this more mesic environment with the expansion of moist vegetation types and associated reduction in the area of vegetation adapted to drought (*Figure 3.5*).

From around 12,000 yr BP humans started to settle in areas that could support the growing populations, which were more or less stable within the given environmental limits. Fishing communities developed near watercourses, such as around a number of permanent lakes within the present-day limits of the Sahara. Rock paintings in the present Sahara depict hippopotamus, elephant and numerous other savannah species, these providing direct evidence of permanent water and catchments characterized by a mesic savannah (*Figure 3.5*). Archaeological evidence indicates a sedentary, non-specialized foraging life style centred close to the water edge of these palaeolakes. The evidence includes finds of a large number of grinding stones and microlithic tools indicating hunting for large prey such as hippopotami and giant buffalo along with smaller savannah game. Fishing appears to have been important, the antiquity of this is most convincingly demonstrated by an 8000-year-old dugout canoe from north-eastern Nigeria, the oldest boat in Africa and one of the oldest in the world (Connah 2001).

The general view is that plant domestication began within the 'fertile crescent' of the Levant Valley of western Asia (*Figure 3.4*). There is on-going debate as to how Africa relates to this domestication. Was there a migration of food production technology or did independent domestication occur? Cattle herding and crop production were present in the Nile Valley, reaching the central Sahara around 9000 yr BP. Archaeological investigations from the Egyptian Sahara have unearthed settled houses with hearths and cooking holes that were occupied about 8000 yr BP. Associated with these are the remains of some 40 plant species (Wendorf 1992). These indicate that the North African plant-food complex developed independently from the Levantine wheat and barley complex. Nevertheless, wheat cultivation was introduced from western Asia, being recorded first around the Nile delta. In the Sudanese lowlands and the Ethiopian Highlands several crops were brought under local domestication, notably sorghum, millet, the banana-like *Ensete* and the oil-yielding noog. Independent agricultural origins in equatorial West Africa appeared much later. The combination of yams and oil palm into an effective system of food production were a prerequisite for life in the humid forest areas; expansion of oil palms is not recorded until after 4000 yr BP. Thus early agriculture has different inception times at different locations, with the domesticated plant types depending on the local environment, which was quite different from the present day at this time. Early in the Holocene period, settlements were established and sedentary populations grew as restrictions on fertility imposed by a mobile life were lifted. Population densities remained low during this period with the associated impact on the extant vegetation being localized and relatively negligible.

Social adaptation among the Mande people (McIntosh 2000a; McIntosh 1988) Nomadic populations have lived in the western part of the Sahara for thousands of years. During the large modal shifts in climate over the last 10,000 years hunters have evolved, according to McIntosh, an elaborate system of myths and symbols to cope with these changes. This allowed them to maintain a kind of heterarchy that provided flexible, responsive adaptations to a mosaic and changing environment. Authority was conveyed to hunters – the Weather Machine – as they gathered secret knowledge about the climate and the rapidly changing environment. The landscape became a grid of nodes of sacrality and information; the important concept was nyama: 'the malign if improperly controlled energy that flows through all animate and inanimate things' (McIntosh, 2000a: 161). Droughts and other unpleasant surprises were seen as signs of perturbations in the flow and nature of nyama. Later, this information and the authority it wielded were transferred to the ironsmiths and, later still, to secular dynasts. It has always remained part of the Mande social memory. In later chapters we will come back to the relationship between the natural environment and the socio-cultural practices and organization of populations.

3.3.2. *Environmental drying about 4000 yr BP and increasing vegetation degradation: the transition to the present*

The mid-Holocene period in much of equatorial of Africa is marked by a relatively abrupt shift toward a drier, more seasonal environment. Lake levels fell sharply (Gasse 2000) and there was an increase of drought-adapted taxa (Elenga 2000). Although this started as early as 8000 yr BP, a particularly strong pulse of aridity is recorded after 4000 yr BP. Several lakes registered minima or completely dried up between 3800 and 1300 yr BP in West Africa (Vincens 1998). In North-west Sudan, reduced precipitation and/or an increased evaporation initiated a shallowing of a lake that continued until approximately 4500 yr BP, at which time the basin was dry (Ritchie 1985). The influx of desert-dust into sedimentary deposits began to increase at other sites in this area about 4700 yr BP, with a permanent rainfall decline after about 4100 yr BP (Street-Perrot 2000). In Central Africa taxa more tolerant of drought appear to have increased in abundance within tropical montane forest after 3800 yr BP (Jolly 1998).

This change in macro-climatic conditions would have impacted on other environmental constraints on the vegetation. For example, it increased the incidence of fire, as detected by an increase in charcoal coinciding with this arid period after 4000 yr BP. The vegetation at this time is shown in *Figure 3.5*. Although the last 4000 years appear to have exhibited much greater climatic variability than the previous period, this may stem from an artefact of sampling resolution and the availability of a wider range of data sources over the most recent geological period (Bonnefille 2000). In northern Nigeria, the relatively arid conditions discussed above were followed by a subsequent wet phase at approximately 1200 yr BP (Holmes 1998). Expansion of moist around Lakes Kitina, Ossa and in the Ngamakala depression at 900, 700 and 500 yr BP all indicate the re-establishment of more humid conditions in western Equatorial Africa during the last millennium (Vincens 1999). Time series records of Nile River discharge, from the Roda gauge near Cairo, identify two distinct epochs of relatively low minima of Nile River levels from 1400 to 1000 and from 650 to 350 yr BP (Fraedrich 1997). In Central Africa, Lake Malawi was at a high level between 1100 and 900 yr BP, and 700 to 500 yr BP, the intervening low stands occurring at 800 and 300 yr BP (Owen 1990). A third phase of increased aridity began around 500 yr BP when there was a major decline in the level of Lake Malawi. Webster (1979) has suggested that these episodes are tied in with famine and drought, although the understanding of the paleological data, chronology and overall interpretations has been questioned. Within the more recent past, within the memory of most people, climatic variations have influenced food production in large parts of Africa.

This period also witnessed a major change in agriculture, organization of settlements and population migration, widely recorded by archaeological sites. The transformation to a pastoral and agricultural economy is thought to be associated with the arrival of people from elsewhere, rather than independent domestication. It is likely that this is part of a general southwards movement of pastoralists from northern and western Africa after 4500 yr BP. This migration may have been facilitated by the expansion of grazing land on the edges of draining lakes and river floodplains as these adjusted to a drying climate. In the area of Africa under review here, one of the main transformations is associated with the migration of populations. One such notable migration is associated with the Bantu from their origin in the grasslands of western Cameroon and Nigeria (*Figure 3.6*; see p. 165). Although there was a general diffusion of Bantu influence, this may have been concentrated along a number of 'migratory pathways' – there is continuing debate as to the timing and direction of these migrations. One appears to follow the Atlantic coastal margins and inland ridges that border the Congolese basin and through the equatorial forest. A second route traverses the southern limit of the southerly expanding Sahara, then goes south down the Nile valley. Whatever the timing and direction of this migration, passage was rapid. The Bantu probably followed river courses, dry ridges within the intervening forest, these not being so dense during this period. From 4400 to 2500 yr BP yam and oil palm spread south and east with the first Bantu migrants, who either replaced, or encompassed, earlier established populations.

On reaching the highlands areas of Central Africa, an interesting focus for settlement of these early populations appear on high ground, as recorded in the Rukiga Highlands (Taylor 1995). Higher altitude sites may have been favoured initially for agriculture because: (a) the land would have been easier to prepare as forest growing on ridge-top locations is less dense than at lower altitudes; (b) the incidence of disease, such as malaria is much less; and (c) the hilltop locations would have offered protection from potentially hostile neighbouring clans or indigenous populations. The interlacustrine region is therefore a contact zone between diverse agricultural traditions as demonstrated by the present diversity of cultivated crops that include millet, bananas, yams and sweet potatoes. These arose from four distinct origin centres: the Sahel, trans-Indian and the latter two on the fringes of the West African forest, respectively. As the population quickly grew during this period, the associated impact on the vegetation was localized, although it would have increased rapidly as livestock levels rose.

A major change that occurred in the Holocene period was the rise in metalworking that has allowed the developing agricultural population to become much more effective in land clearance and subsequent transformation to agricultural land. The spread of iron technology was most likely due to the Bantu, arriving from north-western Africa, although this is under continuing debate. Due to the complexity of the artefacts, Meroe along the upper Nubian Nile is a possible centre of origin for the spread of iron technology throughout sub-Saharan Africa; this was a major centre of iron working with an extensive trade hinterland. Whatever the direction of this import, interlacustrine populations had a sophisticated iron smelting technology by 2500 to 2000 yr BP that has undergone a series of developmental stages. These transitions in metallurgy and pottery style appear to be coeval with a plethora of social, political and economic changes.

Iron and culture   The cultural assimilation of iron technology and agricultural practice should be viewed as more than just simple resource development; there were
important socio-economic connections between the iron smelters/smiths and the
levers of political power (Schoenbrun 1993). Maintenance of power by certain seg-
ments of the population may have been the precursor for the development of organized states such as the major settlement at Ntusi, Uganda, with increased ownership,
stock and defence of pastures with increasing social, political, military and competition
implications (Sutton 1993). The establishment, and maintenance of such sites must
have required the use of organized labour and a transition to a system of governance –
in short a political hierarchy with diversified economies, trade and stronger political
control. However, several of these states declined around 500 yr BP. There is no consensus to explain the abandonment of the earthworks and the rise of the later pre-colonial kingdoms that emerged, such as that of Bunyoro, which were encountered by early
European visitors, although environmental change, disease, slaving, war and famine to
name but a few may have been contributory factors. We will come back to the forces
behind state formation in Chapter 6.

3.4.   Early human-environment interactions: the Americas

In Latin America, as in Africa, the Holocene period is marked by significant phases of
environmental change, these being documented by a developed network of archaeological and palaeo-environmental records. However, these changes differ in direction and
magnitude as the area is under the influence of different climate systems (*Figure 3.2*). We
will now investigate cultural and environmental changes in two regions: coastal Peru and
the Maya lowlands.

3.4.1.   *Environmental and cultural change in western Peru*

Our first focus is on Peru in the northern part of the Andes (*Figure 3.7*; see p. 166).
Although radiocarbon dating of past occupation layers from the western flanks of the
Peruvian Andes indicate inhabitation in excess of 20,000 years ago, these are highly controversial. A more reliable set of dates indicates human occupation back to 12,000 yr BP
with several of these sites concentrated in the lowlands. For example, the archaeological
site of Quebrada Tacahuay (Peru) dates to 10,770 yr BP and contains some of the oldest
evidence of maritime-based economic activity in the New World concentrating primarily on seabirds and fish (Aldenderfer 1999). Rising sea levels recorded thorough the
Holocene would have had direct implications for the use of marine resources. While it

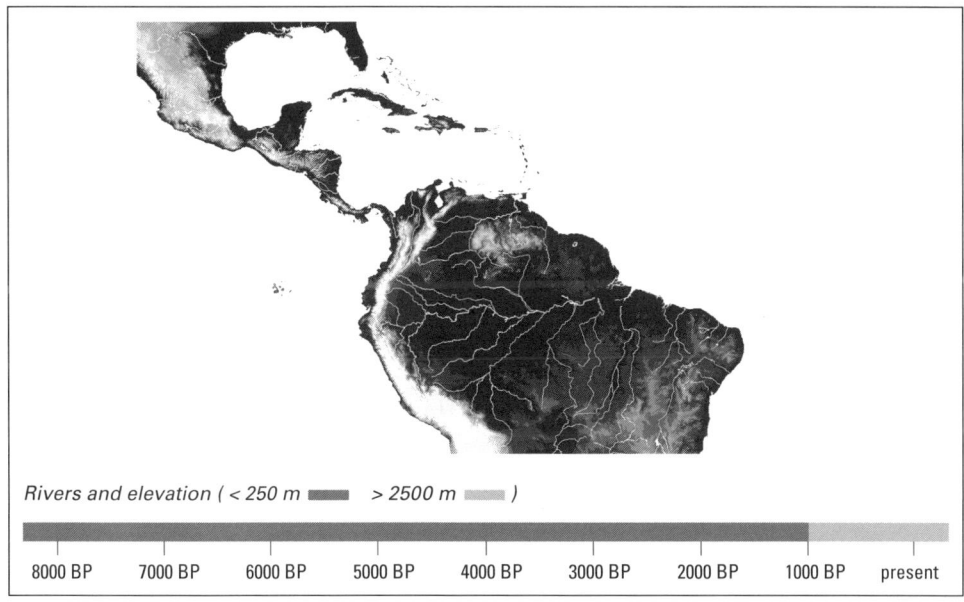

Rivers and elevation (< 250 m ▬▬ > 2500 m ▬▬)

8000 BP   7000 BP   6000 BP   5000 BP   4000 BP   3000 BP   2000 BP   1000 BP   present

was relatively moist in Northern Africa, with the green Sahara, in north-western South America a significant drop (60 m) in the water level of Lake Titicaca occurred from 9000 to 6800 yr BP (Cross 2000) attesting a dry climate (Hansen 1994). Oxygen isotope measurements from an ice core located in highland Peru suggest maximum climatic aridity from 6500 to 5200 yr BP (Thompson 1995).

One of the main climatic variables to impact on the Peruvian resource base, particularly on the Pacific coast, is an increase in ENSO activity. This important oceanic current, which has very tangible impacts on the climate of South America as well as in other areas of the globe, only appears to have been active since approximately 7000 yr BP. A particularly strong period of ENSO activity, likely to be recognizable by Peruvian pre-Inca societies, has been dated to between 3300 and 2300 yr BP. Another series of disastrous El Niño events, which would have caused heavy rains in Peru, happened around 950 yr BP (Chepstow-Lusty 1996). As today there would have been consequential effects of this ENSO activity on the biological food chains in the Peruvian cold current, and disturbances to in-shore fishing communities (Manzanilla 1997).

For example, ENSO events significantly reduce mollusc populations in coastal Peru (Moore 1991), and may have encouraged cultural connections with highland locations. Indeed, Peru was characterized by a wide range of economies, from the hunter-gatherers and pastoralists of montane areas to increased sophisticated agricultural communities. Small indigenous societies are likely to have been involved in minor food production and/or trade with large food-producing societies (Headland 1989). This trade is partly indicated by finds of obsidian from a near-shore environment. These tools came from highland sources some 130 kilometres inland indicating that people either travelled to the highlands themselves or traded with people who did (Sandweiss 1999). A possible stimulus for the growth of trade between maritime hunting and gathering communities to those operating inland and vice versa may have been a sudden disruption of the population/resource balance. Such a perturbation is suggested for coastal Peru where the Humbolt Current yields an extremely resource-rich coastline except during El Niño events (Yesner 1980). The people taking advantage of such a rich resource would have to develop some kind of device to get over a decline in food availability.

As such a variable environment places a premium on the mobility and diversity of resources, and the development of secondary subsistence modes such as connections between Andean and coastal dwellers are likely to have a long history. However, connections cannot just be confined to times of food shortage and it is likely that an exchange of goods developed, including food and locally available goods such as obsidian. For example, Camelid meat from pastoral communities living at high altitude was transportable following preservation by drying into strips called Ch'arki (Stahl 1999). The relationship between these two groups is unlikely to have been solely concerned with food; it is likely there was a myriad of connections at the material, social and spiritual level (cf. Section 3.5). Thus, between 8000 and 3600 yr BP arid conditions prevailed and humans occupied 'ecological refuges' where resources and especially flowing water were locally available in a generally very hostile environment. Thereafter, more complex societies emerged with a diverse lithic industry, domestication (from 4800 yr BP), semi-sedentary agriculture with terracing and channel irrigation (from 3100 yr BP). Although the rate of technological innovation seems rather high during this time of environmental stress, the extent to which the prevailing environmental conditions constituted a trigger for domestication remains debatable. The nature of these connections can only be inferred as these aspects of former cultures are not readily preserved within the archaeological record and modern analogues are not present.

3.4.2.   *Late-Holocene environmental and Mayan cultures*

One of the most startling connections, or coincidences, between a changing environment and culture comes from the Guatemalan lowlands of the Yucatán peninsular, the area of Mayan settlement (*Figure 3.8*; see p. 167). The Mayan occupation stems from about 2000 yr BP with the Classical period lasting from 1750 to 1150 yr BP culminating in a large and highly developed culture that collapsed in a relatively short time, spanning some 50 to 100 years (Leyden, 1987). Throughout the Classical period, slow but exponential growth led to large settlements that then underwent expansion into the less fertile Yucatán Peninsular (Hsu 2000; *Figure 3.8*). Associated with this growth was widespread anthropogenic deforestation occurring between about 2000 and 950 yr BP.

Many reconstructions of the collapse of the Classical Maya political, social and economic systems around 1050 cal AD[7] emphasis anthropogenically induced failure (Santley 1986). Others suggest the collapse was not so catastrophic and the magnitude of population decline not uniform throughout the Mayan region (Rice 1984). The debate as to the nature and duration of the catalyst that precipitated the rapid population decline continues to rage on, this is partly driven as responses appear different in different locations. Palaeological and geological evidence from the Yucatán and the wider area indicate a dry period about 1000 and 500 yr BP (Hodell 1995). Coincident with a shift to a drier environment was the cultural collapse of the extensive Mayan civilization around 1100 ^{14}C yr BP. A series of strong El Niño years around 1050 cal AD resulted in relatively dry environmental conditions in the area inhabited by the Maya. This event may also have been coincident with a period of increased solar activity as part of a 208-year cyclical variation in solar activity. Within the Yucatán peninsula where the ambient environment is already xeric, this appears coincident, and possibly precipitative, of the cultural collapse of the Maya about 900 cal AD (Hodell 1995). However, such a model cannot be applied throughout the area. Environmental stress centred within the Yucatán peninsular may have induced migration and possible political tensions in areas to the south. Indeed, severe soil loss appears to have occurred within the Peten Lakes region to the north. In the Petexbatún areas, where effective land-use management such as terracing was able to prevent widespread erosion, soil loss appears relatively minimal (Beach 1994).

3.5. The Vera basin in Spain: 10,000 years of environmental history[8]

The Mediterranean Basin is the birthplace of many ancient civilizations; in this fourth and last case we will take a closer look at the environmental history of the Vera Basin in south-eastern Spain. As with the previous case studies, climate change has also occurred in the Mediterranean. Some 6000 years ago, winter temperatures were 2-4°C less than at present whereas the water availability was significantly higher than at present (Cheddadi 1997). Recent data from northern Mesopotamia indicate a synchronous warming of exceptional duration in a region controlled by Mediterranean circulation (Leeuw 1998). In the Vera basin a significant destructuration – with loss of permeability – of soil systems occurred around 4200 yr BP in response to an abrupt change in climate. The period was characterized by significant warming, heavy rainfall and strong winds that led to disorganization of the overall landscape.

The environmental history of the Vera Basin indicates oscillations of intense human activity apparently followed by some environmental crisis, after which reoccupation with changed exploitation techniques occurred (*Figure 3.9*). The perceptions of people, and the social and political institutions that guided them, were found to be crucial ele-

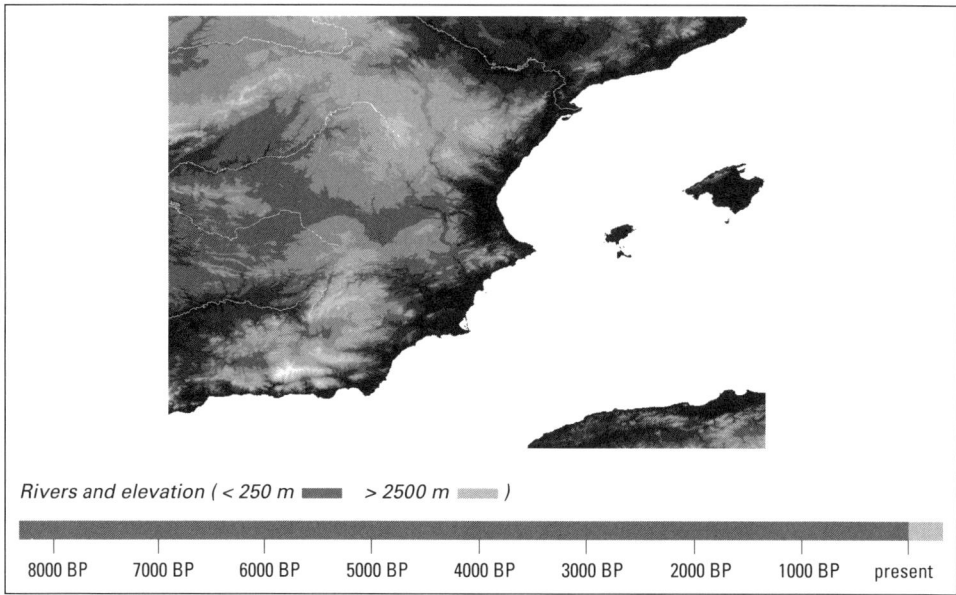

Rivers and elevation (< 250 m ▰▰▰▰   > 2500 m ▨▨▨)

| 8000 BP | 7000 BP | 6000 BP | 5000 BP | 4000 BP | 3000 BP | 2000 BP | 1000 BP | present |

ments in this dynamic. There is evidence of at least four major phases of human occupation and desertion since about 6000 yr BP, occurring on different time-scales. This evidence comes from human settlement remains and burials on the one hand and from environmental data such as hydro-carbonate isotopes, soil micromorphology, pollen cores, charred wood and seeds, and ancient molluscs on the other (Castro 1995; Fedoroff 1995; Leeuw 1998). The two datasets at our disposal indicate the regional socio-environmental history from different perspectives. These data served to reconstruct a general history of the area and to determine the spatial scale of the various phenomena observed. In short, the valley is the meeting point of three fault systems and must have been tectonically active over the period of human occupation. Micromorphological research seems to indicate that until about 10,000 yr BP, a process of deposition of Aeolian sediment continued (Fedoroff 1995). After that date, there seems to have been a phase of approximate stability or very slow erosion of the landscape until about 6000-5000 yr BP. There is some micromorphologica and geological evidence to argue that, at that point in time, degradation accelerated considerably in a process that must be held responsible for the badlands that now make up much of the basin, as well as for the sedimentation of the valley bottom.

Around 6000-5000 yr BP there are traces of the first human incursions into the area. The remains are scant, and do not show any preferential localization. Human activity increases rather rapidly from around 5000 yr BP: people increase in number and the first signs of social and spatial differentiation manifest themselves, with a preference for settlements on fluvisols where the gallery woodland seems to have been cleared. On such soils, settlements are far from evenly spread. Subsistence seems to have been based on mixed farming and animal husbandry. There is some evidence that in sites farther inland, occupation was discontinuous with several breaks in human occupation.

Between 4300 and 3600 yr BP alongside the settlements on the valley floor, which show evidence of continuing cultivation with ample water, we now find settlements higher up the slopes *around* the central valleys. These were not situated on the best agricultural land, hence flocks of sheep and goats must have been an important part of the subsistence economy as they are able to feed on poor quality grazing. From the nature of these settlements, and from the wealth of archaeological finds in the tombs, one must conclude that the area was relatively wealthy at that time. The period shows marked contrasts in social organization with the previous one. Settlement occupation seems to have been continuous. There is clear evidence that the settlements specialize in particular kinds of craft production and that they are part of a regional exchange network with supra-regional contacts. Towards 3800 yr BP, there is a shift towards barley-based monocrop agriculture, general deforestation and desiccation of the valleys. These changes are more easily explained by overexploitation than by climate change.

This was followed by a period of relative desertion (3600-2700 yr BP) of the area and abandonment of many settlements. This begins with a general depopulation of the high-

FIGURE 3.9

Demographic trajectory of the Vera Basin from neolithic times until today (Source: Leeuw 1998)

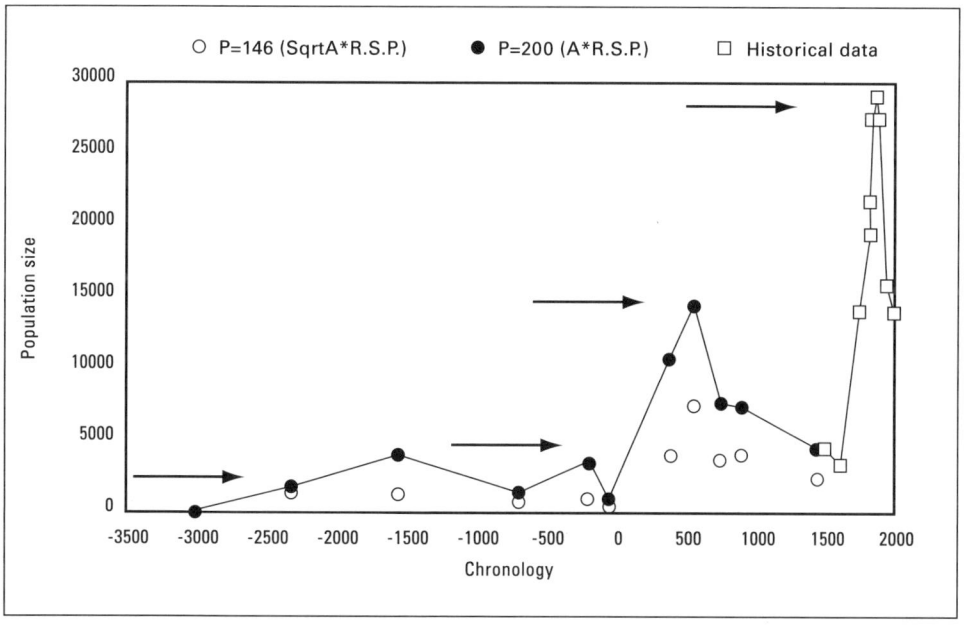

lands that is virtually complete by 3200 yr BP. At that time, only small, dispersed settlements remain in the lowlands. Although the evidence is scarce, it seems that there also was a reduction in the level of socio-economic differentiation and structure, with few people remaining in the highland settlements building the first terraces. The population relies increasingly on a diversity of cultivation strategies and crops. It is at this time – much later than elsewhere – that olive and vine are introduced. Deciduous forest, present in the last period, disappears completely. From 3400 yr BP we observe an increase in shrubs and weeds being used for fuel, which also points to a general scarcity of wood.

In the period 2700 to 2200 yr BP the move is again towards (rapid) population increase and population concentration in larger settlements (at the foothills). By about 2400 yr BP the population concentration is at its peak and is notably located near the coast. The intensity of occupation in these areas surpasses anything the region had previously seen. Social complexity increases, as evidenced by the level of individual inhabitants in cemeteries and settlement differentiation. The economic base also changes, with considerable mining; very quickly, this causes fuel shortages. Dependency on exchange increases and also the export of raw materials. In the charcoal remains, riverine wood species are absent and palms are present. Erosion seems to have been considerable.

After 200 BC a short period of depopulation is observed, followed by the introduction of a spatially and technically different exploitation system by the Romans. We now see many isolated, continuously and intensively occupied farms in the lowlands, which develop into centres for large landholdings exploiting the area for export and applying new technology. The intensity of human occupation exceeds, again, that of earlier periods. Irrigation was probably widespread. Towards 400 AD, this socio-economic fabric collapses; some people move back into the hills. Mining is on the rise, but subsistence production shifts back into a local mode, with diversified dry-land agriculture. The same is true for pottery production. There is some evidence in the coastal settlements for importation of wheat, possibly indicating local overexploitation.

By 750 AD the Arabic conquests introduce another clear change in occupation pattern, introducing the widespread use of irrigated terracing as part of a move of the population land inwards onto the slopes. These are better managed, which improves the balance of the whole region. In the historical evidence there is little sign of a differentiated population: the landholdings are all of about the same (small) size. The local climate seems to be drier, as judged from the vegetation, but surface water management much better. Cultivation is multi-crop, with horticulture alongside cereals and considerable acreages of tree plantations, notably mulberry for silk production. The area as a whole may be said to be heavily, but stably exploited (Leeuw 1998).

Expulsion of the Muslim population by the Christians at the end of the 15th century – and showing up in the first population count since, around 1550 AD – resulted in a rapid decline of the population, with the loss of more than one third in 40 years. Nevertheless, we have evidence of repeated clamour for more land to be released by the state for private use. The landholding system changed: accumulation of land in the hands of the few became possible, leading to considerable pressure in some areas. Depopulation of, notably, the mountain regions of the basin was followed by the collapse of irrigation systems and terraces, initiating major erosion. This prevented the regeneration of wood-land on the higher slopes and started badlands formation. The replacement of mulber-ries by olives along the banks of the rivers indicates – and caused – deterioration of the local hydrological regime. Everything points to the movement of vast quantities of soil,

---

Mediterranean Mountains and the use of the land Latorre (1999) has done inter-esting research into land use in Spain; we present here parts of his abstract. Sierra de Filabres is a semi-arid mountain range in south-eastern Spain, next to the desert of Tabernas and near the Vera Basin. Its highest summits are around 2200 metres. The very irregular precipitation ranges from 300 to 450 mm per year. Old abandoned ter-races cover the mountains from the lowlands to the higher tops. Nowadays Sierra de Filabres is almost totally deforested. However, Spanish place-names referring to ever-green oak, pine, cork oak and strawberry-tree forests, as well as to forest animals such as bear, and deer show that the landscape has changed dramatically since the first Spanish-speaking peasants arrived here around 1580.

In the last thousand years this mountain range has been exploited and shaped by two different societies. During the Middle Ages Muslim peasant communities, organ-ized in a tribal egalitarian structure, developed an intensive agriculture that produced fruits, vegetables and dry fruits in small irrigated plots. They produced perishable prod-ucts that could not easily become the foundation of a typical feudal structure because they are difficult to store. Expansion of irrigated crops was limited by the available water resources. Although dry-farming cultivation of cereals was possible, over 90% of the land remained uncultivated. As a consequence of a land-use system that reflected a social structure, forest ecosystems still covered the mountain range by the time when the Muslims, were expelled in the 16th century.

The newcomers from the north, Christian peasants and landlords, developed a new kind of social relationship and a new land-use system based on the cultivation of dry-farming cereals. As happened quite often with colonists (cf. Chapter 10), the newcom-ers brought their own agricultural and cultural practices with them – which sometimes caused disaster from a mismatch between old perception and new reality. In the semi-arid environment of the Sierra de Filabres, the yields of dry-farming cereals were very low and the peasants tried to compensate this by cultivating more land. Over 300 years cultivated surface increased more than 400%. Forests and forest fauna disappeared and enormous soil erosion took place. Some small forest remains can still be found, with place names referring to forests.

---

causing the coast to extend and depositing, according to one estimate, as much soil in the last 500 years as in the whole of the Holocene period. At the same time, the hydrological research indicates a considerable increase in evapotranspiration from about 400 years ago, possibly pointing to the loss of vegetation cover that is concomitant with such erosion (Leeuw, 1998).

A mining boom in the 19th century caused a brief interruption, by forcing reoccupation of much of the area in order to provide the means to maintain the miners. A new dispersed agricultural settlement pattern sprang up over the whole basin, with terracing and irrigation in the highlands. The difference with the Arabic period is, of course, that this time the investment needed for such terracing was only viable in view of the mining, rather than the agricultural production. The main consequence for the lowlands was increased salinization, and for the highlands total and complete deforestation. As the boom ended, emigration towards the towns initiated erosion once more.

3.6.   Conclusions

Changes in human population and their activities in synchrony with environmental change should not be interpreted in terms of single, unilateral cause-and -effect relations. The interactions were already more complex at an early stage. On closer inspection and with recent insights, the Holocene environment was less stable than had been thought. We should not be surprised to discover influences from climate and vegetation change upon human populations throughout the Holocene period, including their responses and adaptations. In Africa there once was a green Sahara with large animals and hunters. Later, large migrations took place that may have been triggered by environmental change. In South America the variable environment, partly due to the specific ENSO event, stimulated mobility and resource diversity. The environmental history of the Maya in Yucatán and of the Vera Basin in Spain shows clear evidence of environmental feedback loops upon human populations and their organization and wealth – but not in a simple way and with different dynamics at work in different places and at different times.

4

Environment and the Great Transition: Agrarianization

DE VRIES AND MARCHANT

> The next step is to come together in larger numbers, which will increase the size of the communities, and turn to agriculture. This will be at first practiced in the skirts of the hill country; dry fences of a kind will be contrived as walls for defense against savage beasts, and a new and larger single homestead thus erected for the community.
>
> *Plato's Laws Third Book*

4.1.   Introduction

Human-induced modification of the environment started with the use of fire, much earlier than any form of agriculture. Fire opened up the land for hunting and early forms of horticulture and agriculture and pastoralism. The subsequent process of agrarianization has already been described in Chapter 2. The agrarian regime saw a series of tools and practices, including the adaptation of new crops and the domestication of animals. Animal domestication and a more sedentary existence influenced population growth. Parts of the natural environment – good soil, sources of water and wood, mineral deposits – became a 'resource'. New forms of social organization came into existence. Pockets of natural landscapes became dominated by humans as control over the natural environment increased. With populations growing in size, other human groups became the largest adversary and hunting tools and domesticated animals became increasingly also weapons of war, conquest and suppression. More peaceful ways of exchange intensified too: trade.

One of the most immediate and important aspects of the natural environment is the provision of food. Food is the human-environment interaction *par excellence*. As the environment with its geography, climate, water, soils and vegetation is the key factor in the supply of food, the focus on the emergence and forms of agriculture is natural in the present context. There are still many open questions (Messerli 2000; Walker 1993; Gunn 2000; Diamond 1997). Are there favourite sites for human societies to evolve – ecotones, interlocks of environmental zones such as hill-plain areas or river basins at medium elevation? Which factors made certain environments feasible and attractive for human habitation? How did agricultural cropping, animal herding and the use of trees for wood and fodder start – as a response to deteriorating conditions for a gathering-hunting way

---

Microbial life and human populations: the role of diseases[1] Human beings were – and are – to a large degree at the mercy of the age-old microbial inhabitants and have always lived in a complicated interaction with the microbial world. Micro-organisms caused various kinds of infectious diseases: diseases such as cholera and dysentery via food and excreta (faeco-oral), parasitic infections such as bilharzia, and respiratory infections such as diphtheria, tuberculosis and meningitis. All three and the latter in particular tend to have a higher incidence in crowded situations; hygiene and sanitation practices are the most important factors. Man has shown the ability to spread to extremely different environments, adapting to the new habitats as far as his genome permitted. The microbial world threatened his health – is there a relationship with the landscapes?

The tropical forests have always been a rich storehouse full of parasites and micro-organisms of an often vehement virulence. Until recently their large disease pressure kept the population at bay. Many illnesses there are caused by arthropods, such as malaria, yellow fever, dengue, filariasis, onchocerciasis (river blindness) and leishmaniasis. Diarrhoeal diseases such as typhoid and amoebiasis also thrive there, as do tuberculosis and leprosy. Fungi have a reasonable chance in the moist conditions.

The savannahs are an environment favouring Guinea worm infections and trypanosomiasis (sleeping disease). We do not know how old Lyme's disease is, but high grass and deer form a perfect combination for its spread. Mountains mean a decrease of exposure to arthropods that bring malaria, yellow fever or dengue. But altitude sickness and blindness due to cataracts – caused by intense UV light – are new dangers as well as goitre from iodine deficiency – which is rare on sea coasts. Parasites such as giardia can dwell in high regions.

The moderate and cold climate zones offer many micro-organisms an unfavourable environment outside their hosts and victims. This seems to be the main reason why many germs there developed a moderate virulence, since killing off their host too eagerly would mean an ineffective spread. As a result, evolution favoured forms that were less virulent than their like in the tropics. Microbial pressure may have been less in these regions to some degree, but disadvantages were present in the form of cold, food shortages and (vitamin) deficiencies, e.g. scurvy.

of life or simply, in some locations, as a more rewarding alternative strategy, or even both? Did the first farmers clearing 'pristine' forests, for crops, wood and fodder, result in more widespread environmental change? Are there traces of environmental feedback as a consequence of these forms of human interference with natural processes? In the previous chapter, the various stories have already indicated parts of the answer. In this chapter we take a more general approach to these questions. We do not claim our treatment to be complete. It merely probes deeper into facts and forces behind the second major transition process after the control of fire: agrarianization.

4.2.   Environment and human habitat

In the 1960s and 1970s the British anthropologist John Reader travelled widely among a variety of cultures and habitats in the world. His amazing account *Man on Earth: A Celebration of Mankind* (1988) is intended to show the fundamentals of human ecology. It describes peoples who have each found their own way of living in their particular environment: islanders, slash-and-burn agriculturists, pastoralists, nomads, fishermen, hunter gatherers and modern-day farmers. He concluded:

> All mankind shares a unique ability to adapt to circumstances and resolve the problems of survival. It was this talent that carried successive generations of people into many niches of environmental opportunity that the world has to offer – from forest, to grassland, desert, seashore and icecap. And in each case, people developed ways of life appropriate to the particular habitats and circumstances they encountered... Farming, fishing, hunting, herding and technology are all expressions of the adaptive talent that has sustained mankind thusfar. (Reader 1988: 7-8)

This perspective on human ingenuity in the face of environmental change may be incomplete: it is a synchronic view of small-scale, only partially isolated systems. There is vivid evidence of the inability of larger human groups to sustain more complex arrangements amongst each other and with their environment, although this may have had as much to do with social as environmental constraints (cf. Chapter 6). Yet it is amazing how the species *Homo sapiens* has succeeded in using and stretching the opportunities of a huge variety of natural environments.

As indicated in the previous chapter one problem in palaeo-research on vegetation is distinguishing between natural and human-induced situations. There is ample evidence that human groups have changed the natural landscape from the Early Holocene on and even before (cf. Chapters 2 and 3). However, the human habitat was still largely determined by climate, vegetation and geography in these first stages. Obviously, wherever peoples moved in, the environment – its mountains, hills, valleys and rivers, forests and

Human habitats: the Ethiopian Highlands In his book African Civilizations, Connah gives a description of the Ethiopian Highlands that illustrates the many aspects that affect the potential for human habitation (Connah 2001). The heartland of old Ethiopia is a huge area of mountains which compared with the surrounding dry, hot plains, offer a range of relatively attractive environments. Altitude is a major determinant of climate and vegetation: a temperate climate above 2400 metres, a subtropical climate between 1800 and 2400 metres, and a tropical climate with average temperatures of 26 °C and over below 1800 metres. Seasonality is mainly determined by rainfall variation with altering wet and dry seasons. The large variation in climate, even across short distances, is in turn responsible for a large variation in vegetation.

The combination of environmental diversity and fertile soils allowed multi-cropping and a wide range of crops. The large seasonal and altitudinal variation provided good opportunities for pastoralists and agriculturists. A variety of livestock emerged: cattle, sheep, goats, oxen, horses, asses and mules. Their prospects even improved due to deforestation by humans, causing much of the high plateaus to be covered with short grass which provides excellent grazing. Other resources were the variety of animals, minerals such as gold and iron ore, good building stone and, until a few centuries ago, abundant timber. With the nearby Red Sea at its narrowest, this resource abundance gave good trading opportunities with southern Arabia.

There were also obstacles. The plateau was inhabited by many other species that could make life for humans quite unhealthy and risky. Several infectious diseases were present and occasional epidemics swept the region with great severity. Swarms of mice, troops of monkeys, massive locust invasions or extremes of high rainfall or temperature, or both at once, caused a periodic recurrence of famine. The high and open plateau is exposed to wind, making it prone to erosion, and large parts are rocky and obstructed by gorges, hampering communication. Such was the environment in which one of the early African states, Aksum, came to flourish some 2000 years ago.

coasts – has forced them in certain directions. A recurring theme in this research is the importance of gradients in the landscape: in elevation, climate variables, vegetation – and population density. Another element, proposed with great persuasion by Diamond (1997), is the existence of natural corridors along which peoples and their cultural traits could move. Trading routes are one of the important crystallizations of such interactions (cf. Chapter 6). On the other hand, we have to be wary of environmental determinism. As discussed in the previous chapter, scientific evidence in no way always supports explanations of human group dynamics on the basis of environmental change – such as climate change and tectonic activity. Even if the event and the change in the environment have correctly been inferred, dynamic mechanisms proposed on the basis of corre-

Landscape and symbol   Le symbolisme de la montagne est multiple: il tient de la hauteur et du centre. [Elle] est ainsi rencontre du ciel et de la terre. La colline est la première manifestation de la création du monde... elle marque le début d'une émergence et de la différenciation. La plaine est le symbole de l'espace, de l'illimité terrestre. Le symbolisme du fleuve, de l'écoulement des eaux, est à la fois celui de la possibilité universelle et celui de l'écoulement des formes, celui de la fertilité, de la mort et du renouvellement. [La mer est] le symbole de la dynamique de la vie – tout sort de la mer et tout y retourne: lieu des naissances, des transformations et des renaissances. En diverses régions, notamment chez les Celtes, la forêt constituait un véritable sanctuaire à l'état de nature; en Inde, les sannyâsâ se retirent dans la forêt, de même que les ascètes bouddhiques.

Jean Chevalier et Alain Gheerbrant, Dictionnaire des symboles (1997)

lation should be considered with caution. A similar caveat holds for straightforward explanations of socio-political complexity from biogeographical features such as hills, rivers, soils or vegetation.

In the first stages of agricultural development, the geography of a habitat has surely been an important determinant – 'geography is destiny' – but not in simple ways. Here we confine ourselves to rather general associations that have been made between landscapes and cultures. A more in-depth study would have to delve into the insights from economic and cultural anthropology; while the latter are touched upon in subsequent chapters, the former are briefly considered in this chapter.

Vegetation, as a reflection of climate and geography, is a good indicator of the human habitat because it is an important intermediate variable in the provision of food. Using environmental, mostly climate, parameters, 'potential vegetation' maps have been constructed which give a first, crude impression of the human habitat.[2] *Figure 4.1* (see p. 168) shows such a vegetation map for the climate in the early 1990s. It is largely based on satellite data; for agricultural land cover a conversion to potential vegetation has been made on the basis of the BIOME model. This map shows present vegetation and as such is of limited use for insights into mid-Holocene and earlier vegetation. Yet it gives an indication of the potential human habitat.

4.2.1.   *Mountains, hills and plains*

More than 46% of the earth's landmass is elevated 600 metres or more above the present sea level. In the early development stages higher altitude sites have advantages for agriculture: the land would have been easier to prepare as forest growing on ridge-top locations is less dense than at lower altitudes; the incidence of disease, such as malaria is much lower; and the hill-top locations would have offered protection from potentially hostile neighbouring clans. In fact, most if not all of the early forms of agriculture developed in the hills and valleys around the large mountain ridges. Outstanding examples are the Iranian Plateau and its edges with traces of farming 6000-12,000 yr BP and the hilly regions in northern China and Central America. In the discussion on the origins of agriculture, the Russian biologist Vavilov argued as early as 1926 that the centres of varietal diversity, and origin, of cultivated plants were to be found in mountainous regions (Harris 1996). His theory has been modified and refined since, distinguishing for instance between centres of crop origin and regions of crop diversity – but the association with mountainous regions still holds.

Coming down from the mountains and hills, the human habitat expanded: hunting the wild animals, clearing the forests, filling up the swamps, learning to use the river for transport and successfully fighting the disease-bringing insects – many steps had to be

The hills and the plains   A possible account of the Sumerian civilization reminds us of biblical Cain and Abel: 'The creation of an artificial landscape in the southern plain, with the elaborate irrigation systems needed to sustain city civilization, made the Sumerians particularly vulnerable to outside attack. This has been one of the key factors in their history... Hill peoples against peoples of the plain; nomads against sedentary farmers: these are two of the more ancient confrontations in human history.' (Wood 1999: 14)

Braudel has suggested a similar antagonism between the mountains and the plains: '... if social archaisms persisted, it was above all for the simple reason that mountains are mountains: that is, primarily an obstacle, and therefore also a refuge, a land of the free. For there men can live out of reach of the pressures and tyrannies of civilisation: its social and political order, its monetary economy... In fact, no Mediterranean region is without large numbers of mountain dwellers who are indispensable to the life of towns and plains... mountain life seems to have been the first kind of life in the Mediterranean whose civilisation ...barely disguises its pastoral origins... Why was this? Perhaps because of the varied distribution of mountain resources, and also because the plains were originally a land of stagnant waters and malaria, or zones through which the unstable river beds passed.' (Braudel 1947: 51-52) Of course, equally often symbiosis may have existed – as in the case of preferential trade relations between inhabitants of the mountains with particular families in the plains in the Philippines and Arabia.

76

taken. Water often turned out to be an attractor. Rivers and lakes on earth occupy an area of about 1.8% of the surface of the landmass; the area of their drainage basins is at least ten times as large.

4.2.2.   Rivers, lakes and coasts – and the sea

Rivers and lakes in the landscape have many functions: as a source of water and food, a medium for transport and trade, a natural boundary for either unity or separation. 'All four great civilizations of the Old World arose on rivers, all of them in a narrow band around 30 degrees latitude in the temperate zone of the northern hemisphere… In their character they may have differed widely. But in the material basis of their development, they shared very similar conditions and similar concerns.' (Wood 1999: 15). The observation that the large, ancient civilizations originated in the great river plains of the world has led some authors to posit universal theories. Wittfogel called them 'hydraulic civilizations' in his book Oriental Despotism (1957); Mezhenev suggested that civilizations move from river-oriented (Egypt, Indus) to sea coast-oriented (Greek) to ocean-oriented (Portuguese, British). Such sweeping generalizations may be unwarranted and suggest a false causality and simplicity. For instance, irrigation systems in early Mesopotamian times were rather small, weakening the hypothesis that the large-scale irrigation works with their centralized management requirements gave 'oriental despots' their legitimacy. The mechanism may have been more subtle: irrigation may, by means of processes of differential control and wealth accumulation, have induced the social stratification that led to centralized state-level power and controls (Pollock 2001).

Yet the role of water as an environmental determinant is undeniable. As soon as the barriers of dense forests and diseases could be overcome, the river valleys and deltas provided the fertile soils and access to water, which made more intensive farming possible. The majority of civilizations with greatly increased population densities emerged in the alluvial plains near the rivers and in the coastal deltas (cf. *Table 4.1*). Some were small, some were large, depending on several other factors, but there was always a 'Great River': Mesopotamia with its Euphrates and Tigris; Egypt and the Nile; South Asia and the Indus-Sarasvati and later the Ganga; China with the Huang He and the Yangtze He; Europe with the Danube and the Rhône; North America with the Mississippi. All these rivers are in the temperate zone that made them a relatively easy environment to settle. In most tropical river basins, with much larger water flows, high-density occupation never developed. Disease-causing micropredators and poor soils are thought to be two of the major reasons. The exception are rivers in tropical regions in Asia, such as the Mekong, which became the locus of high-density occupation and civilization, probably due to a combination of irrigated rice cultivation and dietary habits (Gourou 1947).

TABLE 4.1   CHARACTERISTICS OF THE MAJOR RIVERS IN PRESENT TIMES

Region	Name	Drainage area (000 km²)	Mean discharge rate at mouth (m³/s)	Name	Drainage area (000 km²)	Mean discharge rate at mouth (m³/s)
S-W Asia	Euphrates/Tigris/ Shatt el Arab	808	856	Indus	955	3850-6700
& N Africa	Nile	3000	2850	Amu Darya (Oxus)	227	1300
Europe	Volga	1365	8200	Danube	85-805	6425
	Dniepr/Don	500/445	1660/930	Po	70	1460
	Rhône	98	1900	Ebro	86	600
	Seine/Loire	200	1400	Rhine	224	2200
	Elbe/Vistula	340	1850	Neva	281	2530
Asia	Huang He	750	1500	Yangtze He	1900	35,000
	Indus	950	6700	Ganga- Brahmaputra	1480-2010	19.300-35,000
	Mekong	795	15,900	Irrawaddy	431	14000
Africa	Niger	1000-2000	6100	Congo	3,800,000	42,000
	Zambezi	1330	2500			
North America	Mississippi-Missouri	3267	18,400	Rio Grande	350-930	82
	Colorado	629	168	St. Lawrence	1030	10,400
South America	Amazon	6600	175,000	Rio de la Plata- Paraná-Uruguay	2650	19,500
	Orinoco	1086	28,000			

(Douglas 1990; www.rev.net)

And then, the *sea*... another obstacle, opportunity, threat. Some peoples became masters of the seas. The Polynesians sailed thousands of miles thousands of years ago. In the Mediterranean the Phoenicians were probably the earliest sea-faring people, travelling to Spanish Galicia and further in 3000 yr BP in search of metals and loot. Their – relatively safe – maritime trade network with strongholds all along the coasts became one of the first in which finished products from a developed region, Phoenicia, were exchanged for

Sea resources In exploring early human-environment interactions, the focus is largely on land. However, the seas have also been exploited since many thousands of years and here too humans have used and impacted upon the natural dynamics (Jackson 2001). A recent detailed survey of archaeological and historical records has been made of human exploitation of coastal resources for food and materials. In some key marine ecosystems the long-term human impact has been investigated. Although these impacts have accelerated enormously in the past few centuries, there are clear signs of early overexploitation that led to changes in food webs with long-term and irreversible impacts. Aboriginal fishing in coral reef environments began at least 35,000-40,000 years ago in the western Pacific, with apparently minor ecological impact until the recent dramatic intensification of human disturbances. Aboriginal fishing in Aleutian Islands in the northern Pacific greatly diminished sea otters as early as 2500 yr BP. This led to a concomitant increase in sea urchins. When the otters were hunted to extinction by the fur traders in the 1800s, the urchins grazed away the kelp forests to collapse.

raw materials. The Minoans and Mycenaeans already had trading posts in the Aegean. Possibly as a consequence of their downfall leading to many refugees, the Greek city states started colonizing large parts of the eastern and, later, western Mediterranean. In addition to the search for raw materials and trade, adventurism and population pressure played a role in this maritime expansion. Surpassing the Phoenicians, they sailed all the way up to the Shetlands or even further. The Irish Book of Invasions – Leabhar Gabhala in Irish-Gaelic and based on orally transmitted myths written down by Christian monks – tells of peoples coming from overseas.

Coastal connections The Greeks, a littoral culture, provide a good example of how geographical features interact with an orientation on commerce and technology. McEvedy applied a simple geographical rule to understand the spread of settlements in ancient Greece. Dividing the area in rectangular cells, he assumed that a straight, flat coastline as in many river valleys would strengthen the relationships between coast and inland, whereas sea-shore communities along irregular coast with many indents would tend to have weak relationships with inland areas and instead sustain relationships with other sea-shore communities. Applying this rule to the colonization of the Mediterranean and Black Sea regions by the Greeks in the 1st millennium BC gives a reasonably good reproduction of the actual location of Greek colonies (McEvedy 1967). Of course, every community needed a hinterland as well as a connection to the sea so this procedure mainly points to existing differences in emphasis.

The coastal seas connecting the Indus and the Euphrates-Tigris plains were sailed as early as 4000 yr BP. In an attempt to explain the rapid expansion of people throughout the Americas and the maritime nature of many early Latin American culture, it has been hypothesized that the earliest colonizers of Latin America arrived by sea routes from the North. A well-known outburst of sea-faring peoples was the Viking period in the 8th to 10th centuries of the Christian era. According to some the Viking expansion was a continuation of earlier outward migrations from Scandinavia, notably of Germanic and Gothic tribes about 1900 to 1800 yr BP and probably motivated by both internal population pressure – and such customs as primogeniture: the eldest son is the only inheritor, the others have to make it for themselves – and the attractiveness of the civilizations to the south. Trade and desire for profit were no doubt an important driving force behind the Viking expansions along the northern European and Russian rivers – and maritime innovations played a pivotal role (Bell-Fialkoff 2000). More than land peoples, it seems, were the sea peoples oriented towards commerce and trade. Water – rivers, seas – thus became a crucial element in another aspect of human development through ecological regimes: exchange, in the form of trade, raid and conquest.

4.2.3.   Steppe and savannah lands

An important category of peoples with a lasting impact on history has been the nomads. Nomads are people who live at the end of the continuum of pastoral nomadism that has been defined as a distinct form of food-producing economy in which extensive mobile pastoralism is the predominant activity, and in which the majority of the population is drawn into periodic pastoral migrations (Khazanov, in Bell-Fialkoff 2000: 181).[3] Such nomadism, which has existed in many regions of the world, leaves little room for specialization and complex economic development. It originated in areas where cattle breeding offered comparative advantages over agriculture. Such areas – steppe and savannah – comprise an estimated 35%[4] of the landmass surface of the earth. The nomads were highly mobile, their habitats extending over distances of 50-1500 kilometres. They often appeared as, in a sense, natural predators with respect to adjacent forest tribes and sedentary civilizations. It would be more correct to view the close development between pastoralist, agriculturist and hunter-gatherer as mutualistic, their resource bases not overlapping too much and therefore possibly promoting inter-cultural trade.

Probably the best known nomads are those of the Eurasian steppes: the Huns and the Mongols. Their history goes back a very long way. The renaissance of Mesopotamia some 4200 yr BP was preceded by a conquest by archers coming from the Arabian steppes. Millennia later, the outburst of nomadic tribes from Arabia in the 7th century led to a great empire – probably initially fed by the need to find an outlet for the martial energies of the Bedouin warriors and less an expression of religious zeal than of the pressures of hunger and want from the barren desert lands (Mansfield 1976).

Nomadic existence has also dominated the savannah lands, Africa's most dominant single ecosystem and stretching across the continent from the Atlantic Ocean to the Gulf of Aden. These savannah lands offer a floral and faunal richness that allows cereal agriculture and livestock rearing. In West Africa they consist along a north-south stretch of only 1500 kilometres encompassing a series of different environmental zones of great complexity and rich in resources. Resources were abundant: 2-3 millennia ago, the West African environment could offer cereals, oils, nuts; meat and milk, hides and skins; wild plants and animals; also ivory, iron ore, alluvial gold, rocks and clays (Connah 2001: 3.3). Moreover, the large ecological gradients provided resilience as inherent or incidental shortages could be alleviated by the exchange of raw materials and products: '...the complexity of [this] environment, as a whole, provided conditions conducive to the development of a complex network of regional trade... (Connah 2001: 112). Why, then, did nomadism persist? One explanation is that in most areas many of the resources were seasonal and available at a low density.[5] It was not until the arrival of crops suited to growing in lowland tropical environments, such as banana/plantain from Asia, that a sedentary existence was possible. Furthermore, the very nature of the trade routes may have supported nomadism, with trade integrated into the pattern of seasonal migration.

A related ecozone inhabited by nomadic peoples is the large basin of the Mississippi, Missouri and Illinois rivers in North America, with a prairie-forest continuum (Nelson 1998). In the pre-colonial period before 1700 AD, the bottomlands near the rivers and the highlands each had their specific ecosystems and their dominant disturbance 'maintenance': fire in the highlands, from lightning strikes and annual fires set by native Americans, and floods in the bottomlands. Although relatively high biomass-density allowed for rather large settlements, the inhabitants of these plains lived an essentially (semi)nomadic life.

4.2.4. *Forest peoples*

About 39% of the land mass is covered with forests and woodlands, of which some 16% in tropical regions.[6] Peoples of the mountains and the plains, peoples of the sand and the steppes distinguished themselves – how about the forest peoples? A large diversity of populations have lived in and from the forests, both in the temperate and boreal forests of northern Eurasia and the Americas and in the tropical forests of South Asia, Africa and the Americas. The forests had diverse functions and connotations: places of hunting and danger, of food and medicinal plants, of shelter and defence. The Celtic tribes in Europe, probably related to the Kurgan culture near the Caspian Sea from where they migrated westward some 4000 years ago, may have been characteristic of early temperate forest peoples, with their warriors, forest sanctuaries and array of nature-inspired gods and goddesses.

Once settled, forest tribes such as the Celts and later the Germans and Slavs in the European forest zones were vulnerable to attacks by nomads, as the latter often had superior war techniques as part of their highly mobile lifestyle. In turn, they were attracted by or driven into the more civilized regions of China and the Mediterranean – of which the Great Wall of China and Hadrian's Wall in Scotland are testimony. The

---

The warm and human tropics as a human habitat   Why have the tropical forests and the great river deltas in the tropical regions not, as far as we know, led to urban civilizations? It seems there are at least three reasons (Gourou 1947). Firstly, *Homo sapiens* prospered and evolved in savannah-steppe environments – not in the forests where much of the fruit hangs too high. Secondly, and most importantly, the forest is an unhealthy habitat for humans because of the many micropredators causing all kinds of diseases. Besides the effects this has on human well-being, it has the consequence that animal herding is also difficult or impossible. Thirdly, and this matters mostly in the early agricultural stages, the tropical soils are poorer in nutrients and more fragile than in the temperate zones. Large changes in water flow sometimes causing huge flooding may also be have played a role: a settlement on the river bank during flood may be tens of kilometres away from the river in the dry season. In a recent study, Weischet and Caviedes (1993) point to restrictive soil properties in the humid tropical warm lowlands to explain the relatively low agricultural population densities, low labour inputs, and low yields per surface unit. In the semi-humid and semi-arid outer tropics, geomorphic barriers to water management often prevented agricultural development.

As a consequence of all these factors, most tropical regions sustain population densities of below 10 people/km^2 under slash-and-burn agricultural practice. More intense cultivation or opening up the land for pastures often caused accelerated erosion. Trading may have been one of the few possibilities for the onset of urbanization (cf. Section 9.3).

Of course, these factors are not in place throughout the tropics. Altitude may decrease the incidence of malaria, volcanic soils provide in some places extremely fertile soils. An interesting question is why some river deltas in tropical Asia have known high to very high population densities. Gourou (1947) suggests two major reasons. One is the availability of wet-rice cultivation with high perennial yields. The other is a low level of need satisfaction and a preference for vegetarian food. It could even be argued that the vegetation-oriented food habit is a cause of the high population densities, not the other way round as is sometimes thought.

---

dynamic interactions between these peoples and the more organized states may have been an important force in history, as Bell-Fialkoff suggests:

> [The] model of the triangular relationship among sedentary empires, nomads, and the forest tribes works better in the Far East... In the West, although the interactions among the three were also a constant factor, they lacked the almost mechanical synchronicity evident in the Far East... The configuration was largely determined by geography... I cannot escape the conclusion that if the core European areas bordered on a wide expanse of the steppe or if China faced a densely forested zone in the north, their histories might have been very different... If the migration confirms the central role played by geography, it also deflates the role of climate as a decisive factor. (Bell-Fialkoff 2000: 276)

This is an interesting complement to other interpretations, for instance, of Keys (1999) who argues that climate change due to a large volcanic eruption triggered the westward Avar migration because the Turkic cattle-based economy was less vulnerable to subsequent severe droughts than the Avar horse-based economy.

What about the tropical forests – can the forest peoples living in the recent past and, though in small amounts, the present tell us about the peoples who inhabited the large forested areas of the Gangetic Plain and the Deccan Plateau in present-day India or the huge tropical forests in the Amazon and Congo basins? Forest peoples in the tropics did not have to migrate across larger areas in response to changing seasons. As the forest provided them with all the basic necessities of life, they could sustain themselves for long periods: it is estimated that the Mbuti pygmies of the Ituri forest in the Congo Basin and the BaTwa pygmees of south-west Uganda have occupied their habitats for 30,000 years (Cunningham 1992; Turnbill 1961). Forest people have become horticulturists and agriculturists in later times when the appropriate tools became available. As Agrawal suggests for northern India:

> ... in the Ganga Valley the urbanisation processes had to wait till the middle of the first millennium BC. The monsoonal forests, mentioned in the epics as mahavana, which were dark even in the day, could be cleared only after the mass production of iron artefacts which alone made it possible to drain the swamps and clear the dense forests to produce the requisite agricultural surplus which alone could sustain towns and cities. (Agrawal 2001: 28-29)

Similarly, in the West African forests peoples living in and on the fringes could more practically exploit the forest once iron tools could be used – although the tropical soils would often only allow forms of slash-and-burn cultivation (Knapen 2001).

4.3. The agricultural transition: some narratives from science

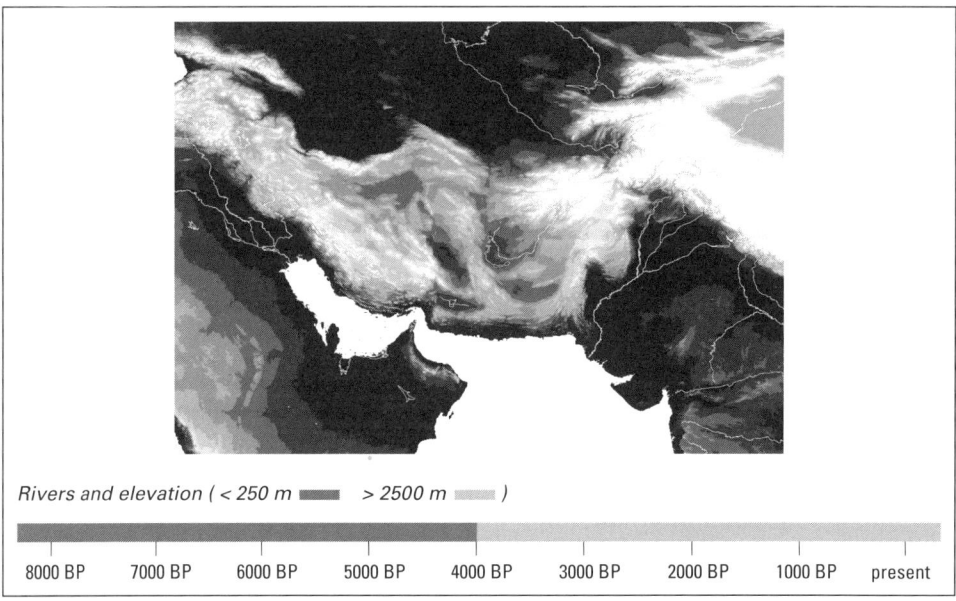

Rivers and elevation (< 250 m ▬▬ > 2500 m ▬▬)

8000 BP   7000 BP   6000 BP   5000 BP   4000 BP   3000 BP   2000 BP   1000 BP   present

Obviously, the biogeography of regions has been a major determinant of how human groups, and in particular their food provision, could develop. The previous chapter has already covered elements of the transition from hunter-gathering to horticulture and agriculture and animal husbandry for parts of Africa and South America. We will continue with a few more, and more detailed, narratives from other parts of the world.

4.3.1. The Iranian plateau and the surrounding plains

The Iranian Plateau is defined in the north by the Caspian Sea and the Kara Kum desert, in the west and east by the Zagros Mountains and the Baluchistan hills, respectively. The Zagros Mountains are topographically complex and support a wide diversity of vegetation with differences in temperature and precipitation across various altitudes. Near the upper parts of the Euphrates and Tigris rivers, villages might have existed as early as 13,000 yr BP at elevations from 300 to 800 metres, with houses and grinding tools but no evidence of domestic animals or cultivated plants (Hole 1996). In a process that lasted at least 3000 years, the hunting and collecting economy underwent a transformation from earlier higher elevation sites – around 16,000-18,000 yr BP – to permanent villages with a mixed agricultural economy based on domesticated plants and animals. The driving mechanisms behind these changes are unclear; climate change probably played a role.

South and west of the Zagros Mountains is the Mesopotamian plain, the basin of the Euphrates and Tigris rivers. These alluvial lowlands are characterized by long and hot summers and little rain. 'Rain comes in unpredictable amounts; neither today nor at any time since the end of the Pleistocene has the average annual precipitation in the area approached the minimum necessary (200 mm per year) for the reliable cultivation of crops without irrigation. On average, there is more than 200 mm of rainfall approximately one out of four years...' (Pollock 2001: 30-31). Another characteristic is the gentle slope, which makes the rivers split into multiple, shifting channels. The unpredictable river movements had a great impact on settlements. Strong annual floods just before or after the harvest made flood control a greater preoccupation than water procurement, or at least an additional one. As the water velocity decreased on the low-gradient plain, levees were formed by the coarsest particles sedimenting; this raised the river water level above the surrounding land, which facilitated channel irrigation. The Mesopotamian lowlands therefore offered an environment with opportunities as well as hardships.

Not surprisingly, *irrigation*, from the simplest forms of flood irrigation to large-scale canals and dams, has always been an important agricultural practice in Mesopotamia (Christensen 1993). On Alexander's conquest of Mesopotamia in 331 BC, the Macedonians were dazzled by the immense system of dikes and reservoirs of Babylon which protected the city against natural disasters. Irrigation may have started with small dammed wadis: sites from Syria indicate an essentially pastoral economy around 5100-3400 cal yr BP in what is now an arid area (Wilcox 1999). Larger-scale irrigation in the Euphrates-Tigris floodplain began in the early days of agrarian colonization around 7000 yr BP and was mainly based on parallel diversions from the Euphrates channels. The early technically uncomplicated inundation irrigation gradually became more sophisticated and intensive. The earliest canals along the Euphrates date from 5000 BP; later on, the focus has shifted towards the Tigris region and some canals connected the two river basins. As has previously been pointed out, unlike the lands of the Nile, the Mesopotamian floodplain is predisposed to salinization because of its soil structure and the gentle slope of the land. Another consequence of irrigation was that, between the 4th and the 3rd millennium BP, the Euphrates began to move westwards due to the sedimentation that was greatly increased by irrigation. It led to the construction of eastward-flowing canals (Christensen 1993).

It has been speculated that progressive salinization of the low-lying southern plains ultimately caused the shift of the political and demographic centre from the south to the north. According to Christensen (1993) the evidence is not convincing: it is likely that salinization had not reached disastrous levels and the move northwards may well be explained by the bitter wars between enclaves for control over the Euphrates, with the north reducing or interrupting the water supply to the south. The resource disparity between the lowland plains and the highland mountains is often assumed to have been a principal driving force in Mesopotamian history. This explanation should not be exaggerated either, according to (Pollock 2001). Besides fertile soils and forested areas providing pastures and firewood, the lowlands mostly relied on clay, reeds, bitumen and palm and poplar wood. However, the inhabitants of the plain made extensive and highly creative use of these limited available resources before more intense contact evolved with the population of the Zagros and Taurus foothills and mountains with their more abundant rain, trees, metal ores, stone and limestone. This suggests that relative resource scarcity can be relieved in an extensive – 'expansion' – but also in an intensive – 'efficiency' – way.

In the relatively narrow zone between the northern edge of the Iranian Plateau and the Kara Kum desert, the first agro-pastoral settlements in the foothills probably date from 8000 yr BP. 'This major physiographical boundary between mountainous highland and alluvial lowland is comparable in scale, and perhaps also in prehistoric significance, to

---

Resource overexploitation may have been around from the earliest times. There is evidence that early 9th millennium BP villages collapsed around 8500 BP, while new settlements were founded in quite variable landscapes in the same period. One of the largest, over 12 ha in size, was Ain Ghazal in southern Jordan (Rollefson 1992; Redman 1999: 107-110). There is evidence that this permanent farming village rose and then was abandoned between the 10th and the 6th millennium BP. Climate change, in the form of less precipitation, may have been one of the factors. However, it has been suggested that a combination of three factors might have caused disruption to varying degrees: plaster technology, animal husbandry and topographic variation. In particular the use of plaster – mud, gypsum, and lime – for housing and the associated use of timber for fuel in combination with goats, may have contributed to the gradual abandonment of the villages. The preparation of lime plaster required an estimated four tons of wood as fuel per ton – and apparently the inhabitants of Ain Ghazal chose to plaster their houses with lime frequently. This might have led to several km^2 of deforested area, of which regeneration was retarded or prevented by grazing animals, particularly goats. Erosion would degrade the already fragile soils. Several villages in the region succumbed to the consequences of this environmental deterioration – Ain Ghazal could sustain its role as a major population centre for a longer period because it was located at a major ecotone of biological resources.

Figure 4.2 gives a causal loop diagram about these interactions. The main, negative feedback loop is from increasing food supply through population growth to deforestation from increased wood for fuel use for plaster which in turn affected soil fertility. Animal grazing, itself contributing to food provision, aggravated this negative loop by disturbing the forest regrowth. This could be one of the early examples in which resource exploitation caused long-term unintended consequences from short-term behaviour – possibly in a process of competitive emulation (cf. Chapter 6).

FIGURE 4.2

Possible dynamic interactions leading to resource overexploitation in near east villages. A + sign near an arrow indicates that an increase in a variable will cause an increase in another variable; a – sign the reverse (after Rollefson 1992 and Redman 1999).

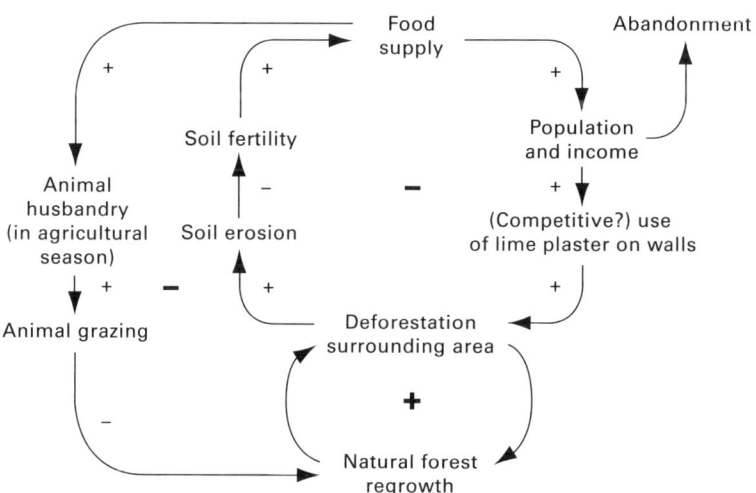

the western and eastern margins of the Iranian Plateau…' (Harris 1996: 372). The whole region may actually have been a vast area of very early cultural interactions, with contacts by land routes across the interior of the Plateau. Southern Turkmenistan is part of the extensive region from which most of the early crops and wild progenitors of several domesticated animals originated. Turkistan, the land of the Amy Darya (or Oxus) and the Syr Darya (or Axartes) rivers, is also an area where irrigated agriculture may have started as early as the 6th millennium BC (Christensen 1995). Although moister conditions may have prevailed some 9000-4000 yr BP, it has always been an area of dispersed oases. Fairly large-scale irrigation has been documented in the deltas of major rivers such as the Murghab and the Tedjen at about 5000-6000 yr BP. It seems that by the early 4th millennium BP all suitable areas had been settled and brought under irrigated agriculture.

On the east of the Iranian plain is the Baluchistan mountain range. Here, the site of Mehrgarh provides the earliest signs of agro-pastoral settlement around 9000 yr BP. Mud brick impressions of domestic barley and wheat and the bones of domestic goats, sheep and cattle suggest that agriculture had started in these lowlands adjacent to the south-eastern edge of the Iranian Plateau by 8000 yr BP, probably largely through diffusion from the west of South-West Asia (Harris 1996). From here, it descended into the Indus valley where several thousands years later also rice was adopted as part of the summer cropping (or kharif) system.

4.3.2.   *Europe*

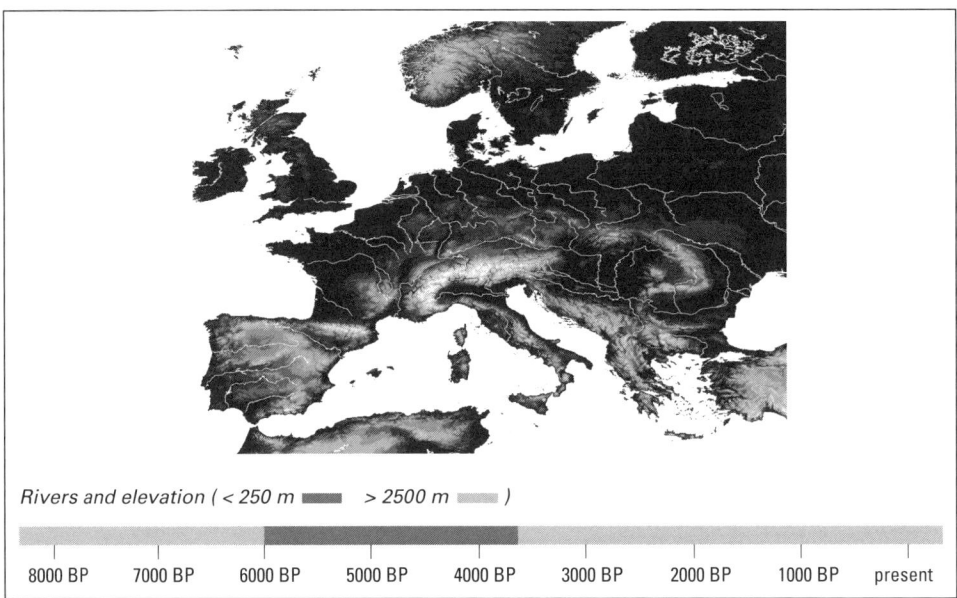

Rivers and elevation (< 250 m ▬▬ > 2500 m ▬▬)

| 8000 BP | 7000 BP | 6000 BP | 5000 BP | 4000 BP | 3000 BP | 2000 BP | 1000 BP | present |

Among the places on earth accessible to early humans, the European Peninsula may have had a favoured position. It has an exceptionally high ratio of shoreline to landmass, its sizes in distances and heights are bridgeable for all types of exchange and its temperate climate favoured the requirements of primitive agriculture. In what sounds like a bout of environmental determinism, the historian Davies writes:

> … Europe's landforms, climate, geology, and fauna have combined to produce a benign environment that is essential to an understanding of its development…. [Its] climate … is unusually temperate for its latitude… under the influence of the Gulf Stream, northern Europe is mild and moist; southern Europe is relatively warm, dry, and sunny…. Extremes are usually avoided. … Most of the Peninsula lies within the natural zone of the cultivable grasses. There were abundant woodlands to provide fuel and shelter. Upland pasture often occurs in close proximity to fertile valleys. In the west and south, livestock can winter in the open…. The extensive coastline… gave fishermen rich rewards. The open plains… preserved the nomadic horse-rearing and cattle-driving of the Eurasian steppes. In the Alps… transhumance has been practised from an early date. (Davies 1996: 47-49)

When and where did the agricultural transition start in this blessed place? In Chapter 3 the story of the Vera Basin in Spain was told; now we explore a few more.

Greece: early farmers and the risks of life

The southern Argolid, the Argive Plain and the Larissa Basin in Greece are alluvial areas that formed the cradle of later Greek civilization and show clear signs of early agriculture. It is thought that the early agriculturists entered the Argive Plain in southern Greece, settling on the edges of valleys near the best soil and water supplies (Andel 1990; Runnels 1995). Numerous finds of artefacts such as pottery, grinding stones and obsidian tools have been made. The hazards of rainless winters, late frosts and so on may have led early Neolithic farmers to adopt subsistence strategies involving a range of crops with different growth requirements and tolerances and an emphasis on sheep as a low-risk 'meat' strategy. Early farming may actually have resembled intensive horticulture rather than agriculture, with human labour as a critical constraint on survival. In combination with the climatic vagaries, this may have induced food overproduction and storage and cultivation of social relationships as responses (Halstead 1996). It is believed, from archaeological and palynological evidence, that grazing and farming were the principal activities on the valley slopes in the 6th millennium BP and that they resulted in one or more episodes of catastrophic soil erosion.

Was there more environmental degradation to come and what were its causes? As much as 2500 years ago, Aristotle claimed that the land had undergone considerable alterations in the millennia preceding the classical Greek civilization of his time. Evidently, the semi-arid valleys and hills of Greece were vulnerable to soil erosion. Research in the southern Argolid plain and the Larissa basin has shown the occurrence of rather brief and widely scattered erosional episodes that cannot be explained primarily by climatic changes (Redman 1999). Apparently, people farmed these lands for long periods using labour-intensive soil conservation practices such as terracing. However, in times of heavy rains population concentration and the abandonment of highland farms triggered cycles of depopulation and slow, natural regeneration. As part of the downturn, poorer soils were left to animal grazing, damage from animals was not repaired, farms and terraces broke down, and gully erosion would deposit large amounts of soil on the valley bottoms. Early agriculture in Greece is also one of the examples of how investments for control could actually make peoples dependent on the means to sustain control or, in other words, decrease resilience: 'Once the Greek landscape had been controlled by soil conservation measures, its equilibrium became precarious, the price of maintaining the equilibrium was high, and economic perturbations were only too likely to disturb it.' (Andel 1990: 383)

Erosion in the Mediterranean

As agriculture intensified from the 4th and 3rd millennia BP onwards into the extensive cereal cropping, specialization into olives and vines and transhumant pastoralism, impacts upon the environment increased in many parts of the eastern Mediterranean. Widespread human-environment interactions have been identified not only in ancient

Greece but also in Italy and Spain (Redman 1999). The history of the Mediterranean contains many stories about the struggle of farmers against the forces of erosion which were sometimes natural, sometimes human-induced, often both. As in Greece, an increase in erosion from a combination of intensifying human population and agricultural pressures and climate changes would set in motion an environmental crisis from which a region would recover only slowly. No doubt the frequency and intensity of these cycles of expansion and contraction were also influenced by 'history' in its well-known appearance of wars and invasions, coastal piracy and foreign occupation, slavery and migration, urbanization and overexploitation for export markets.

The vulnerability of Mediterranean slopes for erosion, especially when denuded by fire, has deeply altered the mountain landscapes in such widely different regions as the southern Taurus in Turkey, the Pindus in western Greece, the Lucanian Apennines in southern Italy, the Sierra Nevada and Alpujarra ranges in southern Spain and the Rif in Morocco – as narrated beautifully in McNeill's book on the Mediterranean mountains (McNeill 1992). Despite the local differences, the impact of humans and their animals have inflicted great damage on these ecologically fragile environments and reduced their carrying capacity for humans. The expansion and contraction rhythms in the population size reflect this fragility as well as the roles of the mountains as a refuge in times of disease and war.

Early agriculture in north-western Europe
A large amount of research has been done on the emergence of agriculture in north-western Europe – Neolithic agro-pastoral farming (Harris 1996). The process has been a complex one, with intense interaction between foraging groups. In most places agriculture appeared first in resource-abundant areas, its spread being mainly through the movement of ideas and products rather than people. Cattle pastoralism with plant gathering has probably been a – rather short – intermediate stage in the transition from hunting-gathering to stable agriculture. The spreading in space may have been driven by an 'agricultural frontier zone' in which agriculture could diffuse in a series of co-operative and competitive processes (Zvelebil 1996).

One of the controversial issues is the 'forest-farming' debate that started in the 1940s with Iversen's *landnam* (Old Norse: land take) model (Walker 1993): what was the nature of the interaction between the early farmers and the natural vegetation? There are four different models, based on palynological research and differing in their emphasis on the role of fire in clearing primeval forest, the extent of pastures, the way in which trees were used for fodder (leaf-foddering, girdling and coppicing) and the rates of abandonment and regrowth. At stake are questions such as whether the observed decline in the elm tree population was human-induced and whether the forest was seen as a malevolent obstacle or as a shelter and resource (Edwards 1993).

Berglund and co-workers (Berglund 1991) have done an extensive study of the land-

Early population-environment interactions   Usually, archaeologists lack the empirical evidence to make robust reconstructions of population-environment interactions in early human groups. Yet illustrative stories can be told – for instance, the outcome of archaeological research in some of the best preserved settlement sites of European prehistory, in the north-eastern part of France (Pétrequin 1998). Excavations of the lake dwellings dated to the period of the Neolithic and Bronze Ages, about 5000 yr BP, indicate distinct changes in the population density during a 300-year period. Tool and pottery analyses suggest a rapid demographic growth as a consequence of the arrival of successive human groups around 3050 BC. There is evidence of a recession and degradation of the local forest. This was, according to the authors, caused by total clearance of the young forest due to shifting agriculture through sequences of 30-70 years. Cultivated land expanded into the primary forest as a result of changing cultivation habits; livestock grazing led to degradation of the woodlands as it hindered regeneration of secondary forest.

Another response to the subsistence problems connected to a growing population was to increase hunting strategies rather than animal husbandry. With the advent of a second wave of immigrants from the south around 2980 BC, products of hunting abruptly diminish, together with evidence of livestock feeding on forest products. Husbandry is now predominant. The consumption of meat, however, is reduced (Pétrequin 1998: 189). It seems that when the limits of the traditional pattern of shifting agriculture and hunting and husbandry based on forest products had been reached, permanent fields and husbandry based on grazing fields were established. After 2970 BC the number of villages decreased and local groups were strongly affected by the climate degradation at the end of the 29th century BC.

scape changes in the Ysted region in south Sweden. Drastic opening of the landscape and recession of broad-leaved tree forest occurred between 5000 and 4600 yr BP, with the dominant underlying causes believed to be sudden climatic/hydrological changes along with other factors such as elm disease. Early agriculture, with rotation cycles of 30-50 years, was indirectly favoured by these changes. Settlements became more concentrated; megalithic graves were erected. In the subsequent millennium, woodland gradually regenerated; coast-concentrated coppice agriculture developed; and houses became bigger. Around 3800 yr BP a new wave of deforestation occurred and the first signs of soil erosion and lake eutrophication emerged. In the period 2750-1250 yr BP, agriculture developed into permanent fields in a grassland landscape. A great deal of deforestation, much through burning, to meet the demand for pastures and wood, larger houses and co-operation to store fodder in winter, and systematic manuring were among the associated phenomena. There are also signs of increasing social stratification, such as fences and more grave goods.

In other parts of Europe, palynological research also traces the Neolithic agrarianization process that occurred around 5000-7000 yr BP and is characterized by animal and plant husbandry (Huntley 1988). Until 5000 yr BP, the Late Mesolithic hunting-fishing-gathering society stayed near some high-productivity lagoons and estuaries. The inland was of marginal importance and landscape changes were largely due to internal ecological processes. Around 5000 yr BP, in just a few generations a distinct change in habitation structure and material culture happens with the advent of Early Neolithic farmers. Tillage in small areas and animal, mostly pig, husbandry emerged.

4.3.3.   *East and South Asia*

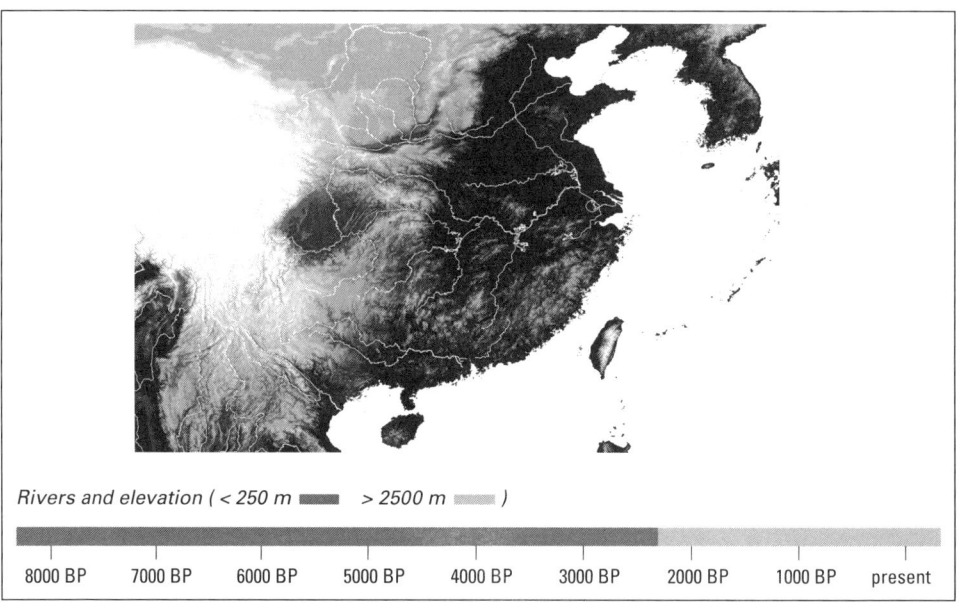

Rivers and elevation (< 250 m ▬▬ > 2500 m ▬▬)

| 8000 BP | 7000 BP | 6000 BP | 5000 BP | 4000 BP | 3000 BP | 2000 BP | 1000 BP | present |

China

The recognition of the very early, probably independent origins of agriculture in China has been one of the important recent archaeological discoveries. Pottery may have preceded agriculture. Present archaeological evidence suggests that rice in south-east Asia was first domesticated and regularly cultivated at least 8000 yr BP, probably behind areas of seasonally receding floodwaters around lakes in the middle and lower reaches of the warm and humid Yangtze He region (Glover 1996). Its subsequent spread was slow and stagnated at about 2500 yr BP until it was spread to the west by Islamic cultures, apparently because of the need to develop varieties adapted to new environmental conditions. Millet was at the base of another origin of agriculture, in the northern Huang He area around 7000 yr BP. The early developments will no doubt have been influenced by significant changes in climate (Ge Yu 1998). Farming in the Guangzhong Basin in the north-west started some 7000 yr BP in warm and wet climate conditions. Recent research in this area shows that between 6000 and 5000 yr BP a rapid climate deterioration with intensive aeolian dust deposition took place, with widespread aridization and a remarkable decline in Neolithic culture (Chun Chang Huang 2000; Zhang 2000).

The Jomon culture in Japan

In 1960 radiocarbon dating of pottery found near Yokosuka in Japan indicated it was older than 9000 years; more recent founds have pushed back the date of the earliest attempts to produce ceramic vessels to 12,700 yr BP. It belonged to what is called the Jomon culture, which flourished in Japan until about 2400 yr BP and became renowned for its technical and artistic ceramic skills. An important archaeological discovery in 1992 showed that this culture was far more sophisticated than previously thought possible for a Stone Age culture not based on a farming economy. The excavated site, covering an area of 35 hectares and occupied from around 7000 to 5500 BP, had food storage rooms, more than a thousand buildings and three separate cemeteries (Rudgley 1998).

This Jomon culture appears to have lasted for over 8000 years without any fundamental changes to its economic hunting-gathering economy – nuts, fish, deer, boar – with pottery and sedentary settlements (Imamura 1996). Its peak was probably around 5000-4000 yr BP in north-eastern Japan. The orderly arrangement of the buildings and burial grounds, the apparent specialization in crafts and the evidence of trade with the outside world in the form of exotic obsidian and amber suggest a complex culture. Ingenious fishing tools were developed – but no stratified social systems or political structures evolved. Why did Japan – where stone tools have been found in large quantities from as long ago as 30,000 yr BP – make the transition to what is known as the Bronze and Iron Ages so late (2400 yr BP)? One explanation may be that the dry-field rice agriculture from northern China was known but more arduous than the Jomon hunting, gathering and fishing strategies. Only when well-developed wet-field rice techniques came in from overseas, full-scale agriculture quickly took over (Imamura 1996).

4.3.4.   *North America: the Anasazi and the Hohokam people*[7]

In the American South-West – roughly the states of Arizona, New Mexico, Colorado and Utah – there is evidence of agriculture from the 3rd millennium BP onwards (Redman 1999). The Colorado Plateau, in the middle of this region, shares some important environmental characteristics with the eastern Mediterranean and the Levant. The complex

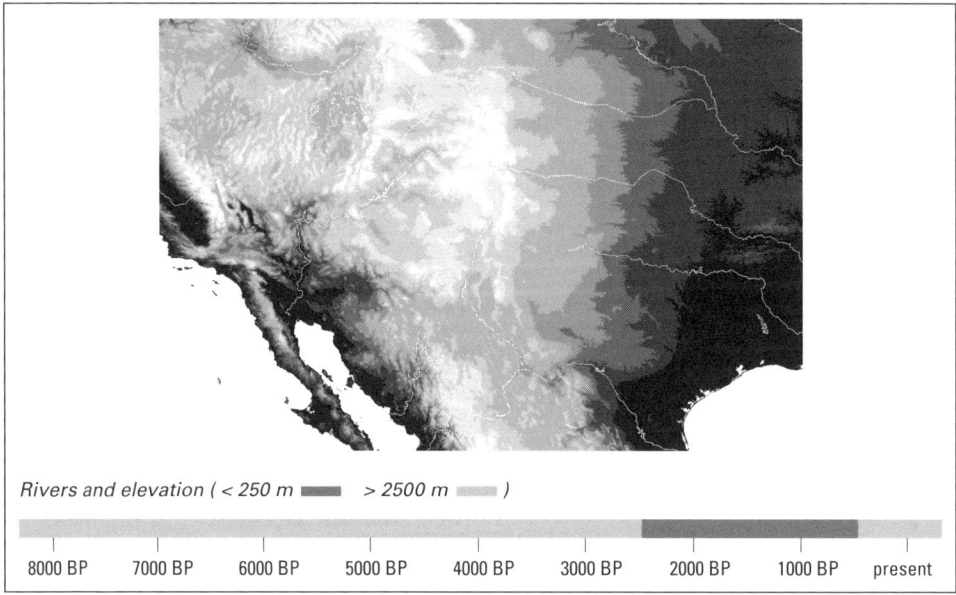

Rivers and elevation (< 250 m ▬▬ > 2500 m ▬▬)

| 8000 BP | 7000 BP | 6000 BP | 5000 BP | 4000 BP | 3000 BP | 2000 BP | 1000 BP | present |

system of coupled human social and landscape changes in this part of the United States is relatively well known because of a great deal of archaeological survey and excavation, and the availability of tree-ring dating and tree-ring-based climatic reconstructions. This region was once occupied by the Anasazi, or ancestral Puebloan, population. The area includes both high mesa tops where dry farming is productive under most climatic conditions, and lowland floodplains, much more limited in extent, where water-table farming was employed. A farming way of life appeared within some parts of this area by about 3000 yr BP, but the region was completely depopulated just before 650 yr BP. Between those two bookends, striking differences in population sizes, the degree of agricultural dependence and the degree of aggregation appear in the various sub-areas in quasi-cyclical patterns that can be linked – in many cases at least – to local changes in temperature and precipitation which assume a magnified importance in this region that on the whole is marginal for agriculture (Dean 2000; Kohler 1996). The coupling between the human and the natural systems is made more intricate by well-documented human impacts on forests and big game in areas with dense, stable populations (Kohler 1993). The link between human systems and climate in particular is strengthened in situations where populations depleted big game and other 'wild' resources such as piñon seeds in their localities, becoming more dependent on agriculture which is very responsive to climate change. In Chapter 8 we present a case study showing how models can be employed to help understand how ancestral Puebloan settlement systems responded to these factors.

Another region of early occupation was the desert region of central and southern Arizona. Here, early in the 3rd millennium BP, maize farmers settled in the river valleys in places suitable for floodwater farming. Some of the settlements lasted for more than a thousand years. Around 700 AD this Hohokam culture had developed irrigation agriculture which tied households together into community networks, and a regional ritual and belief system that included distinctive red-on-buff pottery, iconography and ball courts. By 1150 AD, larger villages with platform mounds were beginning to appear and canal systems were expanding, linking communities into larger networks. These and a variety of other cultural changes mark the beginning of the 'Classic' period. These changes appear to be linked to downcutting and widening of the river valleys which destabilized the existing irrigation systems and everything else that was based on them, and precipitated the construction of new canal systems, and new ceremonial and political organizations. By around 1400 AD the Hohokam culture had disappeared.

The Hohokam depended on the nutrients brought down in flood periods by the two rivers traversing the Phoenix lowland basin. Hundreds of canals led the water and sediments to the fields, thus regenerating soil fertility.[8] The localized nature of accessible surface water and farmland, in combination with the need for labour investments in canals and rising population, made it disadvantageous to move around and forced them to take care of the productive potential of their immediate surroundings: 'The fact that intensive agriculture results in reduced mobility options for human groups is key to understanding the human-environmental interactions of the Hohokam and many other groups around the world.' (Redman 1999: 151). The large empty surroundings provided a sustainable flow of wild food and material resources. Social institutions and community networks were instrumental in providing labour for canal construction and maintenance and in spreading the risks of food shortages.

It appears that Hohokam life was based on principles of sustainability. What, then, caused their disappearance? The Hohokam lived in an unrewarding environment and their way of life – no domesticated animals, modest use of wood – tended to spare the vegetation. Nevertheless and despite their conservation practices, archaeological evidence suggests that the increase in population led to a scarcity of protein-rich food such as fish and rabbits. According to Redman this degradation was probably not the main cause of abandonment. Some older theories accounted for the disappearance of the Classic Hohokam as a result of channel cutting or flooding, but recent research points to general stability of most floodplains in that period. The history of explanations suggests a mystery: 'Each age, it seems, reads something different into the demise of the Hohokam. Not only does each age have an explanation, but each pushes into the shade explanations that had seemed reasonable to their adherents.' (Krech 2000: 71). Yet the outcome of recent research allows a plausible reconstruction, as Redman (1999) convincingly shows. Three factors were at work: environmental change, irrigation strategies and social responses. Tree ring analyses indicate a rather high climate predictability in the period 1250 to 900 yr BP with modest variations in wetness – hence without extreme floods or droughts. Communities developed along the feeder canals that brought the water downstream to the distribution channels; population, organization and trade all increased. When in subsequent centuries flood variability became larger – as the tree ring evidence suggests – these communities were resilient enough to handle droughts and floods through storage, repair and trading. However, after 700 yr BP

> the climatic situation appears to have become even more erratic, with floods or droughts coming at least once every 10 years. This put tremendous pressure on the survival of the entire system. Crop production in the valleys was seriously diminished, and labour required to maintain the irrigation works dramatically increased… it is likely that the valley farmers overplanted in their good fields, extended planting to marginal fields, and cut back on fallow periods. All of these strategies would lead to decreases in soil fertility and subsequent productivity. (Redman 1999: 154)

Because the Hohokam remained in the same location, their activities unavoidably caused environmental changes such as increased runoff volume and velocity and subsequent soil erosion and canal silting. Although they maintained soil fertility through various conservation methods and by supplementing local food with goods brought in by exchange systems, 'when the climate entered a long period of greater variability, including disastrous flooding, it put an additional pressure on the Hohokam system that could not be easily sustained. Their response was to invest more labour in extracting the maximum from the land, but that made the system even more vulnerable to climatic extremes.' (Redman 1999: 155). Socio-political changes towards more centralized control and ceremonial activities may have further weakened the system's resilience. Their disappearance, it seems, was due to a dynamic interplay of environmental and social forces working on different time-scales.

4.4. The agricultural transition: how and why?

The Iranian Plateau was surrounded by semi-arid regions where among the first agro-pastoral economies existed as long ago as 10,000 yr BP.[9] Some four to five millennia BP, the first expansion and contraction cycles of agricultural activity and population density took place in the fragile Mediterranean environments of Europe. Meanwhile, in the rest of Europe the transition process from hunter-gathering to various forms of agriculture and horticulture and livestock raising was well underway. Similar transition processes took place in other parts of Asia and in the Americas – sometimes successful and enduring, sometimes broken off in complex interplays of environmental change and social response processes. Sometimes – as with the Jomon peoples in Japan – the transition never took place or occurred much later because the known forms of agriculture were not an attractive enough alternative. Although our brief overview is incomplete and each place and time surely had its specific characteristics, it appears there were universal forces at work to push the agrarianization process forward. The first main route was plant-food production, from wild plant-food procurement to crop production. The second main route was animal domestication, from predation to taming and protective herding to livestock raising and pastoralism. In the process, the dependence on wild plants and animals continuously decreased.[10] Can we get a deeper understanding of this transition process and its environmental ramifications?

4.4.1. The origins and spread of agriculture and pastoralism

The origins and spread of agriculture and pastoralism – in the sense of plant and animal domestication – has been the subject of intense investigations, as is evident from the previous narratives. The prevailing view nowadays is that agriculture probably originated some 12,000 yr BP in the so-called Levantine Corridor near the Jordan valley lakes in the form of the domestication of cereals and pulses. Within a millennium animal domestication took place: dogs, then sheep and goats[11]. It is hypothesized that preceding hunter-gatherer populations lived in small refuges and that by this time the steppe vegetation started to become richer across the Fertile Crescent as a consequence of climate change.[12] The invasion of annual grasses was followed by oak-dominated park-wood-land and

> increased dramatically the gross yields of plant-foods per unit area, particularly starch-protein staples, that correspondingly led to increased carrying capacity. It is suggested that these increases prompted significant extensions both in the storage of plant-foods and in sedentism, and that the ensuing increases in birth rate eventually produced stresses on carrying capacity, which, in certain locations, led to the cultivation of cereals. (Hillman 1996: 195)[13]

This process of cereal cultivation started spreading to the south and east, accelerated by the increasing climatic seasonality and unpredictability coupled with the dry conditions. The spread of forest reduced the open range that encouraged territoriality and pre-domestication of animals by the protection and propagation of local herds (Hole 1996). It is evident from these facts and explanations that 'climatic and other environmental changes were powerful forces in the spread of agriculture and possibly in the inception of animal domestication.' (Hole 1996: 264)

In any case 'the' agricultural revolution has not been one momentous event – one of the reasons why we prefer to talk about the process of agrarianization (cf. Chapter 2). Instead, it may have been a gradual intensification of the relationship between groups of humans, their environment and each other (Harris 1996). Clearing plots of land, usually

Climate, foraging and agriculture: the role of the steppe Climatic change affected human groups mainly through changes in vegetation: 'The effects of climatic change on the plant-based components of the subsistence economy were mediated principally by changes in the distribution and composition of vegetation, and by concomitant changes in the plant-food resource base.' (Hillman 1996: 159) Climatic change brought increased soil moisture in the Late Pleistocene leading to woodland expansion in the northern Fertile Crescent. Many pollen diagrams testify to this. The same conditions also 'allowed the spread of wild cereals and other herbaceous annuals, which hitherto probably achieved their highest concentrations in the broad woodland-steppe ecotones.' (Hillman 1996: 187) Agriculture became possible as an alternative strategy because, overall, the dry, cool steppe were places of low mean energy yield per unit of area – lower than in the later moister steppe, the woodland steppe with their grasses and the wetlands.

Prior to ca. 15,000 yr BP almost all of the interior of South-West Asia was dominated by steppe and desert-steppe, dominated in part by grasses such as perennial feather grass. A huge number of these steppe plants produce edible seeds or fruits, 'roots', leaves, shoots or flowers that have been used as food by recent hunter-gatherers, pastoralists or cultivators. Some of the starch-rich lowish-fibre 'root' foods have relatively low energy costs of processing, making them prime targets. They also have a high digestible 'net' caloric value for humans. 'During even the most arid and cold episodes of the Pleniglacial (before 15,000 yr BP), therefore, the steppe vegetation is likely to have offered local foragers a diverse array of wild plant-foods that could have provided not only carbohydrates, oil and proteins, but also vitamins, minerals and those miriad 'secondary compounds' that are coming to be recognized as essential to complete human health.' (Hillman 1996: 178) The life of early hunter-gatherers may not have been so bad!

by fire; having animals around, becoming part of their habitat; gathering roots and tubers, gardens emerging. These could have been the slow changes in various places that led to 'agriculture' and its associated phenomena such as sedentarization, domestication and urbanization.

Insidious complementary (sub)mechanisms have been proposed, for instance about the role of micropredators. When the temperature started to rise in the early Holocene, not only wild cereals spread but also parasites:

The climatic amelioration during the terminal Pleistocene was a bonanza for many temperature- and humidity-sensitive micropredators and their vectors. Coastal changes, particularly swamp formation with the rising sea levels, created ideal conditions for anophelene mosquitoes, the vector of vivax malaria, which… would have punished any hunting group wavering near zero growth… Along the protein-rich coasts of western and northern Europe… everyone living near saline swamps would have been particularly at risk… (Groube 1996: 123)

Also in other regions, schistosomiasis and other diseases would have made less spectacular but significant inroads into regions from which they had long been excluded. Many human groups may have moved in response 'beyond the newly extended range of these micropredators; those who could not move were, forced by the increasing aridity into the better-watered areas, trapped in increasingly unhealthy environments.' (Groube 1996: 124). One possible response to the resulting increased mortality may have been reduced birth spacing, which forced populations to become less mobile and intensify food procurement. High-density groups became more common, attracting more micropredators. In this way infectious diseases may have become an important force in human habitats, particularly in situations of failing sanitation, crowding and malnutrition. Could climate change have started up the escalator of food-quest intensification, agriculture and urbanism – which, as Diamond (1997) argues, turned out to be one of the great comparative advantages in the European invasions millennia later? *Figure 4.3*

FIGURE 4.3

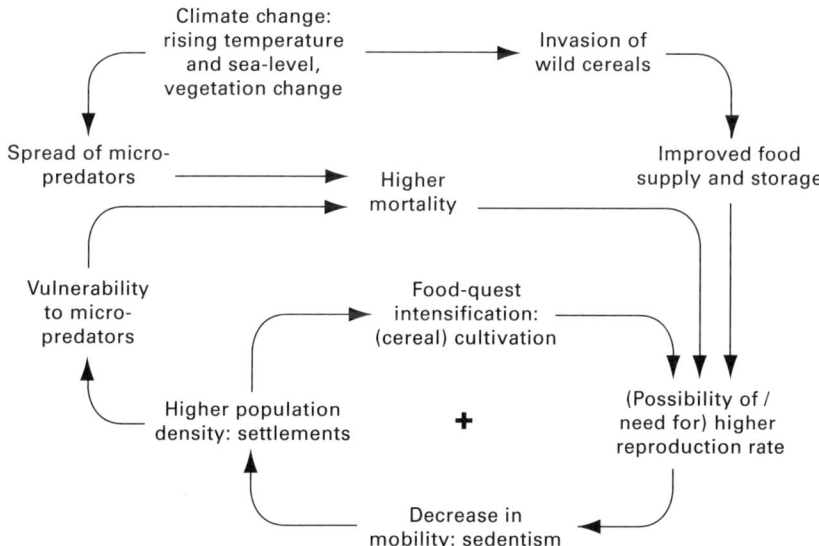

Possible, simplified routes in the early stages of the transition from hunter-gatherers to agriculturalists in the Near and Middle East (after Hillman 1996 and Groube 1996).

schematically indicates some possible mechanisms in the transition from hunter-gatherers to sedentary agriculturists the Near and Middle East (Hillman 1996; Groube 1996). Climate and vegetation change may have improved the prospects for food extraction which in turn led to a process of food intensification through higher net growth rates, sedentism and settlements. The combination of climate change related shifts in micropredator occurrence and heightened vulnerability of dense populations to diseases may have functioned as a second set of intermediate factors influencing population dynamics. The suggestion of a monocausal positive feedback loop is surely a simplification.

4.4.2.   Causes and consequences of agricultural expansion

Why peoples made steps in the agrarianization process is, at least partly, a question about motives and means and as such in the domain of economic anthropology.[14] The transition probably resulted from many, site-specific forces at work, with various options – food gathering, hunting, horticulture, pastoralism, agriculture – making up a locally specific mix of competing or complementary alternative strategies. As it turned out, this process was irreversible (cf. Chapter 2). Several interrelated trends can be seen: an increase and spatial concentration in food production and people, increasing specialization and the growth of organizational systems dealing with the food system – production, distribution, storage, consumption – and increasing differentiation of power (stratification) (Goudsblom 1996). Tools, rules and markets accompanied this process.

Many questions can be asked about why and how. Did people develop tools by chance, out of boredom and surplus labour or out of necessity? Did customs and rules and the associated institutional frameworks regarding, for instance, land access and control reflect survival strategies or mental attitudes or both? Was food produced for direct, own consumption or for (market) exchange in the later stages? Food shortages led to hunger and starvation, in turn, often threatened social organization – as the numerous peasant revolts testify. As a result, the explanation of why peoples shifted to agriculture has wider ramifications.

Virtues and vices of foraging life

One element in the discussion is the interpretation of the pre-agricultural stage: how did hunter-gatherers live? Until the mid-20th century the view prevailed that 'Stone Age' people lived in 'a mere subsistence economy', were incessantly searching for food in a meagre and unreliable environment, and had limited leisure and no economic surplus. In his book *Stone Age Economics* (1972), Sahlins refuted or at least complemented this view with a different assessment. Data on several contemporaneous hunter-gatherer groups – Australian Aborigines, the South African !Kung Bushmen and the South American

The roots of economic behaviour   In search of the foundations of economic theory, great debate has been ranging about the material and social roots of human behaviour. In an attempt to structure somewhat the diversity of (anthropological) thought, several schools can be distinguished, as done by for instance Dupuy (2001) in his book Anthropologie économique. One school are the formalists, who claim universality for the *Homo economicus*, 'cet être générique guidé par le seul goût du profit personnel et pour qui "la fin justifie les moyens".' (Dupuy 2001: 14) It is in the nature of human beings, according to this view, to maximize the use of scarce means in a process of [market] competition.

A second school, the substantivist, is rooted in the work of Polanyi and emphasizes the role of social relationships in economic processes. Reciprocal and redistributive mechanisms did and do co-exist with more or less institutionalized market processes, the latter being cut off from social relation based upon kinship, religion or political power. A third, and related, school is (neo)Marxist, with Sahlins as one of its adherents. Following Marx's analysis of pre-capitalist societies, the emphasis is not so much on the distribution and circulation of goods distribution as on their production. What matters most in economic processes is the mode of production in the sense of productive forces and their organization and of the associated political and ideological relationships. It seems the past two centuries of (European) thinking in the social sciences vividly demonstrate how open our past was, is and possibly always will be to divergent and value-laden interpretations.

Yamana – indicate that their members spent on average between two and five hours of work per day per person on the appropriation and preparation of food. It also showed that they had a fairly varied diet, often underused their economic potential and did not care much for material possessions or foresight. Sahlins suggests several sources of the discrepancy between the prevailing (European) view and these observations. Firstly, the ethnographic records suffer from the naïveté with which European travellers perceived what to them were exotic environments. Moreover, they met mostly hunter-gatherer tribes who had already been forced into a marginal existence by expanding colonialism. The second reason for a distorted view was the European economic context in which these tribes were judged:

Modern capitalist societies, however richly endowed, dedicate themselves to the proposition of scarcity. Inadequacy of economic means is the first principle of the world's wealthiest peoples... The market-industrial system institutes scarcity, in a manner completely unparalleled and to a degree nowhere else approximated... insufficiency of material means becomes the explicit, calculable starting point of all economic activity... it is precisely from this anxious vantage that we look back upon hunters… Having equipped the hunter with bourgeois impulses and palaeolithic tools, we judge his situation hopeless in advance. (Sahlins 1972: 3-4)

Yet scarcity is a relationship between means and ends constructed by people. It can be argued that many hunter-gatherer peoples lived a life of material plenty, highly mobile and therefore without 'big things' that would have to be carried around. They did not store food because it may have given rise to distributional and transportation problems. Besides, why store food and care for the day of tomorrow if nature is experienced as abundant – a view interpreted by Europeans as a lack of foresight and prodigality. Other consequences of such a mobile life were shared property and harsh demographic controls. They probably enjoyed a great deal of leisure time, which was filled with all kinds of ceremonies and rituals. For this reason, they may often have declined agriculture because it required more work. In fact, the most important economic impediment is, in Sahlins' words, the imminence of diminishing returns which forced them into moving around with all the above consequences.

Why, then, did the transition to agriculture occur in so many instances? Apart from considerations such as the quest for more protection from animals, invaders and diseases, one reason may be that in quite some regions life was or became much harder than the life of the hunter-gatherers Sahlins talks about – because of climate change, resource limitations and depletion, population pressure or all of these at once. Listen to the lament of an Eskimo hunter (Rothenberg 1969: 242):

My biggest worry is this: that the whole winter long I have been sick and helpless as a child.
Ay me.
Now with me sick there is no blubber in the house to fill the lamp with.
Spring has come and the good days for hunting are passing by, one by one.
When shall I get well?
My wife has to go begging skins for clothes and meat to eat that I can't provide –
O when shall I be well again?'

The idea that people started farming because they enjoyed leisure time seems erroneous – so is the idea that people were farmers 'by nature' or 'stumbled' upon technological innovations. In her book *Population and Technological Change* (1981), Boserup argued that the transition to agriculture was largely born out of necessity: increasing population pressure forced peoples to produce more food by putting in more labour at a generally decreasing labour productivity rate (cf. Section 5.6). As such it was a response to scarcity: 'progress' born out of necessity (Wilkinson 1973). Without such a response to population growth nor growth-reducing measures or outmigration, a (neo)Malthusian collapse would occur – no doubt this happened occasionally.

What were the most important 'causal' factors? Population – both size and density –

is often mentioned. So is technology – the use of increasingly advanced tools and prac-tices, in response to the rising need for more food. The nature and dynamics of social relationships is a third factor. Trade is proven to be of enormous importance in some regions as a means to reduce vulnerability for droughts and other natural disasters. Vio-lent forms of interactions such as conquest and piracy, and exploitation in the form of tribute and taxes have been other forces in the agrarian regime. Evidently, understanding socio-cultural organization is crucial in understanding human-environment interac-tions.

Peasants, priests and warriors
Sedentation and agrarianization changed the relationship between humans and their environment. With increasing population density, interactions within and between human groups became more important and lower mobility intensified the exploitation of the surrounding environment. Cultivation practices developed in a sequence of inten-sification measures – shorter fallow periods, irrigation, multi-cropping (cf. Section 5.6). As people started to invest more of their labour in harvesting and feeding animals, in irrigation channels and – often indirectly – in soil amelioration, the land became 'value-added'. Accumulation of material possessions became possible and important. Notions of collective – tribal and familial – and individual property became elements of the emerging social fabric (cf. Chapter 2).

Agrarian populations were more productive than foragers – in food per unit land rather than in food per unit labour effort. However, they were also more vulnerable. Along the lines of the 'triad of basic controls' proposed by Norbert Elias, Joop Gouds-blom (1996) distinguishes between dangers coming from the extra-human world – droughts and floods, wild beasts and pests, earthquakes and volcanic eruptions; from inter-human relationships – hostile neighbours, invading warriors; and from misman-agement due to intra-human nature – negligence, ignorance, lack of self-restraint or dis-cipline. In a meticulous sociological investigation Goudsblom relates the rise of social organization to the risks early agrarian communities faced. Priests fulfilled a mediating role between ordinary people and the extra-human world but, Goudsblom argues, they also played a pivotal role in inducing the self-restraint required for a farming life of hard work and for the exigencies of food storage and distribution: '...rites conducted by priests helped to strengthen the self-restraint which could keep people from too readily drawing upon their reserves.' (Goudsblom 1996: 42). Harvest feasts and sacrifices are social institutions to manage the pressures of frugality. Priests are resource-managers *avant-la-lettre* – not a strange idea when one knows about the rules in Christian and Buddhist monasteries.

A second observation is that the priest-led – religious-agrarian – regimes were proba-bly first but came almost everywhere in competition with warrior-led – military-agrari-an – regimes. The latter usually won, a dominant but not universal trend. The emergence of a warrior class, that is, of professional killers and pillagers, should be seen as one stage in the monopolization of violence and cannot be explained solely in terms of their discipline, equipment and organizational skills. It can be argued that the most crucial force behind it was the bonding of warriors and peasants (cf. Chapter 6):

> The warriors needed the peasants for food, the peasants needed the warriors for protection. This unplanned – and, in a profound sense fatal – combination formed the context for the great variety of mixtures of military protection and economic exploitation that mark the history of the great majority of advanced agrarian societies…. wherever in agrarian societies rural settlements developed into city-states which were subsequently engulfed by larger empires, the priests became subservient to the warriors. (Goudsblom 1996: 59)

Increasing population density
Theories about agricultural development and carrying capacity suggest an intimate relationship between the possibilities of the natural environment and the human population density (cf. Chapter 5). Most hunter-gatherer groups have a population density below 0.1 people/km^2, which is representative for the onset of agriculture (Sieferle 1997). Population densities in grasslands and shrublands had similar values; in most tropical regions they seldom exceeded 2 people/km^2 (Gourou 1947). The increased productivity of agrarian communities had major direct and indirect demographic consequences (cf. *Figure 4.3*). For instance, women could have more children as birth spacing became shorter for settled life compared to nomadic life and epidemic diseases may have spread more easily because of the higher population densities and the proximity to domesticated animals.[15] Whatever the details, the opportunity to feed people beyond subsistence needs and the corresponding increase in population density surely added new dynamics to human groups and their natural environment. Besides the socio-cultural dynamics discussed above, there are two other related facets: environmental degradation and urbanization.

More intense exploitation of the local resource base also intensified environmental change. In some cases it was rather direct and visible, for instance erosion from overgrazing or salinization from irrigation. Sometimes, it operated over longer time-scales, such as a change in regional climate as a result of deforestation. In the process populations may have come to be in a better position to manage short-term risks related to frequent events, such as those related to variations in rainfall. Food storage and trade were also key in this respect. However, the associated techniques and practices sometimes had a new, unknown impact on the longer-term future. Learning to cope with such longer-term and less frequent or more erratic events is more difficult. Risk may also have increased because the 'escape space' had become smaller in a broad sense – unexploited resources, the existence of survival skills and the like. Another risk element arose because increased productivity was only possible with investment, i.e. stored labour efforts. These are particularly susceptible to deterioration, catastrophes or destruction. For instance, when a society put in great investment to control the environment, at the same time it became more dependent upon it and upon the means to operate and maintain it. If such activities were undertaken with an improper or incomplete understanding of environmental processes, they could accelerate negative feedback loops. As a result, the values of a society, its past responses to environmental challenges and its capacity to learn from it are part of the human-environment interactions.

As an ever larger fraction of the population could be fed without working the land, physical and social dehomogenization became possible: urbanization. Small settlements of a few families mostly involved in agriculture, grew into villages and towns and expanded further in some places into cities that depended on the surrounding regions for their food. *Figure 4.4* illustrates this point. As peoples developed from one agricultural stage to the next, the potential to sustain a certain population density increased. In certain river plains already millennia ago population densities of several hundreds of persons per km^2 could be sustained. An 'urbanization potential' developed: in certain places and times, leaders, craftsmen, merchants and others started to concentrate around fortified villages which extracted part of the food surplus from the agricultural popula-

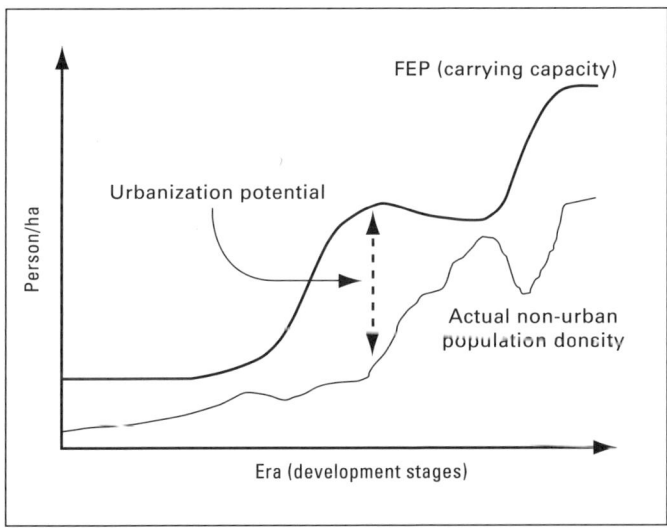

FIGURE 4.4

Illustration of how the food extraction potential (FEP) increases over time with the stage of development. The rises in FEP indicate periods of agricultural innovation, the falls could result from periods of overexploitation. Urbanization uses the difference between the FEP and the needs of the food-providing rural population.

tion, either by trade, tax or take. *Figure 4.5* (see p. 169) gives an indication of the population and area of a few ancient towns and cities – most estimates are surrounded with large uncertainties. The urban populations – to which the ruling classes usually belonged – were more vulnerable for food shortages and their response to such events often made the difference between societal collapse and continuity.

How (un)healthy was settled life?[16]   It is argued that sedentarization exposed humans to many new pathologic germs, mainly from cattle – a large disadvantage of sedentary life and a cradle for the large pestilences (Diamond, 1997). However, such a view neglects the enormous pressure from pathologic micro-organisms on nomadic groups, among which fellow people and a large animal and aquatic reservoir provided all sorts of germs besides domestic animals. In fact, cattle breeding coincided with improving life expectancy of humans.

In prehistoric – and even 20th century – nomadic societies, the median age at death was only a few (1-5) years. Major causes of death were 'natural': heat and cold, floods and drought, fires, hurricanes, volcanic eruptions and earthquakes. Lack of food was always a major cause of death; predators and homicide were not negligible either. Infectious diseases were then, too, the predominant cause of morbidity and mortality, often from the individual's own microflora or contagion from tribe members. Early in life, mothers and others handed down potentially dangerous micro-organisms to the infants, sometimes even before their birth. For instance, bacterial meningitis, which until recently killed 1 out of 10 nomadic children before the age of five, is caused by symbiotic bugs from the direct family.

Early cities provided an enormous advantage to their inhabitants in terms of longevity and comfort. They gave protection against armies and brigands; their centralized food storage was some guarantee against famine; and labour differentiation and specialization may have stimulated proper housing and clothing. These advantages were only partly offset by the hazards of infectious diseases due to high population numbers and crowding. The early cities were islands embedded in their countryside, so their populations were not – yet – easily massacred by bugs arriving from far away. Trade routes provided a way through every now and then for the micro-organisms of smallpox, pestilence and cholera and caused waves of mortality. But this was a haphazard process since long distance transport was scant and quite a few contagions 'on their way' to a city died out before reaching it. The median age of death was well over 20 years in some Sumerian cities. The well-known infectious diseases were still the main cause of death, while other causes were kept at bay to a degree.

However, some cities grew to populations of hundreds of thousands or more inhabitants (cf. *Figure 4.5*) and travel and trade intensified. This made the urban population vulnerable to contagious diseases, as there was a toing and froing of pathogenic micro-organisms in the large centres. Rome, a spider in a vast web of land and sea transport, is a good example of this turning point in city history. Contemporary writers such as Juvenal were amazed by the unhygienic streets, the stench and the enormous risk of acquiring diseases. In Rome one lived much shorter than in the rest of Italy: the median age of death was about 5 years. These conditions would persist for many centuries to come in the large cities, which absorbed rural poverty and overpopulation: the median age of death in 17th century London and contemporary Dutch towns was between 5 and 10 years.

4.5. Mapping the past: Europe in the Late Neolithic[17]

Is it possible to map the anthroposphere in the early days? Because of a paucity of reliable data, such an attempt will be difficult and at best give an incomplete picture full of uncertainties and white spots. *Figure 4.6* (see p. 170) shows such a map of Europe in the Neolithic to Early Bronze Age (7000-4000 yr BP). It was compiled on the basis of the original map 'Landscapes of Europe' using a scale of 1: 5,000,000. Boundaries on the maps are those of natural landscapes identified according to the common lithogenic base (relief and geology), climatic (types of local climate) and biogenic (soils and vegetation) components. The components are closely interrelated, and their spatial variations result in the change of landscapes in the space. Each landscape includes a number of smaller natural geosystems that could not be shown on the map; they determine the inner spatial, or chorological, structure of the landscape. By compiling a series of maps for different periods of landscape evolution, the chronological structure has been studied. The mapping is based on the following principles:
- a map of cultural and economic types for the whole territory of Europe or its regions is compiled using the archaeological, cartographic or published data for the chosen period. The focus is on those economic branches or types of resource utilization that result in the most obvious transformation of landscapes, such as land cultivation, forest cutting, mining, urbanization, etc. Economic objects and systems are represented on the maps.
- analysis of this described map makes it possible to evaluate different types of impact of economic objects on the natural geosystems and the consequences of this impact. Of particular importance are the scope of landscape transformation and the degree and duration of the resulting changes. For example, forest cutting for timber or fuel production may not cause deep destructive processes in the landscape, particularly if it is practiced only once and then natural reforestation takes place. The resulting landscapes are referred to as derivative ones. But in case the forest is cut down and the land is cultivated, such anthropogenic processes as accelerated erosion, deflation

and decrease of soil fertility, become characteristic of the affected natural geosystem and the natural landscape turns into its anthropogenic modification. When all of the natural components are transformed, for example through mining or construction, the term technogenic is applied to such landscapes.

The economic and cultural stage in European landscapes in the Neolithic to Early Bronze Age shown in *Figure 4.6* is a stage characterized by the formation of primeval societies in Europe. Active domestication of animals took place in the south-eastern regions within the forest-steppe landscapes of the Danube plains (Shnirelman 1989), so cattle-raising was the dominant occupation of people there. The most significant event of this stage was the start of the agrarianization process in the Neolithic that took place during the climatic optimum when the climate became more humid and warm. The first areas of cultivation were formed in the south-eastern subtropical parts of Europe, i.e. in Greece, Crete and Cyprus, and then extended over the southern regions of the Apennine and Iberian peninsulas (Shnirelman 1989; Andrianov 1986; Pounds 1973). Cultivation of shifting and slash-and-burn types required extensive forest cutting. Even under favourable agro-climatic conditions, the cultivation of more diverse landscapes was rather slow and usually combined with cattle-raising. But within developed areas the rate of anthropogenic processes was greater than that for natural ones. It is at around this time that the areas of modal landscapes appeared in Europe, i.e. natural geosystems with minor anthropogenic modifications. The most developed economic structures were typical of the eastern Mediterranean (Crete and Mycenae). Within other regions of Europe, cultivation was hampered by the cooler climate and the wide occurrence of wet-lands and boggy plains. The cultivation of temperate landscapes in Europe took about 2000-3000 years (Pierre 1987; Maksakovsky 1997).

In the *Bronze to Iron Age* (4000-2300 yr BP), new forms of interactions between man and nature appeared. Production of metals and iron tools, particularly the plough, development of the wheel and sail transport means, irrigation, separation of land culti-vation from cattle-raising, etc. – all this had made the anthropogenic impact on land-scapes more sophisticated and contributed to the expansion of developed areas. Forests were cut for ploughed arable lands, grazing lands increased in area, towns and rural set-tlements came into existence. Limited areas of derivative landscapes and even anthro-pogenic modifications appeared.

4.6.   Conclusions

Early human-environment interactions were dominated by the search for food. Biogeo-graphical factors and their – direct or indirect – changes have been a dominant force in shaping the first human habitats and, later, the agrarianization process – although one should be wary of simple environmental determinism. Vegetation in particular has been an important intermediate variable in food provision. Other related determinants were water availability, disease occurrence, soil erodability and ecological diversity. Relative resource abundance will also have determined cultural traits: fragile environments may have induced prudent practices whereas resource-rich environments might have led to prodigality.

In exploring and exploiting the environment for food and shelter, humans encountered opportunities and threats. Agro-pastoralism caused erosion, irrigation salinization, investments in terraces could be destroyed: each action induced changes that required further action, usually combinations of adaptation and intensification, if collapse or abandonment were to be avoided. On a larger scale this showed up as cycles of expansion and contraction, as is evident in Mediterranean (pre)history. One set of forces in this dynamic was external, particularly climate change but also for most peasants raids by outsiders or invasions. Other forces were internal, in the sense of being a reflection of people's perception of their environment and themselves and of their value and belief systems. The nature and balance of these forces largely determined the fate of many of the early populations.

The prevailing view nowadays is that agriculture originated around 12,000 yr BP in the so-called Levantine Corridor. In any case 'the' agricultural revolution has not been one momentous event. Instead, it was more of a gradual intensification of the relationship between groups of humans, their environment and each other – which is why we use the word agrarianization. It was in its particulars quite local and there were no simple cause-and-effect relationships. A series of concurrent factors may have induced people to make this transition: climate change, subsequent changes in food opportunities and vulnerability to diseases, population pressure and the limitations and depletion of easily available resources.

Agrarianization had far-reaching, irreversible consequences: it replaced a life of high mobility, modest effort and material ascetism by a sedentary existence with more working hours, goods accumulation, food storage, trade and urban concentrations. The gradual shift from religious-agrarian to military-agrarian regimes was probably a response to inter- and intra-human as well as extra-human risks.

The nature of human-environment interactions became more intense and complex. As the growth in populations and investments in rural and urban areas increased, control increased – but so did vulnerability for environmental change. A proper understanding of and learning opportunities about environmental processes became more important. Resource exploitation intensified in an attempt to deal with short-term risks related to frequent events, such as those related to variations in rainfall. It caused environmental change, often unanticipated and unintended. It sometimes manifested itself rather directly and visibly but also more globally and later. Coping with the latter, which occurred less frequent and/or more erratic, often turned out to be the more difficult one.

In the early stages of agrarianization, deforestation and filling vital functions for human groups, also contributed to the diversification of the landscape. In summary: with agrarianization the anthroposphere was expanding and the human footprint could increasingly be spotted by a lunar observer.

5

Exploring the Past: on Methods and Concepts

DE VRIES, MARCHANT AND DE GREEF

Time present and time past
Are both perhaps present in time future,
And time future contained in time past.

T.S. Eliot

We are changing Earth more rapidly than we are understanding it.

Vitousek et al. in Science *277 (1997)*

5.1.   Introduction

Our perception of the past has changed enormously over the course of time. Early travellers – geographers *avant la lettre* – have contributed to our knowledge by giving descriptions and conceptualizing what they encountered (Lacoste 1996). Much of this knowledge disappeared for long periods. With the 'Golden Age' discoveries of the 15th and 16th centuries and, in its wake, the reinterpretation or outright rejection of religious dogmas – for instance, the claim that the Earth was created in the year 4004 BC – Europe ushered herself, and the world, into the 'scientification' of the past. This process of making empirical observations, interpretations and experiments, i.e. the scientific method, led to the mechanization, then historization of the 'European' worldview, as expounded in Chapter 1. It has led to more efficient use of and increased control over the environment in the form of technology. It has also been applied to understanding and reconstructing the puzzle of our own past. The old sciences – history and geography – regained new vigour, new branches of science emerged – archaeology, palaeo-ecology and palaeo-climatology.

Using available methods and inference techniques, one can attempt to reconstruct 'scientific facts' about the past from what remains of it in the present. In this chapter, we focus on some of the methods to collect such empirical 'facts'. The methods to look into the distant past are still evolving. We see more and realize that what was 'seen' in the past was itself part of that past – as is also true for the present. Our knowledge, both in the form of data and concepts, always came – and comes – through filters and 'scientific' data and theories are biased accordingly. The larger part of historic and palaeo-climatic research, for instance, has been done by European and North American researchers, and ultimately set by their research agendas. This has resulted in relatively more knowledge being available for certain places – and time periods – and in predominantly 'Eurocentric' interpretations. In addition, information about the past may have been or be distorted or withheld for (geo)political reasons. The more advanced societies have left conspicuous and lasting material remains which naturally became the main focus of archaeology. The available methods and the fragmentary evidence are another obstacle in reconstructing past – environmental – changes. For instance, there are fewer traces left from plant foods than from animal foods, hence a bias towards meat-eating habits appears in such reconstructions. In the arid and tropical regions people usually built their houses with materials – mud, wood – that do not last for more than a few generations; this makes inferences about their settlements and society more difficult. Changes in sea-level affect the use of marine resources and the ensuing archaeological records – numerous sites are likely to be below the present sea-level. Indeed, it is not a coincidence that the earliest coastal sites date from 6000 yr BP, precisely the time of the Holocene transgression. In this chapter we discuss these issues in somewhat more detail. As Diamond remarks:

> If it's hard to determine the function of things happening today under our eyes, how much harder must it be to determine functions in the vanished past! Interpretation of our past runs the constant risk of degenerating into mere 'paleopoetry': stories that we spin today, stimulated by a few bits of fossil bone, and expressing like Rorschach tests our own prejudices, but devoid of any claim to validity about the past. (Diamond 1992: 82-83)

Our knowledge of human-environment interactions in the past is the outcome of experiences and notions deeply rooted in that same past. In that sense any narrative, theory or model about the past is itself a myth in the sense of a collectively negotiated, broadly accepted and shared view – as indicated in Chapter 1. As such, it is constantly being renegotiated – this book is itself part of such a process.

5.2. Concepts and categories to organize the knowledge of the past

To acquire knowledge we need an apparatus of concepts to classify and organize our sensory experiences – the more so as the latter become, through all kinds of measuring equipment, elaborate extensions of those experiences. Investigating past societies in recent (pre)history starts by examining patchy observations on material artefacts, food remains, vegetational traces and orally and written transmitted records. These have to be contextualized to become more than an incoherent sequence of material and mental objects. This process involves making associations and inferences to glue the patches together. In this book, the construction of such a fabric is largely undertaken according to the rules of the reductionist-empiricist science. This is by no means the only way: many people did, and do, contextualize the world around them on the basis of different rules. To clarify what we wish to communicate, we will briefly discuss the nature and origin of some concepts that are crucial in this process of scientific contextualization. We explore the concepts of time and space and introduce a few thoughts on the concepts of complexity and resources. But first a note on epistemology and models.

5.2.1.   *An epistemological note*

It may sound trivial but: you can only see what you can see. Yet even in the realm of sensory perceptions philosophical questions may immediately arise about the relationship between those perceptions and the associated experiences, information and knowledge. There is always a lot of filtering and selection going on, followed by complex cognitive processes which add 'meaning' to the perceptions – or simply ignore them.

Human beings have gradually expanded the spectrum of sensory perceptions. After centuries of developing natural science, we are now aware of the narrowness of our 'natural' sensory apparatus. The human eye only sees a tiny part of the frequency spectrum of light – many animals see more or different parts. The same holds for sounds and smells – elephants can communicate across miles by stamping their feet, some fish are able to catch a prey using the smell of a mere few molecules. By now, humans have outperformed most animals in collecting and interpreting signals, by using tools such as telescopes and microscopes to extend their sensory limits. Beyond our immediate sensory experiences, with or without artificial extensions, we use inferences, hypotheses, speculations, conjectures and refutations as part of our genetic and acquired configuration. Concerning these – more subtle – thought processes, we are possibly only at the start of our potentialities and of our awareness of them. To understand and interpret past events, we have to delve into this a little deeper.

Our observations of the real world are derived from a huge array of simultaneous sequences of events or processes. To make it tractable, we delimit them by establishing system boundaries, for example of two systems A and B (*Figure 5.1*). The observations are filtered in a variety of ways, for example by one of the methods discussed below and in association with some kind of 'gauge'. Such a gauge can be as simple as a thermometer or as complicated as in extracting the age of a piece of pottery from thermo-luminis-

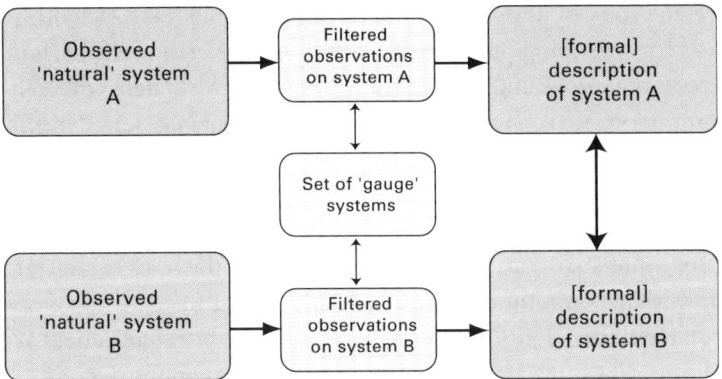

FIGURE 5.1

The translation of observations into explanatory descriptions (hypotheses, theories)

cence data. The filtered observations are then translated in descriptions of the system, for instance an evocative story or a set of differential equations about migration or diffusion. Often in the advance of science, observations about one system are used to infer hypotheses about another system – the use of analogues and metaphors. In the present context, an obvious example is spatial transference in which events in system A are given explanatory meaning in understanding system B. Interpreting the development of early human settlements, for instance, has often been constructed along these lines. Another

Disciplinary filters Recently, a meta-analysis of the proximate and underlying causes of tropical deforestation was published (Geist 2001). From a detailed literature search, Geist and Lambin identified three clusters of proximate causes of deforestation, that is, human activities that directly affect the environment. They also listed five clusters of underlying causes of deforestation: economic, demographic, technological, policy-institutional and socio-cultural factors. For the latter they explored whether the disciplinary background of the scientific authors had an impact upon drivers and causes perceived and reported. It is concluded that there is a significant correlation for political scientists and ecologists between their disciplinary background and the main cause identified – and that research teams which combine natural and social science views show negligible bias. One may subsume that such correlations are also found in questions addressed in this book, such as what drove the process of agrarianization, what led to the rise and decline of social complexity, and how did environmental factors affect cultural orientation and social organization.

one is time transference in which events in system B at some stage of its evolution are understood in terms of observations about system A in a supposedly similar stage. Learning about the old hunter-gatherer populations based on the few hunter-gatherer peoples existing today is an example of this. Such synchronic and diachronic comparative analyses can provide fruitful hypotheses, but they usually are also misleading – which is precisely why they are sometimes fruitful in the formation of more solid knowledge.

5.2.2.   *Models: population-environment interactions*

In the previous chapters and the chapters to follow, we present 'stories' told by climatologists, archaeologists and scholars from other disciplines. The stories themselves as well as their sequence often suggest a kind of trajectory or path. This tells of the rise and fall of human settlements in the early phase of transition to settled agriculture and on to states and empires. However, there is much uncertainty and controversy about how to interpret the empirical evidence squeezed out of scattered bones and pottery, dug-up seeds and the like. Scientific 'stories' appear and attempts have been made to tell such stories in a more formalized way by making a mathematical model. Let us briefly look at the notion of a model and how models are being used to deepen our understanding of past developments, not as a substitute for stories but as a complement.

To understand our ancestral past, scientists put forward qualitative hypotheses and quantitative models – *our* models. Loosely speaking, we may call any mental map representing associations between events a model. Such mental maps in the human mind can be formalized into mathematical models. In the process, the complex forces at work are interpreted and simplified. A part of the experienced reality is delineated as the system under consideration and described in terms of state variables and how it changes as a consequence of forces operating in time and across space.

Scientifically speaking models are more or less formal representations – or encodings – of observations, applying certain rules of inference, and deducing and testing subsequent hypotheses (Rosen 1985). Such models about human-animal-resource-vegetation interactions emerged, possibly for the first time, with European science. Some of them, however rudimentary and simple, have been very influential: the logistic population growth model (Verhulst), the prey-predator ecosystem dynamics (Lotka-Volterra), the mining life cycle of a resource (Harris), the Central Place theorem in geography (Losch and Christaller) and others.[1] Many such 'mental maps' about how humans and their environment have co-evolved still have a limited relation with everyday reality. Despite their sometimes high mathematical sophistication, they are stylized representations of certain observations, often based on metaphors or analogues.

The most important 'system' variable in (mathematical) population-resource-environment models is the population size; modelling population density spatially explicitly is still the exception. A general framework about population growth and resource limits would have to consider the elementary notions of population growth, resources, and technology mediated by organization and culture. More specifically, the dynamic interplay between fertility – regulated through cultural practices such as the postponement of marriage or infanticide – and mortality – with determinants such as diseases, famine and war – is part of this scheme. The population size is the result of fertility, mortality and migration processes. A subsequent extension is to incorporate a resource – fish, soil, trees, copper – and simulate possible pathways: overexploitation followed by famine and population decline, cultural and technical responses to overcome the resource crisis, and the like. Simple 'archetypical' mathematical population-resource models suggest four typical population trajectories, as shown in *Figure 5.2*. Exponential growth without an upper bound can continue indefinitely – and hence does not exist. If there is a limit – and hence a finite carrying capacity – the approach to it can be smooth or with overshoot-and-collapse. However, the limit may also be lifted due to technical ingenuity or behavioural changes. It may also brought down by natural processes or mismanagement. Human actions and the nature of the limits are in continuous interaction.

Science proceeds towards ever more explicit mental map (re)construction. It is important, then, to distinguish 'our' 'scientific' models and the associated perspective from the mental maps of the peoples of the past. In 'our' models there has been, in the last few decades, a tendency towards integration of scientific (sub)disciplines and the use of actor-oriented 'bottom-up' simulation models. However, this demands an explicit formulation of how humans behaved in the past – that is, 'their' models. In such 'agent-based modelling' – agents being the name used for any effective actor in the model, such as individual humans, households or mountain goats – it is found that one cannot easily discern specific causes for specific changes. Changes, maybe even random variability, in actors' behaviour, or in some aspect of the boundary conditions for the model such as the climatic context, may precipitate small but growing avalanches of changes in the system's evolution over time. This is particularly true when agents are modelled in such a way as to be able to alter their sets of behaviours and communication flows, instead of merely reacting to a stimulus with a predetermined, rule-based response. A 'cause-and-effect' approach and explanations in terms of 'variables' abstracted from the model are not very satisfying. The true locus for change in such systems may reside in changes in the network of relationships linking agents to each other and to the boundary conditions of their world. Another trend has been to make more integrated models in an attempt to incorporate crucial – and often ill-understood – interactions between various subsystems.[2]

The deeper understanding which models can give us consists of more general insights at a larger level of abstraction. It is tempting to aspire towards universal laws and theories. Of course, even if our models become more elaborate, they still face serious prob-

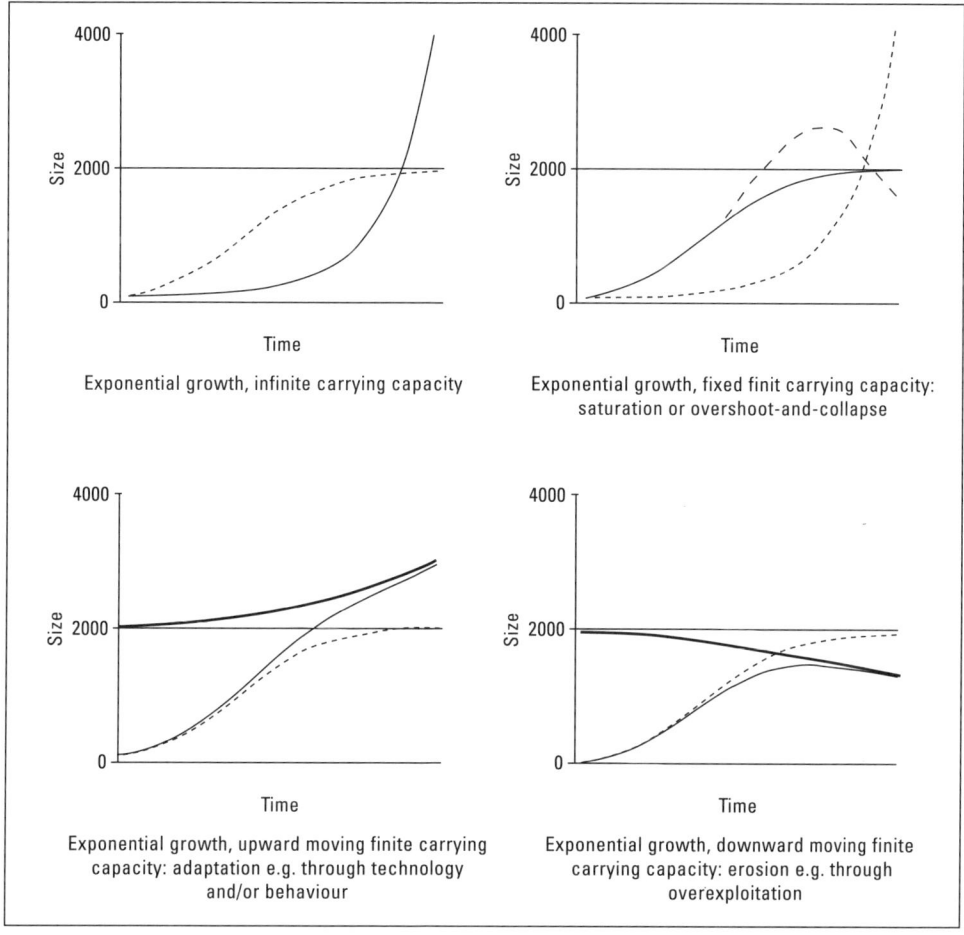

FIGURE 5.2A-D

Archetypical human-environment models. In this illustrative example, (1) an exponential population growth (0.2%/yr) leads to a growth from 100 to over 4000 individuals within 150 timesteps. Logistic growth (2) would slow down the growth at the exogenous carrying-capacity level of 2000 individuals, unless the countervailing forces are not or with a delay working in which case 'overshoot and collapse' occurs. If the level of the carrying-capacity itself changes, possibly because of the growing population, other trajectories (3, 4) will be followed.

lems of validation because controlled experiments such as in physical and chemical la-boratories are not possible. The laws and theories we should expect will be somewhat fuzzy and appreciative, not rigid and formal as in classical mechanics. There will always be room for competing hypotheses and models available and able to explain the empiri-

The mathematical basis To give a flavour of some 'archetypal' population-environment models, let us assume a system of a hunter-gatherer population in interaction with its main food resource, for instance a fish population. It is based on a human population with births, deaths, and a requirement of food which is satisfied by exploiting a local resource. If there are no resource constraints, such a [human] population will grow exponentially (*Figure 5.2a*). Its growth rate will depend mainly on the number of children per woman during her fertile period and on the life expectancy at birth. In its simplest form, the mathematical equation is:

$$dP / dt = bP - P / L$$

where P is population, b is birthrate and L is average life expectancy. Obviously, in the real world a local resource will always have a limited resource provision capacity. For instance, the resource may be a lake where fish are caught, the fish feeding on shrimps – or another ecosystem that can be exploited by a hunter-fisher community. It may also be an area with fertile soils to grow food crops and pastures to keep animals. The mathematical description consists of one additional equation for the renewable resource:

$$dR / dt = \alpha R (1 - R / K) - \beta P$$

in which R is the resource size, α is its recovery rate, K is the carrying capacity of the particular area under consideration and β is the resource extraction per person. If initially the resource system is in dynamic equilibrium ($R = K$), a stable population ($\beta = 1 / L$) with a finite extraction rate will drive the resource to extinction unless its extraction βP is below some level (*Figure 5.2b*). This happens for instance at $R = K / 2$ and $\beta P = \alpha R / 4$. Interesting questions to explore are:

– how will the declining resource size R constrain the extraction rate, for instance through less animals per area, soil erosion and the like;

– how will this in turn effect the population dynamics, for instance through increased mortality and subsequent starvation or violent deaths from mutual competition; and

– how will the human population respond to such an effect on population dynamics, for instance by outmigration, concentration in certain places where chances for survival are highest, infanticide, postponement of marriage or other adjustments of the number of births.

Some of these responses have been discussed qualitatively in previous chapters. Numerous models have been developed to introduce them in mathematical models; one of them is presented summarily in Chapter 8.

cal data. A large part of humanity's past – and future – will always be told in the form of stories. In Chapter 8 we discuss a few attempts to apply these novel approaches in the quest for a more in-depth understanding of socio-natural systems.

5.3.   Time, space and resources

In the local space and the short time-span of everyday life, individuals learn to orient themselves in their environment in a continuous process of interaction. A mental map is built and adjusted on which to base one's actions in known environments and, at least in the first instance, in new environments. How peoples in the past oriented themselves in their world may at first glance be incomprehensible and chaotic in modern eyes – as would be the reverse.[3] Events were organized and recorded according to some external 'clock' such as the moon or the sun. Location was related to landscape features in combination with travel time and means. Although there is still a wide variety of measures in use, 'globalization' has advanced rapidly in the last century and there is an almost uniform use now of the Système Internationale (SI) units of measurement: the metre, gram and second. With the expansion of science and technology, the unit domain is expanding – nm for one millionths of a millimetre, Myr for one million years – and new units or contexts appear, such as Mb and GHz for computers.

Two remarks. First, similar to knowledge, space and time manifest themselves as distinctly 'personal' – or subjective – in our everyday experience but at the same time as evidently 'impersonal' – or objective – in the processes in the world. Time, the 'fourth dimension', clearly exemplifies this apparently unbridgeable gap. Goudsblom (1996)

Perceptions and the environment   How perception affects the interaction of peoples with their environment is illustrated with the example of certain tribes in the Western Highlands of Papua New Guinea (Leeuw 2000: 372). The tendency among these tribes is to view change as degradation and the stable past as ideal – a tendency present in parts of any population. To correct problems, they believe, one should ceremonially go back to the point in time where the root of the problem lies and sort it out. In one well-recorded case, this led to a spiral of environmental degradation. When change was observed, people held ceremonies requiring freshly killed pigs. This, in turn, required deforestation to expand horticulture to provide pig feed. This caused erosion on the steep slopes where the settlements were located and 'slowly, the population cuts away the means of subsistence that surround it and is forced to move downhill.' (Leeuw 2000: 372) They end up in the valley marshes which are partly formed by the washed down soil on which it all started.

---

suggests that a sociological approach can bridge it, by emphasizing that time is 'a socio-cultural construction which aids people in their efforts to collectively orient themselves in the world and to co-ordinate their actions.' (Goudsblom 1996: 20). Secondly, developing quantified measures for orientation and communication has been only successful for relatively simple (sub)systems. More complex (sub)systems can usually not easily be characterized by quantified measures derived from a unique and unambiguous gauge. For example, (past) climate and vegetation changes, the nature of economic transactions or a society's organizational form are most often expressed as relative changes or positions. The climate was 'drier', transactions took place in a 'subsistence economy' and a state was 'more centralized' than another one.[4]

5.3.1.   *Orientation in time*

The perception of time has always been an important aspect of all cultures and is reflected in environmental and social experiences in various ways. In all cultures the notion of time has been used to point to what cannot be experienced by the senses, grasped by the human intellect or said in human words. Often, this is expressed in metaphors, as in the writing of the Persian poet and mystic Rumi:

The world of time[5]

Every instant thou are dying and returning. 'This world is but a moment,' said the Prophet.
Our thought is an arrow shot by Him: how should it stay in the air? It flies back to God.
Every instant the world in being renewed, and we unaware of its perpetual change.
Life is ever pouring in afresh, though in the body it has the semblance of continuity.
From its swiftness it appears continuous, like the spark thou whirlest with thy hand.
Time and duration are phenomena produced by the rapidity of Divine Action,
As a firebrand dexterously whirled presents the appearance of a long line of fire.

Time is not measured as such but is a constructed relationship, a duration between relevant events (Elias 1985). One may assume that there was no abstract notion of 'time' among ancient peoples. Instead, their sense of time was determined directly by their everyday needs. The group, often mediated by a priest, interprets the changes in the environment in order to know the moments and sequences of actions. Only later did more abstract notions of simultaneity and a sequence of past, present and future emerge.

In the modern scientific sense time is measured 'exactly' by relating it to highly regular gauge processes. This exactness became an important step in conceptualizing the past as an ordered, coherent narrative according to the scientific rules of the game. It is a relatively recent development in the history of the concept of time. The 'scientification' of

Science:	Science:	Disciplinary classifications		
cal. yr BP	^{14}C age equivalent	Geology	Archaeology	Sociology
8000	7260	Early Holocene	Palaeolithic (Early Stone Age)	Fire regime
6000	5260	Mid Holocene	Mesolithic (Middle Stone Age)	Agricultural regime
4000	3670	Late Holocene	Early/Middle/Late Neolithic	
2000	2060		Bronze Age	
1000	1120		Iron Age	
500	430			Industrial regime
Present		Anthropocene		

Science:	Historical sequences					
yr BP	Egyptian dynastic	Chinese dynastic	Jewish religious	Christian religious	Islamic religious	India religious
> 4000	Old, Middle and New Kingdom (1-21st dynasty)	Xia Shang	Era Mundi: 1 (3760 BC)			
3000	New Kingdom (22nd-31st dynasty)	Zhou Qin		yr BC		
2000		Han	diaspora	Birth of Christ: 0 AD (Anno Domini) or CE (Christian Era)		Saka Era: 1 (79 AD)
1500		Sui Tang		500 AD Dark Age	Era of Hijra: 0 (622 AD)	
1000		Song Yuan		1000 AD Middle Ages	500	
500		Ming Qing		1500 AD		
Present			5761	1950 AD	1328 AH	Calendar reform: Caitra 1 (Saka Era 1879, 1957 AD)

TABLE 5.1   VARIOUS CLASSIFICATIONS OF TIME

The match between disciplinary and historical classifications and 'scientific' time is not meant to be precise. The name Anthropocene as the last geological period was suggested by Crutzen.

time is a process of narrowing down the older, broader notion – as such it is a mirror as well as a tool of the forces of modernity. More recently, the natural sciences have also recovered more subtle aspects of time – this is beyond the scope of the present discussion.

As explained previously, orientation in time needs some form of gauging system. In ancient times these always originated in the observation of 'natural' recurrent phenomena, such as the cycles of the sun and the moon and using instruments such as a sundial. Gradually, more elaborate time-measuring devices emerged such as the water clock, the hourglass and the mechanical clock. The latest one is the atomic clock, using radioactive

Perceptions of time   In many early agricultural civilizations, time was intricately related to the seasonal cycles (McIntosh 2000b). As an English medieval verse goes (Sisam 1970: 485):

The Months
Januar: By this fire I warme my hands,
Februar: And with my spade I delfe my landes.
Marche: Here I sette my thinge to springe,
Aprile: And here I heer the fowles singe.
Maii: I am as light as birde in bow,
Junii: And I weede my corne well ynow.
Julii: With my sithe my mede I mowe,
Auguste: And here I shere my corne full lowe.
September: With my flail I erne my bred,
October: And here I sowe my whete so red.
November: At Martinesmasse I kille my swine,
December: And at Christesmasse I drinke red wine.

In other societies, low-frequency or other events such as periodic fluctuations in ocean currents as with El Niño may have been more important (Marchant 2002). In traditional African life the linear concept of time is absent: time is a composition of events with a long past, a present and virtually no future – it is actual time and moves 'backwards' rather than 'forwards' (Mbiti 1969). What has not taken place or is highly improbable to take place is part of no-time; what falls within the inevitable rhythm of natural phenomena or is certain to occur is potential time. Time has to be experienced in order to make sense or become real. This shows up in East African languages: they have no concrete words or expressions to convey the idea of a distant future – at most two years. As with many peoples past and present, history and prehistory are dominated by myths that defy any attempt to be described on a mathematical time-scale. Space orientation is

122

similar to time orientation and both are essential in understanding (African) religions and philosophy.

Time is intimately related to the attempt to come to terms with death, a vast topic and beyond the scope of this book. Pre-capitalist Europe was largely 'timeless' – or, in historian Le Goff's words, 'free of haste and careless of exactitude'. As capitalism raised the 'price' of time, people began to think of time as a scarce resource and metaphors emerged such as saving or wasting time. Time and money began to substitute for each other – time itself had become a commodity. More than 150 years ago, Alexis de Tocqueville, the French commentator on life in the colonies, observed that Americans were always in a hurry. Time is intricately related to environmental change through the notion of productivity: large tropical trees in Australia could not be felled before 1910, it took several weeks by 1920 – and only a few hours by 1940.

It would be possible to fill a whole book with thoughtful reflections on time, as it is such an existential aspect of human life. To give just two examples:

'But time is life itself, and life resides in the human heart. And the more time people saved, the less they had,' writes Michael Ende in his book Momo.

'Of time you would make a stream upon whose bank you would sit and watch its flowing. Yet, the timeless in you is aware of life's timelessness, and knows that yesterday is but today's memory and tomorrow is today's dream,' the prophet is saying in Kahlil Gibran's book *The Prophet*.

decay processes as the gauge. In this process of social construction, time is imagined as a linear continuum that can be divided in equal parts and is used to synchronize time measurements anywhere in the world: the 'Global Time Regime' (Goudsblom 2001).

As scientific inquiry proceeds from the simple mechanical systems of early science into the more complex ones of biology, ecology and the social sciences, time as a reflection of a system's characteristic dynamics or 'Eigendynamik' (Bossel 1989) becomes important. Such systems have growth and decay cycles and response times reflecting complex, nested dynamics, and they are not easily linked in a quantifiable way to a gauging system. Whole ranges of phenomena occur interdependently across a wide spectrum of time-scales and spatial scales. Within such a context, time is usually experienced as a sequence of events – for instance in an individual life, an organization or a civilization. Usually some structure is imposed in the form of 'natural' phases of development: the physical and psychical growing up and maturing of human beings, the rise and fall of businesses, states and empires. In most cultural traditions, events and transitions from one characteristic period to another order the dimension of time.

Whereas each scientific discipline has developed its own time classification, based on the phenomena of interest (*Table 5.1a*), most cultures have developed their 'historical' time, (re)constructed from oral or written records (*Table 5.1b[6]*). In the present context where we deal with complex socio-natural systems, we 'date' events based on scientific methods – a chronology – and at the same time position events through association with ecological regimes – a phaseology.[7] The fire regime, the agrarian regime with plant and animal domestication, urbanization, and the industrial regime are each the outcome of human-induced transformations and each has their characteristic events, behaviours and processes, although they cannot be sharply demarcated (Goudsblom 1996: Chapter 2-4).

5.3.2. *Orientation in space*

Interactions between humans and their environment have an important, if not essential, spatial aspect. Space is the mediator between the human needs for food, exchange and meaning on the one hand and the physical landscape on the other. When considering migration, conquest etc., physical geography, climate, vegetation, encounters with large animals, as prey and competitors, and with other groups of humans all incorporate spatial aspects in the co-evolutionary processes. Transport processes and speed relate space to time. An increase in the speed of travel, slow for millennia and accelerating rapidly in the last century, has totally transformed 'physical' or 'Euclidean' space. Until a few centuries ago, physically experienced space was for most people confined to an area of a few hours' travel on foot – an area of, say, 100 km^2. With ships, horses and carriages, later trains and planes it has expanded to the whole globe for a significant fraction of the world's population. Mentally experienced space has expanded even more with advances in communication technology. Like knowledge and time, space has both a subjective and an objective side, as is evidenced in apparently closely related astronomical enquiries on the one hand and metaphorical poems on the other: one measures the distance between starts in light-years, and the other expresses the infiniteness of inner space.

The first attempts of the human mind to bring orientation in space from an individual to a shared, collective understanding were maps. If one understands the word 'map' in a wider sense, maps are all around us: animal drawings and statues, town plans, a horoscope and Tarot are all 'maps' in the sense of simplified, static, symbolic yet material representations of a complex reality. They all tell a story for those who can read them. For instance, some interpretations believe the Giza pyramids to be a map of the constellation Orion; the interpretation of megalith circles, such as Stonehenge and Seahenge, as related to ritual maps is more widely accepted. Maps in a narrower, geographical sense may have started many millennia ago as simple drawings in the sand or on rocks, transmitted in oral traditions and serving as mental maps. These were, one can assume, memorized and transmitted collections of relevant data: on territorial boundaries, on good soils and places to find water etc. The surroundings were the gauge or reference system. These ancient maps were distinctly ethnocentric and an intimate expression of the bond between humans and their habitat.[8] Even when people in ancient times thought they were drawing a map of 'the world', they could not possibly conceive of the entire planet in the way we can, nor could they locate their own position on the planet. They were unable to escape from a thoroughly ethnocentric and hodicentric view of the world. Gradually, maps evolved into ever more elaborate and detailed physical representations of certain areas and regions.

EARLY SUMERIAN MAPPA MUNDI

(ca. 4500 yr BP) (Clay Tablet, Berlin, Vorderasiatisches Museum (VAT 12772)).

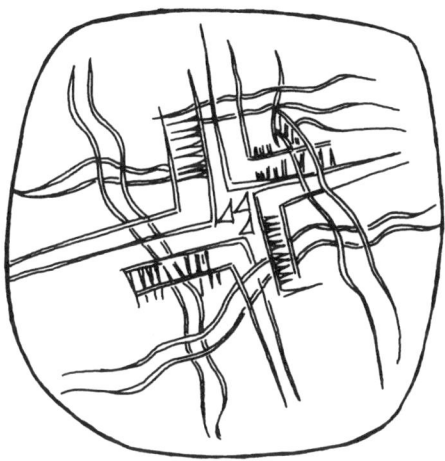

In the middle of the map is the holy city of Nippur, indicated by the three wedges spelling '(primeval) mound', the place where the city was built. The city in the centre is surrounded by four of the cuneiform sign for 'irrigated field'; in Sumerian eyes the production of grain and the consumption of bread and beer distinguish civilization from barbary. The four streams enclosing the land of farmers and cities denote the 'Four Banks', the Sumerian expression for 'inhabited world'. The eight districts outside the four banks must have harboured the barbarians. The text on the other side of the tablet is in perfect harmony with the drawing: it is a list of professional names or, in other words, of the inhabitants of the civilized world. (See F.A.M. Wiggermann, *Scenes from the Shadow Side*, 207-230 in M.E. Vogelaar en H.L.J. van Stiphout, *Mesopotamian Poetic Language: Sumerian and Akkadian*, Groningen (1996))

Simulating the emergence of towns   An example of a model of the simulation of the evolution of a settlement system over a period of 2000 years is SIMPOP, developed at CNRS in France (www.parisgeo.cnrs.fr). It starts with a regular population distribution, its only activity being agricultural. Growth depends only on the ability of the population to use agricultural resources. Sufficient accumulation of wealth leads to the transformation of a settlement to a town, this transformation being associated with the appearance of basic commercial activities. These in turn create possibilities for exchange and further growth. Progressively the system organizes: new towns emerge, some grow quicker than others with more advanced commercial activities and exchange across longer distances. Cities emerge and the settlement system becomes more hierarchical.

From a methodological point of view, SIMPOP is developed with multi-agent systems (MAS) whose protocol of communication makes it possible to simulate the inter-

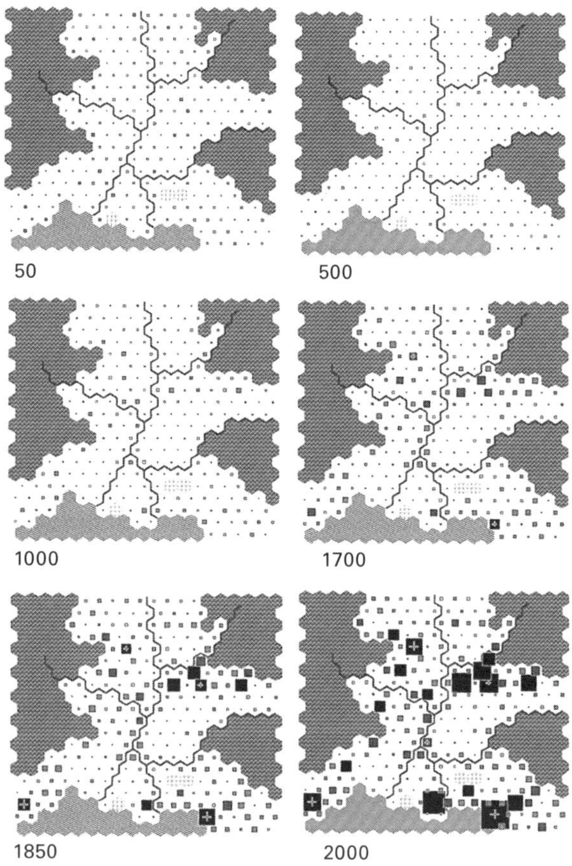

FIGURE 5.3

Simulation of a possible settlement evolution in south-eastern France over the last 2000 years. Map symbols: dark: mountains; grey in lower part: sea; small grey signs: swamps; lines: rivers; squares: settlements, their size proportional to the number of inhabitants; a cross in a square: cities with an administrative function. The colours of the squares are a measure of commercial activity.

50

500

1000

1700

1850

2000

126

actions between places in an interesting way (Sanders 1997; Bura 1996). Without interactions the system stagnates: the total population remains stable and no hierarchy
evolves between settlements.

Figure 5.3 shows simulation results for the Rhône valley in south-eastern France,
with Valence in the north, and the initial population sizes are fictitious. The key point of
interest is the spatial and hierarchical organization as growth and interactions evolve.
The urbanization process has a slow, unstable start. As soon as some hierarchical
organization appears, it tends to be reinforced with time. Although the overall structure
is somewhat independent of the initialization, bifurcations may appear when small differences are reinforced: 'the butterfly creating a storm'. The aim of the model is not to
reproduce the exact location of the cities and towns in 2000, it is to produce a plausible
structure of the urban network in terms of hierarchical organization, city sizes and spac-
ings.

Geographical maps as we know them were known around 2000 yr BP. In ancient times,
the image of the Earth was intertwined with mythological belief systems. The first maps
of the world were probably made in Sumer at around 5000 yr BP. The eastern image of
the Earth as a corpus floating on water was gradually replaced in the Greek civilization
by the notion of a rotating free-floating ball. Chin emperor Shi Huangdi had an enormous tomb built, around 2150 yr BP, on the floor of which was a stone map of the world
with the hundred rivers of the Empire flowing mechanically with mercury (Wood 1999:
106). The Arab cartographer Al Idrisi, after whom the geographical software package
Idrisi is named, was the first to use co-ordinates. By means of a long process of map-
making, the most recent development are the computerized maps using Geographical
Information Systems (GIS) techniques. Vast amounts of data can be stored, processed
and represented in a spatially explicit form: maps. Space, too, has been 'scientificated'. An
example is the research in the framework of the Land Use History of North America
(LUHNA) project, yielding for instance maps of population density in the Washington-
Baltimore region in the USA over the last 200 years illustrating the transformation from
an agricultural to an industrial region (www.luhna.gov). An example in which dynamic
simulation models generate spatial maps to mimic and understand dynamic settlement
processes is the SIMPOP application for Southern France (Figure 5.3). In practical
terms, space will show up in this book in two forms: geographical maps with indicators
such as population density and land cover/land use, and maps representing the outcome
of spatially explicit dynamic models of spatial interactions between humans and their
environment.

5.3.3. Resources

Ecology teaches us that individual living beings are always part of a larger system with which they interact in a variety of ways. Such a system is called an ecosystem and its evolution over time is the result of numerous and complex dynamical processes, among them material exchange processes with the physical environment.[9] The easily observable interactions between humans and their environment takes place at the physical level – breathing, gathering food, hunting and eating, diverting water flows and building settlements. The parts of the environment that are 'used' in this way are referred to as life-support systems or environmental resources. Some call the associated fluxes the – agricultural, industrial – metabolism. Agriculture, in this context, is human interference with natural succession in ecosystems.

Resource shortages have often been invoked to explain the decline of civilizations (cf. Chapter 6). As we will see, this is often an overly simple explanation. What is experienced and exploited as a resource is a reflection of the prevailing values and opportunities, the available technical skills and the organizational capabilities. They tend to develop in a dynamic interplay – as shown by the modern example of uranium which only became a resource once the discovery and control of fission technology had developed. For hunter-gatherers and early farmers, resources were – and are – largely associated with their value on the individual level such as a desire for crops or cattle. At later development stages, desires of more advanced farming communities and of urban elites added a whole array of new resources.

Regarding resources and their exploitation and degradation, it appears to be useful to mention some general aspects of the interference of humans with the material world:
- every transformation of material and non-material fluxes has a 'value-added' character;
- most – but not all – transformations have a 'capital formation' character in the sense that the action may result in a permanent accumulation of effects;
- many transformations have a 'value redistribution' character which is the outcome of social exchange processes.

The first two points express the fact that the essence of a 'resource' is that some part of the natural environment can be changed (transformed, concentrated, transported) in such a way that value is added. If the resultant effect has an enduring capacity to satisfy certain needs, it is a form of 'capital formation'. It incorporates not only materials but also the technical knowledge and skills to actually perform the transformation. At the same time a process of 'capital destruction' takes place as both natural and non-natural capital stocks inevitably degrade at a rate which depends on its composition and management. This aspect of environmental change is associated with resource depletion and environmental degradation. The third point is about whose values and needs are involved. This depends on the ways in which societies (re)distribute the surplus. In early development stages most 'capital' was in the form of individual possessions such as houses, tools and ornaments and collective undertakings such as roads and defence works. In hierarchical societies, the capital often reflected the values and desires of a king-priest elite – as is evident from the palaces, temples and irrigation works in ancient empires. In coastal trading communities, important capital assets were the ships, the harbours and the stocks of goods – goods which often had a high added value per unit of mass or volume because that is what made it worth to transport them across large distances.

5.4.   Complexity

> The world is constantly threatened by two things: order and disorder.
>
> *Paul Valéry*

As humans adapted to a variety of environmental stresses during the evolutionary process, their society became more complex. In this book we use the words social complexity, socio-cultural and socio-political complexity and complex socio-natural systems somewhat interchangeably. But what is complexity and what exactly has become more complex? In the first instance and in the present context it is associated with the familiar items listed in *Table 5.2*: an – incomplete and unsystematic – list of activities that tracks peoples' interaction with their environment.

The notion of complexity is a difficult one; an extensive discussion is beyond the scope of this text (see e.g. Allen 1993; Dean 2000; Leeuw 1998). Recent insights in ecosystem and human-environment dynamics have led to the awareness that many concepts and models from the physical sciences are inadequate to understand more complex systems – for instance, the concept of change as a series of equilibria (Prigogine 1980). Refined notions of stability, predictability and resilience are emerging. More emphasis is given to the simultaneous existence of multilevel dynamics in space and time. These scientific developments are of great importance for the topic under consideration. Often, complexity is the buzzword that unites them.

We will not try to supply a strict definition, merely provide some reflections which serve our purpose in later parts of the book. Let a complex system be any set of elements, material and non-material, interrelationships and procedures. It can be hypothesized that complexity emerges in open systems in which the elements have many and varied degrees of freedom to act and of interactions. However, it is tempting to say 'complexity is in the eye of the beholder'. In other words: saying that something is complex gives it a

TABLE 5.2   DEVELOPMENT PATH OF HUMAN ACTIVITIES

Activity	Relevant aspects
language	communication
control of fire	burning of vegetation
	protection, shelter
	food preparation
hunting, fishing	food
	cutting tools
	extermination of animals
domestication of plants	food: provision/storage
	tree clearing and soil cultivation
	settlements and markets
	food surplus => rituals and priests, urbanization
	trade, 'money'
domestication of animals	food: herding and animal husbandry
	source of power in agriculture
	means of transport in trade, war etc.
	diseases
shelter	dwellings: clay, reed, stone
	clothes: fibres, animal skins
exchange	trading infrastructure: roads, bridges
	market places
war and conquest	weapons, defence works
	palaces
religion	rituals, sacred places
	temples
forestry and mining	construction materials: stone, wood, clay
	pottery: food/water storage, ceramics
	art: obsidian, amber, metals
	hunting, war and conquest: wood, stone, metal tools
control of water	food: irrigation
	source of power
ships	transport and trade
	conquest
writing	communication, organization and administration
	bookkeeping and trade
	dissemination of knowledge

Complexity is a complex concept. It is a property of a real-world system which manifests itself in the inability of any one formalism being adequate to capture all its properties. It depends on the language used to describe it and is the opposite of reductionism. Complexity can be characterized by a lack of symmetry. It is determined by two dimensions: distinction and connection. Neither are objective properties: they depend on what is distinguished by the observer. In anthropology the notions of 'emic' and 'etic' are introduced to differentiate between descriptions of a system as seen from one of its members (emic) as against a description from an outsider vantage point (etic). One measure of complexity, it can be argued, is the number of possible valid descriptions which can be given of a system by observers.

Complex systems may develop self-organizing patterns and thus present surprizing behaviour – occurring in the narrow band between order and chaos, where the information content is highest. Complex systems can acquire emergent properties in their evolution, that is, properties that cannot be defined or explained in term of the properties of its parts or its antecedent conditions. The notion of emergence can thus be considered as a result of the limitations of the Newtonian formalism: it is a response to failure.

In the present context, it is important to realize that socio-natural systems are complex systems. They may exhibit emergent properties which may survive and be reproduced. In this evolutionary process, natural selection will tend to increase control and the action span viz-à-vis environmental change – in other words: the system develops requisite variety.[10] Socio-natural systems co-evolve: the increase in variety in one system often creates an increased need for variety in others. Evolution will tend to irreversibly produce functional differentiation, because breaking down a decision problem into relatively independent sub-problems enhances controllability. A corollary to this statement is that, for near-decomposable systems, the right representation of the underlying, often simple laws may greatly simplify it. Complexity is partly apparent and: 'the central task of natural science is to make the wonderful commonplace: to show that complexity, correctly viewed, is only a mask for simplicity; to find pattern hidden in apparent chaos.' (Simon 1969: 3) It is along these lines that one may argue that reducing the complexity of the environment is what civilization is all about.

Some have stressed the role of communication in complex systems. Members of a human group or society are performing their activities on the basis of shared meanings and communication. '[Luhmann] views society as a self-organizing (social) system of communications, based on complementarity of expectations among individuals... In the process the complexity inherent in social action is reduced by harmonizing the perspectives of the actors.' (Leeuw 1998: 9) Such attempts to organize observations leads to coherent worldviews, for instance the cultural perspectives discussed in Chapter 8.

contextual characteristic. Here, another factor is to be introduced: the (human) observer. There is an increasing awareness of the various ways in which an observer filters information, for instance in decision-making processes (Morecroft 1992). Experiences are organized by several subsequent layers: first, tradition, culture and the like; next, organizational and geographical structure; next, information, measurement and communication systems; then operating goals, rewards and incentives; and, finally, people's cognitive limitations. Complexity is in the interplay between system and observer, the latter operating within the limited domain of possible observations – that is, within 'bounded rationality'.[11] One consequence is that a complex system can be described in many different ways. At each level a complex system is only intelligible in terms of its own ordering principle, that is, from a top-down orientation. Systems theory attempts to generate statements from a higher, 'etic' level, as opposed to the statements generated at a lower, 'emic', level.

In the present context, we use complexity to indicate that a system apparently exhibits complex behaviour that is not easily understood, handled or (re)constructed by (most) observers. Change in such – evolutionary socio-natural – systems consists of a combination of changes: in actions, in characteristics, and in relationships.[12] Relatively low-complexity events, behaviour and structures are those of controlled experiments in physics and chemistry. Of higher complexity are biological systems and their building blocks. Still higher complexity is exhibited by an ecosystem with its inhabitants and their genetic codes and intricate web of connections, which gives rise to overall behaviour to be understood only at the system level. Humans, they themselves usually suppose, are at the highest level of complexity in terms of individual diversity, genetic and cultural codes and interconnections. At the same time, humans – as individuals and as groups – are intricately connected to the lower-complexity systems.

In a somewhat different vein, levels of complexity can be seen as representing an ascending order of intentional consciousness (Vries 1996). Whether this is read as an unfolding, or is pushed from below – as in the materialist-empiricist orientation – or as a teleological drift towards above – as in the metaphysical-spiritual orientation – is as yet an open question, for each individual human as well as for human society at large. It is important to realize that our observations, if not part of an analytical-reductionist experiment, are constructions across all levels – the essence of the systems perspective. At each level also all scales of time and space exist. *Figure 5.4* is an attempt to sketch such a framework; arrows indicate relationships between the material flows, the behaviour and information flows and the value and belief systems.

In the present context, it is possible to interpret a description of a human group in biogeographical terms at the lower plane, for instance a semi-arid steppe or a dense forest. In interacting with local and global causal dynamic and contingencies, such groups develop mutual relationships between its members and with other groups. These can be mapped as representations of information flows and actor rules at the middle plane. To

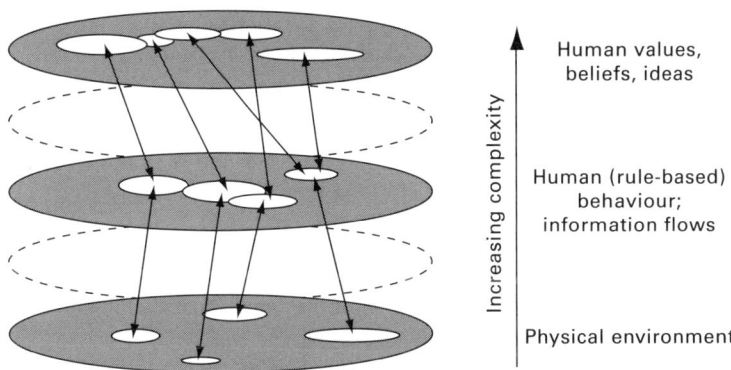

Human values,
beliefs, ideas

Increasing complexity

Human (rule-based)
behaviour;
information flows

Physical environment

FIGURE 5.4

Layers of reality: as the degrees of freedom and variety of and interactions between system elements increase, complexity increases and – relative – ignorance gives room for value-based interpretations and controversies.

satisfy the human search for meaning and understanding as well as to legitimize prevailing social relationships, more elaborate representations come into existence – one may think of the Mother Goddess and Sun worshipping in ancient cultures or the harmony between heaven and earth in Chinese culture. These can be thought to represent the third plane – and still, one may presume, in one way or another reflect the underlying levels. Whether there are universal representations – 'laws' – at the middle or upper planes is one of the lasting quests in the social sciences as well as one of the rationales behind this book's attempt at synthesis. To explore whether and where the Mappae Mundi converge could be one of the greatest tasks for humanity.

This representation could help to communicate that 'strong' science, generating statements on the basis of controlled experiments/investigation only covers a limited domain of the physical environment and an even smaller part of the levels of behaviour and values. For more complex systems, our knowledge will always be approximate. There will always be competing explanations of real-world observations that can be used to support one's behaviour and one's beliefs, values and preferences. Such controversies are, in fact, what drives social structuring. They are an inherent part of the scientific enterprise and will be with us for a long time, if not forever. Indeed, they reflect inherent uncertainties in our knowledge and are used to target areas of present and future research. We come back to this in Chapter 8. After these brief discussion on concepts used in the remainder of this book – time and space, resources and complexity – we now say a bit more about the scientific methods used to uncover the past.

A 'third' dimension   A kind of 'complexity axis' has often been proposed. Maybe it is in the nature of humans to think in terms of hierarchies. Teilhard de Chardin (1963) advances complexity and interiorization as a third dimension alongside the infinitely large and the infinitesimally small; his concept of the noösphere is part of the process of its unfolding. Schumacher introduces it, with reference to Thomas of Aquino, in his book *A Guide for the Perplexed* (Schumacher 1977). Shri Aurobindo perceives an evolution towards an ever higher consciousness (Aurobindo 1998). The Eastern chakra doctrine expresses a similar experience. Jantsch puts forward the same vision but in more recent, scientific terminology in his book *The Self-organizing Universe* (Jantsch 1980). Many authors suggest a similar hierarchy from a more worldly orientation. Besides Marx's distinction between an infrastructure and a superstructure, one may think of the spectrum from 'low' to 'high' human needs proposed by the psychologist Maslow. Daly used a hierarchist spectrum of values, ranging from worldly means to ultimate spiritual goals (Daly 1973); Harman founded the Center for Noetic Sciences to explore the fusing of values and self-image (Harman 1993); recent life-science research points at the existence of three cerebral layers (Vroon 1989).

All religious teachings point at a value hierarchy, often in association with Good and Evil, God and the Devil. As Baudelaire expressed it: *'Il y a dans tout homme, à toute heure, deux postulations simultanées, l'une vers Dieu, l'autre vers Satan. L'invocation à Dieu, ou spiritualité, est un désir de monter en rade; celle de Satan, ou animalité, est une joie de descendre.'* In the Bhagavad Gita Krishna talks about the three qualities of prakritri, the sanskrit word for nature or the basic energy from which the mental and physical worlds take shape (Easwaran 1985: 177-178):

Sattva – pure, luminous, and free from sorrow – binds us with attachment
To happiness and wisdom.
Rajas is passion, arising from selfish desire and attachment...
Tamas, born of ignorance, deludes all creatures
through heedlessness, indolence and sleep...
Those who live in sattva go upwards;
Those in rajas remain where they are.
But those immersed in tamas sink downwards.

5.5.   Methods of acquiring knowledge about the past: setting the clock

As part of the scientific endeavour, many methods of scientific enquiry have been developed and refined which are used to investigate past environments and societies. For the present purpose, we will only give a brief description of the various methods that have been developed to make inferences about the past. There are many excellent texts available on the subject (Roberts 1989; Renfrew 1973; Berglund 1986; Lowe 1999; Bradley 1998; Cohen 1999). Each of these methods explores part of the many 'environmental signatures' to be found on earth – and has it particular limitations. By combining a set of environmental proxies the limitations of the individual techniques can be assessed. For example, information on hydrological variation is available from reconstructed lake-level dynamics, direct discharge records and the remains of aquatic organisms such as diatoms or fish bones. Through indirect and direct combination and inference a variety of information can be extracted from material samples, among which age and climate-parameters and vegetation characteristics are the more important ones. Of course, in the everyday world of the scientists involved in such explorations, life is much more difficult than might be deduced from a dry classification of the various methods. In this brief overview we confine ourselves to a consideration of dating methods.

One of the biggest problems facing the study of past environments, in any sphere, is the establishment of a robust chronology, determining when the changes we observe in the proxy indicators took place. Placing past environmental change in a temporal context can be divided into a series of methodological approaches – those that provide an *absolute date* (radiometric and incremental methods) and those that provide a *relative chronology*. A comprehensive review of these is outside the scope of this chapter; although we do provide a discussion of some of the more common techniques.

Pollen analyses of sediments   The study of past environments often starts by accessing archives of sediments, such as lakes, ice-caps, mires or oceans. These sediments are sumps for a range of environmental information on climatic, biotic and human dynamics. To obtain this information, a core of sediment must be recovered and a suite of increasingly sophisticated analytical techniques applied to the sediments. These techniques concentrate on either the physical/chemical character of or on the biological material incorporated within the sedimentary matrix as it is deposited.

One of the most established techniques to reconstruct past environmental change comes from plant material, and in particular pollen. Pollen retained in sediments is particularly suited to unraveling environmental dynamics as they reflect the local and regional vegetation and are readily preserved. By analyzing fossil pollen, combined with a dating chronology, it is possible to reconstruct past plant communities at specific times in the past. When this is carried out from a number of samples, at a number of different sites, a regional picture of vegetation dynamics through time can be constructed. This animation reflects the environmental controls, both climate and cultural, operating within the area under investigation.

5.5.1. *Absolute dating*

There are two suites of methods that allow the age of the material under investigation to be established in years before the present (yr BP): radiometric dating and incremental dating.

Radiometric dating (using isotopes of carbon, oxygen and other elements)
These dating techniques rely on analyzing the difference in decay rates of different isotopes of the same element. Different techniques and different elements offer a diverse age range, methodology, precision and associated restrictions. Oxygen isotope stratigraphy measures variation in ^{18}O due to seasonal cooling and can be used to provide a correlative chronological framework for many sedimentary records, particularly those from marine environments that stretch back several million years. Lead (^{210}Pb) and caesium (^{137}Cs) dating are concerned with dating isotopes with a relatively short half-life, but can be very useful techniques for determining environmental changes over tens to hundreds of years.

One of the most commonly used techniques is that of radiocarbon dating.[13] Traces of radiocarbon ^{14}C are present in all carbon containing materials – wood, charcoal, peat, seeds, bone, ancient pigments, honey and milk, metal casting ores, cloth, eggshell and groundwater to name but a few. Initially the half-life, i.e. the time it takes for half the sample to disappear, of radiocarbon (^{14}C) was estimated to be 5568 years. The amount of ^{14}C in a sample can be counted to give the so-called ^{14}C age in years before present (^{14}C yr BP). The present is defined by convention as the year 1950 AD because this is when a large number of nuclear bombs were exploded resulting in creation of artificial radiocarbon. For example, if only 25% of the original amount of ^{14}C is present in a sample, a date of 11,136 ^{14}C yr BP is produced. One of the assumptions behind radiocarbon dating method was the constancy of the atmospheric ^{14}C concentration; this has proved to be false with slight variations in the amount of ^{14}C production through time due to changes in solar activity. Indeed, in addition to being able to provide a chronology, ^{14}C variations also provide information on past changes in the cosmic rays, solar activity, the Earth's magnetic field and the global carbon cycle (Geel 1996).

One of the most exciting developments in radiocarbon dating has been the accelerator mass spectrometry (AMS) technique that has allowed for the counting of the actual number of ^{14}C atoms rather than an estimation of the percentage present within a gas. The advantages of AMS are the smaller sample sizes required, shorter measuring times and greater precision afforded (Grove 1992). For example, dates on individual seeds can determine spatial patterning of the spread of agriculture. The method has significantly influenced archaeological and historical insights. It also provides a good example of how human action – in this case, the emission of CO_2 from fossil fuel burning and the testing of atomic bombs – can complicate our efforts to uncover the past. These emissions have altered the atmospheric ratio of ^{14}C to ^{12}C so that the radiocarbon dating method is of little use for samples less than 150 years old. The radiocarbon dating method cannot date anything older than about 70,000 years and gives interpretative limitations on dates in excess of 20,000 years.

Incremental dating

This suite of techniques relies on the regular accumulation of biological or lithological material through natural processes. These are quite diverse, from sedimentary basins that accumulate a layer of sediment following every summer, trees and stalagmites and corals with annual accumulations of carbonate, and lichens with a known growth rate from a central point. By either counting and/or measuring these accumulations one can develop a chronology. One of the best known techniques is dendrochronology or tree-ring counting. This method is based on the natural growth process of trees; by counting the number of growth rings between the bark and the centre of a living tree, the age of the tree can be determined. How far back one can go depends on the tree age. Some trees

---

Age equivalence dating A group of methods are used to determine age equivalence: they are concerned with the recognition of simultaneity of processes. Such 'marker horizons' are quite diverse and can be found under a range of environments. Most systems that involve fluid dynamics result in marker horizons that can provide an insight into past environments and a relative date for an event. Where there is either a well-established chronology or a distinctive stratigraphic marker, these can be used to infer a date or to identify an event across a spatial range. One good example of such an application comes from volcanic ash or tephra. These form around a volcanic source and can be quite extensive for large eruptions. Where these are identified by their composition (Fe-Ti oxide, glass, ferromagnesian, mineralogy) and dated by a radiometric method, tephra layers can provide clearly defined time markers that allow for correlation across broad geological areas. However, multiple dates on a single tephra show considerable intra-sample variation and indicate that obtaining dates for tephra is not a simple process (Newton 1999). If not associated with independent age estimates they can still be a good marker horizon.

These include desert dune systems, river terraces, former coastlines, old shoreline knick points and littoral deposits resulting from Holocene period lake fluctuations. In areas that were subjected to glacial action in the past, such as high latitudes or altitudes, the past action of the ice will leave sediment behind, usually in linear accumulations called moraines. For example evidence from montane glaciation has been successfully used to reconstruct environmental change in tropical Africa, these being placed within a robust chronology (Osmaston 1989).

are very long lived – for example, the North American bristlecone pine lives to 4000 years.

The technique can be extended back in time by accessing trees that have died and become preserved in accumulated sediments or in buildings. Tree ring chronologies from different sources can be matched together like the pieces of a jigsaw to position wood of an unknown date. By cross-dating sequences of tree rings from dead trees or wood, it is possible to push dendrochronological records back far beyond the age of living trees. For example, ancient conifer logs in western Tasmania have provided a 11,600-year span of precise dating at annual resolution. Such records also provide a master calibration curve, which is associated with radiocarbon dates to correct for past atmospheric fluctuations in ^{14}C concentrations and give ages in calendar years. In this way, they give a basic reference for radiocarbon laboratories worldwide. These are used throughout this book. This technique of dating has the added value of providing information on past environmental change. The width, character and chemical composition of the individual rings is an indicator of climatic (temperature, rainfall, seasonality, etc.) and environmental (CO_2 concentration, nutrient status, fire incidence, etc.) circumstances. Stalagmites and coral also develop seasonal incremental growth bands and also contain high-resolution late Holocene palaeo-environmental information for constructing past chronologies and information on past environments.

5.5.2.   *Relative estimates of age*

This suite of techniques is used to establish the relative order of antiquity – it is similar to the previously mentioned phaseology. The relative age of a landform or sedimentary unit can be derived from the degree of transformation resulting from a physical or chemical degradation process operating through time. One of the main areas where these techniques are applied, usually in combination, are cultural development stages. One technique is the direct analysis of past occupation layers and the associated artefacts such as pottery, metal work, clothing and tools. Some of the oldest cultural reconstructions are carried out on skeleton types with the hominid finds being placed into recognizable species groups on skull morphology. Following these developments a chronology of the use of tools has been produced – early pebble cultures were replaced by worked stone, and became more refined and specialized as tool manufacture developed. More recently in human prehistory, artefact styles such as pottery type are often used to trace the transitions for one cultural group, particularly as there is a well-documented temporal succession of pottery styles. Another well-established chronological framework within which to place temporal constraints is derived from characterizing the metallurgy practised. This is well established in Europe with its transition from copper to tin to bronze to iron. Additional sources of information come from the modern composition and distribution of ethnic groups, historical evidence and linguistic analysis. For example, the Bornu chronicles contain information about the Lake Chad region from well before 500 yr BP and can be an excellent source of information on droughts, famines and prosperous periods. Egyptian hieroglyphs, ancient texts of the Maya amongst other prehistoric 'texts' are slowly being recyphered to reveal the information they retain regarding the culture of the time. However, care must be taken to incorporate these records in the light of other available information, as propaganda may have been rife in historical times. More cryptic are the monuments and building structures which themselves are in the process of continual re-interpretation.

The range of archaeological investigations indicates not only the growing tendency to remain in one place but also the growth in ritual, an important factor in social cohesion. Similarly to the record of environmental change, the Holocene period is characterized by recognizable cultural developmental stages; these allow the transition to a centralized, socially structured society observable today to be reconstructed. However, as with the palaeo-environmental information, the amount of information is skewed towards certain locations and time periods. In common with the data from sedimentary sequences, these temporal divisions should be viewed as plastic: the reality is a transgressive development from nomadic, hunter-gatherer populations to a food producing society that is settled and socially structured (cf. Chapter 4). These transitions are riddled with numerous gaps between the living world and the proxy traces, and it is these gaps that fuel ongoing research. As new techniques become available and established techniques develop, new insights into the 'established' reconstruction of the past and the relationship of the present are developing.

5.6.   The potential for human habitation and stages of agricultural development

We end this chapter with an attempt to give a quantitative impression of the density of human populations in the past, using the ideas of carrying capacity and agricultural stages. Carrying capacity is a well-known concept in ecology, defined as the maximum population of a given organism that a particular environment can sustain. It implies a continuing yield without environmental damage or degradation. The concept is not as clear as it may seem: both the organism and the environment, including all other organisms, are usually in a continuous process of mutual change and adjustment. Notably human interventions may change the carrying capacity by controlling other species, influencing soil and river streams. As a result, the carrying capacity for human populations can only be defined in a dynamic context, using a proxy for the 'development stage' to include the appropriate interventions and consequences. *Figure 5.5* is a way of visualizing the dynamic character of the carrying capacity. At a given site a human group may evolve to a situation in which they reach the carrying capacity for a given environment

FIGURE 5.5

The carrying capacity of a region as a sequence of population growth near or above the prevailing value (N1,P1) and a resumption of population growth with new techniques (N2,P2) in a new era.

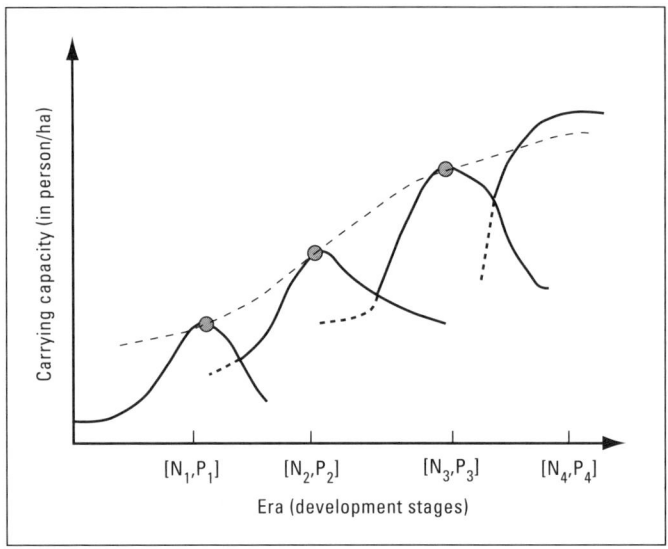

and set of habits, tools and skills: (N_1,P_1). In response to external and internal stresses, such a group may – or may not – make the transition to a next stage where the improved tools and skills in combination with the environment as of then can sustain a larger population. It should be noted that a population may live for long periods below its carrying capacity – as has been observed, for instance, in several hunter-gatherer populations (Sahlins 1972).

The idea of agricultural stages is often associated with Boserup's *Population and Techno-logical Change* (1981), in which she categorized a sequence of stages in agricultural development: hunter-gatherers, pastoralism, fallow forest, bush fallow, short fallow with domestic animals, annual cropping with intensive animal husbandry, and multi-cropping with little animal food. Mixed forms may occur in some areas. The gradual decline in the fallow period is a key determinant of agricultural system evolution in relation to the environmental potential and the available tools. An attempt has been made to correlate various proxies for the development stages – such as the ratio of pasture to arable land and annual cropping frequency – with population density in terms of carrying capacity. As *Figure 5.6* shows, increasing population density goes with a decline in animals and pastureland per person and an increase in the intensity of land use intensity as measured by the number of crops and operations, irrigation, fertilizer, etc. Extensive databases for a

FIGURE 5.6

Indicators of agricultural development as a function of population density (after Boserup 1981, 1965). We use population density classes as proposed by Boserup: class i corresponds with a population density between 2^{i-1} and 2^i people/km².

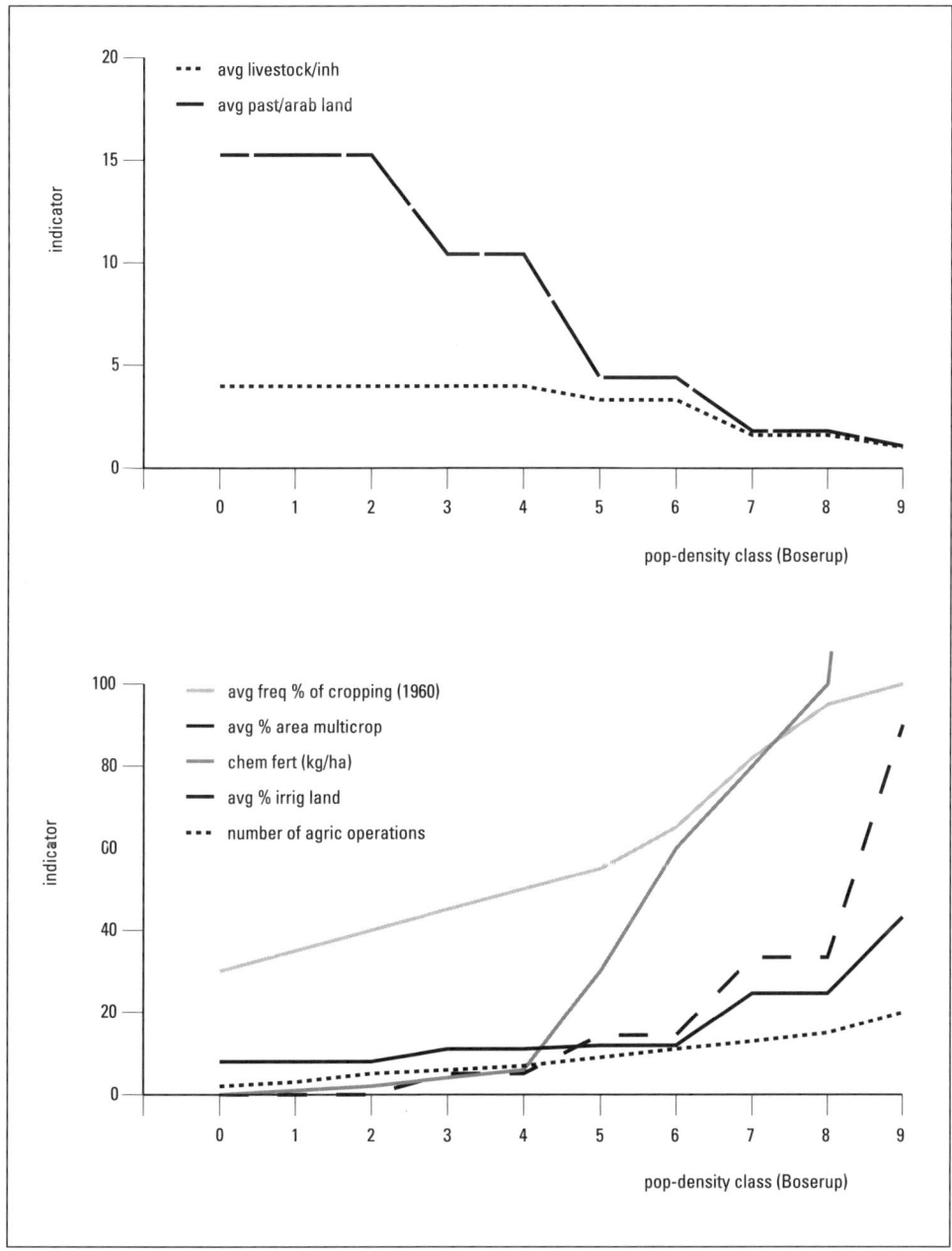

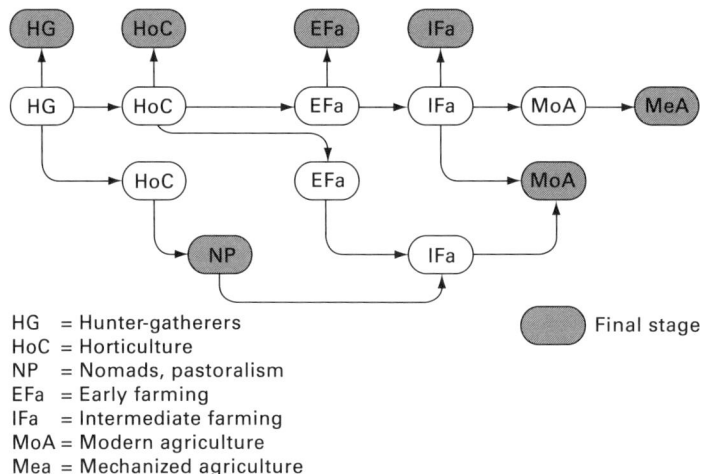

HG   = Hunter-gatherers
HoC = Horticulture
NP   = Nomads, pastoralism
EFa = Early farming
IFa   = Intermediate farming
MoA = Modern agriculture
Mea = Mechanized agriculture

Final stage

FIGURE 5.7

Simplified scheme of agricultural system development

variety of 20th century systems indicate that marginal returns on agriculture, in a subsistence economy, decline with increasing labour input (Tainter 1988 Chapter 6).

For the present purpose we have simplified the possible routes in agricultural developments as shown in *Figure 5.7*. In this figure, agricultural productivity is categorized on the basis of technological advancements, combined in a development multiplier $m(k)$ where k is the development stage. With increasing development and subsequent increase of productivity the need to rely on wild resources decreased. Hunter-gatherers (HG, k = 1) relied completely on wild resources and feed for the largest part on vegetable supplies. Their extraction of natural, i.e. wild or non-domesticated, resources was restricted. Horticulturists (HoC, k = 2) are sustained by their cultivated crops although their diet is supplied by the gathering of wild vegetables and, to a lesser extent, by wild animals. Also, development of husbandry settled secondary production in the human community and reduced the need to hunt. Nomads and pastoralists (NP, k = 3) are assumed to consist of herding groups that subsist from the secundary production of domesticated ruminants (Simmons 1989). They can be considered as gatherers because they depend almost entirely on the supply of converted vegetable material accumulated by domesticated animals. Early farming (EF, k = 4) is the stage where draft animals were not used for tillage and agricultural production depended completely on the human labour force. It is assumed that the farmer's food at this stage consisted largely of yields from agriculture and livestock and that this diet was supplemented by hunting. In the intermediate farming stage (IF, $k = 5$) draft animals (horses, oxen, and the like) were put into action to assist in tillage. Replacement of the human work reserve by the power of animals greatly increased the agricultural potential of the farmers, while at the same time sharply reducing the demand for human labour. Finally, in modern and mechanized agriculture (MoA, MeA, $k = 6$) draft animals were exchanged for engines. The increase in replacement ratios that ensued from this process correspondingly boosted agricultural production, in combination with improved cultivation and breeding techniques, and the development of pesticides.

The next step is to link the (past) environment to the agricultural stages. The question is how to construct from the available climate and vegetation indicators a proxy for the carrying capacity for humans at a given development stage. We use the following expression for the human habitat potential (*HHP*) as function of development stage k and location *I*:

$$HHP[k,i] = \frac{BaseYield[CSI_i] * EnvMult[i] * DevStageMult[k]}{Food\,Re\,q[k]} \text{ (people/ha)}$$

with *BaseYield* being an estimate of prevailing crop productivity at some well-defined stages. We use the crop suitability index *CSI[i]* as calculated in the IMAGE model.[14] It is an aggregate of temperature, rainfall and elevation; on length of growing season; and on soil characteristics as of 1970. *EnvMult[i]* takes into account the occurrence of environmental constraints or opportunities such as elevation and the presence or absence of rivers. *DevStageMult[k]* expresses the factor with which the *BaseYield* is to be multiplied to represent the agricultural practices and technology at stage k. The product of *BaseYield*, *EnvMult* and *DevStageMult* is the food extraction potential *FEP[i,k]* of one hectare in location *i* and development stage k.

Finally, *FoodReq FR[k]* is the food required per individual which is a function of the development stage because the energy requirement for farming changed as a result of the replacement of human labour by draft animals and in later stages by mechanized power. Estimates of *FR* for individuals in a family cluster in various development stages are shown in *Figure 5.8*. The ratio *FEP/FR* is a first approximation of how many individuals can be supported from the agricultural yield of one hectare, given development stage k at place i – to be interpreted as the carrying capacity (or *HHP*) in people/ha. It should be noted that time as such is implicit in this approach.

The procedure outlined above allows us to construct spatially explicit maps of potential population density (or *HHP*) over the past millennia. We start with the first stage, that of hunter-gatherers, for which we have followed a slightly different procedure than in the above equation: the *BaseYield* is assumed to be a function of the net primary productivi-

FIGURE 5.8

Estimates of the food requirement FR for various development stages

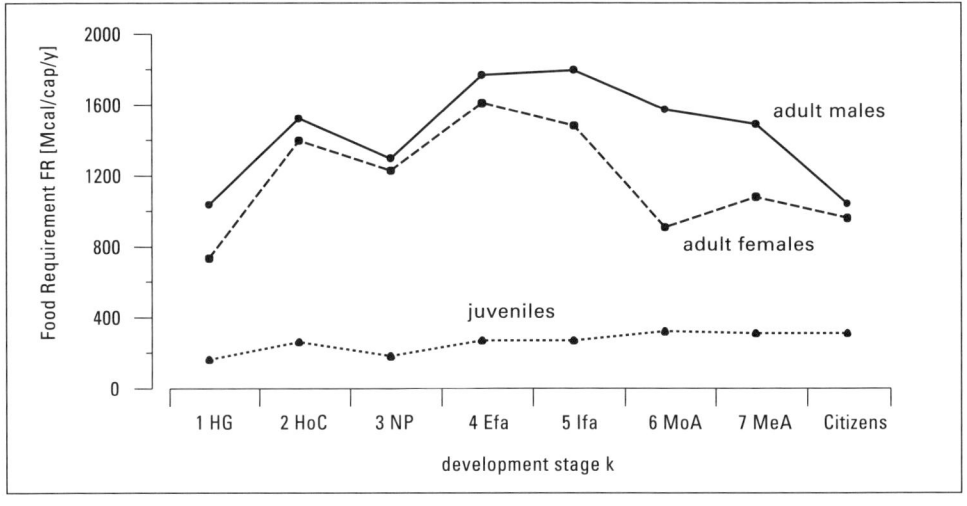

ty *NPP[i]* of the land on location *i*. This function should reflect the relative unattractiveness of the areas with very low (such as tundras) or very high (such as tropical forests) *NPP*-values for hunter-gatherers. Many areas were uninhabitable for humans because they were occupied by inimical species: swamps and river delta by malaria mosquitoes, forests by wild animals. In addition, large trees could not be cut until certain tools were available. The *BaseYield* is therefore assumed to increase until a *NPP* value of about 500 kg/yr/m² after which is declines. We used similar multipliers for elevation and rivers (*EnvMult*) to reflect the relative attractiveness of regions outside the high mountain ranges and near rivers. It was assumed that only 10% of the area of each grid cell was accessible for food extraction by hunter-gatherers. Probably the most serious error is that present-day vegetation, not palaeo-vegetation, is used. For the next stage, nomad-pastoralists, we assume that only the steppes and savannes are suitable for herding by letting the *BaseYield* drop quickly beyond 500 kg/yr/m².

For the subsequent stages of agriculture, we have calculated the *CSI* for the crops cultivated around 1970.[15] We then used estimates for the development stage multipliers *DevStage[k]* (*Table 5.3*). We also made an assumption that about a fraction of a cell area was under cultivation because not the whole area was used for agriculture – there was much uncultivated land occupied mainly by forests and referred to as 'culturable waste' by British observers in India in the 19th century. In combination with the environmental multiplier *EnvMult[i]*, an average potential population density in a grid cell can be estimated.

The results of these crude and preliminary estimates of the Human Habitat Potential are, for three subsequent early stages, shown in Figure 5.9a-c (see p. 171).

Urbanization led to increasing spatial gradients in population density which makes the average population density – in people/km^2 across a cell of about 2500 km^2 – a less interesting quantity. Can we make a link here with the archaeological and historical estimates of city sizes? To this end we estimate in a simple manner the labour requirements for food production, from which then the potential for urbanization – discussed in the previous chapter in qualitative terms – is calculated. It is assumed that for horticulturists – as for hunter-gatherers – everyone is involved in food procurement. However, for later stages we use a labour replacement factor by which the required labour is reduced (*Table 5.3*). This factor accounts for the use of animal and later machine draft power as early farmers developed towards modern agricultural practices.[16] The difference between the potential population density and the required farmer density is a measure for the potential for urbanization. *Table 5.3* gives the range of potential average density of an urban population across a cell.

A comparison with population estimates from archaeologists and historians for some regions with ancient civilizations shows that our results have the right order of magnitude. *Figure 5.10* (see p. 172) shows some population time-series for several states or empires. Presuming some sort of early and intermediate farming systems in these ancient civilizations, a loose link between the development stages and the historical time-axis can be derived. In the Egyptian Nile Valley stage 5 had already been reached by about 5000 yr BP, reaching stage 7-8 around 2000 yr BP. This suggests a combination of

TABLE 5.3   FACTORS USED TO ESTIMATE THE BASEYIELD AND THE REQUIRED LABOUR

Stage	Development stage multiplier	Replacement factor	Fraction of cell (2500 km^2) cultivated	Urbanization potential in people/km^2
Hunter-Gatherer HG	1	1	0.1	0
Horticulturalists HoC	1.8	1	0.12	0
Early farming Ef	3.5	21-42	0.15-0.25	0.5-0.8
Intermediate farming IF	6.8	38-104	0.25-0.4	1.7-2.7
Modern Agriculture MoA	12.8	56-126	0.3-0.5	5-8.4
Mechanized Agriculture MeA	94.6	72-198	0.3-0.6	36-72

higher fertility and more advanced practices than in almost any other world region at the time – the other civilizations were at stages 1-2 and 3-5 respectively in those years.

One serious error in our estimates of population densities at higher development stages is the omission of transport and trade. Whereas in subsistence economies the area for food provision had to be within a few hours walk, the advanced means of transport have increased this to much larger distances (cf. Chapter 6). River valleys and deltas and coastal areas provided opportunities for transport and trade; this often stimulated habitation and settlement formation far beyond the potential for local food extraction.[17] The availability of resources such as wood or metal ores often had similar consequences. In such situations a much higher population density could be sustained and the urbanization was much higher than estimates from the potential for local food extraction would indicate (cf. Section 4.4.2). This situation certainly prevailed in such centres as ancient Egypt, Mesopotamia, Greece and Mexico. It was even more obvious in later metropolitan areas such as Rome, Xi'an, Istanbul and Bagdad. One can get an impression of this effect by associating each development stage with a distance across which bulk transport of food was economic.

5.7.   Conclusions

To acquire knowledge about past human-environment interactions, we need concepts to classify and organize 'the facts' derived from observations using increasingly sophisticated techniques. These scientific facts have to be contextualized to become more than an incoherent sequence of material and mental objects. The analysis undertaken in this book is largely according to the rules of the reductionist-empiricist science and biases are unavoidable. Models in the sense of more or less formal representations of observations – 'mental maps' – are a necessary tool in this process. Some 'archetypical' models about human-environment interactions, such as logistic growth against hard or soft limits, can be helpful in communicating basic ideas. However, they are simplifications and their use may be misleading, like the use of analogues and metaphors.

Two essential concepts in this book are time and space. Both have been and are used by humans to orient themselves. It should be realized that as such they are socially constructed and hence have been experienced differently by peoples in different times and places. As a social construct they bridge the personal, subjective and 'scientific' objective nature of experience of time and space. Another key concept is complexity – socio-natural systems are complex systems. The notion of complexity appears to be at the centre of an attempt to go beyond the limitations of classical Newtonian science. There is not yet a well-defined 'theory of complexity' and knowledge of complex systems will probably always remain approximate. Yet, the inclusion of individual agents with rules and information exchanges into simulation models, possibly thanks to huge increases in computing power, give a deeper understanding in complex socio-natural systems. Relating complexity to an ascending order of intentional consciousness may diminish the mutual misunderstanding and misappreciation of 'strong' natural science on the one hand and 'soft' social sciences on the other – an issue at the heart of this book.

Many of the stories presented in this book are based on scientific evidence. It is therefore important to understand the techniques and methods used, in particular for dating, and their strong and weak points. Only in such a way one can appreciate their relevance in the construction of – sometimes quite divergent – stories and models. A first, tentative sketch of the potential human habitat is given and can possibly serve as an experiment in synthesizing various approaches, insights and data into a broad time-space framework.

6

Increasing Social Complexity

DE VRIES

> ... des populations denses sont généralement douées d'une civilisation supérieure: elles ont en effet su résoudre les problèmes économiques, techniques, sociaux et politiques posés par les fortes densités.
>
> *Gourou 1947: 3*

6.1.   Introduction

One of the great questions about human societies is how they emerged and transformed – and sometimes decayed – in the face of environmental change. With increased capabilities to use animals, store food and manage water supplies came a surplus of food exceeding the needs for bare survival. This allowed the rise of warriors and priests, administrations, palaces and temples – at least so the story goes. It has been related in previous chapters as the process of agrarianization, with many linked driving forces specific to given cultures and ecological regimes. Within each group of humans there would have been individuals with different skills and traits. Each group was confronted with different environmental opportunities and threats – and neighbours – and evolved in a continuous process of response and adaptation. Among some, the dominant trend may have been to live 'the good life'. Among many, the increase in social complexity occurred in response to the need and wish to bring forth food, water and shelter from an exacting and unpredictable natural environment. In the process, some groups settled down and developed forms of agro-pastoralism that developed into large-scale land clearing and irrigation efforts; others never settled down remaining mobile nomads with large animal herds. Often neighbouring groups of humans became an ever greater enemy and war and migrations – as well as trade – intensified.

In previous chapters the natural environment has been described as a background against which the first steps into the second, agricultural regime were set. We now focus

> **Mysteries – science's atrium?** Could it be that, as a convergence of research re-
> sults from geology, astronomy, palaeo-climatology and archaeology suggests to some,
> that there have been grand civilizations as long ago as 12,000 yr BP? At present we are
> largely ignorant, it seems, about their interaction with the natural environment. One
> hypothesis is that the large climate changes coincident with the end of the last glacial
> period have largely wiped out such civilizations. Antarctica may have been involved
> and some of their achievements may have been transmitted to the better known
> ancient civilizations – Atlantis, after all (Hancock 1995). Another hypothesis is that some
> 9500 years ago the rapid rise in sea level caused the Mediterranean Sea to overflow
> into the Black Sea which by then may have shrunk to the size of a rather small lake
> (Ryan 1998). Although controversial, it might explain recent insights into the early cul-
> tures in the Balkans and the waves of immigration into Europe. Enough riddles remain
> to keep future generations of curious scientists at work, if only to refute modern myths.

on the further unfolding of social complexity because it is an essential component of any
meaningful understanding and interpretation of the human-environment relationship.[1]
Both extensive and intensive growth of human populations and their activities led to
more intense and widespread interference with the environment and to the spreading
and spatial concentrations of populations. The natural environment was the setting that
provided the means for such an increase in complexity – or failed to do so. What was
the role of the natural environment as a formative resource and as a constraining
force? What were the effects of environmental change? And what was the role of the
major transmission mechanisms: trade, conquest and migration? Social organization
has partly evolved in response to opportunities for new and improved ways of life and to
natural disasters. Can variation in the environment explain the nature of social organization and symbolic complexity and the associated social stratifications? And to what
extent was the perception of environmental resources and risks a major determinant of
how social complexity took shape? Our approach here is to first present a set of narratives.

6.2.   Manifestations of increasing social complexity

As human groups increased in size, they learned to store food to overcome natural limitations; with it came tools, transport devices and storage rooms. Specialization in certain skills began – fishing, hunting, stone quarrying, house building, pottery, metal-
and tool making, boat construction. Trading along trade corridors evolved, market-
places became nodes in an emerging transport infrastructure. It was often one of the

more feasible and successful strategies to reduce risks – of famine, for instance, and of war. In the process, individual households and villages became more dependent upon each other – an unintended but inevitable consequence of increasing interaction (cf. *Table 5.2*). A concurrent process was social stratification (cf. Section 4.4.2). In the ascent to complexity, bands with familial bonds and common residence evolved into communities with land- or property-holding social units and elaborate ceremonies and rituals. Social ranks with differentiation in ownership and access to resources appeared: the chief was born with acclaimed noble birth, a special relationship with the gods and the right to community support and tribute. These chiefdoms often already had large populations with thousands living in villages. It was only one more step towards the state. At this point came the classes of soldiers, priests and kings, of merchants and administrators, who were given part of the food surplus as a reward for real or imaginary talents: physical superiority for good (protection) or bad (extortion), sacred knowledge necessary for rituals, divine ancestry, goods and means of transport for exchange, procedural or informational power. An urban-rural divide started to develop, with larger variations in population density. Complexity manifested itself in increasing spatial interaction, social stratification and demographic and cultural heterogeneity. Let us take a closer look at these developments and follow some of the traces left: the megaliths, the mines and the deforested lands, and the trading and migration routes, before we engage into a more in-depth exploration of the early states and their relationship with the environment.

6.2.1.   Megaliths

An early sign of humans emerging above mere survival are forms of ritual and art. Constructions of large stones – megaliths – have existed in Africa and the Mediterranean. As recounted in Chapter 3, large megaliths embedded in the Late Neolithic period forming stone circles and aligned to the sun have been found in the western Central Sahara predating most of the megalithic features of Europe. Megalithic cultures were widespread in large parts of Europe, with large mounds and graves built around 5000-7000 yr BP. Many of them are on the island of Sardinia, which must have been densely populated by then – perhaps 200,000-300,000 inhabitants, 10% of its present value (Cavalli-Sforza 1995). The megalith constructions on the island of Malta are well known. The archaeologist Evans suggested that 'no more peaceable society seems ever to have existed' than these Neolithic cultures of Malta, but this peaceful and bountiful life came to an abrupt end around 4500 yr BP.

> The reasons why this flourishing and vibrant civilization disappeared are as obscure and mysterious as those that resulted in the end of Catal Huyuk [in Anatolia]. Evans... sought

to explain this by an invasion of war-like people. Gimbutas has suggested that perhaps the natural resources of the island could no longer sustain its inhabitants and deforestation or crop failure may have brought famine, disease and other disasters in its wake.(Rudgley 1998: 23-24)

The Megalithic cultures do suggest a rather independent development in Europe. This could also be the case for the Balkans, where recent excavations suggest civilizational developments possibly independent of the Mycenaean-Aegean cultures (Bailey 2000; Renfrew 1973). Numerous Neolithic sites have been found in the Danube basin with artefacts with an estimated age of 8000 years. Remains of large shrines have been uncovered. The site of Lepenski Vir near Belgrade is, according to its excavator Srejovic, 'proof that the Mesolithic is not the 'dark age' of European prehistory but only a prolonged period of gestation… and that Europe did not have to borrow from the Near East in order to rise above the past.' (quoted in Rudgley 1998: 26). There has been a long debate about the origin of the Megalithic monuments along Europe's Atlantic Coast. Before radiocarbon and dendrological dating methods, it was hypothesized that these large burial monuments had their origin in the Eastern Mediterranean. It became apparent that they are older than the Cretan and Mycenaean cultures of the 4th millennium BP (Renfrew 1973). It may well be that these monuments originated from Mesolithic people who developed a more elaborate burial ritual in consequence of the evolution of farming communities and the associated increasing population densities.

Whatever the precise origins and meaning, these monuments dated between 7000 and 3000 yr BP stand as durable examples of human artefacts. It seems that the colonists settling on islands such as Malta and Corsica were able to create a surplus sufficient to erect huge temple and grave buildings. In all of these situations, it is the organization of people that is a reflection as well as a determinant of their relationship with the natural environment. The megaliths may be an expression of some sort of more intense – peaceful – competition between neighbouring groups, leading to more elaborate celebrations, gift exchanges and memorials and itself a possible consequence of rising population densities. There are similar peaceful competition examples in history: the medieval towers of San Gimignano in Tuscany or the huge skyscraper office buildings in today's megacities, for instance. Comparison with more recent populations in the Pacific, for instance on Tahiti and Easter Island, and with present-day farming communities in Asia also suggests such social dynamics. It is tempting to compare the organization of the small communities in the Orkney Islands who constructed the Megalithic burial mounds some 5000-6000 years ago with what has been created much later on Easter Island (Renfrew 1973). The scarce historical evidence also suggests that here, too, competition may have been at the root of collapse from environmental overexploitation.

The story of Easter Island A famous example of how a finite island environment posed limits to human expansion and how people responded to the resulting feedback loop is Easter Island, the small island in the Pacific Ocean which was 'discovered' by the Dutch admiral Roggeveen on Easter Sunday 1722 (Ponting 1991; Redman 1999; Renfrew 1973). When he set foot on this small (400 km^2) island in the Pacific Ocean, it had a primitive society 'with about 3000 people living in squalid reed huts or caves, engaged in almost perpetual warfare and resorting to cannibalism in a desperate attempt to supplement the meagre food supplies on the island.' (Ponting 1991: 1) Scattered across the island were over 600 massive stone statues that were on average some 6 metres high. Upon the arrival of the Europeans, the inhabitants of the island seemed incapable of carving and moving statues and indicated they had no knowledge of how to do so. A widely accepted explanation of this 'mystery' is that deforestation for ceremonial purposes led to the collapse of this at one time possibly most advanced Polynesian society with some 7000 inhabitants around 1550.

Ponting (1991) tells the story in a nice, evocative way. Polynesian settlers arrived at around 1500 yr BP. The island had few resources and the inhabitants mainly lived on a diet of sweet potatoes and chickens, which was nutritionally adequate and not demanding in terms of labour. In Ponting's account, it was the combination of plenty of free time for ceremonial activities and enduring competition and conflict between the tribal clan centres and chiefs that led to the achievements and subsequent fall of Easter Island society. Ceremonial activities and the construction of stone statues absorbed enormous amounts of peasant labour – obsidian stone axes were the only tools. To transport these huge statues, wood was required as there were no suitable animals. '... at the time of the initial settlement Easter Island had a dense vegetation... As the population slowly increased, trees would have been cut down to provide clearings for agriculture, fuel for heating and cooking, construction material for household goods, pole and thatch houses and canoes for fishing. The most demanding requirement of all was the need to move the large number of enormously heavy statues... The only way this could have been done was by large numbers of people guiding and sliding them along a form of flexible tracking made up of tree trunks... Prodigious quantities of timber would have been required... As a result by 1600 the island was almost completely deforested.' (Ponting 1991: 5) Social and ceremonial life came to a standstill, wood for houses and canoes became scarce and the soil deteriorated. Fish and crops became more scarce. As chickens became more important, defensive chicken houses were erected. No more statues were built, belief systems fell apart and with them the legitimacy of social organization. Slavery, war and cannibalism followed suit. 'Against great odds the islanders... sustained a way of life in accordance with an elaborate set of social and religious customs that enable them not only to survive but to flourish... But in the end the increasing numbers and cultural ambitions of the islanders proved too great for the limited resources available to them.' (Ponting 1991: 6-7)

Several attempts have been made to enhance the understanding of Easter Island events with help of a mathematical model (Anderies 2000). After all, there are some intriguing questions here. Why did other Polynesian groups who almost always altered their environments equally dramatically not collapse? And, even more importantly, why did the Easter Islanders not respond to the impending catastrophe? Was some form of institutional adaptation prevented by insufficient ecological understanding or conflicts between competing groups, or did the decline occur too quickly for such adaptation? One interesting suggestion from such model explorations is that the very ability of the population to increase its work effort and maintain its material well-being was hiding the feedback loops from the forest resource base so that, when change finally did occur, it was so thoroughly degraded that the change was too rapid and dramatic for effective (institutional) response. Such an explanation is consistent with the archaeological findings.

6.2.2.   Non-agricultural resources

Peoples will consider only those parts of their natural environment as a 'resource' if it somehow fulfils individual or collective needs. Obviously, the existence of available resources in a certain space-time domain has always been a paramount factor in the evolution of human groups. As shown in Chapter 4, location – near a river or a coast, in a hilly area – may be one of the great resources, depending on the context. Obviously, agricultural resources such as good soils and water availability, wild plants and animals and good grazing grounds also make a region attractive. Good places to shelter or materials to build dwellings and make clothes are other necessary 'resources'. Organic resources such as reeds for dwellings, fibres such as cotton and hemp for textiles, and animal skins and bones for various purposes are usually closely related to the agricultural and pastoral activities. The use of forests as sources of food but also of wood for fuel and construction and of medicinal plants applies to all times and places.

The environment provided an initially highly localized but gradually expanding array of inorganic resources: rock and clay for construction, salt, mineral ores (gold, silver, copper, iron) for tools and weapons. All of these have ancient origins. All emerging tribes, states and empires had to produce or procure them in one way or another. In doing so, the natural environment was affected, sometimes in minor and transient ways, sometimes in large and irreversible ways. An increasing number of historical atlases map such resources: limestone, alabaster and granite quarries of the Old and the Nubian gold mines of the Middle and New Kingdom in Egypt (Manley 1996); the bewildering spectrum of raw materials mined and processes in the Harappan culture in the Indus valley (Lahiri 1992); the timber, wool, ivory and metal resources which were the basis of the Phoenician and Greek trading cultures (McEvedy 1967) to mention only a few of the earliest ones. However, most information on the environmental impact of the resource-using activities, such as forest thinning and cutting and stone quarrying, is qualitative and circumstantial. Let us have a brief, closer look at some of these resources and the trading routes that grew up around them.

Mining

Mineral resources have been an important incentive for trade, as they represented goods with an added value either because they came from faraway, because they were processed or both. Mining has a long prehistory. Near Norfolk, in Britain, a Mesolithic mining complex has been found comprising some 200 shafts approximately 20 metres deep and excavated with antler picks and bone spades. Flint of very high quality was exported over a well-developed trade network, some as far as southern Europe. Much earlier even, large flintstone 'blades' were exported from Grand Pressigny and other sites in the 'Bassin Parisien' at different times to large parts of continental north-western Europe. Extensive mining took place in ancient Mediterranean civilizations. Gold, silver, copper and tin mines existed throughout the Near and Middle East, East Africa and South Asia at least as early as 4000 yr BP. There has probably been silver mining in Greece since 3500 yr BP. In the mines of Laureion between 10,000 and 30,000 miners were at work in the 5th century and there is evidence of a transition from surface to underground mining as mining went on (Sonnabend 1999). Other mining areas of known importance were the Ptolemaean gold mines in Nubia, the Spanish mines from Carthaginian times onwards and the tin mines of Cornwall and Devon. These were large undertakings:

> Allein in den Silbergruben von Cartagena sollen zur Zeit der Polybios im 2. Jahrhundert v. Chr. bis zu 40.000 Arbeiter beschäftigt gewesen sein... Die [im Tagebau] angewandten Abbaumethoden... waren technologisch ebenso spektakulär, wie sie sich für die Landschaft und die Umwelt als problematisch erwiesen. Um in Nordwesten Spaniens Alluvialgold, d.h. von Flüssen im Boden Gold zu gewinnen, nutzten die Römer die Kraft von Wasser. Über kilometerlange Leitungen führten sie dazu das Wasser von Flüssen und Bächen der Umgebung ... Nicht nur durch ... rabiate Eingriffe in die Umwelt, sondern auch durch seine räumliche Konzentration gehörte der antike Bergbau – und mit ihm die Verhüttung der Erze – zu den neben Wasser- und Städtebau am meisten die Landschaft beeinflussenden und verändernden Technologien der Antike. (Sonnabend 1999)

The environmental impact often resulted from the large fuel requirements needed for upgrading the primary ore.

Salt – sodium chloride – has always been an important resource for humans: the body needs it and it is a food preservative (Sonnabend 1999; Laszlo 1998). Salt was recovered from salt water by evaporation, but there is evidence of underground mining as early as 4500 yr BP. In Halstatt near Salzburg in Austria great salt mines – as well as copper mines – were exploited in the pre-Roman Bronze and Iron Ages. Major salt deposits existed in China and India; it is said that during the Han dynasty there were over 90,000 salt mines in Szechuan. Since ancient times salt has been an important trade item because of its uneven distribution. For centuries, the Berbers exchanged gold for salt with Africans across the Saharan desert on a 1-to-1 kg basis: salt was a necessity of life and not locally available. Places where salt was produced used to become settlement centres of trade and transport. Sometimes salt was the currency of exchange – it is the root of the word 'salary'. The importance of salt led many states to the establishment of salt monopolies China in 2650 yr BP, Rome in 2500 yr BP; taxing salt became an important source of state revenues. Salt mining appears to have been very important in East Africa with some of the first initial trade route developing to distribute this resource. Its development allowed for the preservation of food and thus the ability of populations to buffer against risk.

Mining and mineral processing had all kinds of impacts on the environment. Copper smelting kilns dating from 3000 yr BP have been found in the Negev desert, producing copper for the Egyptian Pharaohs. As 1 kg of copper required an estimated 10 kg of charcoal to be burnt, huge quantities of wood were needed and these sites may have been abandoned because of lack of fuel. Later, much larger iron mines and smelters sometimes had an equally devastating effect on forests. In some cases the impacts have been traced through measurements of isotopic composition. An interesting case study is the investigation of lead concentrations in dozens of Swedish lakes revealing the history of lead pollution (Renberg 2000). Before 4000 yr BP there are no signs of man-made atmospheric lead pollution – the lead found came from natural catchment sources. In the period 4000-3500 yr BP the first signs of atmospheric lead pollution could be seen in southern Sweden, rising to a peak during the Roman period (2150-1550 yr BP). The Roman pollution peak has also been found in lake sediments on the Kola Peninsula in Russia, indicating the wide area impacted. After the Roman period lead concentrations declined to a low level until the end of the 10th century, after which they started rising again to levels up to ten times the Roman peak in the 20th century. A strong similarity is found between the pollution records of the sediments and the history of metal production in Europe. From at most a few tonnes of lead production around 5000 yr BP, it increased to about 300 tonnes/yr in 2700 yr BP and further to an estimated 80,000 tonnes/yr around 1950 yr BP. Smelting released large amounts all over the northern hemisphere. Lead emissions increased partly due to the growing use of silver coins, as silver production from sulphide ores also releases large amounts of lead into the atmosphere.

Deforestation for ceramic ovens in the Roman era, southern France In spite of high large fuel requirements of most mining and processing, the environmental impacts need not necessarily be devastating. Nature's own adaptive capacity and responsive forest management could limit the damage. Near Béziers, along the Mediterranean coast in southern France, the remains have been found of at least 17 furnaces that were used to fire pottery kilns during the first three centuries of the Christian era. Detailed investigations of the charcoal remains (Chabal 2001) allow a rather detailed reconstruction of environmental change during this period. It started around the year 10 AD in one of the abundantly forested Languedoc plains. Within a few decades the cutting down of nearby forests led to a vegetation change, reflected in the composition of the ashes which changed from almost exclusively elm and ash to oak trees, the latter coming from forests regrown in the deforested areas. Using a simple model and assumptions about kiln use, type of wood and regrowth rate, it is estimated that maximum wood use occurred around 40 AD (1900 m^3/yr) with some 220 ha exploited. Subsequently, use fell to about 640 m^3/yr around 180 AD with 523 ha exploited, the much lower m^3/ha ratio being explained by the increasing use of 'taillis'. The village got its wood from within a circle of at most 2.6 kilometres in diameter and the model suggests that the decline of the ceramic oven works – all kilns were abandoned by 320 AD – had nothing or not much to do with depletion of the local forest – or at least that its role was more insidious. Changing economic circumstances, possibly in olive and wine export, may have played a role.

Deforestation

Large-scale burning of forests and felling of trees may have been one of the earliest and most intense impacts of humans on the natural landscape. There were two main reasons: land clearing and wood. Land clearing as part of agro-pastoral farming, usually with the help of fire, was an intrinsic part of the transition from the fire to the agricultural regime – the term 'slash-and-burn' is quite evocative (cf. Chapter 4). Animals also played their part, eating leaves and young shoots. Equally important was the felling of trees for that magnificent material: wood. Wood for fuel and charcoal, timber for houses, tools, fences, defensive structures and ships. As with so many natural resources, its use had many deleterious and usually unintended consequences – such as accelerating soil erosion and unsettling local hydrology.

Concern about Mediterranean forest destruction has a long history. Plato's lament about the huge deforestation in Attica, where 'originally the mountains were heavily forested' but which had now – 2500 yr BP – become 'the skeleton of a body emaciated by disease' is well known. As the forests near the population centres disappeared and/or degraded under the pressures of agriculture, pastoralism and felling, the forests further away came under threat, making some places into major harbours. When Aegean forests became depleted, timber was drawn from the Caucasian and Black Sea coasts. Pressure further increased during Roman times.

In China forest clearing for agriculture and tree felling for wood and timber has a long and complex history (Elvin 1993). At around 6000 yr BP the climate in most parts of China was warmer and more humid, with forests extending further north and into higher altitude and less taiga and tundra (Ge Yu 1998). A colder period that lasted with fluctuations until the present began around 3000 yr BP. Consequently, changes in forest cover reflect natural as well as anthropogenic processes. During the 1st millennium BC the first signs of erosion appeared in the northern and north-western parts of the country, probably related to forest clearing for agriculture and timber for the cities. This may have led to more irregular and extreme river flows: the Huang He started to rise above the surrounding plain as the first man-made embankments appeared – partly for military reasons. People started to occupy the fertile sediment areas within these levees, necessitating two enduring hardships of Chinese life: flood risk and repair work.

The Japanese have seriously depleted their forests over the last 2500 years (Totman 1989). In the earliest period, around 2250 yr BP, rice culture was well established and caused the first dramatic modifications of woodlands. Bronze and iron products at first came from the continent, but by 1750 yr BP smelting was carried out locally and the demand for high-quality charcoal increased the pressure on the forests. As metallurgy led to new, more powerful tools, the assault on the woodlands expanded in a positive feedback loop. A warrior caste emerged with the need for weapons (charcoal), wooden stockade headquarters, large residences, coffins buried in huge mounds – rivalling the Egyptian pyramids – and pottery (wood for firing). In 759 AD 393 seagoing vessels were built to fight the Koreans. Kings and emperors often had to move, possibly because local wood supplies dwindled. Owing to termites and rot, most elaborate wooden buildings had to be rebuilt every 20 years and so wood demand remained high. Another area of high demand was monasteries, shrines and temples, mostly near Nara and Heian (present-day Kyoto).

Deforestation had all kinds of consequences, such as wildfire, flooding and erosion, often forcing people to move. Farmers also needed wood for fuel, but also for fodder and, most importantly, for green fertilizer material which sometimes relieved cutting pressure. The decline of powerful rulers also eased the pressure on forests as there was no will or capacity to build monumental structures. There were occasional attempts to control the use of woodland on the part of governments and monasteries. Ruling warriors tightened control to assure themselves of resources for military use. It was a history of outright exploitation without concern for preservation or reforestation.

When political struggles subsided in the 17th century, population and construction rose rapidly and the demand for timber soared (*Figure 6.1*). The demands of the peasant families led to widespread but less intensive use than the more concentrated demands

FIGURE 6.1

Areas logged by monumental builders in Japan (Source: Totman 1989)

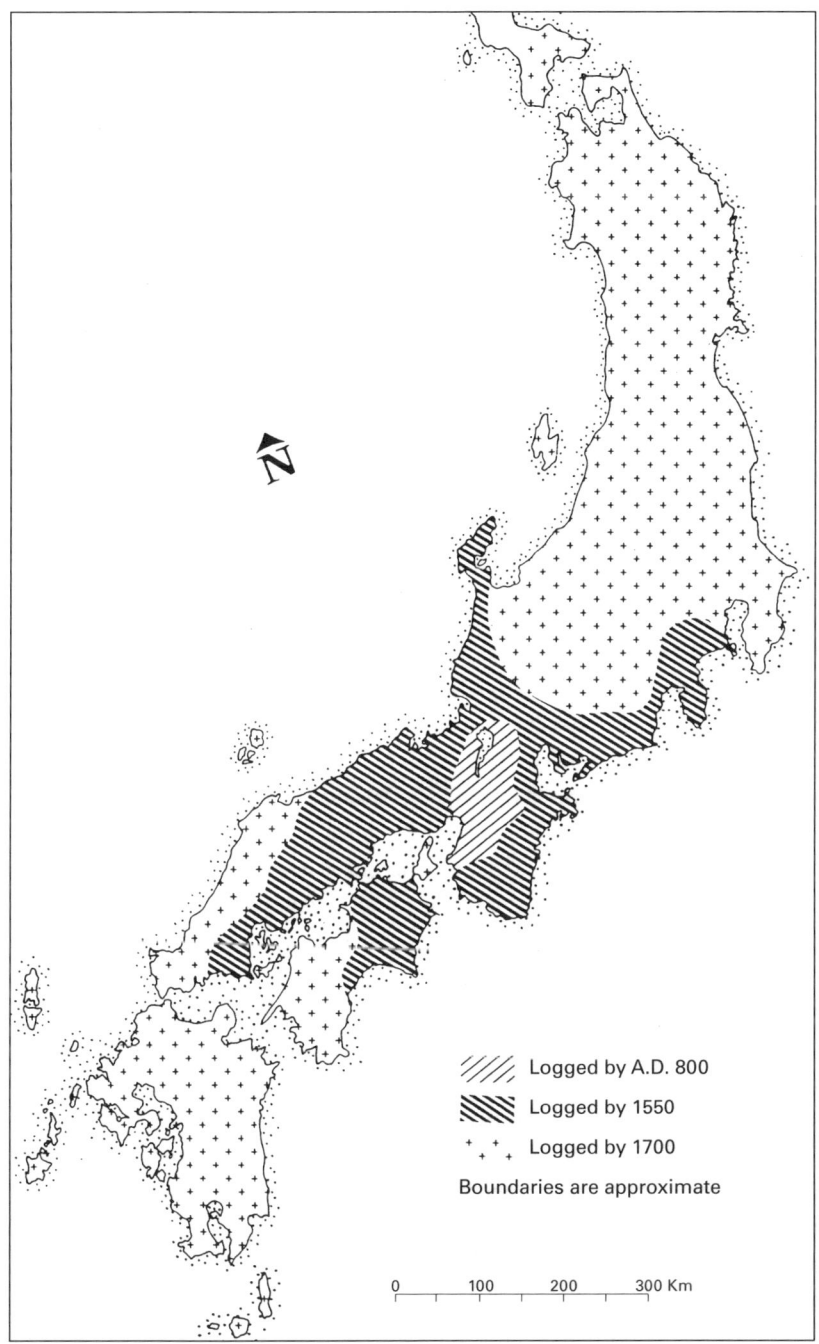

///// Logged by A.D. 800

▨▨▨ Logged by 1550

+ + + Logged by 1700

Boundaries are approximate

0   100   200   300 Km

Rubber in ancient Meso-America[2]   A ball game, invented at least 3400 years ago and played on a court with a solid rubber ball, was a key event in ancient Meso-American societies. The Popol Vuh, the Mayan creation story, captures the game's religious and sacred function by pitting the ball-playing skills of the Hero Twins against those of evil lords of the underworld, using complex imagery of human sacrifice, fertility, and regeneration. By the 5th century AD, many towns had central stone courts, some of which could hold thousands of spectators. Leaders tested prophecies through tournaments, rival cities took out their aggressions on the court, and the rich placed huge wagers. According to a 16th century codex, the Aztec capital Tenochtitlan demanded 16,000 rubber balls each year as tribute from one province. Spanish invaders reported that apart from its religious significance the ball game also was a sporting event in which contenders gambled for land, slaves, and other valuables.

These societies also used rubber for a host of other products, including religious figurines, incense and even lip balm. They made solid rubber balls, solid and hollow rubber human figurines, wide rubber bands to haft stone axe heads to wooden handles, and other items. They used liquid rubber for medicines, painted with it, and spattered it on paper that was then burnt in ritual. Ancient Meso-American peoples were therefore processing rubber by 1600 yr BC; this predates the development of the vulcanization process by 3500 years.

The raw material for most Meso-American rubber balls and other rubber artefacts is a latex acquired from the Castilla elastica tree. The tree is indigenous to tropical lowland Mexico and Central America. Castilla latex is a sticky white liquid that when dried is too brittle to retain its shape. Sixteenth-century Spaniards relate that ancient Meso-American peoples processed the raw material by mixing C. elastica latex with juice from Ipomoea alba. Rubber artefacts are poorly preserved, but archaeologists have recovered a few hundred ancient Meso-American examples. The oldest archaeological specimens are 12-inch solid rubber balls recovered at the Manatí site in Veracruz, Mexico.

from the rulers in the cities. Logging expanded and intensified, erosion denuded mountains and damaged lowlands, and Japanese rulers were forced into a combination of regenerative forestry and imports from the tropical rain forest in nearby regions, particularly in Malaysia and Indonesia. Regulation to restrain consumption was introduced, plantation forestry emerged by the late 18th century and most forested areas came under some sort of management. One consequence is that Japan now remains more forested than nearly any other country in the temperate zone.

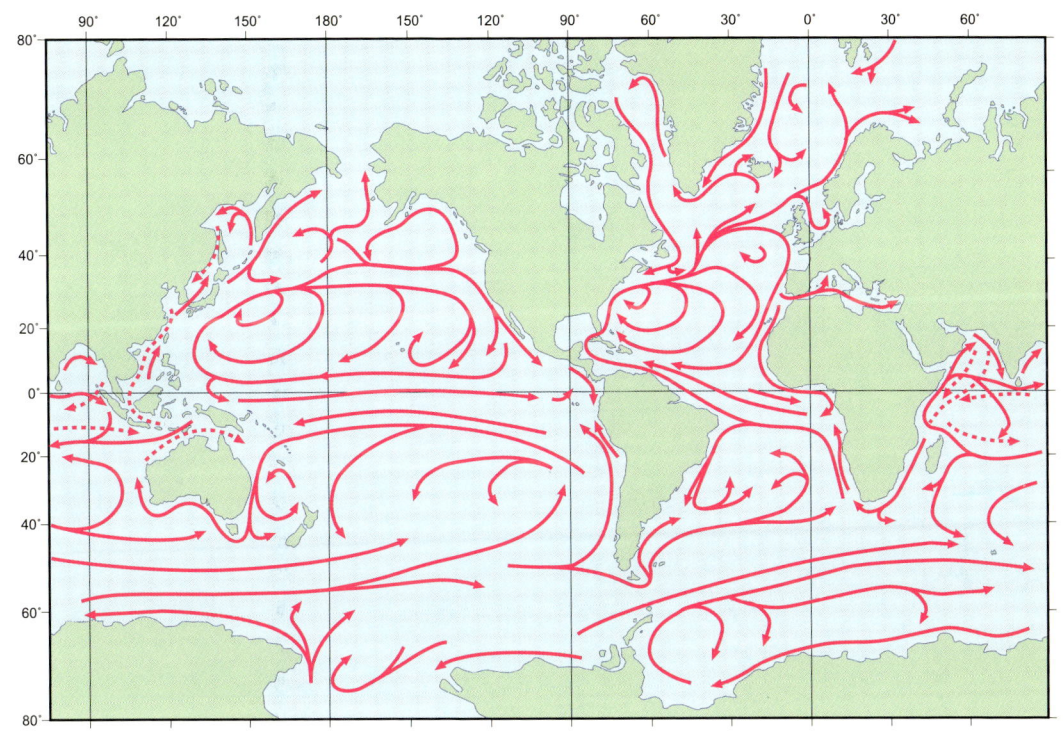

FIGURE 3.2

The world climate system: redistribution of the sun's energy by ocean currents

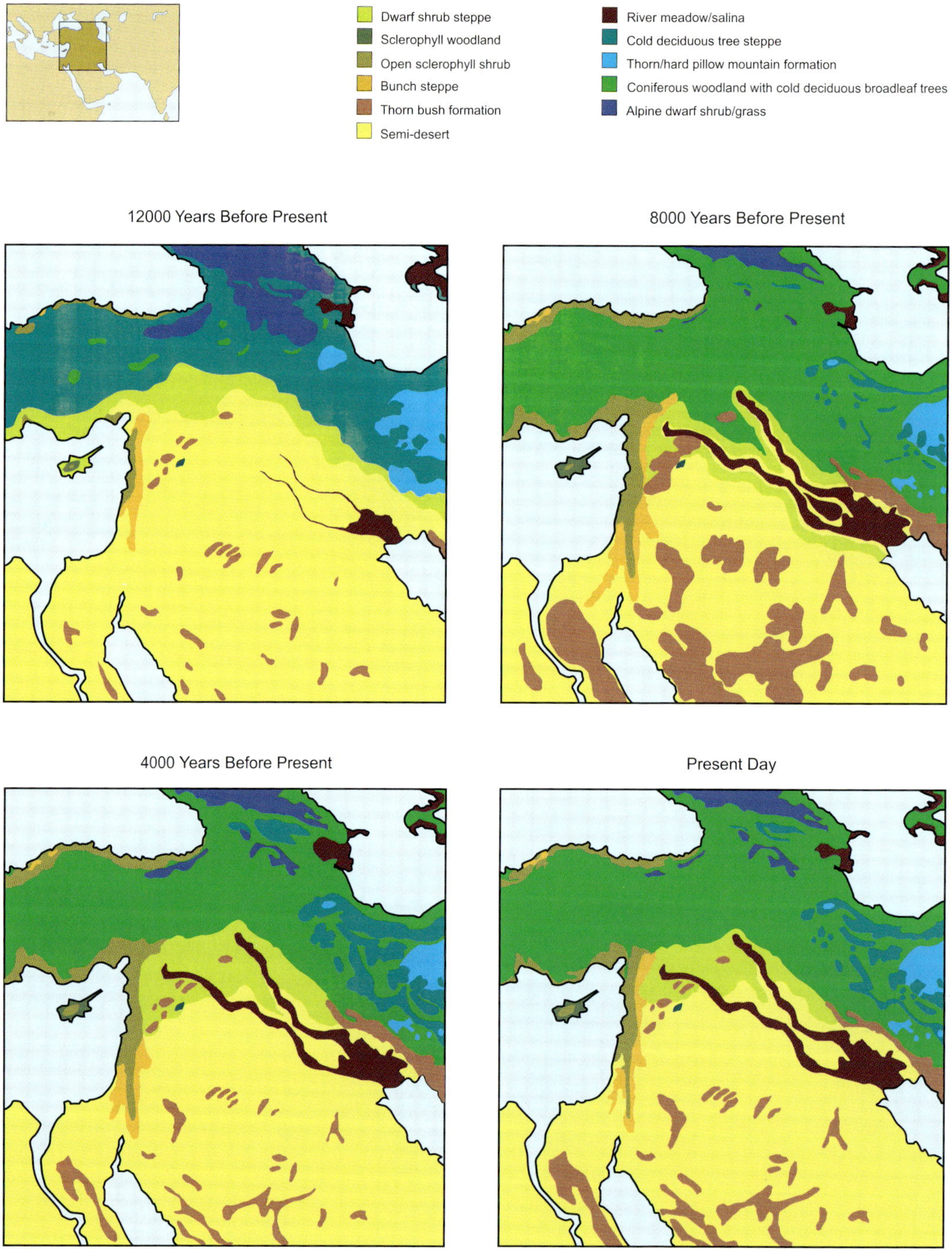

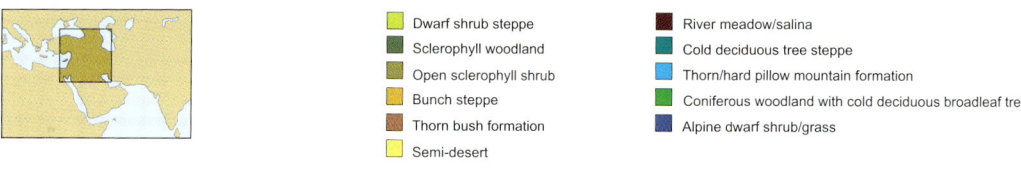

Dwarf shrub steppe		River meadow/salina
Sclerophyll woodland		Cold deciduous tree steppe
Open sclerophyll shrub		Thorn/hard pillow mountain formation
Bunch steppe		Coniferous woodland with cold deciduous broadleaf trees
Thorn bush formation		Alpine dwarf shrub/grass
Semi-desert		

12000 Years Before Present

8000 Years Before Present

4000 Years Before Present

Present Day

FIGURE 3.3

Map series showing the changing distribution of vegetation from the eastern Mediterranean region from the last glacial period through the Holocene. Notable are the increasing expansion of forest following climate warming and the subsequent modification of the area following early agriculture

162

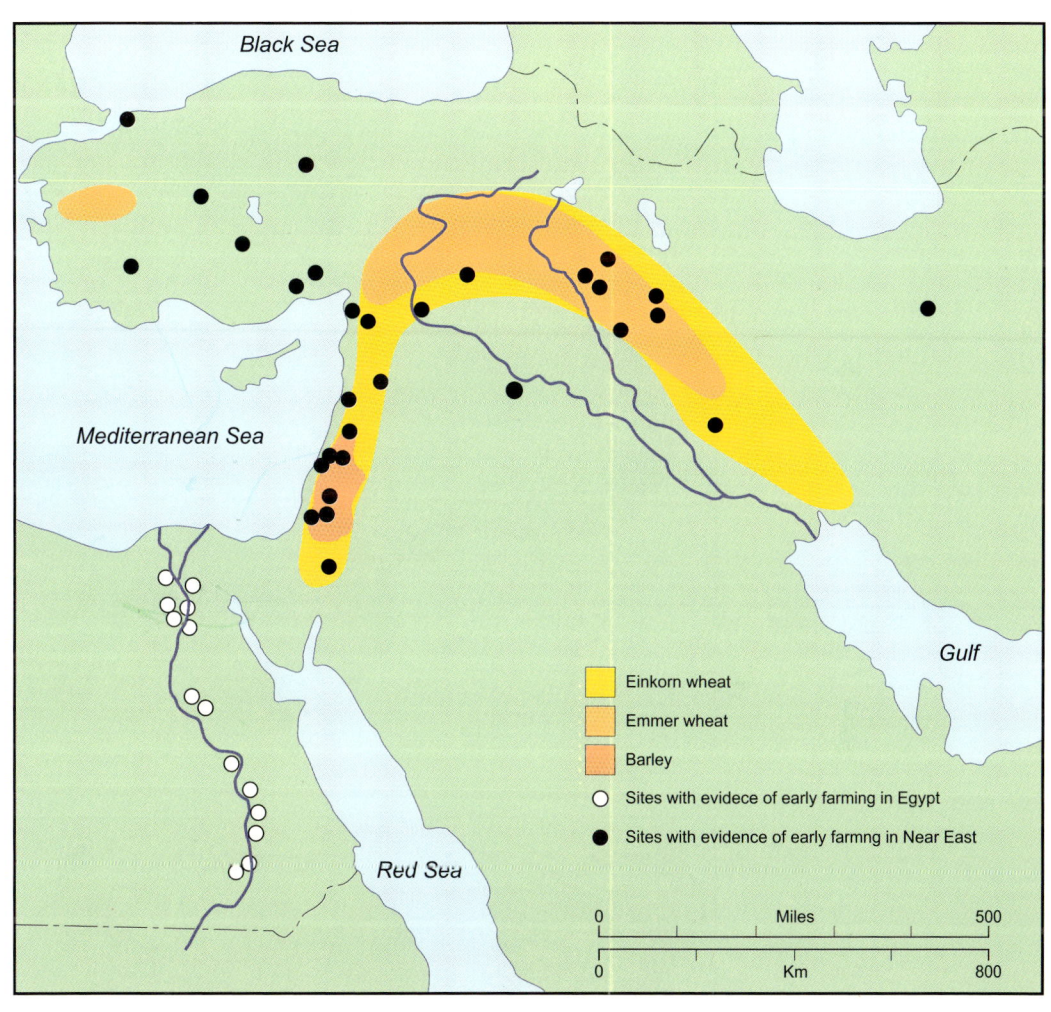

Black Sea

Mediterranean Sea

Gulf

Red Sea

- Einkorn wheat
- Emmer wheat
- Barley
- ○ Sites with evidece of early farming in Egypt
- ● Sites with evidence of early farmng in Near East

| 0 | Miles | 500 |

| 0 | Km | 800 |

FIGURE 3.4

Onset of farming in the Levant Valley

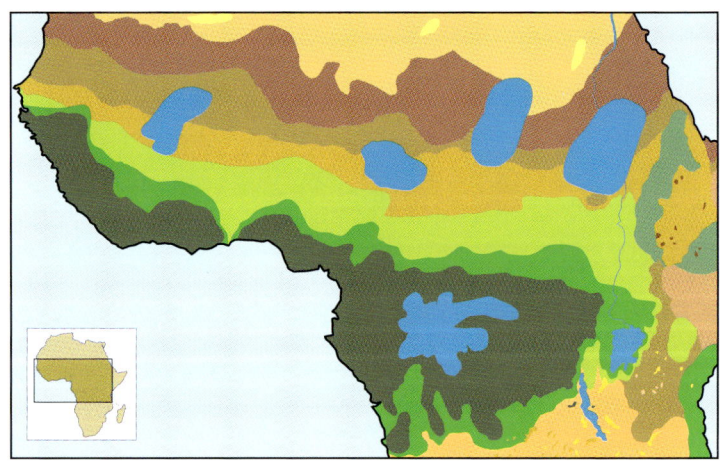

6000 Years Before Present

Tropical rain forest
Tropical seasonal forest
Tropical deciduous forest
Juniperus forest
Montane forest
Savanna
Open savanna
Scrub formation
Open desert scrub
Sand desert
Stone desert
Wetland
Mangrove
Podocarpus forest

3000 Years Before Present

Present Day

FIGURE 3.5

Vegetation maps for Equatorial Africa in the last 6,000 years

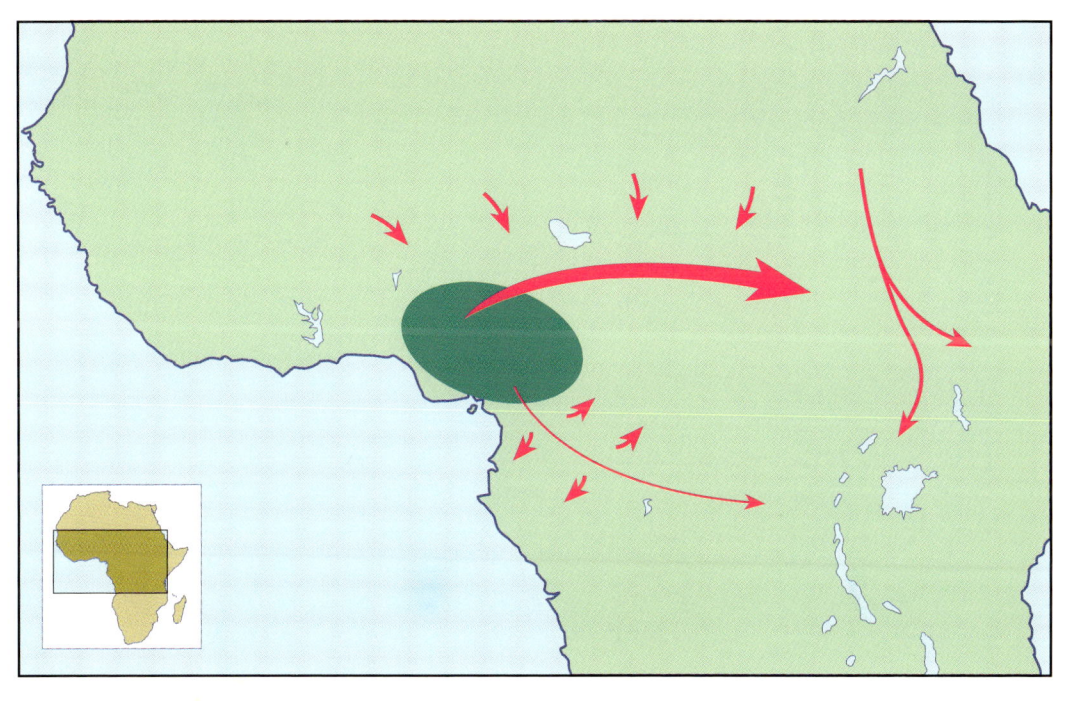

FIGURE 3.6
Human outmigration from the grasslands of western Cameroun and Nigeria

FIGURE 3.7

Map showing the area of western Peru under investigation. The location of archaeological sites, and palaeo-ecological studies mentioned in the text are shown. The extent of land above 3000 m is also showing the close proximity of this to the coast

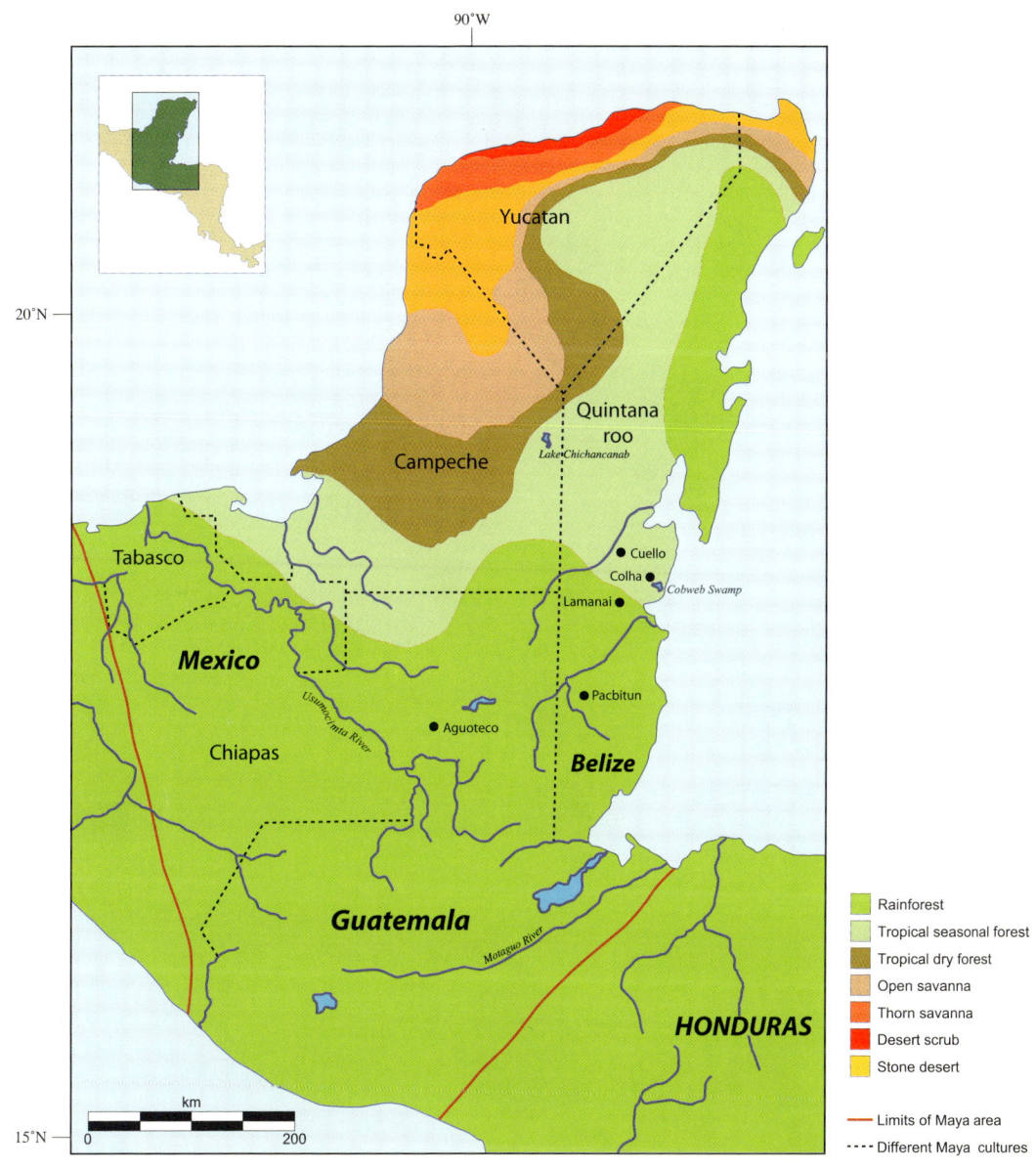

FIGURE 3.8

Map showing the area settled by the Maya detailing the main vegetation units, the archaeological, and palaeoecological sites mentioned in the text

Legend:
- Rainforest
- Tropical seasonal forest
- Tropical dry forest
- Open savanna
- Thorn savanna
- Desert scrub
- Stone desert
- Limits of Maya area
- Different Maya cultures

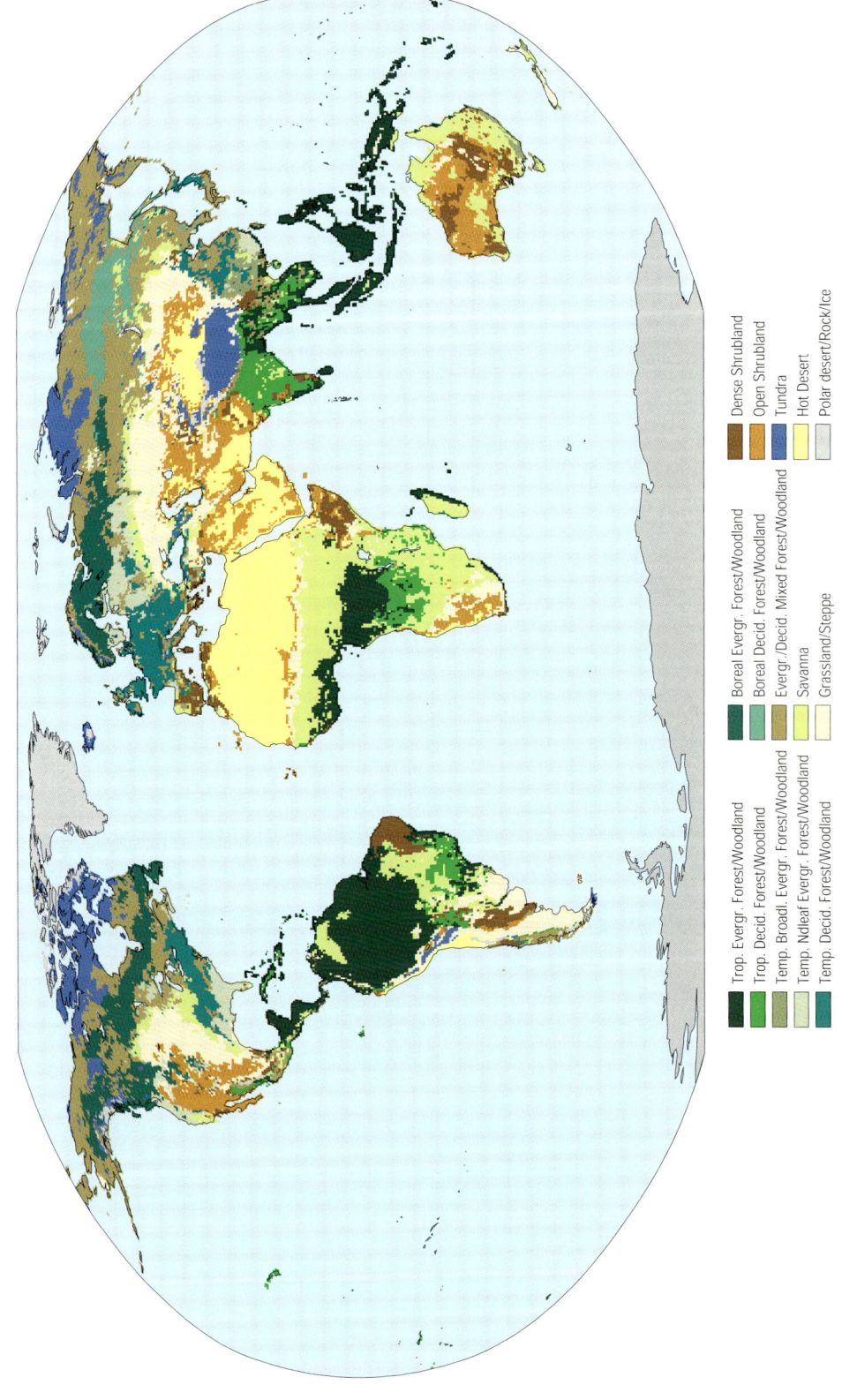

FIGURE 4.1

Potential vegetation with the early 1990s climate from satellite data and BIOME3.5 model-based extensions (Source: Ramankutty and Foley 1999)

Trop. Evergr. Forest/Woodland
Trop. Decid. Forest/Woodland
Temp. Broadl. Evergr. Forest/Woodland
Temp. Ndleaf Evergr. Forest/Woodland
Temp. Decid. Forest/Woodland

Boreal Evergr. Forest/Woodland
Boreal Decid. Forest/Woodland
Evergr./Decid. Mixed Forest/Woodland
Savanna
Grassland/Steppe

Dense Shrubland
Open Shrubland
Tundra
Hot Desert
Polar desert/Rock/Ice

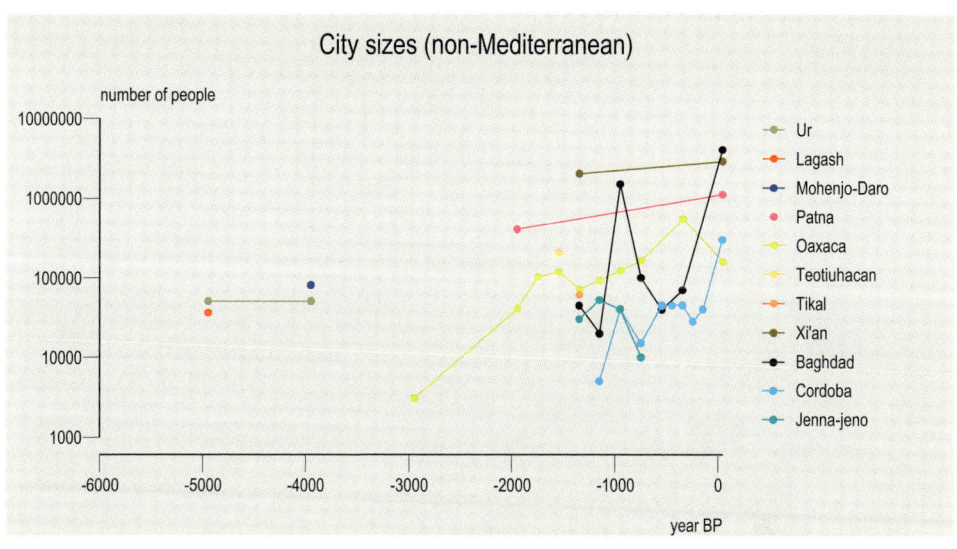

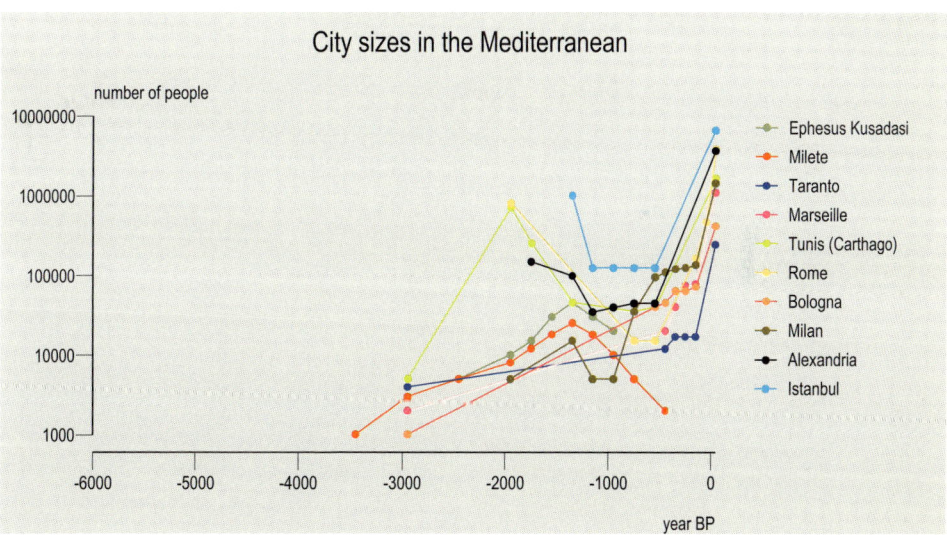

FIGURE 4.5
Ancient towns and cities and estimates of their population (Sources: McEvedy 1967, 1992; Wood 1999; Manley 1996; Vries 1983; Woude 1990; Blanton 1993 and others)

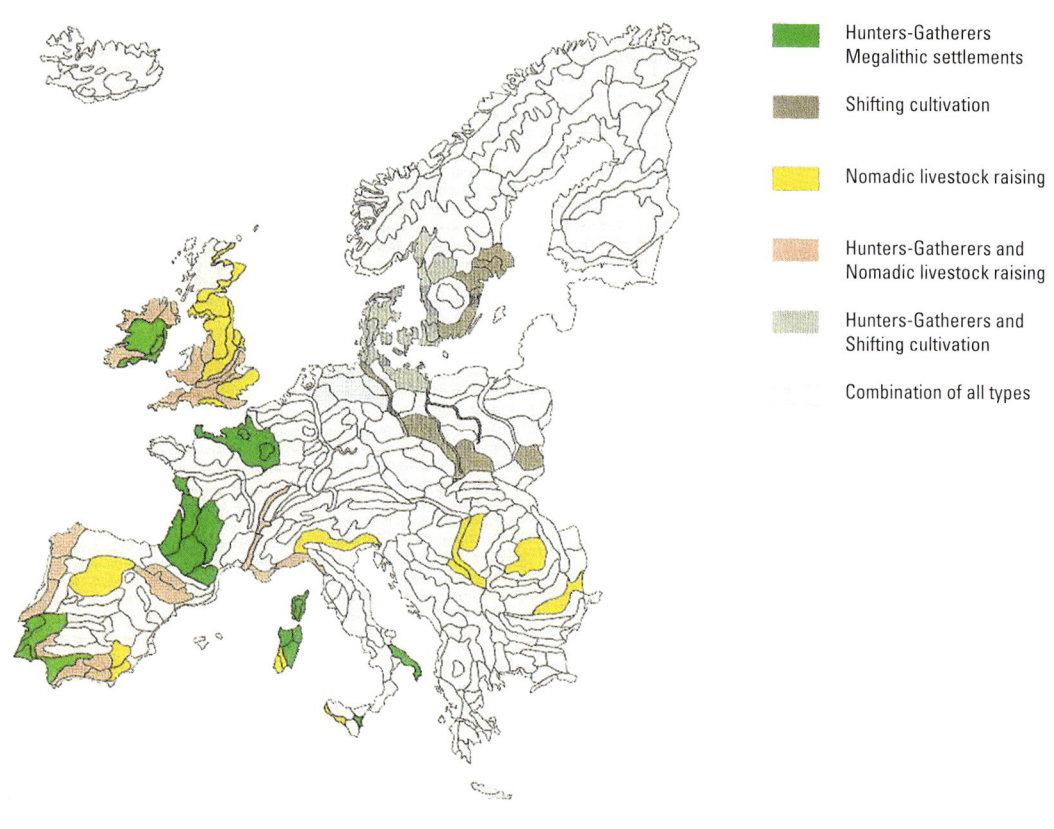

Hunters-Gatherers Megalithic settlements

Shifting cultivation

Nomadic livestock raising

Hunters-Gatherers and Nomadic livestock raising

Hunters-Gatherers and Shifting cultivation

Combination of all types

FIGURE 4.6

Economic and cultural stages in European landscapes in the Neolithic to Early Bronze Ages (7000-4000 yr BP) (Source: Romanova, pers. comm.)

FIGURE 5.9A

*First tentative calculation
of the Actual Human
Habitat (in people/km²)
for the present-day
climate and the hunter-
gatherer development
stage*

hunter/gatherers

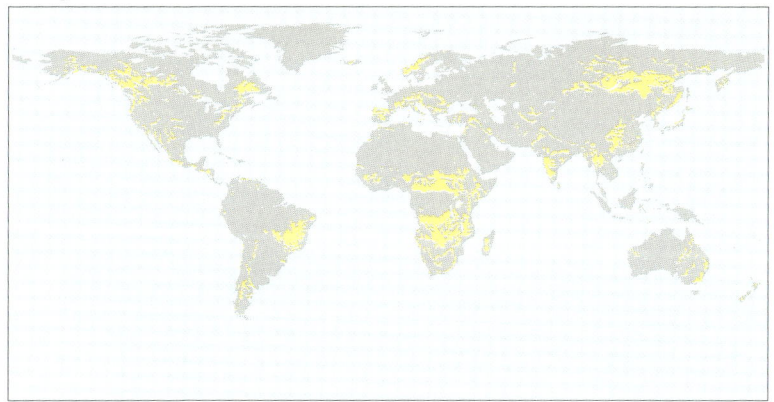

FIGURE 5.9B

*First tentative calculation
of the Actual Human
Habitat (in people/km²)
for the present-day
climate and nomad-
pastoralism development
stage*

nomads/pastoralists

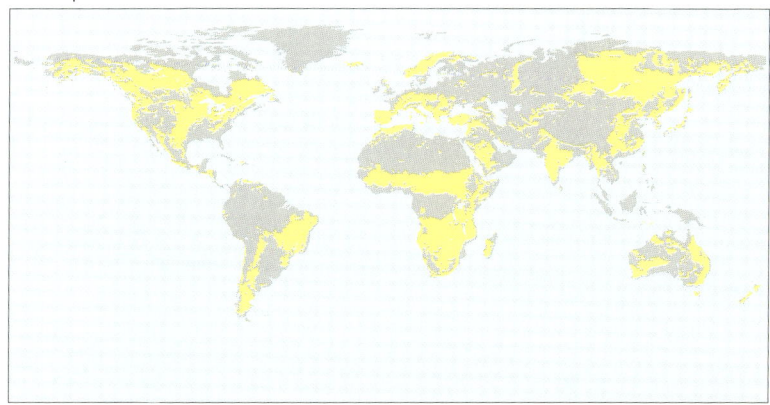

FIGURE 5.9C

*First tentative calculation
of the Actual Human
Habitat (in people/km²)
for the present-day
climate and early farmers
development stage*

early farmers

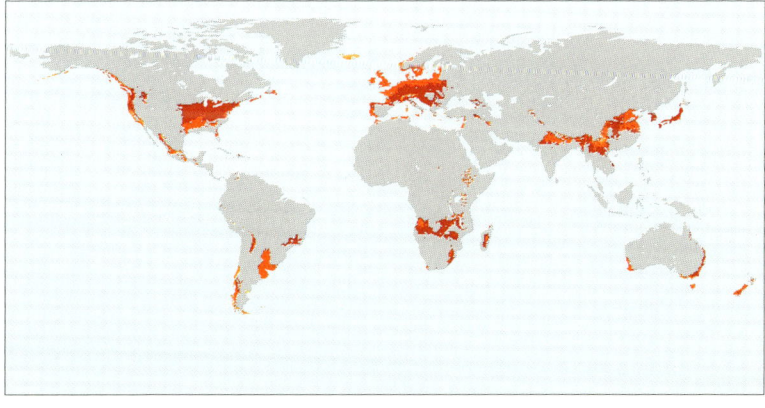

cap/km²

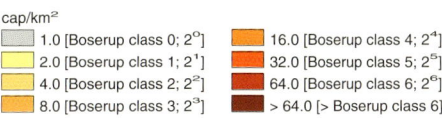

1.0 [Boserup class 0; 2^0]   16.0 [Boserup class 4; 2^4]
2.0 [Boserup class 1; 2^1]   32.0 [Boserup class 5; 2^5]
4.0 [Boserup class 2; 2^2]   64.0 [Boserup class 6; 2^6]
8.0 [Boserup class 3; 2^3]   > 64.0 [> Boserup class 6]

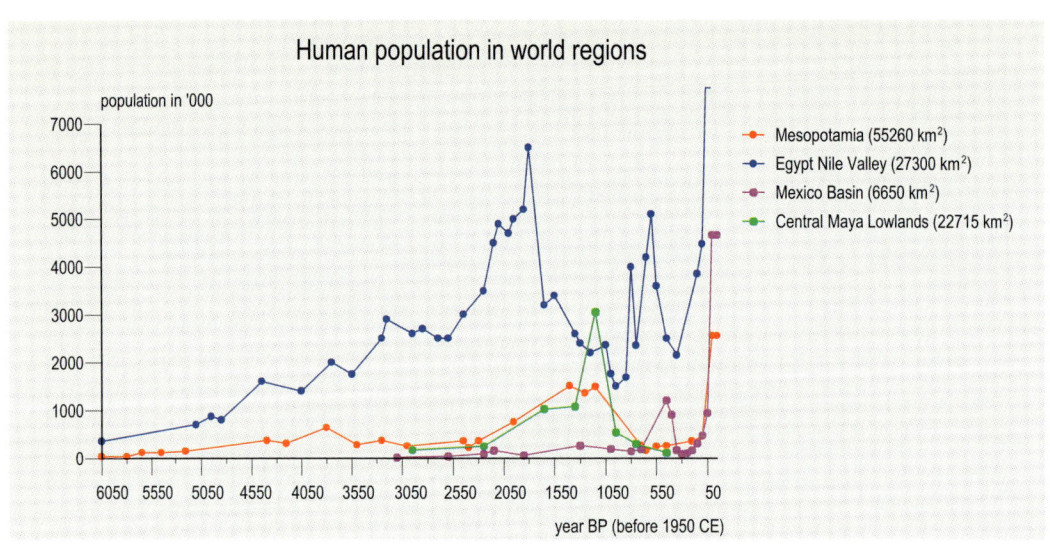

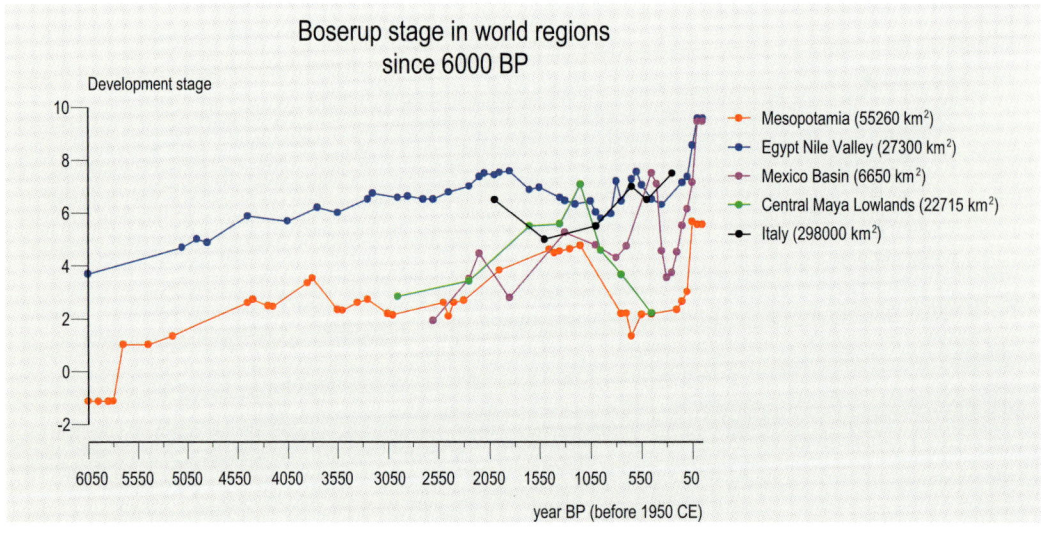

FIGURE 5.10

Population size estimates in some regions over the last 6000 years in absolute numbers and in development stages (Sources: Whitmore 1990, Manley 1996 and others). Development stage i corresponds with a population density classes as proposed by Boserup (cf. Figure 5.6)

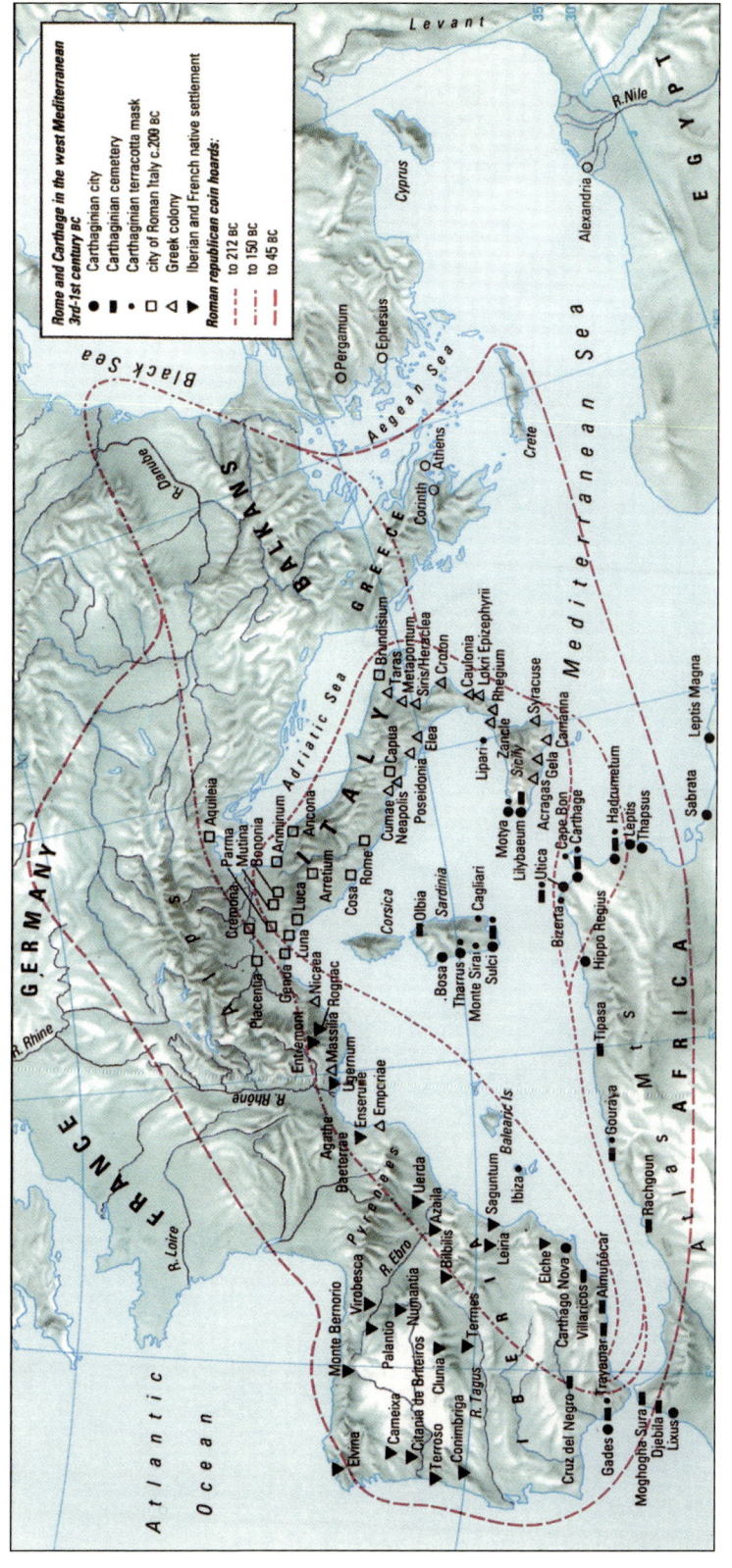

FIGURE 7.2
The spread of urbanization in the last half of the first millennium BC (From: Past Worlds 1988)

173

FIGURE 7.3

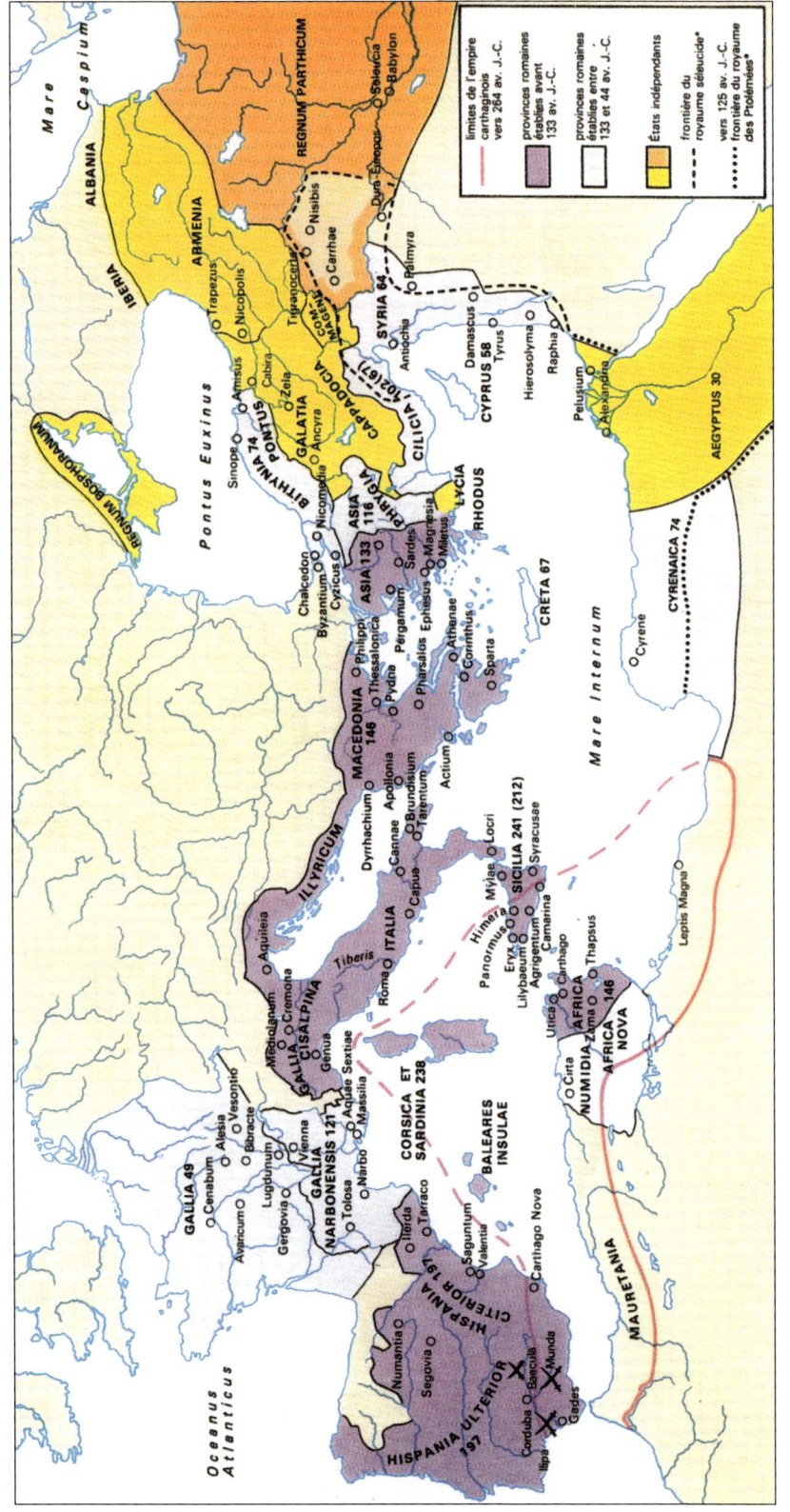

FIGURE 7.3

The extent of the Roman Empire in the 2nd and 1st centuries BC. Note that the boundary essentially includes the urbanized areas (From: Encyclopaedia Universalis Atlas de l'Histoire 1985).

FIGURE 7.4C

Plan of the excavation of a Roman pottery workshop in Sallèles d'Aude, Southern France (Source: Lauben-heimer 1991: 12).

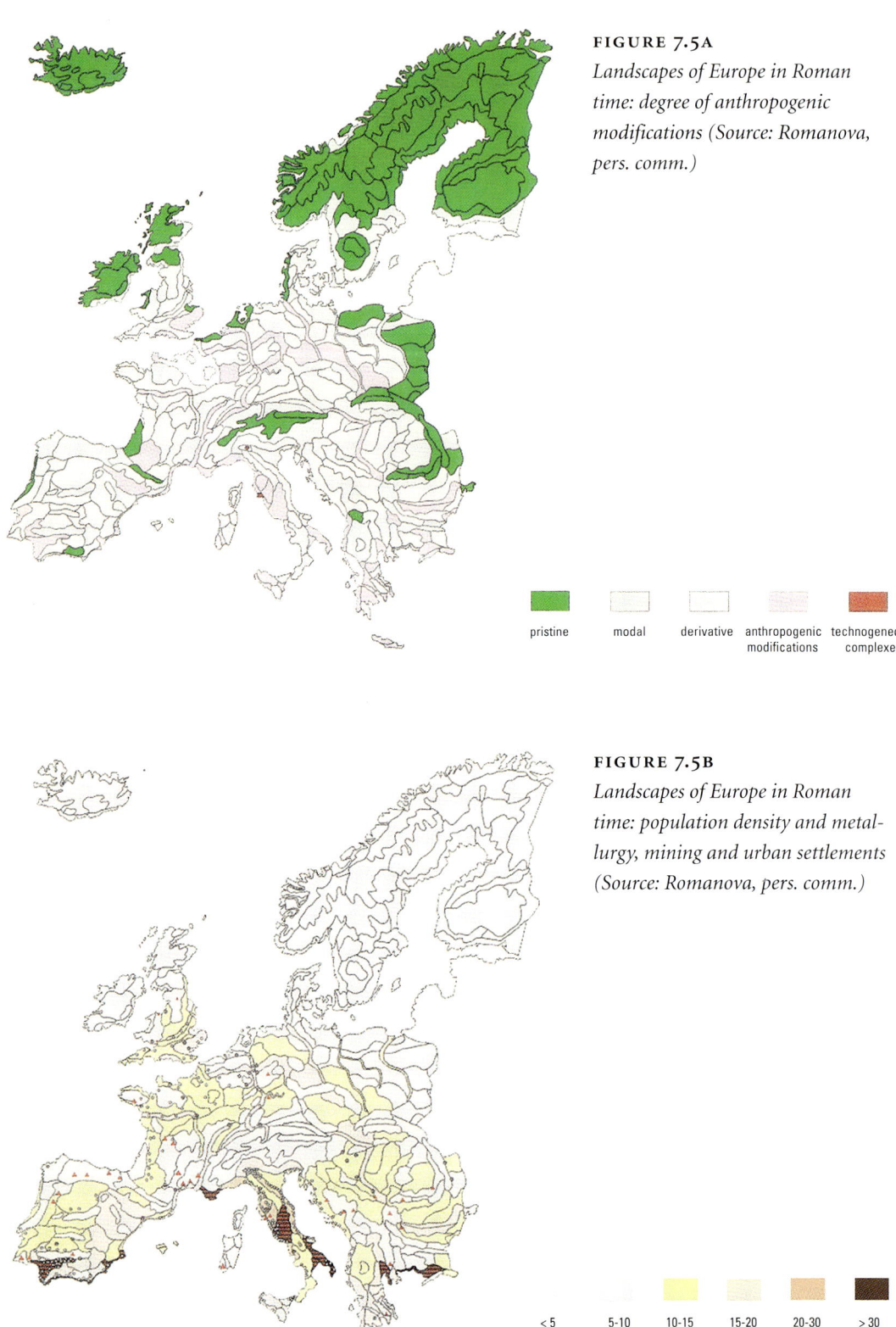

FIGURE 7.5A

Landscapes of Europe in Roman time: degree of anthropogenic modifications (Source: Romanova, pers. comm.)

pristine   modal   derivative   anthropogenic modifications   technogeneous complexes

FIGURE 7.5B

Landscapes of Europe in Roman time: population density and metallurgy, mining and urban settlements (Source: Romanova, pers. comm.)

< 5   5-10   10-15   15-20   20-30   > 30

● Metallurgy   ▲ Mining   ●●● Urban settlement

6.2.3.   *Interactions: trade*

An important element in the development of human groups, once they increased in number and size, has been their mutual interactions. Initially, many human groups may have been self-confined within a wide availability of space, mountain ridges, swamps and rivers barring communication and exchange. It can even be surmised that relative isolation was a precondition for the first stages of development – latecomers may not have been given a chance. Yet interactions of all kinds have probably been an essential component of the extensive and intensive growth process of human populations.

Trade has ancient origins dating back long before the Holocene period. In the earliest agro-pastoral settlements the exchange of ideas and goods was an important dynamic (cf. Chapter 4). Scarce and therefore precious materials have been traded over large distances since at least 8000 years ago. In the Near East obsidian was already being procured over distances of hundreds of kilometres by 9000 yr BP; products from the Mesolithic flint mines in Britain spread throughout Europe via a well-developed trade network. As long ago as 5000 yr BP lapis lazuli was imported from northern Afghanistan into the Indus valley; major trade routes, over land as well as along the coast, connected the Harappan civilization and Mesopotamia as early as 4000 yr BP (Lahiri 1992). The Palermo Stone on which the annals of the ancient Egyptian kings up to the 5th Dynasty (4500 yr BP) are inscribed testifies to trade routes between Egypt and Syria (turquoise) and Ethiopia (oils, ebony, ivory, animal skins and gold). Amber from the Baltic Sea region dating back to 3600 yr BP has been found in Greece (Renfrew 1973). The silk route connected the Roman Empire and China – silk was a luxury in Rome as it was free of lice. The salt/gold trade linked the northern and southern fringes of the Saharan desert and was probably part of a larger chain: an abandoned caravan-load halfway through the desert contained cowry shells of a species found in the Maldive Islands 9000 kilometres away. Colombian peoples formed a complex mosaic of societies linked by networks of communication, trade, alliance and probably warfare. Beginning 3000 to 5000 years ago, these cultures erected thousands of linear kilometres of artificial earthen causeways and canals, large urban settlements and intensive farming systems.[3]

There can be no doubt that trade routes both reflected and affected the natural environment. In western Africa, many savannah urban centres sprang up at environmental interfaces where transportation systems connected: in Timbuktu goods were transferred from camel to canoe, in Kano from camel to donkey, and at forest-savannah junctions the tsetse fly necessitated the transfer from donkey back to human head (Connah 2001: 141). Rivers, coastal hamlets and mountain passes stimulated the growth of trading centres. In these various ways, trade was instrumental in disseminating skills and ideas across the continents – it can even be argued that this gave Eurasia, with its large east-west corridors, its competitive edge in population and economic growth (Diamond 1997).

Trade may have started primarily for its survival value by diminishing the risk of famine and in the procurement of all kinds of resources. Plants, animals, food products and the associated practices will have dominated early, largely short-distance trade. It allowed small communities to spread the risk, as may have occurred along the Mediterranean coasts in early times. Obviously, there were other motives – such as the desire to accumulate items to which personal or social value was assigned. There is widespread evidence of this role of rare materials and exotic goods in ancient cultures. For instance, the Meso-American cultures were formed around an elite prestige system: small, lightweight items made of rare materials used as rewards was a key aspect of a ruler's power. In this way, obsidian, jade and feathers acquired their value. Another motive was profit. The expansion of the Phoenicians and the Greeks along the Mediterranean coast may have been inspired largely by the search for metals and other resources as well as for adventurism, curiosity and conquest. The same holds for the ancient trade routes along the Iranian Makran and Arabian coasts. The fact that the importance of 'market value' has been acknowledge in these times and places can be surmised. Trade was sometimes the only pathway to development for resource-poor regions – the Phoenicians traded cedar wood and wheat for papyrus and gold with Egypt as early as 3000 yr BP.

Trade has an intricate and complex relationship with societal stratification, structuring as well as reflecting social class and power differences via trade monopolies and taxes, for instance. The trading network that sustained a continuous flow of metal, timber, stone, oils and rare items in Mesopotamia was probably a precondition for the emergence and survival of the ruling class (Redman 1999). In Meso-America the Teotihuacan monopoly control of the obsidian trade, mined only in the northern basin of

---

Value and trade   For several millennia people have valued items that became precious because they were from far away or satisfied an urgent need or both – and hence became 'value added'. This is in contrast with most bulk goods. Transporting maize in the Meso-American highlands between two large centres over a distance of 400 kilometres, an 18-day journey, would leave only 20% of the food value as the human carrier would have eaten the equivalent of 80% (Blanton 1993). The use of 'beasts of burden' such as the lama and the donkey could improve this ratio somewhat, adding to the feasible transport distances. The earlier story about Easter Island is a suggestive tale about the possible role of bulk transport in exhausting a society. Large empires could mobilize enough labour to move bulk goods around: Roman Gaul got most of its enormous demand for construction stone from three quarries in France – in the Alpilles, the Pyrénées and the Elzas region – which implied vast amounts of labour and transport.

Mexico and highland Guatemala, seems to have been one of its major economic supports – as was the salt monopoly in China. As social complexity increased, the trading networks became indicators of political (in)stability and of a system's resilience. Maintaining trading routes required investments in and maintenance of roads, bridges, trading posts and security, which were all vulnerable to political instability and conflict. Trading activities across the Eurasian continent have been related directly to the stability and prosperity in the Mongolian Empire around 1000 yr BP; they played a similar important role in the Roman Empire (cf. Chapter 7).

6.2.4. *Interactions: diffusion and migration*

The movement of human groups – fleeing natural catastrophes, in search of better soil or water, expelled or invaded by other groups – have been another integral part of the human adventure. Such movements not only dispersed or diffused peoples, they also spread skills, crops, habits, tools, beliefs and diseases. As such they had all kinds of impacts on the environment, depending on how the new inhabitants – whether humans or animals and plants – exploited their new environments. For the present discourse, we will only briefly touch on questions such as: which role did environmental and/or climate change play in large-scale migrations; whether and how practices and tools to exploit the environment spread from one population to the next; and to what extent the (mis)interpretation of the migrants' new environment led to environmental change.

The answers are part of long-standing and broader issues in archaeology and history. For instance, a major controversy in archaeology is about the origins of prehistoric cultures – not unlike that about the origins of agriculture and pastoralism as discussed in Chapter 4. Were they mainly the result of one or a few older cultures, the diffusion of people, ideas and goods being the transmission mechanism, or were there many more independent ones? Until the 1960s the conventional view supported one version or another of the diffusionist theory. Later on, the existence of independent origins gained importance in archaeological interpretations (Renfrew 1973; Bell-Fialkoff 2000). Processes of diffusion were seen as parallel to processes of differentiation in which the environment, population growth and internal social dynamics were seen as major explanatory factors. As so often, the richness of our past defies simple cause-effect explanations.

A variety of explanations have been suggested for the large migrations – a book on its own. In Chapter 4 some possible mechanisms have been indicated, for instance the nomads oscillating between the Chinese civilization in the east and the Near East and south-western and western civilization and western forest tribes of Europe. The dynamic causes were probably occasional disturbances of the balance between humankind and

Genetic gradients and migration A variety of factors may have triggered migratory waves. Genetic research appears to provide an empirical basis that could clarify at least some of the complex underlying processes (Cavalli-Sforza 1993; Cavalli-Sforza 1995; Harris 1996). One of the major forces leading to outmigration is population growth – or so a widespread conviction holds. If the migration pressure increases in a relatively isolated group and they start migrating outwards, genetic drift among small populations is important and genetic variation can be expected over long distances. Recent genetic research has been applied to establish genetic gradients across the earth's continents and test this hypothesis. The various migrations into Europe can be resolved into its constituent components. In this way, the agrarianization process can be followed in the form of waves of inward migrations, 'impounding' the original Mesolithic peoples: Neolithic farmers from the Near East; a – probably single large-scale – migration of Uralic language people from northern Europe and western Asia; Indo-European language-speaking nomadic herders from the Euro-Asiatic steppes (4500-6000 yr BP) who were probably descendants of the first cultivators migrating to the Steppes north of the area in which agriculture originated, with horse-rearing as a local adaptation; and the Greek expansion of the 2nd and 1st millennia BC. Cavalli-Sforza contends that migration of peoples has been at least as important as exchange via tools and artefacts in the cultural dispersion process (Cavalli-Sforza 1993). Could it be that one of these waves is related to a catastrophic event such as the flooding of the Black Sea region by the Mediterranean waters? (Ryan 1998)

nature. Overpopulation may have stimulated the outmigration waves of peoples of the Eurasian steppes – but this so-called 'Pulse of Asia' (McEvedy 1992: 76) can also be explained by desiccation cycles on the grasslands. Other triggering mechanisms have been suggested: climate change leading to periods with snow cover too thick to allow the nomads to get food may have forced them to move elsewhere; the emergence of a strong leader, such as Genghis Khan, every now and then united peoples which resulted in larger population growth because their normal mechanism of population control by internal strife slowed down – and hence their occasional outward thrust; the differences in drought resistance between cattle and horses. Yet another suggestion has been put forward to explain peoples' move from the steppe to the forest: the discovery and subsequent desire for iron. Ironworks needed charcoal and core analysis of peat bogs in Russia suggests that some 1500 years ago people started burning primary forest, which showed up as a rise in cadmium concentrations in the soil.

6.3.   Early state and empire formation

> ... one might raise the question whether the growing contrast between urban and
> rural lifestyles and perceptions, as well as the growing impact of the former on the
> environment, is not at the root of much degradation.
>
> *Leeuw 2000*

From the earliest stages on, human groups have shown signs of self-organization. This
process gradually intensified with processes such as stratification between the rulers and
the ruled, differentiation into castes and guilds, and the emergence of towns and trade
markets. Tribal chiefdoms evolved into one dominant authority in larger regions, the
state:

> a type of very strong, usually highly centralised government, with a professional ruling class,
> largely divorced from the bonds of kinship... highly stratified and extremely diversified inter-
> nally, with residential patterns often based on occupational specialisation rather than blood or
> affinal relationship. The state attempts to maintain a monopoly of force... while individual
> citizens must forgo violence, the state can wage a war; it can also draft soldiers, levy taxes, and
> exact tribute. (Flannery 1972: 404)

As a social institution, the state is said to exist in societies that have two or more social
strata, an administrative apparatus and revenues from tribute and taxes. Mythical and
legendary charters and war and terrorism are among the methods in which states
enforced legitimacy, displayed power and exerted control (cf. Section 4.4). These 'traditional' states emerged all over the world, under a variety of environmental conditions: in Mesopotamia, in the eastern part of the Mediterranean, in South Asia in the
Indus valley, in China in the Huang He basin and in Meso-America and, to a lesser
extent, in parts of South-East Asia and Africa. They were of limited size and had relatively modest administrations and transport and communication channels. The following gives a 'capita selecta' impression of the human-environment interactions in
this process.

6.3.1.   Early urban centres in Mesopotamia

The earliest urban centres probably developed in the plains of southern Mesopotamia.
As early as the 6th millennium BP the city of Uruk extended over more than 100 ha. The
early towns facilitated all kinds of exchange; indeed, it may have been their natural raison d'être and function. The economy of the Ubaid and Early Uruk culture was a 'tributary economy – one that was dependent to a significant degree on the mobilization of

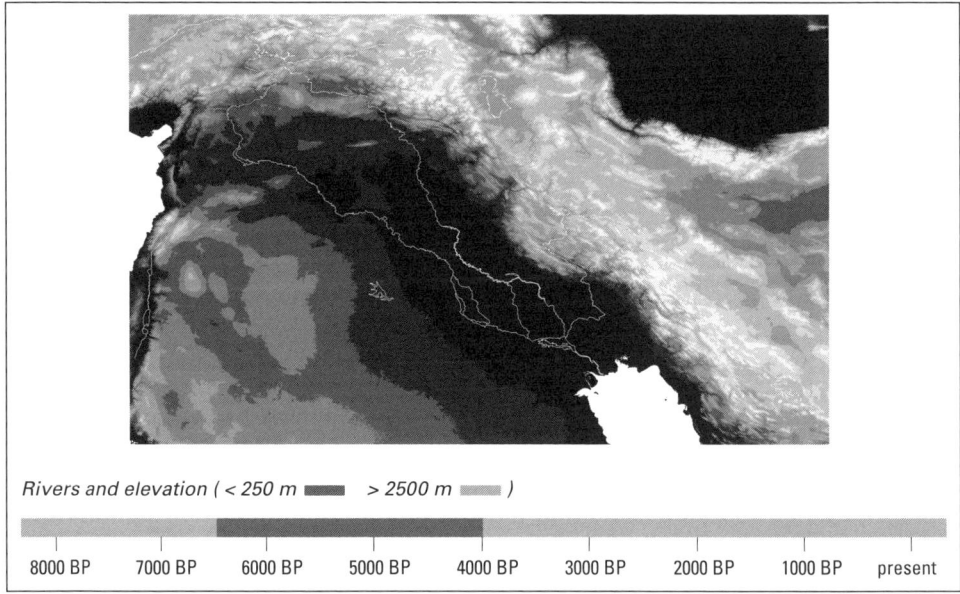

Rivers and elevation (< 250 m ▬▬ > 2500 m ▬▬)

| 8000 BP | 7000 BP | 6000 BP | 5000 BP | 4000 BP | 3000 BP | 2000 BP | 1000 BP | present |

tribute, in the form of goods or the labour used to reproduce them, from producers to a political elite.' (Pollock 2001: 80). The rural peasant families produced the food – wheat, barley, vegetables, milk and meat – and flax, wool, hides, dung, reeds and clay for non-food needs such as clothing and housing. Archaeological analyses show a clear emphasis on the utilization of locally available resources. Initially, it has been suggested, state organization was essentially egalitarian with some but not much economic and social differentiation. Building temple platforms and serving as priests may have been volun-tary while at the same time being a source of social or political prestige and of material gain. However, as time progressed into the Uruk Period (6000 yr BP), there are signs that the elite divorced itself more from the material forms of production, collecting larger and larger portions of the surplus food and goods. Its members started to acquire pres-tige goods for personal use, political support and the purchase of labour. Institutions for political control emerged and long-distance expeditions were set up to procure exotic goods. There is evidence for growing tribute demands during the 6th millennium BP. This may have stimulated debt-ridden peasants to flee into towns. To pay for the grow-ing urban populations and their demands, more tribute had to be exacted – and a cycle of extraction and control evolved as a means of sustaining the centres of power and avoiding social disruptions (*Figure 6.2*).

Although the extent and mechanisms are still debated, there is general agreement that environmental deterioration – mainly in the form of salinization – played a role in the collapse of the later Ur dynasties. Agricultural productivity declined continuously from

FIGURE 6.2

Possible factors in the rural-urban dynamics in Ubaid and early Uruk society in Mesopotamia (after Pollock 2001). Extraction and control, partly as a result of elite desire for luxury and prestige goods, reinforce each other and induce urbanization and land intensification processes.

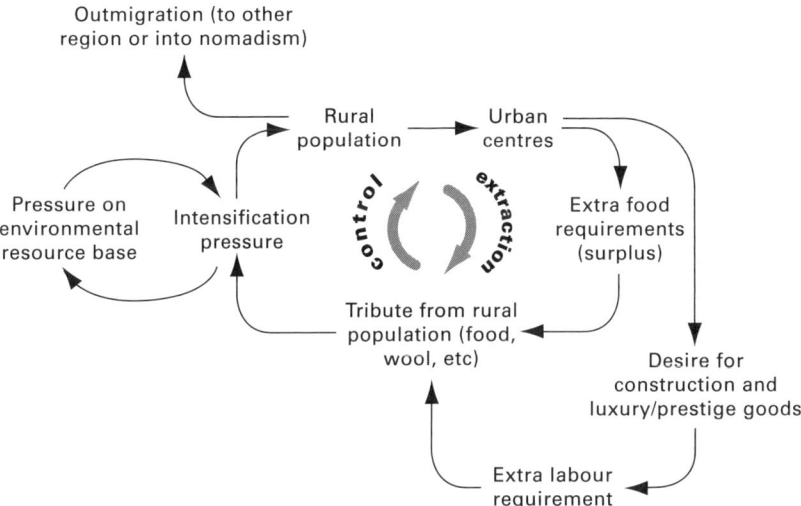

the middle of the 5th millennium BP, with a shift from wheat to more salt-tolerant barley. Deforestation as a result of woodcutting for domestic and industrial hearths, with further destruction by goats, was another detrimental force. Redman (1999) emphasizes that the rise in centralized control was a major force behind the declining agricultural productivity and environmental damage, which in turn brought down the central authority with its surplus maximization policy. More local production modes took over, geared at local needs and resources.

Paradise Lost? Mumford claims that already in ancient Sumer there was a yearning for the bygone pastoral past – the Garden of Eden. The city and its associated exploitative regimes were the main cause: 'Unarmed, exposed, naked, primitive man had been cunning enough to dominate all his natural rivals. But now, at last, he had created a being whose presence would repeatedly strike terror to his soul: the Human Enemy, his other self and counterpart, possessed by another God, congregated in another city, capable of attacking him as Ur was attacked, without provocation.' (Mumford 1961: 64)

6.3.2.   *South Asia: Indus-Sarasvati*

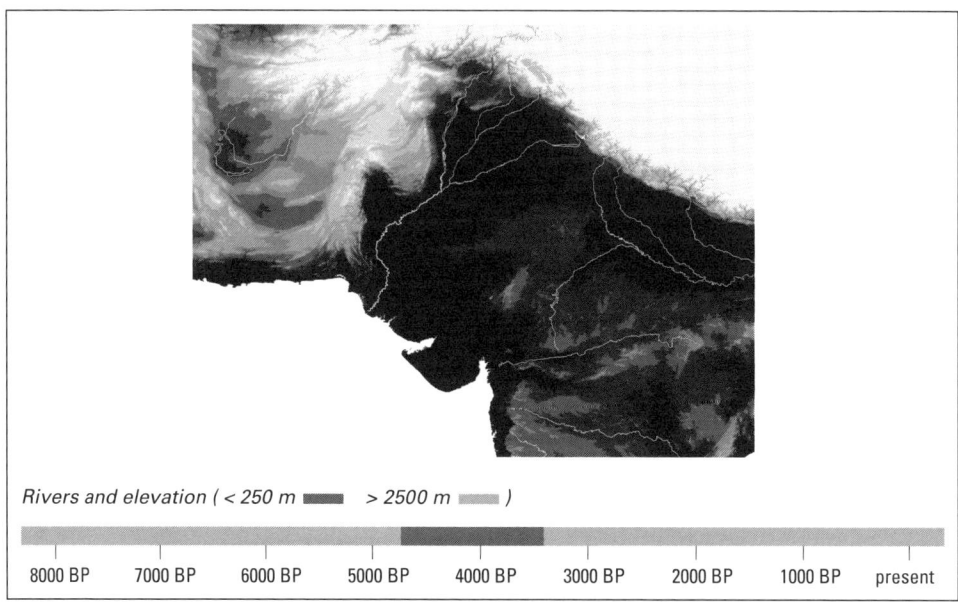

Rivers and elevation (< 250 m ▬▬ > 2500 m ▬▬)

| 8000 BP | 7000 BP | 6000 BP | 5000 BP | 4000 BP | 3000 BP | 2000 BP | 1000 BP | present |

The first signs of an agrarian civilization in South Asia emerged in the valleys of the Indus river and the – now largely dried up – Sarasvati river. Since British explorers discovered the famous sites of Harappa and Mohenjo-Daro, the civilization that flourished here some 4000 years ago has been called the 'Indus civilization'. Its origins can be dated back to ancient settlements in Baluchistan of at least 7000 yr BP (cf. Section 4.3.1). These peoples may gradually have settled into the upper and lower valleys of the Indus and Sarasvati rivers.

In the past decades new insights into the ancient cultures in the Indus valley have been gained from archaeological excavations (Lahiri 2000; Chakrabarti 1999; Dandekar 1982; Misra 1994; Kalyanaraman 1997). Remains of this civilization are found in a much larger area, possibly the size of Western Europe. Recently excavated sites such as Rakhigarhi in Haryana, Ganweriwala in Pakistan's Punjab and the ports of Dhoravila and Lothal in Gujarat were as important as Harappa and Mohenjo-Daro. The large concentration of sites in the Cholistan Desert near the old course of the Hakra river is best explained by taking into account that the important rivers in the region – the Sutlej, the Yamuna and the Sarasvati or Ghaggar-Hakra – have changed course several times. Hence the proposed change of name: the Sarasvati-Sindhu (Indus) civilization.

This civilization of which over 1400 sites were known across an area of more than one million km^2 by 1984 has apparently known three phases. In the Early Phase, 5100-4800 yr BP, it still bore the traces of the early farming communities and pastoral camps. The

184

Mature Phase, 4800-3900 yr BP, is the period of at least a dozen large cities; of interaction with culture-complexes in Rajastan, Central India and Maharashtra; of farming a variety of crops including rice and cotton; of extensive metal mining and smelting activities; and of extensive trade with Mesopotamia through ports such as Lothal. The culture was characterized by sophisticated architecture, a distinctive own writing style, the worship of fire and an absence of personality or ruler cults such as they emerged in contemporary Mesopotamia, Egypt and China. Its sudden rise, within a few centuries at most, is rather mysterious – if Mesopotamia was not the source, was it a jump after centuries of germination?

The Late Phase was around 3900-3400 yr BP. The story of the emergence and flourishing of the Harappa civilization is told in different ways; this is equally true for the tale of its mysterious decline (Chakrabarti 1997: 124; Lahiri 2000). Until the recent finds in the south, it was thought that the Indus civilization came to a rather abrupt end – the causes are still controversial: climate change with increasing droughts and changes in the Saraswati river bed, more or less gradual invasion by northern Aryan nomads or internal erosion. New evidence suggests that a combination of adverse changes in rainfall patterns, a massive earthquake causing river courses to change and a decline in trade due to the downfall of the Euphrates-Tigris civilization led to an eastward migration. Slowly but inexorably the Sarasvati-Ghaggar-Hakra channel dried up. The cities were left:

And like a dying candle, [the civilization] shone brilliantly again but briefly before being snuffed out... There was a breakdown in sanitation and cities like their modern-day counterparts in India simply ran themselves aground. They were replaced by massive squatter colonies and an explosion of rural sites as people, disillusioned with cities, went back to farming communities. A giant step backward. (Chengappa www.itihaas.com/ancient)

Another explanatory factor may be that the Harappan civilization had overstretched itself in thinly spreading itself out over a large number of hunter-gatherer villages. It is also possible that a violent invasion of, but more probably an ordered interaction with, the northern Aryans also played a role.

Some 3500-4000 years ago, the descendants of the Harappan civilization probably diffused eastwards into the Gangetic plain across the Doab and Gangetic valley and southwards into Maharasthtra and Malwa. Their interaction with the hunter-gatherers led to many Neolithic-Chalcolithic cultures and their transition to agriculture. Yet, this post-Harappan period is the start of *siècles obscurs*: although traces of metallurgy and trade have been found and a rather dense pattern of settlements existed, one can only speculate about the period that precedes the kingdoms and scriptures of the 3rd millennium BP. These early Mesolithic cultures of inner India were familiar with the domestication of cattle, sheep and goats and the utilization of plants – why had they not already made the transition to agriculture? One hypothesis is similar to what might have happened in the Japanese Jomon culture: there was no attractive alternative and hence no need. Ethnobotanical/anthropological studies of the Indian forests, among them those on the Deccan plateau which is less rich in vegetation than other parts of India, suggests that there was a wealth of edible forest products known to the local inhabitants – fruit, berries, leaves and mushrooms, but not wild game, honey and the like, nor coconuts. The past is, in this respect, not so far out of sight:

Till recent years there was a marked dependence on wild plant resources in Indian villages and when the grain bins are empty for the poor for two or three months in a year, it is the availability of plant food in the forests which keeps them going till the next crop. A hunting-gathering streak has always run strong through the fabric of Indian subsistence economy and perhaps in various ways through society. (Chakrabarti 1997: 167)

As the population increased and the forests were cleared, this source of resilience readily disappeared – which laid the basis for the later famines (cf. Section 9.2).

6.3.3.   *State formation in the Aegean*

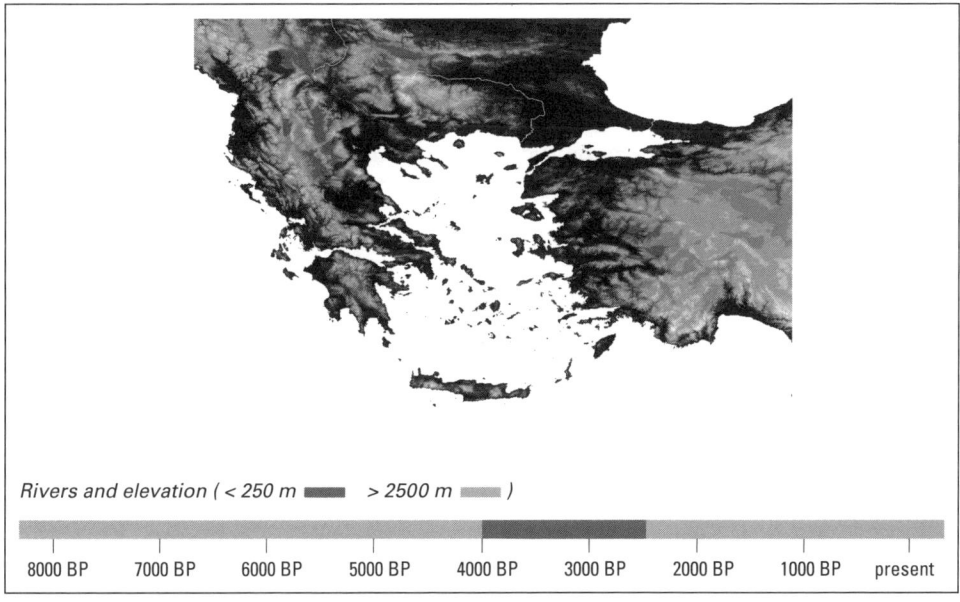

Rivers and elevation (< 250 m ▬▬ > 2500 m ▭▭)

| 8000 BP | 7000 BP | 6000 BP | 5000 BP | 4000 BP | 3000 BP | 2000 BP | 1000 BP | present |

One of the best researched and most interesting areas with regard to state formation, an important step in the rise of socio-political complexity, is the Aegean Sea region (Renfrew 1985; Halstead 1995). It covers mainland Greece in the north and west, the coast of Asia Minor – or Anatolia – in the north-east and the island of Crete in the south. In between are hundreds of large and small islands. Farming spread over Greece from 9000 yr BP onwards, early on in the central lowlands of Thessalia with good soil and moderately reliable rain. The more arid, less fertile south-eastern Aegean was colonized later on, Crete not being inhabited by humans before the 9th millennium BP according to the available evidence. Yet, in these regions complex societies emerged first. On Crete, an 8000 km^2 island of largely marginal mountain country, a major change in the scale and the nature of socio-political complexity had taken place by the end of the 5th millennium BP after the foundations had been laid in the previous millennia. The material expression of this process were the 'Old Palaces' which were destroyed a few centuries later, probably by earthquakes, and rebuilt. The 'New Palaces' were destroyed violently and/or abandoned around 3400 yr BP – probably *not* as a result of the volcanic eruption of Thira.[4]

Characteristic features of this Minoan culture were, amongst others, the conspicuous absence of fortified citadels or defensive walls and earthworks, the large palaces with their peculiar orientations, and the palace-related mountain peak sanctuaries. There was a large degree of cultural homogeneity throughout Crete – its influence reaching out to other parts of the Aegean – with homologous features in pottery skills and designs, in writing and in architecture. The written script, the institutionalized trade and the unverifiable sacred rituals and propositions all gave powers of organizational and psychological control to the classes of priests and kings. They can therefore be interpreted as the consequences as well as the causes of political centralization. Without strong evidence of an overarching, consolidated political system, it has been argued that Crete had a number of regional, political units dynamically bound together in mutual interactions.

Unlike the homogeneous Thessalian plains in mainland Greece, the southern Aegean had a large ecological diversity. To ensure sufficient food in a situation of large and unpredictable interannual harvest fluctuations, trade with neighbouring settlements can

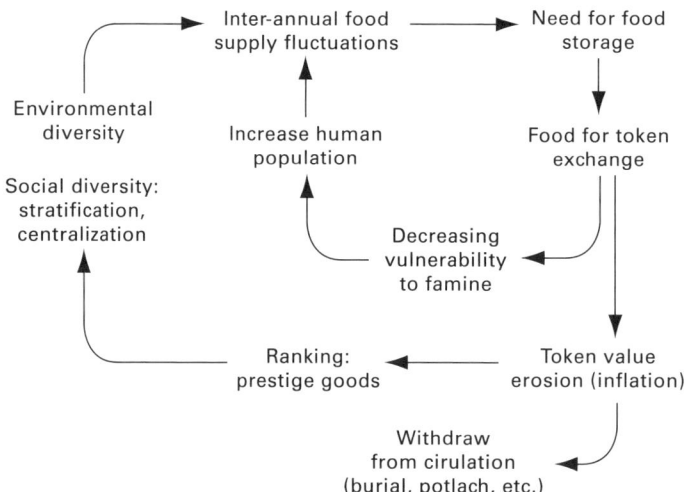

FIGURE 6.3

Possible factors in the emergence of trade in the Aegean Sea (after Halstead, 1995). Trade can mitigate fluctuations in food supply in a region of environmental diversity. The trade system has to be protected against inflation, through withdrawal or upgrading of tokens which gives rise to social ranking.

provide an important buffer as such events tend to be asynchronous in high-diversity regions. As a result, an important stimulus existed for the exchange of food for tokens. To avoid inflation, the tokens have to disappear every now and then – burying them with funerals or destroying them as in the potlach system, for example.[5] Alternatively, they are made into a ranking system of less and more valuable tokens. In this way, ecological diversity may have contributed to the emergence of social ranking, with a prominent role for merchants (*Figure 6.3*). Whatever the details of these explanations, it is tempting to relate this early landscape-inspired evolution to the well-known features of the later Greek city-states: political autonomy and economic autarchy.

6.3.4.   *Meso-America*

The ancient civilizations of Meso-America are among the best researched in the world (Blanton 1993). One of the larger, centralized cultures, the Maya, and the close correlation and synergistic links between climate change, vegetation response, and cultural development have been discussed in a previous chapter (cf. Section 3.4.2). In other places, too, past human activity has left its trace on the present-day landscape and the ecological composition of vegetation communities. For example, the present vegetation of north-eastern Guatemala is predominately tropical semi-evergreen forest interspersed with patches of savannah; some researchers believe these are the relicts of Mayan land-use practices (Leyden 1987). A cooling climate may have allowed the Mayan civilization to prosper as it would have forced the malaria-carrying mosquito to migrate further to the south, allowing extensive farming and the construction of cities (Perry 2000). When the world climate warmed again, the Maya abandoned their fields and moved into the less fertile Yucatan Peninsular (Hsu 2000).

An investigation into social organization in the south-western Mayan lowlands points at the importance of the local geography and resource base (Gunn 2000). South of the Yucatan Peninsula, three river basins with different characteristics have played a major role in the Mayan civilization from 4000 yr BP (Early Pre-Classical) to 500 BP (Late Post-Classical). The three rivers, Usumacinta, Candeliaria and Champoton, formed three different biocultures which together have determined the human-environment interaction in this part of Central America. It has been possible to identify how the river basins responded to changes in important climate parameters (rainfall, temperature) and derived variables (monthly river discharge). The Candelaria River was of crucial importance as an ecotone between the two relatively stable upland and lowland ecozones of the other two rivers.[6] Such an ecotonal river is a generator and reservoir of cultural diversity. The conditions under which Mayan culture could develop can be established, following the various stages of activity. Three interesting patterns emerge: changes in climate parameters have led to population shifts between the three river basins in the Early and Middle Pre-Classical periods; elevated cities were abandoned in a period of great drought (1050-1250 yr BP); and the Champoton river basin was the only one where human activity – deforestation with river discharge volume change – had a serious impact. Mayan cosmology may have provided them with a superior ability to prognosticate patterns of cyclical environmental changes. The investigations of human-environment interactions in this part of Central America confirm, as much other research, that a meaningful interpretation is only possible at a sufficiently desegregated spatial level.

A comparative analysis of the highland valleys – of Oaxaca and Mexico – and the eastern lowlands is quite revealing with regard to the relationship between the environment and social organization (Blanton 1993). The highland valleys have natural barriers, the mountains, which obstruct communication and have limited potential for agriculture. Their agricultural systems tend to aim at the 'replication of uniformity': 'a continual preoccupation with comparatively little horizontal complexity – the vast majority of parts are alike, and they tend to stay that way. The replication of uniformity is usually accomplished by means of a strong vertical differentiation – a powerful hierarchy manages most affairs.' (Blanton 1993: 163). The lowlands, on the other hand, are much more vast and unbounded. It can be hypothesized that people in these circumstances employ a wide and diverse spectrum of production techniques. The diversity entailed co-ordination in matters such as access to resources, allocation of time and labour and exchange of

---

Environmental degradation as a cause of collapse   A good piece of Maya environmental history is based on the pioneering Central Petén Historical Ecology Project (Redman 1999: 141-145). In this region in lowland Guatemala a swidden – or milpa – agricultural system with a 3-5 year fallow period can support population densities in the order of 25 people/km². How did the Maya manage to sustain in some places and times up to 250 people/km², and can the environmental impacts of the required efficient and centralized agriculture be traced back? Examining sediment core from lake bottoms, the researchers found a significant increase in phosphorus and silica deposition during the Maya occupation. Accelerated phosphorus deposition points at more phosphorus in the soil due to human activity (waste, food, disintegration of bodies and stoneworks) and to more soil erosion (*Figure 6.4*). Similarly, silica deposition increased severalfold during the period which archaeologists think had the highest population – another indicator of increased erosion rates. Apparently, the Maya appreciated the tropical forest ecosystem well enough to thrive for centuries by managing land clearance, control water flows and transport food to cope with localized shortages.

However, the lake sediment data indicate that 'the high forest that prevailed in much of [the] region was largely removed by the farming and settlement building activities of the Mayas as early as 3000 to 4000 years ago. This resulted in a shift toward more open vegetation during much of the Mayan occupation with the maximum defor-estation between 1000 and 2000 years ago. The basic drain on the land... increased to the point where the system was no longer sustainable. Declining productivity must have had a multiplier effect, leading to food shortfalls, reduced labour investment, and political instability. By the end of the 10th century AD, most of the large settlements of the Mayan uplands and southern lowlands had been abandoned or at least seriously depopulated.' (Redman 1999: 145) Coincident was a relatively dry period that put crop productivity under additional pressure in an ecosystem already strained by human activities.

FIGURE 6.4

Impact of long-term Mayan settlement on the terrestrial and lacustrine environments of the central Petén lakes (Redman 1999, from Rice 1996)

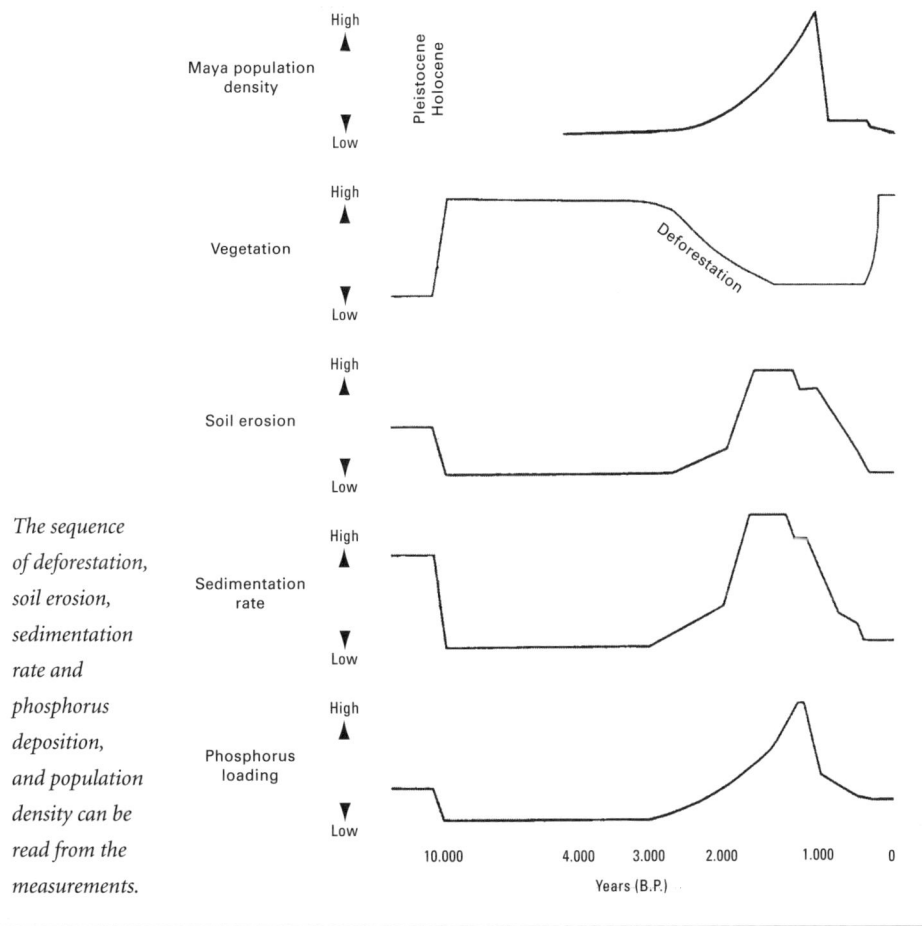

The sequence of deforestation, soil erosion, sedimentation rate and phosphorus deposition, and population density can be read from the measurements.

products. Economic institutions developed early and consistently provided the basis for survival. The evolutionary problem here is the 'organization of diversity': how to keep the components in these horizontally complex systems doing their jobs eventhough they have very different roles and interests. In the eastern lowlands, there were many interacting socio-political units with permeable boundaries or large efforts to regulate flows of things and people across the boundaries. From this perspective, these lowlands resembled more the ancient civilizations in the Near East or Asia than the nearby highland valleys.

6.4. From states to empires

> To read what the 'ecologists' write, one would often think that civilised peoples only ate, excreted, and reproduced; to read what the humanists write, one would think civilisations were above all three, and devoted all their energy to the arts.
>
> *Flannery 1972: 400*

In the previous narratives, we have seen how increasing social complexity manifested itself in the form of hierarchically organized urban conglomerates and exchange oriented trade networks. There is a good deal of evidence that such patterns reflected local and regional biogeography, in the sense of landscapes, soils, rain patterns and corridors. As social complexity further increased, the most impressive and conspicuous development has been the process in which some of the early states expanded their territory and developed more elaborate systems of governance: they became empires. Their administrative bureaucracies became larger, state-controlled trading networks expanded and large urbanized regions with a core-periphery dependence emerged. Of course, there are no sharp boundary lines. These ancient civilizations manifested, as part of their evolution into more urbanized and stratified societies, a further intensification of agriculture and manufacturing. The resulting larger productive surplus was invested into large-scale investments, temples and palaces as well as roads, dams and canals, ships and harbours. Let us look at a few more narratives.

6.4.1. Egypt

The Nile and Egypt are synonymous. The river is Egypt's life vein – and at the root of its economic fragility. Nile water levels mirrored climatic events throughout the region, as is becoming clear from East African lake levels and Indian monsoon patterns (Yasuda 2001, 3.3.2). During the 7th and 6th millennia BP episodes of severe drought, dwellers of the desert drifted towards the Nile valley in search of water, food and fodder. In subse-

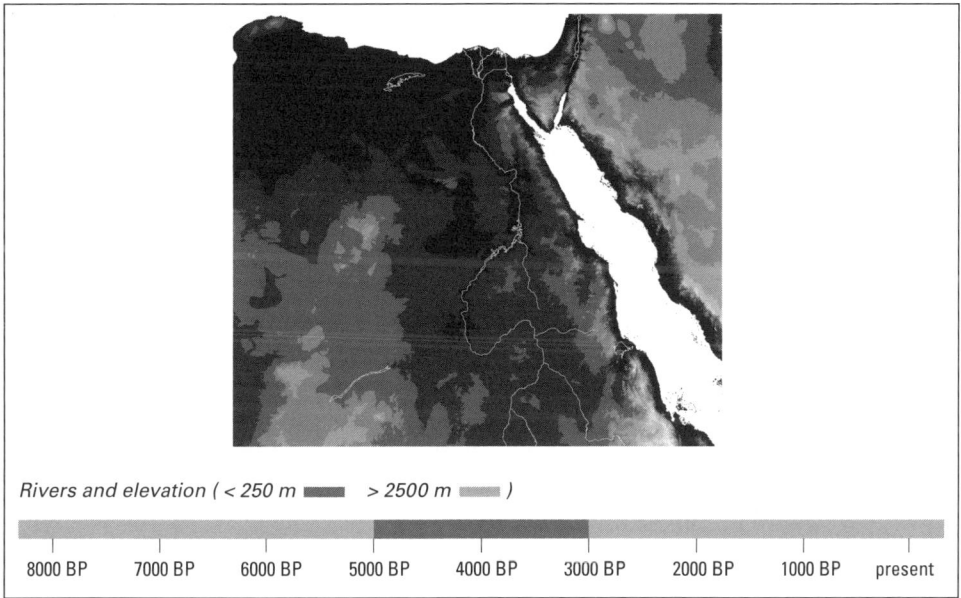

Rivers and elevation (< 250 m ▆▆▆ > 2500 m ▆▆▆)

| 8000 BP | 7000 BP | 6000 BP | 5000 BP | 4000 BP | 3000 BP | 2000 BP | 1000 BP | present |

quent millennia the basis for Egyptian civilization was laid. Spells of hyperarid conditions occurred around 4500 and 3700 yr BP and the savannah vegetation retreated to its
present limit (cf. Section 3.3). Episodes of high Nile flood discharge are correlated with
greater rainfall in East Africa and a warmer climate in Europe; low levels correlate with
cooler temperature and drier conditions in East Africa. Such levels had serious consequences for human populations in Egypt. Very high floods led to the destruction of dikes
and houses and prevented the planting of crops. Very low discharge levels reduced the
cultivable area as natural irrigation failed. Peoples have found a variety of responses to
such risks: building – and maintaining and repairing – dikes, irrigation canals and
drains.

Long-term historical water level records in combination with archaeological finds
provide a unique basis for studying human-environment interactions in the Faiyum and
Nile Valleys and the Nile Delta (Hassan 2000; Hassan 1997). As for Mesopotamia, it is
generally assumed that the increasing irrigation needs and efforts forced the local rulers
to unify peoples in centralized administrative states although the mechanisms may have
been subtle (cf. Section 6.3.1). Droughts in the Nile Valley around 5200 cal yr BP may
have been responsible for the unification of Egypt and the rise of the nation state – the
Old Kingdom. Early documents show administrators shifting from wheat to the more
salt-resistant barley to combat increasing salinization resulting from irrigation, although
eventually much land had to be abandoned through salinization. One millennium later,
around 4200 cal yr BP, low floods with catastrophic droughts have been invoked to
explain the opposite: the collapse of centralized government and the end of the Old

193

Kingdom (Hassan 1997; Fairbridge 1984). The low Nile River levels may have triggered a series of civil uprisings widely recorded during this time and the rule from Memphis broke down at the end of the 5th Dynasty, about 4180 yr BP.

> The Old Kingdom (ca. 4750-4150 yr BP) [in Egypt] was a time of tremendous royal power...
> and it saw a big increase in population... This placed great reliance on maximising the use of
> the land flooded and fertilised each year by the inundations. Around 4250-4150 yr BP the
> same prolonged dry period which caused such problems for the Ur III kings in Iraq brought a
> series of consistently low floods and precipitated half a century of famine. This helped pull a
> declining order. The monarchy was overthrown... (Wood 1999: 141-142)

Unlike in other parts of the Middle East, social order was regained by the end of the 9th Dynasty, about 4000 yr BP, with the administrative centre now at Thebes. Wood (1999) states that it was because the norms and values of Egyptian civilization were so deeply rooted and enduring – which begs the question why they were. During the New Kingdom the population of Egypt as a whole increased again, possibly to as many as 5 million during the 18th to 19th Dynasties (1539-1186 BC). Up to half of the population may have lived in cities such as Memphis and Heliopolis, the former perhaps being the world's first city of over 1 million people (Manley 1996).

What happened to society during these episodes of natural disaster of which the Bible accounts so vividly? As ruling elites were dependent on the tax revenues from farmers, a series of low Nile floods was critical for governance. Farmers were confronted with starvation, urban craftsmen and artisans died in massive numbers – it is reported that less than 10% of the weavers in Cairo survived the 1200-1201 AD famines – and the king saw his income shrink rapidly. In such periods of economic distress, rivals would emerge denouncing royal excesses such as the construction of large monuments with an appeal to ancient, fundamental religious beliefs. The legitimacy of the ruling class was questioned and centralized government weakened. The situation worsened as urban administrators, functionaries, merchants and other non-food producers would try to stick to their 'good life' habits. Because of declining revenues the king could no longer pay for adequate military and political support – nor for large agricultural projects that would redistribute food and secure against future droughts. The 'power range' – an estimated 400 km with the available transport capacities – decreased and the state would disintegrate in smaller, provincial units. At this stage, some people would flee the region while others might invade it. *Figure 6.5* is a schematic representation of some aspects of such a spiral, as one possible intrusion on the positive loops of growth and control. It is quite probable that such a course of events happened during the periods of low Nile discharge around 4200, 3100 and 2700 yr BP.

Let us continue our travel, side-stepping another 'rise and fall of empire' region – the Near and Middle East – and jump towards the Far East: China. Here, too, peoples and

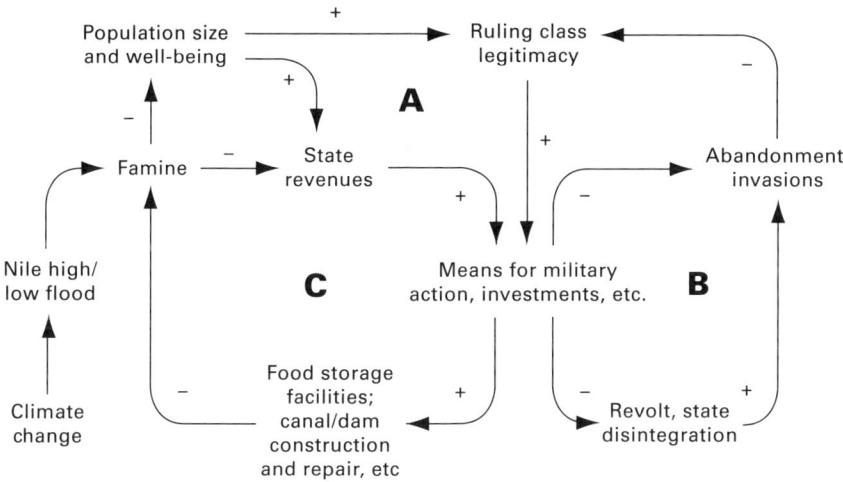

FIGURE 6.5
Environmental change induced forces of decline in Egypt: famine can cause a positive feedback loop towards disintegration (A), accelerated by subsequent tendencies towards disintegration (B). Invest-ment in adaptive capacity and restoring ruling class legitimacy (C) can halt or reverse the decline. A + sign near an arrow indicates that an increase in a variable will cause an increase in another variable; a – sign the reverse (after Hassan 1997).

their rulers experienced the consequences of natural disasters and their ways of dealing with it – another décor against which the human destiny unfolded in tragedy, failure and wisdom. The outcome of such a disintegration process, though, was not necessarily dis-astrous: the newly emergent, smaller units may actually have been more resilient. As Guarnsey and Morris (1986) say in a description of the collapse of the centralized redis-tributive system of the Mycenaean palaces in the 4th millennium BP: it devolved into 'petty lords, practising small-scale redistribution as part of a strategy of ironing out localised shortages.'

6.4.2.   China

China, the land of the Ch'in, has a peculiar geography. From the south-west to the north-west it is surrounded by high mountains, in the north by the cold Mongolian mountain ranges, and in the north-east, east and south-east by seas. Agriculture in China goes back to at least 8000 yr BP (cf. Section 4.3.3). However, Chinese history has been influenced greatly by peoples coming in from the large Eurasian steppes. The

Guangzhong Basin of the Wei He between the Qinling Shan in the south and the löss plateau in the north, in particular, has been a corridor in and from which the earliest – at least recorded – states have come into being: the Xia and Shang dynasties (4200-3100 yr BP) and subsequently the Zhou, Ch'in and Han dynasties. These peoples had a natural outlet into the large Huang-Huai-Hai Plain, covering some 350,000 km^2 and largely built up from 400-500 metre-thick sediment layers from the Huang He.[7]

The natural environment here has always made an impact on humans: 'Frequent major and minor river shifts have affected the geomorphology of the plain; it is recorded that during the past 3000 to 4000 years, the Huang He has broken its banks 1593 times. The general pattern of undulating relief characterized by hills, slopes, and depressions is liable to waterlogging due to irregular drainage.' (Zuo Dakang 1990: 473). Human activities started to add to these natural vagaries but probably not earlier than 2000 yr BP. The area has hot summers and cold winters and the distribution of settlements up to 2000 yr BP – mostly in the hilly areas between the mountains and the plain – suggest the inhospitable nature of the plain as a human habitat. Yet it was here in these northern valleys and plains that, around 1900 yr BP, state development started – much earlier than in south China.

Yates (1990) gives a nice overview of the early developments in China from the perspective of food and famine. From the early Xia period onwards, war has been a most prominent feature of life. Together with the weather fluctuations, it was a major cause of famine. The Shang people practiced a mix of hunting and slash-and-burn farming – the word for hunting and agriculture was the same, t'ien – and they had elaborate rituals related to droughts. There was a close connection between sacrifice, war and agriculture: the king sent out farmer-soldiers to colonize and hunting was a military activity. The state's interest in the welfare of the people goes back to these early peoples. The king had unique divine powers and divined personally about war and agriculture, and the legitimacy of his power depended on his success in manipulating the weather and war spirits.

Much more is known about the later Zhou dynasty and the subsequent Spring and Autumn and Warring States periods and the unification of these parts of China under the Ch'in dynasty. One possibly key aspect is the advent of a colder period around 3000 yr BP which will have been experienced as a traumatic shift. Elvin (1993), in his detailed account of the environmental history of China based upon ancient texts, maintains that the social structure of power was the most important single factor controlling what happened to the environment. In his view the most intriguing aspect of these ancient civilizations was their 'powerless wisdom': a political philosophy which put conservation of a well-ordered nature at its centre and at the same time a political reality which led to warfare in the ruthless pursuit of economic development. Disturbance of the natural order was thought to bring catastrophe and seen as a sign of moral decline – yet:

in order to mobilize resources and build up populations to man the armies that were engaged in warfare that was rapidly shifting from a ritualized combat to merciless destruction… statesmen turned to economic development… [which became] both the consequence and the cause of intensified warfare. (Elvin 1993: 17-18)

In practice, this meant limiting access for commoners to non-agricultural land, creating an advantageous state monopoly and forcing people to settle down and become a source of taxes and soldiers. Taxes on mountains, marshes, dams and reservoirs were under the control and to the benefit of the Imperial Court. Nature conservation regulations were violated and the guardians were the most effective destroyers of the natural environment. Yates makes another interesting statement in view of China's later history: 'Briefly, the Ch'in state only valued agriculture and war, and all secondary occupations, such as trade, were discouraged. Peasants could gain aristocratic rank by cutting off heads in battle: one head gained one rank, two heads two ranks…' – not unlike the contemporaneous Celts in Europe (Yates 1990: 156).

Environmental degradation, rather modest and mostly local, became an important element in the perennial struggle between landlords and peasants (Chang-Qun 1998). Initially, 'migratory farming' with relocalization of centres of civilization, already happening during Xia and Shang times, increased. The introduction of iron farming implements and animal husbandry made agriculture more productive and pressures were reduced. Yet, famines became a recurrent phenomenon due to a variety of factors, many of them linked to the endemic warfare: field abandonment due to corruption and war, physical destruction of the farming population and of harvests in military campaigns (Yates 1990). Another set of factors, most probably often cause and consequence of the wars, were environmental. Higher yields led to higher population growth. In northern China, where the larger part of the estimated 60 million inhabitants of China lived, most cultivable land was used and millions of people were forced or sent away to cultivate grasslands and forests. The surging construction of military and civil works – such as the Great Wall – required massive amounts of timber and brick and led to large-scale deforestation and subsequent desertification and increased flooding. A final and inseparable component was the increasing social stratification and the resulting more complex hierarchy and the accompanying processes of urbanization and commercialization. These created large differentials in access to food supplies – as well as wealthy bureaucrats and traders. In the official response to the famines and disasters one recognizes again the 'powerless wisdom': the rulers were morally obliged to put the people's welfare first and many administrative rules and techniques were introduced, but often only revolt or the fear for it would bring practical relief. Of course, the tension between a society's ideology on the one hand and the reality of greed and power on the other hand are found throughout civilizations. Any judgment is also partly focus and interpretation: whereas Elvin summarizes Chinese reality as 'fine sentiments, dosed action', Yates finds it hard to imagine that the Chinese population could have grown to the present size without the technical and moral foundations for the system of state involvement in providing for peoples' basic needs.

FIGURE 6.6
Forces at work in complex societies: the positive loops of growth and control

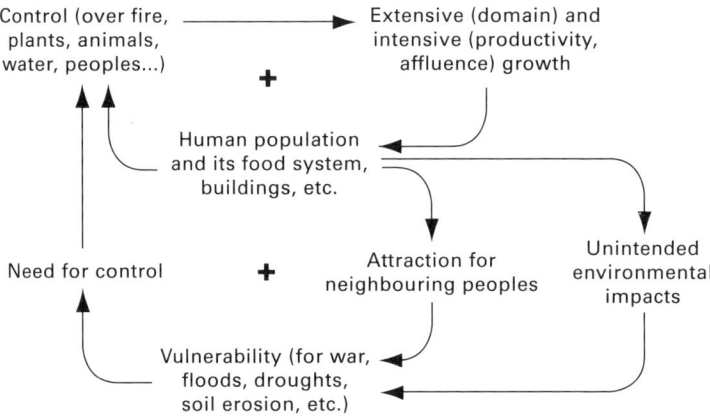

From the narratives in this chapter, it may be concluded that the rise in social complexity was driven by a series of positive feedback loops. At the physical level, they are manifest in the growing size and density of human populations and artefacts. At the informational level, it is the extent and content of information flows and processing capacity in the pursuit of control that matter most. *Figure 6.6* sketches some of the forces at work – suggesting that the threats as much as the opportunities were behind the search for more control of the environment.

6.5.   What happened in the fringes of empires?

'As city states have expanded into nations, kingdoms and empires, civilization has repeatedly become obsessed with the acquisition and wielding of power; an activity that has left millions of people dead in the streets and dominated the pages of history so much that the significance of the substance bases upon which civilizations are founded have all but ignored.' (Reader 1988: 157). Despite the lasting impression that states and empires made on human imagination, it should be noted that the larger part of human life took place outside or in the – spatial and temporal – fringes of states and empires. The true diversity of the processes by which egalitarian hunter-gatherer communities or

Life in the outposts of a declining Empire[8]   At the close of the Late Bronze Age (ca. 3200 yr BP), the whole of northern Mesopotamia had been brought under Assyrian rule. Centuries of warfare had eroded the urban basis of Assyrian royal power; the old provincial centres were abandoned and large tracts of agricultural land had reverted to nomadism. The coastal areas of the Near East were ravaged by the Sea Peoples and an aggressive new tribal federation, the Aramaeans, raided the countryside. Assyria was surrounded by foes, chaos was on the move. The Assyrian King Tukulti-Ninurta I (1233-1197 BC) expressed his worries in a prayer to the state's main god, Assur: 'All the evil-doers await a dark day without sunshine, their threatening fingers are stretched out to scatter the armies of Assur, vilely plot against their benefactor.'

Some 400 kilometres west of the capital Assur lies the Balikh valley, which was governed by members of the royal family. Provincial governors in this period were not funded by the crown, but covered their expenses by raising taxes on the settled population and by producing a grain surplus on the state farms in their territory. Such state farms were founded in abandoned and marginal territories and thus served the economy as well as a resettlement programme.

Tell Sabi Abyad (the modern name) lies halfway down the Balikh in a broad and well-watered part of the valley. Impressive fortifications enclosed an area of some 3600 m^2, the location of the owner's residence, a jail, stores and administrative facilities. The domestic and industrial buildings outside the walls were enclosed by a defensive ditch several metres deep. The written sources, 319 clay tablets with cuneiform writing, indicate a dependent population of around 1000, partly Assyrians brought down from the Assyrian heartlands, partly deported foreigners and prisoners of war. Their tents and mud brick houses must have been scattered around the countryside. About 36 km^2 of land was available for grain, pasture, fallow, and gardens. With a seed corn/yield ratio of 1 to 7, the returns of agriculture could be called fair.

The day-to-day affairs of the state farm were directed by the 'steward', who had full executive powers and interacted not only with the owner but also with the civil and military administration of the region. Regional communication was by mail, slow and dependable. Thus, a regional functionary wrote to the steward: 'What is this, that whatever I tell you to do, you don't do it as I said? Why did you not make a potter available to the brewer in [the town] Dunni-Assur? Now your brewer in [the town] Sakhlalu must be instructed to supply me with both beer and drinking vessels for my banquet with [the representatives of] the Sutû tribe. From whom [else] could I request these supplies? Respond promptly.'

In theory the Assyrian state treats its citizens and dependents according to public law; in practice, however, the administration of justice is unpredictable. Consequently the practice of bribing civil servants to further one's cause is officially frowned upon but in fact condoned. The quid pro quo implied by a 'gift' – as it is called – can even be

199

recorded in a sealed and witnessed contract: 'Damqat-Tashmetu, daughter of Sin-shuma-usur, wife of Sigelda, son of Irrigi, from [the town] Shuadikanni, owes one un-castrated male adult to [the governor] Assur-iddin, son of Qibi-Assur. This male is his gift; he [Assur-iddin] will receive his gift, when he [Assur-iddin] has treated her [Dam-qat-Tashmetu's] case which concerns her [deceased] husband's serfs that must not be given to Adad-shuma-iddina.'

Caravans from the Levant passed through Syria and left Hittite territory at Karkem-ish where they crossed the Euphrates. On the route to Assur 90 kilometres to the west lies Sabi Abyad, which functioned as border town and customs office. A regional office wrote to the steward: 'Formerly I instructed you as follows: 'caravans that come to me from Karkemish must not pass without your consent, and you must [check and] seal all wares.' Now I have heard that caravans in fact are on their way [and I repeat]: 'any car-avan that comes my way, be it of [the governor] Ili-pada, of princesses, or of nobles – seal everything! I have also heard that they carry balsam; if any balsam is missing, you will be executed.' The import tax raised in Assur on luxury items such as balsam was an important source of revenue for the state. It all has a distinctly modern ring.

the survivors of collapsing states and empires developed more complex relationships between its members and with their environment and their neighbours may be severely underestimated (McIntosh 1988; Renfrew 1973). In more heterogeneous landscapes, peoples had motives to develop other forms of organization, reflecting amongst others the (lack of) opportunities for migration, conquest, defence and taxation.

In this periphery of Great History, some populations stuck to or fell back onto earlier forms of organization: bands, tribes, with or without local despots. In some places and times peoples attained and sustained a degree of social complexity different from the social stratification characteristic of states and empires with centralized authority or of trade-oriented city-states with competitive merchant elite.[9] The process of accumula-tion of (access to) resources into fewer and fewer hands may have been halted by the combination of a precarious environment on the one hand and egalitarian distribution schemes on the other. Anthropological explanations tend to give an important role to the local/regional biogeography. The Chimbu tribe in highland New Guinea has hardly any social stratification, yet population densities are up to 250 people/km^2 – a reflection of the ruptured landscape which restricts aggregation into larger units. Their exchange is nearly all reciprocal and interpersonal relationships are regulated by an elaborate ritual system as an alternative to political power and institutions (Flannery 1972). An example from Africa is the Mande people who populated the Middle Niger region in West Africa some 4000-8000 yr BP (McIntosh 1988; McIntosh 2000b). Close seasonal adaptation and high seasonal mobility in combination and articulated specialization may have been at the basis of this heterarchist society:

The salient characteristics of today's climate and flood regime are high interannual variability and the difficulty of prediction from year to year (much less at longer perspectives). Those characteristics can, with some confidence, be extrapolated back into prehistoric time… The lesson for the prehistorian and historian working within these long-term perspectives is that environmental stress, surprise, and unpredictability were constant realities for the inhabitants of the Middle Niger. Do differences in tool assemblages, faunal remains and settlement location reflect a precocious development of specialists linked together by habits of regional exchange? If so, we will have evidence for one quite successful adaptation to climate surprise. If so, and if the emergence of specialists does not entail the emergence of elites, we have the beginnings of a long-successful Middle Niger brand of heterarchy. (McIntosh 1998: 79-80)

East of the river Niger in Nigeria live the Ibo people who in spite of a high population density have apparently developed neither cities nor states and had a dispersed not a concentrated authority – 'as late as the 1930s the Ibo could still boast that 'there is no one who owns us' (that is to say: we have no rulers) and their society remained characterized by [this].' (Connah 2001: 164). On the island of Bali there is an intricate relationship between rice cultivation and social organization (Reader 1988). Wet rice cultivation is labour-intensive, mechanization being difficult. It also has a high and lasting productivity, mainly due to the benefits of controlled flooding on the nitrogen balance. In this situation a form of social complexity has arisen with a strict caste-related hierarchy and an important role for priests – who derive authority from high standards of behaviour.[10] Yet it also has distinctly egalitarian features – as one would imagine to have existed in the early religious-agrarian regimes:

> The Balinese tend to dislike and distrust people who project themselves above the group as a whole, and where power has to be exercised they tend to disperse it very thinly… For the Balinese there is no difference between a person's spiritual and secular life…The devils and demons [in religion]… provide forceful reminders of the obligation to restrain selfish instincts for the benefit of social harmony… Rice cultivation is the ultimate expression of the Balinese readiness to follow the edicts of some greater authority. (Reader 1988: 61)

The complex religion of the Balinese – and other Asian populations – is an excellent example of the functional significance of religion in human ecology, but beyond the scope of this book to deal with in more depth. One is also reminded of the role which monks and monasteries have played in the periphery of large civilizations.[11]

Despite the controversial nature of some of the interpretations of these examples – some speak of a 'heterarchist gang' – these examples highlight that social complexity has evolved in more directions than just secular state and trade regimes. There is another collection of stories that are of particular relevance in the present context and also suggest that state control and trade regimes were not the only organizational forms of human-environment interactions. Ostrom (1990) refers to them as common property regimes. Written accounts show that peoples all over the world have developed institutions which have lasted over 1000 years in some cases and have survived droughts, floods, diseases and economic and political turmoil. Most of these regimes were in highly variable and uncertain environments and resource systems. The appropriators, that is, the individuals who use the common pool resource, have 'designed basic operational rules, created organizations to undertake the operational management of their common property regimes, and modified their rules over time in light of past experience according to their own collective-choice and constitutional-choice rules.' (Ostrom 1990: 58). These self-organizing groups solved the problem of commitment and mutual monitoring – among them the avoidance of free-riders and effective sanctioning – without resorting to centralized power exercised by external agents or to competitive market institutions. According to Ostrom, these regimes were the outcome of a deliberate choice:

> The villagers have chosen to retain the institution of communal property as the foundation for land use and similar aspects of village economies. The economic survival of these villagers has been dependent on the skill with which they have used their limited resources. One cannot view communal property in these settings as primordial remains of earlier institutions evolved in a land of plenty. If the transactions costs involved in managing communal property had been excessive, compared with private-property institutions, the villagers would have had many opportunities to devise different land-tenure arrangements for the mountain commons. (Ostrom 1990: 61)

Who were these villagers? One such a place is the Swiss village of Törbel for which a legal document on the rules for communally owned property dates back to 1224 AD (Ostrom 1990; Reader 1988). Another famous example is the co-management schemes of water resources for irrigation in south-eastern Spain (Ostrom 1990; Guillet 1999). The huerta irrigation systems of Valencia, in operation since at least the 15th century, have been singled out as unusually long-lived and successful, locally managed, common property regimes. Spain also has a rich history of local management for other resources such as forests, land and pastures, possibly related to the practices of Islamic nomads from North Africa (see Section 3.5). However, such systems did not develop in isolation – they worked in conjunction with guidelines and regulations contained in a famous seven volume legal code, *Las siete partidas*, completed in the second half of the 13th century and the epitome of a centralizing state. Other examples are the zanjera irrigation communities in the Philippines, with a central role for the small-scale communities of the local irrigators and rules tailored to its own specific history, and management of over 12 million hectares of common lands in Tokugawa in 17th to 19th century Japan (Ostrom 1990).

6.6.   The decline and fall of social complexity

As can be seen at a glance from *Figure 6.6*, the forces behind a rise in social complexity are interwoven with the forces of decline. What endures are the fringes – but the destruction and collapse narratives usually receive most attention:

> The last heyday of an independent [Sumer] took place between 4150 and 4050 yr BP under the leadership of the city of Ur…. That [the massive and costly administrative reforms and the animal sacrifices] contributed to the dynasty's economic troubles seems likely. The climate of the plain seems now to have been going through a long, dry spell; much agricultural land had gone out of use, and economic documents show administrators shifting from wheat to the more salt-resistant barley to combat salinization. Worse, the perennial raids on the plain from nomadic outsiders grew more and more threatening…. There is evidence that much land by now had been abandoned through salinization. The population could not be fed: prices hit the ceiling with a sixtyfold increase in grain. International trade…broke down… and soon government communications started to fail…. Gloomy oracles prophesied the worst, and the worst duly arrived. (Wood 1999: 33)

This is only one of the many evocative descriptions of what has always been a fascinating subject: the decline and fall of empires and civilizations. Flooding and drought have destroyed empires in a complex process of famines, revolts and migrations. The end of the Harappan civilization in the Indus-Sarasvati valley is associated with tectonic activity:

> Saraswati emerged as a mighty river during the warm spell that succeeded the Pleistocene glaciation some 10,000 years ago… Flowing down the Himalayan slopes, it had coursed through northwestern India and drained into the ancient Arabian Sea… great civilizations had flourished on its banks during the river's heydays. After glorious existence for some 4000 years, the river declined and gradually vanished… spells of intermittent tectonic activities associated with the rise of the Himalayas, neotectonism in the Cutch region, climatic changes and desertification induced by variations in earth's orbit and tilt, diminishing supply of water due to river piracy, all appear to have had vital roles in the downfall of Saraswati river. (Sankaran 1999)

Table 6.1 gives an overview of some of the more well-known 'decline and collapse' stories.

As with explanations of the large Eurasian migrations, many cause-and-effect schemes have been proposed to explain the 'rise and fall of empires'. Most spectacular are the Big Catastrophes, dismissing the possibility that '… the world ends, Not with a bang but a

TABLE 6.1   SOME DECLINE EVENTS FOR WHICH THERE IS ARCHAEOLOGICAL
EVIDENCE

Location	Date	Probable causes
Malta	4500 yr BP	Unknown: a 'mystery'
Ur (Mesopotamia)	4200 yr BP	Drought, salinization, overexploitation of peasants, nomad invasions?
Egypt – Old Kingdom	4130-4080 BP	Climate change with low Nile water levels
Indus-Sarasvati (Harappan)	4000-3600 yr BP	Earthquakes with multiple consequences, in combination with climate change?
Crete (Minoan)	3500-3400 yr BP	Volcano eruption with plural consequences?
Tiryns (Mycenaean)	3200 yr BP	Flooding
Rome	1400-1700 yr BP	Multi-causal (Chapter 7)
Yemen	1300 yr BP	Collapse Marib dam, possibly and partly as result of climate change, caused by volcanic eruption?
Aztec Teotihuacan (Mexico)	1250 yr BP	Mutlicausal but possibly and partly as result of climate change (caused by volcanic eruption?)
Maya (Yucatan)	1000-600 yr BP	Soil erosion, climate deterioration as trigger
Hohokam (Arizona)	650 yr BP	Population pressure: soil erosion etc. in combination with climate change (Section 4.3.4)

whimper,' in the words of T.S. Eliot. In some periods, with influential scholars becoming the spokesmen, climate change and earthquakes have been seen as such causal factors, for instance in the decline of the Harappan, Minoan and Mycenaean civilizations. The collapse of the Egyptian Old Kingdom has been linked to variations in Nile flood levels, the decline of the Peruvian Chimu culture to tectonic uplift. At times, the pendulum

---

Mesopotamia: mud, mud, mud   Byron, on visiting Iraq in 1937, gives in his travel book *Road to Oxiana* a brief account of how he experienced 20th century Iraq: 'The prime fact of Mesopotamian history is that in the 13th century Hulagu destroyed the irrigation system; and that from that day to this Mesopotamia has remained a land of mud deprived of mud's only possible advantage, vegetable fertility. It is a mud plain... From this plain rise villages of mud and cities of mud. The rivers flow with liquid mud. The air is composed of mud refined into a gas. The people are mud-coloured; they wear mud-coloured clothes, and their national hat is nothing more than a formalised mud-pie.' Yet he was visiting one of the cradles of human civilization.

switched to the other side, giving hardly any consideration to climate and environmental change (Meyer, in Bell-Fialkoff 2000). Other 'collapse theories' have suffered similar ups and downs. Population pressure – often incorrectly equated to high population density or growth – has figured prominently in many explanatory theories, although it is at best an indirect association. Resource overexploitation and mismanagement, bringing famine and diseases in their wake, are said to have caused the collapse of ancient Mesopotamian and Meso-American civilizations, the former possibly and the latter probably during periods of environmental change as has been recounted in this and a previous chapter. Human-induced environmental degradation in the form of soil erosion and salinization feature as co-determinants. Interactions with other peoples in the form of wars and invasions have been invoked. A last important group focuses on internal political processes: over-stretch in material and cultural terms, erosion or lack of spiritual values. As the British historian Toynbee states in his last book Mankind and Mother Earth:

> Man is a psychosomatic being, acting within a world that is material and finite… But Man's other home, the spiritual world, is also an integral part of total reality; it differs from the biosphere in being both non-material and infinite; and, in his life in the spiritual world, Man finds that his mission is to seek, not for a material mastery over his non-human environment, but for a spiritual mastery over himself. (Toynbee 1976: 18)

It seems prudent to be aware of the degree to which theories big and small are a reflection of dominant scientific fashions, schools, disciplines and individuals.

The evidence for decline and collapse is sometimes vivid and clear, in other cases indirect and obscure. Using all kinds of information, tentative population estimates have been constructed which reflect such momentous transition periods: populations in Mesopotamia, the Nile Valley and the Mexico Basin have experienced precipitous decline (*Figure 5.10*). In most cases, the population density had risen to levels far above those that could be sustained with early agricultural techniques. As a result, there was a continuous pressure in these societies to extract surplus and to increase the workload and push for innovations among the rural populations. This struggle to lift the carrying capacity to satisfy growing demand has probably been the background to dynamic innovations and expansions as well as to decline and collapse. Which way it would go will have depended on a variety of factors, which can be summarized under the headings of ecological resilience – topography, resource endowments and dynamics, existence of trade routes, etc. – and socio-political resilience – legitimacy of leadership, availability and accessibility of tools and skills, military capacity, etc.

As usual, more investigations make the explanation more subtle and multi-faceted than previously thought. In his book *The Collapse of Complex Societies* Tainter (1988) lists elev-

What can more intensely convey the grief and desperation in such episodes of dramatic decline than this lamentation of an Egyptian king, as quoted by Hassan (2000)?

> I was mourning on my throne
> Those of the palace were in grief,
> My heart was in great affliction,
> Because Hapy had failed to come in time
> In a period of seven years.
> Grains was scant,
> Kernels dried up,
> Scarce was every kind of food.
> Every man robbed his twin,
> Those who entered did not go.
> Children cried,
> Youngsters fell,
> The hearts of the old were grieving;
> Legs drawn up, they hug the ground,
> Their arms clasped about them. Courtiers were needy,
> Temples were shut,
> Shrines covered with dust,
> Everyone was in distress.
> I directed my heart to the past
> I consulted on the staff of the Ibis.

en major themes in the explanation of collapse. They can be categorized into three groups:
- Resource- and environment-related changes, fully exogenous or partly endogenous in the sense of human-induced;
- Interaction-related changes in the form of conquest or other, less penetrating forms of invasion; and
- Internal changes in socio-political, cultural and religious organization and world-view, diminishing the adequacy of response to external events.

If decline happens, if collapse threatens, societies have had a variety of responses. Setting up or expanding trade, technical and social innovations, a change in environmental management practices, migration and conquest and a mix of all these have sometimes postponed, sometimes reverted and sometimes accelerated the processes of decline and collapse. If disintegration occurred, new shoots on the tree of human civilizations got a chance.

Understandably, the kind of explanation given for the collapse of complex societies is often related to the explanation given for the emergence of complexity – as we have seen in the narrative above on floods in Egypt. One can also often recognize at once the disciplinary background or prevailing value orientation behind the explanations. It is only logical, for instance, that Toynbee assigns great value to the erosion of moral and spiritual values in explaining the decline of the Roman Empire and that epidemiologists read great epidemics and geologists read tectonic movements into past collapse. Tainter (1988) in his analysis finds nearly all explanations unsatisfactory: they are either cyclical or superficial or both. Most scholars would now agree that the decline and fall of complex societies can never be explained by a single cause-and-effect chain. Instead, as is the case with explanations of the emergence of complexity, such systems will be in constant structural transformation during which thresholds, non-linear behaviour and feedback loops make their trajectory in time and space a unique series of interconnected, irreversible events. Whether it is nevertheless possible to distil some general features for such processes is the topic of Chapter 8. First, we take an empirical look at one of the most intensely researched complex systems: the Roman Empire.

6.7.   Conclusions

A new stage in the agrarianization process involved extensive and intensive growth of human populations and their activities. It led to more intense and widespread interference with the environment and to spread and spatial concentrations of populations. Resources were used for ritual and art, sometimes causing environmental havoc. Mining and deforestation occurred on ever larger scales, with environmental changes in their wake. Interactions, in the form of trade and migration, intensified and reflected in trade routes and market towns. States emerged, with increasing social complexity in the form of craft specialization and social stratification. Some early states expanded their territory and developed more elaborate systems of governance with large, centralized administrative bureaucracies state-controlled trading networks.

Although environmental determinism in the form of single cause-effect schemes has to be dismissed, the roads towards increasing social complexity were at least partly a reflection of the local environment. Mesopotamian urban centres depended on an extraction and control mechanism, which ultimately destroyed Mesopotamia's agricultural basis and therefore itself. Egyptian civilization proved to be more resilient under such forces, due in part to the lower long-term vulnerability of the Nile valley to environmental disturbances. The Indus-Sarasvati and Aegean civilizations may have had more trade-oriented features, with ecological diversity of their landscapes as one of the determinants. Meso-American civilizations such as the Maya apparently followed also a development path in which environmental resource features and use patterns played a prominent role.

With increasing social complexity came an extension of control over both the natural and the human-inhabited space, in loops of actions with the subsequent need for greater control. Sustaining the more complex physical and institutional arrangements required more extensive information gathering and processing. In this sense, the rise in social complexity can best be seen as a response to as well as a mediating factor in human-environment dynamics. Vulnerability for disturbances increased as existent and new risks for the larger populations with their higher densities and larger fraction of non-food producers emerged. Unintended and probably only partly understood social and environmental consequences tended to undermine response capabilities to its manifestations in the form of increased taxation, famine, social uprisings and wars. Moreover, as the interaction with the environment became more intense and human society itself became more complex, it became more difficult to develop an adequate representation of what was going on – enhancing the possibility of mismanagement.

Historically, most attention has been paid to the more conspicuous form of social organization: the hierarchically structured empires that evolved from military-agrarian regimes and were mainly based on extraction and control with an associated ideology. Trade-based states, formed around competitive markets, have also left clear marks in human history. Both reflected important aspects of their natural environment. In the spatial and temporal fringes of such states and empires, other forms of social complexity have existed with resource management regimes based on local circumstances, co-operation and community control. These various forms of social organization had mutually antagonistic yet complementary relationships. They all have experienced periods of decline or collapse, often as a combination of mutually related external and internal stresses. Internal factors reflect a social rigidity which blocks structural transformation in the face of social disruption. External factors are usually a combination of natural and human-induced changes in the environment as well as attack from groups of outsiders.

Parts of the process towards greater social complexity may be universal, that is, of all places and times, but the particulars of the natural resource base had a great bearing on its actual evolution: similarities everywhere, sameness nowhere. The proximate causes of environmental change came from a combination of population pressure and agricultural intensification, with salinization, deforestation and erosion as secondary events. The ultimate causes were rooted in and became the roots of the quest for power, profits and possessions and all the associated pleasures and pain.

7

Empire: the Romans in the Mediterranean

VAN DER LEEUW AND DE VRIES

> What else, Ophelia dear, happened in the Roman Empire besides Ben Hur, Spartacus and Gladiators?
>
> *Anonymous*

7.1. Introduction: Why the Roman Empire as a case study and from which perspective?

In the previous chapter we focused on what can be said about the interactions between peoples and their natural environment as social complexity increased. In a sense, the Roman Empire can be seen as the culmination of the development towards states and empires in antiquity. But can we add anything to the entire libraries of studies on the Roman Republic and the Empire that followed in its footsteps? Thousands of books have been written on all aspect of Roman society, culture, economics, military strategy and organization, measurements, infrastructures, political history – probably nothing can be added that has not already been said. But let us reverse the argument: because so much is known about the Roman period, it is a good one to present as an example of more general insights into complex socio-natural systems. There is a wealth of data, both written and archaeological, about the course of history – events as well as processes, politics as well as economics, but also commerce, literature, agronomy and almost any subject necessary to gain a thorough insight into what happened. These data have been known for a long time, and much time and effort has been expended in interpreting them. Moreover, it is quite exceptional to be able to study the full cycle of genesis, expansion, contraction and disappearance of such a major historical phenomenon that has dominated a large area of the world for over a thousand years. It allows an uninterrupted perspective on the dynamics concerned at all temporal scales – from the longest to the shortest. And because the Mediterranean basin and its surroundings have been investigated for so long and in such detail, our perspective can also be developed for all spatial scales – from the city of Rome to the entire known world and beyond.

In the study of socio-natural relationships, this possibility of taking all scales into account is of particular importance. Firstly, among the many processes that play a role in the relations between society and the environment some are very long-term, and often cumulative. Among these are the 'unintended consequences' of human interventions in the environment, which often come to light many years after the interventions them-selves. If one is to assess their true importance, a very long-term perspective is essential. Secondly, the Romans are of particular interest to us because their way of dealing with 'their' world in many ways resembles our own in the 16th to 19th century. Many traits of modern society were in effect already part of Roman society some two millennia ago: the rapid colonization of most or all of the known world, an elaborate military and civil organization that managed to control the Empire, an urban base, as well as major invest-ments in infrastructure such as roads, aqueducts, ports and large-scale semi-industrial agriculture organized in *latifundia*. Indeed, one of the most striking parallels between the Roman exploitation of much of Western Europe and the comparatively recent exploitation of North America is the checkerboard of roads and drainage ditches that divides both landscapes into square miles. Last but not least, the scientific analysis of archaeological data from a natural and life sciences perspective has recently provided a much better insight into the ways in which people explored, organized and exploited their environment in the Roman period (Leeuw 1998; Greene 1986; Favory 1998). It is therefore possible to go into considerable detail on the effect they had on their environ-ment and vice versa.

Having decided to look at the Roman Republic and Empire as an example of the evo-lution of the relationship between a society and its environment, we must also justify how we will look at that Empire. What will we try to show and, more importantly, what will we not try to show? To begin with the latter, any complete overview of the 1000 years of Roman history (500 BC to 500 AD) is neither possible nor the purpose. It will even be impossible to even-handedly present some of the debates that are raging about many of the issues we will deal with. We will be unashamedly biased and partisan, telling the story from the perspective of the long-term dynamics of socio-natural evolution – in all of the 1000 years and in all of the Mediterranean basin and the adjacent areas that came to be included in the Empire. Thus, the focus is on the coherence of the large-scale processes of the emergence and decay of Roman society and the role of and its relation-ship with the natural environment within that evolution.

It should be noted that we do not distinguish between a 'natural' and a 'cultural' or 'societal' realm but treat all socio-natural interactions as part of an indivisible whole. The core hypothesis is that, in order to grow to the size it did and to persist as long as it did, the Roman state and the Roman 'way of doing things' had to be highly resilient.[1] Roman organization had to be able to deal coherently with very complex dynamics. It had to be stable yet flexible enough to deal with many profound internal and external changes without losing its identity. What made this possible? And what changed towards the end of the 'Roman millennium' to cause the Empire to disintegrate? What was the role of the natural environment in that process, if any? Could it have been society's impact on the natural environment that in the end sapped the Empire's strength? One way to get at 'what it takes' for a society to be so resilient is to reverse our perspective for a moment, and to look out from inside the society rather than towards the society from the outside. How do we individually respond to problems, to changes in our social or natural environment? Generally, we learn to deal with such 'problems' by means of a mixture of changing our behaviour and changing the dynamics of the environment. Provided that we can do both efficiently enough, and in due time, then we will survive intact – and so will our society. A critical element here is the capacity to collect and process information. If we cannot process the necessary information quickly and effi-ciently enough, we run the risk of seeing our 'way of life' forced out. We may lose contact with our society, it may disintegrate, we may be forced to try our luck elsewhere or we may simply 'disappear'.

Our working hypothesis here is that the key factor limiting resilience in socio-natural systems is the capacity to process information. What constitutes this capacity? Is it a question of brainpower, of know-how? Is it a question of learning, of communication? How about invention and innovation? What about reactivity? Or, looking at it from the opposite side, was there anything particular to the Mediterranean basin or to the Roman period that enhanced the resilience of the system concerned? The short but unsatisfacto-ry answer is 'a little of all of them'. We will attempt to determine, using broad brush-strokes, how and to what extent each of these factors was implicated. Many of the ques-tions raised by our perspective on these matters are not answerable for the moment or the answers are only partial. More complete and satisfactory answers are some years down the line.

7.2.   Critical social and environmental phenomena accompanying Roman expansion

7.2.1.   *An increase in surface and population*

The first striking aspect of the Roman expansion in Western Europe is that both the sur-face area and the population increased extremely rapidly over the few centuries con-cerned, from the 3rd century BC to the 1st century AD. After that, the expansion stalled. *Table 7.1* summarizes the Republic's surface in square kilometres at various crucial points in its earlier history; *Figure 7.1* gives an impression of the trends in population and area. Trying to assess the size of the population is at best a desperate task, only to be

TABLE 7.1   EXPANSION OF THE AREA COVERED BY THE ROMAN REPUBLIC

Time	Surface	Increase factor and growth rate
At the end of the Monarchy	983 km²	(-)
At the start of the war with Latium (340 BC)	3.089 km²	3.14
At the start of Second Samnite war (328 BC)	6.039 km²	1.95 (5.7%/yr)
At the battle of Sentinum (296 BC)	7.688 km²	1.27 (0.75%/yr)
After the unification of Italy (264 BC)	27,000 km²	3.51 (4%/yr)
After the Second Punic war (201 BC)	37,000 km²	1.37 (0.5%/yr)
After the conquest of Cisalpine Gaul (190 BC)	55,000 km²	1.49 (3.7%/yr)
After the Social war (89 BC)	160,000 km²	2.91 (1.1%/yr
After the conquest of Gaul (20 BC)	267,000 km²	1.67 (1%/yr)

approached with extreme care. Some 'order of magnitude' data are available, at least for Italy. Our main source of information consists of the census of Roman citizens, taken about every five years, for the purposes of tax assessment and availability of military manpower. The data that remain are less than satisfactory and their interpretation is fraught with difficulties. The best we can expect for the moment are 'order of magnitude' approximations. Apart from the usual problems of presenting such data – such as divergences of opinion on boundaries – we must also remember the biogeographical diversity: some parts are more mountainous than others, less densely settled and with more difficult lines of communication. Moreover, the area covered at any time is very heterogeneously integrated. The degree of control varied with specific arrangements made between the Romans and the various conquered or defeated enemies. Nevertheless, the Republic and early Empire underwent rapid expansion by any standards. This expansion had several bursts of accelerated surface increase in at first sight potentially critical transition periods.

The data in *Table 7.1* and *Figure 7.1* refer to Roman citizens only and therefore need to be placed against the backdrop of the population as a whole, which is much more difficult to reconstruct. The two main population components to add are the members of other nations and the slaves. The former are calculated to have included about twice as many individuals as the Romans around 225 BC, bringing the total population of Italy (excluding Cisalpine Gaul) at that date up to about 3 million, who were essentially all given civil rights after the Social war. By implication, the citizen population of Italy seems to have risen far from dramatically, if at all, during the last two centuries BC. Concerning slaves, we have even fewer data. 150,000 revolted with Spartacus in 73 BC; and a

FIGURE 7.1

Territorial expansion of the surface colonized by the Roman Republic (logarithmic vertical scale) and growth of the population of Roman citizens during the Republic and early Empire (after Nicolet 1979).

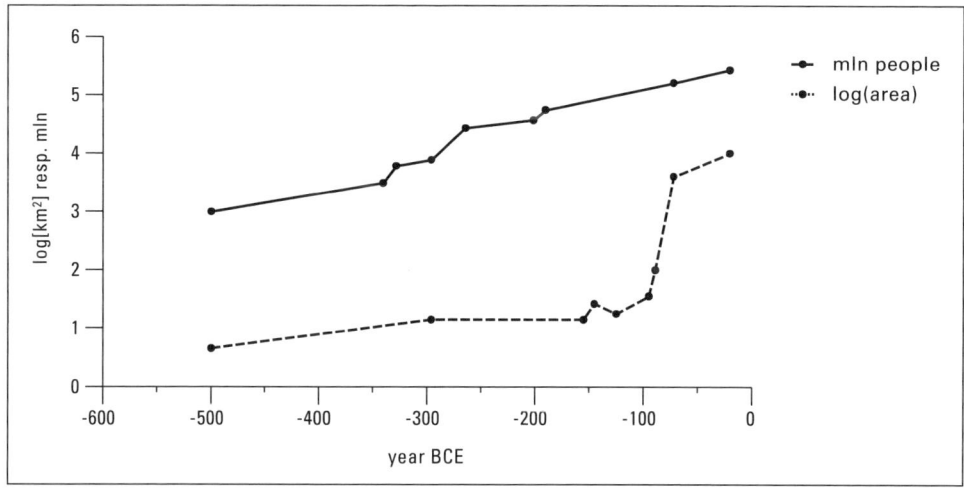

'guesstimate' based on rather vague statements might lead us to suppose about a slave for every two citizens in the Augustean period (Nicolet, 1979: 84 based on Brunt 1971: 124). All in all, Nicolet comments:

> ... Italy seems already to have been [...] very densely populated, equalling the three or four other main foci of the Mediterranean world: the Balkans, Egypt, [North] Africa and the Celtic world. Highly urbanised along Greek lines from the 2nd century BC, its population is highly stable, notwithstanding the fragility of the economy and the impact of offensive and defensive wars, and even shows a slow tendency to increase over the three centuries which concern us. [This increase] is sufficient to feed a certain emigration, as well as maintain numerous armies over the whole world. But, on the other hand, there is a considerable immigration, mainly of slaves, which, notwithstanding high losses, after two or three generations brings the levels of the free population back in line. (Nicolet 1979: 89-90)

We have not been able to come up with any reliable population data for the provinces that were added to the Republic after the middle of the 3rd century BC, so the size data will have to suffice. The average population density of Italy – about 20 inhabitants/km² – was, according to Nicolet, probably of the same order of magnitude as that of other parts of the Mediterranean world. In contrast, for Gaul at the time of Caesar the equivalent number was about 9 inhabitants/km² (ca. 5.7 million people for all of Gaul, including

Population in the Roman Empire and the Umayyad Empire Issawi (1981) is among the authors presenting an overview of population estimates for the Roman Empire in the 1st and 2nd century and the Arab Empire in the 8th century AD. As with all estimates of past populations, they have to be used with caution. The core of the Roman Empire – Italy, Spain, Greece, Egypt, Narbonensis and the islands – had an estimated surface of 1,294,000 km^2 and 22 to 37 million inhabitants. Including more peripheral regions – North Africa outside Egypt, the Danubian and Near Eastern provinces and the Three Gauls – the numbers increase to 3,790,000 km^2 and 54 to 75 million inhabitants. Population densities in 14 AD ranged in Western Europe from an estimated 1.3 (Britain) to 24 people/km^2 (Italy), whereas in parts of the Eastern Mediterranean it reached much higher values. For the Balkans, Egypt and North Africa Nicolet (1979) accords a population of density of some 20/km^2 each. However, in the subsequent 150 years they have more than doubled in the western part while increasing much less in the eastern part of the Mediterranean. Interestingly, the density distribution in the later Ummayad Arab Empire of the 8th century seems not to have been different although its population was much more heavily concentrated in the southern and eastern parts of the Mediterranean.

Gallia Narbonensis). If these estimates are accepted, the conclusion must be that the rapid conquest of Gaul by Caesar doubled the population of the Roman Republic just before it became an Empire in the formal sense. The conquests that occurred in the East a few years later, around the beginning of our era, must have more than doubled it again. Such expansion is, of course, unheard of until that moment in history and has not durably occurred at any other time in the history of the West. It could not fail to have major consequences for its internal structure and functioning, as it increased the flows of energy, matter and information a number of orders of magnitude.

7.2.2.   Urbanization

What enabled this rapid expansion? In order for such large areas to be conquered all at once, and durably so, the conquerors must have been able to establish or control an appropriate infrastructure. That infrastructure depended on the spread of towns. In the Near East and Egypt, the first cities occur in the 4th millennium BC. By the 1st millennium BC they had spread to the Levant and the coastal areas of the eastern Mediterranean, and by the 5th century BC to many coastal areas of the western Mediterranean. The last half of the 1st millennium BC sees them spread inland from the coast, notably in Spain and Gaul (*Figure 7.2*; see p.173). The Roman conquest of the western Mediterranean closely follows the spread of urbanism, which precedes it by at least two centuries (*Figure 7.3*; see p. 174).

We have ample indication that Rome preferably integrated territories that had reached a specific degree of urbanization. They were easier to control, by means of garrisons, etc., but also had in place a mode of administration and commerce that could be connected directly to Rome's own. In fact, urbanization was the groundswell on the back of which Roman colonization rode all over Western Europe.

But control over the towns and other centres should not be assumed to be central-ized. The Romans developed a number of different modes of association with their neighbours, based on leaving existing local institutions intact to varying degrees and on allowing some members of such other groups – tightly controlled – access to their own institutions. This provided them with the means to expand by conquest, and to control the territory thus acquired from the 'bottom up', using local administrative and control structures to integrate these enormous new territories and their inhabitants. As a result, the degree of Roman impact on the various components of its territory was highly vari-able:

> What we see appearing is not a civilian administration which extends its bureaucratic ramifi-cations over all the Roman possessions, but multiple solutions, each born of circumstance, which range from assimilation to exploitation pure and simple. (Rougé 1969: 56)

Italy

Up to around 500 BC Rome was merely a leader among equals (the Latin cities), but all later 'adhesions' to the Republic were directly structured as individual treaties of another city with Rome. This led to what was essentially an exploitative pattern of administra-tion, based on links with the centre of different form and intensity. The centre of Italy was 'allied territory' peopled with individuals who, in a treaty with Rome, had submitted to it rather as 'clients' to a 'patron'. The inhabitants of these cities were 'strangers' (non-citizens) who had a degree of independence (at least *de iure*). Their exact status depend-ed on whether it was the result of a negotiated treaty (*socii*) or a submission (*fœderati*). They had the right to marry Romans and trade with Rome but not with others; their components of the army were directed by Romans and they had to follow the Senate in questions of foreign policy. Internally, they usually ruled themselves.

Both coasts, on the other hand, were quickly made into 'Roman territory' (*ager Romanus*). Within that territory, distinctions were made on the basis of citizenship. The closest ties existed between Rome and the 'colonies' (*coloniae*), founded by groups of Roman citizens (up to 300 BC) in Roman territory. The members of colonies retained full citizenship and were seen as 'a projection of the City' (Rougé 1969: 59). The colonies' administration was originally organized from Rome, but these communities later formed their own administration, modelled on that of Rome, with the same assemblies and magistrates.

Next in line came the *'municipia'*, the cities with obligations *vis-à-vis* Rome. These had their own administrative institutions, even though their inhabitants had full citizenship, including the right to vote when in Rome. These cities often had experienced a phase in which their inhabitants had no full citizenship (*civitates sine suffragio*). In the early days, the municipal form of association originated in a treaty with Rome in which both cities were legally each other's equals. Later, however, the status of *municipium* was unilaterally designated by Rome itself. The institutions of such a city were left intact, and the city governed itself internally. Its inhabitants had the right to marry and trade with Romans, if not that to vote. The main advantage of this status from the organizational point of view was, that it left local channels of communication intact and directed the cities in question towards Rome's aims without burdening the latter's administration excessively.[2]

After the revolt and the defeat of the Latin cities (338 BC), these were not given Roman citizenship, but Latin citizenship was given special status *vis-à-vis* that of Rome. The cities retained their own institutions. Latin citizens had the right to trade with and marry Romans but also with other Latins, the right to move to Rome, and the right to vote in certain Roman councils of government – but in such a way that their vote was hardly effective – when they were in the city. But they could not become magistrates, other than after obtaining full Roman citizenship on an individual basis. Large numbers of new colonies were founded with Latin rights, each with up to 6000 inhabitants.

In conclusion, the Romans controlled Italy in the true sense of the word, politically, economically and judicially, but to varying degrees that essentially depended on the economic importance (coast versus inland), power, degree and efficiency of internal organization and the 'nuisance value' of the different territories. This enabled them to remain on top of a power pyramid with a relatively wide basis, as it limited the amount of energy involved in control while optimising its communication channels by providing incentives for the locally dominant classes to toe the Roman line.

The provinces
The Roman provinces essentially consisted of the territories outside Italy conquered by Rome. They were governed by Roman magistrates, whose efforts were in general single-mindedly aimed at creating optimal (i.e. peaceful) circumstances for draining the areas in their care of as much of their wealth as was possible. The administration put in place to do so was generally based on, as well as limited to, the cities. There was no standing Roman administrative apparatus on which the consuls or *praetors* entrusted with them could count. Instead, they had to depend on their wits, on a small entourage, on some administrative assistants and on about 12,000 soldiers. The magistrates made their own rules at the beginning of their term of office and supported the members of the knightly

order who had formed companies to extract taxes from these territories.

As in Italy, the legal status of the cities in the provinces was decided on a case by case basis. Three types of status existed: 'federated', 'immune' and 'submitted'. The former had a separate negotiated treaty with Rome; they were autonomous – not submitted to the provincial administration – and did not pay tax but had to contribute to the army and provide it with food. The immune cities had submitted to Rome but, at Rome's discretion, were accorded the – immediately revocable – status of federated cities rather than that of 'submitted cities'. The latter formed the third and least enviable category. They were the property of Rome and were allowed to use their lands only in return for a payment. In so far as they kept their own institutions, these were under the control of the Roman provincial administration, which had extensive powers over them, including life and death, and the power to use the army to 'pacify' both within the province and at its borders.

In practice, there were immense differences in the degree of control exerted over and within the provinces. These were largely due to differences in the degree of urbanization. Where that was not sufficient, the Romans found it very difficult to exert any control at all. Thus, Caesar complains that in Belgium 'there is nothing to control – no cities, no forts, no installations' (Roymans 1990).

7.2.3.   Transport and commerce

In order to hold together an Empire the size of the Mediterranean basin, dependable and efficient means of transportation for goods and people are essential. The fact that the Romans managed to create such a system is due to the particular geography of the region, as well as to their organizational talent and technology. We briefly discuss three aspects: location, the road system and commerce.

Location
The location of Rome, at the centre of the Mediterranean basin, almost as far from the coast of Spain as from the Levant and as far from North Africa as from the southern French and Dalmatian coasts, was a major advantage. By facilitating maritime contacts, it allowed the centre to deal efficiently with the outlying parts of the Empire. No one part of the coastal core of the Empire was much further away from the centre than any other. All were within easy reach of Rome. That provided a solid physical-geographical basis for the expansion of the Empire away from its coasts. Moreover, the Mediterranean basin's particular geographical structure – the only one of its kind and size in the world – also provided a relatively homogeneous climate and, therefore, vegetation over the whole of the area. That, of course, facilitated the adaptation of people and the borrowing of techniques across the region. Finally, the geographical structure of the entire

Empire, around a sea, also contributed in important ways to its cultural coherence. By the time Rome conquered the Mediterranean basin, intensive contacts between all Mediterranean coasts had existed for thousands of years. These contacts contributed to the – relative – cultural homogeneity of the Basin. Not only had people from all parts of the Mediterranean previously been in contact, but they had exchanged goods and inventions in all areas of human endeavour. As a result, they were highly similar with respect to their economic basis, their socio-political organization and, in general, in their 'ways of doing things' – in short, their culture.

The road system

In many ways, the road system was the pride of the Empire. As the principal means of communication overland, this system formed the backbone of the expansion during the Republic and the Empire. The trajectory of all the major Roman roads across Europe and the Mediterranean Basin is well-known. The extensive secondary road systems that were linked by the major highways have not been particularly well researched, and it is often extremely difficult to date these roads. Comparing the following two examples may be illustrative. Dowdle (1987: 279), in his study of the roads in Burgundy in France, argues very cogently that a major part of the regional road system in this Gaulish state of the *Aedui* was in place well before the Romans had absorbed the area into their Empire (*Figure 7.4a-b*). After Caesar had broken the back of Gaulish resistance, he moved the capital of the area from *Bibracte* to *Augustodunum* (Autun). As a consequence, we see a number of new sections of road connecting the new capital to the existing road system. Moreover, many of the roads were paved, the network was completed here and there and was extended to include changes in the relative importance of the settlement network, but it was not fundamentally changed. There were, however, major reconstructions of, and additions to, the inter-regional system of major roads connecting the territory of the *Aedui* to other parts of Gaul and beyond (Crumley 1987).

Such road-building activities should in essence be seen as 'streamlining' the position of the territory within a newly created larger context. One of the results was that new conurbations came into existence at junctions or crossing points of the new roads with each other, with old roads and with rivers. Equally, Roman activity greatly enlarged the sub-regional road network, which came to include connections between the many 'villas' that exploited the fertile countryside for the Roman Empire.

The primary *raison d'être* of the road system was, of course, that it provided a dependable and efficient means to move people around all of the area concerned and thus to exchange information and ensure administrative and military control. But its impact was also felt in other ways. Firstly, the trajectory of these roads deliberately broke through the unity of the tribal territories that they crossed. In doing so, they fundamentally changed the patterns of spatial interaction between the indigenous populations. Secondly, from an environmental point of view their most durable impact was probably

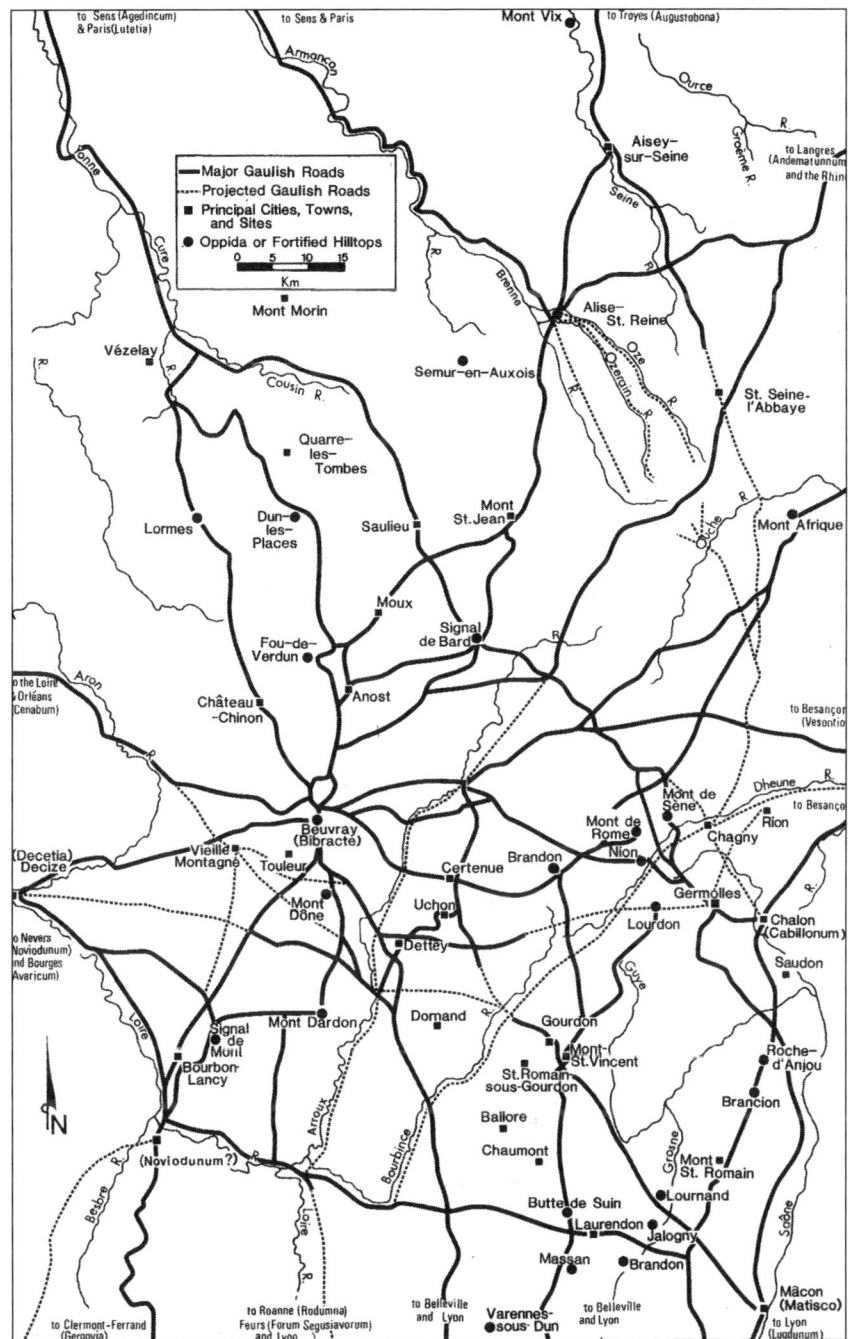

FIGURE 7.4 A

Major Gaulish roads before the Roman conquest (Source: Dowdle 1987)

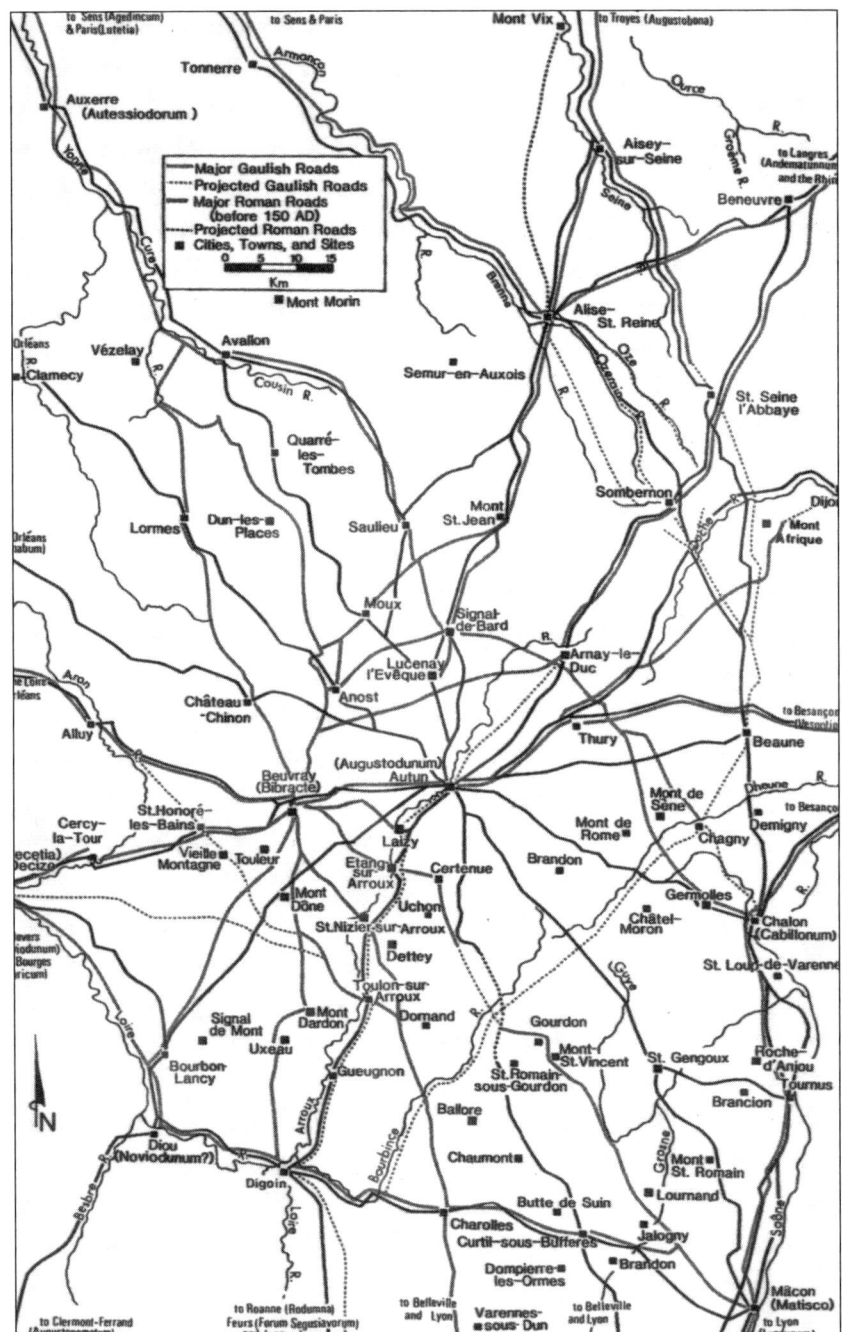

FIGURE 7.4 B

Major Gaulish and Roman roads, 150 years after conquest (Source: Dowdle 1987)

that they facilitated the implantation of a dense network of farms that produced for export. They therefore brought many areas that had thus far led a relatively autarchic life into the mainstream of the then 'world system'.

Commerce

Trade itself is, of course, nothing new – people have traded ever since they produced artefacts and food, and we find traces of such trade from the Palaeolithic period onwards. Moreover, in the two millennia leading up to the Roman expansion, trade in all conceivable commodities had spread to all parts of the Mediterranean basin. According to literary and archaeological evidence, it must have included cereals, olive oil, wine, (dried) fruit, slaves, marble and other kinds of stone, copper, iron silver and gold, etc.

But the scale of trade changed several orders of magnitude. In the Roman period, we observe several new phenomena linked to trade. First of all, we commonly find evidence of the industrial production of trade goods. We know of the existence of pottery and glass factories, for example, that produced tens of thousands of objects a year, principally for export (*Figure 7.4c*; see p. 175). Many of these goods were containers used in connection with the trade in agricultural products such as wine, olive oil and cereals. These exports were found all over the Empire. But that is not all. The Romans also linked into the spice trade with the Middle East and East Asia. Recent archaeological research in the Indian Ocean confirms that Roman goods were traded as far afield as present-day India, Indonesia and East Africa. Throughout the Empire, archaeologists have uncovered the existence of a large number of trading emporia where we find remains of masses of trade goods. Some of these emporia were established before the advent of the Romans, but many new ones were founded during the Roman period, and they can be found literally everywhere. They are located on the coasts, particularly at the mouth of large rivers, along rivers at points where they connected with other rivers or with roads, and at the point where these rivers became unnavigable and goods had to be loaded on to carts or animals.

Another major indicator of the importance of commerce is the widespread use of coins of all kinds of denominations. High-denomination gold and silver coins from the pre-Roman period have been found in limited quantities in parts of Gaul and Britain. But the sheer numbers of coins found in a Roman context overshadow any such evidence from earlier periods. Moreover, the fact that lower denomination coins abound even in rural areas shows the extent to which the monetary system has penetrated those parts of commercial life that were traditionally the preserve of *in natura* exchanges.

Altogether, then, we have clear indications that trade is one of the major economic activities in the Roman world. It can be concluded that the transformations that are expressed in the material culture of the Roman period seem to point in the direction expressed by Dowdle:

It is commonly believed (and rightly so) that Gaul underwent a massive agricultural, industrial, and cultural expansion after its conquest by Rome, to become the most productive, most
industrialised, and indeed most civilised province in the Empire [...]. But it is also true that
such growth could not have happened had not the indigenous people been capable of it and
ready for it. Indeed, we would argue that they were well on their way toward rapid economic
growth and diversification by the time of the conquest. (Dowdle 1987: 291-2)

This seems to apply to the majority of the territories eventually drawn into the Roman
sphere (cf. Rodwell 1976: 310-11). Where it does not apply, the Romans found conquest
difficult, if not impossible, and preferred not to intervene militarily. The territory that
they eventually conquered was prepared for them by the history of the areas concerned,
and in particular by their prior economic relationship with the Mediterranean. The
Romans merely realized a potential that was generated beyond their own control. They
were able to do so for a number of reasons. Firstly the location of Rome in the centre of
the Mediterranean basin is important – the whole of the basin was within reach in a reasonable time. This in turn facilitated the existence of an Empire that was to an important
extent built on trade in raw materials and agricultural products between geographically
highly variable regions, yielding different commodities. The sea provided the Romans,
once they had control over shipping and seafaring and had defeated their principal commercial enemies the Carthaginians, with the means to transport goods efficiently
throughout the centre of the whole region they controlled. All around the Mediterranean basin, coastal cities, particularly at the mouth of navigable rivers, provided the
infrastructure to control and facilitate further transport inland, by boat or over land. But
whilst shipping is an effective way to transport bulk goods, it is much less effective as a
means of communication or the displacement of power. The administrative structure of
the Empire was therefore based on decentralization and overland communication.

In most of the areas the Romans colonized, they were able to take over an existing
infrastructure of power and commerce that was centred on towns. Their success in doing
so was to a large extent due to the very adaptable socio-economic and political framework into which they linked each local unit. Moreover, their technical prowess in surveying enabled them to build a long-distance road network that linked the different regional and local infrastructures, providing a dependable means to move information and
military power, even when weather conditions made seafaring difficult. A third reason
was that the Roman expansion occurred in an era of demographic growth, which
allowed the Romans to harness labour on a large scale all over the Empire. Slaves and
serfs effectively ran the Roman economy from relatively early on, serving as clerks, edu-
cators, stevedores, builders, factory workers and almost everything else. Without an
ample population to draw upon, both inside the Empire and in the areas into which it
expanded, the Empire would never have been able to harness sufficient energy to keep
going.

Mapping the European landscape during the Roman Empire (Romanova 1997)[3]   At the beginning of historic time, the Ancient period (3rd century BC to 5th century AD), the differentiation of the anthropogenic subsystems within European landscapes became more pronounced. Five categories of landscapes are shown in *Figure 7.5a* (see p. 176); estimated population densities, urban settlements and the important mining and metallurgy centres are shown in *Figure 7.5b* (see p. 176). Densely populated areas with developed social, economic and cultural structures were concentrated in the Mediterranean regions of Europe (Pounds 1973). On the eve of the new era, about 29 million people inhabited the European territory (Maksakovsky 1997), of which an estimated 8 million lived in Italy, 7 million within the Iberian Peninsula and 3 million in Greece. It is in these times that the forests, mainly cedar stands, were cut down to satisfy the needs of shipbuilding. Drainage, irrigation and fertilization were practiced within agricultural landscapes, with increasing grain yields (Barash 1989; Samarkin 1976; Pounds 1973). Intensively cultivated landscapes underwent irreversible anthropogenic transformation. Major impacts were associated with settlements (particularly large and very large towns and villages), agriculture (ploughing and hydraulic amelioration), forestry (forest cutting, expansion of *maquis* and *garrigue*) and mining and metal processing (Pounds 1973). Radical changes of natural geosystems resulted in the formation of modal landscapes in remote mountainous areas, while the remainder of Southern Europe was dominated by derivative landscapes, *maquis* and *garrigue*, or anthropogenic modifications of natural geosystems, mainly agricultural and pastoral (*Figure 7.5b*). Central and Eastern Europe were much more sparsely populated (English Landscapes 1985). There were about 5 million people in Gallia and 1 million on the British isles, while the population of the northern regions, Scandinavia and Ireland, was extremely low. The economy of the Celts, Slavs and Germans was poorly developed; crop yields were low and cultivated areas were concentrated around a few settlements linked with trade and migration routes. Forest-steppe landscapes of the Danube plains were mainly used for settled or nomadic cattle-raising (Shnirelman 1989). However, both cultivation and grazing had only a slight and local impact on natural geosystems, so natural landscapes with minor anthropogenic changes dominated the territory.

7.3.   The human environment in Roman times

The central questions of this book concern the relationship between society and its environment. How did the Mediterranean environment change under the impact of Roman colonization? In which ways did the Romans have to change their way of dealing with different environments in order to accommodate these changes? In order to gain a good understanding of these matters, we should first look at the Mediterranean environment before the advent of the Romans.Next, we will look at the changes wrought by Roman colonization, and finally we will look at how these influenced the process of colonization itself.

7.3.1.   *Geography and climate*

The original territory of the Roman Republic was relatively homogeneous from a geographic point of view – the hills and valleys of Latium, Etruria and the other landscapes of central Italy. The diversity of exploited landscapes increased with the conquest of other Mediterranean provinces. Many coastal valleys were added all around the Mediterranean. Some of these were very large, such as the valleys of the Po, Nile and Rhône, but others were small and enclosed by high mountains, such as in southern Greece. Other areas were completely different, for example as the highlands of central Spain and Turkey and the rolling hills and plains of northern Gaul and Belgica. In yet further regions, the climate was the principal difference to the Italian heartland, such as in drought-ridden North Africa and the Near East, not to mention cold and wet Britain. Altogether, it is impossible to generalize about the environment, environmental change, resilience and adaptation of the Roman colonization to these different environments. All that can be said is that the basic environmental differences between the various regions must have triggered many different forms of local adaptation.

At the same time, these geographic differences constituted one of the major assets of the Empire, as they provided a variety of crops under a variety of different conditions, thus spreading risks (cf. Section 6.3.3). It is typical of most Mediterranean landscapes that they are very fragmented – small valleys alternate with hills and mountains to create a spatially discontinuous environment. As a result, the conditions are generally different in closely neighbouring areas. Therefore, these landscapes as a whole lend themselves to the small-scale cultivation of different crops, together with herding, rather than to the large-scale farming of homogeneous crops. For the latter, one has to move away from the Mediterranean rim, and into the large river valleys of the Po, the Rhône, and the Nile. These discontinuities created good conditions for a very wide range of plant and animal products (see below). Maybe even more importantly, due to the variety of environments, most of these products were available most of the time; a poor harvest in one area could often be compensated by a better harvest in another area.

Most suitable Mediterranean landscapes were 'disturbance-dependent' by the time the Romans colonized the region, in the sense that the landscape has become entirely dependent on interruptions of the natural cycli by humans. Seven-and-a-half thousand years of co-evolution between human societies and their natural environment had caused the latter to be so modified as to depend on human dynamics to maintain its condition. Interruption of human activity would have caused profound changes in the landscape – erosion, growth of *garrigue*, recolonization by forest – and would immediately have made these landscapes unsuitable for the human activities that had shaped it. The central position of a large surface of water in the region did to an important extent attenuate differences in temperature and precipitation around its edges, as it does today. Unlike other regions, such as the Andes and California, there are no north-south mountain chains to impede the winter's wet winds from north Atlantic high-pressure zones; they penetrate thousands of kilometres into the basin. Relatively mild winters, hot summers, and precipitation in spring and autumn – between 100 and 400 mm/year – are the dominant characteristics of the climate in the basin itself. Many of the sub-regional differences within it are linked to variations in altitude, or in distance from the coast, rather than to the regional climate dynamics themselves. The one major exception is the proximity of the Sahara making Northern Africa a drier and warmer place than the northern rim of the Mediterranean.

The evidence for climate change is for the moment still fragmentary, based on a wide range of data relative to different spatio-temporal scales, but it is rapidly getting better (cf. Chapters 3 and 4). The evolution of the water level in circum-alpine lakes, the volume of water flowing through the Rhône, oxygen isotope measurements in the atmosphere, and measures of erosion on the slopes of some of the Rhône's tributaries all seem to point to the same conclusion. In areas where these data can be compared – principally in south-eastern France – there are no indications of *major* changes in climate during the period we are considering, from about 400 BC to about 600 AD. But it is possible

---

Did human-induced changes in land cover affect the climate? Present-day climate models make it possible to simulate the extent to which past human actions have led to climate change. Although such endeavours are still full of uncertainties, they can give an impression of when and how human interaction with the environment started to result in larger-scale feedback loops. In a recent paper, Reale and Shukla (2000) have presented the results of an attempt to simulate the impact of humans in the Mediterranean area during the Roman Classical period, around 2000 yr BP. They have organised all available archaeological and historical information into a coherent history of climate and vegetation. It was found that North Africa was wetter than today and that the Mediterranean had experienced a continuous trend towards a 'drier' kind of vegetation. A general circulation model was run to explore the impact of human-induced change in land cover – mainly deforestation – on the climate (a vegetation change experiment). The result suggests that the action of land clearing might have contributed to a positive feedback loop affecting climate and resulting in a drift towards drier conditions.

that at the time of the Roman expansion, in the last two centuries BC and the first two centuries AD, precipitation may have been slightly lower and average temperatures somewhat higher than either before or after that period. This may have facilitated the colonization of otherwise relatively humid areas, such as ancient endorrheic marshes and the flood plains of major rivers (Magny 1992). We will return to the question of what part such an oscillation may have played in the overall history of the Empire.

7.3.2. *Colonization*

Archaeological research undertaken in the last thirty years has provided us for the first time with independent means to corroborate the literary evidence concerning the changes in the countryside that occurred during Roman colonization. The archaeological evidence points to the fact that major changes had affected the Mediterranean countryside for a long time before the advent of the Romans – a definite change in perspective on the Roman period (Greene 1986). A large number of systematic regional surveys in many parts of the Mediterranean have unearthed numerous archaeological remains of all periods. In many places, the evidence points to dense agricultural settlement even before the Roman period. In the Molise valley on the Eastern flank of the Apennines, for example, the number of farming settlements increased from about 4000 BC until, around 1000 BC; even the least 'attractive' land was settled and exploited (Barker 1981). From that point in time onwards, a complete change in the settlement pattern is observed, apparently closely related to fundamental changes in agricultural exploitation.

The most important of these is the introduction of the Mediterranean system of polyculture. This combines the cultivation of cereals with that of olives and vines. Because the latter two grow on different soils to cereals, this system brings different parts of the landscape under cultivation. And because olives and vines are harvested later in the year, it possible for the farmers to harvest three kinds of crops. But polyculture was not used in isolation. The results of palaeo-botanical analyses seem to indicate that a range of new crops was cultivated and a range of new techniques introduced in the first half of the last millennium BC. Although some of the best evidence for new crops comes from Western Europe (Roymans 1990; Jones 1981), the idea that agricultural innovations occurred is systematically corroborated in the Mediterranean wherever the quality of the evidence is sufficient. Among the new crops are new species of pulses, cucumbers, grapes, dates and figs and many kinds of medicinal herbs. In the area of animal husbandry, one of the main innovations is a larger breed of cattle. *Figure 7.6* shows the approximate chronology of a number of new inventions in agricultural techniques documented in Britain during the 1st millennium BC and the 1st millennium AD.

FIGURE 7.6

Chronology of introductions and inventions in British agriculture in the 1ˢᵗ millennium BC and the 1ˢᵗ millennium AD. (Source: Greene 1986: Figure 26)

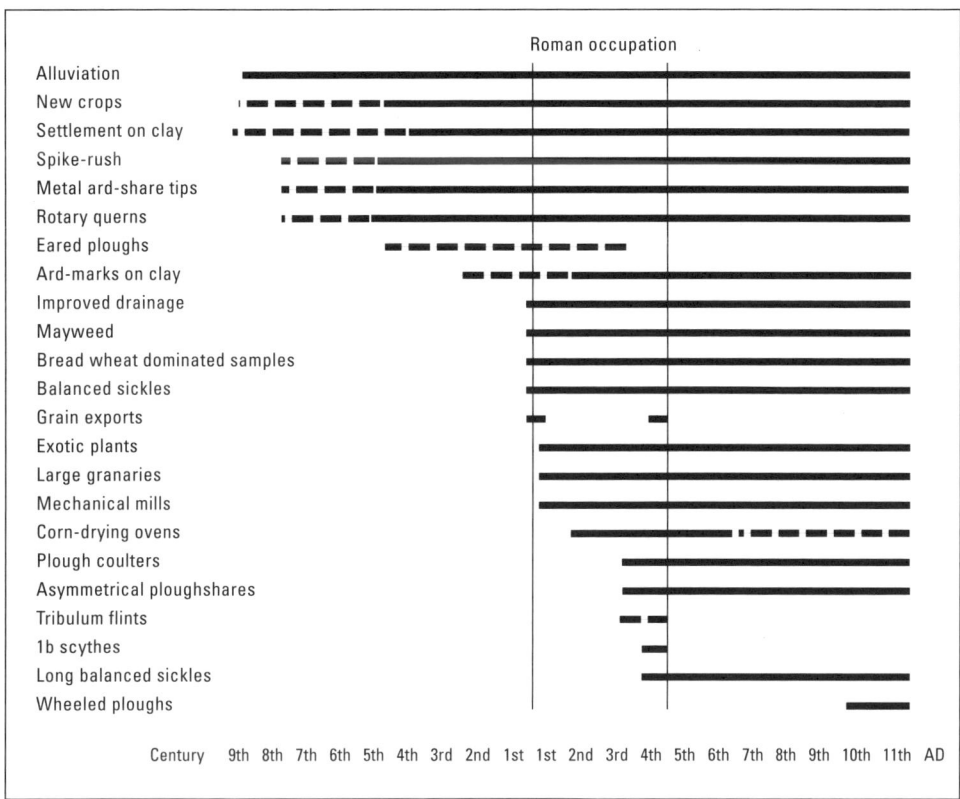

Although new crops, rotary querns and eared ploughs, for example, were available by the middle of the 1ˢᵗ millennium BC, Roman occupation added a whole set of new inventions which predominantly point to the improvement of storage, treatment and trade. Clearly, then, a number of essential techniques were already in place before Roman colonization, and colonization primarily brought an increase in the scale of production. Barker summarizes:

> First in Etruria, then in outlying regions like Molise, we can see how the new society had to be sustained by an agricultural system that brought with it a transformed world of commercial organisation and social differentiation. In an extraordinary reversal of roles, the prehistoric societies [of central Italy] changed in the space of a few centuries from a virtually Stone Age people ... into the central nations of the Roman world. (Barker 1981: 219)

Vindolanda: daily life in an outpost of the Roman Empire[4]   During the reign of Trajan (98-117 AD), northern England was a recently conquered, remote part of the Roman Empire. Vast distances and the limited capacity of wind- and animal-powered means of transportation separated this outpost of the empire from the Mediterranean world. However, numerous wooden writing tablets that have been found at the site of the fort of Vindolanda show that the troops stationed there were not isolated. The fort at Vindolanda was first built about 80 AD. Most of the writing tablets date to the early years of Trajan's reign (98-105 AD) and therefore predate the construction of Hadrian's Wall. A cavalry unit of Roman allies, the Ninth Cohort of Batavians, occupied the fort.

The thousands of wooden tablets provide at least two important insights. Firstly, the tablets, which contain official and private letters and documents – and even a writing exercise from Virgil – reflect the scale and range of written communication on a remote outpost of the Roman world. Secondly, they provide valuable insight into the workings of the Roman Empire, which had to provide for the day-to-day sustenance of a Roman army unit in a barren and unproductive environment. The provisions that arrived at Vindolanda reflect the unit's contact with three different zones: the immediate hinterland of the fort, the rest of the province of Britain, and the other provinces of the Empire, foremost Gaul and Spain.

The unit exploited the resources from the immediate hinterland: the native population cultivated barley, which was used to make beer, which was part of this unit's official rations. The unit had its own herd of swine – pork was an important item of the Roman soldiers' diet. The region also provided fodder and grazing for the horses, mules and oxen. In order to supplement their official rations, officers and common soldiers bought chickens, apples, eggs and other items from the local farmers. However, the most important part of the Roman soldier's diet – wheat to make bread – had to come from the southern parts of the province of Britannia, where it was acquired largely through taxation-in-kind. Other goods also arrived from the South, such as ceramics and textiles that were sent from Londinium. Lists of food include imported goods, for example fish sauce, spices, olives and olive oil. The officers were particularly eager to continue their accustomed way of life. Items of clothing came from Gaul, while taxation in the Spanish provinces provided olive oil to Roman army units throughout the northern provinces. The regular supply of this typically Mediterranean product shows that even a barbarian unit on a remote outpost was not forgotten as part of the Roman Empire.

For the Roman period itself, the intensive surveys of the last thirty years highlight two major differences between the literary and the archaeological evidence (Greene 1986):
– large parts of the Mediterranean basin were much more densely dotted with farm-

steads both before and during the Roman colonization than the contemporary texts seem to indicate; and

- similarly, the Roman countryside was not dominated by villas and latifundia, as the Roman authors would have us believe; these existed alongside a great many small farms and farming settlements.

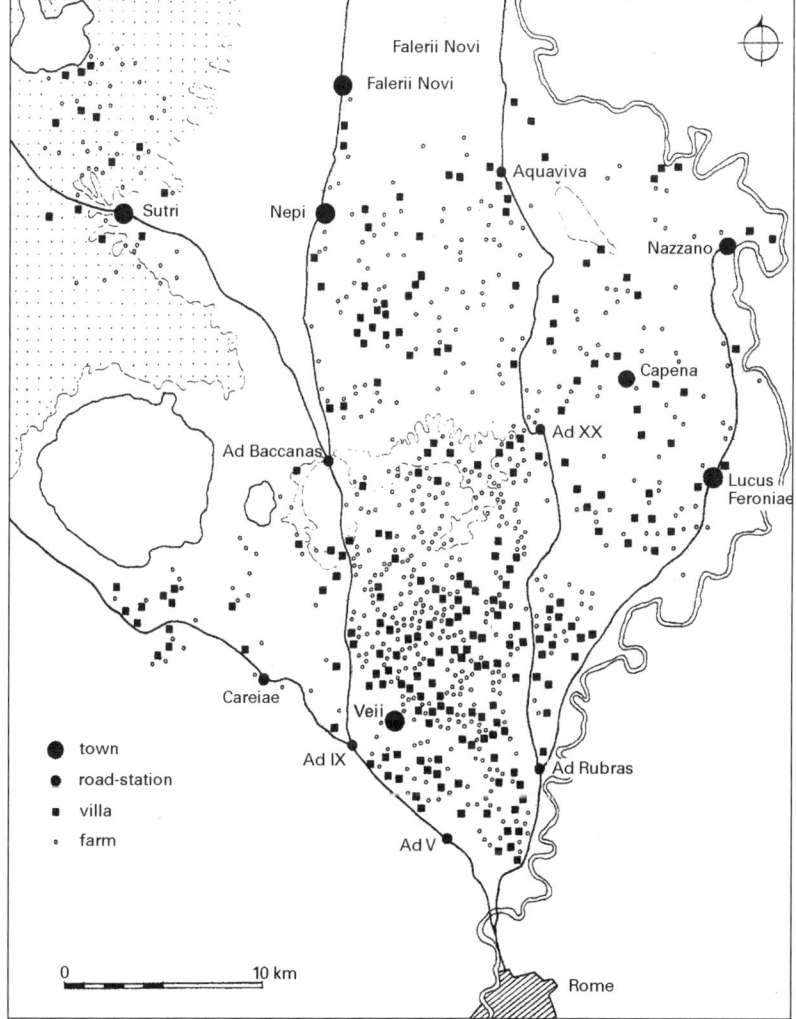

FIGURE 7.7

The results of Potter's settlement survey in Southern Etruria in the 1950's. In the early imperial period, the closer to Rome, the higher the density of villas. Overall, small farms vastly outnumber villas (Source: Greene 1986: Figure 43).

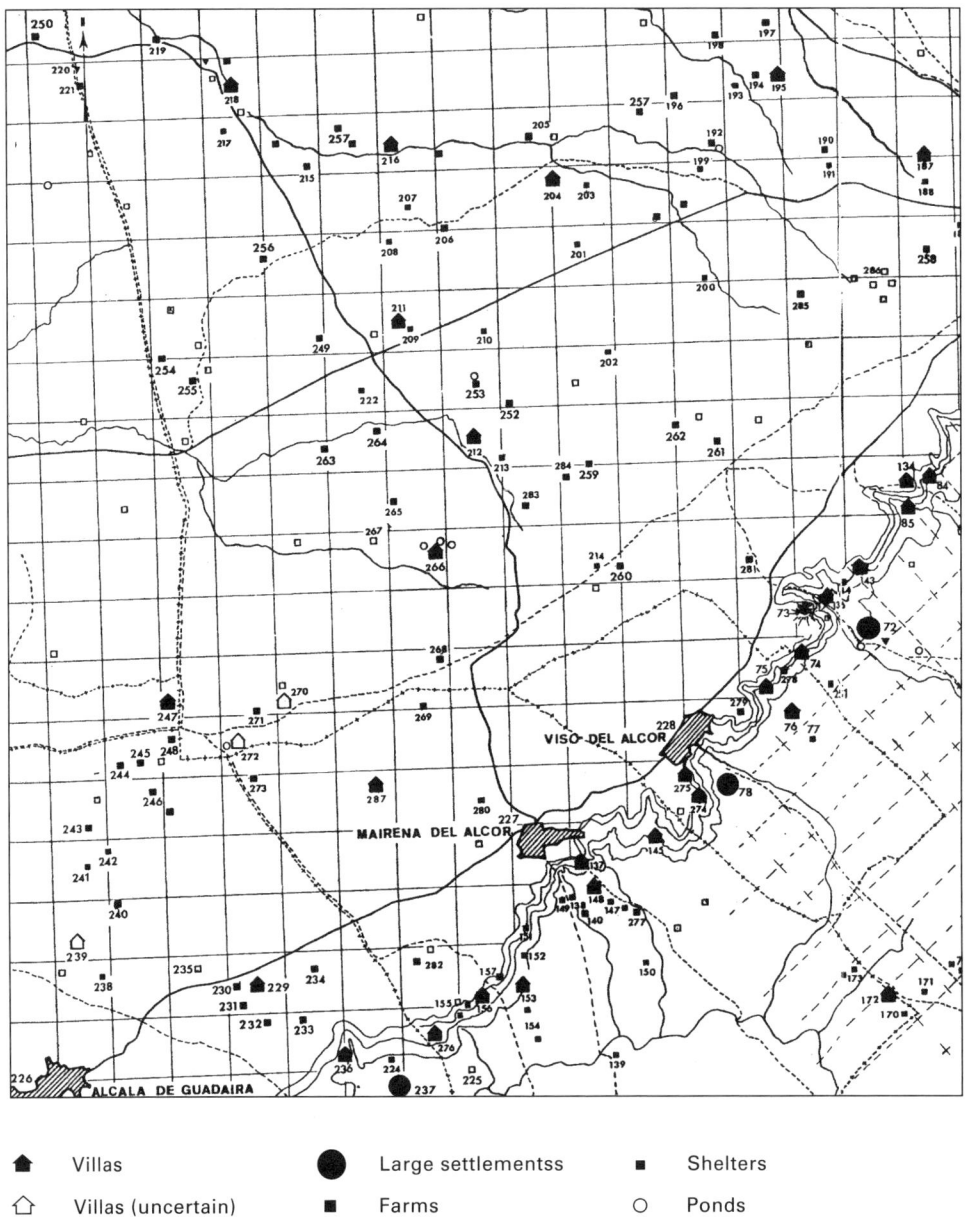

	Villas	●	Large settlementss	■	Shelters
⌂	Villas (uncertain)	■	Farms	○	Ponds

FIGURE 7.8

The results of Ponsich's settlement survey of the Guadalquivir valley. The villas are located on the plateau and along the scarp, within reach of the main roads. Overall, there are many more small farms than villas. (Source: Greene 1986: Figure 46)

The simplest way to corroborate both points is to look at some of the many maps that synthesize the data from surveys in different parts of the Roman world. Results from Southern Etruria (Potter 1979; *Figure 7.7*) and the river valley of the Guadalquivir (Ponsich 1974; *Figure 7.8*) show very clearly that relatively small farms vastly outnumber villas, let alone *latifundia*.

For the more northern parts of the Empire this is less easy to prove, as the nature of the remains of simple farms is more ephemeral. In those areas, most of these would have been built in wood, wattle-and-daub or similar perishable materials rather than in brick or stone as is frequently the case in the Mediterranean area. Wherever settlement data have been collected systematically, a major increase in the number of such settlements just before, during and after Roman colonization is manifest, as in the Somme (Agache 1978), the Lower Rhine (Willems 1981-1984) and the Berry.

7.3.3. *Introducing industrialization of agriculture and commercial exploitation of the land*

In all the areas that have been fully colonized, i.e. the areas in which new settlers exploited the land, exploitation was initially organized in one of three forms:
- a very dense pattern of farms which covered the area before the advent of the Romans; these farms were of variable size;
- villas and the large, highly efficient *latifundia* introduced by the Romans; these were larger than the farms and to a great extent dependent on slave labour and produced mainly for export;
- in some areas, Rome gave smaller plots of land to its veterans, who were put to good use in pacifying potentially rebellious areas and bringing new areas under exploitation.

As time went on, these different exploitation systems became more and more dependent upon each other and had an increasingly large impact on the landscape, as we see in the Rhône valley between about 100 BC and 300 AD. Here, successive waves of colonization (*Figure 7.9*) created many new farms in the 1st century BC, over and above the existing ones. In the 1st century AD, the wave of new farms stops, and by the end of the 2nd century most of them – the smaller ones – had been deserted (*Figure 7.10*). At that point, a rationalization seems to have intervened, which restructures the agricultural landscape profoundly under the influence of the increasing importance of mass-production for the export of agricultural products. Many smaller farms were either abandoned or became part of the larger ones that had grown out of the first established Roman farms in the region, located on the best land and with the most direct access to the markets (Favory 2002).

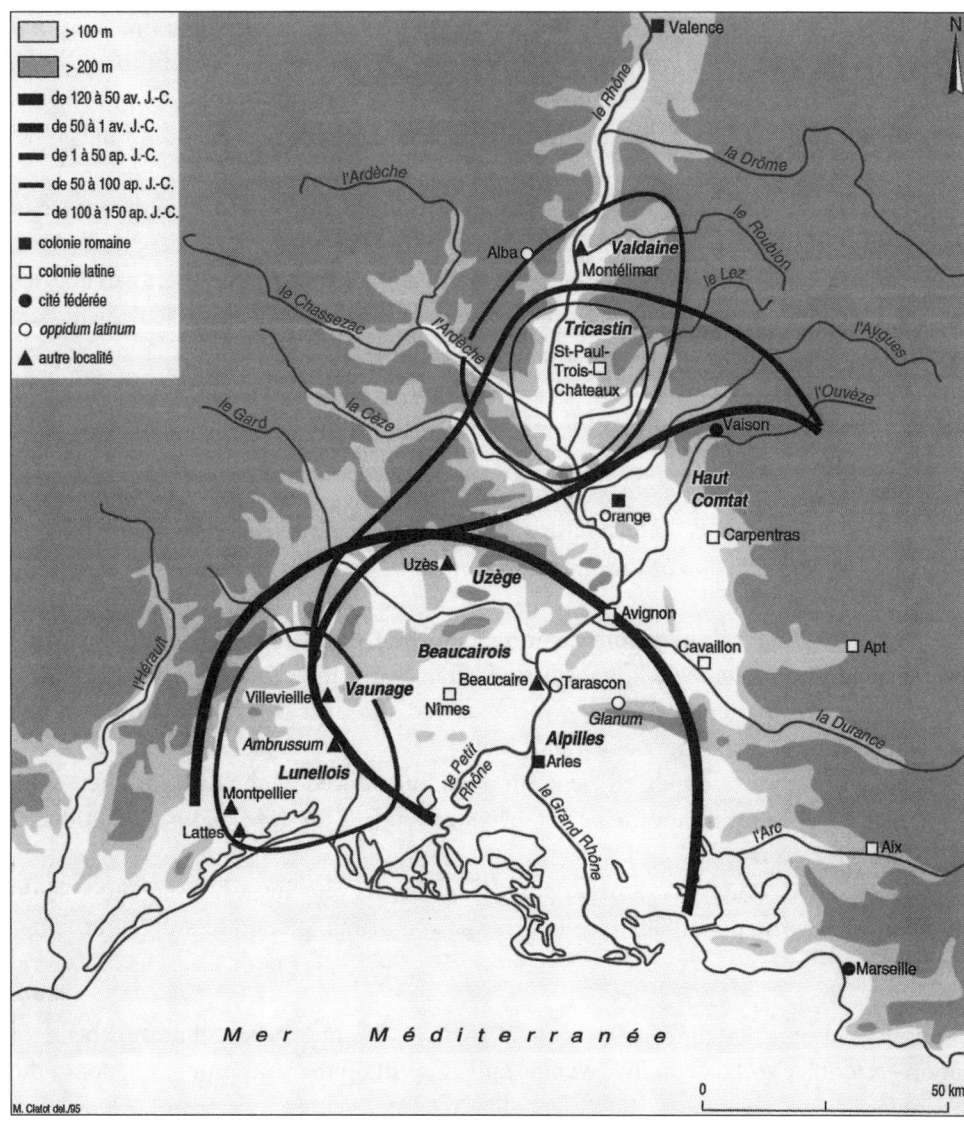

FIGURE 7.9

Successive waves of colonization in the lower Rhône valley. (Source: Archaeomedes 1998)

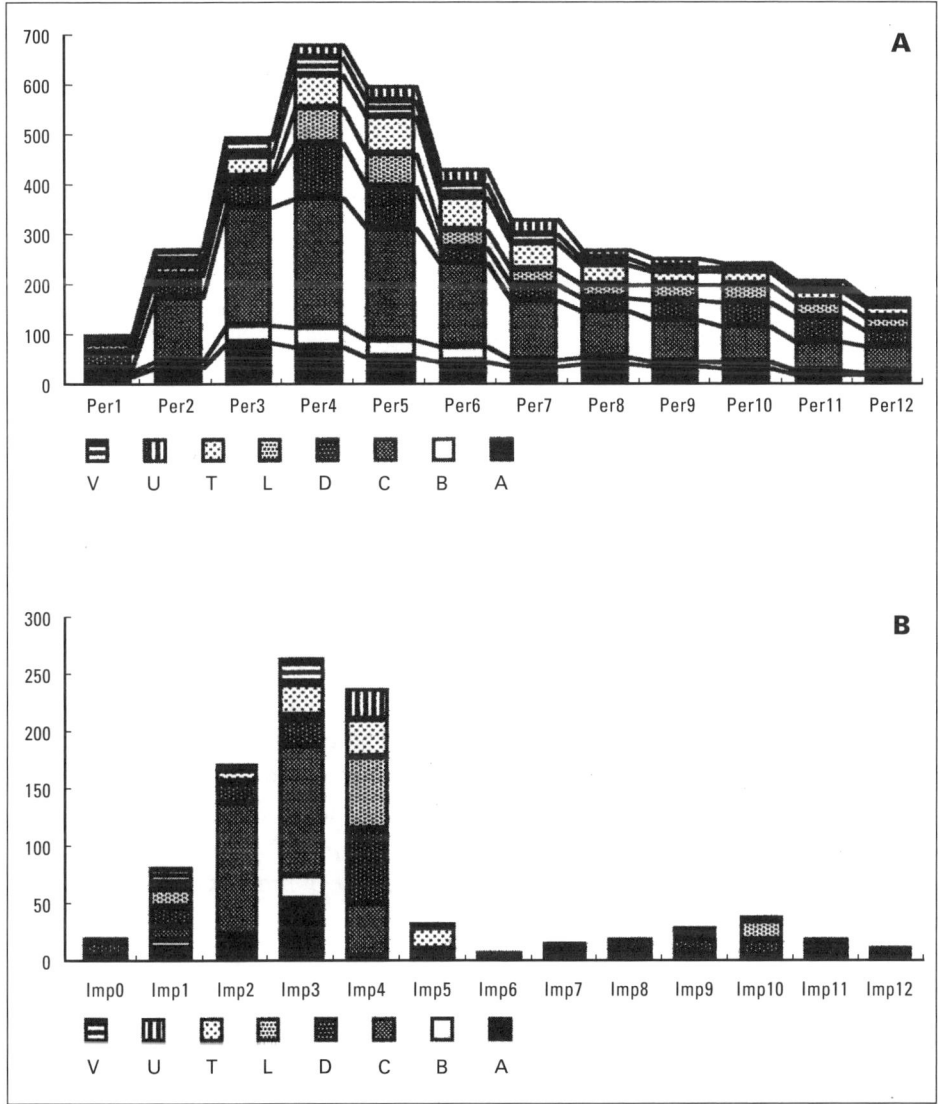

FIGURE 7.10

Graph showing the number of sites (upper) and the number of sites created (lower) in eight sample areas in the lower Rhône valley between the 1st century BC and the 5th century AD. (Per 1-12 refers to periods of 50 years; A-V to the regions concerned; IMP1-12 to periods of 50 years). Note the steep fall-off in farm creations at the end of the 1st century AD and the rapid decrease in farms exploited from the end of the 2nd century AD (Source: Archaeomedes 1998: Figure 2).

But this model is not directly applicable elsewhere: the local circumstances played a predominant role in shaping the dynamics in each colonized region. For example in northern Gaul, the proportion of villas in the total settlement pattern is considerably higher than in areas densely settled before the Roman conquest. On the one hand, the local circumstances were absolutely ideal for a villa-based exploitation system: plenty of rainfall, fertile soils and gently rolling terrain. On the other, the degree of organization of the tribal societies conquered by Caesar in these parts was much lower than that of the societies further south in Italy or in Southern Gaul. Hence, the Romans relied more on their own infrastructure than they would have done in situations where such an infra-structure already existed before they arrived.

Another case altogether is the hinterland of Benghazi in present-day Libya (Barker 1983). On the maps of the shifts in settlement pattern and exploitation strategy in the Hellenistic and Roman periods, the increase of trade in agricultural and other products through the port of Benghazi is seen to link it to an ever growing hinterland, in which more and more simple Roman farmsteads emerge between the 1st and 3rd centuries AD (*Figure 7.11*). This pushed the desert pastoralists further and further away from the coast and reduced the grazing land available to them. Eventually, that forced them to begin herding camels instead of sheep and goats. The increasing contrast in wealth led to increasingly frequent raids on the wealthy Roman settlements, so that eventually these were fortified to protect the colonists. The pre-Roman mode of subsistence is pushed out of the territory occupied by the Romans. These examples reflect the fact that in due time, and with a varying degree of success, the Romans imposed a commercial exploita-tion system on the existing, highly varied ways in which the local populations exploited their lands. Two major factors accompanied these developments and made them possi-ble: land mapping and rationalization and increasing scale of production.

7.3.4.   *A different perception of space and the landscape*

One of the major hallmarks of Roman control over the countryside is that rural areas were effectively administered for tax and commercial purposes. Such administration depended on an effective way to map the land. All over Western Europe, there are traces of this administration in the fact that the Romans organized the land in a system of square-mile blocks (called *centuriations*) which were laid out and mapped by a profes-sional class of surveyors (the *agrimensores*). In the case of the Tricastin, we even have fragments of the resultant map, carved in marble, with the names of some of the landowners and the rate of land tax they paid to the state. It is particularly noteworthy from our point of view that the land was divided into square blocks measuring one by one mile.[5] The boundaries of these blocks were marked by means of roads and drainage ditches. In this respect, the Roman perception of the landscape was very different from

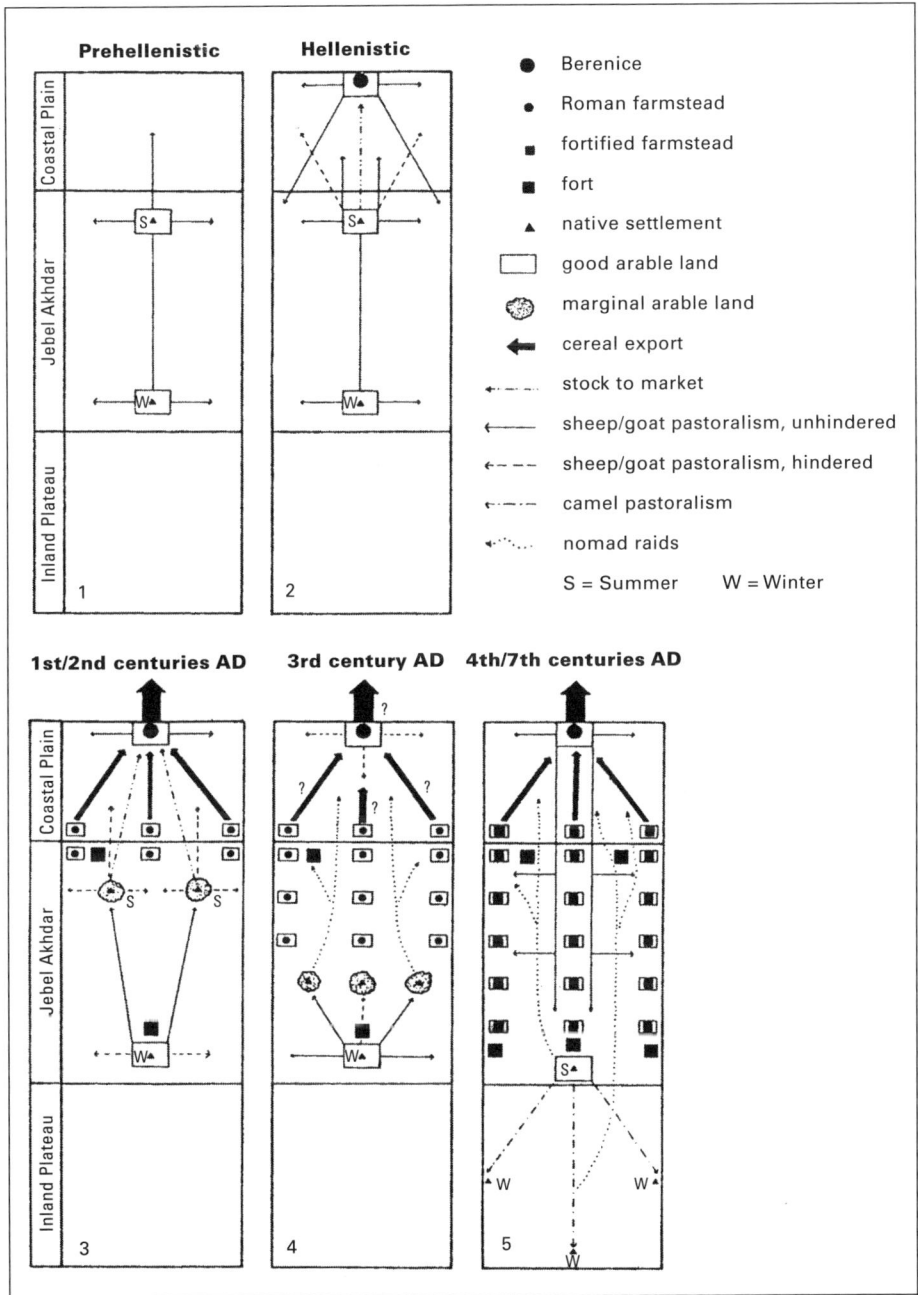

FIGURE 7.11

A theoretical model of the dynamics of the settlement system south of Benghazi (Libya), according to Barker (1983). (Source: Greene 1986: Figure 28)

the pre-existing ones, and because this 'square' administrative point of view often pre-vailed over any practical considerations, the resulting organization of the landscape was regularly at odds with the natural dynamics of an area. In the Tricastin, a large drainage scheme was laid out in the late 1st century BC, in order to provide land for soldiers of the Roman legions when they reached retirement age. The roads and ditches were all laid out in north-south and east-west directions, whereas the natural drainage of the area generally went from north-east to south-west. Unfortunately for the scheme, peace broke out a couple of decades after the scheme was initiated. The first peace dividend was a drastic reduction in the number of soldiers, and thus (somewhat later) in the number of veterans. As soon as there was insufficient manpower to keep the ditches open, the drainage scheme fell apart, and the land became neglected and ultimately it began eroding (Leeuw 1998).

Advantages of scale and rationalization

As we have seen in the case of Benghazi, as exports became more and more important, other considerations gave way in the face of rationalization and other means of increasing yield. In large parts of north-western Europe, the Romans introduced other races of bovines, which were considerably larger than the pre-Roman ones. But this drive towards 'bigger is better' is also found in the size of agricultural installations. In Southern France, Roman wine and oil cellars have been found that are several orders of magnitude larger than was the case in pre-Roman times. In the Donzère, one of these has a capacity of 2800 hl (400,000 modern-day bottles!). Another sign of the changes occurring in agriculture is found in the production of amphorae for the transportation of grain and liquids (again, olive oil and wine). Both the number of such vessels and that of the pottery workshops making them, increase very rapidly during the 1st and 2nd centuries AD.

Of course most of the data on the exploitation of such domains is found in texts, rather than in the ground. We have detailed descriptions of the best ways to run large estates, including many hints of an agronomic as well as a management nature, from several Roman authors, such as Columella and Pliny the elder. For a long time, it was impossible to decide whether their precepts were only applied to large estates in Italy and Southern France, or whether the recommendations in them found a wider audience. Increasingly, the excavation of villas, the reconstruction of their fields and of the crops cultivated upon them, as well as the way these were planted, begins to confirm that the written data may have been applied quite widely. Such research shows clearly that the Romans preferred relatively light, well-drained soil, and that wherever possible, they chose to settle on low slopes facing anywhere but north (Favory 2002). Thus, we find large cultivated areas on the rolling plateaux of northern Gaul, as well as in the foothills of the Haut Comtat, Vaunage and Beaucairois.[6]

When no such land was available, they would go so far as to drain large alluvial areas

to bring them into exploitation, such as the Tricastin plain. In this context, it is important to mention that many such hilly slopes were originally covered with forest. As the
forest was cut down to make place for agricultural crops, these slopes had to be terraced

---

Views of nature in European Antiquity[7] How nature was seen depended in antiquity – and in many places still – on its actual or potential threat to humans. Nature was
in no way always a friend, with her unpredictability and threats. It was therefore permitted and even a duty to fight her, as can be seen in a variety of cultural motives. The
disappearance of forests was seen as a sign of civilization, at least in the dominant
view.

The forests Clearing land for agriculture, wood, firewood and animal grazing have
been the main processes in changing the vegetation. Thirgood (1981), quoting Strabo,
mentions the mountains in south-eastern Spain 'covered with thick woods and gigantic
trees' being cut for shipbuilding. North Africa was an important timber-producing
region for the Romans, leading to temporary depletion of Moroccan forests. Wars had a
devastating effects as it accelerated the felling of trees to be used for the warships and
because the people fled into the mountains and abandoned the land. Mismanagement
may have added to the problems, but variations in aridity make it difficult to distinguish between human and natural factors.

Extinction of wild animals The cultural hero or king had a special role in the civilizing process: Heracles battled with near-invincible mythical wild animals, becoming a
symbol of courage. Whereas this view had limited consequences in Mesopotamian and
Egyptian times, this changed with the advent of the Roman Emperors. Not only slaves
but also wild animals were taken from the conquered lands, to show total dominance
over man and animal. More intense hunting brought some species to extinction. The
enormous demand for animals skins, from as far as the Baltic and northern Russia, further increased the pressure.

The *Pax Romana* acquired a specific connotation through the mass killing of wild
animals. Thousands of wild animals were slaughtered in the *venationes* during the
games or *ludi*. These took place in every garrison town but Rome had by far the largest:
with the inauguration of the Colosseum in 70 AD some 5000 animals were 'used' over a
few days (Auguet 1994). It must have given rise to huge transport problems. Only
recently it has been acknowledged that the grand scale fo these huge killings may have
led to the extinction of some of these species. It has been hypothesized that the games
indirectly contributed to the expansion of agriculture in the Mediterranean by strongly
reducing the threat from wild animals – a view that fits into the view that humans
should 'civilize' the world and was therefore approvingly supported by scholars until
recently.

---

or otherwise protected against erosion. As long as those terraces remained and the land was cared for, this did not cause any immediate problems. It did, however, make these landscapes extremely dependent on human intervention and vulnerable to erosion in its absence.

To facilitate the marketing of their products, as well as support from the army, the villas and *latifundia* concerned were linked into the road system and/or the navigable rivers of Western Europe. That this was essential to their survival is clearly shown by the fact that there is a highly significant statistical relationship between the fact that a site is linked into three or more roads and its survival beyond the end of the 2nd century AD. But in interpreting this relationship we must delve beyond the obvious. The sites that survived were indeed those with direct road access, but these sites were also the earliest among the sites founded by the Romans, and they had the most, and the best, land at their disposal. That in itself should not surprise us, as the first of the new colonists founded their farms in those locations which seemed best to them, and which therefore gave them the best chances of survival. At the same time, these first colonists shaped the landscape, including its spatial structure. They therefore profited from a number of positive feedback loops that did not benefit those who came later. That, in turn, allowed them to overcome the major difficulties involved in any kind of colonization of new lands. What kinds of difficulties were involved? Their exact nature differed from region to region, but a more general description in system dynamics terms may be derived from a study of such 'pioneer' colonization fronts elsewhere.

7.4. The Roman Empire as a self-organizing system

7.4.1. Self-organization

How does all of this relate to the dynamics of the Roman Empire? To penetrate below the surface of what is happening hence and thus to transform our description into an explanation, we must develop a way to conceive of the core dynamics of Roman colonization. One fruitful approach is the theory of self-organizing, complex adaptive systems (cf. Section 8.5). The whole of the Empire is seen as a dynamic dissipative structure, existing by virtue of the fact that it slowly structures an increasing area and a growing number of people into a coherent whole. In return, it draws energy (human and animal) and raw materials (foods, minerals and water) from the area thus colonized. The spatial extension of control manifests itself as longer and longer communication chains in new territory, such as the roads that link all parts of the Empire, the contacts and visits that link people across the whole of the territory, and the exchange of goods between distant communities. But the process of structuration is also evident in many other forms: the spread throughout the Empire of a common language and writing system for the dominant classes, of imperial coinage, of an administrative and judicial apparatus, of citizenship, and so forth. In a different domain, it also includes the spread of compatible agricultural and industrial technologies and of similar settlement systems (*villas*, *latifundia* and towns). Let us look at the developments in more detail from this perspective.

The spread of all the manifestations of integration structures the channels through which raw energy and matter are drawn into the core of the system. Matter and energy are subject to the laws of conservation. Information is not; it can in effect spread and be shared. In this sense, societies can be said to be held together by the information flows and the information processing channels which are created by negotiating shared meanings, ideas and customs. That spread is in practice a question of acculturation, and therefore of collective and individual learning. As such, it has its own, bottom-up dynamic, which can be helped by creating the correct circumstances but cannot be imposed from the top. The resilience of the system as a whole depends on that process of acculturation. If certain sectors of society, or certain areas, do not manage to keep pace with the remainder of the population, they will become isolated and will eventually cause problems. Similarly, if certain groups learn too fast, this will create resistance around them.

How do the dynamics of structuration of the Empire relate to the processes of colonization and exploitation of the countryside? The process of dynamic structuration did, of

---

Conceptual framework: self-organizing open systems   Ecosystems may usefully be considered as dynamic, hierarchically organized sets of relations between different individuals, species and communities. These relations are multi-temporal and constitute a web in space-time. Thus defined, the systems are open and dissipative: their continued existence depends on the dissipation of both their energy and their entropy. All living beings use (solar) energy to transform a limited number of material components into different organic components constituting organisms, and then to disintegrate these different forms of matter into their constituent components. To extents that vary from species to species, and from community to community, the self-organising mechanisms that shape them inform substance (matter and energy) and substantiate form. In doing so, they create organization.

Human beings are an integral part of such systems (McGlade 1995). Due to their capacity to learn, and to learn how to learn (Bateson 1972), they are very efficient at dissipating entropy. In situations where long-term co-evolution occurs between human and non-human species, human beings tend with time to take over more and more of the structuration of the system as a whole. Human groups do so by expanding the scope, depth and reach of their own network of relationships, involving more and more people, bringing them ever closer together – in a physical, social and cultural sense –

and using the emerging structure to enhance their control over their environment. In short, they impose themselves by means of a positive feedback loop between the size and efficiency of their information-processing capacity and the amount of information they process. As a result, they can extend their control over what surrounds them on condition that their efforts to do so do not hit a snag for very long. If that happens, the positive feedback loop turns negative, and the society begins to lose coherence and it may disintegrate, if no remedy is found.

If such a co-evolutionary system is to survive, a dynamic balance needs to be maintained between exploration and/or innovation (enhancing the information-processing capacity to anticipate change) on the one hand, and routine exploitation (dissipating noise or entropy and thereby causing change) on the other. The latter is necessary to maintain the necessary level of energy flow throughout the system, and the former is required to ensure that new forms of exploitable energy are found before the presently available forms are exhausted. Without such a balance, i.e. when the society innovates either too rapidly or too slowly, it is not able to dissipate sufficient entropy and loses coherence. That jeopardizes the equilibrium between adaptedness to the present and adaptability to future circumstances, and the chances increase that when the positive feedback loop hits a snag, no remedy can be found in time to restore the growth dynamic.

A system that maintains such a balance is called *resilient*. It is able to '[...] absorb and utilize or even benefit from perturbations and changes that attain it, and so to persist without a qualitative change in the system's structure.' (Holling 1973) Whether it is able to do so, depends on the nature and size of the perturbations as well as on its own capacity to deal with them. Thus a perturbation of considerable magnitude is necessary to trigger a qualitative change in a highly resilient system. Resilience is not stability. Stability indicates a system's capacity to return to equilibrium upon perturbation whereas a resilient system does not lose its internal structure in a period of perturbation. A system can be highly resilient and yet fluctuate widely, i.e. have low stability. There does indeed seem to be a relationship between the two. The wider the range of fluctuations, the more frequently the system is called upon to adapt and the more practice it gets in doing so.

course, occur at all levels of the society simultaneously, in – partly overlapping – groups of different sizes, with different roles and functions: families, extended kinship systems, trade networks and associations, armies and towns. Of all these different levels, the one that concerns us here most directly is the interaction of individual farms, farming communities and ultimately all farmers in the Empire with their natural and social environment. What kinds of dynamics were involved? To what extent were these constrained by the immediate natural environment or by the social environment in which agriculture was practised? What were its consequences for the environment? What were the difficulties for the farmers? Of course, the answer to these questions will differ from region to region and is difficult to give on the basis of archaeological and documentary data alone, but a more general description of system dynamics terms may be derived from a study of 'pioneer' agricultural colonization systems elsewhere (Duvernoy 1994).

Each basic unit (individual, family, enterprise) deals with its own particular circumstances, including its geographic location, its natural circumstances, the particularities of its human participants and its role in, and links with, the wider socio-economic system. Together, these complex dynamics, with many degrees of freedom, ensure that each entity in the system (farm, settlement or region) operates in a permanently changing environment, and that it maintains both a domain of fluctuation and a domain of stability in its dealings with that environment (*Figure 7.12*). Every once in a while, a fluctuation in the combined environmental and social dynamics will occur that takes the system outside its margin of stability. At that moment, a new domain of stability – and a new domain of fluctuation – needs to be identified.

The way in which the procurement and flow of energy are organized is of critical importance. In order to survive, the socio-natural system must at any time be able to find a viable way to deal with all of the parameters involved if it is to maintain a sufficient flow of energy to guarantee its survival. What enables it to do so?

The number of degrees of freedom of the socio-natural system is so large, that its dynamics can, for the purposes of this argument, be thought of as chaotic. Yet humans

FIGURE 7.12

Bifurcation and qualitative change in non-equilibrium systems (after Laszlo, 1987)

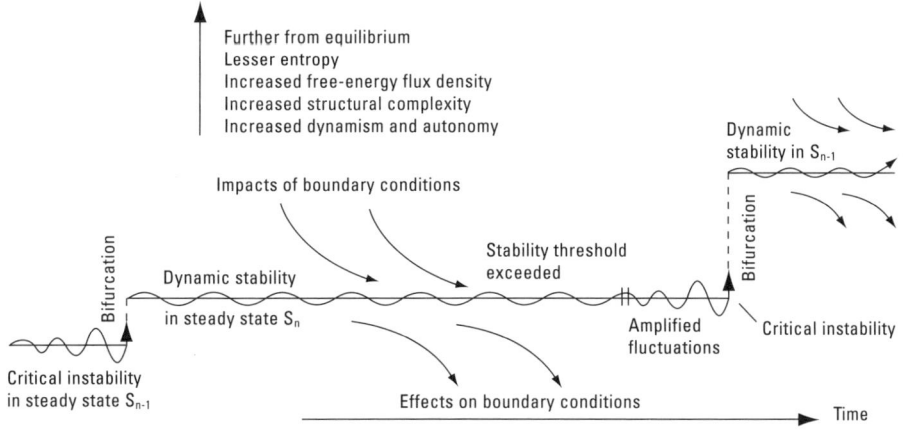

and human societies have generally been able to deal with such dynamics sufficiently well to survive, and eventually to take control of the socio-natural system. Their interaction with the other components of the system must therefore be very efficient and effective. Atlan (1992) argues cogently that all human theories are necessarily underdetermined by the observations on which we think that they are based. Our capacity to conceptualize is therefore a necessity, but not a sufficient condition to explain our effectiveness in dealing with our environment. Our efficiency in doing so may go a long way to explaining our resilience as a species, as it enables us to rethink our concept of what we observe as it changes. As a result, we can – and do – individually adapt rapidly to any change in conditions.

However, there are limits to both our efficiency and our effectiveness in dealing with the environment. Our efficiency is constrained by both our means of communication and our diversity. As the number of people involved in a system grows linearly, the number of messages required to keep all of them in touch grows exponentially, and so does the time involved to reach everyone concerned. As the number of people involved grows, so does their diversity, and with it the time it takes to 'negotiate' collaboration between them. But if size has such important disadvantages, why have socio-natural systems in general, and the Roman one in particular, grown so spectacularly in the course of their existence? The answer lies in the fact that the Roman Empire was dependent on continued expansion for its survival. More and more resources – including raw energy in the form of slaves – were brought from an increasingly distant periphery to the centre and transformed into a growing range of artefacts and other objects. That 'inflation' kept the whole system going. As soon as the difficulties in the sphere of information processing came to weigh more heavily than the need to keep the flows of energy and matter going, the Empire found itself stagnating and eventually in decline.

More generally, the answer is related to the asymmetric relationship between societies and their environments. Not only do they have fundamentally different dynamics, but also society's perception of the environment and its impact on it is governed by the filter of human perception – and not vice versa: the relationship is asymmetric.[8] This perception and subsequent interpretation of the environment is always simplified and incomplete; it is often underdetermined by observations and overdetermined by the cognitive structure that determines our definition of problems. Conquerors' and colonists' experiences are sometimes a vivid illustration of this point (cf. Chapter 10). When deriving a conception from our observations, we simplify the phenomena observed and retain that simplified form in our memory. Our interventions in the environment are therefore based on these simplifications. But as we intervene in the environment, we change it – modifying its dimensionality as well as its qualitative and quantitative dynamics. Our cognitive capacities to observe environmental change may be adequate as long as change is within the variations confronted before, through social memory. For change outside these variations – many environmental processes operate on centennial or millennial scales – the capacity for adequate response is less. This limitation to our effectiveness has important consequences for the way we deal with long-term change in the environment.

7.4.2. *An example: newly colonized environments*

The colonists begin their adventure with inappropriate ideas about their new environment and the way to deal with it, mainly because their perception of what constitutes the natural environment is determined by the area they come from rather than the one they go to. But they learn quickly, dealing with undesirable events and processes as and when they observe them. They will therefore first mitigate the most frequently occurring events that they do not like. As they do, they shift the 'risk spectrum' of their dealings with the local environment, eliminating frequent, minor risks and introducing risks with unknown periodicities. Even if we assume that the latter are normally distributed, the net effect of this interaction over the long-term is a build-up of less frequent but more important risks – 'time-bombs' or 'unintended consequences'. Once their density is sufficiently high, major crises are bound to occur. Such crises have the impact of forcing the colonists either to heavily restructure their exploitation system under pressure or abandon their investment. In general, the ensuing reorganization will spread risks by differentiating the soils exploited and the crops produced, as well as the stages of exploitation, for example exploiting a range of soils from freshly cut forest soils to soils that have been exploited for some time. This is generally achieved by expansion of the exploitation, by inducing more people to exploit it together and, where possible, by introducing technical innovations. It entails the reorganization of the spatio-temporal dynamics of exploitation, the differentiation of the tasks fulfilled by the people working on the exploitation, and investment in installations and equipment. In many cases, the opportunity to achieve economies of scale will also lead to intensification in order to achieve an increase in the volume of goods produced.

On the other hand, the reorganization will generally reduce the system's diversity of species and the complexity of its natural dynamics, while the complexity of the social dynamics increases. As a system's natural resilience in effect depends on the extent to which its dynamics are open to change (Leeuw 2001) and thus on its dimensionality, any human efforts to 'focus' any part of it on a specific function reduces its inherent resilience (Leeuw 1998). As a result, the burden of maintaining the system is increasingly shifted onto the social dynamics: the system becomes truly dependent on human disturbance (Naveh 1984). Moreover, the narrower range of products into which the system is driven by human action will, to a greater or lesser extent, shift the balance between its exploitative and its innovative dynamics in favour of the former. Ultimately, this will often lead to a reduction of the productivity of the system due to resource exhaustion. At any one time, the continued existence of the system will depend on the balance between the risks involved in the dynamics of its natural and social components. Increasing the diversity of the uses of resources, production techniques and products reduces the natural risks but enhances the complexity of management and therefore the risks due to the social dynamics.

Time is of the essence in the ensuing balancing act. Once a crisis looms, the time-span available to find a solution is limited, and the outcome is dependent both on the nature of the solution found, and the efficiency with which it is introduced. Too little is as useless as too late. Very often, whether the system survives or goes under depends on minute differences in external conditions or in the nature of the dynamics involved. In this respect, differences in perception may be just as important as slight differences in precipitation, soil fertility, management efficiency or the price of the products on the world market at any particular time.

7.4.3.   Stagnation is decay: changing settlement patterns in the Rhône valley 100 BC to 600 AD

To explain some of the changes wrought by the Roman colonization of the Mediterranean Basin and Western Europe, and to lay the groundwork for our understanding of the decay of both the environment and the Empire itself, we will look at events in the Middle and Lower Rhône valley. The present perspective there has been brought to bear on a relatively large data-set, comprising more than 2000 settlements dated between 500 BC and the present, some 1000 of which date to the period 100 BC to AD 600 (Leeuw 1998; Favory 2002). It can clearly be demonstrated that the implantation of new Roman colonies in the area increased rapidly between 100 BC and AD 100 but came to a sudden halt after 150 AD. Of course, that did not mean that the number of settlements in active use declined as dramatically after that date, but it is incontrovertible that the settlement dynamics fundamentally changed in the 2nd century AD. *Figure 7.13* sheds an interesting light on why this happened. It shows that by far the largest proportion of the newly founded settlements did not survive more than the first two centuries of colonization, regardless of the environment in which the settlements are located. As these environments are very different, representative of all the natural environments of south-eastern France, this graph suggests that it is highly improbable that the desertion of these settlements was due to changes in the climate or in the natural environment. Such changes would have affected different landscapes differently and would therefore have had a differential effect on the process of abandonment. It seems much more likely that the abandonment of many of the smaller sites was due to socio-economic changes of some kind. This is corroborated by the fact that the deserted settlements were in general those that were among the last to be established. They are located in the least favourable areas and

FIGURE 7.13

Graph showing that, irrespective of their physical environment, most of the newly founded settlements in the Lower Rhône valley were deserted before they were 200 years old (Occ 1-6 refer to the number of centuries that the sites were occupied; Rel1-10 refers to ten different classes of relief-related environments) (Source: Leeuw 1998: Figure 6.6.9)

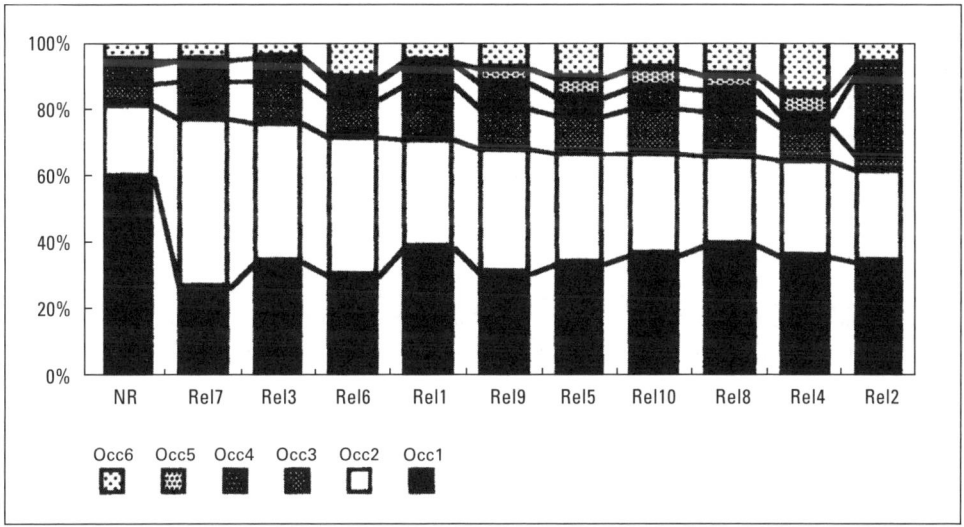

therefore never grew as large as the earlier ones that effectively shaped the geographical structure and the landscapes of the region.

A closer look at what happens in one of the sample areas most thoroughly surveyed by archaeologists, the Lunellois, clarifies the situation. The evolution in size and structure of rural settlement in the area between the 1st century BC and the 11th century AD has been explored in detail. Relative size of the settlements concerned and the links of – economic – dependency between settlements have been reconstructed. In the 1st century BC, there were a handful (8) of major settlements in the area, all of about the same size, and about twice as many small settlements. Most of the larger ones had a number of dependent 'satellites', as did three of the very small ones. Between the 1st century BC and the 1st century AD we see first of all an increase in the number of sites. In addition, the size of these sites is much more variable and many more of the sites have dependent 'satellites'. Altogether, therefore, the settlement system had become much more differentiated and complex. Between the 1st and the 5th century AD, however, although the growth of many of the individual sites seems to have continued, *the degree of integration of the system as a whole – as measured by its rank-size distribution – decreased.* There were fewer differences in size and fewer dependent satellites. Individually, the surviving

245

settlements had grown by absorbing some of the activities of their satellites and *in the process a large number of smaller sites had been sacrificed*. The process is driven by the need to reorganize the economic activities in the area as a whole in such a way as to reduce the exposure of individual settlements to particular risks. The surviving sites are those which have been able to do so by differentiating their *raisons d'être*. Notwithstanding the foundation of a limited number of new settlements in the 5th and 6th centuries AD, by the end of the latter century much of the expansionary drive has probably gone out of the system. It is therefore not surprising that by the 11th century AD there were more, but generally smaller, settlements and even fewer satellites. Whereas the beginning of our era witnessed the transformation of a decentralized, rural system into a much more coherent, partially urbanized one, the 5th and 6th centuries saw the early phases of a return to a rural way of life, an evolution that was complete by the 11th century.

What could have been the increased risks that triggered this reorganization? The first factor that springs to mind is the fact that after two centuries of exploitation of the relatively light soil that the Romans preferred, the soil probably showed some signs of exhaustion. Yields per hectare must have gone down and competition with more recently colonized areas, or richer soil, must have become stiffer. A second contributory factor may have been the slight deterioration of the climate that seems to have occurred from the end of the 2nd century AD onwards. Annual average temperatures decreased by around two degrees, and precipitation also increased somewhat. That may have affected the lowland soils in particular. But we should not exclude another very important, anthropogenic, factor that had a different effect. We have seen that in the 1st century AD the producers in the area significantly increased production and focused more and more on exports to the other parts of the Roman world. As a result, they also became more and more dependent on the economic conditions in faraway regions over which they had no control whatsoever. Together, these factors not only reduced the local system's resilience – reduced yield, worsening climate – but they also increased its socio-economic instability and enhanced the risks to which every exploitation was exposed. In order to avoid high local risks the system had to keep on expanding, but the expansion itself in turn increased the external risks by tying the local system more and more closely into the world system. And in order to compete on that level, the local system had to become more and more efficient, raising its production levels. Of course that had consequences both for the local socio-economic and the environmental dynamics, stretching these to their limits. Once they were thus stretched, further expansion became more and more difficult and eventually impossible unless a major technical or management innovation could be triggered. In the absence of such an event, local stagnation was the result.

Polluted water in the Roman Empire: an environmental challenge[9]   Among the factors contributing to the decline of the Roman Empire, it has been argued, some were related to sanitation and diseases. The possible role of lead poisoning is well known. Local air and water pollution would have been serious in Rome, not unlike metropolis such as 17th and 18th century London and Paris and present-day urban conglomerates in less developed regions.

Cities need systems for water disposal as rain is not easily absorbed and water from sewage and other sources needs to be discharged. Rome already had a large main underground sewage canal, the Cloaca Maxima, with many tributuaries in the 4th century BC. In the 2nd century BC this canal was coated with lava blocks and it served the city well into the 20th century. Venus Cloacina was the goddess of the poor slaves employed in maintaining this underworld.

There is a myth about toilets in the Roman Empire. Quite often the number of public conveniences is exaggarated and the number of house facilities underestimated. Towns such as Pompeii and Herculanaeum in the year of their apocalypse (79 AD) had many private toilets and even the upper stories of the houses occasionally had toilets. These were not always connected with a sewer and the cesspits had to be emptied in the same unhygienic way as can be seen in present-day third world countries.

Public toilets did exist and can still be admired in cities as far apart as Ostia, Aleppo and Efese. Often they comprised two opposite rows and sometimes the excrement was carried away by flowing water, such as the overflow of an adjacent bath house. In front of one was a gutter with streaming water. Sponges on sticks were submerged in these and one could clean one's bottom through a hole in the front of the toilet seat. The sponge was rinsed and left in the gutter for its next user. Water vessels served for washing hands.

Archeologists, historians and classicists are engaged in a fierce debate as to whether the Romans aimed at comfort and relieve of hinder or whether they already had deeper hygienic insights. Whereas archaeology provides evidence of good hygiene practices, contemporary authors such as Juvenal and Martial complained bitterly about the difficulties of life in the overcrowded city of Rome and mention dead bodies, dirt, and animal excreta in the streets. The use of flushing by means of water jars, the slope of the floor towards the drain, the coating with tiles and walls plastered with water resistant coating (opus signinum) and the occasional cesspits situated in sites that guarantees cleaning without polluting the house are signs of good hygiene. On the other hand, many sewers were not covered but open waste canals and the sponges for communal use and open connection to sewers or cesspits were not. Compared to the second – and hopefully lasting – rise of sanitation in the 19th century, ancient Rome did not have a clear idea of the link between waste water and disease.

7.4.4. *What consequences does this have on the level of the Empire – how did it become a 'global crisis'?*

Each different region will, of course, meet its own fate, which depends on its particular natural and social circumstances. But they all will suffer from the fact that their dynamics are more and more dependent on those of other regions. In the end, many of them will hit an invisible barrier, the point at which innovation can no longer keep up with the stress to which the system is subjected. It will manifest itself as a sense of 'crisis', in which things go wrong on all fronts: climate change, soil depletion, price collapse, important social imbalances, etc. Such a sense of stress is clearly present in the Roman world from the 3rd century AD onwards. It is referred to by many of the Roman authors, who apportion blame to very different causes, ranging from bad government to invasions, to widespread lead poisoning, soil exhaustion, famine and possibly climate change (Provost 1982).

In practical terms, regional and local stagnation ultimately affected so many areas that the Empire as a whole could expand no further. Rather than blame this sense of 'crisis' on any particular one of these putative causes, let us turn reverse the issue. The exact domain in which the stagnation – climate, soil exhaustion, social or economic difficulties or invasions – first manifested itself is less relevant than the inability to cope with it. The sentiment that 'the sky is falling in' – which is inherent in any major crisis – is due to the fact that the social system as a whole lacks the information processing capacity needed to deal simultaneously with all these issues effectively. The salient point is that that could have been avoided by innovation, i.e. by an increase in overall information processing capacity. But that argument leaves us with the need to explain why all these things 'hit' at the same time. We argue that is due to the accumulation of long-term risks resulting from the frequent intervention of people in their environment, leading to a shift in the 'risk spectrum' discussed earlier. In each area, that shift occurred in its own way – and the dynamics affected by it therefore differed from region to region. It is, however, significant that their temporal occurrence coincided – it reflects the fact that, irrespective of the local circumstances, a similar amount of time lapsed between the early colonization of the provinces and the crisis.

7.5. The decline and end of the Empire

7.5.1. *The disintegration process*

The last part of this paper is devoted to an outline of the decay of the Empire and the dynamics responsible for it. Our starting point is the fact that, from the late 3rd century onwards, there are a number of important changes to be seen in the interaction between the Empire and its environment, as well as in the Empire itself. Let us begin with a very schematic description of the history of those two or three centuries (300-600 AD). The 'growth crisis' which announced itself in the 2nd century had its full impact in the 3rd. The Roman authors usually blamed invasions, several epidemics, a weak and overstaffed administrative infrastructure, incompetent Emperors and the heavy burdens of maintaining a government and an army over such a wide territory. Most of these factors were real and did contribute to the difficulties. One plague epidemic lasted from 165 AD to about 180 AD, with the loss of up to a third of the population in certain areas. The 3rd century saw a rapid succession of emperors lasting between a few months and three years – 28 of them were anointed in the 75 years between Septimius Severus and Diocletian. In that period, there were always one or more provinces in revolt, independent or out of control – for instance, the Rhine-Danube area in the 230s and 260s, Dacia in the 260s and 270s, Moesia in the 270s, Gaul, Britain and Spain from 260 to 274, Syria in the period 267-273. But it should also be noted that since the early 1st century AD, there were no new territories to be conquered. The significance of this fact becomes clear if we try to quantify the importance of the financial contribution of the different conquests. Tainter gives an interesting set of figures:

In 167 BC the Romans seized the treasury of the King of Macedonia, a feat that allowed them to eliminate taxation of themselves. After the Kingdom of Pergamon was annexed in 130 BC, the state budget doubled, from 100 million to 200 million sesterces. Pompey raised it further to 340 million sesterces after the conquest of Syria in 63 BC. Julius Caesar's conquest of Gaul acquired so much gold that this metal dropped 36% in value. (Tainter 1988: 129)

He concludes: 'By the last two centuries BC, Rome's victories may have become nearly free of cost, in an economic sense, as conquered nations footed the bill for further expansion.'

The fact that after Augustus there were no longer any rich territories to be conquered in the periphery of the Empire therefore amputated the income of the State. Most of the Emperors between Augustus and Diocletian complained of fiscal shortages and/or had to resort to new kinds of taxes. Although the annual non-conquest income of the State since Augustus regularly increased from about 500 million to 1500 million sesterces under Vespasian, seventy years later this was not sufficient to deal with any crises. All of that sum went towards the maintenance of the administration and the army, the dole (to about 200,000 Roman citizens) and the maintenance of the physical infrastructure (roads, wharves, etc.). Yet, overall, the first two centuries of our era were a period of peace and security in which the population and the economy flourished. But that economy could not easily generate added value. 90% of the Empire's economy was agricultural and therefore provided a stable, but not very flexible source of income. Trade and industry were small in scale. Notwithstanding the good roads, the means of transportation – beasts of burden, carts and small ships – remained relatively small and did not favour bulk trade. Transport overland was particularly expensive: a wagonload of wheat would double in value over 500 km, and it was cheaper to cross the Mediterranean by ship than to haul a load over 120 km overland. Bulk trade was therefore confined to essentials, mainly cereals, to coastal regions and to the shortest possible distances. Almost the only long-distance trade was in high-value, small items: precious stones and gold, perfumes and jewellery. All in all, the economy was low-margin, highly decentralized and locally based. Emperors faced with crises or ambitious to leave their mark on history resorted to the debasement of the currency. Between Nero (54-68 AD) and Septimius Severus (193-211 AD) the silver content of the denarius (four sesterces) dropped from 91.8 to 58.3% (Bolin 1958: 211, cited in Tainter 1988: 135). Inflation must have demanded a heavy toll.

Diocletian (AD 284-305) was the first to restore a semblance of order. His reign initiated half a century of relatively stable government and a century of relative wealth. The administration was completely reformed into a larger, more complex and more powerful apparatus. In doing so, Diocletian broke with the tradition of minimalist administration that went back to the Republic. He divided the Empire in two parts: East and West, with a separate administration, different languages – Greek and Latin respectively – and different cultures. The provinces were subdivided into smaller ones, breaking the power of the provincial governors and imposing an Imperial administration. The army was reformed and doubled in size; taxes were augmented and people conscripted to perform duties in the maintenance of infrastructure and many other activities. Diocletian also attempted to reform the coinage.

In spite of this, the structure of the Roman Empire collapsed in 395 AD. Of the two parts the West was by far the most vulnerable as it did not have the same degree of cultural and linguistic homogeneity as the East. The latter was essentially co-terminous with the Greek-speaking world and had shared a common destiny for about a millennium, whereas the Western Empire consisted of a hodgepodge of semi-integrated nations and cultures with a lower overall level of structuration. The West therefore collapsed very rapidly, in less than a century, while the Eastern Empire was able to maintain itself for another millennium.

The written documents of the period give the impression that the structure of taxation – in essence tax-farming – is to blame, as well as the increasing independence of large *latifundia*, and the loss of administrative control over the countryside. This is corroborated by archaeological evidence. An analysis of the deposits of scale on the inside of the Nîmes aqueduct, for example, proves that from the 4th century the town no longer cleaned the aqueduct regularly, so that all kinds of small plant remains are embedded in the calcium deposits from that century. At the same time, large landowners illegally diverted part of the flow by making holes in the sides of the channel – indicating that the town no longer had control over its hinterland.

On the scale of the Western Empire, we see that the periphery increased in independence as the core began to lack the means to impose itself. The areas around Soissons and Trier, for example, became highly active regions that developed their own independent identities around the urban centres. Other such areas sprang up in southern Britain and southern Spain. Everywhere else, the cities retracted within their walls, and the flow of trade goods and people to areas farther from Rome began to dry up. Once that happened, peoples outside the Empire who were attracted by its relative wealth and its fame, and who did not find any armies standing between themselves and the core of the Western Empire, increasingly raided the areas where wealth could be found.

7.5.2. *Causes and effects: on the centre-periphery information gradient*

What was cause, what was effect, what contributed to this disintegration and what was the underlying dynamic (cf. Section 6.6)? By far the most cogent explanation for these – and many other, simultaneous – phenomena comes from the work of Tainter (1988). He is one of the very few archaeologists who has seriously studied the collapse of complex societies from a systemic point of view. Although particularly interested in the Western Roman empire, he has studied it in a comparative perspective that takes many other complex societies into account, such as the Maya, China and Japan, the prehistoric complex societies of the South-Western USA and others. The core of Tainter's argument is akin to that developed here and hinges on two observations:
– socio-political systems require energy to maintain the investment in infrastructure that keeps the members of the society acting together,
– increasing socio-political complexity as a problem-solving and risk-spreading response in a variable environment often reaches a point of declining marginal returns.

In the case of the Roman Empire, the infrastructure costs of integrating Spain, Gaul and other territories were relatively low, because that integration was deliberately based on incorporating existing infrastructures of local origin. Spreading risk over a wider range of environments and circumstances therefore initially provided the required stability and control over the destiny of the population that was sought. Nevertheless, at most a couple of centuries after the beginning of our era, the total costs reached a point of declining marginal returns, so that further expansion – and the tapping of new sources of energy – became unprofitable. Once expansion had halted, the Empire lacked sufficient reserves of energy to maintain the existing infrastructure when it came under pressure. At the same time, further increases in complexity became less attractive, so that organizationally simpler solutions were favoured. As such solutions are all those that involve fewer people and fewer organizational links, this shifted the balance in favour of

251

local solutions, and resulted in loss of coherence at the level of the Empire as a whole. Eventually, the sheer variety of local solutions so increased the diversity of spatio-temporal rhythms in the societal and socio-natural dynamics that the system fell apart and society approached a chaotic state.

We differ from Tainter only in one fundamental aspect. In our opinion, the lack of sources of energy cannot explain the disintegration of a social structure because, as long as such a structure is viable, it will always find ways to tap the energy that it needs in order to remain resilient. The reasons for the disintegration have to be sought in the domain responsible for the integration in the first place: they are linked to insufficiencies in the capacity to share and negotiate information between the members of the society.

On the most global scale, world systems are based on the creation of structure, on the information of matter and energy. Raw matter and energy are taken out of the environment – both social and natural – and transformed into structures that further facilitate the extraction of raw matter and energy. Such structures are nothing more than organized forms of matter and energy, forms that have a meaning for the actors concerned and can be manipulated with respect to that meaning. In this way, the world system of the time – and all subsequent ones – was dependent on whether or not the Empire managed to keep creating sufficient structure of the appropriate kind to drain enough energy and matter from its environment – whether inside or outside its boundaries – to keep itself running. Moreover, to contribute to the survival of the Empire, such matter and energy as it extracted had to be of the right sort, to help the existing structures to survive or even flourish. That meant they had to be of a form that the structure that extracted them could also 'deal' with, so that they could (be made to) contribute to the growth of the structure. As a result, it was not the energetic and/or material nature of the substrate that was important, but the information it carried and its suitability for processing by the structure concerned. Energy and matter are everywhere, in all conceivable forms. However in order to be able to harness them, structures must be put in place that can deal with them. From the 3rd century onwards, these structures seemed to be less effective, so that the cost of feeding the necessary energy and matter into the system became too high relative to their yield.

In the first part of this chapter, we saw how in many ways the Romans transformed the Mediterranean basin. How they managed to enhance its integration and reduce local risks by setting up a road network, controlling local élite groups and integrating them into the Empire, organising a bureaucracy and a monetary system and regular flows of goods to all parts of the Empire. All these innovations were directed towards facilitating the flow of goods, energy and information throughout the system, but notably from the periphery to the centre and vice versa. They were crucial elements in the republic's strategy of conquest and integration, serving to facilitate control over a large number of locally organized socio-political entities by enabling the Roman authorities to rapidly convey messengers or armies from one part of the Empire to another. But they also facilitated the spread of Roman ideals, techniques, goods, attitudes and concepts to the periphery.

Around the beginning of the 1st century, the early Empire linked a highly organized centre to a completely unstructured periphery. In the two centuries that followed, that situation dramatically changed as the Romans themselves 'organized' many provinces not only physically, but also culturally and socially according to their ideas. Hence, the centre became more and more dependent on interaction with the periphery and vice versa. At the same time, as others learned Roman ways and means, Rome no longer had the same advantage over the periphery in terms of information processing that it once did and the periphery came to be more difficult to control. In more abstract terms, the 'information gradient' across the Empire, from the centre to the periphery, levelled out. As that happened, the periphery became more difficult to control. In other words, the fragmentation of the 3rd century was inevitable as the different political and cultural entities within the Empire came to deal with Rome on a more and more 'equal' basis.

Towards the end of that period, this levelling of the 'information gradient' finally forced Diocletian and his successors to abandon the original underlying philosophy of Roman control, based on minimal interference in local matters and reliance on the superior 'ways of doing things' of the Romans. They diminished the difficulties inherent in controlling the huge geographical space concerned by cutting the Empire into two – and later four – parts each of which had its own system of control. They reinforced the administration and the army by doubling the personnel involved in each, and in doing so doubled the 'overheads' needed to ensure the *pax romana*. That staved disintegration off for another century or so but based on effective administrative control, rather than on the earlier, relatively light-handed, exploitative approach. With the level of overhead now involved, the economy's reliance on agriculture and its lack of capacity to generate added value became major constraints, themselves due to the nature of Roman technology. Moreover, taxing an agricultural system demands spatial and temporal flexibility from region to region and from year to year, adapting rates to the ways in which local circumstances influence yields. Diocletian's reforms had to reduce flexibility to reassert control, but in the process eroded the population's capacity to pay tax by pushing the system permanently too close to its carrying capacity.

It is therefore not surprising that incontrovertible evidence for an important increase in erosion in the 4th and 5th centuries has recently been brought to light in the South of France by one of the members of the ARCHAEOMEDES team, Berger. This peak is the only one in the Holocene history of the area that does not coincide with one of the 'normal' cycles of the global and/or the western Mediterranean climate, as documented in glacier dynamics, oxygen isotopes in the polar ice-cap and water levels in circum-alpine lakes. As a result, it can not be attributed to any external dynamics and requires another explanation. This element in the debate is too recent to be assessed on its merits, but Berger argues (2001, personal communication) that it is a clear instance of anthropogenic degradation of the regional climate, as was predicted by the models presented almost two years earlier by Reale and Shukla (2000). If that is correct, the 'crisis of the 3rd century' is in essence a societal crisis, which rapidly triggered local overexploitation, as indicated by, for example, Groenman van Waateringe (1983). But in other areas, the reverse is the case. The changes we see at the same time in southern France, for example, are corollaries of the fact that the agricultural system became industrialized and increased its efficiency. It took a much longer time, and different societal circumstances, for environmental degradation to become so general in the core of the Empire as to severely hamper the resilience of the Empire as a whole.

Why was the Empire unable to adapt by innovation and structural transformation? Tainter observes several times that the validity of his explanation is dependent on the absence of innovations (e.g. Tainter 1988: 122). Yet he does not explain this absence. Instead he argues (Tainter 1988: 105) that:

> As Elster has pointed out, 'Innovation and technical change are not universal phenomena, but are restricted in time and space to a very small subset of historical societies'. In this light the question 'Why didn't Rome develop economically?' can be rephrased 'Why wasn't Rome economically abnormal?' Viewed thus, the question of Rome's economic development becomes substantially less problematical. (Tainter 1988: 152)

It seems to us that even if Elster's remark may be true for historical societies as a whole, it is not for Empires and other very complex societies. Indeed, all major states and empires have invented such things as writing, commerce, coinage and laws (cf. e.g. Claessen 1978; Wesson 1967; Leeuw 1981). Innovation is recognized as the main driver behind the long-term existence of all urban systems (Guérin-Pace 1993).

Science and technology in the ancient Mediterranean   As a matter of fact, steam power was known to scientists such as Hero of Alexandria (around 60 AD) and used to construct 'toys', in this case a 'fountain'. Similarly, Plutarch recounts how Archimedes invented a system of pulleys to launch a huge ship that could carry 3000 tons of freight. Whereas the scientist himself regarded such efforts as 'geometric games, that he had played to amuse himself', king Hiero II of Syracuse, for whom it was constructed, gave it away to one of the Ptolemaic kings of Egypt. From geography to algebra, from astronomy to architecture, innovations were many and in all areas of life, as is clear from the works of van der Waerden (1954), Clagett (1955) and other historians of classical science. It is tempting to speculate what would have happened if the Empire, for example, had adopted steam engines.

Adapting the structures could have saved the day if it had happened in time – and we need to explain why it did not. Interestingly enough, the Mediterranean basin was a breeding ground for innovation throughout most of its history, from the earliest Egypt to the end of the Greek period. What if the Empire had been able to exploit new sources of energy and power? But such 'what if' questions are not what this is all about. The core questions are the ones Tainter asks, but does not answer: 'Why did not Rome develop economically (by innovating)?' (Tainter 1988: 152), 'Why did not the system as a whole engage in 'scanning behaviour', seeking alternatives that might provide a preferable adaptation?' (Tainter 1988: 122). Why did it not implement the enormous advances made by the scientists of the classical world? In our opinion the collapse of the Empire was not due to the declining marginal returns on further investment, but to the fact that the structure itself weighed too heavily on the Empire's capacity 'to think the unthinkable and do the undoable' when that was required. Declining marginal returns were in our opinion an effect and not a cause. The economist's view is incomplete in this respect, and it would be interesting to be able to devote a study to these questions from a more anthropological and sociological perspective.

7.6.   Conclusions

Being well-documented and covering many spatial and temporal scales, the Roman Empire is a good case to study the evolution of socio-natural systems. The rapid expansion of its territory and population was possible due to adequate control and infrastructure. Only regions with some infrastructure were conquered and their local institutions were used in governing them. Italy's central position and the Roman engineering skills – as evidenced in the road system – were important aspects, as were commerce and trade. The 'readiness' for development of regions such as Gaul played a role too.

The Roman Empire was characterized by a large geographical, ecological and cultural diversity, with local adaptation and global resilience. After several millennia of human activities the landscape had become highly dependent on human interference with the natural cycli. Colonization, polyculture and new crops and techniques intensified this dependence. Small farms, efficient *latifundia* and lands for veterans made up an interdependent mix. Pre-Roman subsistence modes were pushed out and rural lands were effectively administered for tax and commercial purposes, aided by good landmapping and economies of scale and rationalization. The large estates were sited near roads and rivers in order to be protected by the army and to have good access to markets; the local landscape was often severely altered.

Viewed as a self-organizing system, the Roman Empire showed a capacity for conceptualization and information processing that was at the essence of its resilience. However, it had to expand for its survival and increasingly suffered from the inherent limitations in correctly observing and interpreting environmental change and the exponentially increasing demands on handling complex networks. Several narratives illustrate this. Decline set in, apparently because many things went 'wrong' simultaneously: climate change, soil depletion, price collapse and important social imbalances. A sense of stress is clearly present in the Roman world from the 3rd century AD onwards. One reason why all of these problems may all have hit at the same time is the accumulation of long-term risks resulting from the frequent intervention of people in their environment. Another element was the declining marginal return in problem solving and risk-spreading responses which may have showed up not so much in the scarcity of resources as in an insufficient capacity to share and negotiate information between the members of the society. In particular, the levelling out of the earlier 'information gradient' between rulers and ruled, core and periphery may have contributed to the final fragmentation and disintegration: a societal crisis which then triggered local overexploitation in the already highly human disturbance dependent Mediterranean basin. Bluntly stated, then, the lesson from this story is that the resilience of social structures is determined by their capacity to innovate in response to the changes in circumstances that they themselves generate.

8

Understanding: Fragments of a Unifying Perspective[1]

DE VRIES, THOMPSON AND WIRTZ

Concepts of past cultures have probably changed as much in the last thirty years as have ideas of the earth system. The two massive data sets await reconciliation.

Gunn 2000: 227

The normal sense of a satisfying explanation in archaeology is that it makes a set of facts in some sense intelligible by demonstrating that they seem 'natural' when viewed from the perspective of a certain framework of thought.

Cherry 1985: 44

8.1.   Introduction

The previous chapters have given various illustrations of how socio-natural systems evolved within their environment as they developed collective and individual habits, techniques, rituals and more elaborate ways of communication and organization. These developments are sequences of processes of exploitation and adaptation. Simmons (1989) lists elements and stages of these multi-faceted interaction processes: domestication, simplification, diversification and conservation. Goudsblom (1996) stresses the differentiation in behaviour and power between people and animals and between people; increasing numbers and concentrations of people; and the specialization, organization and stratification with its interdependencies. In investigating aspects higher on the scale of complexity, there is kind of a trade-off: the distant past is badly observable but fairly simple, the near past is better communicated through writing and art but – if only for that very reason – more complex. As Roberts remarks: 'Because information shrinks rapidly backwards through time, historical myopia is created...'(Roberts 1989: 193) The scientific evidence, particularly regarding human-environment interactions, is also biased in other ways as explained in Chapter 5.

From all the pieces of the puzzle, hypotheses and theories have emerged to put the archaeological and historical findings and facts about past societies into a more universal, abstract perspective. They are buildings blocks towards a more comprehensive and satisfactory theory of socio-natural systems – this has not been constructed yet and possibly never will. It is worthwhile inspecting the building blocks, some of which come from the natural sciences and some from the social sciences. The hypotheses and theories often start off in a qualitative, descriptive form. In a next stage, attempts appear to mould them into the language of the natural sciences, mathematics. A system boundary is defined, relevant system elements are identified and models are constructed to explore dynamic interactions between these elements. The models, in turn, can serve as heuristic tools in further investigations. In this chapter and following up on what was said in Chapter 5, we first illustrate how models may help us to ask the right questions, sharpen controversial issues and deepen understanding. Next, we explore several theories about social complexity and human interaction with the – increasingly human-shaped – environment. We end with an attempt at integration from two recent contributions from social and ecological science: Cultural Theory and ecocycles.

8.2. Modelling the Neolithic transition: a global dynamic model

In Chapters 3 and 4 we gave an overview of scientific narratives about how early Holocene human populations may have made the transition from hunter-gatherers to agriculturalists in the face of environmental opportunities, threats and changes. In a recent paper, Wirtz and Lemmen (2002) describe the building of a dynamic model simulating this transition for populations around the globe. It is highly instructive to have a closer look at this model as it attempts to put many of the pieces of the puzzle into a theoretical frame with great heuristic value. In this sense it tries to mediate between the many descriptions selectively unfolded in this book – and often dedicated to individual communities – and the more general theories. The next section gives an account of how this modelling attempt structures and couples the space and time dimensions of human-environment interaction.

8.2.1. Spatial dimension: recovering effective projections of the environment

The model starts with the construction of a world map of 196 land units or regions, constituted from 0.5 x 0.5 degree grid cells and each comprising about 10^5 to 10^6 km^2. For each of them, the potential to provide hunting-gathering and agricultural subsistence is estimated from environmental conditions that are supposed to be inherent to the mid-Holocene distribution of vegetation types. The latter are to that end projected onto two quantitative biogeographic characteristics: the net primary productivity (NPP, see Chapter 5) and a temperature limitation index that is zero at permafrost conditions and unity in warm climates. Their values should not be taken literally since they serve as a bridge to two other indicators acting much more directly on the Neolithic transformation. First, the local natural food extraction potential (FEP, see Chapter 5) becomes a linear function of the temperature limitation index and a parabolic function of NPP, reflecting the low caloric return achievable in marginal ecozones as well as the notion that the amount of unusable biomass increases when going from temperate zones to the tropics. Secondly and akin to the Boserup stages discussed in Chapters 4 and 5, each regional NPP is transformed to the number of locally available agricultural strategies. This quantified agricultural potential represents the natural occurrence of domesticable plant and animal species in a habitat and, thus, peaks in open woodlands while approaching zero at either marginal (low NPP) or too densely forested (high NPP) ecozones. In order to obtain a more realistic estimate, the calculated diversity in domesticables/agricultures, however, has to be further processed to account for faunal and floral differences between continents: if the local agricultural potential weighted by the region area is integrated over each landmass separately, a set of continent-specific overall potentials emerges. Each of these overall values is then multiplied by the regional numbers of agricultural diversity on that same continent. The outcome of the projection of vegetation types and subsequent transformations is represented in *Figure 8.1* (see p. 305).

It is intriguing to inspect the distribution of agricultural potential since it carries some essential spatial gradients visible in world prehistory and even modern times. Except for the Yangtze He river basin in China, all Neolithic hot spots are already roughly confined. As these can be connected to later early civilizations, subtle links between biogeography and state formation emerge. Regarding the prevalence of centres, we observe a subdivision in three distinct suitability classes: the huge Eurasian landmass, the Americas and sub-Saharan Africa and a group of large islands and small continents.

8.2.2.   *Time dimension: socio-economic and technological evolution*

Using the maps of NPP, FEP and agricultural strategies, a dynamic model is constructed to simulate the evolution and spread of population characteristics. The kernel of this dynamic model part is constituted by an array of four state variables covering main aspects of human exploitation of natural resources in prehistory. These are: (i) the relative effort put into agricultural food production with respect to foraging; (ii) the fraction of realized agricultural strategies relative to the habitat-specific potential; (iii) the degree of subsistence effectiveness reflecting the application of technological and organizational innovations; and (iv) the population density. Population growth is supposed to be a linear function of the FEP and the temperature limitation index and also depends on all four state variables, in particular those capturing the multidimensional macro-economic and technological development (i)-(iii). Modification by secondary effects of technology, overexploitation of resources and crowding are mathematically integrated.

Through the sum of all dependencies the 'carrying capacity' of a human population (sf. Chapters 4 and 5) becomes highly variable in space and time, affected both by exogenous and endogenous factors. The intrinsic dynamics of a developing community are represented by variations in the effective variables (i-iii). Deterministic rules for their propagation with time are found by means of analogues, with adaptation being the keyword. In the present context, adaptation is described with a set of differential equations

---

The microbial analogue   While anthropologists have long been familiar with the comparative approach in the context of past and present foragers (cf. Section 4.4.2), Wirtz and Lemmen (2002) stress an analogue much more beyond the obvious. They assert that past hunter-gatherer populations do not behave differently to microbial cultures or higher plant organisms when exposed to changing environmental conditions. As a consequence, the same equations used and tested for species such as *Escherichia coli* or *Fagus sylvatica* should apply to actions of *Homo sapiens*. But can a modelling attempt guided by an uneven isomorphism mean anything more than just a naive undertaking?

The central keyword in this debate is again adaptation. On a phenomenological level of description, adaptation by behavioural optimization defines a universal interaction mechanism of living systems. In Section 8.5 we will briefly meet the frame of complex adaptive systems as an alternative modelling approach assuming optimal self-control of human behaviour in confrontation with new challenges – applied to human as well as non-human organisms. It can be shown on pages of endless, complicated calculations that the modelling method used here represents an aggregated version of a complex adaptive systems, with effective variables defined as ensemble averaged traits of adaptively behaving agents.

One of the major opportunities arising from the exclusive dependence on growth rate differentials lies in the disentanglement from the population pressure theory. Most anthropologists working on the Neolithic transition favour the hypothesis that intensification resulted from a mere people 'overhead' after a change from feast to famine conditions, and their hunger for new calorie sources (see Section 4.4.2). However, in analogous situations, ubiquitous species such as *Escherichia coli* also have to adapt, and do so independently from their population density. Density as such or overpopulation stress is no prime mover for the invention of intensification strategies in many natural systems. Up to now no evidence for the 'overhead' theory can be given. Evidently, there is more to work out here.

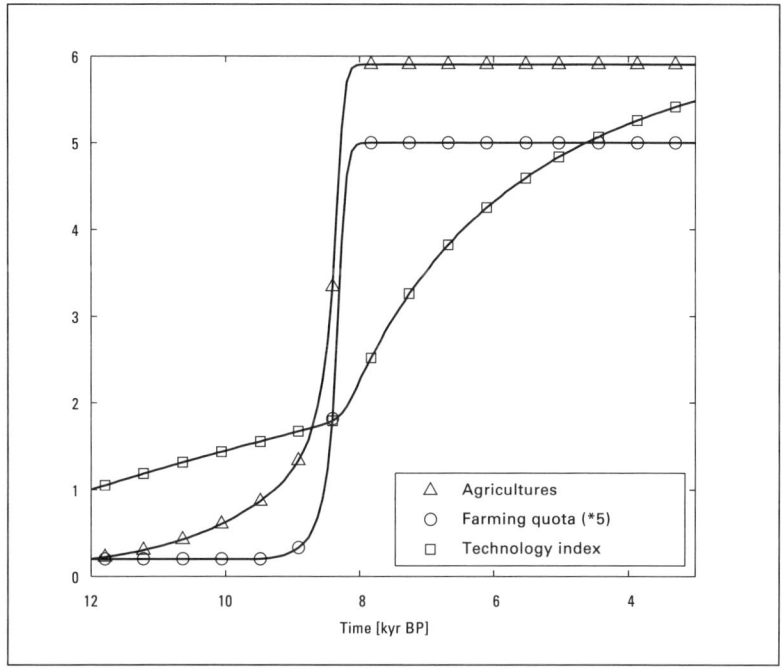

FIGURE 8.2

Model projection for the number of agricultures, the farming quota and the technology index for a generic region with favourable conditions for agriculture (variables have no physical units, see text for definitions). The effects of changing climate or exchange with other regions are excluded in this simulation so that the apparent state transition at 9000-8500 yr BP is entirely endogenous.

expressing the change in the effective variables (i)-(iii) in terms of the degree with which the population density growth rate changes with a change in each of these effective variables. This formulation mimics the dynamic response behaviour that under certain circumstances leads to the transition to more intense food procurement strategies.

The differential equations of the model split the transition into three phases, each built on another. A proto-type result of their numerical integration is shown in *Figure 8.2*. Overall simulated development in the first stage proceeds slowly, at the scale of several millennia and corresponding to the 'slow birth of agriculture' recently recovered by some archaeobotanists (Smith 2001; Pringle 1998). The main dynamics in this phase is the continuous addition of new agricultural practices. As soon as a critical number of production methods are brought under control by the local community, a new attractor – in a mathematical sense – in the system emerges and the second phase can be launched. Within a few centuries the relative effort allocated to these new subsistence methods rises rapidly until their exploitation reaches natural limits. At this point, the transition is completed if the community lives in an isolated habitat. Only the combined technological-organizational effectiveness index continues to increase at a higher rate, levelling off after a number of millennia due to the pay-offs of maintaining higher technologies and diversification of labour. These pay-offs characterize the appearance of limits to further development – or organizational down-regulation – and are the major objects of study in the non-mathematical frameworks of this chapter.

8.2.3. *Integrating space and time: agrarianization, migration and climate change*

This mathematically explicit modelling frame offers several benefits, following from the compatibility with the world-wide habitat characterization as visualized in *Figure 8.1*. The dynamics projected for an exemplary region in *Figure 8.2* can be run under the boundary conditions varying within and between world regions, leading to a mosaic of different development velocities. The main differentiation occurs in the first domestication phase, since habitats with lower agricultural potential need many more millennia to reach the critical value for full transition compared with the suitable kernels which all reside on the Eurasian continent. More generally, the more domesticables there are the faster a region's integration into the human food economy proceeds. The environment yields opportunities which, in turn, determine the intensity of human innovation. This simple rule put forward by the model may explain the significant differences in the onset of full-scale farming between the Americas and Eurasia despite the success of early Holocene domestication on both continents. The dramatic consequences of the lag for the American Indians for several millennia are vividly recounted in Diamond (1997).

Secondly, the spatially explicit nature of the approach forms the basis for a key mechanism in human development: long-range spreading. In the model, a set of diffusion equations is applied through which a flux between two adjacent regions is determined from the regions' boundary length and area and the gradient in a kind of 'index of influence'. This index is defined as the product of population density and the technology/organization level. This influence from growth sustaining neighbouring regions is switched off under negative population growth rates in order to emulate crisis-induced outmigration. In any situation, the resulting flux comprises diffusing populations, plant and animal 'materials' and information.

To explore this behaviour we have undertaken simulations with crises in the form of global deteriorations in the FEP due to, for instance, climate change. As a proxy for the Holocene climate variability (cf. Chapter 3) an oscillation of the FEP with a 1200-year period is imposed, which leads to significant oscillations in population densities and migration rates – but not in the effective variables, as explained above. The effect on population density of the main parts of Asia Minor for two different spreading scenarios is illustrated in *Figure 8.3*. In the 'fast spread' simulation the specific migration velocity is a hundred times larger than in the 'slow spread' case. Short-term, crisis-induced migration waves leaving or entering the region are only visible in the first case. This supports the reality of large crisis-induced population movements as discussed in Chapter 6. Notably, massive abandonments even occur at imposed climate optima at 5400 and 4200 yr BP, which indicates a density close to carrying capacity. The irregularity of the waves can be attributed to the complicated interrelations with the surrounding neighbouring regions (for region boundaries see *Figure 8.1*). A further interesting result is that climate change and population growth are out of phase. Resettlement in the depopulated regions starts before favourable conditions have been restored.

The two trajectories in *Figure 8.3* are even more revealing. A comparison of the slow- and fast-spread scenarios pinpoints the relevance of long-range transport for the local

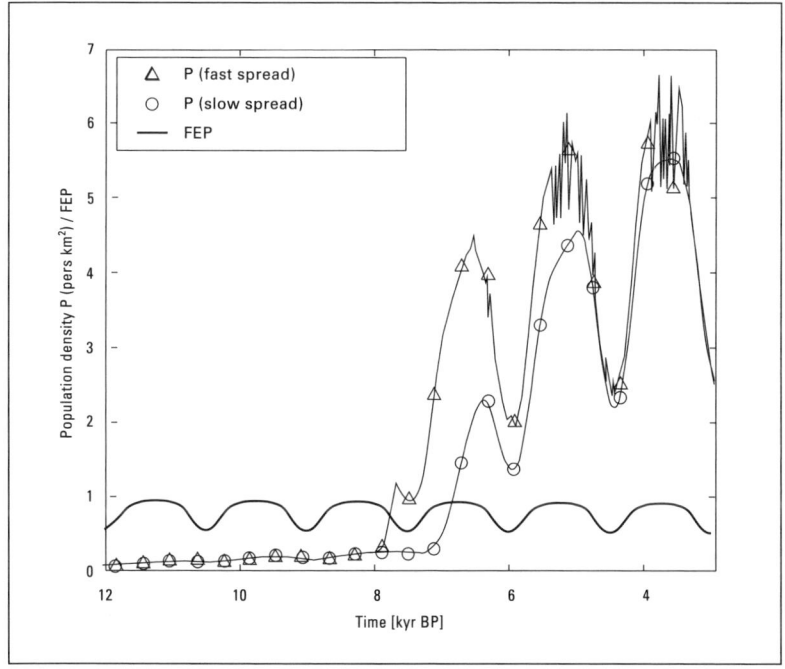

FIGURE 8.3

Fluctuations in population density triggered by varying FEP and subsequent migration events. Simulation results as shown for Asia Minor are obtained with two different values of the specific exchange coefficient, one describing a scenario of fast and the other of slow overall spreading.

development, as in the first case the transition to agriculture accompanied by a step increase in population density lags behind the second case for almost one millennium. For regions more distant from one of the Neolithic centres, the lag interval obviously becomes much greater.

8.2.4. *The computerized emergence of spatio-temporal patterns*

Standard model runs are performed with an intermediate spreading intensity. It is fascinating to follow the resulting global dynamics made visible by a continuous sequence of maps. *Figures 8.4* and *8.5* (see p. 306-307) give a time discrete example for the two model variables: actual agricultures, that is, the actually available agricultural strategies, and population density. The time slices show the where and when of the local Neolithic transitions and their first order effect on the human population, and how agricultural subsistence strategies diffused from the independent centres. In the early Holocene period, nowhere does the population density exceed the level of 0.08 people/km^2, which is characteristic for hunter-gatherer communities. Some 2000-3000 years later, it has increased considerably to a range of 5-10 people/km^2 in several Eurasian regions. Most densities turn out to be reasonable if compared to published estimates. By 3500 yr BP large parts of the Eurasian continent have reached the levels of population density associated with the Boserup stages 4-7. Prominent pioneer areas are North China and Near East/ Mesopotamia, later followed by the western Mediterranean, Central Mexico, two Andes regions and the Pampas. Except for the latter region, and in some respect also the Mediterranean one, the correspondence between these farming kernels and their development timing and current knowledge as surveyed in Chapters 4 and 6 is striking. In addition, the emergence of a corridor around the Silk Road, with dense populations oscillating and migrating between China and Europe, mirrors some of the destiny connected to early nomadic invaders. We can hence speculate that the model might have hit relevant key processes acting on an aggregated level in real prehistory.

Of course, the spatio-temporal patterns could be used as a treasury full of expected and unexpected details, especially in zones where finds are rare. We limit the discussion to two foci that appear naturally when the two maps' potential agricultures (bottom in *Figure 8.1*) and their actual value at 6000 yr BP (*Figure 8.4*) are confronted. Firstly, the Indus valley is missing in the phalanx of farming centres, and even in the list of secondary farming regions, despite its relatively high potential. This phenomenon can be traced back to one mechanism included and one missing in the model. It turned out that the development in the Indus valley suffered more from the neighbourhood than the more fertile but agriculturally more backward forest region to the east. Negative gradients together with lower influence induce a net loss in agricultural advancement. Contrary to the 'normal' case shown above, diffusion can reveal its unpleasant sides. Furthermore, the situation to the west is equally uneven for the valley region as the desert zone acts as a border for agricultural technology and livestock of the Near East. Generally, regions with a low NPP do not sustain significant populations and therefore impede exchange passages. The second part of the explanation is that the mechanism presumably correcting for geographical/demographic land barriers, i.e. seafaring along the coast, is neglected in the model. The second region whose development is restricted by contact with a forest neighbour is the eastern edge of Brazil. The projected absence of Neolithic farming there is in agreement with the lack of archaeological evidence of early domesticates. No overseas transport seems to have existed which could have brought domesticated species or related skills from Meso- and South-American centres, as was the case in the Indus valley.

Obviously many questions need to be raised about this complex model, for instance about model initialization and parameterization. There are still a number of difficulties with the biogeographical maps (*Figure 8.1*) arising from, for instance, the compilation of input maps and the many local uncertainties therein. Nevertheless, filling the gaps of *terra incognita* brings the advantage that many world regions that are sparsely investigated by scientists or for other reasons offer a small amount of finds are now treated the same as prominent zones such as the Mediterranean or the south-west of North America. The outcomes of the model have to be interpreted in the light of the spatio-temporal scales for which it has been constructed. Short-term outbreaks of non-adaptive strategies such as the maintenance of a large urban and associated negative feedback loops on wealth and development are clearly filtered out.

The global dimension of the simulation study should be understood as an extremely hard test of the model's generic nature. Parameters, initial values and evolution equations do not carry site-specific modifications. One question arising from these simulations is whether commonly attested world-wide patterns of human-environment interaction during the Holocene period can be reproduced by means of a deterministic rule system and whether they lose their 'contingency'. No clear answer to both questions is presently ready for presentation, However, the model provides a clear context for raising these questions and reflects the growing possibility of linking theories of the macro-evolution of humanity to models which in turn can be more easily subjected to a critical validation using the increasing amount of archaeological and archaeobotanical fragments. It should be clear that the applicability of global simulation studies as instruments for hypothesis testing is not confined to the model presented here, as the latter may soon open the way to alternative formulations, input data sets or employed mathematical methods.

Finally, these analyses may foster a slight change in our perception: explanations for the spatio-temporal outlook of the Neolithic transition must not rely on external change-triggering factors or contingency arguments. The concluding but still preliminary hypothesis, then, is that the globe offers a highly diverse potential for agricultural practices in the different regions that was exploited by culture-bearing humans in a process of steady innovation and competition between different ways of life.

8.3.   Humans and their environment: a few more modelling exercises

As we hope to have shown in Chapter 5 and the previous section, dynamic models can deepen our insights into how socio-natural systems have evolved. In this section we briefly discuss a few models with the emphasis on the role of human values, habits and rituals, that is, on local micro-dynamics. The first model, Lakeland, illustrates the importance of modelling explicitly human behaviour.[2] The second model investigates population growth dynamics among the !Kung San people in South Africa. The third model discussed is an elaborate simulation of the social organization of the Hohokam peoples in the south-western part of the United States. Evidently, it is only one particular choice from the many modelling efforts currently underway.

8.3.1.   *Lakeland: fishing and mining strategies*

In most models, behaviour is simulated in the form of one aggregate actor described by one or a few differential equations for e.g. resource use. To give a more realistic picture, a more comprehensive actor representation can be used in which people engage in cognitive processes such as social comparison, imitation and repetitive behaviour (habits) (Jager 2000). A small group (16) of individuals – or consumats – is placed in a microworld, Lakeland, consisting of a lake and a gold mine. Lakeland gives access to two natural resources: a fish stock in the lake and a gold mine. The lake is being modelled as a simple ecological system of fish and their food: shrimps. Exploiting the gold mine causes water pollution in the lake, which in turn reduces the lake's carrying capacity for fish. The money earnt from gold mining can be spent on fish imports and/or non-fish consumption 'luxury' goods.

The consumats determine how they allocate their time to leisure, fishing and mining. They are equipped with certain abilities for fishing and mining and want to satisfy their four needs: leisure, identity, subsistence and freedom. These needs, which are supposed to play an important role in this case, are selected out of a larger set of needs as described by Max-Neef (1991). The satisfaction of the need for leisure is related to the share of the time spent on leisure. The need for identity is satisfied by the relative amount of money the consumat owns in comparison to consumats with similar abilities. The need for subsistence relates to the consumption of food, i.e. fish. The need for freedom is assumed to be related to the absolute amount of money the consumat owns, which can be spent on whatever assets the consumat prefers. A multi-agent simulation program has been developed to study how the micro-level processes affect macro-level outcomes.

All consumats have to satisfy their personal needs by fishing and/or mining, whereby they find themselves in a common dilemma facing the risk of resource depletion. They can choose different strategies which have been identified on the basis of psychological theory. Depending on the desired level of need satisfaction and behavioural control – which is linked to (un)certainty – of the consumats, they follow different cognitive processes: deliberation (reasoned, individual), social comparison (reasoned, socially determined), repetition (automated, individual) and imitation (automated, socially determined). If their performance falls below expectation – as recorded in a mental map with memory – agents will switch strategy. Two archetypical consumats have been created: *Homo economicus* and *Homo psychologicus*, to study the effects of various assumptions. The former tends to favour deliberation as he or she operates with high levels of need satisfaction and uncertainty reduction, whereas the latter tends to be quickly satisfied and uncertain which induces imitative behaviour.

One finding is that *Homo psychologicus* makes a very different transition from a fishing society to a mining society than *Homo economicus,* who could engage only in the 'standard' mode of rational deliberation. The introduction of mining means less time spent on fishing. Because *Homo psychologicus* spends less time fishing than *Homo economicus,* the latter depletes the fish stock to a greater extent. Yet *Homo psychologicus* depletes the fish stock at a higher rate than before the mining option was there. A major reason for this is that the slow but persistent move towards mining causes water pollution, which in turn negatively affects the fish stock by causing it to decrease *(Figure 8.6).* This further accelerates the transition to mining as the fish catch per hour keep decreasing. This in turn leads to a different resource exploitation pattern (fish population, gold depletion, water pollution). A second finding is that the population and resource use trajectory over time depends on the diversity in agents' abilities: for *Homo economicus* it leads on average to a decrease in time spent working, as opposed to an increase for *Homo psychologicus.* This result suggests the importance of a sophisticated understanding of peoples' motives and habits in exploiting environmental resources. In another experiment, it is assumed that deliberation leads to fish-catching innovations and that mining is not possible. Not surprisingly, the fish resource is more rapidly overexploited. However, the lower level of satisfaction and the more rapid diffusion through social comparison processes in a *Homo economicus* population causes a much faster collapse than in a *Homo psychologicus* community, where people are basically content and stuck in repetitive behaviour for a while without noticing the innovation *(Figure 8.7).* This underlines the ambivalence of technological progress in issues of (un)sustainable patterns of resource use; it also suggests a possible dynamic in the confrontation of relatively advanced societies with traditional ones: living a satisfied life and having a low-risk alertness makes populations easy prey for more capable groups.

A more general conclusion is that the incorporation of a micro-level perspective on

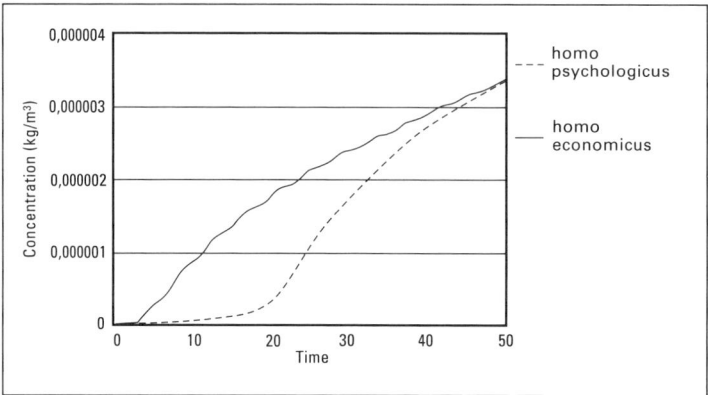

FIGURE 8.6

Pollutant concentration in the lake for both conditions for t = 1 to t = 50. The slower shift of Homo psychologicus to mining causes a slower rate of pollution than for Homo economicus (Jager 2000).

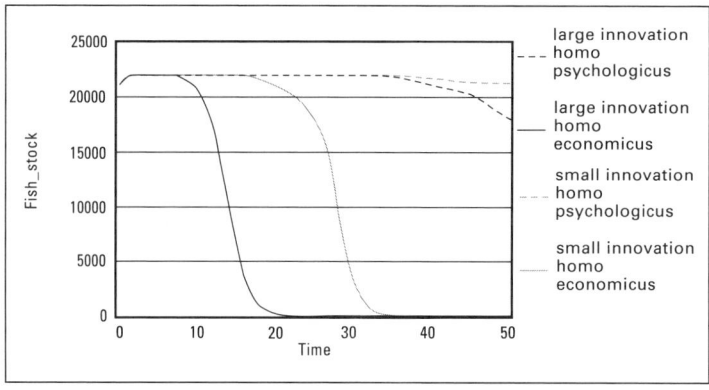

FIGURE 8.7

Fish stocks in the lake under conditions of small and large technological innovations. Innovation, particularly for Homo economicus, accelerates fish stock depletion (Jager 2000).

human behaviour within integrated population-resource-environment models can contribute to a better understanding of micro-level dynamics and hence to more adequate top-down representations. In the present context, the Lakeland simulations suggest that the value orientation ascribed to human beings in their interaction with the environment and with each other may significantly affect the outcome. This makes it an urgent need to collect existing controversial interpretations about peoples' motives and means and incorporate them more explicitly in population-environment models.

8.3.2.   *Population growth among the !Kung San*

Another approach to understanding elementary aspects of the interaction between humans and their environment is the simple population-resource model by Dwight Read (Read 1998). Three models to simulate population growth in hunter-gatherer communities, in particular the !Kung San in South Africa, are described. Such populations are limited by resource availability as the resource base is assumed to be fixed regardless of the intensity of foraging and hunting. The first model (Model 1) is built around the 'textbook' logistic growth equation (cf. Section 5.2.2), which assumes a population density-dependent fertility rate. In such a description of a human population, each individual is characterized by the same parameter values and the mechanism by which women adjust the fertility rate is implicit – hence such a model 'explains' nothing. Read therefore explores two adjustments, based on a minimum specification of !Kung San women's behaviour: (i) they want as many children as possible, and (ii) they are concerned for the well-being of their family and act accordingly in deciding how much time and energy to spend on children and how much on family-support related activities.

The first model adjustment (Model 2) makes the fertility rate dependent on the energy expenditure of a !Kung San woman; if this exceeds a threshold value, the fertility rate drops to zero. The energy expenditure is assumed to be linear in the number of children below a certain threshold age and in the population size. Model 3 is similar to Model 2 but the threshold age – and hence energy expenditure – is assumed to increase with population size, which stimulates birth spacing under scarcity. It thus takes into consideration what ethnographers found about !Kung San women: that they did not want additional children unless they could care for them properly and that birth spacing decreased with lower resource procurement efforts.

A series of simulations was run using an initial cohort of 80 adults. Some ageing, kinship and stochastic aspects are also included. Whereas the logistic model shows a fluctuating population growing toward the carrying capacity, Model 2 generates a crash-and-boom peridiodicity in the population size for a low energy expenditure per child – a pattern that may have characterized the Netsilik Eskimo with periodic starvation from unexpected and substantial changes in their resource base. If the energy expenditure per child is given a high value, that is, if women are assumed to take into account the time and energy requirements for caring for offspring, there is still boom-and-bust behaviour but of a much lower amplitude (*Figure 8.8a*). In Model 3, a woman's decision on how to allocate her energy between the well-being of the family – searching for food etc. – and the desire for (more) children is further tilted towards the former. This results in an even more adequate tracking of population size and resource adequacy, resulting in a further stabilization (*Figure 8.8b*).[3]

269

Model 2b: Threshold Fertility
(r = r$_0$ if E < T, O otherwise; T = 16, Wt = 3)

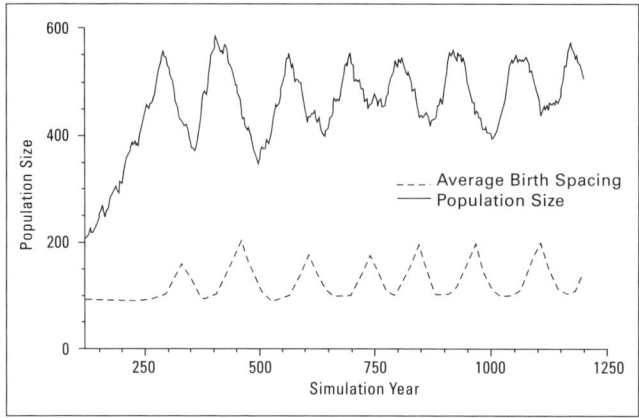

FIGURE 8.8A

Typical population growth trajectories for a !Kung San tribe as simulated for an initial population of 80 adults, a constant threshold age and a simulation period of 1200 years (Read 1998)

Model 3: Birth Spacing

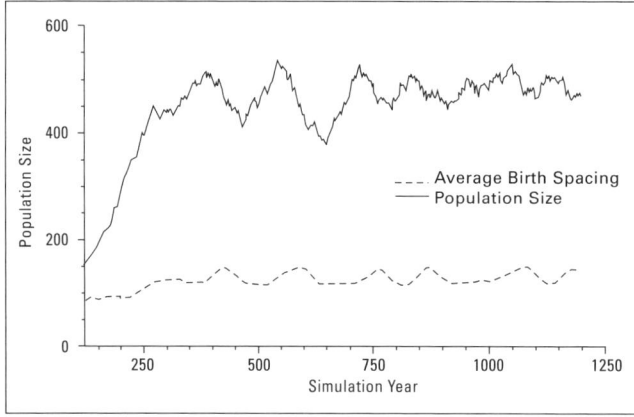

FIGURE 8.8B

As Figure 8.8a but with a threshold age – and hence energy expenditure – increasing with population size, which stimulates birth spacing under scarcity (Read 1998)

In the present context a few interesting observations can be made. Firstly, it is of great importance for population dynamics whether females place high priority on the well-being of the family or instead focus on their desire for more children. Birth spacing is an

The blessings of scarcity? These modelling exercises can also assist in interpreting archaeological finds, for instance with regard to the relationship between resource abundance and culture. In populations in the resource-rich Murry and Darling River valleys in Australia, Harris lines have been found in human bones indicating food shortages. As these are not found in the bone remains of populations in the dry interior lands, they indicate that populations in resource-abundant areas live closer to the carrying capacity than in resource-poor environments. The !Kung San model experiments indicate that a foraging group in a low-density resource region is less at risk than one in a high-density resource region, because women will make decisions to increase the spacing of offspring much sooner under low-density conditions than would be predicted from the change in resource density alone. Why would they do so? As the resource density decreases, the travel and search times required per forager for resource procurement increase more rapidly than would be expected from the decrease in resource density alone. Groups in high-density resource regions will probably be much nearer the carrying capacity – expanding their catchment region is then one possible response. This is the substance of a myth in system dynamics terms: a population is lucky enough to be borne in Paradise, erodes its sources of wealth and, as a consequence, has to expand and develop the tools and tactics of war – Paradise Lost.

important control option, unlike the time spent on procuring resources. In this way, culturally mediated individual behaviour gives depth to a model and brings us from a descriptive model – such as logistic growth – to a model with explanatory power.

8.3.3. What happened to the North American Pueblo Indians in the period 900-1300 AD?

What were the causes and consequences of the contraction of community territories noted for the Pueblo III period in the Mesa Verde region in the final 400 years of pre-Hispanic agricultural society in the Mesa Verde region? (Kohler 2000a). There are clear signs of climate change during this period (900-1300 AD), stress showing up as less protein, possibly cannibalism, receding dwellings, etc. 'There is obviously much that we still don't know about major classic questions [on the Pueblo Indians] but the possibilities are narrowing in tantalizing fashion.'

After a short cold period around 900 AD, the plateau climate and the potential for agricultural production improved. The site distributions suggest a rather high rate of population increase for the period 950-1050 AD (0.5%/yr). People were living in small, dispersed communities of less than 100 individuals. The 50-year period from 1130-1180

AD was very unfavourable for agriculture, and local expressions of the 'Chacoan Phenomenon' – which itself is to the south of this area – disappeared. By the end of the 11th century, the climate became colder again – the potential for maize production was low and population growth was slow – about 0.3%/yr following negative growth in the mid-12th century. With the exception of a few decades in the late 12th century, potential agricultural productivity on the plateau was low and became worse. The region gradually became depopulated and an increasing fraction of the people lived in larger settlements of up to 400 individuals. It is possible that people's farming methods became less efficient because of reduced fallows, greater distances to fields, larger investments in water-harvesting technologies or all three. Hunting increasingly yielded lower-ranked game, suggesting protein shortages.

By 1250 AD a period with changing precipitation patterns set in which added to the already existing uncertainties in food supply. Ever more people lived in large sites, many of them now being in canyon environments. The scarcity of big game may explain the large role of turkey in the diet – although it may also reflect the high value of feathers for rituals. The deteriorating quality of life shows up in low survival rates (41-57% above the age of 20), high incidences of infant mortality and disease and a decline in the status of women and children. The men were probably better fed because they went on long-distance hunts necessitated by local depletion; the hunts were increasingly associated with ritual even as they became decreasingly successful. The people increasingly became inwardly focused in this last stage and may have filtered out real-world data signals in order to retain social coherence. The social logic may have become out-of-step with environmental opportunity – maladaptation. Alternatively, or simultaneously, the threats from other Puebloan or non-Puebloan peoples may have led to increased warfare.

These patterns are all reconstructed from archaeological excavation and survey data for this region. Recently, however, there has been an attempt to see the extent to which it is possible to construct an agent-based model – in which households are the agents – that generates these same patterns working from the first principles of human adaptation in conjunction with the climatic conditions reconstructed for this period and the subsistence technology that was available. Such first principles of human adaptation are: minimization of energy expenditure, population growth responsive to resource conditions, and the possibility of subsistence intensification. An agent-based model has been constructed, with simulations showing how the settlement configurations changed through time in one instantiation of the model.[4] The problem facing households in this simulation 'film' is simply where to live in order to maintain an acceptable standard of living as farmers when climate conditions are changing, in the ways we believe they did between 900 and 1300 AD (*Figure 8.9*; see p. 308). We can draw tentative conclusions about how well this model works by comparing the site distributions it generates with those known from the archaeological record.

Of the many observations drawn from this preliminary work, one of the most

remarkable is the tendency, known from archaeological records, for the latest occupations to be concentrated in a small portion of the apparently farmable area – based on
the simulation. Although this could be due to an error or omission in reconstructing
potential maize productivity from tree-ring data,[5] it is also possible that some other
cause not included in the model, such as widespread violence, was responsible for this
dramatic contraction.

In general, there appear to be three very important and related roles for models in such
situations. The first is to suggest hypotheses that can be tested by other means. Each run
of the simulation can be viewed as generating a series of testable implications – in this
case for settlement size, location and duration – this should be true if the model underlying the simulation is correct. The second is to examine the effects of varying agent
behaviours, such as the exchange of maize, that are difficult or impossible to view directly in the archaeological record but which ought to have measurable effects on settlement
behaviours that *can* be seen in the records. The next phase of this simulation work, for
example, will examine whether the patterns of aggregation (village formation) seen in
the record can be explained, at least in part, by changes in the amount of maize exchange
among households – which itself should change in response to climatic conditions.

Finally, there is the sense that we get much closer to an explanation of phenomena
such as settlement behaviour when we can generate or 'grow' it, working from a small set
of rules and boundary conditions and acting through low-level agents, than when we
derive statistical, system-level correlations between, for example, agricultural productivity and the density of households. One reason for this could be that we have been tuned
by evolution to understand processes that are presented to us as agents in a disaggregate
form. From this perspective these simulations provide a 'crutch for our imagination' and
help us to predict the long-term consequences of processes that operate over long periods of time, large areas and have complicated boundary conditions – such as changing
climates.

8.4.   Social science perspectives on state formation and environment

> Complex societies, it must be emphasized again, are recent in human history. Col-
> lapse then is not a fall to some primordial chaos, but a return to the normal human
> condition.
>
> *Tainter 1988: 198*

After this discussion on simulation models of socio-natural systems, it is time to have a
look at some more qualitative 'pre-modelling' notions and approaches of complex socio-
natural systems. In previous chapters it has been argued that the increase of social complexity in various places and times was both a consequence of and a reason for a more

intricate relationship between human populations and their environment. Populations and in their wake the use of resources expanded and intensified. Resource procurement and management strategies became more elaborate as reflected in more stratified and specialized societies and more sophisticated worldviews and rituals. The emergence of states and empires as well as other forms has been extensively studied as an important and conspicuous phenomenon in this evolutionary path.

Within the social sciences, several theories have been proposed to gain a fuller understanding of the rise and fall of complex societies and, in particular, states. According to Tainter (1988) there are two main schools of thought about state emergence. The first is the conflict school, which asserts that the state emerged out of the needs and desires of individuals and subgroups of a society. Governing institutions are essentially coercive mechanisms to resolve intra-societal conflicts arising out of economic stratification. They exist to maintain the privileged position of a ruling class. Historically, this interpretation is associated with the Marxist view, amongst others. The second school – integrationist or functionalist – argues that complexity in all its manifestations of intensification, specialization and stratification arose out of the needs of society. Governing institutions, in this view, came into existence to centralize, co-ordinate and direct disparate parts of complex societies in response to stresses.

Is the evolution from simple, tribal to complex societies a one-way evolution or are the cycles of rise and fall most characteristic? Surely complex societies were preceded by tribal societies in which

> Leadership ... tends to be minimal. It is personal and charismatic ... Hierarchical control is not institutionalised ... Equality ... lies in direct, individual access to the resources that sustain life, in mobility and the option to simply withdraw from an untenable social situation, and in conventions that prevent economic accumulation and impose sharing ... Personal ambition is either restrained from expression, or channelled to fulfil a public good ... (Tainter 1988: 24-25)

Evidently, tribal society imbues the low-level enclaves with egalitarian tendencies. The conflict school interpretation is recognized as an often pejorative description of how these human groups lost their innocence – Paradise Lost – to either the rationalized authority of priests and kings or the greed of and exploitation by a merchant class (cf. Section 4.4.2). The institutionalist school, on the other hand, tends to see the move to hierarchy as an inevitable event collateral to the increasingly complex challenges and achievements of populations – an irreversible, one-way process. Most large-scale 'successful' civilizations did indeed follow the path towards integration into larger systems, but many of them fell apart into smaller clusters – the 'fringes of empire' discussed in Section 6.5.

In the decline of the larger, more integrated systems, the characteristics of and changes in the natural environment played an important role – but equally important was the societal response. How much information was available on the environment, how much could it process, how was it interpreted and valued and how much capacity for novel, adaptive responses and structural transformation was at its disposal? It is interesting to look at the ideas of environmental historians such as Blanton (1993) and

---

Complexity, risk and social memory   Some environmental archaeologists and historians assign an important role for the features of the local landscape, focusing on ecological diversity and the management of risk (cf. Section 4.4). As populations occupied larger territories and did so more intensely, they became more vulnerable to large-scale environmental change. It became more difficult to develop an adequate representation of what was going on – enhancing the possibility of mismanagement. Long-term large risks replaced short-term risks, the latter being more easily memorized, controlled and/or adjusted because of their higher frequency and locality.

Examples have been given in previous chapters. Another telling example is from a well-researched situation in southern France (cf. Section 7.4): 'The central focus of the roman history of the Tricastin plain seems to have been water management. The system which the Romans conceived and implemented... relied heavily on artificial drainage... But before settlement of the whole area could be completed... the changes in natural circumstances increased pressure on manpower and investments, so as to maintain control over the land. At that point, the colonization ran out of steam, so that there were not enough colonists to keep the drains open over the whole area.' (Leeuw 1998: 10) Similar events happened in later periods of colonization (cf. Chapters 9 and 10).

An interesting question in this context is what role social – or collective – memory plays. Having a large 'social memory' is not always good for being adaptive because it may obstruct the acquisition of new, better fitting interpretations. There is a trade-off between adaptative capability to, for instance, new climates/habitat conditions on the one hand and culturally imprinted response options on the other. In addition to the above example, other examples are given in this chapter. The Anasazi exodus out of the Long House valley mentioned in the previous section was triggered by severe droughts, but ultimately seems to have been motivated by endogenous, cultural determinants – as it appears that occupation of the valley at lower densities remained as a realistic alternative option. The Christian symbolic – and organizational – system created fatal barriers for a more adapted foraging strategy among the mediaeval Norse settlers on Greenland, a story narrated in the next section. Such 'stiffness' of human adaptation might be incorporated in models with a cost function accounting for the energy required to re-establish and inherit knowledge from one generation to the other. Such cost take the form of (attachment to) sunk-cost investments, vested interests of urban administrations and the like.

Renfrew (1985) for whom the natural environment plays a prominent role in the description and explanation of societal evolution. The state is said to exist in societies which are territorially organized, have two or more social strata, an administrative apparatus and revenues from tribute and taxes. Mythical and legendary charters and war and terrorism were among the methods by which states enforced legitimacy, displayed power and exerted control. As we saw in Chapter 6, these 'traditional' states emerged all over the world under a variety of environmental conditions, in some cases to become empires. They were of limited size, had relatively modest bureaucracies and rather weak transport and communication channels. Which factors prevented their further expansion or led to their decline? One, for sure, was negative economies of scale: upon expansion states are confronted with the increasing size and complexity of their institutions. This, in combination with the environmental features such as the existence or absence of natural barriers, may explain why in certain periods and places larger states did not evolve or declined.

Many other theories have been put forward to explain the decline and collapse of hierarchist states and empire, as Chapters 6 and 7 have shown. After a careful investigation of a series of historical cases and explanatory theories, Tainter concludes in his book *The Collapse of Complex Societies* (1988) that, with the exception of mystical explanations, none of the explanations of collapse fails entirely. Cessation or change in access to vital resources, natural catastrophes, social conflicts or malfunctioning, confrontation with other societies or intruders, economic factors have all happened and contributed to collapse. In Tainter's opinion, the economically oriented notion of declining rate of return on increasing complexity is the most general and satisfactory framework. His analysis of the collapse of the Roman Empire, the Mayan civilization and the Chacoan society in north-western New Mexico give a novel and enlightening perspective.[6]

Human societies, it is argued, are problem solvers requiring energy for their maintenance and therefore need increasing investments for information processing and socio-political control. Such investments in 'complexity' have initially positive returns: economic productivity rises, administrations become more efficient and knowledge levels increase. However, beyond a certain point investments face declining or even negative returns, as the empirical data and Boserup's development theory indicate for farming: less and less output per additional hour of labour – although not per hectare. As rulers have to legitimize their power and urban mobs have to be appeased with 'bread and circuses', a larger part of society's resource base goes into maintaining the status quo. At some point, a further increase in complexity not only becomes less effective but also less attractive as a problem-solving strategy. Resilience declines and 'ultimately, the society either disintegrates as localized entities break away, or is so weakened that it is toppled militarily, often with very little resistance. In either case, socio-political organization is reduced to the level that can be sustained by local resources.' (Tainter 1988: 122). Collapse is not a necessity – technological or social innovations or new energy resources may prolong a society's survival.

Whenever centralized state power faded away or became ineffective, competing organizational forms could evolve, such as market institutions and communal regimes. Well-developed exchange systems, markets being one of them, can supply a broad range of goods and services at a variety of locations, volumes and prices. Markets tend to be horizontally integrated; their territories overlap and suppliers and consumers easily cross boundaries. In contrast, state territories and administrative districts are non-overlapping and exclusive. Strong states will exert vertical control by installing trade monopolies, employing or outlawing guilds and the like. The interaction between these two forms of societal organization, for instance when state decay leads to innovations and revitalization of market institutions, is an important aspect of the human-environment dynamics (Blanton 1993). Market institutions are also vulnerable: the basic rules have to be enforced by an overarching agreement or power and their institutionalized greed may cause everlasting struggle and conflict. In periods of decline and disorder, neither state nor market institutions were viable. Politically or religiously inspired leaders, tribalism, anarchic banditry or a combination of all these took over in the scattered remains. Sometimes, in the midst of it, peoples successfully designed and sustained their own local institutions (cf. Section 6.5).

8.5. Perspectives on states and environment: insights into system dynamics

> … if in a society dominant trends can be observed tending in a certain direction, we are always well advised to look for countervailing trends as well, pulling people in other directions, and to inquire why the countervailing trends were outweighed by the trends that turned out to be dominant.
>
> *Goudsblom 1996: 54*

As the previous section shows, a variety of explanations for the emergence and decline of socio-cultural complexity have been given. In some the role of and effect upon the natural environment is thought to have been important. However, in-depth thinking from a systems dynamics perspective about these issues is less abundant. In this section we briefly inspect some explorations from such a systems perspective. Doing justice to the rich and expanding literature on the subject is beyond the scope of this book.

8.5.1. *About processes, mechanisms and pathologies*

Since the advent of systems theory, there have been attempts to understand the emergence of socio-political and cultural complexity in terms of system dynamics. An early and influential contribution has been made by Flannery (1972). In discussing the various 'prime movers' proposed to explain the evolution towards states – irrigation, warfare, population growth/pressure, trade – he advocates the view that rather than a 'prime mover' there is a series of system variables with complex inter-relationships and feedback loops. The important role of information exchange and processing is emphasized: 'One of the main trends in the evolution of bands into tribes, chiefdoms, and states must be a gradual increase in capacity for information processing, storage, and analysis.' (Flannery 1972: 411). In his rudimentary theory, he suggests two processes, two evolutionary mechanisms and three pathologies that could qualify as universal. The driving processes are increasing differentiation and specialization of subsystems (segregation) and increasing linkages between the subsystems and the highest-order controls (centralization). The mechanisms are:

– *promotion*: a special-purpose institution rises in the hierarchy to a higher level, becoming a general-purpose institution. For instance, military institutions often seized power in this way; and
– *linearization*: lower-order controls in the system are repeatedly or permanently bypassed by higher-order controls. An example is when local irrigation is increasingly regulated by a higher-level institution in order to facilitate information exchange and reduce the risk of harvest failure.

Both mechanisms cause transformations in response to socio-environmental stress – and it is not difficult to recognize them from the previous narratives. Institutions may only serve their own interests rather than those of society and bypassing lower-order controls may destroy the resilience of a system – both features well known to hierarchical systems. As a result, there are always pathologies associated with the emergence of civilization, causing further stress which in turn often accelerates the disintegration process:

– *usurpation* occurs when a subsystem's purpose starts to dominate the objectives of the larger system. This is a corollary to the promotion of the military class and is evident, for instance, in periods of the Roman Empire;
– *meddling* is the other way around: higher-level controls take over what ordinarily is best regulated locally. Stifling controls on trade have been proposed as an explanation for the inertia of the Sumerian and Chinese empires;
– too great a degree of subsystem coherence leads to *hypercoherence* which may, in Rappaport's words, be as lethal as too little coherence. Nepotism resulting from marriage alliances between ancient Akkad and Classical Mayan urban centres may have caused such hypercoherence.

This list is not exclusive. The phenomena of hypertrophy and atrophy (Chapter 2) and the difference in pathologies in land-based versus sea-based empires may deserve attention in this respect.

Colonists, Inuit and the church   Danish colonization of Greenland started in 1721 (Marquardt 1999). However, a Norse colony in west Greenland had already been an outpost of Europeans throughout the period 985-1500 AD and the scene of contact between North American hunters and European farmers (McGovern 1981). Excellent conditions for organic preservation and high-quality archaeological research make for an intriguing story about the early Norse settlers and their interaction with the Thule-Inugsuk Inuit peoples. It seems that the Norse community managed quite well for the first 150 years, with a maritime-terrestrial economy with small animal herds, seasonal hunting of walrus, polar bear and seals and occasional trading with Iceland. However, they were living on a knife edge, with great skills being required to survive the long cold winters. There is ample evidence that the Little Ice Age fluctuations in temperature, sea ice conditions and faunal resources put the communities under stress from 1270 AD onwards. Moreover, the southward migration of the Inuit – in response to climate change – and the decline in trading relations with Europe further complicated their subsistence strategies. The western settlements seem to have collapsed rather suddenly around 1350 AD.

In this story, as McGovern convincingly argues, one should not treat the human response to climatic stress as a minor and dependent variable. The Inuit peoples survived these harsh times. The Norse farmers had several options to adapt, for instance orienting themselves more towards the oceanic resources and de-emphasizing pasture and cattle-rearing. They also would have benefited from Inuit practices and technology related to boats, fishing gear and clothing. 'Rather than exploring the possibilities of new technology and searching out alternative resources, Norse society in Greenland seems to have resolutely stuck to its established pattern, elaborating its churches rather than its hunting skills.' (McGovern, 1981: 425) Whence this conservatism and loss of adaptive resilience in the face of rising economic costs and declining returns?

Under the influence of Iceland, the mediaeval church in the Norse communities in Groonland had become more powerful spiritually as well as materially in the 12th century. Between 1125 and 1300 AD, spectacular church construction had taken place, small communities building among the largest stone structures in the Atlantic Islands. Economic, political, religious and ideological authority appear to have come into the hands of a lay and clerical elite. If a society such as this is confronted with increasing fluctuations in resource abundance and use, it has to invest in additional data collection and improve its interpretation of these data in order to survive. This constitutes an overhead cost which is often resisted by the population and has to be enforced by military force or by ideology.

The elite-sponsored expensive elaboration of ceremonial architecture and ritual paraphernalia in Norse Greenland may indicate the successful ideological conditioning of the population. Administrators may not only have declined Inuit superior technology but also have sustained erroneous beliefs – for example that lighting candles had more impact on the spring seal hunt than more and better boats. As stresses mounted, elite groups may have pushed up the necessary overheads in their obsession with conformity and the suppression of dissenters and detached themselves further and further from the phenomenal world, adding Flannery's pathology of hypercoherence to the pathology of auto-mystification. This sounds like the Easter Island narrative. Whether or not this explanation is accepted, the failure of the rulers in the Norse communities in Greenland clearly shows how important the institutions and belief systems of a society are in the face of environmental stress.

8.5.2. *The importance of interactions*

Autonomous political units do not generally exist in isolation, an observation that has led to increasing attention for the role of dynamic interaction among similar and more or less equal units:

> The process of [structural] transformation is frequently brought about not simply as a result of internal processes tending towards intensification, nor in repeated and analogous responses to a single outside stimulus, but as a result of interaction between the [autonomous socio-political units or] peer polities. (Renfrew 1985: 8)

Starting from a given ecological diversity, such structural transformations coincided with the means to increase production beyond the subsistence level and with a large role for exchange systems and, in particular, information exchange. Peer-polity interactions have been proposed as a compromise between pure exogenous and pure endogenous explanations, and there are a number of them to be considered (Renfrew 1985: 8):
- *warfare*, which may intensify both resource use and social stratification – unless catastrophic warfare results in total collapse;
- *competitive emulation*, a process in which polities compete by means of displaying wealth and power, using 'Great Buildings', symbols of deterrence and the like;
- *symbolic entrainment*, not unlike the previous two but now in the realm of symbolic systems where the more-developed one absorbs or influences the less-developed one;
- *transmission of innovation*, during which a specific invention becomes accepted and henceforth imbued with social or religious status;
- *exchange of goods* which are part of the more general process of economic growth with concomitant phenomena such as the rise of a merchant class and specialized skills.

In the present context, the relevance of these socio-political processes that they often

Threat, exchange and integration There have been several attempts to assess human evolution in a broader systems-oriented fashion, for instance by Jantsch and Boulding – these are present-day, 'scientific', cosmologies (Jantsch 1980; Boulding 1978). Like ancient cosmologies they tell a great deal about how present-day people experience the world in all its facets and attempt to give meaning to it. 'The watchword of evolution is interaction, not causation,' says Boulding in his book Ecodynamics (p. 211). He distinguishes three classes of major social organizers: threat, exchange, and integration. The threat system, based on fear, is easily recognized in the narratives on states and empires and has in the past – and the present – led to one of the foremost pathologies in history, the arms race. The second one, exchange and material reward, is based as much on relationships between people as fear. It is the kernel of economic dynamics: (un)employment, accumulation, profits, taxes and prices and its laws – and the misunderstandings about them – have also been a major factor in the rise of social complexity.

Boulding associates the third social organizer with the vast array of other human relationships – love and hate, dominance and subordination, legitimacy and illegitimacy, pity and envy, to mention just a few – and calls them 'the integrative system'. The central concept is an individual's image of his personal identity and the identity of others. Its messengers are symbols, its dynamics the permanent learning processes of socialization or acculturation. In the present context, this most difficult of social organizers gets its relevance from the observation that the legitimacy of any authority ultimately comes from integration and not from the other two systems.

have a large bearing on how environmental resources are used. Warfare has been a perennial phenomenon in the early civilizations in the Middle East and Greece and often led to accelerated deforestation:

> During campaigns, wood foraging parties were sent out. An extreme example was at the siege of Lachish, in 588 BC, by Nebuchadnezzar, King of Babylon. After 2500 years, layers of ash several metres thick still remain, higher than the remains of the fortress walls. The hills for miles around were cleared of trees. The wood was piled outside the walls and fired. Day and night sheets of flame beat against the walls until eventually the white-hot stones burst and the walls caved in. (Thirgood 1981: 58-59)

One consequence was often a decline in population – which somewhat alleviated the pressure on the forests – and an increase in pastoralism as populations sought refuge in the more secure mountainous areas – which could further degrade the environment if intensive grazing occurred. Competitive emulation may have featured in – and exhausted – Megalithic and Meso-American cultures, with Easter Island probably as the example par excellence. Cultural, technological and economic diffusion, exchange and invasion processes have affected almost every civilization in its incipient stages.

8.5.3. Humans and their environment as complex adaptive systems

More recently, the systems approach has gained importance with the availability of theoretical and computer simulation advances leading to the theory of complex adaptive systems. This approach sees behavioural and structural transformations as emerging from the rules of individual system entities – individuals or groups of individuals. Chapter 7 shows how this approach can be applied to understanding the rise and fall of the Roman Empire. Its proponents argue that there has been a tendency in the past to explain the development processes of human societies from an evolutionary framework based on the 'organic analogy' and that this view of a society as a large organism in equilibrium with its environment stemmed from a top-down 'centralized mindset' approach (Lehner 2000). Dissatisfaction with such approaches also originated in the use of analogues from physics and chemistry, positing equilibrium and homogeneity:

> By way of contrast to conventional, equilibrium-based analyses, many [complex systems approaches] emphasize the fact that ecological and human systems are often in transient states, are inherently non-linear, and are metastable; i.e. there are two or more domains of attraction to which the system may converge. Moreover, within these stable domains, the system may fluctuate wildly, but so long as it remains within the boundaries of the domain, it is resilient; it is thus able to persist despite a high degree of disturbance… Importantly, the stability domains themselves may expand, contract or disappear in response to both internal structuring processes or external perturbations. (Leeuw 1998: 11)

Equally important in the study of complex socio-natural systems is to take into account that causes and effects operate at various time- and spatial-scales, each with their own dynamical characteristics. The availability of powerful simulation tools has stimulated a bottom-up approach in which the focus is on individuals with their motives, habits, rules and forms of co-operation and conflict. Such models – also called multi-agent models – are interpreted as 'worlds' that can deepen our understanding of past and present 'real' worlds because they supposedly resemble them in useful respects. They are according to some the best tools we have to study co-evolutionary systems, that is, systems for which traditional one-way cause-and-effect analyses fail. The models based on complex adaptive systems theory were originally conceived as groups of agents engaged in a process in which adaptive moves by individuals have consequences for the group. Under certain circumstances they may exhibit remarkable abilities for self-organization.

Whether these should be interpreted, in the case of human beings, as macro-behaviour without internal hierarchy or as an implicit class structure remains an open question.

One interesting element in socio-natural systems is the role of *surprise*. If external events occur or internal dynamics operate which escape the observation of the agent, there is surprise. These are the periods of environmental and social crises to which agents can respond in a variety of ways: decline, outmigration and concentration in places better suited for survival. In the process, the (group of) agents develop a new mental representation of their environment – a social or collective memory. To learn and evolve a new, more adequate representation of the (same) environment is an important ingredient of a group's resilience and adaptability. We will come back to this in Section 8.6 on cultural dynamics. Another important ingredient is to *make the environment more controllable* by acting upon it. Such action will be associated with as yet unintended consequences that lead to the necessity for subsequent adaptations – which is what makes human history contingent. From these reflections one can posit a sequence of co-evolutionary processes between humans and their environment. Human representations become more complex and the environment becomes at least locally and temporarily more manageable. One may posit the higher fitness of certain representations over others as an evolutionary mechanism (social/individual, genes/ memes). What matters here, too, is the mechanisms and rate of dissipation of the more fit representations. One important element of resilience can now be identified as the ability to sustain – maintain, uphold – and adjust the mental representations and the physical structures upholding its associated regime. As the study of complex adaptive systems is in its infancy, there is a variety of approaches. We will not go into any detail here (Kohler 2000b). We hope the previous chapters and sections have given a flavour of how this approach can come up with new interpretation of the evolution of the socio-natural systems that are the topic of this book. Let us now try to go one step further in the search for synthesis.

8.6. Change and complexity in socio natural systems

8.6.1. Cultural Theory and ecocycles

The 1980s saw an acceleration in interdisciplinary thinking about the relationship between human groups and their natural environment, culminating in books such as *Sustainable Development of the Biosphere* (Clark 1986) and *The Earth as Transformed by Human Action – Global and Regional Changes in the Biosphere over the Past 300 Years* (Turner 1990). One of the interesting results has been the merger of ecological theory and cultural anthropology, leading to the *Cultural Theory* (Thompson 1989). Can these theories from ecology and anthropology be used in our quest for a better understanding of complex societies and their relationship with the environment?

283

Cultural Theory   It is proposed that human beings can be classified according to four worldviews, each associated with a certain way of structuring the relationship between man and nature and between fellow men. According to the societies and individuals involved, this is expressed in quite different judgements about technology, environmental risks and the distribution of prosperity between now and the future and between here and elsewhere.[7] Together these four 'myths' of the world form multiple rationalities. The two axes differentiating the four worldviews are the group axis and the grid axis.

The group axis is associated with the (non)existence of a collective, shared set of values. The grid axis represents the degree of ranking and stratification in a society. The resulting four perspectives are related to their position along these two axes: hierarchist (high on both), individualist (low on both), egalitarian (high in 'group', low in 'grid') and fatalist (low in 'group', high in 'grid').

Needless to say, it should be borne in mind that people seldom express these paradigms in their extreme form – nor should one give in to the temptation to make caricatures. A more controversial question is whether the four worldviews are a mere classification of individuals/groups or, as its proponents claim, archetypical mental reconstructions of how the world functions and hence should be acted upon.

The *Cultural Theory* distinguishes four cultural perspectives, based on the degree to which individuals behave and feel themselves part of a larger group of individuals with whom they share values and beliefs – the 'group' axis – and the extent to which individuals are subjected to role prescriptions within a larger structural entity – the 'grid' axis (*Figure 8.10*). The interpretation of past events and the response to present events are both filtered through the diverse rationalities of each of the four myths – hierarchist, individualist, egalitarian and fatalist – to make their lives liveable. This is illustrated in *Figure 8.10* with a metaphorical landscape in which the position of the ball and the landscape represent the mental map according to which a person interprets and behaves. For the individualist (lower left) the ball rolls in a world of inherent stability and what counts is individual skill and courage. The world is seen as full of opportunities, challenges, and profit; problems are 'challenges', fear paralyses; and humans have enormous capacity for adaptation. For the hierarchist (upper right) the ball may roll over the limits of what is considered to be acceptable, thus threatening social stability which is usually perceived in terms of the status quo. Information and regulation are needed; state laws are enforced by state power. The prevailing rationality is not one of maximizing personal gain, as with the individualist, but administrative and procedural. In Cultural Theory two perspectives on how the world functions are added. One is the egalitarian (lower right) for whom the situation is always precarious: any move of the ball can lead to

284

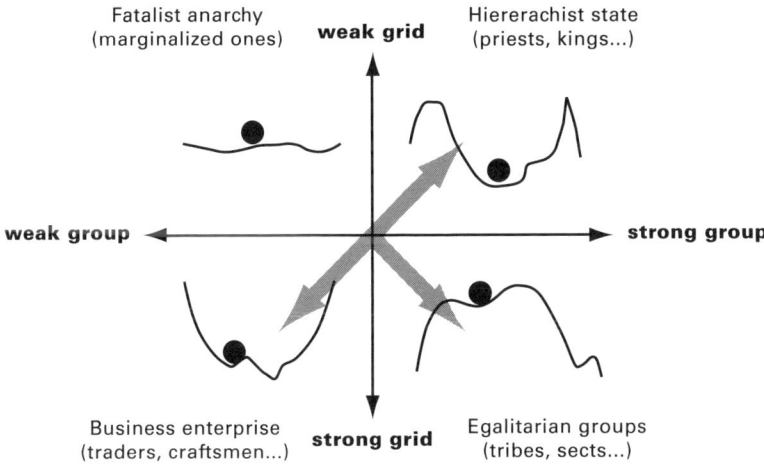

Fatalist anarchy
(marginalized ones)   **weak grid**

Hiererachist state
(priests, kings...)

weak group

strong group

Business enterprise
(traders, craftsmen...)   **strong grid**

Egalitarian groups
(tribes, sects...)

FIGURE 8.10

The four worldviews – or cultural perspectives – proposed in the Cultural Theory

unavoidable catastrophes. The other is the fatalist (upper left) whose social isolation readily comports with the conviction that the situation is beyond control anyway. Both may often have prevailed in a variety of forms in the spatial-temporal 'fringes of empire' discussed in Chapter 6.

Each worldview tends to maintain a related explanation of the world. Whereas the hierarchist places the emphasis on control and expertise in order to guarantee stability within a world of limits, the individualist is convinced that the world has inherent stability and abundance. The egalitarian emphasizes the fragility of nature and the probability of irreversible destruction. The fatalist experiences the world as determined by pure chance. These two constructions of human nature and (the perception of) the natural and human environment mirror the hierarchical state-empires and the market-oriented trade regimes. In the fringes of empire, millions have been living as fatalists whereas egalitarianism is found in political and religious revolt as well as in common property regimes.

These four paradigms interact dynamically and none of them can exist without the other three (*Figure 8.11*). Individuals alter their worldviews when they are no longer reconcilable with their experience – surprise. On the collective level this leads to fluctuations in how events are interpreted and responded to, excessive swings to either side being corrected – although with differing time delays and 'hidden costs'. Such complex institutional arrangements can be recognized in the narratives of emergence and decline in previous chapters. Excessive hierarchism leads to legalism with ever lower marginal

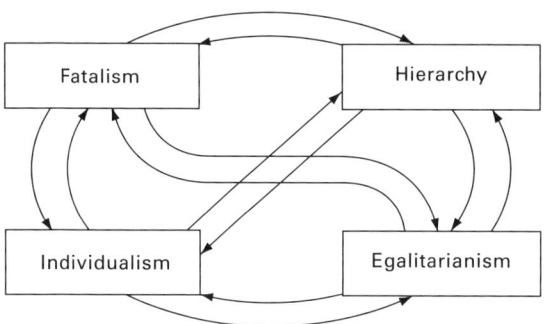

FIGURE 8.11

Transitions between solidarities and their associated transactional realms. Individuals are able to move without causing change. It is when some transactions are shifted from one realm to another that we get change.

returns, containing the seed of decline and eventual disintegration. Extreme individualism ends in perpetuating conflict and marginalization, which feeds the desire for social stability and justice. Egalitarianism, arising from the desire to purify society from extortion and greed, destroys itself in sectarian self-righteousness and religious wars if pur-

---

Mr. López the entrepreneur   There is a story about an entrepreneur that nicely illustrates the interaction in terms of worldviews. One way to sustain an egalitarian regime is with ceremonies in which those who accumulate inordinate amounts of land or other property are compelled to give it away. However, a smart individual can always bypass such a system and create structural change.

In the 1890s Mr. Lopez subverted the old mechanism of wealth levelling in the Mexican village of San Juan Guelavía. Traditionally, only rich people would be designated as major-domo, that is, the one who has to sponsor for the village fiestas and festivals and gains prestige from it. However, with help of the clergy Mr. López forced the village council to designate less wealthy people – who then could not refuse – and offered the insolvent sponsors a loan with their land put up for collateral. By the eve of the Mexican revolution, Mr. López owned most of the community's best land: by 1915 his Big Family owned 92.2% of the arable land and an even larger part of the irrigated land and, with the support of the church, strongly opposed any censure. Thus, equal access to strategic resources had disappeared by the perversion of a ritual regulatory mechanism – an example of the vulnerability of egalitarian co-operative regimes to individualist interference.

---

sued to its extremes. Fatalists are always at the disposal of the other three worldviews, as converts for the egalitarians, as cannon fodder for the hierarchist or as cheap labour for the individualist. *Table 8.1* is an attempt to capture the essence of a particular worldview with regards to nature, people, resources and fairness.

TABLE 8.1   CHARACTERIZATION OF THE FOUR CULTURAL PERSPECTIVES

Worldview:	Individualist	Hierarchist	Egalitarian	Fatalist
Nature is:	benign	perverse/tolerant	ephemeral	capricious
People are:	self-seeking	malleable: deeply flawed but redeemable	caring and sharing	inherently untrustworthy
Resources are:	infinite because they are dependent on human genius	finite and to be managed efficiently based on control and knowledge	finite and to be managed with respect and frugality	what can be grabbed
Fairness is:	who puts in most gets most out	rank-based distribution by trusted, long-lasting institutions	what matters is equality of result, not opportunity	non-existent

Cultural Theory has one of its roots in a theory about the dynamics of ecosystems, developed by Holling and his colleagues (Holling 1986; Gunderson 1997). This should not be too surprising; after all, humans are an integral part of ecosystems. From empirical observations it has been found that ecosystem succession is controlled by two functions: exploitation, in which rapid colonization of recently disturbed areas is emphasized, and conservation, with an emphasis on the slow accumulation and storage of energy and materials. The species in the exploitative phase have been characterized as exploring *r-strategists* and in the conservation phase as consolidating *K-strategists*. The latter live in a climax community, the former in a pioneer community. Revisions in ecological understanding indicate that two additional functions are needed to adequately explain ecological change. One is a stage during which tightly bound biomass and nutrients that have become increasingly susceptible to disturbance – overconnected, in system terms – are released. The resulting debris is then reorganized in a series of soil processes, which makes it available again for a renewed cycle of exploitation. In other words: the complex system becomes compost, which in turn undergoes renewal into low-level energy enclaves, which are the seeds for the rapidly expanding pioneer communities.

Although this 'ecocycle theory' is a simplification of the complex processes in real-world ecosystems, it provides a helpful scheme for thinking about complex system dynamics. For instance, the parallel with economic and political systems is an interesting one. The entrepreneurial market represents the exploitation phase, with innovations, conquests and rapid expansion – on horseback, ship or whatever. Nature is seen as essentially boundless, not unlike some early hunter-gatherer tribes (cf. Chapter 4). With rising expansion, specialization and stratification, an administrative and bureaucratic hierarchy emerges: this is the conservation phase during which states and empires are moulded. Nature or, more adequately, the socially constructed environment has now become part of the conscious worldview and is something to be managed within the confines of past experiences and the resulting insights. The release phase is one of 'creative destruction' – a term borrowed from the economist Schumpeter – and of decline and fall in a

---

Rural-urban landscape dynamics Another fragment of theory suggests an ongoing unification of thinking about complex socio-natural systems. In the ARCHAEOME-DES project (Leeuw 1998) a detailed investigation of land degradation has been conducted in several parts of the Mediterranean. Building on the insights from systems theory, an innovation-communication (or reaction-diffusion) dynamic process is proposed to interpret the changes in rural and urban landscapes. The human component has a few rhythms and a capacity for change through learning. The environmental – or natural – component is a complex composite with links throughout the food webs. In rural situations the relatively fast human processes are tied in to the relatively slow environmental processes: people have adapted to nature and stability is provided by natural diversity. In urban areas all processes have been accelerated and the relation is reversed: the pace is set by the fast processes of human life and stability is linked to value differentiation – or cultural diversity.

These differences are reflected in the corresponding communication structures: hierarchical in small settlements, more distributed heterarchical in towns. The latter have a relatively high connectedness and energy flows and adapt more easily to structural change which in turn accelerates change. In this way multi-nodal adaptive heterarchies can quickly spread along the natural corridors such as valleys, roads and coastal waters. To enhance their stability, they will differentiate along the lines of task and role specialization and local hierarchies emerge in the search for a balance between efficiency and adaptability. If rural areas with a traditional lifestyle are penetrated by urban ideas and ways of life, they can either isolate themselves by barring communication or become urbanized.

historical context. In the subsequent phase of reorganization and restructuring, complex societies decompose into small bands some of whom are absorbed in coping with their own situation – the fatalists – while others start a new cycle by grasping the opportunities that always go along with the threats – the egalitarians and individualists. The dynamics is highly non-linear, consisting of nested cycles, each occurring over its own range of scales and resulting in an ecosystem hierarchy in which each level has its own distinct spatial and temporal attributes. There is also a remarkable similarity between the theory of collapse as induced by the rising marginal cost of complexity as proposed by Tainter (1988) and the ecological and economic notions of increasing instability and subsequent creative destruction of complex hierarchical systems.

8.6.2.   *Complexity in socio-natural systems: the need for requisite variety*

One of the questions posed in this book is whether the pathways towards increasing social complexity are a long progressive march forwards, fluctuate between two alternatives, are essentially cyclical or are even more complex. Cultural Theory and ecocycle-theory encourage us to have an open eye towards 'requisite variety' in human action perspectives. It suggests that peoples did not choose a single trajectory or were forced onto one, but rather have always operated throughout the cycles of rise and fall from multiple worldviews and management strategies. The analogue or metaphor of the ecocycles suggests a 'natural' sequence of state emergence from tribal egalitarian communities, followed by pioneer expansion into a consolidated hierarchist society, and dissolution into shattered remnants either because of external disruptions or internal dysfunctioning or both. At the root of all this is an evolving paradigm about complex non-linear systems which may be essential for a more in-depth understanding of past – and present – human-environment interactions.

The classic assumption, in both ecology and social science, is that there is a one-way transition from state A to state B – say, from a simple (tribal) to a complex (state) society. In ecology, the process of succession (Clements 1916; Odum 1969) ensures that an initially unstructured state of affairs – one huge niche filled with anarchic, opportunistic and competitive organisms (the *r*-strategists) – is steadily transformed into a climax community: a structured and stratified arrangement of diversified niches, with clearly defined inter-relationships between the species (the *K*-strategists) that occupy them. In social science, this predictable, linear and equilibrium-seeking model of change is paralleled by a number of 'grand theories' in which some inexorable logic moves us all from mechanical to organic solidarity (Durkheim 1893); from community to society (Gemeinschaft to Gesellschaft, Tönnies 1887); from traditional to modern (Weber 1958); from status to contract (Maine 1963); from capitalism to communism (Marx 1859/1967); or, as modern theorists of institutions put it, from markets to hierarchies

(Lindblom 1977; Williamson 1975). Different 'masters' may define their As and their Bs differently, but all subscribe to a twofold scheme and to some driving force – such as rationalization (Weber), internal contradiction (Marx), or spiralling transaction costs (Williamson) – that carries the totality from A to B.

These transitions, whether ecological or socio-cultural, are all in the direction of more orderliness, more differentiation, more connectedness and more consistency and, once they have gone as far as they can go in that direction, that is that. In other words, these models of change end up making change impossible. Of course, something on the outside may intervene and mess things up, thereby setting the whole thing in motion once more but, left to themselves, these models get ecosystems and socio-cultural systems from A to B and then stop. Change, these models tell us, is a temporary phenomenon.

There is clearly something less than satisfactory about these models – they explain change by getting rid of it, and they are increasingly incapable of making sense of what is going on – but how can we do better? By understanding Man and Nature as a single but complex system, is our concise but rather opaque answer: an answer we will now try to clarify by looking at the – social and ecological – transactions that sustain a Himalayan village.

8.6.3.   *Cultural dynamics and environmental (mis)management: always learning, never getting it right*

Himalayan villagers parcel out their transactions with their physical environment to four distinct *solidarities* – which we will explain in a moment – each of which is characterized by a distinct *management style*. Agricultural land, for instance, is privately owned whilst grazing land and forests are communally owned. But grazing land and forests do not suffer the 'tragedy of the commons' (Hardin 1968) because transactions in their products are under the control of a *commons managing institution*. Villagers appoint forest guardians, erect a 'social fence' – a declared boundary, not a physical construction – and institute a system of fines for those who allow their animals into the forest when access is forbidden or take structural timber without first obtaining permission. If the offender is also a forest guardian the fine is doubled; if children break the rules their parents have to pay up. There is fragmentary evidence that such regimes have occurred at least since 600 yr BP.

Informal though they may seem, and lacking any legal status, these commons managing arrangements work well in the face-to-face setting of a village and its physical resources. Drawing on their 'home-made' conceptions of the natural processes that are at work – their *ethnoecology* – the forest guardians regulate the use of these common property resources by assessing their state of health, year by year or season by season. In other words, these transactions are regulated within a framework that assumes firstly that you can take only so much from the commons and secondly that you can assess where the line between so much and too much should be drawn. The social construction inherent to this transactional realm is that nature is bountiful within knowable limits. This, to make a link with the ecological theories of Holling (1986), is the myth of *Nature Perverse/Tolerant* (*Table 8.1 and Figure 8.11*).

With agricultural land, however, decisions are entirely in the hands of individual owners and fields, unlike communally owned resources, can quite easily end up belonging to the money lenders. In recent years, when forests and grazing lands have suffered degradation for a variety of reasons, not the 'tragedy of the commons', villagers have responded by shifting some of their transactions from one realm to the other. For instance, they have allowed trees to grow on the banks between their terraced fields, thereby reducing the pressure on the village forest, and they have switched to the stall-feeding of their animals, thereby making more efficient use of the forest and grazing land *and* receiving copious amounts of manure which they can then carry to their fields. In other words, transactions are parcelled out to the management styles that seem appropriate and, if circumstances change, some of those transactions can be switched from one style to another.

Since they are subsistence farmers, whose aim is to remain viable over generations – rather than to make a 'killing' in any one year and then retire to Florida – their transactions within their local environment can be characterized as *low risk, low reward*. However, during those times of the year when there is little farm work to be done, many villagers engage in trading expeditions, or in migrant labour in India. Trading expeditions are family-based and family-financed, and highly speculative: *high risk, high reward*. So a farmer's individualized transactions, when added together over a full year, constitute a nicely spread risk portfolio. The attitude here – and particularly at the high-risk end of the portfolio – is that 'Fortune favours the brave,' 'Who dares wins,' 'There are plenty more fish in the sea'. Opportunities, in other words, are there for the taking. The idea of nature here is optimistic, expansive and non-punitive: *Nature Benign* (*Table 8.1 and Figure 8.11*).

Social scientists in general, and institutional economists in particular, would see these two realms as corresponding to their classic distinction between *hierarchies* and *markets*. They would have no difficulty in explaining the processes by which some transactions are switched this way or that – although they would be surprised to find that the hierarchy was a village level commons managing institution and not the state. But, and this is the essence of the answer we are trying to explain, hierarchies and markets do not exhaust the transactional repertoire of the Himalayan villager. Some collectivized transactions do not involve formal status distinctions – such as those between forest guardians and ordinary villagers – that characterize the *hierarchical* solidarity and some individualized transactions are marked by the absence of bidding and bargaining – an essential characteristic of the markets that are generated by the *individualist* solidarity.

291

The plurality, in other words, is fourfold, *not* twofold (Thompson 1989). Let us observe events in the Himalayas from this perspective.

In many parts of the Himalayas, especially the Indian Himalayas, village autonomy is always under threat because powerful external actors also lay claim to the forest resources that are so vital to Himalayan farming systems. One highly effective response to this external threat is the *Chipko* movement. This is a grassroots and highly *egalitarian* social movement in which women – who are largely responsible both for fodder gathering and fuel wood collection – predominate. *Chipko* means 'to stick', and the Gandhian strategy is to physically hug the trees, thereby preventing them from being appropriated. Those villagers of a slightly less non-violent disposition actually chase the logging contractors – and the government forestry officers who have been corrupted by the contractors – out of the forest with their *kukris* (long curved knives).[8] So far as these threatening external transactions are concerned, it is certainly not a case of 'plenty more fish in the sea', nor is there even a 'safe limit' within which the commercial extraction of timber would be sustainable. *All* external predation is seen as catastrophic in its consequences. Hence the spectacularly uncompromising collectivist response of the tree-huggers, whose idea of nature is one in which any perturbation of the present low-key regime is likely to result in irreversible and dramatic collapse: *Nature Ephemeral (Table 8.1 and Figure 8.11).*

But there is more. In every village, we can be sure that there will always be some people who sneak produce from the forest when no one is looking, or who can never quite get together the capital, the contacts and the oomph to go off on trading expeditions, and manage somehow not to be around when it is all hands to the tree-hugging. These are the *fatalists*: people whose transactions are somehow dictated by the organizational efforts of those who are not themselves fatalists. Theirs is a life in which the world is always doing things to them – sometimes pleasant, sometimes unpleasant – and in which nothing that they do seems to make much difference. 'Why bother?' is their not unreasonable response. If that is how the world is, then learning is not possible and even if it were, there would be no way of benefiting from it. The idea of nature here is one in which things operate without rhyme or reason: a flatland in which everywhere is the same as everywhere else: *Nature Capricious (Table 8.1 and Figure 8.11).* Completing the typology with these two solidarities – egalitarianism and fatalism – makes some important differences for a theory on socio-natural systems.

8.6.4.   *Complexity and the importance of being clumsy*

Change, in the conventional theory, is deterministic. If you're knocked out of hierarchy you'll end up in the market and vice versa. But add in the other two solidarities and change becomes indeterministic: leave A and you can end up at B, C or D, and when you leave whichever one of these you have arrived at there are three possibilities, and so on. Conventional theory treats human systems as *simple* (linear, deterministic, insensitive to initial conditions, equilibrium seeking and predictable); ours treats them as *complex* (non-linear, indeterministic, sensitive to initial conditions, far-from-equilibrium, and unpredictable). Using the example of the Himalayan village, we argued that the interaction of human and natural systems is *complex*: ordered – in that the four forms of social solidarity, and their associated styles of management, spring eternal – but unpredictable – in that, though the failure of any one of these styles inevitably results in the success of one of the other three, there is no way of knowing which of those three it will be. Simple systems are *manageable* in the sense that, once we understand enough about them, we can define some desirable state of affairs – 'sustainable development' is the current favourite – and then steer the totality towards it. If the system was *simple* a clever mathematician could write the relevant differential equations and solve them for equilibrium conditions – which is what conventional modelling does.[9] But this cannot be done this with complex systems because there *are* no equilibria in them.

Treating what is in fact a complex system as a simple system – by ignoring at least two of the solidarities, and then using that model as a management guide – is therefore a recipe for disaster or, at the very least, for surprises that could have been avoided. But, just because conventional modelling is not the way to go – is the way not to go – it does not follow that there is nothing useful we can do. We can make ourselves *clumsy*, and we will now try to explain, with the help of an additional example – a Swiss village – what clumsiness is, and what is entailed in achieving it.

Moving from the Himalayas to the Swiss village of Davos in the Alps, we find much the same fourfold allocation of transactions, with agricultural land being privately owned and grazing land – and sometimes the forests – being communally owned (cf. Section 6.5; Ostrom 1990). But the Swiss forests, unlike those of the Himalayan villagers, are physically sandwiched between the high pastures (communally owned) and the valley floor (privately owned fields, houses and hotels). Over the centuries that the Davos valley has been settled, both the fields and the grazing land have expanded at the expense of the forest, but the trees on the steeper slopes have stayed in place, acting both as a source of timber and as a barrier against avalanches. However, it is difficult, impossible perhaps, to achieve both these functions simultaneously and, in managing the forest for timber production, the Davosers have often set in train changes in the forest's age structure which, decades later, have resulted in exceptional avalanches reaching the valley floor and threatening the destruction of the entire community.

Every time this unpleasant surprise has befallen them the Davosers have responded – through a discordant, noisy and inevitably messy process of deliberation – by switching their forest management onto the all-in-the-same-boat, egalitarian style. Later, it has sometimes shifted, again thanks to the discordant voices and their constructive engagement, to the hierarchist style, often to the individualist style – with farmers owning long thin strips of forest running all the way from valley floor to alpine pasture, and sometimes to the fatalist style – as happened, for instance, when the avalanche danger was clearly perceived yet extraction continued in response to the demands of various mining booms and, in more recent years, the demand for ski-runs.

Surely, you might think, they would have got it right by now. But to think that is to assume that there is *one* right way, and that, as our fourfold scheme shows us, is not the case. There is no way of ever getting it right, because managing one way inevitably changes the forest, eventually to the point where that way of managing it is no longer appropriate. This would happen even if there were no exogenous changes – such as the mining and tourist booms – which of course there always are, even in seemingly remote places such as the Himalayas. *Viability* can only be achieved, therefore, by 'covering all the bases': by the villagers ensuring that they have the full fourfold repertoire of management styles, and by their being prepared to try a different one whenever the one they are relying on shows signs of no longer being appropriate. The Davosers, like their Himalayan counterparts, have now been in their valley for more than 700 years without destroying either themselves or their valley in the process: an achievement that would not have been possible if they had opted for just one management style, or even for the two that the prevalent orthodoxy allows.[10]

Himalayan and Alpine villages, with their transactions parcelled out in these four very different ways, are impressively *multi-vocal*. More than that, as is evident from the examples of stall-feeding and trees on private land (in the Himalayas) and of alternative forest management styles (in the Alps), they have the ability to switch transactions from one method to another whenever it seems likely that this might be more appropriate. Since the behaviour of the villagers continually alters the resource base on which they depend, their villages would not be viable if they did not have this in-built – and messy, noisy and argumentative – mechanism. Schapiro (1988) has dubbed this sort of set-up, in which each conviction as to how the world is – each myth of nature – is given some recognition, a *clumsy institution*. This is in contrast to those more elegant, and more familiar, arrangements – tidy, quiet and suavely consensual – in which just one conviction holds sway. The terminology is deliberately counter-intuitive, clumsy institutions having some remarkable properties that are not shared by their unclumsy alternatives.

To understand just *how* remarkable clumsy institutions are, imagine for a moment that you are a God-like experimenter, able to reach out and change this is or that variable in a Himalayan village's environment, or to move it bodily east or west, north or south, across the convoluted landscape. As you bring in the logging contractors, or take it 100 kilometres eastwards or 1000 metres higher, the village will shift its transactions this way or that between its four options until it has adapted itself to its changed circumstances. In other words, it will maintain its viability thanks to the very practical *learning* system that is part-and-parcel of its fourfold plurality. If the village did not have this plurality, and was an elegant and unclumsy institution – like many national forestry services – it would not be able to do this. Something along these imaginary lines, it turns out, is what has actually happened, and continues to do so.

As we go from one Himalayan village to another, the relative strengths of the four ways of organizing vary. Egalitarianism, for instance, is strongest in those parts of the Himalayas that are most prone to commercial logging. As one moves eastwards, from India – with its powerful centre and its colonial heritage of Reserved Forests – into Nepal and Bhutan, so the Chipko movement and its counterparts become less of a force to be reckoned with. If the inequitable external threat is absent then so too, it seems, is the communitarian response to it. However, the most dramatic of these variations is north-south: between the strongly individualized Buddhist villages and the strongly collectivized Hindu villages around two day's walk downstream. These are Fürer-Haimendorf's (1975) 'adventurous traders' and 'cautious cultivators', respectively: apt characterizations which readily map onto two of the four 'social beings' – individualists and hierarchists, respectively – that we have described above. Fürer-Haimendorf also shows how the small agricultural surpluses of the cautious cultivators become the payloads of the adventurous traders' yaks as they set off on their journey into Tibet, and how the salt they bring back eventually finds its way to the cautious cultivators who cannot produce this vital commodity.

A Swiss villager's day   During the growing season, an individual may, on one day, milk his cows, cut hay, thin saplings, maintain an avalanche control structure and wash dishes in a restaurant. The cows, although privately owned, are grazed on pasture owned by a specific set of long-established families; the hay is on his own private field; the saplings are part of a forest owned by another set of families; the avalanche control structure is on private land but maintained, by agreement, by the village; and the restaurant is owned by a multinational hotel chain.

This framework is fairly stable from season to season, but the individual has a very different pattern of activity in the winter, when the cows live in his private byre and much of the land is snow covered and barely used, unless the valley includes a ski resort. If it does then he has opportunities for work without leaving the valley. If not then he may leave to work elsewhere, thereby reducing the use of scarce resources at home. Thus, in winter, the human ecosystem centred on the valley is concurrently simpler and wider.

So our Swiss villager has a 'portfolio' of transactions and management styles that fluctuates with the seasons and also with the longer-term dynamics (such as those that, in altering the forests' age structure, can eventually shift a whole category of transactions from one style to another).

–   Like his Himalayan counterpart, he owns his hayfields and cows. These are private property; he can buy or sell them, acting as an individualist and subscribing to the myth of Nature Benign.

- Coming from a long-established family, he is a member of a forest co-operative (Waldgenossenschaft) that gives him specific rights to cut trees and imposes a duty to maintain the forest. He is also a member of a pasture co-operative (Alpgenossenschaft) which annually decides the grazing season and the number of animals he may graze, and requires him to contribute to the cowherd's upkeep. These are small-scale hierarchical institutions that have developed over the generations (between the periods when the forests were privatized and their associated transactions transferred to the more exploitative individualist management style) in response to the limitations, as well as the opportunities, imposed by the natural environment: Nature Perverse/Tolerant.

- As a voting member of the commune, he also has a duty to maintain resources that contribute to its survival, such as the avalanche control structures that protect houses, fields and roads from damage. This tends to be an egalitarian involvement which recognizes that, when it comes to these sorts of hazards, all the members of the community are in the same boat and that each should contribute his equal share: Nature Ephemeral.

- Lastly, as a dishwasher in a multinationally owned restaurant, he is effectively a replaceable fatalist. His involvement is necessary if the enterprise is to continue but he has no interest in its future, nor it in his, and he can be paid off at any time (he will almost certainly lose his job at the end of the summer season).

8.6.5. *Theories of change that make change permanent*

The examples above illustrate how 'social beings' in complex socio-natural systems interfere with the environment and each other according to one of the four management styles which belong each to a particular solidarity. The term 'social being' is used here to describe the behaviour to which an individual must conform, and the convictions that he or she must espouse, to help maintain the form of social solidarity to which he or she belongs. The 'prime mover', therefore, is not the individual – the psycho-physiological entity – but the form of social solidarity. Therefore, the terms hierarchist, individualist, egalitarian and fatalist denote available roles – or management strategies – that individuals step into, or out of, as their daily lives, or the changing seasons, take them from one transactional realm to another (*Figure 8.12*). The distinctive strategy of each makes the others viable, and in this way each village, in adjusting to its circumstances – which include the other villages – creates and takes its place in a social and cultural 'ecosystem', in which the marked divergence of the parts sustains the whole.

We have argued that change occurs because the four forms of social solidarity are not impervious to the real world. Just because people insist that the world is as their myth of nature tells them it is, it does not follow that the world really is so. If it is, that is fine, but if it is not, they have an uphill struggle. *Surprise* – the outcome of the ever-widening discrepancy between the expected and the actual – is of central importance in dislodging people and their transactions from their form of social solidarity. And it is these various mismatches between what a way of life promises and what it delivers that continually tip people – and transactions – out of one form of social solidarity and into another. Of course, this hypothesis does require the world, at times and in places, to be each of these possible ways – otherwise we would all eventually end up surprised into the single true way. And it would help the surprises to continue indefinitely if the world itself kept changing the way it was.

Neither of these suggestions, some ecologists would argue, is particularly far-fetched. Holling (1986; Gunderson 1997) for instance has elaborated the notion of requisite variety into a powerful critique of the conventional idea that the *climax community* – the ecosystem in which each specialized species has its stable and ordered niche – is the end of the organizational road. This critique exactly parallels our dissatisfaction with the conventional hierarchies-and-markets account of things, in that it argues that there must be four, rather than just two, destinations. Holling's critique is that the climax community eventually makes itself so complex that it undermines its own stability: an inevitable collapse which has been proved mathematically by May (1972) and resembles Tainter's argument about state collapse (cf. Sections 7.4 and 8.4). This does not mean that an entire climax community – the Amazonian rain forest, for instance – will suddenly disappear, but it does require any climax community to be 'patchy': to always include some localized areas in collapse – as happens, for instance, when a mature tree crashes to the ground. At this catastrophic moment, all the energy that is tied up in all the niches and interdependencies of the climax community is released. Holling, well aware of the parallel with Schumpeter's (1950) theory of economic maturity, collapse and renewal, calls this transition from the climax community to compost 'creative destruction'.

Nor, he argues, is this the end of the road. With the whole place suddenly awash with 'capital' – loose energy – the challenge is to fix it before it all disappears, by soil leaching for instance. This, of course, is where the unspecialized and co-operative fence-builders – mostly micro-organisms– come into their own, gathering up the loose energy into small bundles that have no connections with one another as yet. But even this is not the end of the road, because the stage is now set for the appearance of yet more different ecological actors. These are the unspecialized but opportunistic, fast-breeding and highly competitive '*r*-selected' species. These generalized exploiters – weeds, rodents and so on – are able to harness all the 'energy gradients' that are now in place between all these unconnected bundles of energy. But these *r*-selected species, as they exploit and colonize

this environment, inevitably begin to push it into a rather more patterned and interconnected state, thereby making it less conducive to their way of doing things and more
suited to the sort of energy-conserving strategies that characterize the 'K-selected
species' – those specialized, slower-breeding and often symbiotic plants and creatures
that are the vanguard of the complex and increasingly ordered whole that constitutes the
climax community (*Figure 8.12*).

In other words, once you bump up the number of ecological strategies from two to four,
there is no end to the road. Instead, the system is always in transition – twelve in all. This
exactly parallels, in terms of dynamics but not substance, the social transitions by which
our Himalayan and Alpine villagers 'clumsify' themselves and, in so doing, relate themselves to one another and to their physical surroundings: Man and Nature as a single but
complex system. The adventurous trader's strategy matches that of the omnivorous and
opportunistic *r*-selected species; the cautious cultivator's strategy matches that of the
specialized and niche-dependent *K*-selected species; the fatalists do for social systems
what compost does for natural systems (provides a generalized resource for renewal);
and the egalitarians, through their small-scale communal fervour, create enclaves of low-
level energy (what Marx called 'primitive capital') in places where neither the *r*-selected
nor the *K*-selected species can make any form of impression (Holling, 1986; Thompson
1989; Holling 1993).

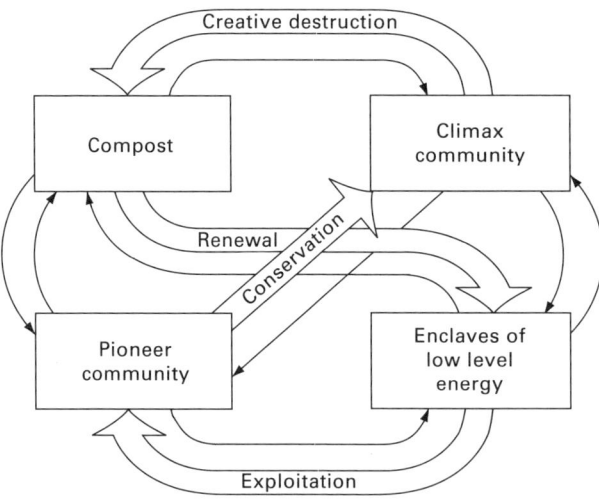

FIGURE 8.12

*The complex critique of the conventional assumptions about natural systems: the set of twelve transi-
tions (redrawn from Holling 1986 to be homologous with Figure 8.11).*

The ambitious hypothesis being sketched here is very different to the way people usually think about the interactions of social and natural systems. There is, from this point of view, no way of ever getting it 'right': of bringing the social into long-term harmony with the natural, which, of course, is the whole idea behind 'sustainable development'. Instead, each is a fourfold and plurally responsive system, and their time-lagged interactions ensure that there can be no steady-state outcome. The whole system is in a perpetual unsteady state: changes at each level – the social and the natural – adapt to the other and change it in the process, thereby setting in motion another set of changes. And so on. Order without predictability – as opposed to transition from A to B or oscillation between A and B – is the crucial idea behind our Himalayan and Alpine stories.

8.7. Conclusions

Understanding of complex socio-natural systems is, and may always be, incomplete. However, empirical observations from various disciplines, each using its own apparatus of methods and concepts, have given rise to fragments of theory.

Going from observations to qualitative theories to quantifications in 'formal' models is not an easy path. Yet it provides important heuristics – 'ask the right questions', falsify hypotheses and the like – and also deepens our insights. The Neolithic Transition model shows that biogeographical factors such as agricultural potential and diffusion corridors are an integral part of the evolution of the population-environment-technology-culture system. It also underlines the importance of spatial explicitness in modelling such systems. The Lakeland model and the simulation models on the Anasazi and !Kung San populations indicate the importance of introducing variety at the micro-level of human behaviour if one is to get a deeper insight into 'emergent' macro-behaviour in these complex systems. Behavioural rules and habits, information collection and exchange processes are, after all, the essence of humans.

Social science perspectives of a less formal nature offer a variety of explanations of the rise and fall of social complexity. Tainter's 'law' of diminishing returns and enhancing complexity suggests an economically oriented cause of state collapse. In Meso-America Blanton and colleagues found ecological diversity to be a key element in understanding state-market interactions. Flannery listed the processes of segregation and centralization of the subsystems and mechanisms of institutional control to explain the creation of order and hierarchy – and added the pathologies that bring them down. Renfrew focused on peer-polity interactions as a crucial element in understanding the spread of populations and the associated transformation processes.

Most of these endeavours are on the edge of a new paradigm with regard to the investigation of complex (socio-natural) systems. The theory of complex adaptive systems appears to be most explicit in this respect. Cultural Theory and ecocycle theory also put forward insights verging on a new paradigm. They propose that the dynamic interplay between four different perspectives on how the world functions and, accordingly, should be acted upon is essential. It transforms the idea of smooth transitions from or oscillations between two states – hierarchies and markets – into one of a complex socio-natural system with order without predictability and never-ending transitions in a continuous process of learning, adaptation and responses. Clumsy institutions, in which each conviction about how the world is given recognition, are identified as a key element of enduring resource management schemes.

9

Population and Environment in Asia since 1600 AD

REVI, DRONIN AND DE VRIES

9.1.   Introduction

Given the limited time and the clearly overly large ambition to sketch Mappae Mundi for all places and times in human history and pre-history, we now take a big leap and focus on the last 400 years. Around the year 1000 AD about two out of every three human beings lived in Asia and some 70% of economic activity took place there (Maddison 2001). The larger part lived in the densely populated plains of China and India. By the year 2000 AD still about 60% of the world population lived in Asia but its share in economic activity had declined to 37% – at least when measured as the gross domestic product (GDP). Probably the dominant phenomenon of the intervening millennium has been the expansion of European peoples and their activities to most of the 'empty' regions of the world. This is the topic of Chapter 10. In this chapter we attempt to give an impression of how the two-thirds of the human population in Asia was doing, with an emphasis on population-environment interactions.

There are two reasons why the population-environment dynamics in Asia are important. Firstly, as the anthroposphere is expanding extensively and intensively, the population in Asia – and its socio-economical and cultural patterns – will have an enormous impact on how the world population will move to the next ecological regime because of its sheer momentum and its relatively low level of economic activity. Secondly, the population in several parts of Asia was confronted in this period with the limits of the carrying capacity of the environment. This manifested itself in famines and revolts whenever and wherever the socio-economic and institutional mechanisms used to sustain the rather large population densities were inadequate. As such they provide valuable insights in the various ways people coped – or failed to cope – with such pressures in these regions and probably in similar situations earlier and elsewhere.[1] Our accounts will be about India, Indonesia and Siberia; we failed to receive one about China. We are fully aware that this eclectic approach with regard to this important part of our Mappae

Mundi is far from satisfactory. However, even finding these tiny pieces of demographic and environmental history turned out to be a tedious task.

In both South Asia and China, multiple episodes of considerable population decline have been reported since the 18th century. Although short-term fluctuations due to armed conflict, migration, famine and epidemics have had an impact on the population, in the long run population growth was exponential as it was dominated by the internal dynamics of trends in fertility and mortality. *Figure 9.1a* (see p. 309) shows population estimates for some of the major regions of the world; the earlier ones in particular are

Population in Asia in ancient times The first evidence of Chinese culture goes back some 4000-5000 years in the upper Huang He (Yellow River) region. Some 2000-2500 years ago present-day China emerged as more or less a unity in the sense that also the southern regions became part of the Chinese Empire (cf. Section 6.4.2). At about 1000 yr BP the Wei He and the city of Xi'an were the centre of Chinese culture. Later, the population increased and shifted to more southern and eastern regions. *Figure 9.2* (see p. 310) shows the population density as estimated and made available by Dr. Man Zhimin of the Institute of Historical Geography of Fudan University in Shanghai. In combination with a series of maps of population density for other periods in the last 2000 years, one can get an impression of the gradual shift in population concentration from the northern to other parts of China.

In Indian history there is a gap in historical knowledge between the decline of the Indus-valley civilization around 3500-4000 BP and 2500 BP (cf. Section 6.3.2). Several invasions from the west and the north changed Indian civilization but most of them were assimilated. The invasions from the north-west around 800 yr BP eventually led to the Mogul Empire. India's population estimates are highly uncertain. For the first millennium Maddison (2001) gives ranges of 34 to 112 million people; it varies between 100 and 150 million for the year 1600 AD. Despite this large number – almost twice as much as in Western Europe – Lord Cornwallis, Governor-General of India, could still state in 1789 '... without hesitation that a third of the [East India] Company's lands in Hindustan are now a jungle, inhabited only by wild beasts.' (Braudel 1975: 239-240)

Indonesia also had a long development process for indigenous tribes who were confronted with foreign peoples, initially from India and later from Europe. Its population is estimated to have grown from 10 to 40 million people in the period 1600-1900. In Russia, the process of eastward expansion in the last centuries was the equivalent of Western Europe's expansion into the Americas and Australia. Its growth from 7 to 136 million people in the period 1600-1900 was more of an extensive than an intensive nature.

contentious. The populations of India and China were roughly on a par at the beginning of the 17th century. Both were then about twice the population size of Western Europe. Japan experienced explosive growth over the 17th century and then evidently settled to a stable population for nearly 150 years during the later years of the Tokagawa Shogunate. Russia similarly saw a rapid population expansion over the 18th and 19th centuries due to a mix of both natural growth and the assimilation of vast new territories. The beginnings of the demographic transition in Europe were laid at this time. The 'New World' experienced explosive growth rates as the European expansion gained momentum: the population of the United States of America (USA) kept growing with an estimated European immigration of some 23 million people between 1600 and 1913; Brazil and Australia absorbed some 5 million immigrants in this period; and an estimated 9.4 million Africans were brought to the Americas as slaves in the period 1500-1870 (Maddison 2001).

Trends in economic activity over the last few centuries have also been estimated by Maddison (2001) and are shown in *Figure 9.1b* (see p. 309). With the onset of the 'Industrial Revolution', Europe and its colonial offshoots experienced a large and lasting economic growth – as is described in the next chapter. The most dramatic economic growth happened in the USA. However, at the beginning of the 18th century, China was still the largest economy in the world by far; the size of the Indian economy was about two-thirds that of the European one. The rapid economic growth of the UK, continental Europe and the USA resulted in the emergence of a new world order that played itself out during the two World Wars of the 20th century. The USA emerged as the largest economic power by 1913 and then proceeded to become the dominant economic power of the 20th century. The Soviet Union more than trebled its economic output over the latter part of the 20th century before descending into economic turmoil in the 1990s; Japan increased its economic output by a factor of almost 50, China by almost 18 and India by about 10 in the period 1900-1990. The trends in population and economic activity are reflected in the increase in GDP per capita, a widely used measure to express welfare and one component of well-being (*Figure 9.1c*, see p. 309).

The trends of economic and population growth within the industrial regime appear to indicate that primary driving forces are able to dampen other shorter-term fluctuations which are consequences of traditional constraining factors such as epidemics, famine, wars and economic cycles. The regional realities are far more complex than these simple trends indicate, but on a general level, the heightened 'metabolic' activity of the industrial age along with its greater economic and material efficiency have enabled a quantum leap from the regime of the pre-Industrial world.

9.2. South Asia: population and environment in a geopolitical context[2]

There is a great deal of evidence that environmental conditions and changes have been an important driving factor in the long-term population-resource-environment dynamics and the economy of South Asia. This interaction was accentuated by a number of factors in the post-Mogul colonial period (ca. 1750-1950). Eventhough objective historical data are too weak to establish proximate causal links between environmental factors and quality of life, a strong causal linkage via the drought-famine-disease-linked mortality cycle has been reported by contemporary observers since the 18th century. Recent analysis hypothesizes that the decline in the total South Asian population of the late 18th century was closely linked to an interaction between factors such as colonial wars of conquest, disruption in regional agricultural production, trade and finance simultaneously with severe episodes of drought, famine and disease (Guha 2001). Most of these factors were anthropogenic or potentially within the span of human control: colonial security, fiscal and trade policy, infrastructure investment, land use, water and forest resource regulation and management practices. Many of these 'driving forces' were operational during the Mogul era, but their combined 'entrainment' to meet the economic objectives of colonial India led to a number of perverse structural changes in the landscape and the economy. As a result they occurred in a lethal combination, decimating the capacity of the peasantry and communities to reinvest local surpluses and cope with the stress induced by recurrent events such as drought.

It is our contention that it is difficult to attribute these events simplistically either to *force majeure*, overshooting beyond carrying capacity or poor 'native' technology, institutions or management practices (see e.g. Myrdal 1977). Rather a wider geo-political canvas may be required to examine the relative impact of the process of imperial expansion in facilitating the colonization of both peoples and nature, and indirectly financing the industrialization and developing large markets and raw material reserves in the pre-industrial colonial economies. The environmental sciences have traditionally tended to play down the importance of historical and political factors in what are seen as rather concrete processes. Unfortunately, for this worldview, geo-political factors have been crucial in determining the long-term dynamics of population and natural resources in colonial South Asia. Changes in the trade regime and political boundaries were not new to the subcontinent before the colonial period. Local cultures adopted successfully to more or less changing fortunes of trade with the Romans, Arabs and Chinese and early European traders with the development of new trading partners and routes and the diversification of products. Territorial boundaries changed constantly in the mediaeval period during the interregnum between large imperial powers. Warfare between contending Muslim and Hindu states was relatively common and yet a radical restructuring of agrarian relationships or the economy is not reported, although the volume of tribute

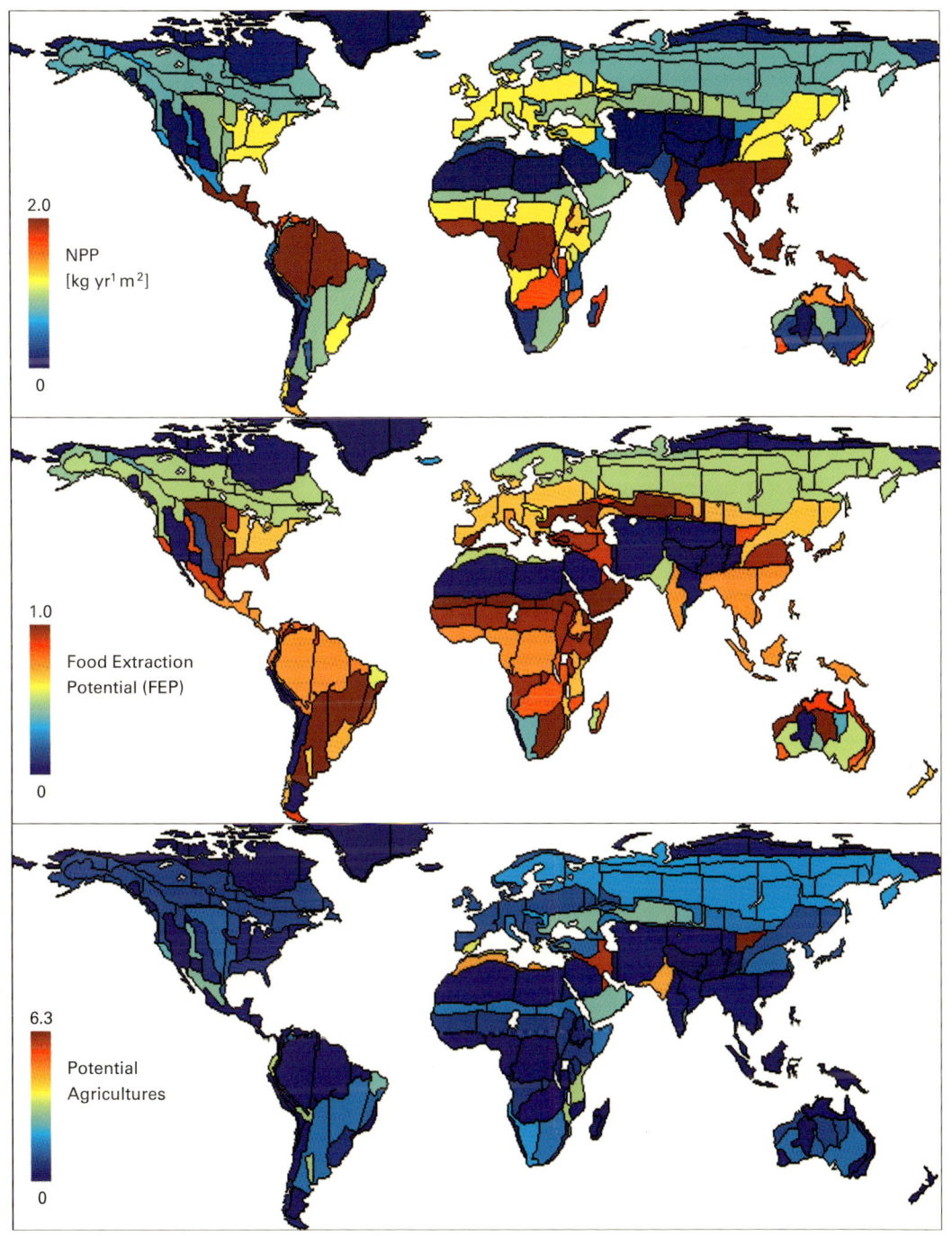

FIGURE 8.1

Maps of vegetation types and subsequent transformations. The graphs show the net primary production (NPP), food extraction potential (FEP) and potential agricultures which are the basis for the dynamic simulations.

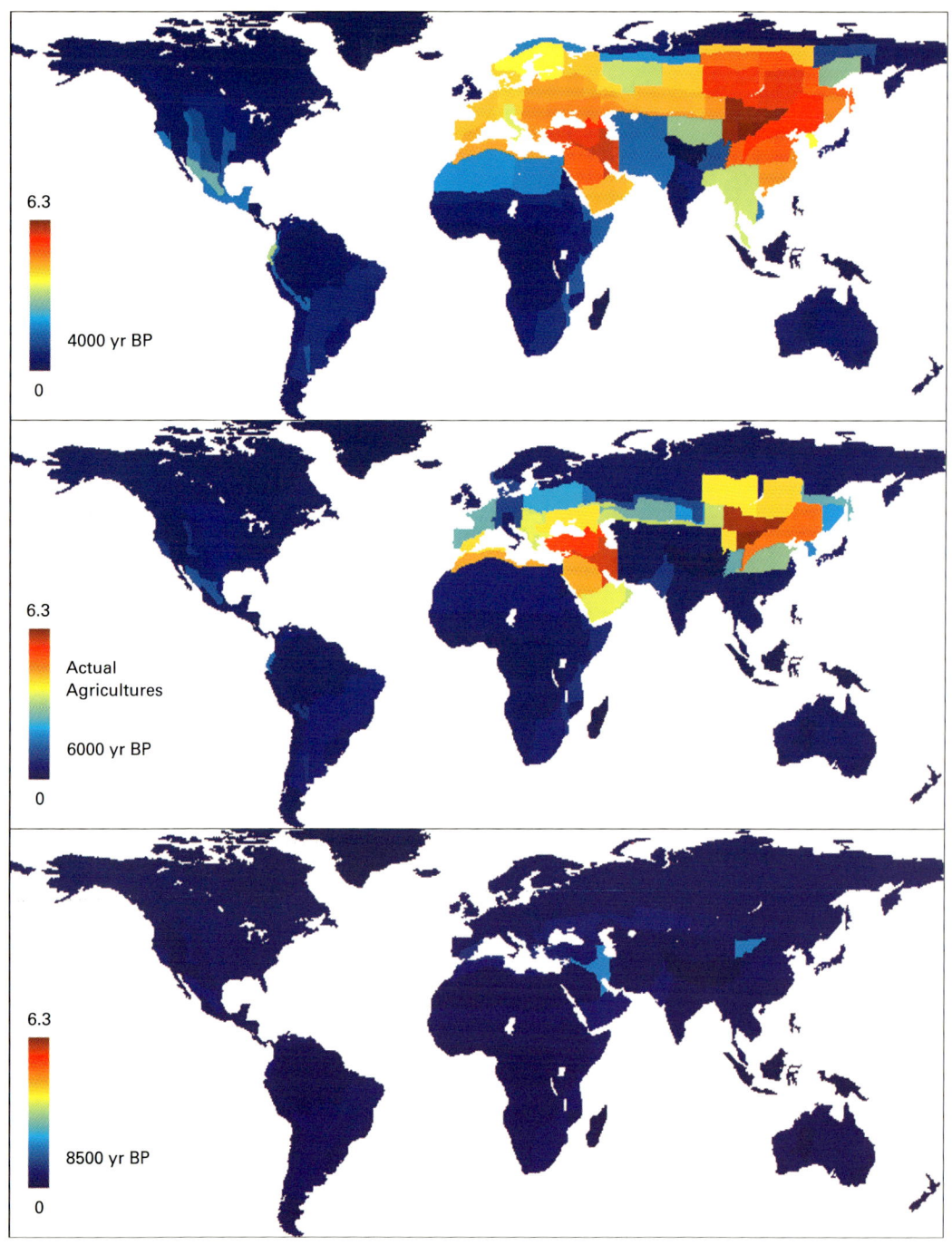

FIGURE 8.4

Discrete examples for the model variable actual agricultures for 8500, 6000 and 4000 yr BP in the dynamic simulation.

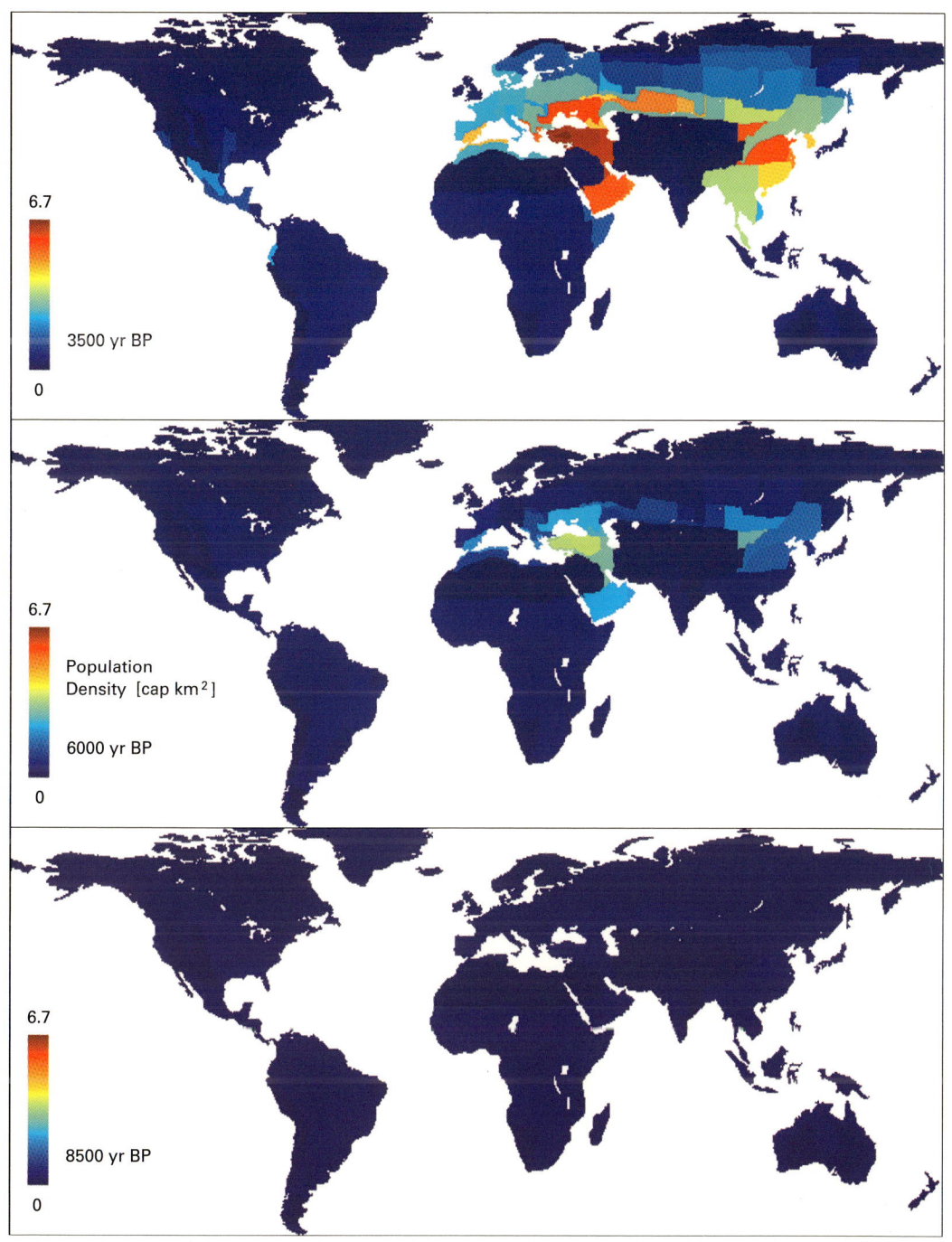

FIGURE 8.5

Discrete examples for the model variable population density for 8500, 6000 and 4000 yr BP in the dynamic simulation.

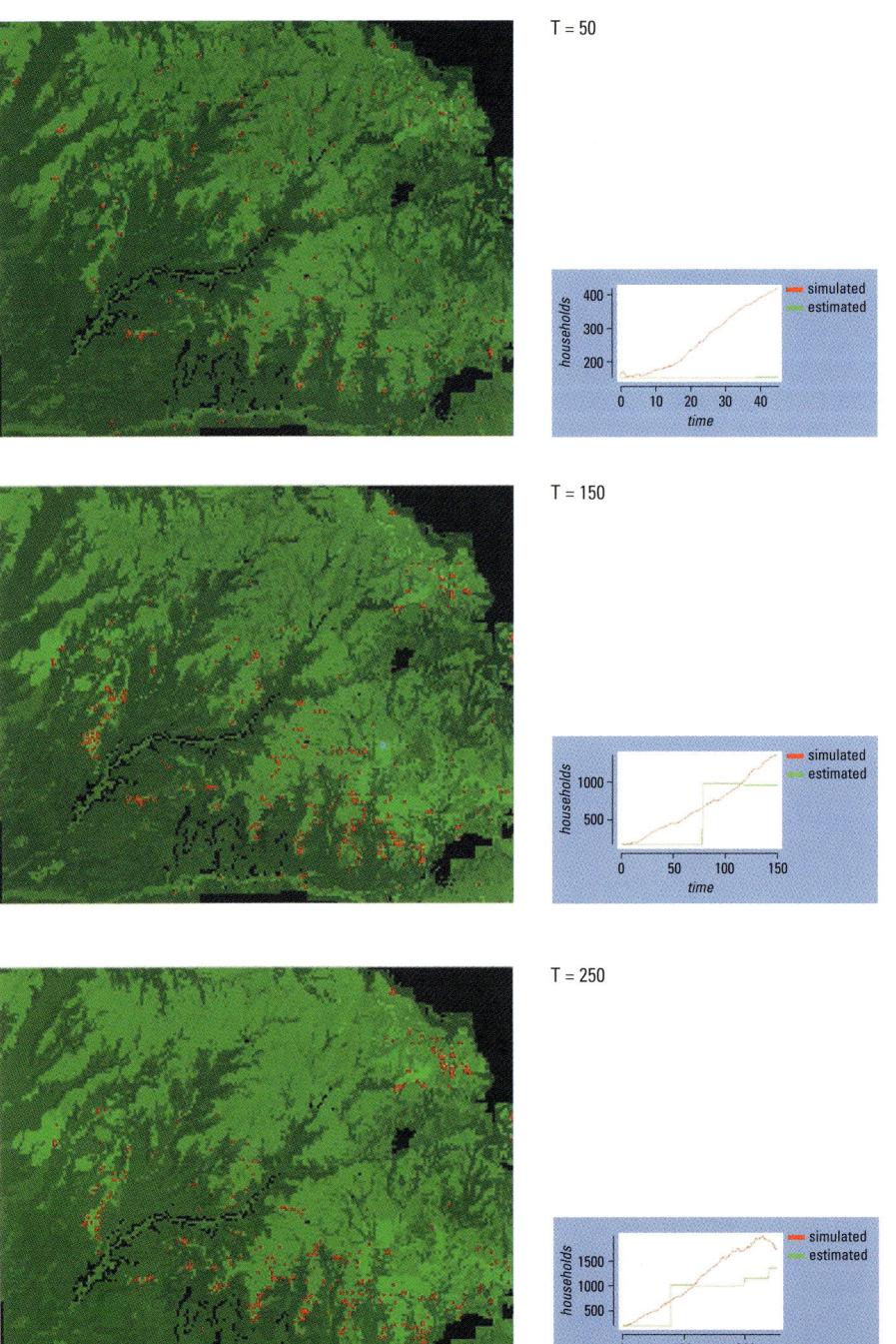

FIGURE 8.9

Settlement patterns in the simulation of the Hohokam people. The graph shows the Mesa Verde region and the simulated settlements for three subsequent years in the simulation. The small graph at the lower right end indicates the population size as simulated and as estimated from archaeological research. (Source: Kohler, pers. comm.)

308

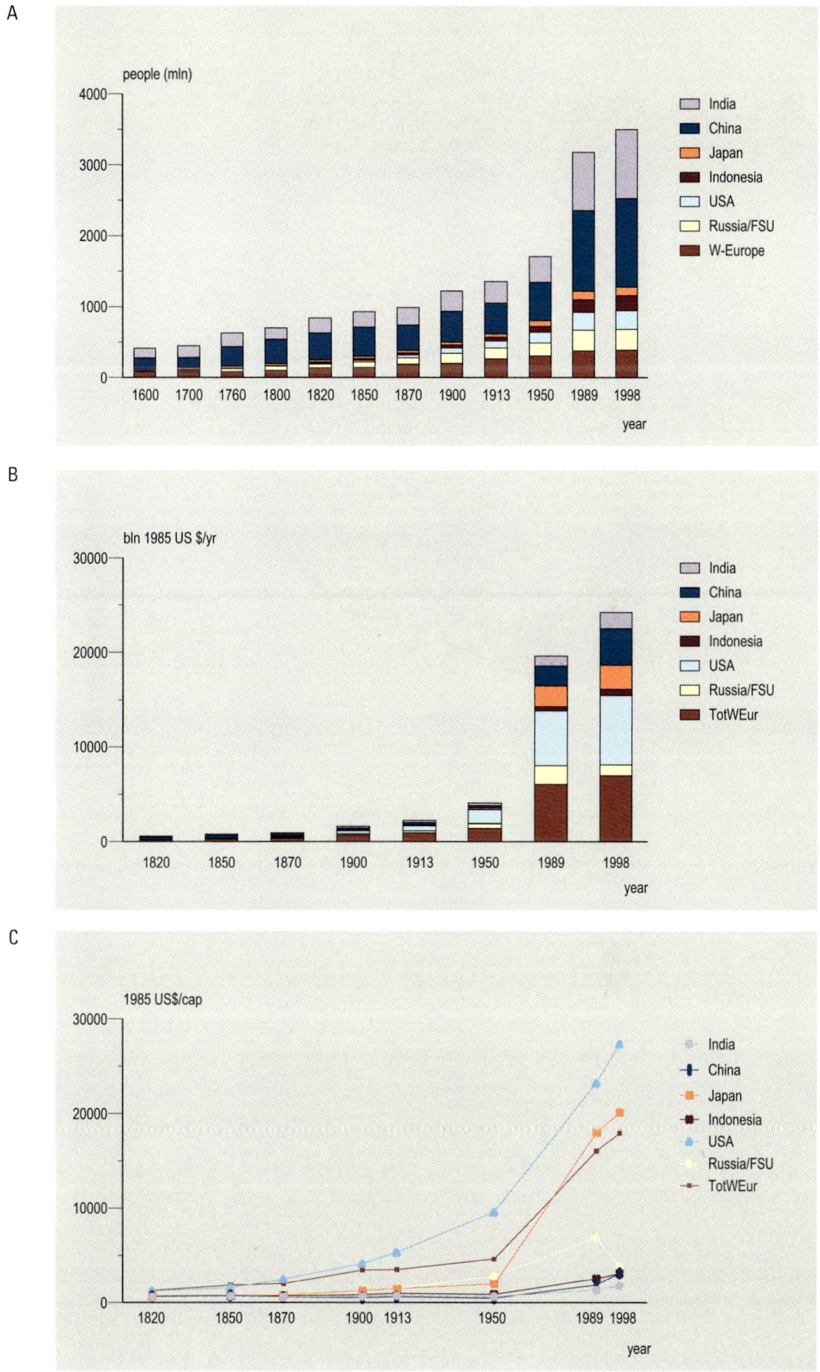

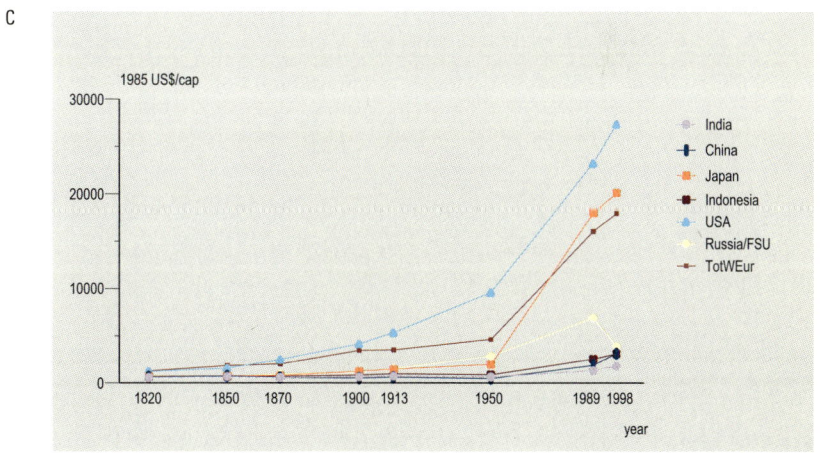

FIGURE 9.1

Population growth (A), economic (GDP) growth (B) and income (GDP/cap) growth (C) in seven world regions during the last 3-4 centuries (Source: Maddison 2001)

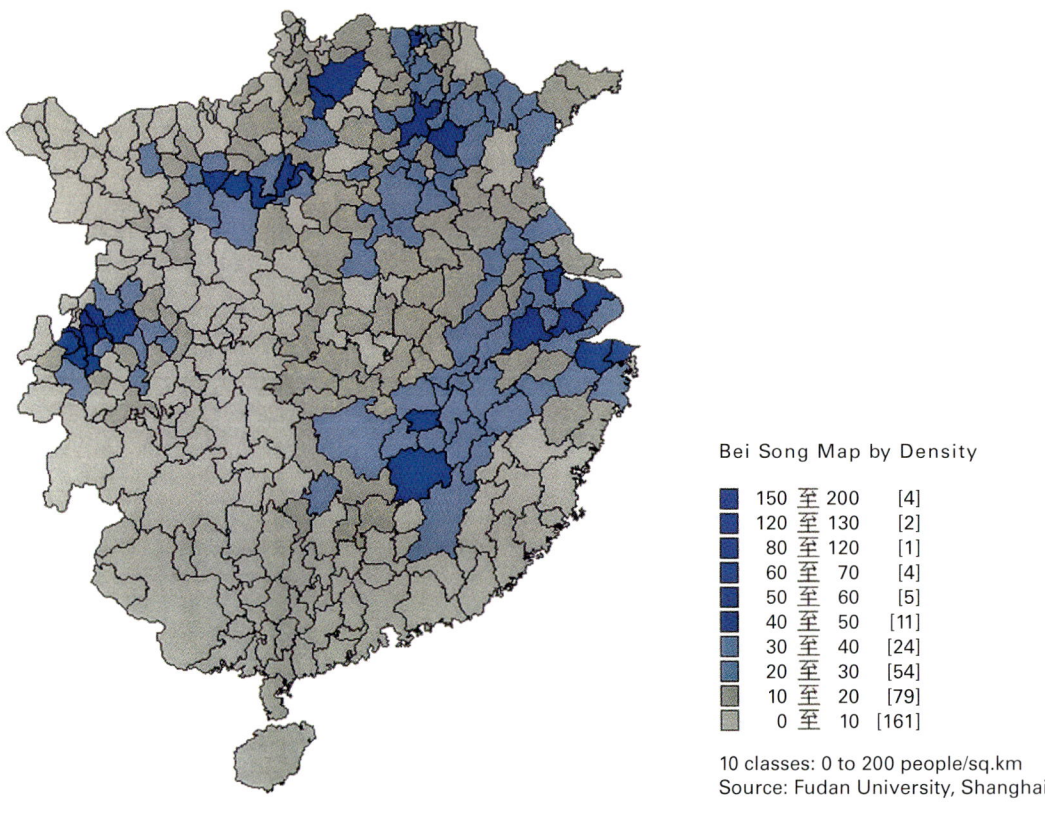

Bei Song Map by Density

■	150 至 200	[4]
■	120 至 130	[2]
■	80 至 120	[1]
■	60 至 70	[4]
■	50 至 60	[5]
■	40 至 50	[11]
■	30 至 40	[24]
■	20 至 30	[54]
■	10 至 20	[79]
□	0 至 10	[161]

10 classes: 0 to 200 people/sq.km
Source: Fudan University, Shanghai

FIGURE 9.2

Population density estimate for administrative units in China in the year 1102 AD (898 yr BP) (Source: Institute of Historical Geography, Fudan University, Shanghai).

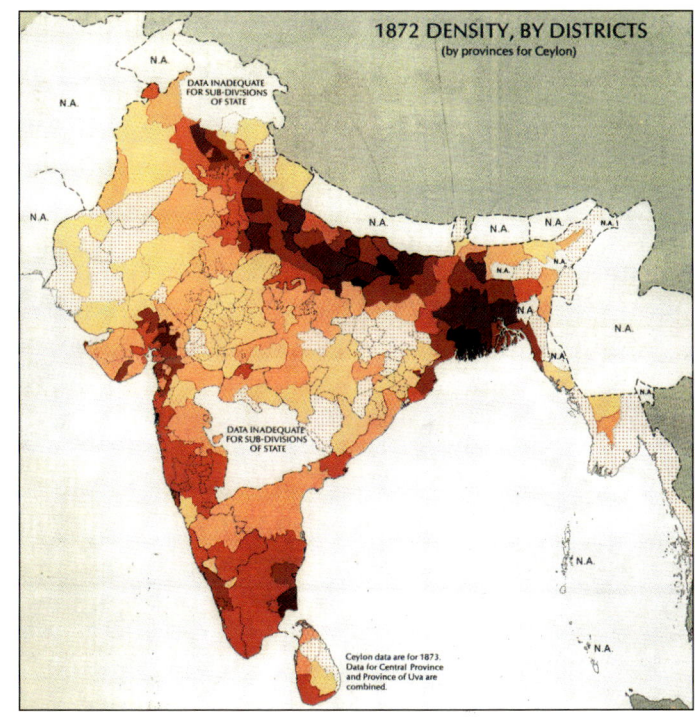

1872 DENSITY, BY DISTRICTS
(by provinces for Ceylon)

DATA INADEQUATE
FOR SUB-DIVISIONS
OF STATE

N.A.

DATA INADEQUATE
FOR SUB-DIVISIONS
OF STATE

Ceylon data are for 1873.
Data for Central Province
and Province of Uva are
combined.

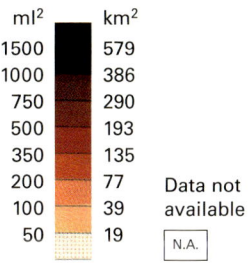

Population Density

Persons per square mile
and per square kilometer

ml²		km²
1500		579
1000		386
750		290
500		193
350		135
200		77
100		39
50		19

Data not
available

N.A.

FIGURE 9.3

Population density estimate for administrative units in India in the period 1872-1961 (Source: Schwartzberg 1992)

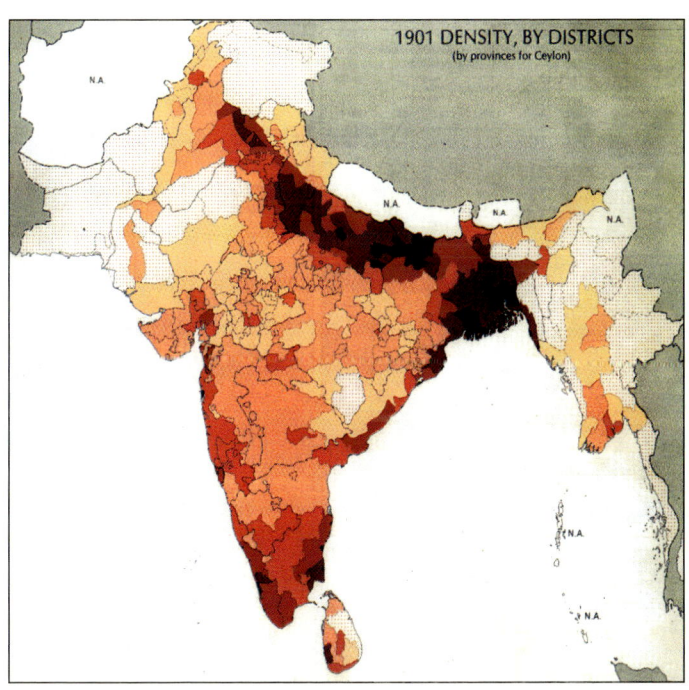

1901 DENSITY, BY DISTRICTS
(by provinces for Ceylon)

N.A.

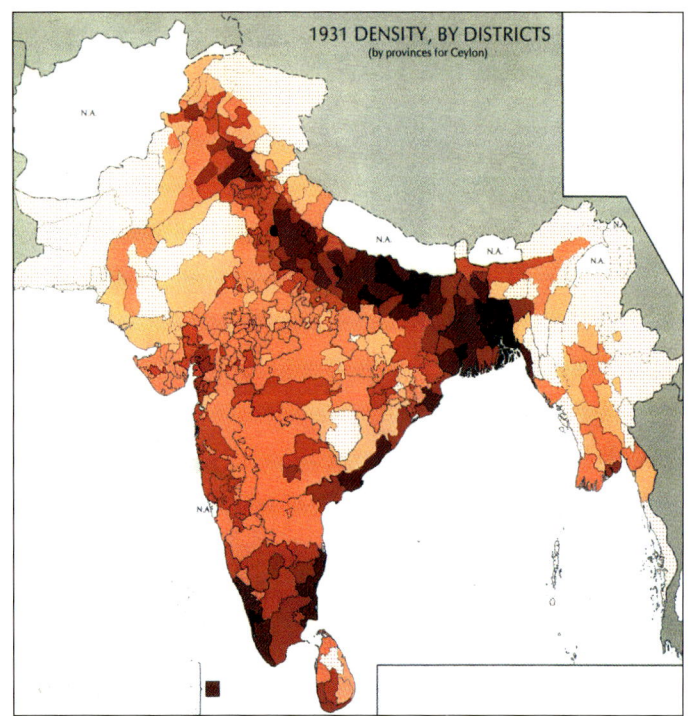

1931 DENSITY, BY DISTRICTS
(by provinces for Ceylon)

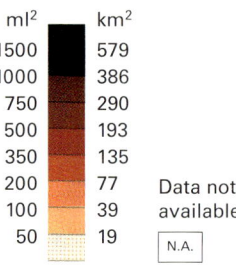

Population Density

Persons per square mile
and per square kilometer

ml²		km²
1500		579
1000		386
750		290
500		193
350		135
200		77
100		39
50		19

Data not
available

N.A.

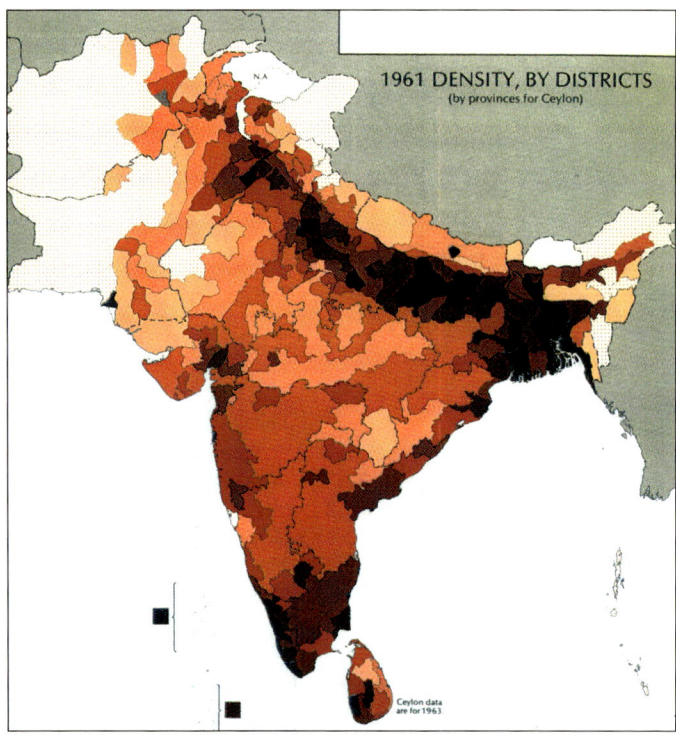

1961 DENSITY, BY DISTRICTS
(by provinces for Ceylon)

Ceylon data
are for 1963

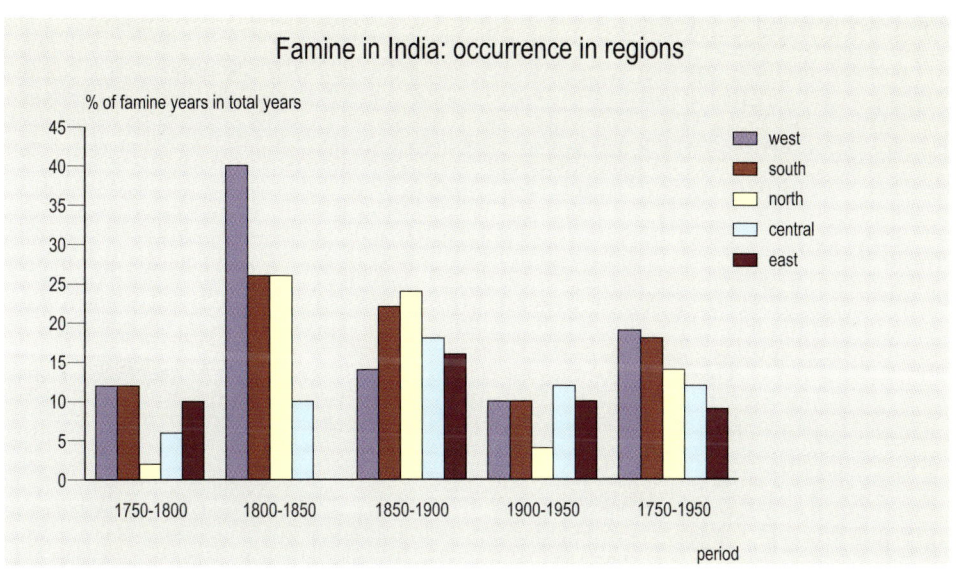

FIGURE 9.4A

Regional profile of famine frequency in South Asia in the period ca. 1750-1950 (Source: Visaria 1984 and various reports of the Indian Famine Commissions)

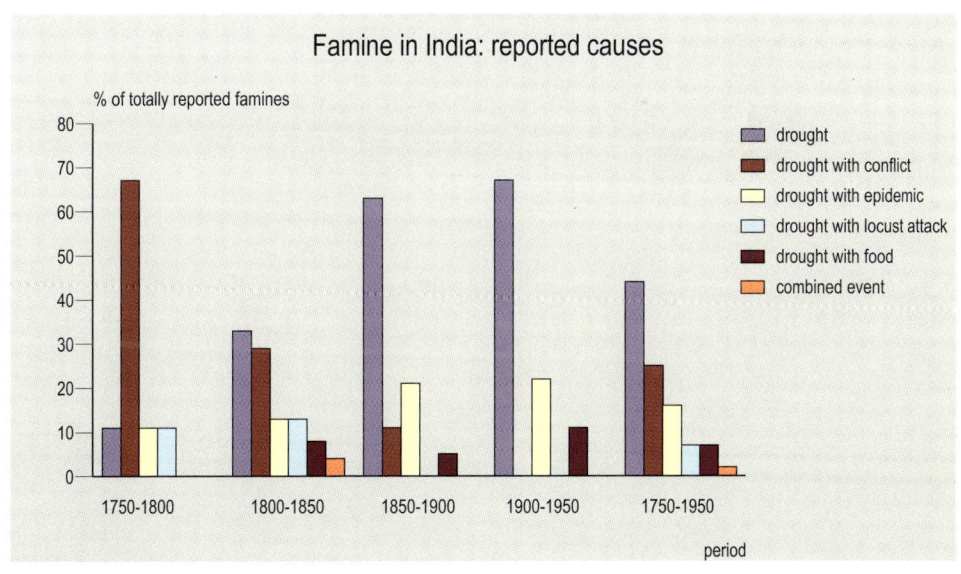

FIGURE 9.4B

Reported causes of famine in South Asia in the period ca. 1750-1950 as a proportion of period events (Source: Visaria 1984 and various reports of the Indian Famine Commissions)

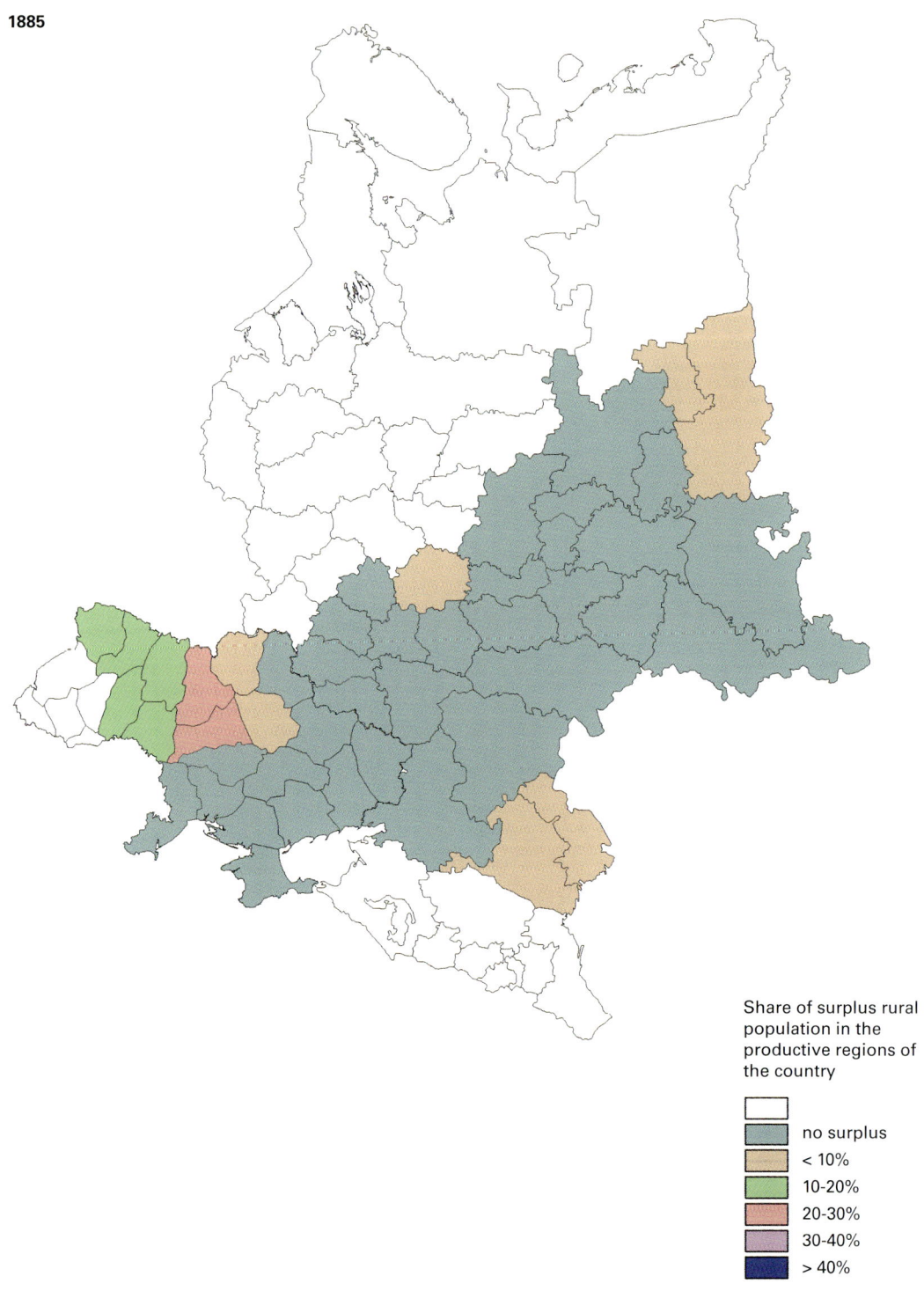

Share of surplus rural
population in the
productive regions of
the country

- [white] no surplus
- [teal] < 10%
- [tan] 10-20%
- [green] 20-30%
- [pink] 30-40%
- [dark blue] > 40%

FIGURE 9.6A

*Change in the population pressure from European Russia towards the south and the east in the period 1885-
1914. Rural overpopulation is calculated as the ratio of population and productive capacity of the land*

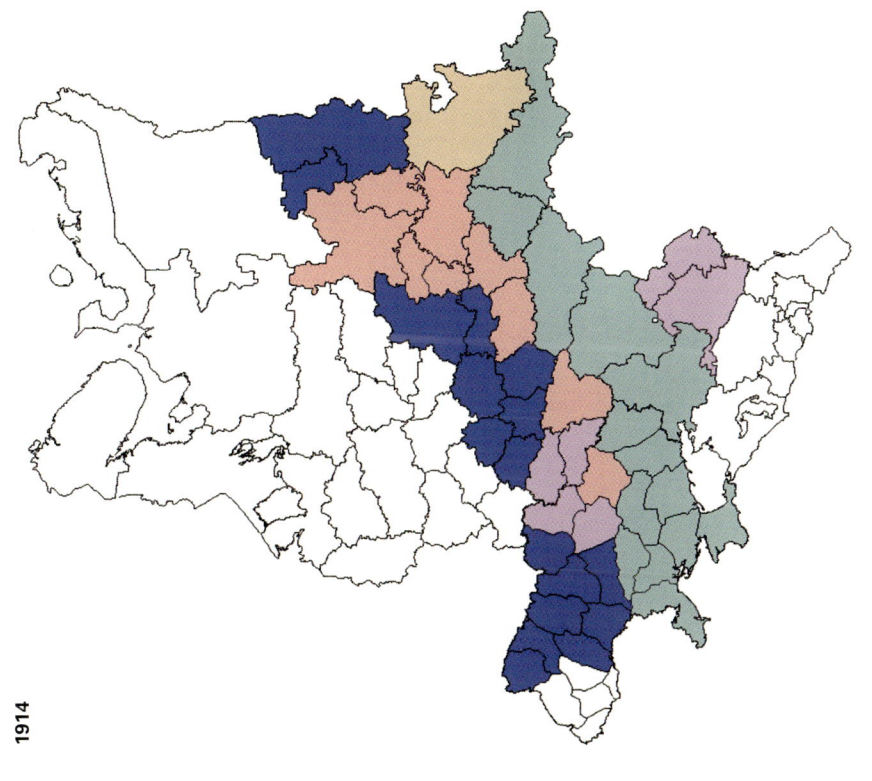

1914

FIGURE 9.6C

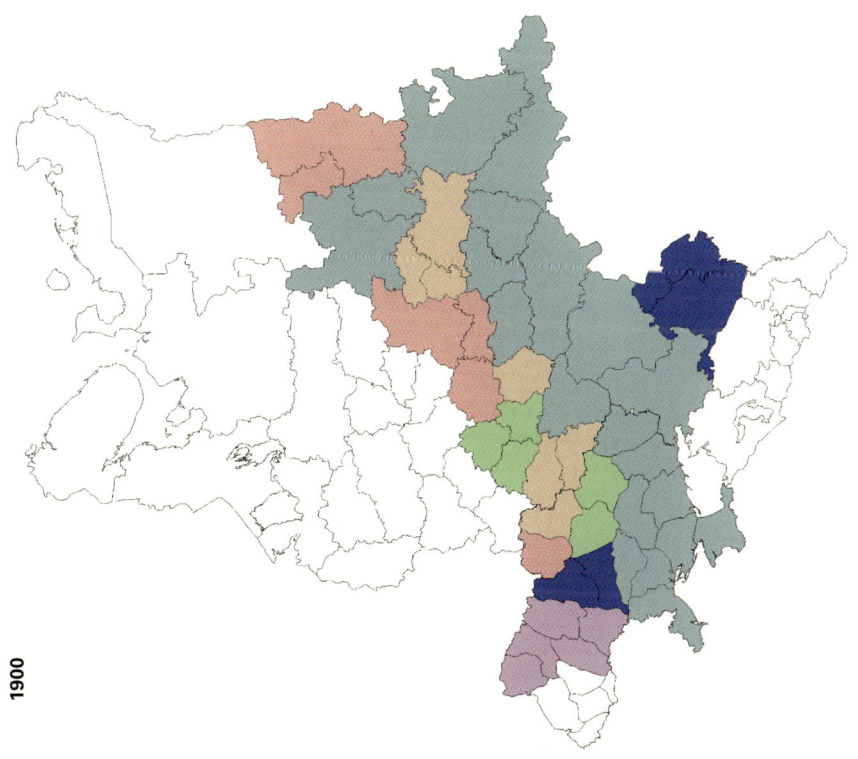

1900

FIGURE 9.6B

315

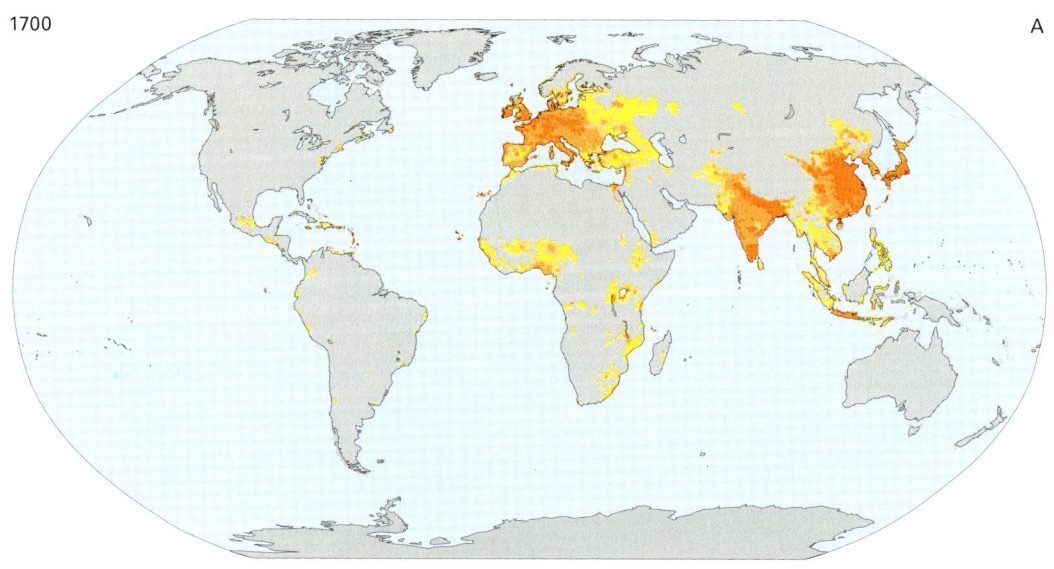

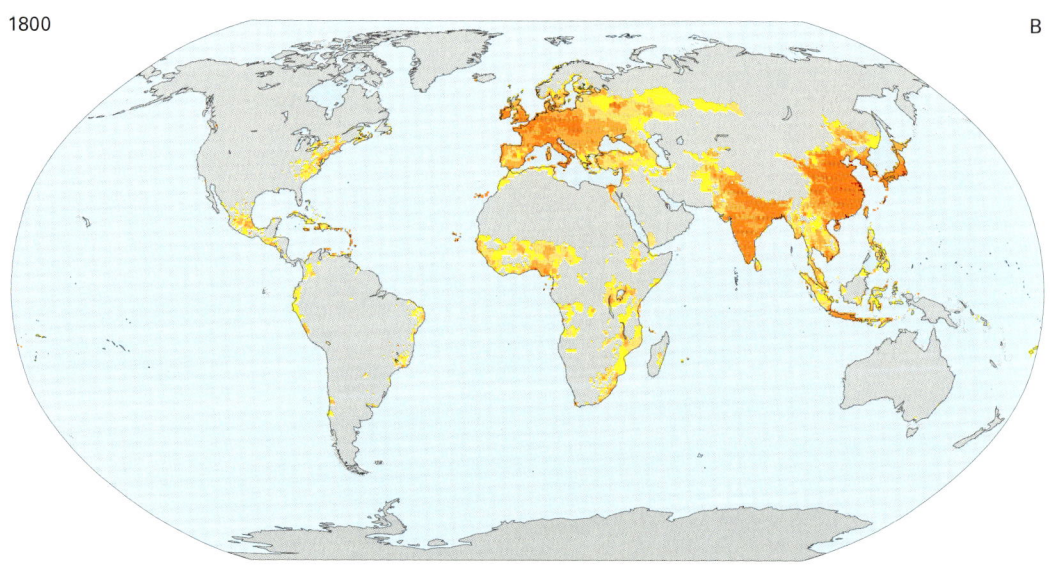

FIGURE 10.1A-B

*Estimate of population density in people/km² at the 0.5° by 0.5° spatial grid cell for the years
1700 and 1800 (Source: Klein Goldewijk 2001)*

1900   C

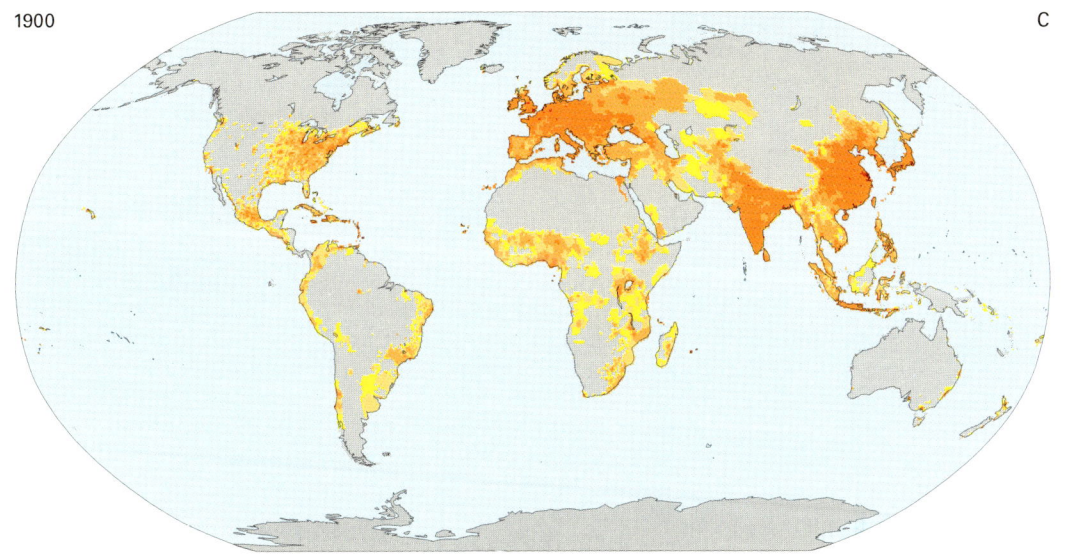

1990   D

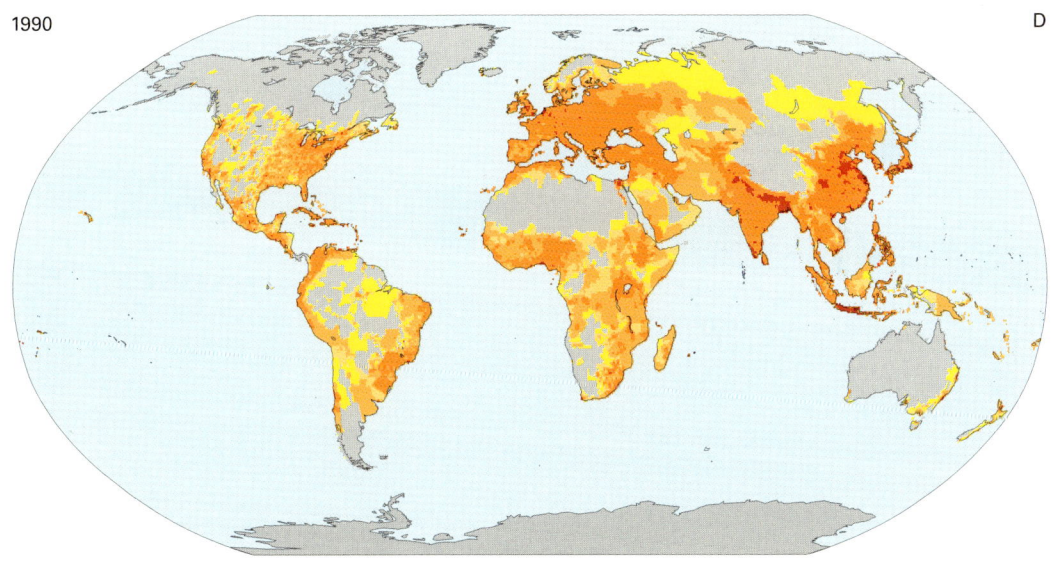

inh. / km2

0
1
2
4
8
16

FIGURE 10.1C-D

As previous figure, for the years 1900 and 1990 (Source: Klein Goldewijk 2001)

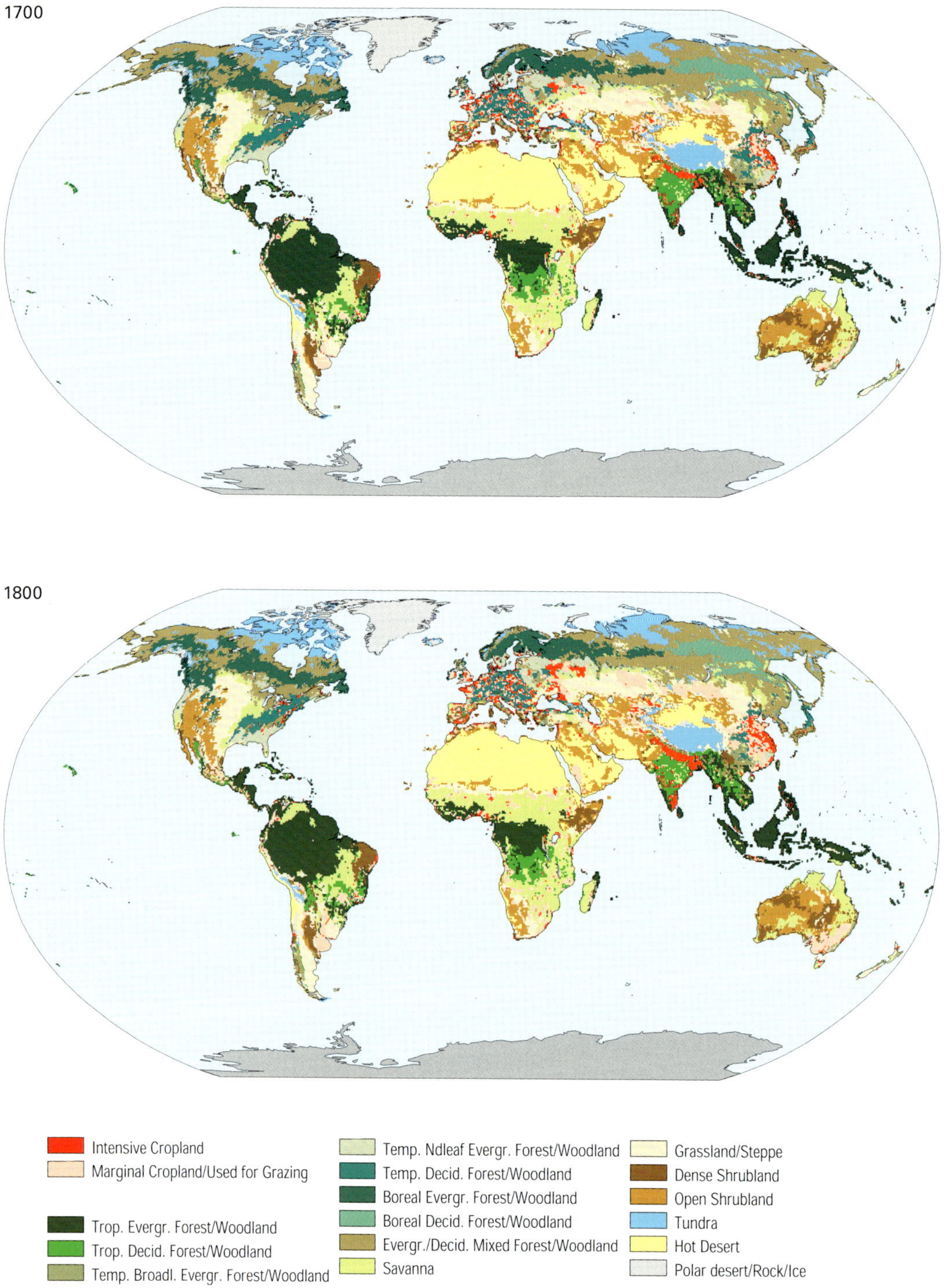

1700

1800

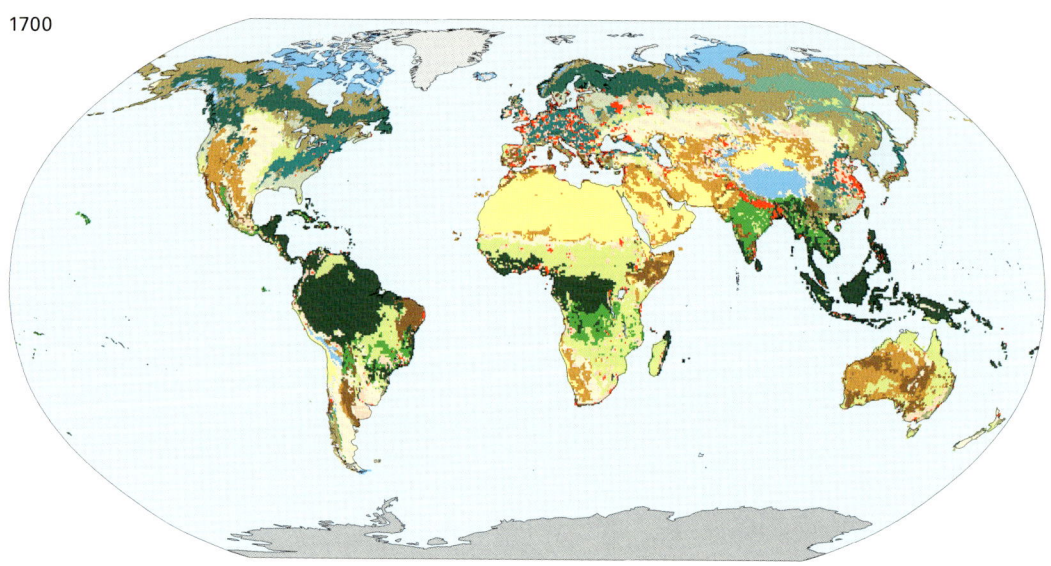

■ Intensive Cropland	■ Temp. Ndleaf Evergr. Forest/Woodland	■ Grassland/Steppe
■ Marginal Cropland/Used for Grazing	■ Temp. Decid. Forest/Woodland	■ Dense Shrubland
	■ Boreal Evergr. Forest/Woodland	■ Open Shrubland
■ Trop. Evergr. Forest/Woodland	■ Boreal Decid. Forest/Woodland	■ Tundra
■ Trop. Decid. Forest/Woodland	■ Evergr./Decid. Mixed Forest/Woodland	■ Hot Desert
■ Temp. Broadl. Evergr. Forest/Woodland	■ Savanna	■ Polar desert/Rock/Ice

FIGURE 10.2A-B

Land cover land use at the 0.5° by 0.5° spatial grid cell for the years 1700 and 1800 (Source: Klein Goldewijk 2001)

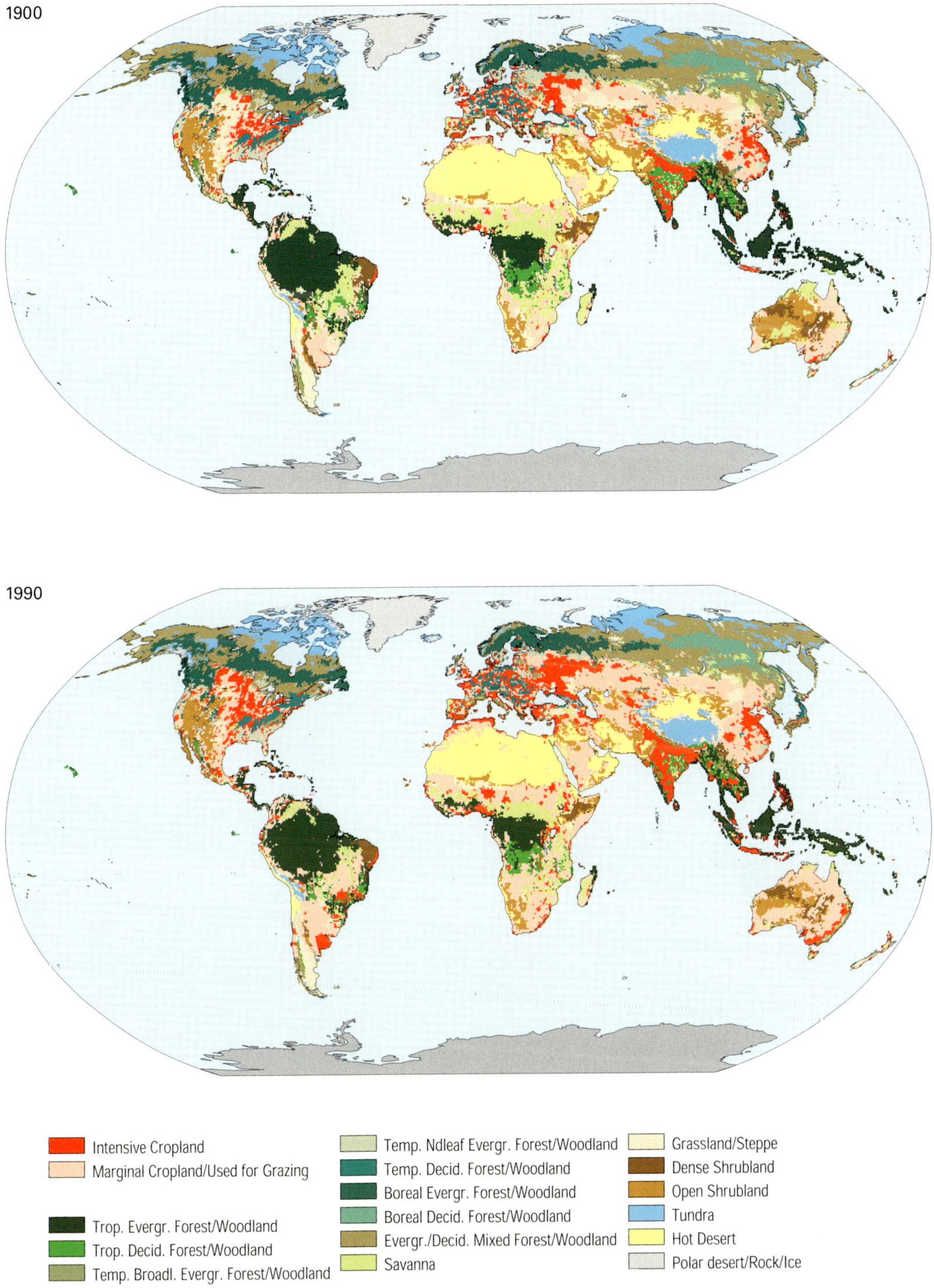

1900

1990

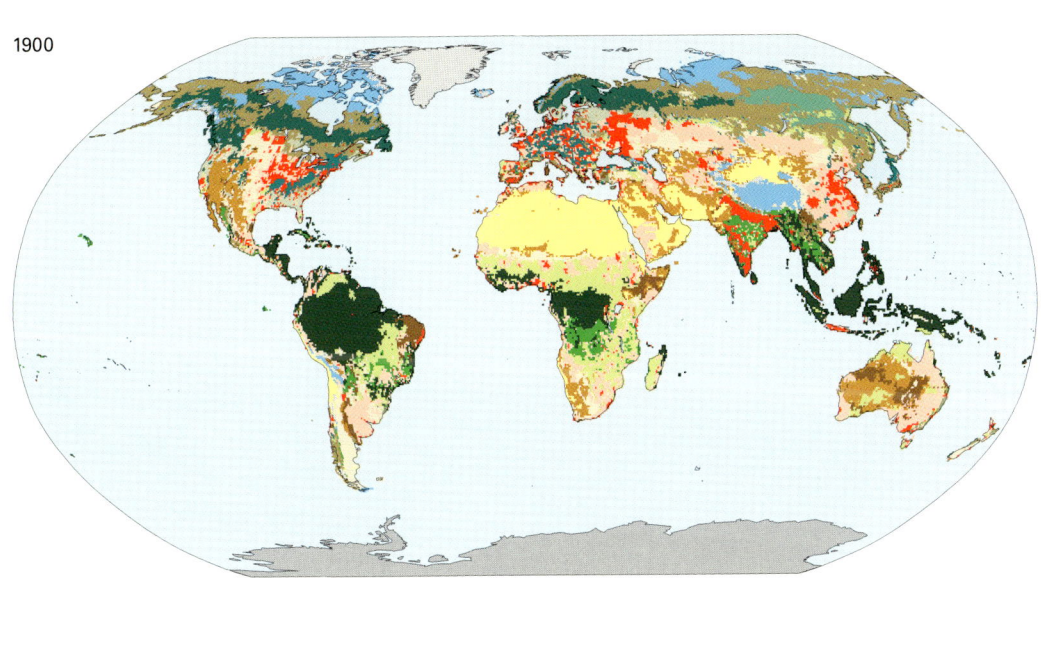

■ Intensive Cropland	□ Temp. Ndleaf Evergr. Forest/Woodland	□ Grassland/Steppe
□ Marginal Cropland/Used for Grazing	■ Temp. Decid. Forest/Woodland	■ Dense Shrubland
	■ Boreal Evergr. Forest/Woodland	■ Open Shrubland
■ Trop. Evergr. Forest/Woodland	■ Boreal Decid. Forest/Woodland	■ Tundra
■ Trop. Decid. Forest/Woodland	■ Evergr./Decid. Mixed Forest/Woodland	□ Hot Desert
■ Temp. Broadl. Evergr. Forest/Woodland	□ Savanna	■ Polar desert/Rock/Ice

FIGURE 10.2C-D

As previous figure, for the years 1900 and 1990 (Source: Klein Goldewijk 2001)

FIGURE 11.6

Jan Hendrik Weissenbruch: View of Noorden

extraction and exploitation fluctuated from regime to regime.

The colonial period represented a clear discontinuity with the past. The fundamental change was that the ruling elite was located abroad and was largely answerable to an overseas constituency highly focused on tangible economic gain via rent extraction, trade and resource exploitation. This resulted in the millennia old South Asian strategy of the assimilation of invading elite groups failing. The battle for control over local and

---

Political periods in India   The four-and-a-half centuries from 1500 to 1947 saw four broad 'periods' of geo-political hegemony in South Asia (Schwartzberg 1992):

1. the period 1504-1757 where the Moguls emerged as a pan-India power only in the late 16th century after a seesaw battle for supremacy in north India. They subsequently provided a strong-handed but relatively stable administration, that expanded by the turn of the 17th century to the bulk of the South Asian landmass. The empire then went into rapid decline as peripheral provinces asserted their independence and overextended the centre;

2. an interregnum from 1758 to the early part of the 19th century, when regional powers: the Marathas, French, Nizam of Hyderabad, Mysore and Sikhs vied for political control over with the rapidly expanding territory of the British East India Company (EIC). Even although only six decades (1710-40 and 1770-1800) were marked by the lack of a pan-Indian power (Schwartzberg 1992) the transition between the Moguls to the Marathas and the British was more disorderly than often reported, severely affecting both economic activity and well-being, especially in the form of population decline (Guha 2001). This culminated with the closely fought First War of Independence (1857-58) – or the Indian Mutiny, depending on one's frame of reference – between the EIC and a coalition of regional interests in north India led by the figurehead last Mogul emperor of Delhi;

3. the patchwork of the crown-administered British Raj (1858-1947) and its 565 subservient princely states that terminated in the Transfer of Power and Partition of India and Pakistan in 1947, following almost 50 years of political struggle for self-determination; and

4. contemporary South Asia made up of India, Pakistan, Bangladesh, Nepal and other smaller nations, faced with endemic cross-border conflict partially due to the ethic and religious nature of the Partition, contending geo-political alignments and the immense pressure of a poor and rapidly growing population on limited land-based resources.

Despite the importance of understanding the geo-political context for the present discussion, we refer to other literature for more details.

---

regional natural resources, economic and social networks of production and exchange was therefore a key factor in the struggle for colonial independence. Against this background, we first explore the population dynamics in India, to be followed by a biogeographical sketch. Next, we discuss the role of some environmental factors for population size and well-being within this broader political and biogeographical context.

9.2.1.   *Population dynamics*

India's population dynamics have been regulated by a number of unique factors, apart from traditional demographic variables. In essence, population growth results from the difference between average fertility and mortality rates (cf. Chapter 5). Demographers have found that in India fertility had been rather stable and then slowly declined; hence the mortality rate appears to be the more important explanatory variable (Guha 2001). Unfortunately, quantitative estimates of the population in India are scarce. Only since the beginning of 10-yearly censuses by the British Government in 1881 have consistent time-series been available. Despite the difficulty of scientific analysis, events over the last 200 years provide insights in the population-resource dynamics that are most relevant in the context of this book. Let us first have a glance at *population densities* in India, which are presented in *Figure 9.3* (see p. 311-312) for four years in the period 1872-1961 (Schwartzberg 1992). The densest regions in the late 19th century were the Gangetic plain, particularly Bengal, parts of Gujarat, Malabar in Kerala and areas around Madras in Tamilnadu. By the turn of the century, Kerala and parts of the eastern and western coastal plains experienced increasing populations that were connected by both road and rail links. Significant density increases occurred by 1931 throughout the Indo-Gangetic plains, especially in East Bengal, irrigated areas in the United Provinces and Punjab. An almost continuous ribbon of dense settlement had developed along the eastern seaboard with the expansion of irrigated delta agriculture. The southern tip of India including most of Tamilnadu and Kerala experienced considerable growth.

The impact of Partition[3], regional development and infrastructure investment are evident in the density map of 1961. A much larger area within Central India, Assam and former East Pakistan – now Bangladesh – shows significant densification. The expansion of irrigation projects, roads and industrial development also contributed significantly to a patchwork of new centres of growth. The differential distribution of the population across the Indian landmass is a reflection not only of the food extraction potential in various regions but also in the level of investment in infrastructure. The Partition of India is an important example of how geo-political changes can influence the redistribution of the population and food extraction. The bulk of the irrigated areas in pre-Partition India went to Pakistan leading to a massive programme of dam building in India with both positive and negative impacts.

A number of factors are mentioned in the literature as having been important determinants of the (changes in) *mortality rate* that was probably less amenable to direct human control than the fertility rate. Mortality rates are estimated at between 45 and 50 per year per thousand people over the period 1750-1850 (Visaria 1984). During the 18th and early 19th century in the run-up to the consolidation of the British Raj, war casualties, widespread famines and epidemics especially in contended territories were key factors behind these high values (Visaria 1984). In the 19th century and the 1st quarter of the 20th century the population was still regularly ravaged by famines and epidemics. The semi-arid region of Rajasthan was notoriously famine-prone, with a dramatically population fluctuation as a result. Four southern states may have lost up to 40% of their population during the famines of the 1890s. Travellers were witness to villages filled with the dead and the dying in the Madras (*Chennai*) region during the famine of 1833. Mortality increases due to famine may have mainly hit the lower classes coping with poverty and economic stress. Consumption of rotten grain during and after a famine and increased exposure to disease vectors from large infected migrant populations in search of employment and food were a subsidiary cause of mortality.

The role of *infectious diseases* has been central to the population dynamics of South Asia. The subcontinent was well-established as the seat of a number of epidemic and endemic diseases. The most important among them include plague, smallpox, cholera and malaria. Exposure to foreign contact, limited preventive medical assistance and changing ecological circumstances – which altered disease mobility – are reported to be key factors that led to high mortality during the colonial era. A major cholera pandemic accompanied British troop movements in 1817-20. Low levels of *nutrition*, especially of women and children, are expected to have been important factors in their vulnerability to infectious disease, which was clearly heightened during periods of drought and famine. Although some of the most serious epidemic outbreaks – for example the cholera pandemic of 1817 and the plague epidemics of 1904 and 1907, which killed 2 million people – did not coincide with famine, rather a number of famine events were followed by serious outbreaks of plague, cholera and smallpox. Cholera following the severe famine of 1833 in Guntur district led to the death of half the population (Visaria 1984). Smallpox was also a great killer, especially of children. The great Bengal famine of 1770 was followed by a massive smallpox outbreak, which killed nearly one third of the population. The famine of 1896 was also followed by outbreaks of smallpox and cholera. Vaccination was confined to small areas and populations, in spite of having been rediscovered in 1796. Appreciable progress in controlling smallpox in South Asia was only made in the 20th century, not far behind some European countries such as Spain and Italy (Guha 2001).

The link between malaria and the mosquito was not established by that time, but sanitation engineers had established the empirical relationship between *canal, road and railway expansion and poor drainage* with the disease (Visaria 1984). It was reported across

Bengal, Uttar Pradesh and Punjab. Endemic malaria increased the death rate and depressed the fertility rate, as it differentially affected pregnant mothers already experiencing haemoglobin deficiency. Malaria was estimated to have caused over 20 million deaths over the period 1895-1920 alone. Typhoid, diarrhoea, tuberculosis and respiratory infections worked steadily in the background, but only emerged as great killers following the decline of plague, smallpox and, to a lesser extent, cholera and malaria in the post-Independence period.

In the background, there was a trend of declining mortality rates that gradually became more important and for which economic development on the one hand and the advent of modern medical services on the other are seen as causative factors. According to Guha (2001) the mortality rate was more strongly linked to nutrition and personal hygiene levels than to advances in medical practice. The former had to do largely with improvements in agriculture, such as irrigation, roads and railways etc. The latter consisted of a multitude of factors, from improved water supply and sanitary conditions to the growth of biological immunities. Nevertheless, diseases remained a major cause of death until well into the 20th century. The first outbreak of the deadly falciparum malaria was in 1924 in Jessore. Cholera deaths reached a peak around 1900 and again in 1906-1907 after which decline set in. Plague was spread all over the country. The reason why India was the home of great epidemics in these times may have been 'that she was being exposed to foreign contact for the first time on such a great scale... India's medieval stagnation was broken down later than that of Europe, so that her period of virulent epidemic disease occurred much later.' (Guha 2001: 70). In the course of the 20th century, a further rapid drop in death rates occurred due to better nutrition, water, public health and access to medical services. This was only appreciated slowly, which is one of the reasons for the rapid population growth in the second part of the 20th century.

A careful analysis supports a link between mortality and *climate* in the late 19th to mid-20th century (Guha 2001). The period 1900-1924 in India was characterized by large fluctuations in rainfall patterns and consequently in harvests, whereas before and after this period production of food grains was on average not higher but more stable. Most experts agree that inadequate diets tend to increase the vulnerability to infectious disease. More particularly, a weather-induced harvest would hit the poorer classes through a general reduction in employment and earnings. One way for them to adapt was to reduce food intake, which in turn would make them more vulnerable to infection. On the other hand, food stability could have the reverse effect of lowering mortality. Thus, after the terrible 1st quarter of the 20th century

as the causes of mortality were inoperative, the population resumed the upward course that it had maintained through much of the 19th century... the Indian population in the 2nd quarter of the 20th century lived longer because the weather gods enabled it to maintain a stable level of malnutrition rather than alternatively plunge between adequate nutrition and severe malnutrition as it was doing earlier. This basic improvement was supplemented by the withdrawal of the plague, the non-recurrence of the lethal influenza, and perhaps by public health measures... but climate change was the most important source of improvement in mortality. (Guha 2001: 83-86)

If this statement survives closer scrutiny, it is a modern example of how environmental factors have a large-scale bearing upon human events.

The other component of population growth was the *fertility rate*. Near-universal marriage, joint and extended families with a strong preference for sons combined with the early age on marriage and linked high infant mortality have historically maintained fertility and birth rates at a relatively high level. Nevertheless, fertility levels in India did not approach potential biological maxima in sizeable populations until the 20th century. This was largely because of a number of fertility control measures, some of them different to those enabling the demographic transition in western Europe. These include permanent celibacy and strong restrictions on the remarriage of widows in an environment where the mean age of marriage was low and the mean life expectancy at birth was under 30 (Visaria 1984). One factor in the rather high and stable birth rate has been the poor status of women and their limited access to education – this declined further with the collapse of traditional systems in the early 19th century. It maintained large male/female differentials and kept both reproductive and productive decisions outside the control of women in the colonial period – a situation that is changing only slowly in contemporary India.

At times of famine, population regulation mechanisms such as female infanticide, fraternal celibacy and the control of marriage were applied among the higher classes, where and how depending on the social structures and values. The regulation of population growth by controlled *migration* was a widespread practice that persists in parts of modern India (Dasgupta 1995). The migration flows were sometimes a response to drought, famine and starvation, making some arid areas primary sources for the outmigration of indentured labour. This happened first within India to support the expansion of commercial crops such as opium, tea, coffee and cotton. Over 1.2 million people moved permanently to Sri Lanka (tea and coffee), Malaysia (rubber), South Africa, the West Indies and other locations in 1896-1928. Most were from agriculturally distressed and drought-prone regions in Tamil Nadu, Gujarat, Sindh, Bengal, Orissa and Uttar Pradesh. This brief account reveals a complex pattern of interdependent factors behind changes in the rates of mortality and fertility. Some of them, such as famines, have an obvious environmental side; others such as people's response to famine and the colonial regime are socio-cultural and political in nature. Food and famine are looked at more closely in the following section.

The rise of foreign maritime powers India was no stranger to maritime trade and even regional conquest with a long history of engagement with European, Middle Eastern, Chinese and South-East Asian powers dating to before the Christian era. The significant difference during the colonial era, however, was the dominance of maritime rather than just land-based powers. The British, French, Portuguese and Dutch colonial powers were miniscule in number compared to the estimated South Asian population of 180 to 200 million in the late 18th century. Even in 1947, the British were less than 0.5% of a total population of roughly 350 million, who were subservient to their interest (Schwartzberg 1992).

The British were the first 'coastal' power to achieve pan-Indian hegemony and unlike previous migrants and invaders were not assimilated into the dominant subcontinental culture in nearly two centuries of contact. They achieved this through a number of 'comparative advantages' including: superior military and industrial technology, trade monopolies, 'superior' organization, aggressive statecraft and the systematic co-opting of local interests. All these factors rendered many of the historic geographical and ecological constraints to conquest and control in South Asia redundant. Part of this was derived from the ideological basis of European imperialism, the strong mercantile and economic rationale for British India and the effectiveness of colonial policies to control and reduce a previously prosperous and viable region into a peripheral dependency and source for cheap raw materials.

This transition from imperial Mogul feudalism to a protectorate of the Queen Empress Victoria had a profound impact on the population-resource interface. Part of this was linked to the process of maximizing land revenue extraction from EIC-controlled areas and throttling Indian manufacturing exports. Among its consequences were breaking into the lucrative Chinese trade via opium cultivated in India and breaking the American South's stranglehold on commercial cotton production with Indian substitutes, which led to a short-run cotton boom in the mid-19th century. The jute industries of Bengal also flourished under colonial patronage.

9.2.2. Agriculture and food

Geographical land barriers

The Indian subcontinent has powerful geographical and ecological barriers that have been an important 'defence' against the mass migration of people, biological material and 'external' powers into South Asia. The arid highlands of Afghanistan, the Himalayan mountain arc and the Great Indian (Thar) desert provide an impressive set of land barriers from the north-west to the north-east, with the exception of a few strategic passes and entry points which have been the traditional locus for trade routes, migrants and invading forces. The Arabian sea, Bay of Bengal and the Indian Ocean with their monsoon winds have also been – except for the colonial powers – a rather effective barrier against invasion, and yet permeable enough to permit lucrative trade and cultural contacts and the import of exotic species.

The primary historical movement of masses of people into the subcontinent has been across its north-western and western boundaries (e.g. Mongols, Afghans, Iranians, and Turks) and to a limited extent on its north-eastern borders (e.g. the Ahom and other tribal groups). But in the pre-colonial period most of these populations tended to be integrated into the cultural mainstream of the regions that they chose to rule or reside in, even though some form of independent religious and community identity was sought to be maintained. In addition, intra-regional population movements continued as a refuge from war, famine and change of power centres, on top of migration in search of livelihood opportunities and land for cultivation. Some castes and communities became particularly mobile during the Mogul era with land-based trading and commercial networks extending from Central Asia, Tibet and China to locations across the subcontinent.

Rainfall, soil and temperature
Large areas of South Asia appear to be conducive to extensive agricultural development and hence human settlement. However, the variation in mean precipitation is extreme ranging at one end from the hot desert of Sindh and Rajasthan to the high altitude Himalayan desert of Ladakh, with an annual rainfall of less than 10 centimetres, to the high monsoon rainfall areas of the Western ghats and the Shillong plateau where annual precipitation can exceed 300 centimetres. Soil types vary considerably across the subcontinent, from the fertile deep alluvium of the Indo-Gangetic, Brahmaputra and coastal plains, the rich black soils of the Deccan to the desert soils of Rajasthan and Sind and the fragile Himalayan soils. Local communities and peasants have attempted to adapt to the soil, but poor management practices often led to extensive soil loss, gradual desertification and irreversible changes in fragile hill and mid-slope environments. The pace of these changes accelerated with the population expansion and agricultural extensification associated with the later colonial and post-Independence periods.

Temperature variations are considerable across South Asia. Long-term temperature changes, as observed from changes in Himalayan glaciation, have also been significant but their impact on the rest of the region is unclear. It is possible that such changes have had an impact on critical insect vectors such as mosquitoes, thereby opening or closing certain areas to settlement (Guha 2001). The length of growing period (LGP), an important factor in the net primary productivity (NPP, cf. Section 5.6), is in South Asia on average longer that in regions such as Europe. However, LGP variations within South Asia are high and change with latitude, altitude and local climatic conditions to provide a wide range of potential habitats and biological niches. Added to these are local soil and ecological and cultural practices that create a huge diversity in land-based community livelihood strategies that persist to the current day.

Landscape change

The Indian subcontinent witnessed large-scale anthropogenic landscape change during the colonial era, with most rapid changes being reported from the mid-19th century. Previous to that, populations of various origins, ethnicities and persuasions had both created and responded to 'environmental' changes in a slowly changing social and economic landscape. Nevertheless, simultaneous long-term ecological, social and economic sustainability eluded even the 'high' agricultural practice of the river deltas, especially as throughput demands increased cyclically with an increasing population being associated with periods of relative peace and prosperity.

Reports from the Mogul era indicate a slowly changing but complex mix of agrarian, pastoral, forest and aquatic cultures and survival strategies. The land-use mix typically depended on the regional climatic conditions, resource base and local response to the promotion of agricultural extensification by the dominant states of the time, either Hindu (e.g. Vijaynagar empire) or Muslim-led (e.g. the core Mogul state). The ideology of the colonial expansion, mixed with the need for the commercial success of state-sponsored enterprises, the immense resource demands of the Industrial Revolution and an expanding population united to ensure rapid irreversible changes in the Indian landscape, at a rate never experienced before. Population densities rose from around 35 people/km^2 in 1650 to over 300 at the end of the 20th century 'accompanied by agricultural clearance and settlement, that would significantly modify the landscape over large areas of the subcontinent' (Guha 2001). Forests, grassland and aquatic and marine habitats across a wide range of ecological conditions rapidly gave way to 'managed' environments centred around subsistence and sometimes commercial agriculture. Fire, clear cutting, irrigation, poor drainage and overexploitation of soil and habitat were the most common instruments of environmental change. Other influences ranged from land management practices such as the flood irrigation of rice, the use of preferred biological stock such as the introduction of melons by the Moguls and chillies by the colonials, and the mass hunting of wildlife – a Mongol tradition that was practised by the royalty well into the 1950s – to perceived 'fair' levels of land revenue.

Agriculture

India had not witnessed agricultural modernization until well into the 19th century and

> ...her technology – in agriculture as well as manufactures – had by and large been stagnant for centuries. For a country so advanced in civilization, technology was rather primitive... in the long run the manual skill of the Indian artisan could be no substitute for technological

progress... No scientific or geographical revolution formed part of eighteenth-century Indi-an's historical experience... it appears to have stabilized for centuries, fluctuating within nar-row limits in response to non-economic factors like the level of peace and security and adjust-ing with ease to limited expansion in demand. (Raychaudhuri 1984)

Five generic cultures of food production strategies have dominated the historical Indian landscape:
1. dry land rain-fed agriculture practiced by peasant farmers was the most common across most of central, northern and north-western India; followed by
2. irrigated agriculture in many areas of the Indo-Gangetic and coastal plains using dug wells, tanks and the occasional canal;
3. slash-and-burn agriculture across most of the hill areas of central, eastern and north-eastern India;
4. pastoralism in high mountain and arid desert terrains which overlapped in range with the other land-based systems; and
5. fishing communities that survived by managing aquatic and marine resources.

Until colonial expansion and the introduction of large-scale plantation 'cash' crops such as tea and coffee, opium and indigo along with exotic cultivars such as maize, tobacco and potatoes, the total range of traditional agricultural crops had been diverse but rather stable for over a millennium. Traditional staples of rice, wheat, millet, cotton and various tree fruits were well-established before the Mogul period. The Moguls introduced crops from the Afghan and Central Asian highlands, but these were not subsistence crops. Agricultural productivity could be high in spite of 'primitive' technology and sensitive to local factors, because of irrigation, the reinvestment of surplus – after taxes and war – in primary production and an enabling land-tenure regime with a peasantry which was – in spite of endemic disease – able and skilful enough (Raychaudhuri 1984). In this 'low-level equilibrium' situation, a few factors determined the difference between prosperity,

---

Rainfall variability and famine in India   One of the most important factors that has historically influenced species choice and food security in rain-fed areas is the coefficient of variability of precipitation. Most of the subcontinent was rain-fed before the development of large-scale irrigation systems since the 19th century and electric power driven groundwater extraction of the 20th century. There have been at least two periods of aridity (cf. Chapter 3). Analysis of more recent rainfall data is more conten-tious, with the bulk of reports showing little or no secular trends of changes in precipi-tation. High variation in mean precipitation led to recurrent cycles of drought, moisture stress and decline in food production in many rain-fed areas.

---

starvation and migration – which still holds to a limited extent to the present day. The most important among them were the variability of rainfall, the size of land holdings, taxes and prices.

The pressure on land has been historically high in most of South Asia (cf. Chapter 4). A strong preference for sons and a patriarchal system of inheritance ensured a continual fractionation of holdings, with few traditional mechanisms of consolidation other than conquest, migration, death and abandonment. Changes in crop mix and irrigation were the primary historical defences against uneconomic holding sizes. The dominant crop mix in most long cultivated areas changed slowly until the expansion of canal irrigation and the introduction of exotic and commercial crops by the British in the 19th century. Irrigation made a significant difference in 'drought-proofing' small and marginal holdings and increasing their surplus value. However, the forced cultivation of certain crops – such as indigo and opium by the British East India Company (EIC) – in the 19th century adversely affected this balance, often making prosperous areas unfit for cultivation.

The prosperity of both the medieval-feudal and colonial economies was closely tied to the *monsoon* – a material fact that the 21st century Indian economy has still not broken free of. Precipitation and its variation closely influenced the crop-mix and its productivity and irrigation was primarily a defence against drought and moisture stress, rather than a means to multiple cropping. Nevertheless, drought was a recurrent annual reality in one region or another of British India. The rehabilitation and expansion of canal irrigation networks in northern India was an adaptive response to declining revenue realization in the region by the EIC in the early 19th century. The commercial success of these canals led to the development of a number of others in coastal and other areas. The canals brought with them the potential of protective irrigation and increased productivity, but also the promise of a shift of crop regime.

A critical factor in the late Mogul and colonial periods was the rate of land revenue through *taxation* – the 'income tax' on net surplus produced by agriculturists. During the Mogul period taxation levels ranged from 25-33% depending on land capability and irrigation. During the British rule, Indian farmers were among the highest taxed in the world, with the floor on taxation at 50% and rising as high as 78% when all surcharges were counted. This hugely exploitative rate of taxation undermined the basis of much of traditional agriculture as reinvestment in maintenance – e.g. of tank systems – and inputs – e.g. regular manuring and seed stock – was no longer possible. Land of farmers unable to pay taxes was often repossessed by the colonial state, leading to large-scale pauperization. This was derived not only from the mercantilist revenue maximization policy of the EIC but also from a misapplication of mind to the pre-existing Mogul system of land revenue that was formalized during the time of Mogul Emperor Akbar (16th century). The EIC and later the Government of British India introduced a system of periodic and in some cases permanent land settlement to determine the local levels of taxation and index them to inflation and revenue requirements. British India was run on the principles of a commercial enterprise, and as such had not only to pay for itself but also for the services of Pax Britannica and investor interests in Britain. As a result, land revenue was a crucial element in the struggle for the control of India between the British Parliament and the EIC. The fiscal deficit of British India due to poor land revenue was often one of the subtle forces that tilted the balance in favour of further territorial expansion to balance the books – apart from the reigning imperialist doctrine of the mid-19th century. This is an independent area of historical research but has had considerable impact on the natural resource-environment dynamics.

Other elements were *food prices and trade*. India had a long history of food grain trade and movements between regions organized by traditional mercantile communities via large land-based caravans. Movement of food between surplus and deficit regions of the Mogul Empire is well documented, as is tax relief in times of distress and drought. Manipulation of food prices and stockpiling by traders and speculators was not unknown. As Mogul market, transport and credit systems went into decline, food prices soared during India's famines, including that of coarse grain consumed by the poor. EIC policy favoured a *laissez faire* approach to the price regulation, importation and interregional movement of food at times of famine and drought. This is reported to be the cause of a great deal of suffering, migration, death and the depopulation of many districts. Famine mortality was very high in the 18th century. Grain movements and public 'relief' measures were constrained because organized regional markets developed only later with the expansion of road and rail systems. An intense debate on State responsibility for intervention continued over the 19th century and became a critical concern of British administrators. In order to reduce the burden of famines on state finances, considerable energy was expended on increasing the efficiency of relief operations.

Famine 'There were no ripening fields to be seen anywhere. On the march from Deeg to Agra five or ten villages showed a few fields of wheat and barley among the wilderness. The rest was wilderness covered with grass...The local administration was already oppressive – on top of that came the failure of the rains and the peasants died en masse, so that entire villages were left uninhabited. Entire households of ten to twenty persons all died! No one remained to dispose of the corpses! Heaps of bones lay in the houses! This is the condition of the country from the Chambal River to the borders of Kashmir and Lahore in the west; in the east to Lucknow... Many have perished. The survivors are those who abandoned their homes early and emigrated to other provinces.' (Report of a Maratha official on the famine of 1784, Itihasa Samgraha, Vol 6, nos 1-3 (1914) quoted in Guha, 2001: 36)

9.2.3.   *Famines*

Drought and famine were no strangers to Mogul India, even in the relative prosperity of the reign of Akbar (1556-1605). Few records of the extent of mortality and loss survive. Besides the monsoon, war and speculation in food grains were reported as critical factors. Disastrous events include famine in Gujarat and the Deccan (1629) that caused widespread depopulation and cattle death – so much so that taxes were remitted for two years and cattle imported to make up the loss. During the reign of Aurangzeb (1673-1767) a great famine in 1659 ravaged much of the country; another in 1685 forced him to raise the siege of Golconda. Resident populations both created and adapted to the changes, sometimes unsuccessfully – as the oral and recorded history of famines in India indicates. They also exposed themselves to a range of health risks ranging from malaria to cholera that came with expansion into particular environments. Before the advent of modern roads, railways, medicine and the widespread deforestation of the 19th century, the forest and hill borders of India probably were invisible lines of inaccessibility and endemic disease that effectively constrained large-scale population expansion in many areas in the Himalayan belt, parts of the Deccan and western and eastern Ghat regions (Schwartzberg 1992).

Nevertheless, a combination of war, rack rent extraction by local and colonial elites, increasing population pressure on moisture-stressed marginal lands and less conducive regions – with high health risks – are reported to have increased the frequency of famine from 1 in 5 years in the 18th century to 1 in 3 years during the 19th century. This was in spite of the fact that considerable energy on the part of local landlords, British overlords of the EIC – greatly concerned about declining returns in London – and Indian Civil Service bureaucrats was expended on addressing the 'Indian famine problem'. Frequent population fluctuations linked to periods of famine, epidemic and natural disasters and political unrest are reported locally or regionally, especially in arid and semi-arid terrains. The human toll of these may add up to over 30 million people over the 18th and 19th centuries, quite apart from the population 'missing' due to fertility depression caused by malnutrition and disease.

In the pre-colonial period the most long-lasting changes centred around the locus of political power, religious ascendancy and control over surplus and trade within a largely feudal community and caste-dominated framework of governance. The decline of Buddhism and Jainism in the face of Islam and a Hindu revival – starting in the 9th century – were among the most important secular trends. Hindu kingdoms across the Indo-Gangetic plain and Central India were slowly displaced by a succession of Islamic dynasties. The backbone to this was a relatively stable agrarian culture, integrated within a highly stratified social and economic structure and tied in to a mature network of urban centres and trade and credit systems to absorb and distribute surplus.

The transition between Mogul and British supremacy in the late 18th century, however, was a major discontinuity. It was marked by a series of catastrophic famines, in which up to 30% of the population of some regions perished. Drought, disruption of trade and credit due to a changing political environment, military confiscation of food stocks and the depredation of EIC traders are important factors behind these catastrophes (Guha 2001). The wars (1779-83 and 1791-92) between the British alliance and Haider Ali and Tipu Sultan, the battle between the British and the Marathas (1782-84) for the supremacy of parts of northern India and internecine conflict within the Maratha confederation all contributed to this discontinuity. This left many regions depopulated and lands fallowed, and led to the return of agricultural land to forest, shrubs and grassland.

Famine has traditionally – and officially – been attributed to monsoon 'failure' or variability in precipitation which led to reduced or no harvests depending on its intensity. Often, hungry peasants consumed the seed stock and cattle death was very high, leading to a shortage of draught power – the primary energy source of the rural agrarian economy – and affecting subsequent agricultural seasons. The reality is more complex, as reflected in a vast strategic armoury of the Indian peasant: from mixed cropping, protective irrigation, the use of a diversity of drought- and pest-tolerant species and a range of food and employment sources to migration as the last resort. A complex pattern of causally linked factors is behind the devastating series of famines across colonial India: the colonial regime, insufficient maintenance, high taxation, wars, malnutrition and diseases. The imperatives of the *colonial state* appear to have had a strong influence on the cycle of drought-famine-epidemic. Part of this was due to the unsustainable 'ecological footprint' of the dominant modes of agricultural production: the colonial pressure to cultivate cash crops such as opium and tea to meet export and balance of trade deficits. Another key factor was the *inability* of the peasantry *to maintain their land*. The reinvestment of surpluses in land development activities, of which water conservation – via tanks and small- and medium-scale irrigation systems – was critically important, is reported to have broken down. This was a result of the *excessive rents* imposed by the various forms of Land Settlement introduced by the colonial administration, changing the nature of property relations between various communities, castes and classes in an irretrievable manner.

Further causes of famine were *war* and *territorial expansion,* which were unavoidable elements of the South Asian landscape, particularly from the 1750s to the 1860s. Some of the worst famines can be directly traced to such conflicts in combination with multi-year drought. The combination of horrendous famines in eastern, southern and western India, the depredations of the Maratha confederacy's struggle for pan-South Asian dominance and the rapid and bloody expansion of British power led to a drop in South Asia's population to about 160 million in 1800. This was close to the 1700 AD population estimate and considerably below the estimated 187-200 million in the mid-18th century (Guha 2001). This 'loss' of between 25 and 40 million people was more than twice the British population at the time and had a considerable demographic impact. Over a decade of conflict in eastern India, rack rents and a severe food shortage combined with a smallpox epidemic led to extensive depopulation and the beginning of the economic decline of one of the most prosperous regions of Asia. The great Bengal famine of 1770 alone carried off one-third of the region's population, an estimated 10 million people. The extraction of surplus for many generations from the treasuries of Indian kingdoms, together with punitive taxes, charges for good governance and the systematic destruction of a relatively large pre-industrial manufacturing sector – particularly in textiles – had the collapse of secondary industry as one its side effects. This is well-documented for the late 18th and early 19th centuries and created large landless service castes.

Growth reasserted itself through the early 19th century as the frequency of serious conflicts declined and the EIC emerged as the single largest pan-Indian power. The only other major demographic discontinuity was around the period 1857-1861 after the First War of Independence, when a combination of armed conflict in northern India and famine caused over 2 million deaths. This was reported to be partially mitigated by the recommissioning of large-scale irrigation systems between the rivers Yamuna and Ganga at that time. The typical colonial state response to the need for famine mitigation measures was to promote commercial canal irrigation schemes – that also provided handsome returns – and the extension of railways – which were promoted by private capital with guaranteed returns of 5% at state expense. Canal and railway expansion unfortunately introduced malaria to new regions, through a significant change in the drainage regime and local habitat.

Other related causes are *deficient nutrition* and *infectious diseases*, in part consequences of economic forces. The impact of reduced nutrition due to recurrent drought and under-nourishment is well recognized, especially among children and women. Settlement of marginal forest, wetland or *tarai* lands and the expansion of roads and railways, which altered the drainage regimes in these areas, led to increased incidence of malaria, diarrhoea and gastro-intestinal diseases. Epidemics contributed to an increasing fraction of famine events over the colonial period, providing some degree of justification to the reports of the negative environmental and health impacts of colonial road, railway and plantation development. The population expansion into these areas during the colonial period coincided with the rapid growth of tea, coffee, cotton and opium plantations under the influence of market forces. Indentured labourers were often transported in great numbers and over vast distances to cultivate these new crops. They suffered greatly due to the poor living and working conditions, apart from the new endemic health risks. Simultaneously, the immense requirement of timber for railways, mines and new industries led to extensive deforestation of vast areas in the Himalayas and central, eastern and southern India. These fragile areas then became the basis for marginal agriculture for immigration populations.

Population kept growing steadily in the late 19th and early 20th centuries. Despite peace and rapid growth of irrigation and road, rail and communication infrastructures in the British Empire, the scourge of famine continued. The two most devastating were those of 1876-1978 with 37 million affected and 4.3 million deaths and the years 1896 and 1899 with a combined mortality of 6.65 million people. The combined impact of improved economic conditions and food production, better governance and public health lead to a sharp decline in famine frequency from the early parts of the 20th century. The closing days of the British Raj would have been 'famine-free' were it not for the infamous Bengal famine of 1943 which affected 60 million people of whom about 3.5 million died. This was in spite of the high-level of mobilization of the war economy, an overall food surplus in South Asia and over 150 years of experience of 'managing famine' in the same region of the world. Economic forces, disentitlement of the poor, hoarding spiralling food prices and a complete breakdown of the community support and public rationing systems signalled the beginning of a new era of 'development' and 'food aid'.

The great 'success' of Independent India has been its 'famine-free' history with a strong emphasis on national food security and productivity at the cost of other priorities. It happened in spite of long-term drought and large-scale refugee influx. This in no means implies that malnourishment and hunger have disappeared from the land, but the widespread loss of millions of lives appears to be an occurrence of the past. Important factors were the abolition of Land Revenue, land reforms and the abolition of landlords and intermediate tax collectors, irrigation, the development of an effective public distribution system, new highly productive crop species and the input of fertilizer and new farming techniques.

Causes of famine
The occurrence of famine and the extent and nature of its consequences is a multi-causal phenomenon and defies any simple explanations. *Figure 9.4* (see p. 313) shows some of the quantitative data available: the number of regional famine trends in India and the reported causes of famines in the period 1750-1950. There may have been under-reporting in non-British controlled areas in the 18th century. As regards the *regional famine trends*, the highest famine frequency over this 200-year period is reported from western India with its large desert and arid areas, followed closely by southern India with its high proportion of rain shadow and semi-arid rain-fed areas (*Figure 9.4a*). Northern India with its mix of semi-arid to moderate rainfall areas and central India with its recurrent drought had a similar frequency of famine. Eastern India with its heavy monsoon, vast rivers and fertile soils reported the lowest frequency – roughly one in ten years – in keeping with its history of better rainfall distribution and lower meteorological drought.

The higher relative famine frequency reported during the early years of colonial territorial expansion and the consolidation of administration and land revenue in each of these regions stands out. Eastern India experienced a devastating famine in 1770 within two decades of the assumption of EIC management of the province of Bengal. The highest famine frequency – one in two-and-a-half years – was reported from western India during the final years of the power struggle between the EIC and the Maratha Confederacy, and also during the expansion and consolidation of the Land (Revenue) Settlements in southern and northern India.

A decline in famine frequency should have been expected in northern and southern India during the latter part of the 19th century with considerable investments in irrigation projects, roads and the first colonial railway systems. Unfortunately, the collapse of the traditional systems of water management, such as tank irrigation in Tamilnadu and Mysore in southern India, rack rents and increased mortality due to both epidemic (smallpox, cholera and typhoid) and endemic (malaria and diarrhoea) disease appear to have constrained this improvement. Improvements in public health (e.g. vaccination), better nutrition derived from improved entitlement and a more effective public distribution and relief system resulted in a sharp decline in the incidence of famine during the early part of the 20th century. In fact, the famine of 1907 was reported to have affected over 50 million people but mortality was very low due to a 'great success' in decentralized relief and the curtailment of the impact of disease (Visaria 1984).

Regarding the *reported causes of famine*: about 45% were primarily caused by drought over this 200-year period; about one-quarter were caused by a mix of conflict and drought conditions, and slightly more than one-sixth by a mixture of drought, food scarcity and linked epidemics (*Figure 9.4b*). A combination of drought and locust attack or flooding made up 7% each. Extensive flash flooding, especially in arid areas, is often caused by a mixture of exceptional meteorological conditions combined with environmental degradation – especially deforestation, change in vegetative cover and soil erosion – due to poor management. This could be traced to insufficient ability to invest by debt-ridden peasant farmers. Locust attacks were reported as an important cause of famine in northern and western India up to the middle of the 19th century. The time trends are remarkable: the importance of drought as the sole cause increased significantly, the other causes having a lower occurrence. This can be related to the decline of serious conflict in South Asia with the establishment of British hegemony by the mid-19th century. It is notable, however, that the famine frequency increased considerably synchronously with the expansion of British administrative boundaries and growth in land revenue collection across the subcontinent.

9.3.   Population and environment in South-East Asia – a historical view with particular reference to Sulawesi (Indonesia)[4]

Causes of low population density
The central problem in the environmental history of South-East Asia is that of what Anthony Reid (1987) has called 'low population growth and its causes' in this region in pre-colonial times. In the era before modern plantation agriculture or mechanized log-

ging, the human impact on the natural environment was in the first place a matter of the amount of food that had to be grown to feed local populations. The total human population of South-East Asia in the year 1600, Reid calculates, was about 22 million, and the average population density little more than 5 people/km². While these are crude and highly questionable estimates, it is clear that South-East Asia at that time was sparsely populated compared with China, India or Europe, and the scale of agricultural deforestation was correspondingly smaller. Equally certain is that very rapid demographic growth during the colonial and postcolonial periods has now brought South-East Asia's total population to over 500 million, a number perhaps 20 times that which it supported four centuries ago and as great as the current population of Europe.

These observations have led many writers to conclude that pre-colonial South-East Asia was for the most part an 'open frontier' (Reid 1988-93 I: 26) in which population densities 'remained far below the carrying capacity of the environment' (Knapen 2001: 390-91). Demographic trends, in other words, bore no relation either to economic constraints or economic opportunities. Explanations for low pre-colonial population growth have often been sought in essentially non-economic factors such as epidemic disease (Knapen 1998: 87; Wylie 1993: 276), internecine warfare (Metzner 1982: 90-91; Reid 1987: 17-18), or cultural idiosyncrasies affecting the age at which people married, the number of children they wanted and the frequency with which they resorted to abortion and other types of pre-modern birth control (Knapen 2001: 391-6; Shepherd 1995). The modern population boom, in these analyses, is interpreted respectively as a consequence of public health measures, military pacification or foreign cultural influences – interpretastions consistent with pessimistic early post-colonial theories of underdevelopment which saw demographic growth as a more or less uncontrollable force acting to cancel out aggregate economic gains and impoverish the population (May 1978: 395; Myrdal 1977: 277).

There are problems, however, with any model of South-East Asian population history in which demographic processes operate independently of their ecological and economic settings. The most obvious is that the distribution of the region's population has always been a rather close reflection of its economic geography, which in turn has reflected variations in the natural environment. Take, for instance, the population geography of the largest South-East Asian country, Indonesia, around 1930. The first and best-known environmental association here is that between population density and volcanic activity, which enriches the soils of densely populated Java and Bali with fertile ash. The colonial soil scientist Mohr (1938: 493) once famously went so far as to state that 'in the Netherlands Indies the population density is a function of the nature of the soil, and this is a function of the presence of active volcanoes.' A second correspondence, classically described by the geographer Robequain (1946: 107-8), is with dryness. South Sulawesi and the Lesser Sunda islands, such as East Java and Bali, have an average of at least five dry months – in which potential evapotranspiration exceeds precipitation – each year (Huke

1982), and this enables them to support moderate densities of population. The benefits of a pronounced dry season for tropical farmers include the reduction of soil degradation by nutrient leaching and mechanical erosion (Dobby 1956: 349) and the facilitation of vegetation clearance by burning during the opening of new swidden fields (Reid 1997: 78-9). The lowest population densities, in contrast, have always been found in those areas that lack either seasonal aridity or volcanic soils, such as Borneo or eastern Sumatra.

If demographic patterns in space have been initially determined in the first place by the economic potential of the land, demographic patterns in time seem to have been determined in the first place by the volume of external *trade*. A recent historical study (Henley, in press) of the relationship between population, economy and environment in various parts of northern Sulawesi (*Figure 9.5*) between 1600 and 1930 indicates that local demographic changes were associated above all with changes in the extent of import and export commerce. Episodes of economic expansion, stimulated by demand for export products such as coconut oil, rice, coffee and copra, were usually accompanied by rising population totals, while economic dislocation, often resulting from changes in overseas demand, was associated with low or negative population growth. Although migration from poorer to richer areas was sometimes an important factor here, demographic change usually also seems to have involved *in situ* processes affecting fertility and mortality. These processes operated despite very low levels of occupational specialization, and despite the universal persistence of a subsistence-focused economic system. They also predated colonial intervention: medical and hygiene improvements under colonial rule, although sometimes effective and in one case (vaccination against smallpox) extremely so, were not necessary preconditions for demographic growth.

Evidence from other parts of South-East Asia supports the idea that commerce and population growth were linked even in apparently unlikely settings. The population of South-East Kalimantan, for example, appears to have doubled during a period of expanding rattan exports and general commercialization of the economy between 1840 and 1900 (Knapen 2001: 135). The population of Java, according to Ricklefs (1986: 30), 'was almost certainly growing at a rate in excess of 1% per annum, and perhaps substantially in excess of that rate, already in the third quarter of the eighteenth century'. In the Philippines, too, there is evidence that sustained growth set in at the end of the 18th century rather than during the intensification of colonial government in the 19th (Cullinane and Xenos 1998: 94; Vandermeer 1967: 334). Commodity export statistics recently assembled from a wide range of sources by Bulbeck and others (1998: 15), correspondingly, show that the period from 1780 to 1820 was one of very rapid commercial growth in most parts of South-East Asia. Fragmentary evidence from the Philippines, the Moluccas, and Java, conversely, suggests a widespread decline in population between 1600 and 1700; this demographic crisis coincided not only with the global climatic perturbation which produced the 'Little Ice Age' in Europe, but also with a marked downturn in the volume of maritime trade (Reid 1990: 649-51; 1988-93 II: 286-91).

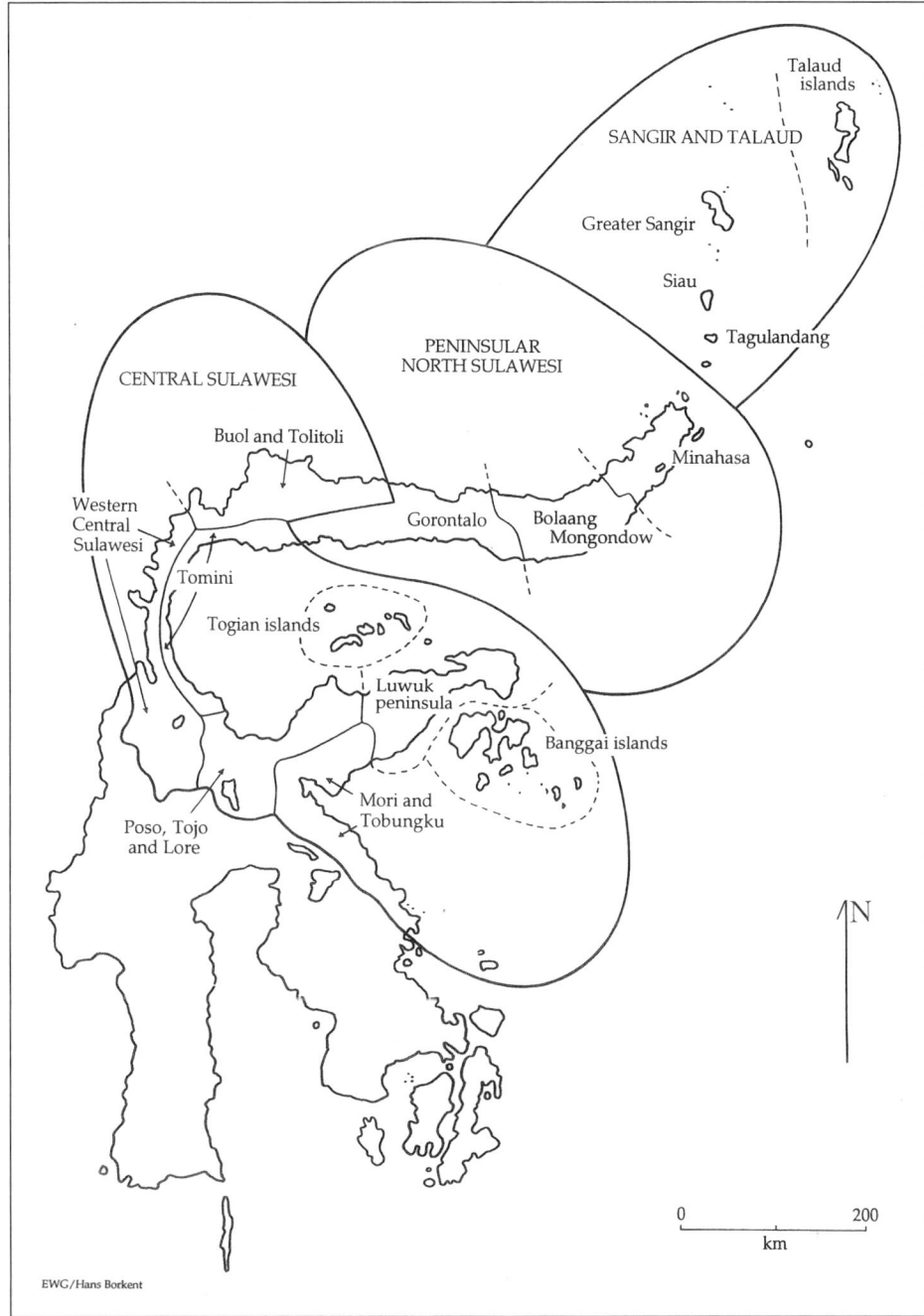

FIGURE 9.5
Northern Sulawesi

Mortality and fertility

The articulation between economic and demographic conditions seems to have worked via effects on both mortality and fertility. On the mortality side, one positive effect was that of improved nutrition. In 19th century Minahasa (peninsular North Sulawesi), a marked drop in the background death rate after 1860 coincided with an increase in per capita food production stimulated by the growth of an internal market for rice and maize (Henley 1997: 117-20). Those writers who dismiss the possibility of an articulation between population and the resource base via the food supply often do so because as far as some sparse populations in ever-wet rainforest areas are concerned, they fail to find much evidence in the oral or historical records for actual famine or starvation (Levang 1997: 105-6; Schefold 1988: 68-9). But this is a naive interpretation of the Malthusian 'positive check' which, under most circumstances, as Malthus himself noted (1976: 36), 'is not so obvious to common view' as the 'preventive check' of fertility control. The demographic impact of malnutrition works mainly via enhanced infant mortality, and in the more remote communities of Borneo it has been observed that the normal situation is one in which 'few persons go hungry but poor nutrition reduces the strength of adults and has more serious effects on the very young and very old' (Alexander 1993: 258). Medical research on Madura in the 1980s confirmed that even where 'real hunger' was never evident, infant death rates still reflected variations in the availability of food (Kusin 1994).

That subsistence-oriented communities sometimes suffer from food shortages due to inadequate production incentives, so that participation in commerce may improve rather than jeopardize levels of food consumption and nutrition (Pinstrup-Andersen 1985: 56-7), is well documented both in Indonesia (Seavoy 1986: 9-27) and elsewhere (Sahlins 1972: 51-74). This is one reason why the potential 'carrying capacity' of uninhabited or sparsely populated frontier areas in pre-colonial South-East Asia was effectively much lower in the past than we now tend to assume; another is that subsistence economies were particularly vulnerable to the El Niño-related climatic fluctuations to which we now know the region is subject (Grove 2000; Harger 1995). Even in the 20th century efforts at frontier colonization often failed, and where they succeeded it was typically thanks to fundamental changes in the economic environment: either the transformation of existing landscapes by means of labour- and capital-intensive irrigation, drainage and terracing or, more often, the cultivation of new commercial crops for previously inaccessible or non-existent markets (Levang 1997; Uhlig 1984). Particularly crucial in facilitating the settlement of formerly empty areas has been the spread of industrial tree crops such as copra (coconuts), rubber and palm oil which, unlike food grains or tubers, allow farmers to profit from the biomass-generating heat and humidity of the wet equatorial environment without making unsustainable demands on infertile rainforest soils (Scholz 1984: 366; 1988: 213). Above all, successful colonization has occurred in the context of a general expansion of commercial exchange, which reduces the impact of harvest failures and frees producers to a greater or lesser extent from the geographical and social constraints to which they are subjected when they have to produce a full range of food and other subsistence goods themselves.

As well as lowering the death rate, economic growth also tended to boost the birth rate. Low birth rates in affluent post-industrial countries, and rapid population growth in the developing world, have accustomed us to associate reproductive fertility with poverty rather than wealth. In the past, however, the reverse was more often true, partly because both the actual and the opportunity costs of childrearing were lower (Lee 1997: 1074). That fertility was low in many traditional South-East Asian societies is certainly well established (Reid 1987: 40-41). Historical research suggests that in 19th century Java, rising fertility was often associated with economic improvement via increases in nuptuality (Boomgaard 1989: 197; Elson 1994: 289-90). Evidence from Minahasa confirms that as in Europe, delayed marriage, the classical form of the Malthusian 'preventive check', formed one link between low population growth and limited economic resources under traditional conditions. Up to the mid19[th] century Minahasan women seldom married before the age of 20; during the period of commercial expansion after 1850, in contrast, marriage at a younger age became more common. One reason for this was the colonization of previously uninhabited marginal land which was unsuitable for rice or maize cultivation but could be planted with coconuts yielding a new industrial export product, copra; another reason was the increased availability of cash and trade goods with which to make brideprice payments (Henley, in press). Rates of deliberate and direct birth control by means of abortion and infanticide were also affected by economic conditions. Abortions, notes a reconstruction of the pre-colonial Philippines from early Spanish sources, 'were a common form of family planning, practiced by ranking ladies to limit their lineage and preserve their heritage, or by others because of poverty or poor prospects for their children.'(Scott 1994: 118)

Labour burden and slavery
Adam Smith (1976: 98) declared that 'the demand for men, like that for any other commodity, necessarily regulates the production of men'. Indonesianists, noting that the population boom in 19th century Java coincided with a period in which Javanese households were subject to a greatly increased labour burden as a result of compulsory agricultural and road-building work, have played an important role in linking demographic growth with the demand for labour (Alexander 1979; White 1973). Evidence from Minahasa, where the population was likewise subjected during the 19th century to corvée labour in connection with the cultivation of coffee under a state monopoly system, provides strong support for the labour-demand theory of population growth. When the average number of children born into each household is compared with the size of the compulsory labour burden for a number of Minahasan districts in the 1870s, a clear positive correlation emerges (Henley, in press). It is not clear whether this resulted

directly from an increased demand for children to share the burden or whether, as Paul Alexander (1984, 1986) has suggested for Java, it was the unintended consequence of reduced lactational amenorrhoea – the temporary infecundity associated with breast-feeding – among hard-worked women with little time to attend to their children.

One very widespread pre-colonial South-East Asian social institution that seems to have had a negative effect on the birth rate is *slavery*. Missionaries working in remote parts of Central Sulawesi before the colonial conquest reported that the incentives to practice birth control by means of abstention, abortion or infanticide were strongest in those communities that contained the most slaves. One reason for this was that children were less economically important to slave owners than to free couples without access to slave labour (Adriani 1915: 458). Since slave children were often taken away from their parents at a young age and put to work for their masters, conversely, many slave women had 'no desire to bear and raise children for other people' (Kruyt 1903: 201). These observations accord with, and partly inspire, recent interpretations of Indonesian histor-ical demography that proceed from the assumption that slavery and childbearing can be regarded as economic alternatives (Boomgaard 1997: 8; Knapen 2001: 394-5). While the quantitative evidence for the relative infertility of slaves in Sulawesi is somewhat ambiva-lent, the association between slavery and low fertility is commonplace in the literature on traditional slavery in Africa (Meillassoux 1986: 79-85; Robertson 1983) and is also attested to in the Indonesian context by early Dutch sources from Ambon (Knaap 1987: 132) and Batavia (Raben 1996: 128).

Analyses of South-East Asian slavery tend to focus on the demand for slaves rather than their supply and to view slavery primarily, in the tradition of H.J. Nieboer's *Slavery as an industrial system* (1900), as a means of forcibly extracting surplus labour in a resource-rich but people-poor environment that ruled out territorial control in the form of tenancy or serfdom (Reid 1983: 8, 22-3; Warren 1998: 39-40). In most cases, however, traditional slavery in South-East Asia was in fact a more or less voluntarily accepted obli-gation based on debt. Often it originated in subsistence crises which forced the poor to borrow food from the wealthy, and both in Sulawesi (Henley, in press) and in the Philip-pines (Barton 1969: 28) there is evidence that geographical variations in the prevalence of slavery were related to differences in levels of economic security – that is, that slaves were more numerous in poorer than in richer communities. In this light slavery, like delayed marriage, can be seen as a negative feedback mechanism that automatically tended to adjust population levels to economic conditions. To put it crudely, the fewer the resources the greater the debt, dependency and slavery, and consequently the fewer children born. The disappearance of slavery from South-East Asia in the 19th and 20th centuries, correspondingly, was very likely brought about partly by increases in wealth and economic security – an interpretation consistent with the ease with which it often seems to have occurred – and the accompanying rise in the birth rate can be viewed as an indirect consequence of commercialization and economic growth.

Conclusion

Partly because population densities adjusted themselves to local economic conditions, agricultural practices were typically sustainable in the sense that average yields did not decline over time – although bush-fallow slash-and-burn, probably the most widespread farming system, was nevertheless highly destructive of natural forest. Episodes of sustained population growth, powered by increases in commerce, mostly took place in relatively favourable agricultural environments and were accompanied by capital and labour investments which made possible higher – and often no less sustainable – yields per hectare of farmland. In Minahasa, episodes of population growth in the 18th and late 19th centuries were respectively associated with a transition from dibbling to hand-tillage and broadcast sowing in swidden farming, and with a dramatic expansion of wet-rice cultivation, an ecologically very stable agricultural system (Geertz 1963: 29) which may well have increased labour efficiency as well as yields (Hunt 2000). The positive relationship between population growth, per capita income and sustainable use of the environment that emerges under favourable conditions has been described in an African context by Tiffen, Mortimore and Gichuki in *More people, less erosion* (1994). Further South-East Asian parallels are suggested by the work of Metzner (1982) and Nibbering (1991, 1997). Unsustainable or expansionary shifting cultivation, in so far as it occurred, was associated with the exploitation of poor soils by sparse populations practicing slash-and-burn farming in combination with livestock grazing (Terra 1958: 170-75). The greatest risk of land degradation may well have come not in times of economic and demographic growth, but rather in periods of disengagement from commerce, when populations which had previously imported some of their food were thrown back on local resources.

Historically speaking, in conclusion, both the size and the distribution of South-East Asia's human population have been determined mainly by economic factors. The best answer to the question of why the South-East Asian countries are now so much more populous than in the past is ultimately that given by Malthus (1976: 31) when he posed the same question in relation to the Western European nations two centuries ago: 'that the industry of the inhabitants has made these countries produce a greater quantity of human subsistence'. The sparseness of settlement in most parts of South-East Asia up to recent times resulted not from warfare, an exceptionally hostile disease environment or cultural idiosyncrasies affecting reproductive fertility, but rather from a combination of natural conditions relatively unfavourable to agriculture, and economic conditions unfavourable to exchange, export and investment. These conditions limited the supply of food and the demand for labour, the two variables that controlled long-term changes in the birth and death rates, albeit often via complex intermediate processes. When the economic situation improved sufficiently to overcome the existing environmental obstacles, for instance by creating a market for tropical tree crops or by causing the productivity of the land to be raised by investments of surplus labour and capital, population growth and the progressive destruction of South-East Asia's natural vegetation were the inevitable results. The wet rice fields and tree plantations that replaced the rainforest, on the other hand, were typically rather stable man-made ecosystems which preserved soil quality and provided sustainable yields of food and export products.

9.4. Russian expansion: eastward bound

European expansion has dominated the last 500 years of world history. Usually, the focus is on the large outward migrations from Western Europe – the topic of the next chapter. However, there was also a huge eastward expansion that was largely dictated by the natural resources abundance and scarcity. During the last millennium, the population of Russia as a political unit increased significantly (*Figure 9.1a*). Statistical data on the population of Kievan Russia are scarce; the size of the Kievan Russian population may have been some 1.9 million in 1000 AD and had grown to 3.3 million by 1300 AD (Population of Russia 2000) – thinly populated in comparison with medieval European countries such as France and Germany (Vernadsky 2001). Using the fraction of the urban population as an indicator of well-being because it shows how many people could afford to be free from subsistence farming, Kievan Russia was rather affluent: its 13% urban population on the eve of the Mongol invasion (1236 AD) was only reached again in Russia at the end of the 19th century. The many treasure-troves with Byzantine silver coins found by archaeologists is another sign of prosperity in the trade capitalism of Kievan Russia (Vernadsky 2001).

9.4.1. *Medieval Russia and the trade in forest products*

Kievan Russia was situated in two geographical zones: forest steppes and forest (taiga). In the 8th to 10th century most Russians settled in the area of rich black soil in the middle of the Dniepr basin. The Kievan economy depended on trade, in particular furs. From the 9th century the Viking traders (the 'Rus') at Kiev developed an extensive trapping network for furs, particularly sable, black fox, ermine, beaver and squirrel. They used the nomadic tribes to do the collecting, just as the Europeans were to do later in North America. The furs were sent southwards to the Byzantine Empire and by the 10th century the Dniepr river was the main trade artery. Although they also tried to control the route to the Caspian Sea, access to the Black Sea was most important. Since the first Crusader's invasion into the Byzantine Empire (1096-1099 AD), the trade situation in the basin of the Black Sea had been deteriorating and weakened Kiev's position. After the breakdown of trade with the south, trade activity switched to Central Europe where the Baltic region was becoming an important trading area under the German Hansa merchants – about

Political periods in Russia   Russian history can be divided in four periods:

1. Kievan Russia, from the Viking invasions to the rule of the Rus and the subsequent Mongol invasion from the 9th to the 13th century. It culminated as a unified state in the 11th century, with the city of Kiev located in the forest zone in the basin of the Dniepr River as its main centre. During succession struggles, the city of Novgorod entered into its golden age and received the right to elect its own archbishop through the veche or popular assembly from Kiev in 1156 AD. While the remainder of Russia suffered from the Tartar-Mongol conquest, Novgorod's willingness to buy off the invaders with tribute, its distance from the main body of the horde and its marshy surroundings all contributed to its autonomy, which continued until it surrendered to Moscow in 1478 AD – which was the start of

2. Muscovy Russia from the 14th to the 17th century. After a refusal to pay tribute to the Mongol Golden Horde and failed attempts of the Mongols to invade the Muscovy lands, Russia became the ideological successor to the Byzantine Empire. The city of Moscow claimed all Russian lands should be under its power. Independent Novgorod remained one of its main political adversaries, until it was defeated in 1478 AD and the merchants from the German Hansa cities were expelled and their goods expropriated. In 1493 AD Ivan III was named 'Tsar' and the next Tsar, Ivan IV and also called Ivan the Terrible, completed integration of the Russian lands under the superiority of Moscow.

3. The epoch of the Russian Empire started in 1721 with an act of the Russian Supreme Council (Senat) revoking the title 'Tsar' and awarding Peter the Great the title of Emperor of Russia. This act marked two decades of radical political and administrative reforms initiated by Peter the Great, in an attempt to transform Russia into a western-style secular state as soon as possible. Since the 18th century, the Russian Empire has seen itself as a state that belonged culturally and politically to Europe, with a rapidly growing military power and great geo-political ambitions.

4. The Soviet Union, a period of transformation of the traditional Russian economy.

three-quarters of the Hansa trade was in fur. Kievan Russia exported mainly raw materials to Europe whereas processed materials and metals were imported. Novgorod concentrated on the flourishing squirrel trade, which became its economic foundation. The value of land was reckoned in thousands of pelts and rents were paid in furs. Until the 14th century all taxes were also paid in fur (Economic History of Russia 2000). As Ponting notes:

The size of the Russian medieval fur trade and the extent of the corresponding slaughter of animals was huge, as a few surviving documents reveal. The best estimate is that at the height

345

of the squirrel trade Novgorod was exporting about 400-500,000 skins a year... Hundreds of millions of animals were killed at an unsustainable rate both in Russia and western Europe. As early as 1240 AD in the Dniepr basin around Kiev, the original centre of the trade, no fur-bearing animals were left and Novgorod merchants were already trading 1000 miles away beyond the Urals in an attempt to find adequate supplies. From the early 15th century imports into London were waning and Russian prices started to rise as the animal population declined. By the 1460s London merchants were complaining about inadequate supplies and the volume of exports from Novgorod had fallen by about a half, though they were still at the substantial level of some 200,000 skins a year. (Ponting 1991: 179)

This decline in economic activity of Novgorod marked the beginning of Muscovy Russia.

9.4.2. *Muscovy Russia and the Russian Empire: extensive not intensive growth*

Muscovy Russia saw a rapid expansion of its territory to the south-east: it increased 5.5 times between 1460 and the end of the 17th century. The Khanates of Kazan and Astrakhan on the Volga were conquered in 1552 and 1554, opening up the regions to the south and east of Moscow to settlement. In 1582 a small troop of Cossacks led by Ermak invaded West Siberia, a military action dictated largely by economic reasons in contrast to the campaigns against Kazan and Astrakhan. Ermak was engaged by rich Russian merchants to protect their fur business in western Siberia, because their trapping network was periodically threatened by the people of a khan named Kuchum (Gumilev 1992). By 1585 the vast territory of the West Siberia was annexed by Russians. In 1676 Ukraine joined Russia, which brought in another 2 million km^2 of new land with the rich soils of the Dniepr basin. Expansion into the Baltic region brought Russia access to the sea; in 1703 Sankt-Petersburg was established at the Finland bay. The most impressive but easiest expansion was to the East. Peaceful annexation of central and eastern Siberia took place in 1689, a period during which the border with China was also established. By 1707 Kamchatka was conquered and thirty years later settlements in Alaska were established. According to Ponting (1991), 'This process was nominally under state control but in practice, especially outside the towns, Russia was as much a frontier society as the United States.'

Initially the Russian population grew only modestly: in 1645 there were 6.7 million people living in Russia according to the first census. Only 4% lived in urban areas by the end of the 17th century, a sign that Muscovy Russia was poorer than Kievan Russia (Population of Russia 2000). Early 18th century, the Russian Plain was inhabited by 17 million people of whom 15 million lived in the territory of the Russian state – the largest population within Europe but at a density of only 3-4 people/km^2. The areas most densely settled were the centre around Moscow and the zone of mixed and broad-leaved forests (12 people/km^2), where population was distributed across the area. In the taiga, the population was concentrated around a few settlements. As the inroads of nomadic tribes and other enemies diminished, the steppe was colonized and the centre of gravity started to shift. Not unlike the situation in Western Europe, the major push factor was economic in combination with the desire of the government to settle thinly populated lands. In the late 17th and the 18th century, more than 2 million serfs moved south while 0.4 million people went east to Siberia and the Urals. From 1724 to 1859, the number of Slavs in the New South – roughly corresponding to the Pontic steppe – increased from 1.6 million to 14.5 million, while the number in Siberia went up from 0.4 to 3.4 million (Bell-Fialkoff 2000). Russians from the north and Ukrainians from the west moved into this wooded steppe area and by the early 18th century a quarter of the Russian population was living in these regions. By the end of the 18th century the defeat of the Turks opened up the grass steppes around the Black Sea for settlement. In the first half of the 19th century an area the size of Czechoslovakia and Hungary combined (50 million acres) was brought into cultivation by farmers in the Ukraine and Volga areas.

The *fur trade* kept its significance for the economy of Russia. By the 16th century the only remaining area untrapped was Siberia and the continuing demand for furs from Western Europe drove the Russian merchants further east into this largely unexplored area, using native and Russian trappers. As in the mediaeval period in western Russia, furs rapidly became the main trade in Siberia and the main currency. By the mid-17th century, over a third of the income of the Russian state came from the fur trade (Ponting 1991). In the

The 'pacification' of the steppe While it was expanding east, Russia was also engaged in a continuous struggle against the Crimean khanate to the south. Originally part of the Golden Horde, it was an independent entity for a generation until it became a vassal of the Ottoman Empire in 1475. The khanate proved to be a persistent and dangerous foe. The Crimean Tartars burned Moscow at least twice, in 1382 and 1571. Even worse were the incessant slave raids deep into Russian territory. Trade in slaves was the cornerstone of the Crimean economy. The last raid into Russia took place in 1769. Ultimately, only the conquest of the Crimea could eliminate this constant drain on Russian human resources. Azov, a key fortress at the mouth of the Don, was captured in 1637, lost again, and finally captured for good in 1696. Towards the end of the 17th century, an insecure 'Belgorod line' near the present Russian-Ukrainian frontier was established. The incorporation of the Crimea in 1774-83 finally eliminated the menace and the pacification of the remaining nomadic tribes opened vast stretches of the Eurasian steppe to Russian settlement.

early 18th century the total population of Siberia was about 250,000, with the European settlers already outnumbering the natives. Expansion towards the Pacific coast was dictated by economic reasons: fur-bearing animals were virtually exhausted and

> by the end of the eighteenth century the fur-bearing animals of even such a vast area as Siberia were virtually exhausted and the Russian traders were turning their attention to the sea otters. Between 1750 and 1790 about 250,000 otters were killed before the trade collapsed because of overhunting. This industry soon showed the same characteristics as the fur trade – rapid exploitation of an area until the seals were either extinct or so reduced in number that it was no longer economic to hunt them, followed by a move to a new area. By the 19th century the heyday of the Russian fur trade was almost over. (Ponting 1991: 180)

Although the early years of the Russian Empire saw the first signs of industrialization, agriculture still dominated the economy: in 1725-27 90% of national income still came from peasants as agriculture kept growing and wheat became an import export product after the 1780s (Chronology of Russian History 1994). In 1700 there were 253 settlements with the status of a town on the Russian Plain, but all of them other than Moscow were small and their 600,000 inhabitants represented no more than 4% of the total population. The peasantry heavily relied on subsistence farming. In 1719 a law allowing everybody to search and extract metals and fossil fuels was adopted. The first coal mines came into operation in 1722 and by the end of the 18th century the Russian Empire had become a leader in the production of iron, cast iron and copper.

9.4.3. *Land scarcity and rural overpopulation as the motor for expansion*

By the 15th century the upper Volga river region with poor forest soils became the most populated and Russian people started to plough these lands intensively – a somewhat paradoxical course of events (Vernadsky 2001). Some natural factors were limiting effective agricultural development in this Russian forest zone. The poor podzolic soils could produce high harvests if they were well-fertilized with manure. Unfortunately, the number of cattle needed for this never reached the critical amount for several reasons. First of all, supporting a big herd in the severe climatic conditions of Russia required the storage of a large amount of fodder during the winter season that lasted 200 days, as against 160 days for the European steppes. Russian peasants were physically not able to produce enough straw and hay to support a large number of cattle (Getrell 2000). It was a vicious circle. Any additional acreage of arable land demanded producing more and more fodder for cattle feed and at some moment in time the expenses for keeping cattle as a 'manure-producing machine' made the whole venture unprofitable. Secondly, Russian peasants only had relatively small plots to rely on and, although in good years it might give enough food for a peasant's family, there was no potential for expansion and pro-duction for the market. Perhaps, this explains the modest growth of the Russian popula-tion during this period because having a big family was a risk, not an advantage. Some researchers believe that the two periods of economic growth in Russia –1718-22 and the 1780s – both took place when the vast uncultivated territories of the southern steppes became accessible for cattle breeding for Russian peasants (Getrell 2000).

Agriculture expanded but productivity remained very low: 0.5 to 0.7 tonnes per hectare. One indicator of slow development is energy use: this increased only by an esti-mated 40% between the 17th and mid-19th centuries (Getrell 2000). Growth of cultivated area went along with population growth: food shortages had been solved by cultivating new land and not by increasing productivity. In the newly colonized areas of European Russia – or 'Central Russia' – it seems that large families had a bigger income than small ones (Population of Russia 2000). In the second half of the 19th century the population of European Russia had increased considerably and the birth rate approached its biolog-ical maximum. In the productive zones, the highest growth rate (2.4%/yr) in the history of the Russian Empire was reached and the population increased from 49.6 million in 1885 to 67.3 million in 1900. The next 15 years there was still an average growth rate of 2%/yr and in many regions of European Russia scarcity of cultivable land reached dra-matic proportions. It caused serious social and economical problems for the whole country.

The main agricultural product of the Russian Empire was cereal, occupying 89% of the total agricultural land. In the last quarter of the 19th century the cereal market deter-mined the agricultural activities of millions of Russian peasants. In 1912-1913, one-quarter of the cereal production was produced for export to the world market. Only 6.5% of cereal production was consumed in the domestic market (Popov 1925). If a peasant had a large enough area to get a decent income and cover his family's needs from the production and sales of cereal crops, there was no reason to change the direction of the farming development. The family would be fully employed, at least during spring and summer, due to the large area of arable land under cereal crops. For peasants with only a small plot of land, cultivation of cereal crops did not give sufficient income even to meet the family's demand. Millions of Russian peasants were forced to leave their vil-lages out of poverty and to search for seasonal work in towns or other regions of the country. The seasonal employment of peasants in towns can be regarded as an indicator of the deep crisis. On the one hand, the peasants failed to change their unprofitable way of farming; on the other, they did not have the resources to migrate to new regions. Instead, they tried to solve their problem by searching for temporary jobs in the towns and soon became used to their poor standard of living (Report of the Imperial Russian Geographical Society 1882).

Seasonal employment of peasants in urban areas is also one measure of rural over-population (*Figure 9.6a-c*; see p. 314-315). In early 1890s the number of peasants looking for seasonal job in towns and other regions of the country reached 6 million a year; by the end of the 1890s this number had reached 9 million (Vilensky 1980). A special commission under the government of the Russian Empire estimated the rural overpopulation to be 23 million in 1901, i.e. 16% of the population – it is hardly surprising that 670 peasants' riots in the European part of Russia were observed in the years 1902-1904.

One way to alleviate overpopulation was to resettle Russian peasants from the European part of the country to the southern areas of Siberia and Central Asia. By the end of the 19th century, these vast territories were still barely populated. By the end of the 20th century, 5.8 million Russians were already living in the four Siberian provinces and in the four provinces of the Far East, according to the census of 1897. During the years 1896-1913, 5.2 million people resettled from European Russia to Siberia, the Far East and Central Asia (*Figure 9.5*; Population of Russia 2000). This trend peaked in the period 1906-1914 when 4 million peasants were resettled into the Siberian provinces. Many of them returned, though, because of the physical and economic hardship: between 1907 and 1914 about 1 million Russian peasants returned to European Russia (Vert 1995). Despite the large migration flows, the problem of rural overpopulation in European Russia was not solved: the total number of migrants from European Russia reached approximately 5% of the population, while overpopulation was an estimated 16%. The First World War practically put an end to peasant outmigration.

The resettling of peasants in Central Asia was associated with numerous problems. Unlike Western Siberia or the Far East, Central Asia was already densely populated and resettlement happened at the expense of the local people who were nomads and already faced a shortage of pastureland. Nomadism is a land-extensive way-of-life: a Kirghiz family needed between 200 to 500 hectares while a peasant family was given 45 hectares in the same region. Immigration of Russian peasants was one of the main factors of the transition of Kirghiz peoples in northern Kazakhstan from nomadism to agriculture (Report of the Imperial Russian Geographical Society 1907).

During the World War, the Socialist revolution and the civil war the country lost more than 12 million of the employable population (Population of Russia 2000). The sowing area decreased, reaching the 1913-level again only in 1925. Redistribution of arable land among the poor peasants after the Socialist revolution undermined agriculture's productivity. Markets declined, there were severe droughts (1921-22, 1924-25) causing mass famine and ravaging many farms. Yet, even after these social and natural catastrophes, the problem of the rural overpopulation and the shortage of arable land in many regions of the European Russia still existed. Before the First World War, 5 million Russian peasants left their farms for towns looking for seasonable jobs. In 1923-24 this number was still 1.7 million, and in subsequent years it increased to 3.2 million in 1926-27. According to the State Planning Committee of the USSR, the total rural unemployment of the country reached 8-9 million people in 1928; in Central Asia and Kazakhstan overpopulation reached 2-2.5 million people. This rural overpopulation manifested itself in periodically emerging food problems and even famine. Peasants owning small plots of lands were worst hit. Other signs of overpopulation were general instability in agricultural production and uncontrolled seasonal migration of peasants. Because the Soviet economy was totally depended on cereal production in the 1920s, at least two of the four governmental crises were associated with failures in cereal production (Economic History of Russia 2000). The Soviet authority was forced to break down the traditional economy and the way of life of millions of Russian peasants. Collectivization of the peasants' farms started in 1928 and was completed by 1932. This collectivization ended ever further fragmentation of peasant land, but it also forced millions of peasants to leave their villages for new industrial centres and towns forever. More than 16 million peasants are estimated to have migrated into towns on the period 1926-37, which is more than any estimation of the size of rural population excess in the 1920s. In 1932 the Soviet authority had to adopt a special resolution forbidding Soviet peasants to leave their villages and collective farms. The urban population rose from 18% in 1932 to 34% by 1940. Thus, in combination with an ambitious programme of industrialization, the Soviet Union had been transformed from a largely rural economy with severe overpopulation into an industrialized power that started to rapidly exploit its huge fossil fuel and forest resources. This transformation happened in a short period, had many victims and was one of the largest population resettlements ever.

9.5.   Conclusions

In the last millennium about two-thirds of the world's population lived in Asia, notably China and India. Their share in the world economy has declined, however, from roughly two-thirds to one-third. To investigate their environmental history is important because in several places these large human populations were living close to the carrying capacity and it may give comparative insights into developments earlier and elsewhere.

The last four centuries of Indian history indicate that environmental history has to be understood in a larger geo-political context. Until the 17th to 18th centuries the rather large population lived in a rather low-level equilibrium, with high pressure on the land due to a variety of socio-cultural factors. Variation in rainfall – sometimes as part of larger climate/monsoon changes – occasionally triggered a cycle of bad harvests, famine and disease. With the advent of the East India Company and British colonialism, these cycles appear to have been negatively influenced by high land taxes due to far-away pressure for profit, lack of re-investment for land maintenance and wars, to mention the most important ones. Famine incidence increased, disease epidemics often followed. Only by the late 19th/early 20th century did better nutrition and hygiene and more effective relief measures lead to a decline in mortality.

Indonesia had a relatively sparse population around 1700 AD. This is often interpreted in socio-cultural terms, but there have also been important geographical and economic constraints. Early spatial patterns were related to (the absence of) seasonal aridity and volcanic soils; temporal patterns show a clear link with (opportunities for) trade and commerce. Relatively sparse population density in most parts of South-East Asia up to recent times, then, resulted not so much from warfare, disease environments or cultural idiosyncrasies, but rather from natural conditions relatively unfavourable to agriculture and economic conditions unfavourable to exchange, export and investment. These conditions largely controlled via complex intermediate processes long-term changes in the birth and death rates.

Finally, the narrative on Russia indicates how a combination of political and environmental factors caused an increasing outmigration from the Russian heartland, first towards the south-eastern steppes, subsequently into Siberia. This, one may presume, was the Eastern part of the European expansion in the last three to four centuries – the topic of the next chapter.

10

The Past 250 Years: Industrialization and Globalization

GOUDSBLOM

A quick look at maps *10.1a-d* and *10.2a-d* in the colour section of this book shows some remarkable changes. Maps 10.1a-d show changes in population density all over the world. Around 1700, there were only four large areas with a density of over 8 people/km^2 (East Asia, South-East Asia, India, and Western Europe), and none with a density of over 16 people/km^2. There had been some growth by around 1800, but it was of an incremental nature: the high-density areas had expanded somewhat, but hardly any other large areas had been added to the list. The map of 1900 shows a very different picture: spots of density of over 16 people/km^2 become visible in the original high-density areas, while new areas with a density of over 8 people/km^2 appear in the Americas and Africa, especially along the coasts. Around 1990 areas with a density of over 16 people/km^2 were found in several parts of Eurasia, and the interiors of the Americas and Africa were beginning to fill up with densities of over 8 people/km^2.

Maps *10.2a-d* show comparable changes in land cover or vegetation. Around 1700 and 1800, intensively cultivated cropland was mainly restricted to areas of concentration in Asia and Europe. By 1900, great changes had occurred and intensively used cropland now also covered large parts of North America. Marginal cropland and land used for grazing were also expanding, especially in South America and Australia. These processes of change continued through the 20th century, as shown in map *10.2d*, which represents the situation in 1990. By that time, the areas covered by forests and woodlands had also diminished considerably.[1]

The picture emerging from these maps is one of an anthroposphere that is expanding at an increasingly rapid pace. The earth has become more densely populated by humans and this is reflected in land cover. In this chapter we point to some of the processes behind the changes that have been made visible in the maps. Some of these processes have already been noted in Chapter 9, on Asia. Here the focus will be on industrialization and globalization.

10.1. Early industrialization[2]

10.1.1. *The meaning of industrialization*

As already suggested by the maps, the time span of the past 250 years for this chapter was not arbitrarily chosen. Around 1750, a new ecological regime was formed: the industrial regime, based on fossil fuel as its main source of energy. Its beginnings were small and hardly noticeable to most contemporaries, but in retrospect we can recognize how consequential they were. Humanity and the biosphere would never be the same again.

While human history over the past 10,000 years has been the history of the agrarianization of the world, the history over the past 250 years has been the history of industrialization. In the process, the anthroposphere has become one global constellation extending all over the planet, and its impact on the biosphere has become more and more intense.

In line with the approach to the domestication of fire and agrarianization outlined in Chapter 2, we define industrialization as the formation of a socio-ecological regime structured around a new source of energy: fossil fuel – first in the form of coal and later also oil and gas. The nature of this new energy source has made the industrial regime different in a basic way from the earlier socio-ecological regimes. Unlike plants and animals, and even wood, fossil fuels are not directly connected to the continuous flow of solar energy. They are a residue of solar energy from a remote past, contained in geological formations. The energy stocks are not diffuse like sunlight but concentrated in particular locations from which they can be extracted through concerted human effort. They have two seemingly contradictory properties: they are abundant and finite.

The abundance is indeed great. Coal, oil and gas represent the remains of unoxidized biomass – in other words, unburned fuel – from many hundreds million years. When people began exploiting those enormous reserves they entered, in the words of the environmental historian Rolf Peter Sieferle (2001), a subterranean forest of inconceivably large dimensions which, moreover, in the course of 250 years of exploitation and exploration proved to contain far more riches than was originally expected.

Yet no matter how large, the hidden stocks are also finite. In contrast to plants, which are the direct 'autotrophic' products of the photosynthetic conversion of solar energy, and to animals, which are the 'heterotrophic' consumers of plant and animal food, geological stocks of fossil fuel do not partake in any living metabolic processes. They are incapable of growth or reproduction, are irreplaceable and non-renewable, and, as is becoming more and more evident, their use generates combustion products that enter the biosphere.

10.1.2.   Connections and continuities with the earlier regimes

The beginning of industrialization heralded a new era in human history. Yet it was clearly a continuation of the fire regime, as every industrial process rested on the controlled use of fire in burning fossil fuel. Industrialization also presupposed agrarianization: it could never have started without a strong agrarian basis that was able to feed numerous people who were not engaged in agriculture themselves and who could therefore be recruited for work in industry. Once the industrial regime was established, new forms of fire control as well as new forms of food production were created; while the two older regimes were thus modified, they continued to bolster the industrial regime. From the very beginning, the industrial world has co-existed and co-evolved with the agrarian world, in close interdependence and symbiosis, culminating in our time in forms of industrial farming or agro-industry that lean as heavily on the use of fossil fuel as any other form of industrial production.

10.1.3.   Origins and antecedents

Like the original domestication of fire and the initial emergence of agriculture, the genesis of industrialization raises a whole array of intriguing questions, concerning its preconditions and its immediate causes as well as such issues as why it started at all, and why in Britain around 1750 in particular. These are in principle the same questions that can be raised about the control of fire and agriculture. Because industrialization began only recently we have the benefit of far more and far more precise empirical evidence; nevertheless, the problems remain puzzling. Any answer that comes to mind can only be tentative and subject to caveats.

One thing at least is certain: industrialization was not triggered by a major change in climate. At most, its beginnings more or less coincided with the end of the most recent secular dip in temperature in Europe, from 1550 to after 1700, known as the 'little Ice Age'; but no relationship with this climatological episode was evident. Industrialization was a completely anthropogenic transformation, brought about by humans in societies which were fully equipped with fire and agriculture.

Industrialization, like agrarianization, is probably best understood as having sprung from a combination of scarcity and opportunity. Again, as with the beginnings of agriculture, the scarcity factor may – seemingly paradoxically – have had something to do with the fact that, through a preceding period of extensive and intensive growth, the population had increased in certain privileged areas and had even attained a measure of affluence and prosperity. By the mid 18th century, Britain and the Netherlands were relatively rich and densely populated countries – the Netherlands mainly as a result of its commercial and military successes during the 'Golden Age' of the previous century, while Britain was currently the scene of accelerating growth. Among the effects of extensive and intensive growth in both countries was an increasing need for, and scarcity of, wood for fuel or timber. In the Netherlands timber was imported from Scandinavia and fuel was provided through the exploitation of peat – a relatively young fossil fuel that was cut in rural regions and carried to the cities by boat. In Britain, where no comparable system of inland waterways yet existed, the solution for the fuel problem was found in coal.

Coal had long been known as a fuel in several parts of the world, from early dynastic China to ancient Rome. It was considered inferior to wood, however, because of its foul smoke; moreover, it was much less easy to obtain in most places. Under the pressure of wood shortage in 18th century Britain, means were sought to overcome these difficulties. On the one hand, chimneys were improved, enabling the consumers of coal to relieve the rooms in which they burned their fires from the worst immediate effects of smoke. Far more important were new techniques on the production side, in the digging and processing of raw coal. Greater quantities could be made available, meeting higher standards of quality.

The story has often been told of how the steam engine was initially developed primarily as a device for pumping water from the coal mine shafts. The coal that was made more easily accessible with the aid of steam engines was used to power other steam engines which came to be deployed for a variety of purposes, some of which were again somehow 'self-serving': to propel steam ships and locomotives for the transport of practically any commodity, including coal. A primary element in the production of coal was iron, needed to build the engines, locomotives, railways and, in due course, ships that formed the material basis of the early fossil fuel economy. The coal and iron industries thus developed 'separately and jointly', 'in an upward-spiralling, symbiotic process' (McClellan and Dorn 1999: 285).

10.1.4.   *The early industrial archipelago*

Just as agrarianization must often have begun in small farming enclaves, carved out in an environment that continued to be the domain of foragers, industrialization started with single steam-powered factories – often called 'mills' as if they still were driven by wind or water – standing apart in the agrarian landscape. In order to indicate their initially semi-isolated position, the image of industrial archipelagos is appropriate (see Sieferle 1997: 162-3).

From the very start, however, even as 'islands' in an agrarian landscape the factories had an ecological impact stretching beyond the land on which they stood. To begin with, considerable amounts of energy and materials went into building them. The usual construction material was partly timber and, to a greater extent, brick, the manufacturing of which involved huge quantities of fuel. The engines were made largely of metal, also in a highly fuel-intensive fashion. Then, brick and timber were needed for the houses to accommodate the workers. Thus, even before the factories began to operate, their 'tentacles' were already reaching into the environment.

Once in operation, the factories had to be supplied with a continuous stream of materials, such as iron and cotton to be processed, and of fuel to keep the engines going. The need for fuel explains the location of the early industrial plants: close to coal-mines and, in the case of heavy industry, sites of iron ore deposits. Of course, a nearby sea or river port facilitated transportation; failing that, canals were built and, later, railways, connecting the islands of industrial production with the areas where the raw materials were found and with the markets where the products were sold. In 19th century Britain, an ever more extensive and intricate network of canals and railways was formed through which the industrial regime spread its reach over the entire country.

The effects on the local landscape were soon noted by travellers from abroad – sometimes with great appreciation (*see box*). In retrospect, we may find the emphasis on the beauty of early industry somewhat surprising and showing a lack of concern, not only for the miserable conditions in which the workers and their families had to live, but also for the ecological damage caused by the industrial operations. The interest expressed by these travellers referred only to the pictorial aspects of the scenery.

The entrepreneurs who ran the factories probably shared this indifference to ecological consequences. Their attitude could only be primarily commercial, conforming to a process characterized by the Dutch sociologist Kees Schmidt (1995) as 'economization'. As Schmidt cogently shows, the social pressures to think in purely economic terms were very strong, leaving little room for environmental considerations.

Even contemporary observers who were to become deservedly celebrated and influential, from Adam Smith and David Ricardo to Karl Marx and Friedrich Engels, did not always fully grasp the ecological impact of the introduction of steam engines. Their acumen was focused on human relations, on the division and exploitation of labour, rather than on the physical environment.[3] Since all the direct impressions that have reached us came from a literate elite, we can only guess how the early industrial workers and the farmers perceived the changes in the landscape. A sense of pride in the successful conquest of nature prevailed among the entrepreneurial classes in Britain, with occasional misgivings about the damage done to the countryside.

10.1.5. Coal exploitation as intensified land use

Our earliest human ancestors treated the land they lived in as essentially all of the same nature – a territory for both collecting and hunting, for foraging food as well as fuel. In agrarian societies, most of the land was parcelled up into three distinct parts with dis-

The impact of early fossil fuel industry on the landscape was registered in many forms: in paintings and drawings and in literary descriptions and factual reports. Rolf Peter Sieferle quotes the impressions of the German author and artist Christian August Gottlieb Goede who travelled in Great Britain in 1802 and 1803. On the road between Birmingham and Shrewsbury, Goede passed through a valley that struck him as 'a surprisingly marvelous spectacle. For miles around near Oaken Gates and Ketley mountain and valley are in flames. A hundred different fires are burning on the fields, and wherever the eye looks it sees brilliantly sparkling lights radiating from steam clouds. Two main points in the whole, however, appear as open craters of two big fire-spitting volcanoes. Here the glow flares up in high columns of fire like an immense multitude of large furnaces, and colours the horizon purple red for miles around. In front of them, in the open field, bright sparkling fires are burning in an interminable variety of colour nuances. One cannot imagine more magnificent lighting; for the whole resembles a large city, burning at all sides, and having set the adjacent regions ablaze as well. Many groups of busy people move to and fro in these fires, beautifully lit by the gleaming glow of coal. One might believe oneself to be in Vulcan's workshop. The multitude of these picturesque scenes is undescribable.' Sieferle quotes similar impressions from other German travellers, including Prince von Pückler-Muskau who was in Yorkshire in 1827: 'Very different from the impressions of the day, but no less beautiful was the evening. With the falling dusk I reached the big factory town Leeds. The wide space which it occupies upon and amidst several hills was covered by a transparent cloud of smoke. A hundred red fires shone up from it, and as many tower-like chimneys emitting black smoke were arranged amongst them. Standing out delightfully in the scene were huge five-storey high factory buildings in which every window was illuminated by two lights, behind which the industrious worker finds himself engaged until deep in the night. In order to add a touch of romance to the bustle of enterprise, two old gothic churches arose high over the houses, on the spires of which the moon poured its golden light while, in the blue firmament, with the vivid fires of the busy people underneath, it seemed to repose in majestic rest' (Sieferle 1997: 165-6).

A very different impression was given by the French writer Alexis de Tocqueville after his visit to Manchester in 1835: 'Look up and all around this place and you will see the huge palaces of industry. You will hear the noise of furnaces, the whistle of steam. These vast structures keep air and light out of the human habitations which they dominate; they envelop them in perpetual fog; here is the slave, there the master; there is the wealth of some, here the poverty of most; there the organized efforts of thousands produce, to the profit of one man, what society has not yet learnt to give. [...] Here humanity attains its most complete development and its most brutish; here civilization makes its miracles, and civilized man is turned back almost into a savage' (Quoted in Clayre 1977: 118-19).

tinct functions: fields or arable planted with crops; pastures or meadows where cattle and horses grazed; and heath and wood land providing fodder for pigs and sheep and, even more importantly, fuel and timber. All three areas were controlled by humans, who were able to make the land thus divided up more productive for their own specific purposes, but who also found themselves in a predicament:

> … a fundamental problem existed here: more arable and more forest products were needed in proportion to population growth, in other words the demand for wood grew at the same rate as forests decreased. If this process is considered more closely, it is essential to view arable, pasture and wood land as alternative forms of land use that were in principle substitutable to some degree without one form displacing the other entirely. It was important to create a sensible balance between them (Sieferle 2001: 52).

Maintaining this balance generally put a constraint on the tendency to growth in agrarian societies – although the examples of wet-rice agriculture in South-East Asia discussed in Chapter 4 show that it did not always bar high population densities. However, industrialization offered an opportunity to lessen the constraint. The exploitation of coal was a highly intensified form of land use that relieved the pressure to use large areas extensively for growing wood for fuel. Reckoned in this way, 'already in the 1820s, British coal production freed an area equivalent to the total surface of Britain' (Sieferle 2001: 103).

Between the late 14th century and the mid 18th century the population of England and Wales steadily increased, from 2.5 to 6 million. Then, in the second half of the 18th century, growth accelerated rapidly, owing to a drastic decline in mortality. Relief for the rising pressure on the land was found in a variety of ways: emigration, more intensive methods of cultivation, food imports from abroad and, to a large degree, the conversion of woodland formerly used as a source of fuel into arable and pastures.

Table 10.1 shows the increased use of land for agrarian purposes between 1700 and 1850 and, by implication, the decrease in land use for fuel (for a similar trend in Japan, see Chapter 6, *Figure 6.1*). This shift occurred during a period when the total population almost trebled from about 6 to 18 million, and demand for firewood would have increased proportionally had there not been the substitute supply of coal.

The virtual land gains attained through the use of coal help to explain the unstoppable advance of industrialization, once it was underway. Like the agrarian regime, the industrial regime made 'offers' that were disagreeable in many ways to a great many people, but in the long run for all of them impossible to ignore or to refuse. The huge gains in energy could be transformed into economic, political, and military advantages that proved to be irresistible. All over the world, societies without fossil fuel industry made way for societies with fossil fuel industry – a process that could not fail to have profound consequences for the biosphere.

TABLE 10.1   LAND USE IN ENGLAND AND WALES (% OF TOTAL AREA)

	1700	*1800*	*1850*
arable	29	30.1	39.1
pasture, meadows	26.3	45.4	42.8
woods, coppices	7.9	4	4
forests, parks, commons, waste	34.2	16.8	8
buildings, water, roads	2.6	.3	5.8
total	100	99.6	99.7

Source: Allan 1994: 104; Sieferle 2001: 101

10.2.   Globalization and European expansion

10.2.1.   *European expansion as an episode in human history*

There are several ways of coping with problems of serious land shortage. One strategy, highlighted in the previous section, is trying to raise productivity by making more intensive use of the available land. Sometimes, however, historical circumstances allow for the possibility of simply adding new territory.

From the 15th century onward, people from Europe began colonizing large portions of the earth, conquering the territories and subjecting the native inhabitants to their dominion. In a few rare cases the land they colonized was empty of people. More often, it was unjustly perceived as being empty of people and appropriated on those grounds, and in many cases some sort of settlement was reached with the people living in the colonized area, usually on terms that were largely dictated by the colonizers.

European expansion in the modern age is sometimes considered to be a unique and entirely unprecedented phenomenon. This is of course correct inasmuch as every single event or process is in its own way unique. However, just as no two events are completely identical, no single event is ever in every sense unique. European expansion in the modern age was preceded by numerous other great waves of expansion, from the times of the Assyrians to the Aztecs and the Incas – as discussed extensively in Chapter 6.

In his pioneering study *The Rise of the West. A History of the Human Community* (1963), William McNeill treated European expansion as an episode in the context of world historical processes. The first part of the title alludes to the famous two-volume-work by Oswald Spengler, *The Decline of the West* (1918-22), which gained renown in the years following the First World War. McNeill opposes the view, expressed by Spengler and by Arnold Toynbee, that human history consists of a mere succession of independent civilizations that emerge and decline, in a cyclical movement. According to McNeill, that view underestimates the continuity in human history – a continuity that is based on people's ability to communicate with and learn from each other. Thus, even while great empires may collapse and their cultures disintegrate, many ideas and skills are not lost and enter into the repertory of later societies (as shown in Chapters 6 and 8). New centres of political power and cultural efflorescence arise, not as completely self-contained historical entities, but taking over the heritage of predecessors – casting that heritage in a new shape, and adding new elements. In this 'ecumenical' perspective, Europe's recent global dominion was 'simply the most recent example of a recurrent phenomenon,' (McNeill 1986: 63) and should be seen in the same light as the dominance of earlier centres, from Mesopotamia (3000-1800 BCE) to China (1000-1500 CE). What made the modern 'West' exceptional was not so much its rise as its reach: for the first time, the centre exerted its influence into almost every inhabited corner of the earth.

10.2.2. *A theoretical interlude: figurational dynamics*

The issue of why globalization began in Europe is interesting and intriguing. It figures prominently in the scholarly literature – but it can easily lead us into endless discussions about allegedly unique features inherent in Europe, ranging from its special geographic location, shape and climate to its history, religion, economy, political structure, technology, scientific tradition and military force. All these features contributed to Europe's rise to temporary hegemony, to 'the rise of the West'. But they were shaped, in turn, by the part played by Europeans in the wider social figurations that they formed with others.

The 'figurational' argument works in two ways. First of all, the features inherent in any social group are, and always have been, shaped by its interactions with other social groups. This has been made brilliantly clear by Arnold Toynbee (1972: 41-2) in his 'encompassing comparison' (Tilly 1984; Pomeranz 2000) of Sparta and Athens, and illustrated in an entirely different setting by the anthropologist Eric Wolf (1982: 158-94) in his historical study of the encounters between American Indians and Europeans. As these and numerous other examples show, when social groups come into contact, they can emulate each other and become increasingly similar, resembling each other more and more; or they can further cultivate initial differences. In either case, interdependence plays a part in what may seem, when viewed from the inside, to be a purely 'intrinsic' development. Once two groups are connected by ties of interdependence, the way group A develops cannot be understood in isolation from group B – and vice versa (cf. Section 8.5.2).

Secondly, as an implication of the previous point, it should be noted that from the moment groups A and B enter into relations with each other, the dynamics of the new figuration they form together are strongly influenced by the conditions prevailing when they first established contact. Initial differences in power are particularly liable to endure, and even become magnified, in the process of increasing interdependence.

In all such cases, we are dealing not with fixed 'laws' but with general tendencies that can be observed again and again, and that can be made understandable.

The basic principle is extremely simple, and yet it tends to be overlooked in discussions about social and cultural development. Cultural features in particular are often regarded as if they are somehow 'given', immune to change. This is, of course, in line with the dogmatic interpretation of any 'revealed' religion; but it does not correspond to the reality of social and cultural dynamics.

Change generates change. This includes growth. When two groups are, or become, interconnected, growth in group A can either stimulate growth in group B or stifle it. In either case, however, it will not leave group B unaffected. This principle of 'figurational dynamics' applies to the relationships between different biological species as well as to those between different social groups within humankind.

Discussions about social and cultural development are too often dominated by a search for first 'origins' – which, in turn, is often inspired by an implicit yearning for fixed features that may prove the inherent superiority of specific groups *vis-à-vis* others and justify either their claims to privileges or their right to revolt against the holders of those privileges.

From the perspective of human history, the question when and where something started is interesting, but usually it is not the most important and by no means the only pertinent question. The most fruitful questions relate to impact rather than origins. How did an innovation, once it was introduced somewhere, spread and affect people's behaviour, power, mentality? How can we account for its appeal? These questions are patently relevant to the many innovations that have modified the relations between humans and the biosphere.

10.2.3.   *Agrarian expansion: sugar*

European expansion preceded industrialization. From the end of the 15th century onwards, encounters between Europeans and people in other parts of the world became more frequent and more intensive, often with fatal consequences for the others. The most extreme consequence was the virtual extinction of entire societies and cultures, as in great parts of the Americas and Australia – in Tasmania eventually none of the native population survived; the same fate befell many Amerindian groups. Another fatal consequence was the transatlantic deportation of millions of slaves from Africa to the Americas. Even where such extremes did not occur, the encounters with Europeans left no people – and therefore no region – on earth unaffected, including European society itself.

With European expansion, more and more regions all over the world were transformed and incorporated into the 'modern world system' (Wallerstein 1974). Tropical crops such as cotton, tobacco, coffee and tea became staple products grown on a huge scale for the international market dominated by Europeans and their 'Neo-European' (Crosby 1986) descendants in North America. Forests were turned into plantations.

Like any sweeping long-term process, the growth of the global economy began in a small way. On a few occasions, European ships arrived at the shores of lands without previous human habitation. This happened in the early stages of globalization when Portuguese sailors set foot on the island of Madeira. Soon after the arrival of these pioneers the indigenous forests were all burnt down, and the settlers introduced European domesticated crops and animals, followed by sugar-cane. By the end of the 15ᵗʰ century, Madeira had a population of approximately 20,000 people, almost all of whom were engaged in the production of sugar. 'Madeirans had plumped solidly for monoculture, had chosen to devote themselves utterly to pandering to Europe's sweet tooth' (Crosby 1982: 77).

Sugar is not generally regarded as a major factor in human society and history. Yet its cultivation and consumption has had enormous demographic, ecological and social consequences over the past four centuries. The monograph *Sweetness and Power* (1985) by the American anthropologist Sidney Mintz gives a vivid account of the crucial role this particular crop has played in modern history.

Sugar-cane originated as an indigenous plant in East Asia. Its human-processed product, refined sugar, reached Europe via India and the Arab world in the 10th century. 'Sugar,' as Mintz notes, 'followed the Koran', but then also entered the Christian world. It remained a precious luxury item for several centuries, used only by the rich in minute quantities as a spice or a medicine, or to decorate, sweeten or preserve food. As a tropical plant, it did not thrive well in the Mediterranean area; consequently, sugar continued to be a rare and expensive commodity.

This ceased to be the case, when, from the 15ᵗʰ century onwards, Europeans found new trade routes across the Atlantic and were able to colonize new lands with climates highly favourable to sugar-cane. Madeira and the Canary Islands were the first regions where the indigenous vegetation was cleared away and replaced by sugar plantations; soon much larger islands in the Caribbean and coastal areas on the South American mainland were to follow suit. Sugar became the single most important export product from these areas, linking them with Western Europe and Africa in a triangle of trade in which European ships carried finished goods from Europe to Africa, slaves from Africa to America, and sugar from America to Europe. Throughout the next four centuries, sugar imports into England rose almost uninterruptedly. One of the first manifestations of 'intensive growth' in the sense of a general rise in the standard of living in Western Europe was the spread to all social classes, from the aristocrats to the workers, of the habit of using sugar in substantial quantities; 'a rarity in 1650, a luxury in 1750, sugar had been transformed into a virtual necessity by 1850' (Mintz 1985: 148).

In the 17th and 18th centuries, sugar ranked first among the crops grown in tropical and semi-tropical climates for export to Europe, exceeding the monetary value of all comparable products such as tobacco, coffee, tea, cacao or spices. The division of labour at the plantations and the technology used in the refinery process were already 'proto-industrial', but the setting was still agrarian. That remained typical of the entire first stage of European expansion, during which land in tropical and semi-tropical regions was converted for cultivation of crops grown for overseas trade. Production took place within a commercial network, backed by military and political support. As local economies were thus made part of the emerging 'modern world system', landscapes were adjusted to the needs of the larger economy, even if in the eyes of Europeans they remained 'exotic'.

The environmental impact was often great, but should be assessed in comparison with the phases preceding and following it. Except for islands such as Madeira which had not been inhabited by humans before, the lands where European colonists settled were never 'pristine' or 'virgin territory'. The 'old world' of Africa and Asia had long been exposed to human interference, especially along the coasts and riverbanks first visited by Europeans. Australia and the Americas were 'new' continents; but there, too, the Europeans did not bring the first but rather, at the very least, the second wave of invasions by human groups.

Nor was the influx from late agrarian Europe during the 16th, 17th and 18th centuries the last wave. It merged into the next surge of emigration from an industrializing Europe, starting in the 19th century, encompassing far greater numbers of people, and everywhere making much further reaching inroads on the environment.

10.3.   Accelerating expansion[4]

The history of the interactions between humans and the biosphere in the 19th and 20th centuries is marked by the accelerating expansion of the anthroposphere. In this process, extensive and intensive growth have become more and more interconnected. The same holds true for the factors that may be distinguished as the major conditions for growth – technology, organization and civilization. These factors too have increasingly come to form intricately complex nexuses in the expanding anthroposphere.

10.3.1.   *Extension and intensification of agrarian regimes*

Nitrogen and European agriculture: clover
The history of agriculture in Europe since the early Middle Ages has been one of progressive intensification, interrupted by periods of economic recession and imminent

ecological crisis (see Slicher van Bath 1963). Attempts to raise the yields of crops and dairy products made heavy demands on soil nutrients such as nitrogen and phosphorous. Through the 17th and 18th centuries, agriculture in many parts of Western Europe became trapped in a process of diminishing returns: reduction of soil nutrients in crop fields led to a growing need for manure and hence for grazing areas (see Sieferle 1997: 135-6). An ecological crisis was looming which, according to the Danish agrarian historian Thorkild Kjaergaard, was averted by the successful cultivation of a small new crop – clover.

Clover was first cultivated in Europe in Moorish Andalusia in southern Spain, at the turn of the first millennium a great centre of agricultural innovation. Domesticated clover offered two great advantages: it had a high nitrogen-assimilating capacity and its cultivation required relatively little labour. Thanks to these qualities, the diffusion of clover helped ecological crisis to revert into ecological recovery. It changed agriculture: the amount of fallow land decreased as clover was incorporated in the rotation cycle; the balance between arable and grazing land was restored; and more forage production permitted more cattle and thus more milk and butter. Altogether it is difficult to overestimate the importance of the introduction of clover:

> ... to forget about the nitrogen factor when discussing agriculture is like forgetting about coal when dealing with the industrial revolution. Indeed, nitrogen and coal were the two driving forces between the agricultural and industrial developments of the 18th century (Kjaergaard 1995: 11).

The northerly diffusion of clover from Andalusia was at first slow, reaching Lombardy and Flanders in the 16th, Britain in the 17th, and Denmark in the early 18th century. According to some agronomists, it was only thanks to the nitrogen-enriching qualities of clover that potatoes could be grown in large quantities on European soil and could consequently become Europe's most popular staple food. Clover fields had the additional effect of attracting bees, and therefore of boosting the production of honey. In Kjaergaard's view, its overall impact on North-western Europe was wholly beneficial, with high yields, no pollution, and a pleasing visual appearance:

> The white and the red clover fields gave new colours, just as they gave new smells. In June, when clover blossomed, the countryside was transformed into a flower garden. The fertile Romantic nineteenth century landscape with red, white and green fields, with humming bees and endless herds of cattle was created by clover and the measures connected with the introduction of clover (Kjaegaard 1995: 13).

In the early 20th century, techniques were developed for the industrial production of nitrogen through ammonia synthesis. Figures cited by John McNeill in his environmental history of the 20th century indicate that by 1940 the world used about 4 million tons of artificial fertilizer, mostly nitrogen and superphosphate. By 1965 the world used 40 million tonnes, and by 1990 nearly 150 million. 'This development was and is a crucial chemical alteration of the world's soils with colossal economic, social, political, and environmental consequences.' With regard to the latter, McNeill notes that 'fertilizers mostly miss their targets and become water pollutants' (2000: 24-26).

After the Second World War, cheap energy made artificial fertilizers so easily obtainable that clover could no longer compete. Land where clover used to grow was now directly cultivated with crops. This step toward greater economic efficiency had detrimental ecological consequences. Instead of a shortage, farmers now have a surplus of nitrogen, which is leaking away into the environment: 'for centuries agriculture has suffered from the lack of nitrogen – now we are being suffocated by it' (Kjaegaard 1995: 13).

European land use in North America

Visitors arriving from Britain in North America in the 17th century were deeply impressed by the abundance of easily accessible forest they encountered. They seemed to be entering virgin territory with unlimited possibilities for harvesting wood for timber and fuel and with excellent opportunities for arable and pasture. Game and fish were also plentiful.

Of course, the land was not really virgin territory: it had already been inhabited by Native Americans for thousands of years. They had 'domesticated' the forest to suit their purposes of gathering and hunting and of slash-and-burn agriculture. It was thanks to

---

Sugar-beet One of the new crops cultivated in Europe in the era of industrialization was beet sugar. It was introduced as a substitute for cane sugar when, during the reign of Napoleon, a British blockade cut off the European continent from transatlantic imports. Ever since, the producers of sugar-cane and sugar-beet have competed in the rich markets of the northern hemisphere. Each in their own way, sugar-cane plantations as well as sugar-beet fields represent typical cases of agrarian monoculture. While the final products in the form of refined sugar do not differ much in quality, the annual yield per hectare of cane sugar in tropical zones exceeds the yield of beet sugar in temperate zones by at least a factor two – in spite of intensive use of fertilizers to stimulate the growth of sugar-beet. Yet in the 1980s and 1990s the rich world has pursued policies of tariffs and subsidies resulting in a huge production of beet sugar and a drastic decline of the world price of cane sugar – thus, as Vaclav Smil (1993: 201) argues, contributing to further environmental degradation in the north and continued economic stagnation and social misery in the south.

---

their time-honoured burning practices that the forests in southern New England were clear of undergrowth and easily accessible. 'Here was the reason that the southern forests were so open and park-like; not because the trees naturally grew thus, but because the Indians preferred them so.' (Cronon 1983: 49)

Most of the British settlers were oblivious to the fact that the Indians were actively managing the land. According to their European understanding, they were the first occupants to really work the land and on that account felt themselves entitled to own it. After a protracted series of struggles the Indians were forced to give up their claims. Forests were cleared altogether, and the land was parcelled up in lots for sedentary cultivation, mostly of crops grown for the market. The result was a thoroughly transformed landscape, 'a world of fields and fences' populated by the colonists and their livestock (Cronon 1983: 127-41).

Once New England was fully settled, European colonists slowly began migrating further west. This movement received new stimulus in the 19th century, when steamships brought a growing influx of immigrants, and railways greatly facilitated transportation over the continent. From the beginning, the railways linked the pioneers to the industrializing hinterland back East from where they were provided with tinned food and all sorts of amenities such as barbed wire and pistols. In this way, 'the West', where American Indians had only recently established new modes of subsistence with horses of European origin, was 'won'. Prairies were converted into grassland for fully domesticated cattle and into cropland for wheat and maize. These conversions were entirely market-driven. They led to one of the great environmental crises of the early 20th century when erosion and economic depression coincided during the 1930s, and large parts of the American Midwest were turned into a dismal 'Dust Bowl' from which farmers fled in despair. Astonishingly, 'wheat cultivation rebounded quickly after the 1930s as war demand took effect' (Riebsame 1990: 564).

Disasters of large-scale commercial farming such as the Dust Bowl episode could give credence to the idea that, in contrast to the shortsighted 'Western' methods of exploitation, ancient Indian land management was guided by the ideal of sustainability. In order to test this idea, the anthropologist Shepard Krech III has subjected the available empirical evidence to careful scrutiny. His conclusion is that the Indians did not leave nature undisturbed, and their reputed conservationist attitude is largely an artefact of Western ideology. The moving speech of Chief Seattle, which is often quoted as testimony to that attitude, has been exposed as a fabrication written in 1970 by a freelance speechwriter for the American Baptist Convention. Such disclosures do not detract from the fact, however, that in our day, as a result of extensive and intensive growth, the land in what is now the United States of America is put under far stronger ecological strain than it ever was before the arrival of the European colonists. Moreover, the same applies for several Indian territories today as in other parts of the world: the land of the poor is often used as a sink for the wastes of the rich (see Krech 1999: 211-15).

Further European expansion: Siberia

More or less synchronously with the westward overseas expansion into North America, an eastward expansion took place from Eastern Europe into Northern Asia, reaching in the 18th century across the Bering Sea as far as Alaska and Northern California. Chapter 9 deals at greater length with this episode. Under the Russian Soviet regime, agrarian expansion in Siberia was carried on in direct connection with industrialization, causing some of the most infamous environmental calamities of the 20th century such as the near-destruction of the Aral Sea and Lake Baikal (see Lincoln 1994: 406-7). The chemicals applied to the cotton fields around the Aral Sea turned the entire region into desert, while diversion of its tributary rivers made the sea itself shrink to a fraction of its former size. Lake Baikal was sacrificed to wood pulp-processing industries.

Tropical forests

In the second half of the 20th century, great inroads were made into the tropical rainforests of Africa, South-East Asia, and South America. In *The Primary Source*, the British conservationist Norman Myers gave a survey of the damage that is annually being inflicted. One of the causes is the need for fuel in the Third World; in many densely populated areas, fuel for the fire to cook on has become as proverbially scarce as the food to be cooked. In addition, there is a rising demand for timber and pulp from the most highly industrialized countries. The greatest threat to the continued existence of the rain forests does not lie in felling the trees, however, but in the indiscriminate burning down of entire tracts in order to clear the ground for raising crops and cattle for commerce. As Warren Dean noted in his book on the destruction of the Brazilian Atlantic forest, 'there is no tool readier to hand than the matchbox for establishing a coffee plantation' (Dean 1995: 190).

Around 1980, according to Norman Myers's conservative estimate, about 20,000 km² of forest (mostly in South America) were sacrificed to cattle-raising each year, and over 80,000 km² worldwide to agriculture, while another 80,000 km² were seriously damaged. Most of the fires that collectively destroyed the forests were started individually by small drifting farmers – whose numbers were estimated at 800 million in 1980 – who saw themselves forced to leave their homesteads and move into the forest. Myers calls them 'shifted cultivators'; he finds that today's typical forest farmer is to be regarded as

> … an unwitting instrument, rather than a deliberate agent, of forest destruction. He is no more to be blamed for what happens to the forest than a soldier is to be blamed for starting a war. The root causes of his lifestyle lie in a set of circumstances often many horizons away from the forest zones. Far from being an enthusiastic pioneer of forest settlement, he finds himself pushed into the forest by forces beyond his control (Myers 1984: 150).

The circumstances indicated by Myers are primarily economic and demographic. The world economy generates a rising demand for products of tropical agriculture. In order to meet this demand, garden plots are converted into plantations and the small farmers have to leave. At the same time, the population continues to grow, so that pressure on land becomes even greater. As a result, the contradictory situation arises that in a world suffering from a severe shortage of wood, many tens of thousands of hectares of forest are set on fire each year.

In contrast, anthropogenic fire has greatly diminished in Australia since the establishment of a European colonial regime. From the time of their first arrival, the British had a sensation of the Aborigines going about 'burning, burning, ever burning', as if they 'lived on fire instead of water' (Flannery 1995: 217). The British took every measure they could to repress these burning practices – with such success that, exceptionally, rainforest has been regaining ground again in Australia over the last 200 years. Another effect was the increasing incidence of large wildfires during dry seasons, for, as Tim Flannery (1995: 236) observes, 'by lighting many small, low-intensity fires the Aborigines prevented the establishment of the vast fires that stripped soil and nutrients most dramatically', and that now, when they are raging, constitute a serious threat to the suburbs of Sydney, Melbourne and Brisbane.

10.3.2.   *Extension and intensification of industrial regimes*

Something new under the sun
It has sometimes been suggested that in the late 20th century some of the technologically most advanced societies entered a 'post-industrial' era. The main reason for using this label is a change in occupational structure: the proportion of people engaged in mechanical industry has fallen, following the earlier decline in numbers of people engaged in agriculture. This trend is real and important; but it does not imply that any contemporary society is really 'post-agrarian' or 'post-industrial'.

The global production and consumption of both agrarian and industrial goods are continuing to grow annually. In this respect, the past decades appear to have merely continued the same trends that have become dominant since 1750. However, as John McNeill (2000) suggests in the title of his impressive environmental history of the 20th century, that century also produced 'something new under the sun'. There are two reasons, in particular, to agree with his assessment. The first reason is that the sheer quantitative increases in certain areas are so staggering as to make the very idea of further growth questionable – humanity may be approaching thresholds beyond which growth will no longer be possible, or where it will produce results that are considered unacceptable. Awareness of this fact has led to a second reason why the contemporary world may represent something really new: proposals and attempts are being increasingly made to give deliberate direction to processes that, until now, have by and large proceeded more or less automatically.

369

In this section we discuss some relevant aspects of these contemporary developments, under the headings of 'means' and 'motives'. We concentrate on the social forces behind continuing extensive and intensive growth. We shall turn to the emerging counter-trends in Chapter 12.

Our main thesis is that, until recently, ecological regimes have been losing ground *vis-à-vis* some other regimes in human society. We shall argue this thesis with regard to two regimes in particular: the money regime and the time regime. Both have, each in their own way, turned people's attention away from the natural environment, and from ecological issues, toward more purely social aspects of the anthroposphere. If the reader is puzzled by the tenuous link between money and time and the biosphere that is precisely the point we wish to make.

Means of exchange: the money regime
An obvious and fundamental condition for economic growth in the era of industrialization has been the availability of cheap energy, cheap water, and free air (see McNeill 2000). The major variable of the three was cheap energy, which was gained through the exploitation of fossil fuels with the aid of rapidly developed new techniques and vast networks of transport and distribution. Cheap energy also made it possible to provide entire cities, industrial plants, and isolated farmsteads with seemingly unlimited quantities of clean water. For the first time in history, cities could become places where mortality did not exceed fertility. The spectacular rise in life expectancy that was part of the first stage of the demographic revolution would have been well-nigh impossible without improvements in public hygiene – improvements that were sustained by an infrastructure of industrially produced pipes for the waterworks and drainage systems.

Urban history is littered with complaints about stench, soot, and smoke and with attempts to do something about it. While in the 19th century the demolition of city walls and the construction of sewers brought relief, the emissions caused by factories and by households using coal for heating were new sources of air pollution. It became increasingly evident that the air could be kept clean only at a cost in densely populated and congested areas.

When we speak of energy as being 'cheap', or say in the same vein that air is 'free', we are referring to the fact that in affluent societies today fuel can be bought at a relatively low price, and that there is no financial charge for air. The self-evident criterion for 'cheap' and 'free' is money.

During the period of the Cold War, the world was divided into a 'capitalist' and a 'communist' bloc. The distinction was predicated on basic differences in the organization of economic relations. Yet the two types of economy still had one thing in common: they both relied on money as the primary means of exchange.

In highly industrialized societies, whether of a 'capitalist' or 'communist' persuasion, people rarely produce themselves what they eat, wear, or use – they buy it, for money.

Even if they still cook their own food, they will have bought most of the ingredients.

Adam Smith was already explaining the benefits of trade and commerce in the late 18th century: trade enables people to profit from the inventiveness and the labour of unknown thousands. According to a more recent formulation, 'the development of markets and money set people free from the need to be self-sufficient, enabling them to benefit from division of labour and specialization' (Grübler 1998: 38).

There is also another side to these advantages. Many a critic has pointed to drawbacks in the market mechanism (for example, Sahlins 1972). The 'invisible hand' may be performing a sleight-of-hand. Trade is predicated on a balance between abundance and scarcity. One party lacks what the other party has in a surplus. We need only to visualize a big super market in an affluent society to see the point: there is an abundance of goods for sale – to be bought by customers who are incapable of producing those goods themselves and who are therefore wholly dependent both on the existence of well supplied shops and markets and on their own financial means without which they could only fulfil their needs by begging or stealing.

Markets thus create scarcity as well as abundance; ideally they keep the two in balance. The balance is maintained and measured by means of money.

Money, in another metaphor, is the grease that keeps industrial society going. It is sometimes said that money brings out the worst in people. But it may well be the other way round. In the first instance, money consists of small objects (coins, notes) that are of no use to anybody but that everybody likes to have. And the only reason why everybody likes to have them is the simple fact that everybody else likes to have them. As soon as this collective desire stops, money loses its value. This value is purely social: every monetary transaction is based on trust – the mutual expectation that the chain of desire will not be broken.

Like most objects that people handle nowadays, money itself in its concrete form of coins and banknotes is an industrial product. In its more abstract form of credit cards and bank accounts, too, it is completely enveloped in the system of the industrial production of electricity, computers, silicon and plastics. Technology, organization, and civilization have become equally important components of one pervasive figuration in which money circulates as the most general means of exchange and, perhaps surprisingly, a symbol of common trust.

That figuration now spans the globe. All currencies are connected; there is no escape from the transnational monetary system. This system, with its variety of national and super-national currencies, belongs to a part of the anthroposphere which seems to exist independently of the natural environment, and which has become highly 'de-ecologized'.

Means of orientation: the time regime
Globalization manifests itself not only in the glaring commercial guises of Coca Cola and McDonald's. It operates less conspicuously but all the more pervasively in such

371

international arrangements as postal services or air traffic regulations. And in what is perhaps an easily overlooked, but for that very reason most interesting aspect of global society: the international regime of time, to which everybody who consults a clock or a calendar submits (see Elias 1992; Goudsblom 2001).

The time regime exists only in the anthroposphere. It is a completely socio-cultural construction, based on human inventions, as discussed in Chapter 5. Like all human inventions, it originated in natural processes that occur independently of human purpose – in the case of clocks, the alternation of day and night caused by the rotation of the planet around its axis. On the basis of this natural 'given', people have developed the notion of 'hours' into which the day (and night) can be divided, and of minutes and seconds to make increasingly finer measurements. In 1884 an international agreement was made by 25 national states to co-ordinate their time schedules. Since then, all states in the world have joined this agreement, so that now hours everywhere have exactly the same length and begin synchronously at exactly the same moment (except for a few countries that deviate by exactly 30 minutes). The system functions smoothly, and few people know or care that the division of the day into 24 hours is based on the duodecimal counting system used in ancient Mesopotamia, present-day Iraq.

The technology of time measurement is seeping into human organizations across the world, and causing people more and more to orient themselves toward the socio-technical division of the day rather than to the natural 'movement of the sun'.

Time and money are social institutions. They both exemplify how the symbolic dimensions of the anthroposphere can become as it were emancipated from the constraints of local environments. In Alaska as well as in Ecuador, an hour is an hour and a dollar is a dollar; the symbols retain their significance and value, regardless of climate and latitude – unless the entire network of social interdependencies happens to break down.

The current time regime transgresses not only geographic distances but also the distinction between day and night. In temperate zones, hours are equally long in summer and winter, even though the actual daylight time may be twice as long in summer as it is in winter. With electricity, enclaves of light can be created everywhere.

While the colonization of the night represents one more aspect of the sheer extension of the anthroposphere, it is at the same time a function of intensive growth. It is made possible by the increasing complexity of the socio-ecological regime, enabling people to penetrate into the darkness and to treat 'the whole world' as a 'hominid cave' (Pyne 2001: 25).

Means of energy use
The same homogenizing effect that the time regime has in our age of globalization, is evident in the field of energy use. Wherever electricity is available, it is the favourite means of generating light and combustion engines are, along with electricity, the favourite means of generating motion.

372

The shift from steam engines to electricity and internal combustion is reflected in the changed industrial landscape, which in the Western world is no longer dominated by endless rows of factory chimney stacks. Yet the methods of production in modern industry, and in agriculture as well, continue to be highly fuel-intensive. Most of the energy consumed – including most electricity – is derived from the fossil fuels coal, oil and gas. Combustion processes still play a central role, but they are relegated to special containers so that most people are not directly confronted with them. Soot, smoke and the risk of fire are reduced to a minimum. The furnaces and combustion chambers in which enormous heat is concentrated remain cool on the outside.

Typical products of modern fuel-intensive industry are motor cars, with engines designed to be propelled by finely tuned and minutely controllable combustion processes. Indeed, the motor car may almost serve as a symbol of the highly complex and differentiated ways in which, in our day, thermal energy is being used. Cars are set in motion by burning fossil fuel. They are made of steel, plastic and glass – materials that are produced and processed at high temperatures. Yet no one who gets into his or her vehicle and turns on the electrical ignition to start the engine needs be consciously aware of using fire and products of fire. When driving, people do not perceive the processes of combustion that keep their car going; they do not see the petrol gas burning under the bonnet, nor have most of them even remotely sensed the fire in the factories and power plants without which their cars would never have been produced at all.

A very different example to the same effect is farming. In the early 19th century, when Britain was already beginning to industrialize, practically all the energy consumed on the farm was still produced within the confines of the farm and its fields, in the form of human and animal labour; the open fire that was burning in the hearth was fuelled with wood from the immediate surroundings. By the turn of the 21st century, the situation has become very different, with practically all the energy used now brought in from outside the farm, in the form of fertilizer, oil, petrol and electricity (see Simmons 1996: 250-55).

A major advantage of the new sources of energy is their flexibility. The fuels are easier to transport and to distribute than wood or coal and combustion can be regulated more precisely. Given the technical facilities, gas, oil and electricity provide for very even and accurately controllable flows of energy. Electricity has the additional advantage of being totally 'clean' at the place of destination. Domestically, a few simple actions and a negligible risk suffice to provide people with an immense array of services: some substituting for old chores such as cleaning the floor and washing dishes, others based on entirely new appliances such as television sets and computers. Industrially, the same advantages apply at a much larger scale, permitting a far more diversified use of power than was possible with steam power (see Grübler 1998: 220-3).

The impact of electricity and internal combustion engines makes itself felt in every sector of social life: in agriculture, industry, traffic and transportation, domestic work and leisure. Everywhere it is possible to mobilize large quantities of energy with very little physical effort. The result is to make life more comfortable in many respects, enhancing the sense that physical processes can be mastered and also, at times, fostering the illusion of independence.

An illusion it clearly is. Regardless of whether people can avail themselves of energy in the form of a petrol engine, a battery, or a connection to an electric circuit or a gas main, in each case they are able to do so only because they are part of a complex and far reaching network of social interdependencies, connecting them eventually to the energy stored in fossil fuels. As long as the supply lines are functioning, and as long as people are able to meet their financial obligations, they do not need to bother much about the entire constellation. They are immediately confronted with it, however, the moment something goes wrong with any of the conditions.

In this way the exploitation of the new sources of energy clearly continues a trend that first began with the domestication of fire. Dependence on the forces of nature has become less direct (which is not to say less important), and by the same token dependence on cultural and social resources has increased. A complicated technical and organizational apparatus is needed in order to continuously maintain the supply of energy. Most of this apparatus is located 'behind the scenes' of industrial society, invisible to the ordinary consumer.[5] Energy is made available in such a convenient fashion that it is easy to forget the social effort required to produce it.

That social effort is spent, first of all, at the drilling wells and in the mines where the energy is won and, next, during the operations of processing it into consumable gas, oil, or electricity, and of transporting and distributing it. And while the many provisions needed for the undisturbed flow of energy are often taken for granted, they cannot fail to exert permanent pressures on those who benefit from it as customers. The bills have to be paid – financially and otherwise.

The permanent availability of electricity, at all hours, in many parts of the world, has led to a diminution of the contrast between day and night (see Melbin 1987). By the middle of the 19th century, the large investments made in their factories impelled many owners to let the engines run day and night. Gaslight illuminated the work place. In the 20th century, nightlife has steadily extended, especially in the cities. Water mains, sewage, gas, electricity, telephone, fax, internet, radio, police, fire brigade, hospitals – all such services are generally expected to operate day and night. International interdependencies never come to a halt. This is one of the reasons why many people turn on the news as soon as they wake up in the morning: before resuming their daily activities they wish to learn what has happened while they were asleep – in their own country, where it was night, and elsewhere, where it was day time.

Once in a while there is a hitch. Sometimes the local supply of electricity breaks down, as happened for a number of hours in the 'blackout' in New York on July 13, 1977, and for a longer period on a regional scale in California in 2001. In New York the failure was due to technical causes, in California its primary causes lay in disturbances in the financial sector. A combination of economic and political complications brought about the international oil crisis of 1973, when the majority of oil producing countries jointly managed to enforce a drastic increase in the world price of crude oil (Yergin 1991: 588-652).

Disturbances are remarkably rare in view of the prodigious growth of energy consumption since 1950. The industrial economy is a fuel economy, revolving around the regular supply of fuel that can be easily converted into energy. The increase in productivity has led to intensive growth, concentrated in the centres of industrial production and consumption, and to extensive growth that at present is mostly confined to the poorer parts of the world. Even more than extensive growth, intensive growth today has all the characteristics of a largely autonomous, self-propelling force. Light, warmth, motion, and even coolness are produced with fuel. The rising supply of all these fuel-intensive amenities in turn constantly stimulates demand from customers, who are eager to enhance both their physical comfort and their social status.

In a large part of the world access to the benefits of modern technology is still restricted to a small upper crust of society. Moreover, while in the western world and Japan effective measures have been taken to reduce the polluting effects of industrial and domestic fuel use in densely populated areas, the quality of the air has only deteriorated in the rapidly growing megacities of Africa, Asia and Latin America. As a consequence, according to an estimate of the World Health Organization in 1997, air pollution killed about 400,000 people annually worldwide (McNeill 2000: 103).

Still, extensive growth has continued in the poor parts of the world, and this is bound to affect the rich countries as well. Wealth attracts poverty; history abounds with examples of this general rule. When the opportunity offers itself, many people from poorer regions will try to migrate to regions with a higher standard of material comfort.

Meanwhile, the combined pressures of intensive and extensive growth continue to push up global fuel consumption. In rich countries, advanced technologies permit customers to enjoy the use of their appliances and vehicles without any physical inconvenience caused by the combustion processes. Poorer people generally are prepared to put up with noise and smell to profit from fossil fuel energy. Nevertheless, there are some signs that the upward trend in energy use is slowing down, and even reverting in some branches of industrial production. We shall turn to those signs in Chapter 12.

Means of violence

With growing interdependence among people, dependence on natural forces has become more indirect: longer and more ramified social chains are formed between the production of things and their use. Even the threat of violent destruction of lives and property comes far less often from natural forces than from forces unleashed by one human group against another. The most powerful groups are those that command the

375

organizational and technical means to mobilize huge amounts of energy and matter against their enemies.

In our day, the search for the most effective means of violence has led to the exploitation of a new source of energy: nuclear fission. For the first time in human history, a new source of energy was first applied at a large scale in war, with the sole intent of massive destruction. If anything deserves to be called 'something new under the sun', it is the ability to generate nuclear energy. It was the result of an enormously concentrated accumulation of technical, scientific, and economic capital, invested in a single one-purpose enterprise: the production of an atomic bomb.

But no matter how single-minded the effort, the invention of the atomic bomb followed a general rule in the history of technology, and produced unintended side-effects. One of these was that the development of the bomb by the United States became the first step in a process of escalation and proliferation, which has engendered a global 'arms race'. Another unintended consequence has been the rising level of risk of fatal consequences in case of a breakdown in any of the nuclear plants that were built in the second half of the 20th century.

War has always been an important factor in the relations between humans and their physical environment. In most cases, it was directed at destruction of a part of the anthroposphere: especially that part in which the organizational basis of the enemy was supposed to be most vulnerable (see Collins 1990). The more investments a group made in controlling its environment, the more susceptible it became to losses through violence. Advanced agrarian communities could suffer a severe setback in case their rice fields, vineyards or terraces were destroyed. Many cities in agrarian societies underwent drastic reduction or were even totally annihilated after military surrender: the greater the concentration of physical wealth, the more irreparable the destruction – a theme that is also dealt with in Chapter 6.

In industrial society, enormous means of destruction were developed even before the invention of the atomic bomb. During the Second World War air raids brought devastation to a great many cities. Global industrial society proved to be sufficiently resilient and affluent, however, so that after the war every bombed city was rebuilt at its original site.

An important segment of industrial production is the arms industry, manufacturing not just weapons but also military vehicles, ships, and aeroplanes. Many other branches of industry, and agriculture, are engaged in supplying the armed forces with equipment, clothing, and food. For this reason the historian John McNeill (2000: xxi) reckons military security to be one of the driving forces behind contemporary economic growth.

Motives

With 'driving forces' we have reached the realm of human motives. What motivations can be discerned behind processes of extensive and intensive growth, behind the forma-

The spiral of desire Desire is usually experienced as a purely individual impulse, but it contains a strong social component. The French philosopher-anthropologist René Girard (1977) has spoken in this context of mimetic or emulating desire. He points out that things in themselves are not especially desirable once people are able to meet their fundamental vital needs. A thing then becomes desirable only when another person has it – in Girard's view, by having that very thing we believe that we can be like that other person.

We need not follow Girard's profound anthropology into every detail to recognize the mechanism of mimetic desire and to acknowledge its importance. We see it demonstrated every day on billboards and in TV commercials displaying goods and services in the expectation that 'seeing is buying'. The mechanism to which an appeal is made here appears to be deeply rooted in the human psyche; we can already observe it among young children in a playground. A toy may be lying unnoticed in a corner for hours, until one child picks it up and starts playing with it. Now suddenly all of the children only want to play with this particular toy.

The mechanism can be explained not just psychologically but also sociologically. As long as something is present somewhere and nobody is paying any attention to it, it is in principle freely available to everybody. As soon as one person starts showing an interest, there is a reason for all others around to be alarmed. Their desire is aroused, and for good reasons: for by letting this chance pass they would put themselves at a disadvantage. The opportunity not only 'makes the thief', it also stirs the desire.

This simple mechanism helps us to comprehend the social psychology of economic growth. It brings us nearer to understanding the collective game people play that results in a continuous increase and differentiation of goods and services. 'Why do they work so hard?' the sociologists Robert and Helen Lynd asked about the citizens of a town in the American Midwest that they studied in 1928. Their answer was as simple as it was intriguing: everybody was working so hard to make money only because everybody else was also working so hard (Lynd and Lynd 1929: 73-89). 'Keeping up with the Joneses' it is sometimes called; but that phrase fails to express clearly that the Joneses themselves find themselves caught in exactly the same spiral movement as all those who wish to keep up with them. Mimetic emulation is mutual (see also Frank 1999).

tion of agrarian and industrial regimes? In response to this highly general question we submit that the answer is to be found in the interaction of human nature and figurational dynamics.

It is in the nature of every human individual to take care of himself or herself and to seek a way of surviving. The only way of surviving is by somehow being social and staying within the flock represented by a human group. The relations between people in a group, and even more so interactions between groups, can lead to situations that no one in particular ever intended nor desired – this is where figurational dynamics enter.

In the complex structures of advanced agrarian and industrial societies, every so often situations arise in which people find themselves faced with a social challenge: to conform or not to conform, to compete or not to compete. The challenges may be subtle and need hardly be perceived consciously; but they are unavoidable, and in the long run they shape, and change, attitudes and behaviour.

Some social relations take place, of course, in a setting that is explicitly competitive. Sports are the best example, but many relationships in the fields of economics and politics come close. In all these areas – sports, economics and politics – competition between individuals can become engrossed in competition between larger collective units: clubs, firms, parties.

Neither individuals nor clubs, neither firms nor parties are supposed to settle their competitive contests by force of arms. That, in most contemporary societies, is a prerogative of one particular type of organizations – states, which officially and legally hold the monopoly of organized violence. Groups defying this system and employing large-scale violence against particular states without a state organization of their own are known as terrorists; since their violence is directed against states, they become part of the state figuration and affect its dynamics – as happened after the terrorist attack on the Twin Towers in New York on September 11, 2001.

This is not the place for a substantive analysis of the political and economic situation of the world today. Evidently, that situation is highly relevant for the relationships between humanity and the biosphere. We need only to think of access to, and use of, energy resources, to see how strong the link is. Political and economic developments will continue to affect people's relations to the biosphere, and they will continue to be affected by them. We shall return to this point in our final chapter, on the future.

Here we wish to point only to a peculiar mechanism in the interaction between human nature and figurational dynamics: the 'spiral of desire' (*see box*).

Competition and co-operation – the key processes in inter-species relationships at the time of the original domestication of fire – continue to be key processes in intra-species relationships in the contemporary world.

11

Back to Nature?
The Punctuated History of a Natural Monument

WESTBROEK

> A painting by Mauve, or Maris, or Israëls is more telling than nature itself.
>
> *Vincent van Gogh*

> If anybody taught me to see nature, it was our old masters. But I learned most from nature itself.
>
> *J.H. Weissenbruch*

11.1.   Introduction

Jan Hendrik Weissenbruch (1824-1903) was one of the most distinguished Dutch painters in the 19th century. Skies, shores and landscapes were his passion, in particular the wide, wet 'polders' – stretches of land reclaimed from the ravaging waters in Holland. He never had to travel far because all this beauty was abundantly available around The Hague, the town where he had lived all his life. From his home he could walk to the famous collection of Dutch paintings at the Mauritshuis Museum in five minutes, and as a young man he spent many hours there contemplating and even copying the works of his 17th century idols, Johannes Vermeer and Jacob Ruisdael. But although he remained faithful to these great examples until the end of his days, his unrestrained abandonment to nature forced him to develop his own look at the world. 'At times, nature gives me a real blow,' he used to say. At such moments drawing and painting was easy. He jotted down his impressions in charcoal so that later, at home, he could work on them in paint. Over the years, his style changed from more meticulous rendering to a highly personal impressionism. What strikes the eye is the subtle balance between joyful and sponta-neous virtuosity and compositional grandeur. In particular his monumental skies are unforgettable, with their infinite variety of blues and greys. He brought the polders to life and taught us to feel at home in this flat, green land of mud and water.

Although public recognition only came towards the end of his life, Weissenbruch was one of the most prominent members of the 'The Hague School,' a rather loose association of painters, which had its heyday in the years 1870-1900. Jozef Israëls, Jacob Maris and Anton Mauve were other well-known representatives. For many years, the 17th century artistic blossoming in the Low Countries had paralysed rather than stimulated painting in this country, but the The Hague School brought a revival. Inspired by the same nationalism that held all of Europe in its grip, these people rediscovered the beauty of the Dutch landscape and everyday life. With their characteristic approach, ranging from realism to impressionism, they gave us a nostalgic view of Holland, not as it really was but how they wanted to see it. It was a period of industrialization and burgeoning tourism, but in those paintings chimneys or trains at the horizon, or swimmers in the water are rarely to be seen. Neither were portraits a favourite subject. People were mostly part of the landscape, together with their villages, houses, cattle and implements. They were farmers or fishermen, resting in the fields or in their humble dwellings. Cities and towns were shown from a distance, or as peaceful street corners and intimate gardens. These painters abhorred glamour and avoided the dynamics of modern life.

Little wonder they soon found The Hague too busy a place for inspiration. To find the peaceful environment of their liking, they had to move out into the surrounding countryside. One such a place was the township of Noorden, at lake Nieuwkoop. Towards the end of his life, Weissenbruch lived there during the spring and autumn months, and it is in Noorden that he produced his finest works. Much of that landscape is still intact. Over all these years, Weissenbruch's paintings appear to have exerted a curious power over this land of pastures and waters: they contributed to its preservation, although their original purpose was merely aesthetic (cf. *Figure 11.6*, p. 320).

Was it really nature that Weissenbruch looked for in Noorden? Now, after a century of unparalleled and world-wide human intervention with the environment, millions of people experience the same nostalgia that brought Weissenbruch to these peaceful surroundings. An excursion to the area will reveal that what we perceive to be our natural environment may be something quite different. With all our longing for nature, it is good to realize what we really ask for.

11.2.   On a rowing boat

A good way to approach the area is from the south-west. A little stream, the Meije, winds through the meadows. One can ride a bicycle atop the bordering dike. The Meije is on the left, and on the right, at the foot of the dike, is a long string of farmhouses, many of which are beautifully preserved specimens from the 17th century. Several of them have

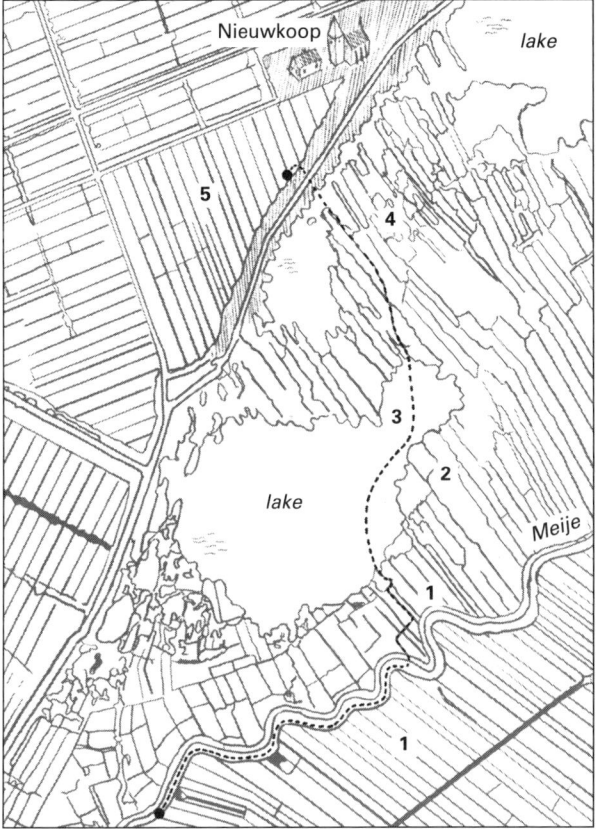

FIGURE 11.1

Map of the surroundings of Meije and Nieuwkoop, with five characteristic landscapes: (1) farmlands exploited since the Middle Ages; (2) reed lands exploited since the 19th century; (3) a lake; (4) the remains of peat exploitations (18th to the beginning of the 19th century); (5) the 19th-century polders at Nieuwkoop. Peat exploitation in the 17th century had left a large lake.

thatched roofs and are surrounded by pleasant orchards, shrubs and vegetable gardens. Beyond the farmhouses, narrow canals separate long, green meadows, forming parallel rows that stretch away from the road. The meadows are often about 100 metres wide and one kilometre long. At their far end, away from the road, rows of trees pleasantly interrupt the otherwise monotonous landscape. Then follows another row of meadows, trees, and so on. In the distance you see the towers of Woerden and Bodegraven.

To the left, on the other side of the Meije, a similar pattern of elongated meadows and canals trends away from the river (Fig. 1). The landscape here is more loosely organized. The bushes at the end of the meadows are more haphazard than the trees on the other side, and the canals are not so straight. Reeds grow along the watercourse, together with patches of pollard willows and a wealth of water flowers. Cows peaceably stare at infinity.

Do not forget to drink a cup of excellent coffee with Jaap Schutter at café De Halve Maan. Rowboats can be rented everywhere, and so it comes that we continue over water, across the Meije and along one of the canals towards the bushes and the lake beyond. The meadows are soaked and nearly level with the water in the canal. They give way to fields of reeds, moss and flowering plants: real bog lands. A rectangular network of canals, ditches androws of alder, birch and willow divide the area into a system of regular patches. The flowers bloom and the birds sing their song – this is nature at its best ...

The canal now widens and ends up in open water, one of the many lakes in the region. This one is two kilometres or so across, and about four metres deep. Reeds and clusters of trees line the shore. Across the lake we float into another new world, a complex labyrinth of narrow ridges of land alternating with waters up to a hundred metres wide. Again, the land ridges are covered with reeds and trees. Then comes the dike that cuts off the bog area. And Nieuwkoop, 700 years old: dignified buildings, small houses, old and new, sailboats, restaurants and hamburger palaces. The village forms a long ribbon along the dike and merges, several kilometres further, into Noorden, where Weissenbruch used to stay.

Look for a spot on the dike from where you can view the polder beyond. The difference in height makes you dizzy, however flat this land may be. The polder is at least four metres below the surface of the waters we have just crossed. It was a lake until two centuries ago. Blocks of rectangular meadows are separated by meticulously arranged sets of perpendicular roads, dikes, rows of trees and large farmhouses. The scale is larger and the planning more efficient and modern than the historic panorama where we started our trip.

This little excursion allows one to cross five types of landscape characteristic of the western region of the Netherlands: farmlands exploited since the Middle Ages; reed lands that originated in the 19th century; a lake; peat exploitation (mainly 17th century); and the 19th-century polder at Nieuwkoop. It is a carefully designed system of multilevel waterways, polders and dikes – the result of a struggle of centuries between humanity and the elements. This is Weissenbruch's nature. Yet there is nothing purely natural here. If left unattended the whole area would soon be underwater.

An interesting paradox underlies these terrains. A thousand years ago this was the 'wilderness', a virtually impenetrable and uninhabitable region between the sandy hills to the east and the low sand dunes along the coast. In the 17th century, however, this very area provided the economic basis for a mighty empire: Holland in the 'Golden Age'.

11.3. Natural causes

To understand the development of this region one must go back more than 10,000 years when the last ice age ended and the present warmer period, the Holocene, began. Fig. 11.2 shows the area in the larger geographical context. A major part of the Dutch territory can be viewed as a river delta merging into the North Sea. The area has already been subsiding for a long time and over the past million years, the rivers that flow down into this delta, particularly the Rhine and Meuse, have filled the space that became available with sands and clay, debris from the Alps and other high regions upstream.

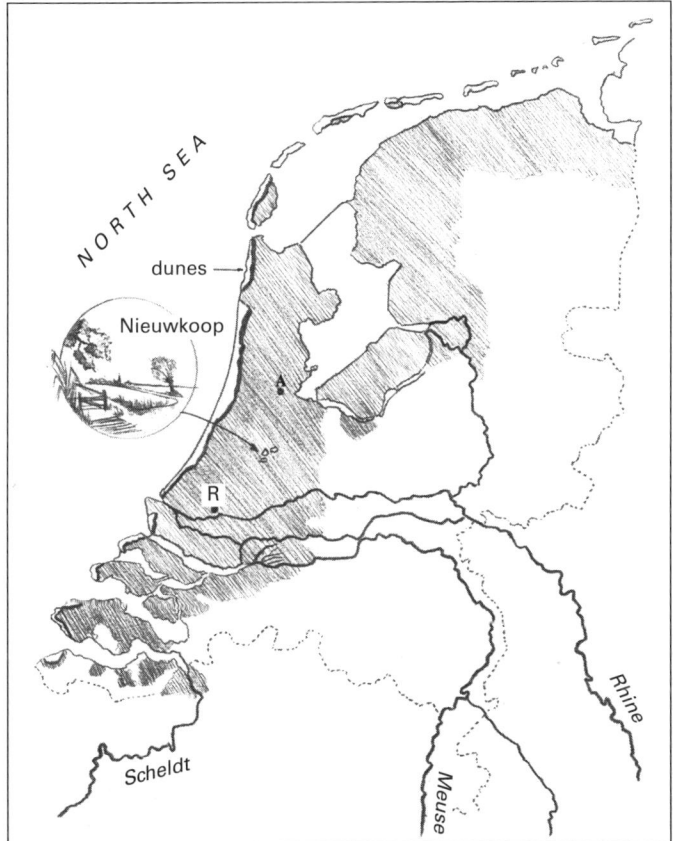

FIGURE 11.2

Map of the Netherlands, including the delta of the rivers Rhine, Meuse and Scheldt. The shaded area is lower than the mean sea level plus 1 metre and would flood if left unprotected. Note the position of the dunes along the coast, the mud flats between the string of islands in the north and the mainland, and Nieuwkoop.

383

During the last glacial period, ice covered large continental areas around the Arctic; the southern boundary of that ice sheet ran across northern Germany and southern Denmark and into the North Sea. So much water was tied up on land as ice that the level of the sea was some hundred metres lower than today. Much of the North Sea was dry, and in the Netherlands a polar desert or a tundra-like regime prevailed. Most of the land was covered with sand brought down by the rivers and tossed around by the wind.

When temperatures moderated at the beginning of the Holocene period, the ice caps started to melt. The sea level rose, and reached the present Dutch coastline about 7000 years ago. The sea went even further inland and was then pushed back again by the steadily accumulating sediment. The rivers brought down huge masses of clay that were swept into the sea and accumulated there in a thick blanket along the coast – a huge mud flat that widened over time, edging toward the land.

About 3000 years ago, low sand dunes started to develop along the western and northern coast of the Netherlands, protecting the original mudflats from marine incursions. At this stage a zone behind the dunes, 20 to 40 kilometres wide, was transformed from mud flats into a huge marshland where large masses of peat could accumulate. The 'wilderness' was born. All that is left of the original mudflats is now in the north of the country, between the string of islands and the mainland. Fig. 11.3 is an east-west cross-section through the Holocene sediments in the middle of the country; from it you can deduce this sequence of events. First, the marine clay expands over the sandy underground, separated from the coast by a narrow strip of peat. The thin peat deposit at the

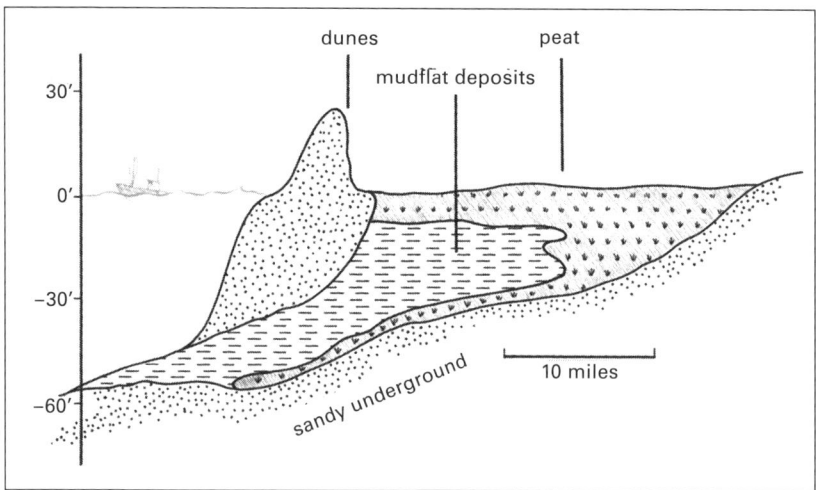

FIGURE 11.3

Cross-section through young sediments in the western part of the Netherlands, showing extensive peat development behind coastal dunes.

base of the Holocene sediments is the result. Then come the dunes and the peat that covers the clay.

Peat is essentially a water-soaked mass of plant remains. When its production exceeds its decomposition, large deposits may form. Just underneath the plant cover, proliferating bacteria and fungi attack the black sludge and convert it into carbon dioxide and water. The oxygen required is poorly soluble in water, and so it happens that the water in the pores becomes anaerobic, oxygen depleted. The consumers suffocate, so that their work has to be taken over by bacteria that thrive in this anaerobic environment. Because anaerobic breakdown yields less energy, it is less efficient. Organic acids and carbon dioxide accumulate and then the same happens as in the production of yoghurt – the breakdown comes to a standstill. Throughout the Holocene period, the conditions in large parts of Holland were highly favourable for peat accumulation. In this deltaic area, rivers and rainfall provided abundant water. Temperatures were moderate under the prevailing marine climate and drainage was poor.

In this region a lake will fill up by itself with peat and change into land. The types of life that grow change in a well-defined sequence. In general, floating water plants and algae form the first debris to be accumulated in the lake. When the water is less than 2 metres deep, reeds can take over, and at a depth of half a metre, sedges dominate. Finally, the ground is high enough for trees to develop, leading to a type of peat full of roots and stems.

These successive plant communities all depend on groundwater for their development and cannot grow much above the surface. With enough rain, however, peat moss or sphagnum may dominate the scene. It has a very peculiar structure that allows it to hold water. In hot dry periods it uses up its water reservoir and appears brown and dead. But during a shower it soaks up large quantities of water and appears green and healthy again. Sphagnum also recycles its food very efficiently because it can grow high above the groundwater level, fed only by the nutrient-poor rainwater. It even stores large quantities of extra nutrients in its cell walls, depriving its competitors from essential foodstuff. This peat moss may rapidly outgrow and suffocate the trees and shrubs that were forming the wood peat. As it does it can produce mossy cushions up to seven meters high covering hundreds of square kilometres. These are curious constructions: gigantic water mattresses, pervaded and kept in place by a fine network of organic remains and forged by a thin veneer of living, teeming tissue on the surface.

This is what happened on a huge scale in Holland. The principle of the distribution of the different types of peat is shown in Fig. 11.4. The zones bordering the rivers and streams were regularly flooded and received a good share of nutrients and clay. Under these conditions, wood peat dominated. Close to the river mouths, where the sea turned the water brackish, reed peat was laid down, while sphagnum cushions developed in the large areas in between. This rather astounding development of peat clearly illustrates the role that life has played in this area over the last few thousand years. There are few other

385

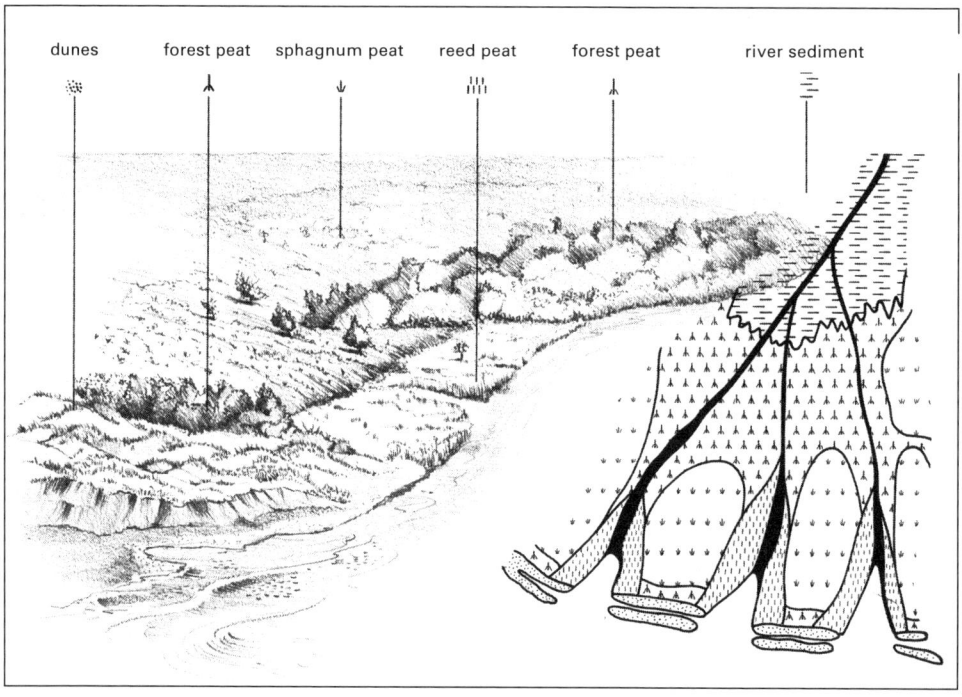

FIGURE 11.4

Distribution of various types of peat in a deltaic area such as Holland.

geological forces that rival life in raising a stretch of land of this size by several metres in such a relatively short period of time.

Some 1000 years ago, this terrain was wilderness. The Meije was just one of many streams in the region that removed superfluous water from the peat lands. Away from its banks, the surface gradually rose and was covered with swamp woods. Then, at about the present location of the open lakes, a huge sphagnum cushion with very few trees started to form, just as would be expected. The contrast with the present is dramatic (see Fig. 11.5). The only thing that seems the same is the course of the Meije. How did the present situation evolve from the earlier, natural one?

11.4.   The impact of culture

The wilderness used to be a forbidding place; even the Romans avoided it. Their settlements were only along the sandy levees of the main rivers. At the beginning of the 13th century, however, the increasing population made exploitation inevitable. The area was brought under feudal control of the Counts of Holland and the Bishop of Utrecht, and a methodical cultivation system was initiated. Colonists were recruited from among the serfs and in exchange for the heavy life they were exempt from feudal obligations. Thus, a spirit of liberty and enterprise was born in the Dutch swamps while everywhere else in Europe bondage was still the rule.

Right from the start, drainage was the major problem for cultivation. But at Nieuwkoop, at the edge of the sphagnum cushion, this was easily overcome and it is here that local exploitation began. Farmhouses were built in a row along the edge of the cushion, and narrow plots, 100 to 200 metres wide and separated by ditches, were extended into the bog for a stipulated distance, generally 1250 to 2500 metres. Reclamation started from the farmhouses as the first settlers dug drainage ditches to lower the water level. The peat excavated from the ditches was mixed with manure and spread over the land, and the vegetation was burnt for fertilization. The settlers cultivated grains and kept sheep, not only for their own consumption but also to sell to the growing wool industry in nearby towns such as Leiden. More than a generation elapsed before a single row of fields was brought into cultivation. When the terminal line was reached, it became the starting point for a second generation of exploitations. As a result, the countryside was divided into a remarkably uniform sequence of parcels. Even now, this is a very characteristic feature of the Dutch landscape – we saw it at the beginning of our trip, on either side of the Meije.

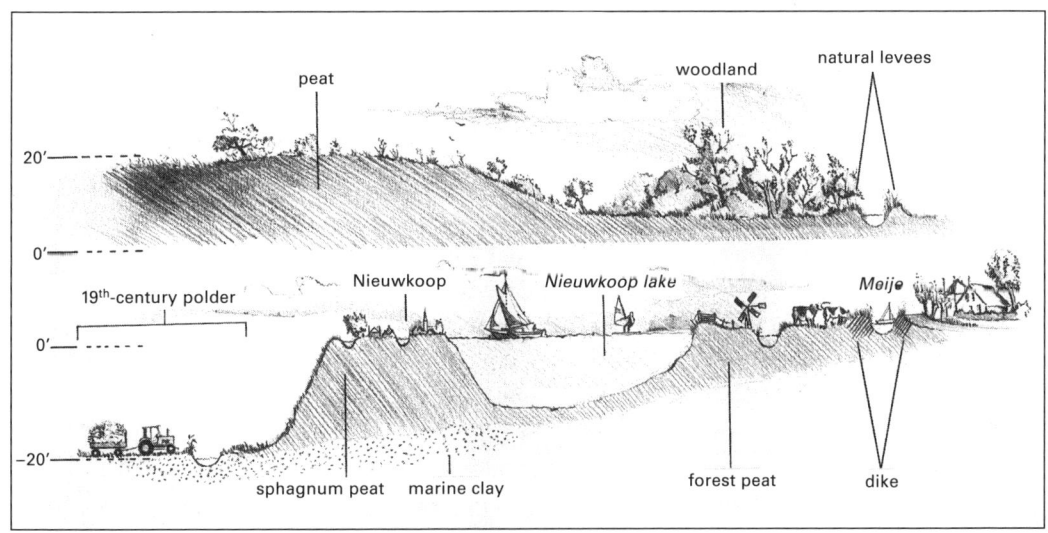

FIGURE 11.5

Cross-sections through the Nieuwkoop and Meije areas 1000 years ago and at present. Redrawn from J. Teeuwisse, De ontwikkeling van het landschap van 1000 tot 2000; in Nieuwkoop, Beelden en Fragmenten (Noorden: Post, 1982).

A large part of peat – as much as 80% in sphagnum peat – is water. Drainage causes a swamp to shrink, accelerated by the increased exposure to oxygen, which stimulates the breakdown of plant debris. The settlers soon discovered that their activities caused their lands to subside and be drowned to an ever greater extent. They deepened the ditches several times and removed water from the surface using manual labour. A vicious cycle began: the improved drainage caused further collapse, forcing the peasants to take more severe measures. The existing swamp streams, such as the Meije, could not remove all of the excess water. Drainage works in one area brought flooding elsewhere, which caused many skirmishes between local landlords. But the flooding also imposed the construction of an intricate system of land drainage and reclamation and, concomitantly, led to the creation of novel technologies in water management. A complex network of new waterways, canals, ditches and dikes appeared in the landscape and, as a result, new exploitations became feasible. By the end of the Middle Ages, the whole region around Nieuwkoop was in cultivation.

The invention that revolutionized the development of the Dutch landscape was the wind-driven water-pumping mill. The earliest version appeared in Alkmaar in 1408. It was small, driving a paddle wheel or a scoop wheel, and could carry water some two metres upwards. A series of two to four such mills was needed to drain deeper water. More sophisticated and much more efficient windmills using Archimedean screws superseded the older types, and were a common feature by the 17th century. They made it possible to drain large terrains that would otherwise have fallen victim to occasional incursions of the sea. New types of polders came into being. They were surrounded by 'ring dikes' and outside these, ring canals into which the windmills discharged their surplus water and from which the water could be transferred to the main rivers. The improved drainage allowed the polders to be used as grasslands, which made cattle farming profitable. The development of Dutch cheese went hand-in-hand with the introduction of the windmills.

One important element in the development of this landscape has not yet been mentioned. The peasants lived atop a thick peat blanket of excellent fuel. Originally, they dug some of it away to satisfy their own needs, and it was readily replenished by renewed peat accumulation. But the demand for fuel increased as the population grew. More fuel was needed, in particular to support the growing towns in a wide variety of industrial activities: beer brewing, pottery, metal and cement industries, brickworks and so on.

In the early days, only a superficial layer of peat was dug away, but in 1530 an important innovation was introduced that would leave deep scars in the Dutch landscape. It was the 'baggerbeugel', a long-handled metal net that allowed peat to be dredged from several metres below the water level. Figure 11.7 shows peat mining in operation. Large and deep rectangular pools were excavated, and the peat was spread out as a slurry on narrow strips of land in between, dried, and carved into blocks. The complex labyrinth of land ridges and waters near Nieuwkoop are the remains of just such an exploitation.

One reason for the resounding success of peat mining was that the fuel could be transported very cheaply by boat over the elaborate system of canals. Peat ecology supplied the energy that stoked the industrial centres of the 17th century, what is known as the Golden Age in Holland. If horsepower had been needed for transport, the enormous feeding expenses would have precluded the development of this remarkably prosperous industry.

Unfortunately, the hunger for fuel in the cities of Leiden, Gouda and Amsterdam also led to widespread destruction of the land. The skeleton of narrow strips of land left in the wake of the underwater excavations was an easy target for wave erosion in stormy weather. Poverty encouraged the rural population to sacrifice the meagre long-term benefits of the land for attractive short-term profits. For the majority of people, the consequences were detrimental. Poverty increased and depopulation of the area followed. Regulations issued by the local authorities to curb the destruction were circumvented. Large territories laboriously brought into cultivation in earlier days gave way to steadily growing lakes that could barely be kept in check. The advent of the more powerful windmills in the 17th century meant that some of the water could be reclaimed as polders; the last remains of turf were sold and the exposed marine clay used for agriculture or grassland for cattle. But it was only in the 19th century, with the introduction of the steam

Afbeelding van de Hollandsche Veenen na 't Dorp AMSTERVEEN te zien, met de wyze van het Turf maken.

FIGURE 11.7

The peat mining operation in Holland. The man in the rowing boat is digging for peat with a net on a long pole: the baggerbeugel. The peat is spread out over elongated strips of land, dried and prepared for transport by boat. Engraving by J.C. Philips (1741).

pump, that the deterioration of the landscape could be brought under control.

Nowadays, the country is drained by an elaborate system of electrical pumps. Large polders have been reclaimed in recent years, and there are only a few major works that remain to be carried out. Some lakes, such as those between Nieuwkoop, Noorden and the Meije, were preserved – their exploitation would not have been profitable. In the 1930s, the local government decided to use the Nieuwkoop lake as a dump for the rubbish of the towns and cities in the area. In a 'Guide for Nieuwkoop and Noorden' of 1935 we read that no harm was done. 'Only a little rubbish is dumped, but we cover it up with peat so that nobody can see it. And best of all, it gives work to quite a few people.' Although this activity met with growing opposition by the nascent movement for environmental protection, dumping continued until the 1960s. Cleaning is underway now – at an estimated cost of 10 million euros.

11.5.   Uneasy compromise

What Weissenbruch perceived as 'nature' is the remains of an extensively excavated mining district and, at the same time, a landscape that has for centuries been the scene of careful and parsimonious cultivation and water control. Nothing here was left to chance. Even the reeds nearby have been maintained over the centuries for the construction of roofs and to supply the tulip fields near the coast with a protective covering during the winter months.

The result of this human involvement is a pleasurable homeland where we can enjoy the interplay of water, wind, life and history. It is this compromise between nature and artifice that Van Goyen, Hobbema, Ruisdael and, later, Weissenbruch captured in their visionary paintings. They grasped what we now recognize as the landscape of Holland – a friendly place and a delight for the city dweller.

Today, the integrity of Nieuwkoop's surroundings is under renewed attack. Since Weissenbruch's time, the population of the Netherlands has increased from 4 million to 16 million inhabitants. People have not only become more numerous, but in addition their wealth and mobility have vastly increased. Airplanes draw their chalk stripes on the sky and you can scarcely avoid the sound of motorcars. In the west of the Netherlands, fragmented urban centres are combining to form a new, embracing construction, the 'Delta-Metropolis.' It is a ring-shaped region of 6 million inhabitants, comprising the 'main ports' Amsterdam and Rotterdam as well as several middle-sized cities, such as The Hague, Utrecht, Leiden and Gouda. This urbanized ring surrounds the 'Green Heart of Holland,' with Nieuwkoop right in the middle. This constellation is thought to favour living conditions in the emerging metropolis. To reach the countryside, you don't have to travel through endless stretches of suburbia, like in London or Paris. You can just take your bicycle.

Clearly, further development of the Delta-Metropolis requires coherent planning and leaves little space for local initiatives. The metropolis is conceived as a major centre within north-western European economic networks. Large-scale amplification is foreseen for the existing facilities for transport and communication, both between the urban centres within the ring and with other agglomerations. Intellectual centres of excellence have to create a favourable climate for international investment. To accommodate the expected growth in population, innovative architecture will bring new life to expanding agglomerations. The execution of these plans is well underway and should be completed within a few decades.

What, in all this turmoil, is to become of Nieuwkoop, Noorden and the Meije? When looking around, it is noticable that the rural character of Weissenbruch's days is already disappearing. Sewage, local industries and tourism are causes of this, and encroaching urbanization undermines the comfortable peace of former times.

The present population is older and richer than in the past. While the youth escapes to the cities, retired citizens move in. They build comfortable imitation farmhouses, or transform the old ones into cosy homes and weekend cottages. Farmers, once central to this community, now see their position marginalized. A large part of the countryside has received the status of natural monument. In the past, hundreds of reed cutters used to work around the lake. Now, only ten of them are left to supply the roof-building trade and keep the landscape open. The old villages are becoming city districts and the area is changing from a productive landscape into a consumptive commodity. It is unlikely that this land can sustain these changes for long without losing its intimate dignity.

The Green Heart of Holland is literally central to the scheme of the Delta-Metropolis. Judicious exploitation of the area's natural amenities must boost the quality of life for the entire population. In contrast to the urban ring, the Green Heart must bring home the delightful peace of the Dutch landscape. And so it comes that a new balance is being forged between human demands and the natural environment.

A 250 million euro project has been adopted to protect the remaining wetlands from deterioration and to reinforce its infrastructure. It has been estimated that twenty years will be necessary for its implementation. Extensive agricultural domains are converted into natural parks and recreational areas. Elsewhere, modern combinations of agrarian and natural management are implemented. The quality of environment and water are improved, and existing natural centres combined into larger reserves, capable of supporting the unique vegetation and fauna. On the other hand, spontaneous associations between local farmers and citizens bring the deteriorating landscape back to life by judiciously combining ancient and modern farming practices. The soils, meadows and cows become healthy and vigorous again, pollution disappears and the waters are drinkable. Such bottom-up initiatives are essential for the future of this area and deserve to be fully supported at the governmental level.

11.6. Nature

What kind of nature did Weissenbruch look for in Noorden? The question raised at the beginning at this chapter is timely. Society today is obsessed with nature, more so than ever before. The environment is being converted from a natural to an artificial world on an unprecedented, global scale. The outcome is highly uncertain and casts doubt on the future of humanity. The environmental movement thrives on a widespread awareness that the natural world was beneficial and that we should try and find a way back. At this juncture, we need some enlightenment on what we really want.

The story of Nieuwkoop with its 800 years of environmental management has wider connotations that we should not ignore. Human society has subjected the inhospitable wilderness, once formed by the unbridled geological forces, to one of the most telling examples of interference with the environment. This area became an artifact, an environment adapted by human shrewdness to human demands. Change was not instantaneous. Instead, we discern a regular pattern in the area's history. Human interference was destructive as soon as it began. The earliest attempts at cultivation brought about a dangerous imbalance in the natural equilibrium. Later, the ruinous effects were curbed by protective countermeasures and, in time, a new human-maintained balance was achieved. This country has gone through a long succession of such cycles of destruction and reclamation. Its history is punctuated with alternating times of change and stability.

The environmental problem is no longer localized but affects the planet as a whole. It is widely felt that further human interference with nature will lead to disaster, and that the idea of global management is a dangerous and misguided illusion. But the story of Nieuwkoop may inspire a more optimistic vision. It shows us that unbridled nature is not tailored to human demands and can only support very few people. Unavoidably, nature must be brought under control if we wish to survive. The result can be delightful. If our ancestors could forge new alliances with nature so well, why couldn't we do it again? If they managed to create delightful surroundings locally, why could we not do so on a global scale? It certainly is a risky enterprise, but this has always been the case. The idea of a cultivated earth is not illusory, it is a matter of common survival. We must not go back but further ahead, cautiously.

Nevertheless, when we row between the flowering meadows, reeds and dikes of Noorden and Nieuwkoop, we can enjoy the silent glory of Weissenbruch's world. He captured its essence and made it available to us all. His paintings give us a reference by which to value our impressions. The forces of art are cunning and powerful. Millions of people see this country through Weissenbruch's eyes, even if they are unaware of his work. This is why it could be preserved for so many years.

But times change. Inevitably, Weissenbruch's world is a vanishing one. Even the Delta-Metropolis cannot sustain it. Something new is in the air. Let us hope for new artists of Weissenbruch's calibre to change this new world into a homeland we like.

Acknowledgements

I am greatly indebted to Dr. Siebrand Tjallingii for introducing me to the story of Nieuwkoop and to Dr. G.O. van Veldhuizen, the present Mayor of this municipality, for explaining the newest developments. Bram van der Vlugt made me aware of inspiring initiatives by farmers and citizens to keep the Nieuwkoop area a wonderful place. I would like to thank Claartje de Loor and Mariette Jitta (Gemeentemuseum, the Hague) for introducing me to Weissenbruch. Judith de Jong and Kees Pleij made highly valued suggestions and Edwin Jacobs, of the Museum Jan Cunen in Oss made the reproduction of Weissenbruch available. This paper is based on Chapter I of the book: P. Westbroek, 1991. Life as a geological force; dynamics of the Earth. Norton, New York, London.

12

Conclusions: Retrospect and Prospects

GOUDSBLOM AND DE VRIES

> After ten thousand years of breaking the soil, after a hundred thousand years of setting fire to the forests and the plains, after a million years of chasing game, human influence is woven through even what to our eyes are the most pristine landscapes.
>
> *Budiansky 1995: 5*

12.1.   The discovery of the biosphere

The interaction of humans with the biosphere is as old as the human species itself. It has acquired a new momentum over the past 250 years when, in the course of industrialization, people developed new means of technology and organization which enabled them to reach further and deeper into the natural environment than ever before and to incorporate more and more 'nature' into their societies.

Social trends rarely occur without eliciting counter-trends. The rise of modern industry in the 19th century was generally hailed as progress, but from the very beginning it also met with protest and resistance. Resistance was at first mainly directed at the social but from early on also to some extent at the environmental consequences. These were noted with most alarm in two very different contexts: in the urban centres, where the massive burning of coal for industrial and domestic purposes vitiated the air and caused serious health problems, and in rural areas, where people felt that the last vestiges of unspoilt nature were being destroyed.

Concern about the quality of air and water in cities is probably inherent in city life. The high concentration of people and domesticated animals has always created problems regarding the regular supply of food and water as well as the disposal of waste. In the 19th century, the situation was deemed more and more unbearable in many European cities – perhaps in part because objectively the level of foul emissions exceeded all earlier records, but certainly also because people were becoming more sensitive to health hazards and began to see the possibility of amelioration. Motivated by a combination of observed facts, plausible theories and sentiments of alarm, the Public Health Movement set out to reform the sanitary conditions in cities. Scientists and scientific ideas have played an important role in the movement from the beginning (see Porter 1997: 397-427).

The rural conservationists were at first more romantically inclined. What they perceived as nature was, almost without exception, a landscape that already bore the imprint of long-established human interference but was still free from the scars of industrialization. Like modern industry, conservationism started as an archipelago of modest local initiatives, which soon assumed regional and national proportions. As the movement grew, it attracted support from scientists, particularly from biologists and geologists. An impressive intellectual manifestation of the new outlook was *Man and Nature; or Physical Geography as Modified by Human Action* by the American naturalist George Perkins Marsh (1864); this book is generally recognized today as the first comprehensive study viewing the relationships between humanity and the natural environment from a truly global perspective.

In 1875 the Austrian geologist Eduard Suess coined the term biosphere, in passing, in order to refer to the geographical region of the earth where life is found. It was taken up in the early 20th century by the versatile Russian biologist and geochemist Vladimir I. Vernadsky, who published a book in French entitled *La biosphère* in 1926. He made the term biosphere into a central technical concept referring to 'the area of the Earth's crust occupied by transformers which convert cosmic radiations into effective terrestrial energy: electrical, chemical, mechanical, thermal, etc.' (quoted by Lovelock 2000: 10). For many years, the work of Vernadski and like-minded 'holistic' theorists remained largely unnoticed in the scientific community, but their reputation rose rapidly in the second half of the 20th century, when a general awareness dawned that all forms of life on earth partake in one great ecological system and that people are perhaps tinkering with this system in a manner that may prove fatal.

In the years after the Second World War, an increasing number of individual scientists addressed the public with warnings about the unbalanced relation between humanity and the natural environment. Concern about this issue became so widespread that, in 1968, a group of influential industrialists, scientists, and politicians (the 'Club of Rome') commissioned an international research team to draw up an authoritative report. The team, led by Donella and Dennis Meadows, published in 1972 the report *The Limits to Growth* which presented global trends in five areas: population, food production, industrialization, exploitation of non-renewable resources and pollution. On the basis of the evidence then available, the report concluded that if growth in each area were to continue at current rates, the world's population would experience 'overshoot and collapse' within a few generations, owing to a combination of resource depletion, soil degradation and environmental pollution.

Limits to Growth?   A comparison of the computer simulation results of the World3-model in the report *The Limits to Growth* with the historical trends since 1971 indicates that population and economic production trends roughly followed the model projections. However, natural resource degradation and the associated environmental pollution are significantly below the levels predicted. This is for several reasons. Firstly, the estimate of metal and energy resources was too low and the technological potential to reduce their costs was equally underestimated. Secondly, the oil crises in the 1970s induced large efforts in the industrialized world regions to bring down the energy – and material – intensity, that is, the amount of energy or material used per unit of economic output. As a result, demand increased much more slowly than before despite continuing economic growth – although this effect has become weaker since the oil price dropped in the mid-1980s. A third factor is that, owing to the pressure of citizens who wanted clean air and water to be part of their emerging affluence, governments and industries in the industrialized regions of the world have introduced numerous measures to reduce environmental pollution. It is hypothesized that presently less industrialized regions will undergo a similar 'transition' once their income levels rise. A fourth, overarching reason why the calculations in *Limits to Growth* turn out to be at least partly wrong is that the report itself was among the factors that caused response action – the 'self-denying prophecy'.

This is not to say that mankind will not experience anything like the catastrophes of some model forecasts. However, it will require a far better understanding of the world system than the World3 -model if they are to be anticipated and averted. An attempt at constructing a more complex model and using it in a broader context of divergent worldviews and management styles is the TARGETS -model of RIVM (Rotmans and De Vries 1997, De Vries 2001). It is shown that the most widely published result of the *Limits to Growth* report – catastrophe – is in fact one of the many possible outcomes: the one in which egalitarian environmentalists are right about the fragility of the natural system and the power is in the hands of those who act upon the opposite assumption.

Many events following publication of *The Limits to Growth* seemed to be in line with the bleak prospects it sketched (*see box*). Within a year, the Organization of Petroleum Exporting Countries (OPEC) implemented price increases and boycotts. The resulting international crisis reminded people all over the world, and especially in the richer countries, of their strong dependence on the limited and regionally concentrated stocks of fossil fuels. Throughout the rest of the century, the world's population continued to grow, mostly in the poorer countries. And while agriculture penetrated into forest areas, industrial and commercial activities caused some enormous disasters that made several names ignominious for decades – such as Bhopal (the town in India where a factory of

Union Carbide exploded in 1984), Chernobyl (the site of a nuclear plant breakdown in 1986), and Exxon Valdez (the oil tanker that was wrecked at Blight Reef in Alaska in 1989).

Environmental history since 1972 does not, however, amount to a mere succession of catastrophes confirming the report's predictions of exponential growth and imminent collapse. Several trends of environmental deterioration were in fact reversed. This was partly thanks to the report itself and to a swelling avalanche of publications with a similar tenor, including the equally well-known report *Our Common Future* (1987) by the Brundtland Commission. Their combined impact was to serve as a 'self-denying prophecy' (Merton 1957: 421-36). As most futurologists are well aware, the primary function of predictions based on the extrapolation of current social trends is not so much to give a prophecy of what is bound to happen inevitably, but rather to serve as a warning of what is likely to happen unless attempts are made to curb the trends and to prevent the 'predicted' events from happening. Any scenario of future developments in human society, no matter how strongly it is based on empirical evidence, is partly a forecast and partly a cautionary tale.

Once the message has got through that certain human activities seriously impair the biosphere, there is a chance that people will change those activities. Since the early 1970s history abounds with examples of deliberate attempts to redress damage wrought through careless human intervention in natural processes. In a number of cases, measures were taken after considerable damage had already been done and registered. Impressive results were obtained in purifying the water of some rivers such as the Rhine and the Thames, which had been used for years as 'open sewers' and were devoid of fish life. Fish are once again plentiful. In other cases, early warnings were taken seriously. For example, after a near-disaster in the nuclear plant at Three Mile Island in Pennsylvania in 1979, the United States government introduced stringent safety measures that made the cost of building new reactors practically prohibitive.

A turning point was also reached in the industrial production of CFCs (chlorofluorocarbons), which were built into a variety of appliances, from refrigerators to fire extinguishers. In 1974, a paper appeared in the prestigious journal *Nature* that argued that CFCs were critically reducing stratospheric ozone concentrations. This was a highly technical thesis about which not all experts immediately agreed, although it was later unequivocally confirmed by ground-based and satellite measurements. In 1987 an international agreement was signed in Montreal to reduce the production of CFCs drastically. A combination of factors facilitated its speedy implementation: (a) the causal chains were demonstrated in due course: there was proof of the impact of CFCs on the stratosphere; (b) some detrimental effects were evident to scientists and laypeople alike (skin cancer in Australia, blind penguins in Antarctica); and (c) technology provided alternatives for CFCs which for most practical purposes were satisfactory to all parties concerned – producers as well as consumers. The only negative footnote to this story of the successful formation of a human 'ozone regime' appears to be the fact that 'past emissions have left an environmental legacy that will remain in the stratosphere for many decades to come' (Grübler 1998: 218; see also Lovelock 2000: 154-61).

A far more complex issue than 'the hole in the ozone layer' is the problem that was first known as 'global warming' or 'the greenhouse effect' (see Gore 1992) and is now mostly referred to under the general heading of 'climate change'. Although scientists have discussed this problem for several decades, it is relatively recently that it has become a cause for public concern. Between 1945 and 1975, global temperatures were declining, and some experts held that humanity was accelerating the coming of the next Ice Age by emitting aerosols into the atmosphere which would hinder the radiation of the sun (see Schneider 1976). Since 1975, however, empirical measurements have shown a steady rise in temperature. Although it is difficult to establish exactly to what extent this trend is caused by human action, there is strong evidence that gases emitted by the large-scale use of fossil fuels are contributing to it heavily. Even according to the 'skeptical environmentalist' Bjorn Lomborg, 'some sort of anthropogenic greenhouse effect is fairly uncontroversial' (Lomborg 2001: 260).

In the last quarter of the 20th century, the use of fire in rich industrial societies has been made less perceptible than it ever was before: most of it now takes place in well insulated containers ranging from the furnaces in power stations to the almost silent internal combustion engines in motor cars. Yet to a far greater extent than any preceding socio-ecological regime, the industrial regime is dependent on fire; it has an extremely fuel-intensive infrastructure. The issue of climate change has strengthened public awareness of this fact and fostered the recognition that, while fossil fuel burning is concentrated in specific areas, its effects constitute a truly global problem.

The industrializing world of the 19th century created many environmental troubles. These were perceived as concrete local issues. The atmosphere was regarded as a free sink into which waste vapours could be emitted. If smoke could be sent up high enough, it was believed to have been got rid of. In the course of the 20th century, an awareness has grown that the emissions spill out far beyond their original locality and their full impact can only be grasped by highly technical scientific monitoring on a global level. This awareness is supported by facts, theories, and sentiments. These three elements are fused: the facts become significant in the light of theories, the theories gain credibility on the basis of facts, the sentiments are aroused by the information implied in the facts and the theories, and their arousal stimulates further research.

The diagnosis of climate change involves a plethora of confounding problems in the human realm: economic, political, moral. Because industrial societies are so profoundly committed to the use of fossil fuels, their very texture is impregnated with it. Attempts to reduce the emission of greenhouse gases therefore take many different forms. They range from international treaties culminating in the 1997 Kyoto Protocol signed by the governments of 177 countries to changes in individual consumers' attitudes and, less noticeably, behaviour (Aarts et al. 1995). The history of the Kyoto Protocol testifies to the difficulties surrounding the issue. Although its terms reflect protracted negotiations, with attempts to satisfy many diverse ideals and interests, it still has not yet received the minimum ratification of 55 co-signers which is needed for it to become officially operative.

While climate change ranks high in the international agenda of environmental research and policy, it is far from being the only issue that is causing concern. In *The Limits to Growth* the depletion of resources was given priority; the report stated that the earth's stocks not only of fossil fuels but also of metals such as copper and aluminium were limited, and that humankind was heading toward the depletion of many of these resources in the near future. Developments since 1972 have in many respects been reassuring: huge new deposits of gas, oil and coal have been discovered and even according to conservative estimates today, the supplies are sufficient to provide for human needs in the next four or five centuries (see United Nations 2001). The earth has also been found to contain far greater supplies of most metals than were known in 1972, while synthetic oil-based alternatives have been invented for some other materials. Moreover, by the 1990s, in the richer countries more than 50% of industrial production involving copper, lead and steel has come to be based on recycled materials (Grübler 1998: 245). At the turn of the millennium, the major environmental problem seemed to lie less in scarcity of resources than in the scarcity of 'sinks (*see box*).

Another good that is perceived as becoming increasingly scarce is unspoiled nature. One of the foci of discussion in this context is biodiversity (see Wilson 2002). This is a recently coined concept; the facts to which it refers, however, were among the first signs of environmental decay to be observed and cause alarm. When certain species of plants or animals disappear from a particular site, that is directly visible to expert naturalists and easily understood by laypeople. Loss of vegetation was already observed and bemoaned in antiquity, by Plato as well as by ancient Chinese writers who complained

---

A recent outlook on the future: the IPCC scenarios   In 1992, the Intergovernmental Panel on Climate Change (IPCC) published six alternative emissions trajectories for the main direct and indirect greenhouse gases (CO_2, CH_4, N_2O, CFC_s, SO_2, NO_x, VOCs, CO). In 1997 the IPCC planned the development of a Special Report on Emissions Scenarios (SRES), to review prior scenarios from the literature and to develop a new set of IPCC reference emissions scenarios. The new scenarios should not only cover the full range of emissions but also allow regional desaggregation and span a wide spectrum of alternative futures, structural changes and uncertainties. The new set of scenarios, published in 2000 (IPCC 2000), uses divergent assumptions on population, economic activity and technology, and measures and policies with regard to the North-South income gap, poverty and trade issues, and environmental problems such as acid rain.

The starting point for each of the scenarios was a thoroughly discussed qualitative 'storyline', subsequently quantified by several modelling groups. They were grouped into four scenario families that differ in their outlook on globalization and international governance and on societal values about equity and environment issues. Globalization was loosely defined as a trend towards intensified trade, traffic and communication and as such both a cause and a consequence of processes referred to as 'modernization'. It can be interpreted as a continuation of the industrialization process described in Chapter 10, with a continuation of the trends towards markets and trade liberalization, consumerism, dissemination of technical innovations and expansion of capital flows. Values show up in the degree of social and environmental awareness as they express themselves in widespread support for, for example, solidarity between the rich and the poor, 'green' lifestyles and technologies and community-oriented experiments towards a more sustainable future.

Four scenarios can be distinguished on the basis of these criteria. The two 'globalizing' scenarios differ in the degree of social and environmental awareness, and hence in the corresponding policy actions. In both scenarios population increases to 9-10 billion people by 2050 after which it declines to 7-8 billion by 2100. A future oriented towards markets, materialist values and high-tech consumerism is expected to have the highest economic growth: Gross Domestic Product (GDP) increases at the average 20th century growth rate. Most 'official' scenarios by government agencies belong to this 'reference' – or 'conventional world' or 'business-as-usual' – category. In a more equity and environment oriented scenario, economic growth is also high but less energy- and material-intensive. In both scenarios the emissions of greenhouse-gases increase, fourfold in the first and twofold in the latter. In both cases the atmospheric greenhouse gas concentration will continue to rise to levels well above double the pre-industrial value of 280 ppmv.

In the 'non-globalizing' futures, the world population is assumed to increase to 10 à 14 billion people by 2100. Trade protectionism and limited technology transfer and co-operation hamper economic growth and the modernization process is slowed down. This, it is argued, will in turn retard the demographic transition. How would such a more fragmented world with a focus on regional economic issues and on cultural identity look like? Its very diversity, with cultural and economic pluralism, defies global description. If a materialist outlook and traditional practices prevail, a large and rather poor world population may be confronted by cultural clashes and conflicts because of increasing disparities and scarcities in crucial resources such as clean water, affordable energy and productive land. With a – regional – focus on equity and sustainability, the world population may be smaller and its basic needs better satisfied – but even then, the negative impacts of for instance climate change may exceed the present adaptive capacity of quite a few regions.

about the deforestation wrought by human action (see Elvin 1993: 17-21). Still, their perceptions differed in at least two respects from present observations. They were limited to a particular region and did not refer to anything like global extinctions. Moreover, they reflected innocence on the part of the observers: Plato held others responsible for the destruction of the forests in Attica and did not feel himself to be implicated.

In our era of industrialization and globalization we know of many species which have not only disappeared from certain sites, but have become extinct, either through human killing or because their habitats were destroyed by humans or invaded by competitors or predators who came in the wake of humans. Some of the most famous examples of total extinction in modern times concern bird species, such as the dodo and the passenger pigeon (see Ponting 1991: 168-70). Their losses were rightly seen as irreparable, and when a similar fate threatened large mammals, from whales and seals to tigers and elephants, world-wide campaigns were initiated to protect these animals. Among the sentiments to which the campaigns appealed was a sense of responsibility for other creatures that share the same biosphere. Thanks to these campaigns, the anthroposphere now extends over nature reserves in which several species of wild mammals find refuge.

12.2. *Historical and theoretical reflections*

No matter how far the anthroposphere may expand, it always will be, as it always has been, part of the biosphere. As such, it is dependent on the conditions of climate and on the composition of the air, water and soil. The rhythms of human life are embedded in the motions of the earth, and the resulting cycles of days, seasons and years. Cosmic events such as the impact of a meteorite can disrupt human life, as can terrestial events such as a volcanic eruption, a hurricane, an earthquake, a flood or a drought. The biosphere itself can generate such disruptions, when crowds of visible or invisible parasites invade a human domain and cause a 'plague'.

Like all other animals, humans have to adapt to the circumstances in which they find themselves. Every society in the past developed stable patterns of behaviour ('traditions') that helped its members adapt to recurrent conditions, as well as more flexible procedures for dealing with sudden challenges. For a long time, the most immediate concerns of humans in their interactions with the biosphere must have been finding food for themselves and not becoming food for other creatures (see McNeill 1976: 5-6).

Humans are also similar to all other animals in that they feed directly or indirectly on plants. Plants tap small quantities of solar energy which they assimilate in combination with other substances into organic matter through the process of photosynthesis. In this book we have come across several examples of how changes in vegetation, triggered by changes in climate, forced human groups to change their ways. As described in Chapter 3, there was once a green Sahara with large animals and human hunters. When the climate became dryer and hotter, the habitat ceased to be hospitable to these populations. Other examples, relating to South and Central America and to the Vera Basin in Spain also show human responses to disturbed environmental conditions.

In spite of many such setbacks, there has been a general trend of expansion of the anthroposphere. Starting with the domestication of fire and continuing, at an accelerating pace, with agrarianization and industrialization, more and more human groups came to avail themselves of means of technology and organization which helped them to build 'buffers' or 'dikes' to shield them from at least some of the vicissitudes of the natural environment. If we take a very long-term global view, expansion appears to be a continuous process; if we look more closely, we see that it occurred in leaps and bounds, at different times in different regions.

We have distinguished between extensive and intensive growth as two general aspects of the expansion of the anthroposphere. Roughly speaking, the key words for extensive growth are 'more and more' and 'further and further'. The key term for intensive growth is 'greater complexity', structured by more information. Perhaps extensive growth may be conceived of as a sheer extension of human biomass, physically and geographically. Intensive growth may then be regarded as an increasing capacity to collect and to process information and, thus, to mobilize energy and matter.

In theories about economic history, where the terms originated, extensive and intensive growth are usually seen as contrasts: as mutually exclusive and even opposing trends (see Jones 2000). In this project we have come to the conclusion that, more often than not, the two trends have been mutually supportive and reinforcing. We even suggest as a general hypothesis, ensuing from our inquiries, that *intensive growth has always been a condition for, and even the driving force of, extensive growth*.

The expansion of the anthroposphere has been marked by three major 'leaps', in which distinct socio-ecological regimes were successively formed: the fire regime, the agrarian regime and the industrial regime. With each new regime, humans gained greater control over energy and matter, and thus strengthened their position in the biosphere. Control over the non-human environment may appear primarily in the guise of technology. However, technology cannot exist in a social and cultural void: it can only function in a context of social organization and civilization. Each advance in technology therefore involved changes in organization and civilization.

Throughout this entire process, human life has remained dependent on the resources provided by the natural environment, notably food, water and air. Climate and soil have continued to be the major natural conditions determining access to these primary resources. While the major variable in the provision of food has always been vegetation, the presence of other species has been a crucial intervening variable. Those other species include large animals – in their capacity as potential food or as predators or competitors – as well as insects and microbes. The relationships to other animals and to microbes have largely determined human *access* to vegetation. This is why the domestication of fire has been so vitally important: it has helped human groups to clear bushes, ward off other animals and kill microparasites in food.

The transition to agriculture implied deliberate manipulation of vegetation. It altered the environment, to suit human purposes. In many cases, it also led to an increasing human population ('extensive growth'). This in turn elicited intensification of agriculture, often leading to unintended changes in the environment such as erosion or salinization and inevitably always involving greater vulnerability to destruction – through natural causes, human negligence or violence or any combination of these factors. It created a landscape of fields and meadows that belonged visibly to the human realm, the anthroposphere.

In the agrarian regime people created an ecological niche under human surveillance, in which certain selected plants and animals received special protection because they were valued as contributing to human survival and comfort. In early agrarian society the constraints of this ecological regime were omnipresent and everybody could feel and appreciate their force. These constraints are clearly reflected in the entire structure of agrarian and pastoral societies: in their technology, organization and civilization.

With further intensification, social organization became more complex, and the new social and cultural structures left a strong mark on the human condition. An individual's chances in life came to depend more and more on his or her position in networks of social stratification. Although vegetation continued to be the prime material basis of society, as food and fodder, the ruling elite became primarily concerned with other interests than raising crops or tending domesticated animals.

The great agrarian empires such as ancient Rome and China experienced long periods of both extensive and intensive growth (see above, p. 209-56 and 301-3). The cultivated areas were expanded and used more intensively to feed a growing population. The organization of the production and distribution of food grew more complex, leading to the formation of increasingly larger and more robust inter- and super-regional networks. If, in some cases, these networks had been preceded by networks primarily oriented to the pursuit of exchange and trade, in the great empires those economic networks were superseded and absorbed by military and political organizations.

Much of the evidence collected in this book suggests that environmental pressures in agrarian empires continued to weigh heavily on the majority of the population whose lives were, in Thomas Hobbes's famous words, 'nasty, brutish and short'. The elite groups were only one step removed from these pressures. If a climatic disaster struck, as is likely to have happened to the Maya' around 700 CE, this could lead to the collapse of the empire (see p. 65). In such cases, even if the elite groups were primarily concerned with inter-human relationships rather than with relationships with the non-human environment, the ultimate downfall of the overarching social and cultural structures was precipitated by the failings of an insufficiently resilient socio-ecological infrastructure.

These examples support what seems to be a general rule: societies that stretched their control over energy and matter further also became more dependent on both the resources that were thus being controlled *and* on the entire socio-cultural apparatus involved in their control. We have encountered this unintended side-effect throughout the book and need not elaborate it again here.

The same gains in control that gave humans more power *vis-à-vis* the non-human environment also influenced inter-human relationships, giving groups with superior technology and organization an advantage in confrontations with other groups as well. Here a flywheel effect would often occur so that, in a process of 'figurational dynamics' (see above, p. 361-2), initially small differences would lead to major social inequalities between the mighty and the weak, colonizers and colonized, rich and poor, masters and slaves, each having their own peculiar relationships with the natural environment.

In the modern era, two developments have changed the constraints of the agrarian regime: industrialization and globalization. In the process of industrialization, huge deposits of fossil fuel have been opened up for human exploitation and, with the aid of rapidly developing new forms of technology and organization, are now being used for the provision of food, the extraction of metals and minerals and the production of countless goods and services. Globalization is fostered by, and fosters, the circulation of the products of industrial enterprise across the world. As a result, the very notion of human habitat potential at local or regional or even national levels has become questionable, because the exchange of energy, matter and information is able to sustain high population densities at sites such as Brasilia or Phoenix, Arizona that would be barely capable of sustaining any human life at all without imports of energy and matter. With the emerging global division of labour, the only realistic unit for measuring human habitat potential is therefore the earth.

12.3.   Prospects

12.3.1.   *Paradoxes of prediction*

Images of futures have always been part of the present, in every period of human history. Anticipation belongs to the very essence of life; it is a feature of life in general and is a particularly strong feature of human life. The farmer who plants seeds in the ground, the warrior who sets out for a campaign, the trader who stocks goods, they all gear their behaviour toward goals that fit into a pattern of expectations. The expectations are based on past experience and learning: lessons from the past shape the images of the future.

Members of a society with little social and cultural change could entertain an image of the future that would be largely a replica of the present (see Heilbroner 1995). They knew that they themselves would grow older and would die one day; but their children would follow in their footsteps and carry on the same sort of lives. Although the details of an individual's fate were uncertain, the future in general was somehow predictable: it would unfold in the familiar setting of monsoons or seasons, interrupted from time to time by unforeseen events: a hurricane, a drought, an epidemic or an invasion by foreign raiders.

As societies became more dynamic and more susceptible to change, the patterns of expectations also changed. Foresight and planning became more important and, by the same token, more difficult. This is our present predicament, alerting us to our complex and, in some respects profoundly paradoxical, relationship with the future.

The most basic paradox about the future as we perceive it today can be stated as follows: *we are unable to predict the future and we always will be.* On first sight this statement seems self-contradictory; but it is not. It merely points to the fact that our relationship with the future is diverse and heterogeneous. There are some things about it that we know with reasonable certainty and other things that we do not and, in many cases cannot know at all. If we conceive of 'the future' in a holistic sense as the totality of all events that lie in store for us and for posterity, we are clearly not in a position to predict it. On the other hand, there are a great many things that can be predicted with a high degree of certainty: that the sun will rise again tomorrow, that next winter will be colder than next summer, that the tides will come and go, that water from the sea will be salty.

We can safely make these predictions because they concern regularities that exist independently of human interference. Here we encounter yet another paradox. On the one hand, by exerting control over nature people try to make natural processes more predictable. However, the very processes over which they can exert most control may also be the most difficult to predict – precisely because people are able to influence these processes. The movement of prices at the stock exchange is a good example: this movement is through and through a function of human actions and yet it is essentially unpredictable: its rationale is its unpredictability.

Not only are human beings as individuals in some important ways unpredictable, certain mechanisms in their social interactions add to this unpredictability. We have already referred to the principle of self-fulfilling and self-denying prophecies. A self-fulfilling prophecy occurs when, for example, word gets around that a bank is insolvent. This may prompt people to withdraw their accounts, leading to actual bankruptcy. In contrast, rumours of insolvency may also be taken as a warning and a reason for wealthy investors to support the bank. In that case the prophecy is self-denying.

A related issue is known as the dilemma of collective action (see De Swaan 2001: 91-98). Its relevance to environmental problems has been made famous in the parable of the 'tragedy of the commons' and in the concept of the 'free rider'. The image of 'the commons' refers to a pasture used by herders who each have the right to let their own animals graze on the communal ground. If no limits are set, each herder will be motivated to add more and more animals, especially if his fellow-herders do the same. The inevitable result is overgrazing. An obvious parallel is overfishing; we came across the same mechanism in the 'spiral of desire' discussed in Chapter 10 and in the resource management regimes discussed in Chapters 6 and 8 (see also Ostrom 1990).

In all such cases, the tendencies toward the depletion of resources are undisputedly present. The outcome, however, is not necessarily predictable disaster. For a realistic prediction, we need to know more about the social context in which the dilemma of collective action is set, including political and economic relations as well as the prevailing attitudes and mentalities.

There seems to be no end to the paradoxes of prediction. The discovery of the biosphere has made us aware of the problem of sustainability. Once again we seem to be confronted with paradoxes. To begin with, the need for sustainability has arisen in a world that is perceived to be inherently dynamic and continuously changing; sustainability is predicated on change. But applying the notion of sustainability to a rapidly changing world is almost like adding insult to injury, as it compels us to consider the need for introducing yet another new element in the dynamic relationships between humans and the biosphere. As John McNeill points out in his environmental history of the 20th century, one reason why the environment changed so much is that prevailing ideas and politics changed so little (McNeill 2000: 325). The dilemma was summed up neatly by Giuseppe Tomasi di Lampedusa when he had the main character in his great novel *The Leopard* remark: 'if we want things to stay as they are, things will have to change' (Lampedusa 1960: 21).

12.3.2. Scenarios

To orient ourselves to an unknown future, the simplest procedure seems to be to observe current trends and examine how they are likely to develop further in mutual interaction. Computer models greatly facilitate such exercises and make it possible to construct scenarios in which variable weight is given to many diverse trends. Numerous complications and uncertainties remain, however, especially concerning the future of intensive growth.

With regard to extensive growth there are already signs of deceleration, and in some parts of the world stagnation – or even, as in many regions of the former Soviet Union, regression. Demographers now generally assume that global population growth will continue to slow down and will reach a turning point around 2050, when the total number of people will be somewhere between seven and fourteen billion, most probably close to ten billion (*see box*). It is conceivable that, in geographical terms, large numbers of people may one day migrate into territories such as the Sahara or Antarctica that are as yet largely uninhabited. This may become possible as a consequence either of changes in the climate or of human inventions. The latter case would be one more example of

FIGURE 12.1

World population 2000 BCE-2000 CE and beyond

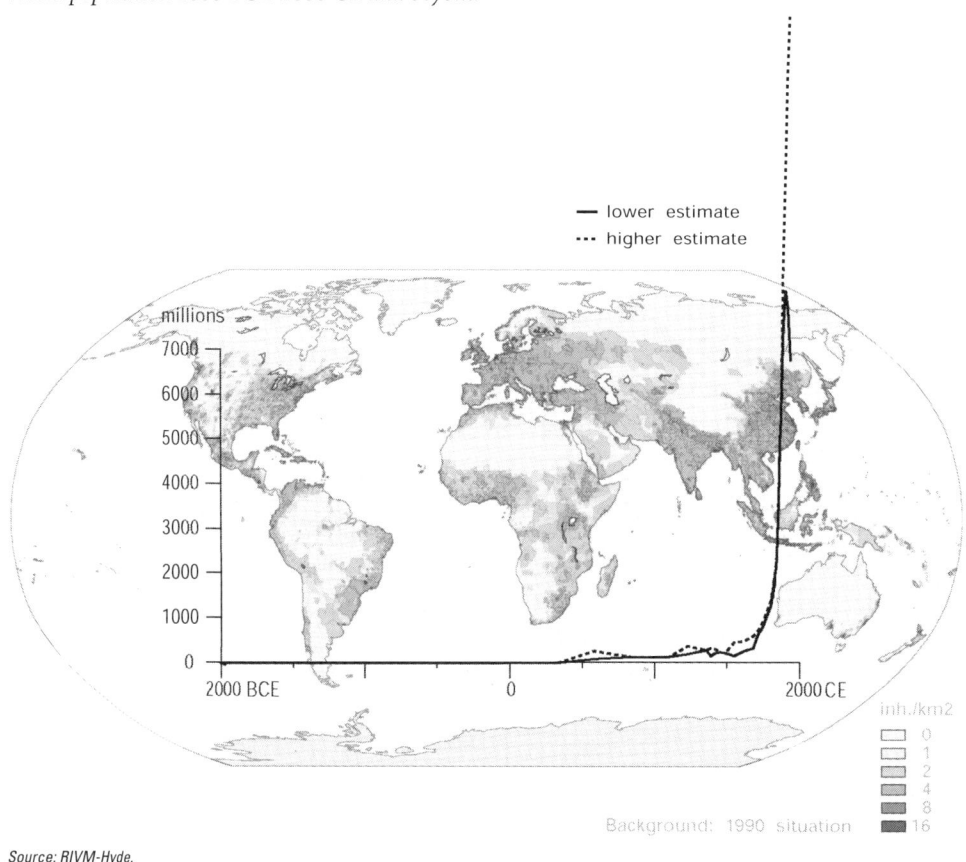

— lower estimate
··· higher estimate

Source: RIVM-Hyde.

intensive growth facilitating or even stimulating extensive growth. In general, however, there appear to be reasonably firm grounds to predict that, in the 21st century, extensive growth for humanity at large will reach its zenith and cease (*see box*).

It is virtually impossible to make any specific predictions for intensive growth, because intensive growth – defined above (p. 27-8) as an increasing capacity to collect and process information and therefore mobilize energy and matter – is strongly dependent on developments in technology and knowledge. As the philosopher Karl Popper (1957: v-vii) demonstrated in a neat syllogism, the development of knowledge cannot possibly be predicted, for if we knew what we will know in the future, we would already know it. Since intensive growth is inconceivable without advances in knowledge, the logic of this argument should make us wary of predictions in this field. An empirical example to support such scepticism is the recent rise of personal computers and the

Anything new under the sun? During a slow, steady and irreversible process of agrarianization, human groups have developed ways to cope with their natural environment both in terms of opportunity and constraints, abundance and scarcity. Forms of societal complexity tended to reflect biogeographical factors – such as climate and vegetation – in combination with rather universal mechanisms of social organization. The social memory built up from generations of past experiences provided a repertoire of responses to the vagaries of nature. With the increase of human control, societies became more dependent on the skills they developed and sustained, on the ways they organized themselves, and on how they managed information flows. This is most obvious in the hierarchically structured empires evolved from military-agrarian regimes and the trade-based states formed around competitive markets.

The loop of control and dependency led to the need for more control and more understanding of the surrounding natural systems. The resulting socio-natural systems mastered the better-known short-term and local risks at the cost of leaving at the time less well-known, longer-term and wider risks to future generations. With the European-led industrialization and globalization process of the last three or four centuries, the control loops have expanded and intensified to the extent that most of the planet is now under some form of management. At the same time, the capability to acquire and process information has grown enormously – providing the conditions for the 'discovery of the biosphere' as a necessary complement to globalization and complexification.

In the 1990s the annual increment of the human population amounted to some 90 million individuals. Most demographers anticipate a gradual slowdown in population growth, stabilizing somewhere in the 21st century at levels between 7 and 14 billion people (Figure 12.1). Intensive growth continues unabated and will lead to future situations as yet difficult or impossible to anticipate. Hierarchies and markets are still the dominant ways in which societies, now on an ever larger geographical scale, organize themselves. The capacity to process the necessary information flows to sustain this latest phase in the human adventure has increased enormously – will it be enough? As in other historical times and places, limits have been – and are – announced: limits to available resources and to the necessary transition periods and efforts, limits to the absorption capacity of the natural environment, limits to institutions and governance – even to happiness.

One lesson from this book is that the limits posed will be a mixture of natural and social limits – nature has become an integral part of the socio-natural system Planet Earth. Undoubtedly, great challenges are ahead because the human race will experience the end to continuing extensive growth. Will it be a process in which such limits make themselves felt in unpleasant and abrupt ways, or will the coming structural transformation be a smooth one helped by corrective anticipation? In any event, it seems wise to be well-prepared by an adequate understanding based on scientific investigations. It may be equally wise to engage in socio-cultural experiments, so as to sustain not only biodiversity but also access to the wealth of human experience in various local settings. For instance, the less conspicuous but probably numerous resource management regimes based on local circumstances, co-operation and community control deserve full attention, as complements to the prevailing forms of hierarchies and markets. It may widen our view on a sustainable future for all of humankind, maybe in the form of clumsy institutions, in which a variety of convictions about how the world functions is given recognition.

internet – a form of intensive growth that had not been predicted in advance (see Margolis 2000).

The future of both extensive and intensive growth is further complicated by the current distribution of wealth and poverty in the world. Access to resources, and to means of exchange and means of violence, is very unequally divided among, and within, nations. At the turn of the millennium, the gross domestic product per capita in the rich 'Neo-European' states (the United States, Canada, Australia and New Zealand) exceeded that in Africa by a factor twenty and that in Asia (excluding Japan) by a factor eight (Maddison 2001: 28). Intensive growth is continuing in the richer part of the world, and although several important poorer regions, including China and India, are beginning to catch up, the general gap between rich and poor is widening. This inequality is the cause, and legitimization, of tensions that can easily erupt into war, as they actually did many times, in many regions.

While wars are, in their own way, also highly unpredictable, they rarely fail to have an impact on the natural environment. Certainly in our day and age, wars cause severe disturbances. In the years between 1950 and 2000 there were numerous oil spills, causing great ecological damage. By far the greatest in this series was due to the destruction in the Gulf War of 1991 (see Oil Spills Website). The planting of landmines in many regions is also an environmental disaster. We have no neat syllogism from which we can infer why both the outbreak and the outcome of war are unpredictable; but we do know on empirical grounds that once started, wars are hard to contain and not only destructive of human lives but also highly detrimental to the physical environment – especially those parts of the environment that people cherish most.

Even apart from war, political and economic developments may defy our expectations. Few observers foresaw the collapse of the Soviet Union from 1989 onwards; nor did many futurist scenarios include the terrorist attacks on the United States on 11 September, 2001. Against the backdrop of these various uncertainties, related to the nature of the development of knowledge as well as to political vicissitudes and the risks of war, scenarios can be no more than explorations of possible futures. As the President of the World Watch Institute and the Executive Director of the United Nations Environment

Programme state in their foreword to *Vital Signs 2001-2202. The Trends That Are Shaping Our Future*:

> If there is one lesson of this extraordinary half-century [1950-2000], it is that most trends defy prediction by experts. The most important changes have generally come abruptly, with little warning. We never seem to know where the latest economic crisis or ecological catastrophe will come from, but we do know that the projections of smooth, gradual change that computer models churn out are almost always wrong. (World Watch Institute 2001: 12)

These are the words of professionals experienced in the art of social forecasting. However, as the authors themselves realize, we all are hostages of the future – our own future and that of later generations. There is no escape from our position in historical time. In that position, we can either relinquish all claims to know anything at all about what lies ahead and enter the future with a blank mind; or we can admit that such an attitude of total agnosticism is also only a pretence. We do anticipate; the question is how far we can go in our anticipation without losing touch with reality.

12.3.3.   Towards a fourth regime?

We find ourselves today in a unique historical situation. Amidst all uncertainties about the future one fact stands undisputed: the age of fossil fuel energy in which we are living will come to an end. The stocks are rich, but limited and not renewable. For this reason the environmental historian Rolf Peter Sieferle (1997, 2001) calls the era of industrialization an age of transition.

Does it also spell the end of industrial production? That is highly unlikely – just as the rise of agriculture did not spell the end of the domestication of fire and industrialization did not put an end to agriculture. It is far more probable that a new socio-ecological regime will emerge (and may already be emerging) which will absorb the earlier fire, agrarian and industrial regimes.

The realization that the stocks of fossil fuel are exhaustible has occasioned some severe shocks, such as the international oil crises of 1973 and 1979. These crises have added to the sense of alarm about the strong reliance on fossil fuels in contemporary society. This reliance feeds not only environmental trends such as global warming but also social and political unrest. It engenders very uneven economic dependence and extreme differences in wealth, in turn leading to strained political relations and escalating military tensions.

The urgency of economic and political problems easily turns public attention away from ecological issues. The major regimes in the world today are formed around political and economic centres. This may be a reason why the fourth socio-ecological regime,

411

if indeed it is already in the making, is still largely unrecognized and nameless.

In the meantime, the population is still increasing in most poor countries. Industrialization and the intensification of agriculture combine to confront those countries with the same two environmental problems experienced, albeit on a much smaller scale, in the industrializing regions of Europe in the 19th century: urban congestion and decay of traditional agrarian communities. Deforestation and the growth of megacities are two aspects of the same overall process. Extensive growth is a driving force; it therefore stands to reason that a lowering of the birth rate would be a prime factor in reducing environmental stress. Although fertility is not an independent variable, as the Canadian geographer Vaclav Smil notes, 'vigorous population control measures are in the best interest of the worst affected countries' (Smil 1994: 215).

If in earlier periods intensive growth was indeed the prime mover of extensive growth, then today and in the near future it will have to be the prime brake. A higher standard of living, better economic prospects and a stronger position for women are aspects of intensive growth that may be expected to contribute to the slackening of extensive growth. Technologically, convenient means of birth control are now available; the obstacles impeding their use lie mainly in the spheres of organization and civilization.

Biotechnology   An important aspect of technological change derives from molecular biology and involves the techniques known as genetic engineering or genetic modification (GM). Human exploitation of plants and animals is rapidly becoming more and more intensified and diversified. As the sociologist Joanna Swabe (1992: 192-205) notes, these developments represent the continuation of 10,000 years of 'biotechnology' under agrarian and pastoral regimes; on the other hand, they bring about 'brand new' circumstances. The prospects of genetic modification include the possibility of bacterial production of meat-like tissues. According to the sociologist Steve Quilley, 'such an in vitro, industrial (rather than agricultural) closed-system, GM trajectory would effectively constitute the greatest ecological and evolutionary transformation since the Neolithic revolution. It might offer a real possibility for a more 'wild' or unmanaged nature to emerge from under the stifling grip of agriculture. For the first time, humanity might be able to allow trees and forests to start winning succession struggles with grasses. Vast tracts of agricultural land could be returned to 'a state of nature'. Such wild nature would no doubt be just as artificial in the broader scheme of things. However, it might allow the planetary mechanism to resume a series of functions that have been temporarily disrupted or usurped by humanity and its allies: soil formation, carbon fixation and climate regulation amongst others' (Quilley, forthcoming: 20).

412

Technology, organization and civilization are the major factors shaping the relationships between humans and the biosphere and determining whether intensive growth will continue, and in which direction it will veer. They reflect the 'triad of human controls' over nature, society and self (see above, p. 28), and as such are intricately interconnected.

Technology is most clearly directed to physical nature. Aided by technology, humans made their position in the biosphere from early on more secure and more comfortable and, in doing so, sometimes wrought havoc with other species. But they have also always used technology when they tried to repair the damage and to stabilize their relationship with the environment. In the same vein, modern methods of recycling and 'waste mining' and more efficient uses of energy and materials have been introduced. There is a continuing search for alternative energy sources: wind, water, biomass, solar power, nuclear fission and fusion, each with their own promises, costs and risks.

The importance of social organization has come to the fore many times in this book; it underpins the very notion of socio-ecological regimes. As John McNeill wisely observes, 'of course, well organized societies always enjoy an edge over the badly organized.' (McNeill 2000: 200) Defining what 'well organized' would mean in the world today easily leads to a catalogue of hackneyed epithets: resilient, flexible, sustainable, grounded on the local level and in touch with the global level. Indeed, the nature of our environmental problems calls on the one hand for a global orientation and the possibility of integrating and co-ordinating activities worldwide. On the other hand, differentiation into a great variety of finely textured webs is also needed. On each level, people have to be prepared for the possibility of unintended and unforeseen developments. An integral part of a 'fourth regime' will be the continuous monitoring of its own impacts.

An index of civilization can be found in manuals for good behaviour, in the form of either ethics or etiquette (see Elias 2000). Until recently, these manuals paid only scant attention to environmental issues. What mattered was how humans treated other humans, not how they treated plants and animals, water and air, the soil and the sea. Those matters were relegated to separate technical treatises. In the 20th century, a new genre emerged, of moral-ecological discourse, as exemplified in Rachel Carson's well-known book *Silent Spring* (1962). The message in this genre is an appeal to people's responsibility as citizens of the earth. They should be aware of ecological chains and cycles and think of the long-term effects of present actions. Both personal behaviour and political decision-making must be guided by foresight. The best strategies on both levels are 'no-regret strategies', inspired even in the context of uncertainty by a willingness to subordinate short-term gains to longer-term interests.

These strategies are in line with the general conclusions that emerge from this book. A pervasive theme is the trend toward the increasing scale of the interactions between humans and the natural environment. The scale has increased in space and time, from local to global and from short-term to very long-term. The extension in scale has been accompanied and, we suggest, propelled, by a concomitant trend toward greater interdependence and complexity.

Information has played a pivotal part in the process of increasing interdependence and complexity. In the past, a major handicap of the regimes in agrarian states and empires was their limited capacity to recognize and understand the dynamics of socio-ecological relations. Attention tended to focus on restricted, short-term issues, especially in times of crisis. A better understanding of the predicaments of the past may enable us to deal in a more enlightened manner with the problems facing us today. In the absence of reliable long-term forecasts flexibility is continuously needed. But short-term alertness should not blind us to the recognition that resilience is best served by recognizing the entire vital network of interdependencies in which human lives evolve – in other words, the dynamics of the anthroposphere within the biosphere.

Notes

Notes to Chapter 1

1 Alexander Pope, 'Proposed Epitaph for Isaac Newton'. Quoted by Prigogine and Stengers 1984: 27.
2 It remains to be seen to what extent the change in world view was an autonomous 'mental' transformation. Much is to be said for the idea that it reflected more general changes in culture and society at large. From the seventeenth century onward, the urban elites in Europe increasingly found
   themselves living in conditions that were different from those of their parents and ancestors. This
   created a sense of perpetuating social and cultural change. When, in the nineteenth century, the
   process of industrialization gained momentum, this only added to the overwhelming experience of
   contemporary witnesses that they were living in a protean age.

Notes to Chapter 2

1 This section is based on Margulis and Sagan 1997: 99-114 and Westbroek 1991: 170-2 and 183-203.
2 For an account of research into early human development with references to recent findings and
   ideas see McBrearty and Brooks 2000.
3 CE stands for Contemporary Era, BCE for Before Contemporary Era. These notations are equivalent to the traditional Christian notations of AD (Anno Domini) and BC (Before Christ) which are
   used in some chapters of this book.
4 This section is largely based on MacDougall 1996 and Roberts 1998.
5 This and the following paragraphs are based on Goudsblom 1996: 31-62.
6 The term functions is used here along the lines of Elias 1978 and Goudsblom 1977.

Notes to Chapter 3

1 There has also been a great deal of 'environmental change' for other species and for less dominant
   offspring of the species *Homo sapiens*, as touched upon in Chapter 2. We will probably never hear
   their story as they would have told it.
2 For research and discussions see Bradley 1995; Lamb 1988, 1995; Jones 1996; Roberts 1989; Prentice
   1998; Houghton 2001; Dunbar 2000.
3 The Nilometer is a stone gauge at Roda near Cairo where the level of the Nile is recorded. Superim-
   posed on the annual high flows that follow rains in the East and Central African highlands are sustained periods of high or low flows that correlate with wet or dry periods, respectively.
4 The Quaternary is the period of geological time that forms the last 2 million years. It is character-

ized by a series of large swings in temperature that form glacial periods (*Figure 3.1*).

5 All chronological indications in this chapter are in years before present (yr BP), i.e. the year 1950 AD, unless otherwise indicated. See also *Table 5.1*.

6 The thermohaline circulation refers to the ocean water fluxes resulting from the input of cold water from the Poles into the Atlantic; the cold, relatively fresh water is denser than the water within the Atlantic and therefore sinks; this movement then sets up a circum-polar gyre.

7 We use cal AD to indicate that the radiocarbon dates have been 'calibrated' to take into account changes in the amount of radioactive carbon present in the atmosphere over time. Calibrated dates are equivalent to calendar years and often accompany the notation AD or BC. See also *Table 5.1*.

8 This contribution was written by Sander van der Leeuw and is based on research within the ARCHAEOMEDES project, a large-scale effort to investigate the human-environment interaction in regions in France, Spain and Greece (Leeuw 1998).

Notes to Chapter 4

1 This textbox is a contribution from Pieter Bol.

2 The IMAGE model developed at the Dutch National Institute of Public Health and the Environment (RIVM) is one of the models in which such maps are used to explore climate change impacts and policy options (Klein Goldewijk 1997, 2001; IMAGE team 2001). It uses the BIOME approach discussed in Chapter 3. See also Ramankutty and Foley 1999 and Section 3.2.

3 A special form of seasonal migration in which full use is made of variations in opportunities for food supply is transhumance, which is widely practiced in the Mediterranean and Alpine countries in Europe.

4 Based on Ramankutty and Foley (1999) *(Figure 4.1)*, representing present areas of the categories Savannah, Grassland/Steppe and Dense and Open Shrubland. Numbers such as these are rather dependent on biome definitions. In the Early-to-Mid Holocene period (8000 yr BP) the steppe and savannahs would have been larger (Adams, 1997).

5 McIntosh (2000, 1988) gives an account of the climatic fluctuations in the Middle Niger floodplain during the Holocene period and indicates how the very old social construction of reality of the Mande people is a reflection of thousands of years of human existence in a highly unpredictable and changing natural environment (cf. Section 3.3).

6 In the Early Holocene period (8000 yr BP) the forested area may have been 10-20% larger than at present (Adams, 1997).

7 This section is largely based on a contribution from Professor Tim Kohler and on Redman's clear account in his book *Human Impact on Ancient Environments* (1999).

8 The relationship of Hohokam cultural change and their irrigation system has been investigated in detail by Waters (2001) and Huckleberry (1999).

9 Agrarian settlements also spread over the entire Plateau itself, near places with accessible surface water (Christensen 1993).

10 See Mazoyer 1997 and Harris 1996 for elaborate evolutionary classifications of plant and animal exploitation by human groups.

11 There is evidence that dogs were domesticated much earlier.

12 See *Figure 3.5* for the palaeo-vegetation in the Levantine corridor and probable places of origin of agriculture.

13 Climatically, the Near East is a highly complex region, conditions were continually changing in the early Holocene period and none of those conditions exist today anywhere in South-West Asia.

14 Contributions about the underlying processes can also be expected from the emerging field of evolutionary economics, but this is beyond the scope of the present discussion.

15 It has been argued that this has also led to an increased immunity of Eurasian populations which caused the large-scale death of native Americans upon the arrival of the Europeans (Diamond 1997).

16 This textbox is a contribution from Pieter Bol.

17 This section is a contribution from Emma Romanova and colleagues at the Department of the Physical Geography of the World of the Lomonosov Moscow State University in Moscow (Romanova 1997).

Notes to Chapter 5

1 The Russian physicist Kapitza suggests that hyperbolic growth for the human population, of the form $P = a/(b-t)$ where P is population and t is time, is the more meaningful because the growth rate then depends on the square of the number of people. As the square is related to the number of connections, it emphasizes the role of interaction and co-operation in the growth process (personal communication; cf. Chapter 2).

2 An early example of an integrated system dynamics model is World3 used in the report Limits to Growth to the Club of Rome (Meadows 1972, 1991). A more sophisticated approach along these lines is the TARGERS model (Rotmans and De Vries 1997). The relationship between models, scenarios and stories is dealt with in detail in the recent Special Report on Emissions Scenarios (SRES) for the Intergovernmental Panel on Climate Change (IPCC) (Nakicenovic *et al.* 2000).

3 The origin of measures constructed for orientation and communication is quite revealing. Distance measures were often related to some part of the body or the local environment: the Roman mile equals a thousand double steps. The unit of 847 grams used by the Harappan peoples in the Indus valley for weight may have a similar origin. A more in-depth treatment is beyond the scope of this study.

4 One may also think here of the plethora of indicators that are being proposed to adequately characterize 'sustainable development'.

5 Quoted from Rumi, Poet and Mystic (1207-1275), Translated from the Persian by R. Nicholson, Allen and Unwin Ltd., London 6th impression 1973 p. 117.

6 This overview is in no way complete; for instance, the elaborate calendar used by the Maya is missing. See http: //astro.nmsu.edu for a discussion of calendars in various cultures.

7 As a matter of convenience, we will use in this book the notation of years before present (yr BP) in a scientific context. In specific historical contexts we also use other time notations. See Roberts 1989 for the conversion and its background.

8 The ethnocentricity is not specific to the past. Chinese people call their land the 'Middle Kingdom' and the eastern Mediterranean is almost always referred to as the *Near* East.

9   Simmons uses the ecosystem as a conceptual tool and quotes Odum's definition: 'Any unit that includes all of the organisms in a given area interacting with the physical environment so that a flow of energy leads to … exchange of materials between living and non-living parts within the ecosystem … is an ecosystem.' (Simmons 1989)

10 Ashby's Law of Requisite Variety states that 'in order to achieve complete control, the variety of actions a control system should be able to execute must be at least as great as the variety of environmental perturbations that need to be compensated.'

11 Complexity is often also value-loaded. For instance, in constructing an apparatus or a set of procedural rules, low-complexity is often appreciated and associated with elegance and effectiveness if it satisfies the objectives for which it is designed. The word 'complicated' has acquired a pejorative connotation precisely for these reasons. The other way around, perceived complexity might give a structure or a person a much-appreciated depth.

12 For more detailed discussions see the Journal of Artificial Societies and Social Simulation (http://jasss.soc.surrey.ac.uk).

13 See Mook and Van de Plassche (1986) for an excellent overview of this important technique in terms of inherent and incidental problems and uncertainties.

14 Place j is within the IMAGE framework one of the 66,000 gridcells of 0.5° by 0.5° and a longitude-dependent area size S of the order of 2500 km^2.

15 For crops $j=1...n$, CSI is calculated as the … mean: $CSI = [CSI1*CSI2*...*CSIn]**(1/n)$.

16 This is a crude representation of the process in which declining yield per labour-hour was counter-acted by substituting human labour for animal and later mechanical power. As such the freeing up of farmers' labour was a direct consequence of using other energy sources with a net energy gain.

17 Trade matters also in a different sense: even in ancient times long-distance transportation of food has in some instances been important, the best known example being the Mediterranean trade during the Roman Empire. Food storage techniques have been a crucial aspect in this respect. In the last few hundred years there has been a general rise in long-distance food transport.

Notes to Chapter 6

1   See Section 5.4 for the notion of complexity. We use the words social complexity, socio-political complexity and socio-cultural complexity interchangeably.

2   This textbox is a contribution from Rob Marchant.

3   For reasons that are still not completely understood, the whole social network unravelled about the time of Columbus or soon after. Smallpox may well have visited the area – many researchers think that an epidemic of the disease greatly weakened the nearby Inca empire in about 1525 AD.

4   At least, according to Cherry (1986). Recent investigations support, according to some, the theory that the huge volcano eruption on Thira – modern Santorini – wiped out the Minoan civilization on Crete in a complex interplay of factors each operating on different time-scales: flood waves, interruption of trade, climate change and erosion of dominant belief systems and invasions.

5   The potlach system is an exchange system to achieve and maintain rank; the word 'potlach' means 'gift' in the language of the Chinook Indian people in North West America (Reader 1988).

6   An ecotone is a narrow and rather sharp defined transition zone between two ecological communi-

ties; they are usually species-rich and may have come into existence either from natural or anthropogenic processes.

7 Yellow River

8 A state farm owned and operated by the governing family is presently being excavated by a Dutch team funded by the National Museum of Antiquities Leiden and the Free University of Amsterdam. This textbox is written by Frans Wiggermann.

9 The fringes of the European colonial empires have been extensively discussed by Wallerstein in his book *The Modern World System* (1974), among others.

10 The process in which a culture turns inward and weaves ever more complex patterns of rituals and social interactions has been called 'cultural involution' by the anthropologist Geertz (1963), with particular reference to Asian island cultures. Such a form of increasing social complexity is one of the – less easily recognized and appreciated – forms of intensive growth (cf. Chapter 2).

11 A telling example are the Cistercienser monks who started convents in medieval France.

Notes to Chapter 7

1 Resilience is the capacity of a system to respond to perturbations with structural transformation. See further on and Chapters 5 and 8 for a more in-depth discussion.

2 It is tempting to draw a comparison with the later Spanish and British Empire, the latter being so similar and the former so different in its governance and control structure to the Roman Empire.

3 This textbox is a contribution from Emma Romanova and her colleagues at the Department of the Physical Geography of the World of the Lomonosov Moscow State University in Moscow – see Section 4.6. See also http: //darkwing.uoregon.edu/~atlas/europe for similar maps.

4 This textbox is a contribution from Paul Erdkamp.

5 Mile comes from *milia*, thousand – one mile being a thousand steps with a Roman step being two of our steps: left-right.

6 All three are regions in the Rhône valley.

7 This textbox is largely based upon a contribution from Dr. Jan Boersema.

8 This is expressed in the two words for environment in French, *milieu* and *environnement*. The asymmetry implies that what is degradation of the *'environnement'* from an environmental perspective can be a socialization of the *'milieu'*.

9 This textbox is a contribution from Pieter Bol.

Notes to Chapter 8

1 We gratefully acknowledge the discussions with and contributions from Timothy Kohler, Dwight Read and Sander van der Leeuw in parts of this chapter.

2 See also the modelling approach to the events on Easter Island (Chapter 6; Anderies 2000).

3 The complex kinship relationships among !Kung San have been explored by Read (1998) and parameterized for operation within the model to test hypotheses about the role of incest rules. It is found that strict rules actually imply that women – or men – have to find a partner outside their

camp group, thus mitigating resource issues. However, it is also found that the model correctly explains the camp size distribution, which suggests that no other explanation – e.g. leadership conflicts – is needed.

4   A preliminary report on this project was issued in 2000 Kohler (2000a) and the project will be finalized in 2003. The CD-ROM accompanying this volume has a film drawn from the work reported in Kohler (2000b).

5   The authors are currently investigating whether including the role of temperature change improves the fit more explicitly.

6   See Chapter 7 for an evaluation of this theory with regard to the Roman Empire.

7   The basis of Cultural Theory in anthropology is work done by Douglas (1978) in which peoples' belief systems are interpreted as reflections of social relationships; in ecology by Holling's work (1986) on the stability of ecosystems and the cycles within them. A fifth worldview, that of the *hermit*, is postulated outside the plane of the grid-group axes and not considered here despite its possible historical relevance. Interpretations of complex phenomena such as discussed in this book can often be traced at least partly to a prevailing worldview and an associated scientific discipline (see e.g. Keyfitz 1993 and Section 5.2).

8   In the Narmada Valley further to the south, where a vast 'development' project is under way, they have now done the same to the representatives of the World Bank. In fact, the World Bank pulled out in 1993, but the project is still being promoted, by Indian state governments and market borrowings.

9   Unlike 'agent-based' (or 'bottom-up' or 'a-life') modelling which is not predictive (cf. Section 8.3). Such unconventional modelling is of great value, precisely because it is not predictive, when we set about making ourselves clumsy.

10 Such an explanation also appears valid for the common property regimes discussed in Section 6.5.

Notes to Chapter 9

1   In an analysis of fertility behaviour in Punjab, India, Dasgupta (1995) notes that her findings '… bring out the commonalities of peasant life and demographic behaviour between this less-developed country [India] and those of historical Europe. Secondly, it throws light on which aspects of developmental interventions are most crucial for enabling people to reduce their fertility.' (Dasgupta 1995: 498)

2   As this section deals largely with the period before 1950, we refer rather loosely to India and South Asia as the entity under consideration.

3   Partition refers to the 1947 division of the South Asian subcontinent into India and West and East Pakistan; East Pakistan later became the independent state Bangladesh in 1971.

4   This section is a contribution from David Henley who works as a researcher at the Royal Institute for Linguistics and Anthropology (KITLV) in Leiden. He has a background in geography and is author of several books on the historical geography of Indonesia.

Notes to Chapter 10

1   The population map is part of the History Database of the Global Environment - HYDE (Klein Goldewijk 2001). Starting point for a global georeferenced historical population map is the 0.5* x 0.5* degree longitude / latitude population density map of 1994 from the National Center for Geographic Information and Analysis (NCGIA; see Tobler et al. 1995). The NCGIA data set was overlayed with country borders from HYDE, and population numbers in grid cells of the NCGIA database belonging to countries as defined by HYDE were aggregated to country totals. The HYDE country totals for 1994 were adjusted in order to equal the country totals of the United Nations population database (United Nations 1997). Finally, the current population densities were scaled down to a same population distribution as in the NCGIA database, under the assumption that high population density areas remain in the same place over time.

   Please note that the average population densities in the map are valid for whole grid cells, which have roughly an area of 2500 km2 (at the equator). The unit given is a logarithmic scale, in order to facilitate comparison with the Boserup classification scheme discussed in Chapters 4-5 (Kees Klein Goldewijk).

2   There is a huge literature on the early stages of industrialization. For this section we have drawn especially on concepts and data from Simmons (1996), Sieferle (1997; 2001) and Grübler (1998).

3   An interesting parallel can be noted between the interests of the early economic theorists in the generation of Adam Smith and the early political theorists Plato and Aristotle. Plato and Aristotle lived at a time when the ancient city states were absorbed by larger political units, such as the kingdom of Macedonia. Their theories pass over this crucial fact, and form brilliant epitaphs to the ancient city state, just as the theories of Smith and his contemporaries and immediate successors are brilliant analyses of a passing pre-industrial and proto-industrial economy. Fossil energy and industrialization are also hardly mentioned in the excellent recent re-interpretation of these early economic theories by Emma Rothschild (2001).

4   Some parts of this section are based upon Goudsblom 1992: 164-83.

5   On the general sociological significance of the 'behind the scenes' metaphor, see Elias 2000: 103.

Bibliography

Aarts, W., J. Goudsblom, K. Schmidt, and F. Spier (1995). *Towards a Morality of Moderation*. Amsterdam, Amsterdam School of Social Science Research

Adams, J. M. (1997). *Global land environments since the last interglacial*. Oak Ridge National Laboratory, TN, USA

Adriani, N. (1915). 'Maatschappelijke, speciaal economische verandering der bevolking van Midden-Celebes, sedert de invoering van het Nederlandsch gezag aldaar', in: *Tijdschrift van het Koninklijk Nederlandsch Aardrijkskundig Genootschap* (2nd series) 32, p. 457-75

Agache, R. (1978). *La Somme pré-romaine et romaine*, Amiens, Société des Antiquaires de Picardie

Agrawal, D. P. (2001). *Holocene Climate and Man in India: Monsoon and civilization*, Pune, January 2001, Roli Books

Aldenderfer, M. (1999). 'The Pleistocene/Holocene transition in Peru and its effects upon human use of the landscape' in: *Quaternary International* 54, p. 11-19

Alexander, P. (1984). 'Women, labour and fertility: population growth in nineteenth century Java', in: *Mankind* 14, p. 361-71

Alexander, P. (1986). 'Labour expropriation and fertility: population growth in nineteenth-century Java', in: *Mankind* 14, p. 361-71

Alexander, J. and P. (1979). 'Labour demands and the "involution" of Javanese agriculture', in: *Social Analysis* 3, p. 22-44

Alexander, J. and P. (1993), 'Economic change and public health in a remote Sarawak community', in: *Sojourn* 8, p. 250-74

Allen, P. M. (1993). *Evolutionary complex systems: models of technology change*. Amsterdam Conference on Developments in Technology Studies, Evolutionary Economics and Chaos Theory, Amsterdam

Andel, T. van, E. Zangger and A. Demitrack (1990). 'Land Use and Soil Erosion in Prehistoric and Historical Greece', in: *Journal of Field Archeology* 17, p. 379-396

Anderies, J. (2000). 'On modeling human behavior and institutions in simple ecological economic systems', in: *Ecological Economics* 35 (3), p. 393-412

Andrianov, B.W. (1986). *The World of the first farmers*. Moscow, Science (in Russian)

Archaeomedes (1998). *Des Oppida aux métropoles*. Paris, Anthropos/Economica (collection 'Villes')

Atlan, H. (1992). 'Self-organising networks: weak, strong and intentional. The Role of their Underdetermination', in: *La Nuova Critica* N.S. 19-20 (1/2), p. 51-70

Atlas van Tropisch Nederland (1938). Batavia: Koninklijk Nederlandsch Aardrijkskundig Genootschap/ Topografischen Dienst in Nederlandsch-Indië

Auguet, R. (1994). *Cruelty and Civilization: the Roman Games*. London, Routledge

Aurobindo, S. (1998). *Le Cycle humain*. Pondicherry, Sri Aurobindo Ashram

Bailey, D. (2000). *Balkan Prehistory*. London, Routledge

Barash S.I. (1989). *History of the crop-failures and weather in Europe*. Leningrad (in Russian)

Barker, G. (1981). *Landscape and Society: Prehistoric Central Italy*. London: Academic Press

Barker, G. (1983). 'Economic Life at Berenice: the animal and fish bones, marine molluscs and plant remains', in: J. Lloyd (ed.), *Excavations at Sidi Krebish, Benghazi (Berenice)* 2. Libya Antiqua suppl. 5. Tripoli, p. 1-49

Barton, R.F. (1969/1919). *Ifugao law*. Berkeley, University of California Press

Bateson, G. (1972). *Steps to an Ecology of Mind*. New York, Ballantine Books

Beach, T., and N. Dunning (1994). 'Ancient Maya terracing and modern conservation in the Peten rainforest of Guatemala', in: *Journal of Soil and Water Conservation* 50, p. 138-145

Bell-Fialkoff, A. (ed.) (2000). *The role of migration in the history of the Eurasian steppe: Sedentary civilization vs. 'Barbarian' and Nomad*. London, MacMillan Press Ltd.

Berger, J.-F. (1995). 'Facteurs anthropiques et naturels de l'évolution des paysages romains et protomédiévaux du bassin valdainais (Drôme)', in: *L'Homme et la dégradation de l'environnement. Actes des XVe rencontres internationales d'histoire et d'archéologie d'Antibes* (S.E. van der Leeuw, ed.), p. 79-115. Juan les Pins, APDCA

Berglund, B.E. (1986). *Handbook of Palaeoecology and Palaeohydrology*. Chichester (U.K.), Wiley and Sons

Berglund, B.E. (1991). *The cultural landscape during 6000 years in southern Sweden: the Ystad project*. Copenhagen, Munskgaard International Booksellers and Publishers

Blanton, R., S. Kowalewski, G. Feiman and L. Finsten (1993). *Ancient Mesoamerica*. Cambridge, Cambridge University Press

Bolin, S. (1958). *State and Currency in the Roman Empire to 300 AD*. Stockholm, Almquist and Wiksell

Bonnefille, R., and Chalié, F. (2000). 'Pollen-inferred precipitation time-series from equatorial mountains, Africa, the last 40kyr BP', in: *Global and Planetary Change* 26, p. 25-50

Boomgaard, P. (1989). *Children of the colonial state: Population growth and economic development in Java, 1795-1880*. Amsterdam, Free University Press [CASA Monograph 1]

Boomgaard, P. (1997). 'Introducing environmental histories of Indonesia', in: Boomgaard, P., F. Colombijn and D. Henley (eds.), *Paper landscapes: explorations in the environmental history of Indonesia*. Leiden, KITLV Press, p. 1-26 [VKI 178]

Boomgaard, P., F. Colombijn and D. Henley (eds.) (1989), *Paper landscapes: explorations in the environmental history of Indonesia*. Leiden, KITLV Press, p. 92-120 [VKI 178]

Boserup, E. (1965). *The Conditions of Agricultural Growth: The Economics of Agrarian Change under Population Pressure*. London, G. Allen and Unwin

Boserup, E. (1981). *Population and Technological Change: A Study of Long-term Trends*. Chicago, University of Chicago Press (*Population and Technology*. Oxford, Basic Blackwell)

Bossel, H. (1989). *Simulation dynamischer Systeme*. Braunschweig/Wiesbaden, Vieweg

Boulding, K. (1978). *Ecodynamics: A new theory of societal evolution*. Beverly Hills, SAGE Publications

Bradley, R., and P. Jones (ed.) (1995). *Climate since AD 1500*. London, Routledge

Bramwell, A. (1989). *Ecology in the Twentieth Century*. New Haven, Yale University Press

Braudel, F. (1947). *The Mediterranean and the mediterranean world in the age of Philip II*. Glasgow, Fontana/Collins

Braudel, F. (1975). *A History of Civilisations*. London, Penguin

Broecker, W.S. (2000). 'Abrupt climatic change: causal constraints provided by the palaeoclimate record', in: *Earth Science Reviews* 51, p. 137-154

Brunt, P. (1971). *Italian Manpower 225 BC-14 AD*. Oxford, Oxford University Press

Budiansky, S. (1995). *Nature's Keepers: The New Science of Nature Management*. London, Weidenfeld & Nicolson

Bulbeck, David, Anthony Reid, Lay Cheng Tan and Yiqi Wu (1998). *Southeast Asian exports since the 14th century: Cloves, pepper, coffee, and sugar*. Leiden, KITLV Press [Sources for the Economic History of Southeast Asia, Data Paper Series 4]

Bura, S., F. Guérin-Pace, H. Mathian, D. Pumain and L. Sanders (1996). 'Multi-agents system and the dynamics of a settlement system', in: *Geographical Analysis* 28 (2), p. 161-178

Carson, R. (1962). *Silent Spring*. Boston, Houghton Mifflin

Castro, P.V., E. Colomer, T. Escoriza et al. (1995). 'Terrritoires économiques et sociaux dans le bassin de Véra (Almeria, Espagne) depuis c. 4000 cal. B.P. jusqu'à nos jours', in: S.E. van der Leeuw (ed.), *L'Homme et la dégradation de l'environnement. Actes des XVe rencontres internationales d'histoire et d'archéologie d'Antibes*, p. 299-314. Juan les Pins: APDCA

Cavalli-Sforza, L.L., P. Menozzi and A. Piazza (1993). 'Demic Expansions and Human Evolution', in: *Science* 259 (29 january), p. 639-646

Cavalli-Sforza, L.L., and F. Cavalli-Sforza (1995). *The Great Human Diasporas*. Reading, Mass., Addison-Wesley

Chabal, L. (2001). 'Les potiers, le bois et la foret à l'époque romaine à Salelles d'Aude (Ier-IIIe s. ap. J.-C.)', in: *20 ans de recherches à Salelles d'Aude*, p. 93-110

Chakrabarti, D.K. (1997). *The Archaeology of Ancient Indian Cities*. Delhi

Chakrabarti, D.K. (1999). *India: An Archaeological History: Palaeolithic Beginnings to Early Historic Foundations*. Oxford, Oxford University Press

Chang-Qun, D., Gan Xue-Chun, J. Wang and P. Chien (1998). 'Relocation of Civiization Centers in Ancient China: Environmental Factors', in: *Ambio* 27 (7), p. 572-575

Cheddadi, R., G. Yu, J. Guiot, S. Harrison and I. Colin Prentice (1997). 'The climate of Europe 6000 years ago', in: *Climate Dynamics* 13, p. 1-9

Chepstow-Lusty, A.J., K.D. Bennett, V.R. Switsur and A. Kendall (1996). '4000 years of human impact and vegetation change in the central Peruvian Andes: events paralleling the Maya record', in: *Antiquity* 70, p. 824-833

Cherry, J.F. (1985). 'Polities and Palaces: some problems in Minoan state formation', in: A.C. Renfrew and J.F. Cherry (eds.) (1985)

Christensen, P. (1993). *The Decline of Iranshahr*. Copenhagen, Museum Tusculanum Press, University of Copenhagen

Christensen, P. (1995). *Technology transfer and sustainable agriculture: Third World Irrigation in Historical and Environmental Perspective*. Copenhagen, Draft Report, Institut for Historik, University of Kobenhavn

Chronology of Russian History (1994). Moscow (in Russian)

Chun Chang Huang, J.Z., Jiangli Pang, Yuping Han and Chunhong Hou (2000). 'A regional aridity phase and its possible cultural impact during the Holocene Megathermal in the Guanzhong Basin, China', in: *The Holocene* 10 (1), p. 135-142

Claessen, H.J.M., and Skalnik, P. (1978). *The Early State*. The Hague, Mouton

Clagett, M. (1955). *Greek Science in Antiquity*. Freeport, Books for Libraries Press

Clark, W., and R. Munn (eds.) (1986). *Sustainable development of the biosphere*. Cambridge University Press, Cambridge/International Institute for Applied Systems Analysis (IIASA), Laxenburg, Austria

Clayre, A. (ed.) (1977). *Nature and Industrialization*. Oxford, Oxford University Press

Clements, F.E. (1916). *Plant succession, an analysis of the development of vegetation*. Carnegie Institution of Washington Publication 242 (1916), p. 1-512

Cohen, A.S., M.R. Talbot, S.M. Awramik, D.L. Dettman and P. Abell (1997). 'Lake level and palaeoenvironmental history of Lake Tanganyika, Africa, as inferred from late Holocene and modern stromatolites', in: *Geological Society of America Bulletin* 109, p. 444-460

Collins, R. (1986). *Weberian Sociological Theory*. New York, Cambridge University Press

Collins, R. (1990). 'Violent Conflict and Social Organization', in: *Amsterdams Sociologisch Tijdschrift* 16

Connah, G. (2001). *African Civilizations: An archaeological perspective*. Cambridge, Cambridge University Press

Coppens, Y. (1994). 'East Side Story: the Origins of Humankind', in: *Scientific American* 270, p. 88-95

Cronon, W. (1983). *Changes in the Land. Indians, Colonists, and the Ecology of New England*. New York, Hill and Wang

Crosby, A.W. (1986). *Ecological Imperialism. The Biological Expansion of Europe, 900-1900*. Cambridge, Cambridge University Press

Cross, S.L., P.A. Baker, G.O. Seltzer, S.C. Fritz and R.B. Dunbar (2000). 'A new estimate of the Holocene low-stand level of Lake Titicaca, central Andes, and implications for tropical palaeohydrology', in: *The Holocene* 10, p. 21-32

Crumley, C., and W. Marquandt (ed.) (1987). *Regional Dynamics: Burgundian Landscapes in Historical Perspective*. San Diego, Academic Press

Cullinane, M., and P. Xenos (1998). 'The growth of population in Cebu during the Spanish era: constructing a regional demography from local sources', in: Daniel F. Doeppers and Peter Xenos (eds.), *Population and history: The demographic origins of the modern Philippines* (Madison, University of Wisconsin Center for Southeast Asian Studies), p. 71-138 [CSEAS Monograph 16]

Cunningham, T. (1992). *People, Park and Plant Use research and recommendations for Multiple Use Zones and development alternatives around Bwindi-Impenetrable National Park, Uganda*. Report prepared for CARE-International, Kampala, Uganda

Daly, H. (1973). *Toward a steady-state economy*. San Fransisco, Freeman and Company

Dandekar, R.N. (1982). *Harappan Bibiography*. Pune, Bhandarkar Oriental Institute

Dasgupta, M. (1995). 'Fertility Decline in Punjab, India: Parallels with Historical Europe', in: *Population Studies* 49, p. 481-500

Davies, N. (1996). *A History of Europe*. Oxford, Oxford University Press

De Swaan, A. (2001). *Human Societies. An Introduction*. Cambridge, Polity Press

Dean, J., G. Gumerman, J. Epstein, R. Axtell, A. Swedlund, M. Parker and S. McCarroll (2000). 'Understanding Anasazi Culture Change Through Agent-Based Modeling', in: T. Kohler and G. Gumerman (eds.), p. 179-206

Dean, W. (1995). *With Broadax and Firebrand. The Destruction of the Brazilian Atlantic Forest.* Berkeley, Univ. of Cal. Press

Diamond, J. (1992). *The third chimpanzee: The evolution and future of the human animal.* New York, HarperPerennial

Dijksterhuis, E.J. (1969). *The Mechanization of the World Picture.* London, Oxford University Press

Dobby, E.H.G. (1956). *Southeast Asia.* London, University of London Press [3rd edition]

Douglas, M. (1978). *Cultural Bias.* London, Royal Anthropological Institute, Occasional Paper No. 35. Reprinted in Douglas, M. (1982). *In The Active Voice.* London, Routledge and Kegan Paul

Douglas, I. (1990). 'Sediment transfer and siltation', in: Turner, B.L., W.C. Clark, R.W. Kates, J.F. Richards, J.T. Mathews and W.B. Meyer (eds.) (1990)

Dowdle, J.E. (1987). 'Road networks and Exchange Systems in the Aeduan Civitas, 300 B.C.-A.D. 300', in: Crumley, C.L. and Marquardt, W.H. (eds.) 1987, p. 265-294

Dunbar, R. (2000). 'Climate Variability During the Holocene: An Update', in: McIntosh, R., J. Tainter and S. Keech McIntosh (eds.) (2000b) 413

Dupuy, F. (2001). *Anthropologie économique.* Paris, Armand Colin/VUEF

Duvernoy, I. (1994). *Diagnostic de la pérennisation de l'activité agricole dans la frontière agraire de Misiones (Argentine): une méthode de généralisation spatiale.* Toulouse, Institut National de la Recherche Agronomique, unpublished Ph.D. Thesis

Easwaran, E. (1985). *The Bhagavad Gita.* London, Arkana Penguin Books

Economic History of Russia (XIX-XX) (2000). Modern View, Moscow (in Russian)

Edwards, K. (1993). 'Models of mid-Holocene forest farming for north-west Europe', in: F.M. Chambers, *Climate Change and Human Impact on the Landscape.* London, Chapman & Hall

Elenga, H., O. Peryon, R. Bonnefille, I.C. Prentice, D. Jolly, R. Cheddadi, J. Guiot, V. Andrieu, S. Bottema, G. Buchet, J.L. De Beaulieu, A.C. Hamilton, J. Maley, R. Marchant, R. Perez-Obiol, M. Reille, G. Riollet, L. Scott, H. Straka, D. Taylor, E. Van Campo, A. Vincens, F. Laarif and H. Jonson (2000). 'Pollen-based reconstruction for Southern Europe and Africa 18,000 years ago', in: *Journal of Biogeography* 27, p. 621-634

Elias, N. (1978). *What Is Sociology?* London, Hutchinson

Elias, N. (2000). *The Civilizing Process. Sociogenetic and Psychogenetic Investigations.* Oxford, Blackwell [Rev. ed.]

Elias, N. (1992). *Time: An Essay.* Oxford, Blackwell

Ellenberg, H. (1978). *Vegetation Mitteleuropas mit den Alpen.* Stuttgart

Elson, R.E. (1994). *Village Java under the Cultivation System, 1830-1870.* Sydney: Allen and Unwin [Asian Studies Association of Australia Southeast Asia Publications Series 25]

Elster, J. (1983). *Explaining Technical Change.* Cambridge, Cambridge University Press

Elvin, M. (1993). 'Three thousand years of unsustainable growth: China's environment from archaic times to the present', in: *East Asian History* 6, p. 7-46

Encyclopaedia Universalis Atlas de l'Histoire (1985). Paris

English Landscapes: Past, present, future (1985). Oxford

Fairbridge, R.W. (1984). 'The Nile floods as a global climatic/solar proxy', in: Morner, N.A., Karlen, W. (eds.), *Climatic changes on a yearly to millennial basis*, p. 181-190. Dordrect, Reidel

427

Favory, F., and J.-L. Fiches (eds.) (2002). *Les campagnes de la France méditerranéenne dans l'Antiquité et le haut Moyen Age, Études microrégionales.* Paris, Maison des Sciences de l'Homme [Documents d'Archéologie Française 42]

Favory, F., and S.E. van der Leeuw (1998). 'Archaeomedes, une recherche collective sur la dynamique spatio-temporelle de l'habitat antique dans la vallée du Rhône: bilan et perspectives', in: *Revue Archéologique de Narbonnaise* 17, p. 33-56

Fedoroff, N., and M.-A. Courty (1995). 'Le rôle respectif des facteurs anthropiques et naturels dans la dynamique actuelle et passée des paysages méditerranéens. Cas du Bassin de Véra, sud-est de l'Espagne', in: S.E. van der Leeuw (ed.) *L'Homme et la dégradation de l'environnement. Actes des XVe rencontres internationales d'histoire et d'archéologie d'Antibes*, p. 115-142. Juan les Pins, APDCA

Flannery, K.V. (1972). 'The cultural evolution of civilizations', in: *Annual Review of Ecology and Systematics* 3, p. 399-426

Flannery, T. (1995). *The Future Eaters. An Ecological History of the Australasian Lands and People.* New York, George Braziller

Fraedrich, K., J. Jiang, F-W. Gerstengarbe and P.C. Werner (1997). 'Multiscale detection of abrupt climate change: applications to River Nile flood levels', in: *International Journal of Climatology* 17, p. 1301-1315

Frank, R.H. (1999). *Luxury Fever. Why Money Fails to Satisfy in an Era of Excess.* New York, Free Press

Fuhrer-Haimendorf, C. Von (1975). *Himalayan traders: life in highland Nepal.* London, John Murray

Gasse F. (2000). 'Hydrological changes in the African tropics since the Last Glacial Maximum', in: *Quaternary Science Reviews* 19, p. 189-211

Ge Yu, I.C.P., S. Harrison and Xiangjun Sun (1998). 'Pollen-based biome reconstructions for China at 0 and 6000 years', in: *Journal of Biogeography* 25, p. 1055-1069

Geel B. van, J. Buurman and H.T. Waterbolk (1996). 'Archaeological and palaeoecological indications of an abrupt climate change in The Netherlands, and evidence for climatological teleconnections around 2650 BP', in: *Journal of Quaternary Science* 11, p. 451-460

Geertz, C. (1963). *Agricultural involution: The process of ecological change in Indonesia.* Berkeley, University of California Press

Geist, H.J., and E.F. Lambin (2001). *What Drives Tropical Deforestation?* Louvain-la-Neuve, CIACO

Girard, R. (1977). *Violence and the Sacred.* Baltimore, Johns Hopkins University Press

Glover, I., and C. Higham (1996). 'Early rice cultivation in south, southeast and east Asia', in: Harris, D. (ed.) (1996), 600

Goldstone, J.A. (2000). 'The Rise of the West - or not? A Revision to Socio-Economic History', in: *Sociological Theory* 18, p. 157-194

Gore, Senator A. (1992). *Earth in the Balance. Ecology and the Human Spirit.* Boston, Houghton Mifflin

Goudsblom, J. (1977). *Sociology in the Balance.* Oxford, Basil Blackwell

Goudsblom, J. (1992). *Fire and Civilization.* London, Allen Lane

Goudsblom, J. (2001). 'The Worm and the Clock: On the Genesis of a Global Time Regime', in: W. van Schendel and H. Schulte Nordholt (eds.), *Time Matters: Global and Local Time in Asian Societies.* Amsterdam, VU University Press, p. 19-36

Goudsblom, J., E. Jones and S. Mennell (1996). *The Course of Human History. Economic Growth, Social Process, and Civilization.* Armonk, NY, M.E. Sharpe

Gould, S.J. (1996). *Full House. The Spread of Excellence from Plato to Darwin.* New York, Harmony Books

Gourou, P. (1947). *Les pays tropicaux.* Paris, Presses Universitaires de France

Greene, K. (1986). *The Archaeology of the Roman Economy.* London, Batsford

Groenman-van Waateringe, W., 'The disastrous effects of the Roman Occupation', in: R.W. Brandt and J. Slofstra (eds.), *Roman and Native in the Low Countries: Spheres of Interaction,* Oxford, British Archaeological Reports S 184, p. 147-157

Groube, L. (1996). 'The impact of diseases upon the emergence of agriculture', in: Harris, D. (ed.) (1996)

Grove, H.E. (1992). 'The history of AMS', in: Taylor, R.E., Long, A. and Kra, R.S. (eds.), *Radiocarbon After Four Decades: an Interdisciplinary Perspective.* New York, Springer-Verlag

Grove, R. H., and J. Chappell (2000) (eds.). *El Niño: history and crisis.* Cambridge, The White Horse Press

Grübler, A. (1998). *Technology and Global Change.* Cambridge, Cambridge University Press

Gruyter, J. de (1968). *De Haagse School,* deel 1. Rotterdam, Lemniscaat

Guérin-Pace, F. (1993). *Deux siècles de croissance urbaine.* Paris, Anthropos

Guha, S. (2001). *Health and Population in South Asia from earliest times to the present.* London, Hurst & Company

Guillet, J.-P. (1999). 'Co-management of Natural Resources: the Long View from northwestern Spain', in: *Nature, Society, History: Long Term Dynamics of Social Metabolism, September 30-October 2.* Vienna, Austria, Department of Social Ecology of the Institute of Interdisciplinary Studies of Austrian Universities (IFF)

Gumilev, L.N. (1992). *From Rus to Russia.* Moscow (in Russian)

Gunderson, L., C. Holling, L. Pritchard and G. Peterson (1997). *Resilience in Ecosystems, Institutions, and Societies.* Stockholm, Beijer International Institute of Ecological Economics/Royal Swedish Academy of Sciences

Gunn, J., and W. Folan (2000). 'Three Rivers: Subregional Variations in Earth System Impacts in the Southwestern Maya lowlands (Candeliaria, Usumacinta, and Champoton Watersheds)', in: McIntosh, R., J. Tainter and S. Keech McIntosh (ed.) (2000b)

Halstead, P. (1996).' The development of agriculture and pastoralism in Greece: when, how, who and what?', in: Harris, D. (ed.) (1996)

Halstead, P., and J. O'Shea (1995). 'A friend in need is a friend indeed: social storage and the origins of social ranking', in: C. Renfrew and S. Shennan (eds.), *Ranking, resource and exchange: Aspects of the archaeology of early european society.* Cambridge, Cambridge University Press

Halstead, P., and J. O'Shea (eds.) (1996). *Bad year economics: Reponses to risk and uncertainty.* Cambridge, Cambridge University Press

Hancock, G. (1995). *Fingerprints of the Gods.* London, Mandarin

Hansen, B.C.S., G.O. Seltzer and H.E. Wright Jr. (1994). 'Late Quaternary vegetational change in the central Peruvian Andes', in: *Palaeogeography, Palaeoclimatology, Palaeoecology* 109, p. 263-285

Hardin, G. (1968). 'The tragedy of the commons', in: *Science* 162, p. 1243-1248

Harger, J.R.E. (1995). 'ENSO variations and drought occurrence in Indonesia and the Philippines', in: *Atmospheric Environment* 29, p. 1943-55

Harman, W. (1993). *Global Mind Change: The promise of the last years of the twentieth century*. San Fransisco, Knowledge Systems Inc./Institute of Noetic Sciences

Harris, D. (ed.) (1996). *The origins and spread of agriculture and pastoralism in Eurasia*. London/New York, UCL Press

Harris, M., and E.B. Ross (1987). *Death, Sex, and Fertility. Population Regulation in Preindustrial and Developing Societies*. New York, Columbia University Press

Hassan, F. (1997). *Nile Floods and Political Disorder in Early Egypt. Third Millennium BC Climate Change and Old World Collapse*, NATO ASI Series I: Global Environmental Change

Hassan, F. (2000). 'Environmental Perception and Human Responses in History and Prehistory', in: McIntosh, R., J. Tainter and S. Keech McIntosh (eds.) (2000b)

Headland, T.N., and L. Reid (1989). 'Hunter-gatherers and their neighbours from prehistory to the present', in: *Current Anthropology* 30, p. 43-66

Heilbroner, R. (1995). *Visions of the Future: The Distant Past, Yesterday, Today, Tomorrow*. New York, Oxford University Press

Henley, D. (1997). 'Carrying capacity, climatic variation, and the problem of low population growth among Indonesian swidden farmers: evidence from North Sulawesi', in: Boomgaard, P., F. Colombijn and D. Henley (eds.) (1997)

Henley, D. (in press). *Population, economy and environment in North and Central Sulawesi, c. 1600-1930*. Leiden, KITLV Press

Hillman, G. (1996). 'Late Pleitocene changes in wild plant-foods available to hunter-gatheres of the northern Fertile Crescent: possible preludes to cereal cultivation', in: Harris, D. (ed.) (1996)

Hirschman, C. (1994). 'Population and society in twentieth-century Southeast Asia', *Journal of Southeast Asian Studies* 25, p. 381-416

Hodell, D.A., J.H. Curtis and M. Brenner (1995). 'Possible role of climate in the collapse of Classic Maya civilisation', in: *Nature* 375, p. 391-394

Hole, F. (1996). 'The context of caprine domestication in the Zagros region', in: Harris, D. (ed.) (1996)

Holling, C.S. (1973). 'Resilience and stability of ecological systems', *Annual Review of Ecology and Systemstics* 4, p. 1-23

Holling, C.S. (1986). 'The resilience of terrestrial ecosystems: local surprise and global change', in: Clark, W. and R. Munn (eds.) (1986)

Holling, C.S., I. Gunderson and G. Peterson (1993). *Comparing ecological and social systems*. Stockholm, Beijer International Institute of Ecological Economics [Beijer Discussion Paper Series No. 36]

Holmes, G., H. Berke and F. Laarif (1998). *Civilization and Climate*. New Haven, Yale University Press

Houghton, J., et al. (ed.) (2001). *Climate Change 2001: The Scientific Basis*. Cambridge, Cambridge University Press [Working Group 1, IPCC Third Assessment Report]

Hsu, K.J. (2000). *Climate and Peoples: A Theory of History*. Zürich, Orell Fussli

Huckleberry, G.A. (1999). 'Prehistoric Flooding and its effect on indigenous agriculture in the Northern Sonoran Desert', in: *Journal of Arid land Studies* 9, p. 277-284

Huke, R.E. (1982). *Agroclimatic and dry-season maps of South, Southeast, and East Asia*. Los Baños, International Rice Research Institute

Hunt, R.C. (2000). 'Labour productivity and agricultural development: Boserup revisited', in: *Human Ecology* 28, p. 251-77

Huntley, B. (1988). 'Europe', in: B. Huntley and T. Webb III (eds.), *Vegetation History*, p. 341-383. Dordrecht, Kluwer Academic Publishers

HYDE Website: http://www.rivm.nl/env/int/hyde

IMAGE-team (2001). *The IMAGE 2.2 implementation of the SRES scenarios*. Bilthoven, The Netherlands, National Institute of Public Health and the Environment (RIVM)

Imamura, K. (1996). 'Jomon and Yagoi: the transition to agriculture in Japanese prehistory', in: Harris, D. (ed.) (1996)

Issawi, C. (1981). 'The Area and Population of the Arab Empire: An Essay in Speculation', in: L.A. Udovitch (ed.), *The Islamic Middle East 700-1900: Studies in Economic and Social History*. Princeton University Press, Princeton, p. 375-396

Jackson, J., M. Kirby, W. Berger et al. (2001). 'Historical Overfishing and the Recent Collapse of Coastal Ecosystems', in: *Science* 293, p. 629-637

Jacobs, E., H. Janssen and M. van Heteren (eds.) (1999). *J.H. Weissenbruch, 1824-1903*. Waanders Uitgevers

Jager, W., M. Janssen, B. de Vries, J. de Greef and C. Vlek (2000). 'Behaviour in commons dilemmas: Homo Economnicus and Homo Psychologicus in an ecological-econimic model', in: *Ecological Economics* 35 (3), p. 357-379

Jansen, G.C.M. (2000). 'Studying Roman hygiene: the battle between the "optimists" and the "pessimists"', in: G.C.M. Jansen (ed.), *Cura aquarum in Sicilia*, p. 37-49. Leiden, Stichting Babesch

Jantsch, E. (1980). *The self-organizing universe: Scientific and human implications of the emerging paradigm of evolution*. Oxford, Pergamon Press

Jolly, D., S.P. Harrison, B. Damnati and R. Bonnefille (1998). 'Simulated climate and biomes of Africa during the Late Quaternary: comparisons with pollen and lake status data', in: *Quaternary Science Reviews* 17, p. 629-657

Jones, E.L. (2000). *Growth Recurring: Economic Change in World History*. Ann Arbor, University of Michigan Press [2nd ed.]

Jones, M. (1981). 'The development of crop husbandry', in: M. Jones and G. Dimbleby (eds.), *The environment of man: the Iron Age to the Anglo-Saxon period*, p. 95-127. Oxford, British Archaeological Reports 87

Jones, P., R. Bradley and J. Jouzel (eds.) (1996). *Climatic Variations and Forcing Mechanisms of the Last 2000 Years*. Heidelberg, Springer Verlag

Kalyanaranam (1997). *Sarasvati river*. Chennai, Sarasvati Sindhu Research Centre, www.investindia.com

Kapitza, S.P. (2000). *Information Society and the Demographic Revolution. The Nonlinear Theory of Growth of Humankind*. Moscow, Institute for Physical Problems

Keyfitz, N. (1993). *Are there ecological limits to population?* Laxenburg, Austria, International Institute for Applied Systems Analysis (IIASA) IIASA Working Paper WP-93-16

Keys, D. (1999). *Catastrophe*. London, Arrow

Kjaergaard, T. (1995). 'Agricultural Development and Nitrogen Supply from an Historical Point of View', in: Journal (A B Academic Publishers)

Klein Goldewijk, K., and K. Battjes (1997). *A Hundred Year Database (1890-1990)*. Data Base for Integrated Environmental Assessments (HYDE, version 1.1, www.rivm.nl/env/int/hyde). Bilthoven, RIVM

Klein Goldewijk, K. (2001). 'Estimating Global Land Use Change over the Past 300 Years: The HYDE Database'. *Global Biogeochemical Cycles* 15, p. 417-33

Knaap, G.J. (1987). *Kruidnagelen en Christenen: De Verenigde Oost-Indische Compagnie en de bevolking van Ambon 1656-1696*. Dordrecht: Foris [VKI 125]

Knapen, H. (1998). 'Lethal diseases in the history of Borneo; mortality and the interplay between disease environment and human geography', in: V.T. King (ed.), *Environmental challenges in South-East Asia*, p. 69-94. Richmond, Surrey, Curzon

Knapen, H. (2001). *Forests of fortune; The environmental history of Southeast Borneo, 1600-1800*. Leiden, KITLV Press [VKI 189]

Kohler, T.A. (1993). 'News from the Northern American Southwest: Prehistory on the edge of Chaos', in: *Journal of Archaeological Research* 1, p. 267-321

Kohler, T.A., and C.R. Van West (eds.) (1996). *The Calculus of Self-Interest in the Development of Cooperation: Sociopolitical Development and Risk among the Northern Anasazi. Evolving Complexity and Environmental Risk in the Prehistoric Southwest*. Reading, Mass., Santa Fe, Institute Studies in the Sciences of Complexity Proceedings/Addison-Wesley

Kohler, T.A., J. Kresl, C. Van West, E. Carr, and R.H. Wilshusen (2000a). 'Be There Then: A Modeling Approach to Settlement Determinants and Spatial Efficiency among Late Ancestral Pueblo Populations of the Mesa Verde Region, U.S. Southwest', in: Kohler, T., and G. Gumerman (eds.) (2000)

Kohler, T., and G. Gumerman (eds.) (2000b). *Dynamics in Human and Primate Societies: Agent-based modeling of social and spatial processes*. The Santa Fe Institute Studies in the Sciences of Complexity. Oxford, Oxford University Press

Kortlandt, A. (1972). *New Perspectives on Ape and Human Evolution*. Amsterdam, Stichting voor Psychobiologie

Krech III, S. (1999). *The Ecological Indian. Myth and History*. New York, W.W. Norton

Kruyt, A.C. (1903). 'Gegevens voor het bevolkingsvraagstuk van een gedeelte van Midden-Celebes', *Tijdschrift van het Koninklijk Nederlandsch Aardrijkskundig Genootschap* (2nd series), 20, p. 190-205

Kusin, J.A., and Sri Kardjati (1994). 'Summary and overview of main findings', in: *idem* (eds.), *Maternal health and nutrition in Madura, Indonesia*, p. 23-36. Amsterdam, Royal Tropical Institute

Lacoste, Y. (1996). *La légende de la terre*. Flammarion, Paris

Lahiri, N. (1992). *The Archaology of Indian Trade Routes upto c. 200 BC: Resource use, Resource access and Lines of communication*. Oxford, Oxford University Press

Lahiri, N. (ed.) (2000). *The decline and fall of the Indus Civilization*. New Delhi, Permanent Black

Lamb, H.H. (1988). *Weather, Climate and Human Affairs*. London, Routledge

Lamb, H. (1995). *Climate, history and the modern world*. London/New York, Routledge

Lambert, A.M. (1971). *The making of the Dutch landscape: an historical geography of the Netherlands*. London, Seminar Press

Lampedusa, G.T. di (1960). *The Leopard: with a memory and two stories*. London, Collins Harvill

Laszlo, E. (1987). *Evolution: the grand synthesis*. Shambala, New Science

Laszlo, P. (1998). *Chemins et savoirs du sel*. Paris, Pluriel/Hachette Littérature

Latorre, J.G. (1999). 'Muslims and Christians in a Mediterranean Mountain: Two ways of using and shaping the land', in: *Nature, Society, History: Long Term Dynamics of Social Metabolism, September 30-October 2*. Vienna, Austria, Department of Social Ecology of the Institute of Interdisciplinary Studies of Austrian Universities (IFF)

Laubenheimer, F. (1991). 'L'atelier de Sallèles d'Aude et son évolution dans le temps', in: F. Laubenheimer (ed.) (1991)

Laubenheimer, F. (ed.) (1991). *20 ans de recherches à Sallèles d'Aude*. Besançon, Presses Universitaires Franc-Comtoises

Lee, Ronald D. (1997). 'Population dynamics: equilibrium, disequilibrium, and consequences of fluctuations', in: Mark R. Rosenzweig and Oded Stark (eds.), *Handbook of population and family economics*, Vol. 1B, p. 1063-1115. Amsterdam, Elsevier

Leeuw, R. de, J. Sillevis and C. Dumas (eds.) (1983). *De Haagse School. Hollandse meesters van de 19de eeuw*. Parijs, Grand Palais/London, Royal Academy of Art/Den Haag, Haags Gemeentemuseum

Leeuw, S.E. van der (1981). 'Information flows, flow structures and the explanation of change in human institutions', in: S.E. van der Leeuw (ed.), *Archaeological Approaches to the Study of Complexity*, p. 230-329. Amsterdam, University of Amsterdam Press, IPP [CINGVLA VI]

Leeuw, S. E. van der (ed.) (1998). *The Archaeomedes Project: Understanding the natural and anthropogenic causes of land degradation and desertification in the Mediterranean basin*. Luxemburg, Office of Official Publications of the European Union, Commission Report EUR 18181 EN

Leeuw, S. E. van der, and the Archaeomedes Research Team (2000). 'Land Degradation as a Socionatural Process', in: McIntosh, R., J. Tainter and S. Keech McIntosh (eds.) (2000b)

Leeuw, S.E. van der, and C. Aschan-Leygonie (2001). 'A long-term perspective on resilience in socionatural systems', in: *Working Papers of the Santa Fe Institute*, n° 01-08-042 (www.santafe.edu/sfi/publications/01wplist.html)

Lehner, M. (2000). 'Fractal House of Pharaoh: Ancient Egypt as a Complex Adaptive System, a Trial Formulation', in: T. Kohler and J. Gumerman (eds.) (2000)

Lenski, G., and J. Lenski (1987). *Human Societies: An Introduction to Macrosociology*. New York, McGraw Hill [5th ed.]

Levang, P. (1997). *La terre d'en face; La transmigration en Indonésie*. Paris, Éditions de l'Orstom

Lewin, R. (1999). *Human Evolution. In Illustrated Introduction*. Malden, MA, Blackwell Science

Leyden, B.W. (1987), 'Man and climate in Maya lowlands', in: *Quaternary Research* 28, p. 407-414

Lincoln, W.B. (1994). *The Conquest of a Continent: Siberia and the Russians*. New York, Random House

Lindblom, C. (1977). *Politics and markets: the world's political-economic system*. New York, Basic Books

Livi-Bacci, M. (1992). *A Concise History of World Population*. Oxford, Basil Blackwell

Livingston, J.A. (1994). *Rogue Primate: An Exploiration of Human Domestication*. Toronto, Key Porter Books

Lomborg, B. (2001). *The Skeptical Environmentalist. Measuring the Real State of the World*. Cambridge, Cambridge UP

Lovelock, J. (2000). *The Ages of Gaia. A Biography of our Living Earth*. Oxford, Oxford University Press [2nd ed.]

Lowe, J.J., and M.J.C. Walker (1999). *Reconstructing Quaternary Eviornments*. Longman, London and New York

Lynd, R.S., and H.M. Lynd (1929). *Middletown*. New York, Harcourt, Brace and World

MacDougal, J.D. (1996). *A Short History of Planet Earth: Mountains, Mammals, Fire, Ice.* New York, Wiley

Maddison, A. (2001). *The World Economy: A Millennial Perspective.* Paris, OECD

Magny, M. and H. Richard (1992). 'Les fluctuations des lacs jurassiens et subalpins', in: *Les nouvelles de l'Archéologie*, 50, p. 32-36

Maine, H. (1861/1963). *Ancient law.* Boston, Beacon Press

Maksakovsky, V.P. (1997). *Historical geography of the World.* Moscow (in Russian)

Malthus, T.R., (1798/1976). *An essay on the principle of population* (P. Appleman, ed.). New York, W.W. Norton

Malville, R. (1998). 'Early megalith sites in the Eastern Sahara', in: *Nature* 342, p. 675-677

Manley, B. (1996). *The Penguin Historical Atlas of Ancient Egypt.* London, Penguin Books Ltd.

Mansfield, P. (1976). *The Arabs.* London, Penguin Books

Manuel, F.E. (1962). *The Philosophers of Paris: Turgot, Condorcet, Saint-Simon, Fourier and Comte.* Cambridge, MA, Harvard University Press

Manzanilla, L. (1997). 'The impact of climate change on past civilisations. A revisionist agenda for further investigation', in: *Quaternary International* 43, p. 153-159

Marchant, R.A., Boom, A. and H. Hooghiemstra (2002). 'Pollen-based biome reconstructions for the past 450,000 yr from the Funza-2 core, Colombia: comparisons with model-based vegetation reconstructions', in: *Palaeogeography, Palaeoclimatology Palaeoecology* 177, p. 29-45

Margolis, J. (2000). *A Brief History of Tomorrow. The Future Past and Present.* London, Bloomsbury Publishing

Margulis, L., and D. Sagan (1997). *Microcosmos: Four Billion Years of Microbial Evolution.* Berkeley, University of California Press [2nd ed.]

Marquardt, O. (1999). 'Demographic consequences of cultural change: Demographic profile of the indigenous population in Greenland from the early contact phase and until the present', in: *Nature, Society, History: Long Term Dynamics of Social Metabolism*, September 30-October 2, Vienna, Austria, Department of Social Ecology of the Institute of Interdisciplinary Studies of Austrian Universities (IFF)

Marx, K. (1859/1967). *Capital.* New York, International Publishers

Mauné, S. (1991). 'Les ateliers de potier d'Aspiran dans l'Antiquité (Ier-IIIe s. ap. J.-C.): Bilan et perspectives', in: F. Laubenheimer (ed.) (1991)

Max-Neef, M. (1991). *Human scale development: Conception, application and further reflections.* New York and London, The Apex Press

May, B. (1978). *The Indonesian tragedy.* London, Routledge and Kegan Paul

May, R. (1972). 'Will a large complex system be stable?' *Nature* 238 (413), 14

Mazoyer, M., and L. Roudart (1997). *Histoire des agricultures du monde.* Paris, Éditions du Seuil

Mbiti, J. (1969). *African Religions and Philosophy.* New York, Anchor Books

McBrearty, S., and A.S. Brooks (2000). 'The Revolution That Wasn't: A New Interpretation of the Origin of Modern Human Behaviour', in: *Journal of Human Evolution* 39, p. 453-563

McClellan, J.E. III, and H. Dorn (1999). *Science and Technology in World History.* Baltimore, Johns Hopkins University Press

McEvedy, C. (1967). *The Penguin Atlas of Ancient History.* London, Penguin Books

McEvedy, C. (1992). *The New Penguin Atlas of Medieval History.* London, Penguin Books

McGlade, J. (1995). 'An Integrative Multiscalar Modelling Framework for human ecodynamic research in the Vera basin, south-east Spain', in: S.E. van der Leeuw (ed.), *L'Homme et la dégradation de l'environnement. Actes des XVe rencontres internationales d'histoire et d'archéologie d'Antibes*, p. 357-386. Juan les Pins, APDCA

McGovern, T. (1981). 'The economics of extinction in Norse Greenland', in: T. Wigley, M. Ingram and G. Farmer, *Climate and History: Studies in past climates and their potential impact on Man*. Cambridge, Cambridge University Press

McIntosh, R. (1988). *The Peoples of the Middle Niger: The Island of Gold*. Oxford, Blackwell Publishers Ltd.

McIntosh, R. (2000a). 'Social Memory in Mande', in: McIntosh, R., J. Tainter and S. Keech McIntosh (eds.) (2000b), 413

McIntosh, R., J. Tainter and S. Keech McIntosh (eds.) (2000b). *The way the wind blows: Climate, History, and Human Action*. New York, Columbia University Press [The Historical Ecology Series]

McNeill, J.R. (1992). *The Mountains of the Mediterranean World: An Environmental History*. Cambridge, Cambridge University Press

McNeill, J. (2000). *Something New Under the Sun. An Environmental History of The Twentieth Century*. New York, W.W. Norton

McNeill, W.H. (1963). *The Rise of the West. A History of the Human Community*. Chicago, University of Chicago Press

McNeill, W.H. (1976). *Plagues and Peoples*. Garden City, NY, Anchor Press/Doubleday

McNeill, W.H. (1986). *Mythistory and Other Essays*. Chicago, University of Chicago Press

Meadows, D. and D., and others (1972). *The Limits to Growth. A Report to the Club of Rome's Project on the Predicament of Mankind*. New York, Signet Books

Meadows, D., D. Meadows and J. Randers (1991). *Beyond the Limits*. London, Earthscan Publications

Meillassoux, C. (1986). *Anthropologie de l'esclavage; Le ventre de fer et d'argent*. Paris, Presses Universitaires de France

Melbin, M. (1987). *Night as Frontier. Colonizing the World After Dark*. New York, Free Press

Menocal, P.B. de (2000). 'Cultural responses to climate change during the Holocene', in: *Science* 292 (2001), p. 667-673

Merton, R.K. (1957). *Social Theory and Social Structure*. Glencoe, Ill., The Free Press [2nd ed.]

Messerli, B., M. Grosjean, T. Hofer, L. Nunez and C. Pfister (2000). 'From nature-dominated to human dominated environmental changes', in: *Quaternary Science Review* 19, p. 459-479

Metzner, J.K. (1982). *Agriculture and population pressure in Sikka, Isle of Flores; A contribution to the study of agricultural systems in the wet and dry tropics*. Canberra, The Australian National University [Development Studies Centre Monograph 28]

Misra, V.N. (1994). 'Indus Civilization and the Rgvedic Sarasvati (Gharrar-Hakra River)', in: *South Asian Archeology. Proceedings of the 12th International Conference of the European Association of Archeologist. Helsinky July 1993*. Helsinky, Asko + Koskikallio II

Mohr, E.C.J. (1938). 'The relationship between soil and population density in the Netherlands East Indies', in: *Comptes Rendus du Congrès International de Géographie Amsterdam 1938*, Vol. 2, *Géographie Coloniale*. Leiden, E.J. Brill, p. 478-93

Morecroft, J. and J. Sterman (1992). 'Modelling for Learning (Special Issue)', in: *European Journal of Operations Research*, 59-1

435

Mumford, L. (1961). *The city in history: Its origins, its transformations and its prospects*. London, Penguin Books

Myers, N. (1984). *The Primary Resource: Tropical Forests and Our Future*. New York, Norton

Myrdal, G. (1977) [1971]. *Asian drama; An inquiry into the poverty of nations*. London, Penguin Books

Nakicenovic, N., et al. (2000). *Special Report on Emissions Scenarios (SRES)*. Cambridge, Cambridge University Press

Naveh, Z. and Lieberman, A.S. (1984). *Landscape Ecology: theory and applications*, New York, Springer Verlag

Nelson, J., L. DeHaan, L. Sparks and L. Robinson (1998). *Presettlement and Contemporary Vegetation Patterns Along Two Navigation Reaches of the Upper Mississippi River*. http://biology.usgs.gov/luhna/chap7.html

Newton, M. (1999). 'Relationship between century scale Holocene arid intervals in tropical and temperate zones', in: *Ecological Monographs* 39, p. 121-176

Nibbering, J.-W. (1991). 'Crisis and resilience in upland land use in Java', in: Joan Hardjono (ed.), *Indonesia: Resources, ecology, and environment*, p. 104-31. Singapore, Oxford University Press

Nibbering, J.-W. (1997). 'Upland cultivation and soil conservation in limestone regions on Java's south coast; three historical case studies', in: Boomgaard, P., F. Colombijn and D. Henley (eds.) (1997)

Nicolet, C. (1979). *Rome et la conquête du monde méditerranéen. Vol. I: Les structures de l'Italie romaine*. Paris, Presses Universitaires de France [3rd ed.]

Nieboer, H.J. (1900). *Slavery as an industrial system; Ethnological researches*. 's-Gravenhage, Nijhoff

O'Brien, P.K. (2000). 'The Reconstruction, Rehabilitation and Reconfiguration of the British Industrial Revolution as a Conjuncture in Global History', in: *Itinerario* 14, p. 117-34

Odum, P. (1969). 'The strategy of ecosystem development', in: *Science* 164, p. 262-270

Osadin, B.A. (1995). 'Energy Crusader Campaign', in: *Energia* 4, p. 20-27 (in Russian)

Osmaston, H.A. (1989). 'Glaciers, glaciation and equilibrium line altitudes on Kilimanjaro', in: W.C. Mahaney (ed.), *Quaternary* and *Environmental Research on East African Mountains*, p. 7-30. Rotterdam, AA Balkema

Ostrom, E. (1990). *Governing the commons. The Evolution of Institutions for Collective Action*. Cambridge, Cambridge University Press

Owen, R., R. Crossley, T. Johnson, D. Weddle, I. Kornfiled, S. Davison, D. Eccles and D. Engstrom (1990). 'Major low levels of Lake Malawi and their implications for speciation rates in Chiclid fish', in: *Proceedings of the Royal Society of London*, p. 519-553

Past Worlds: The Times Atlas of Archaeology (1988). Times Books, London

Perry, M. and K.J. Hsu (2000). *Climate and Peoples: A Theory of History*. Zürich, Orell Fussli

Petit, J.R., Jouzel, J., Raynaud, D., Barkov, N.I., Barnola, J-M., Basile, I., Bender, M., Chappellaz, J. and Davis, M. (1999). 'Climate and atmospheric history of the past 420,000 years from the Vostok ice core, Antarctica', in: *Nature* 399, p. 429-436

Pétrequin, P., R.-M. Arbogast, C. Bourquin-Mignot, C. Lavier and A. Viellet (1998). 'Demographic growth, environmental changes and technical adaptations: responses of an agricultural community from the 32ⁿᵈ to the 30ᵗʰ centuries BC', in: *World Archaeology (Special Issue on Population and Demography)* 30 (2), p. 181-192

Pierre A. (1987). *Le climat en Europe au moyen âge.* Paris

Pinstrup-Andersen, P. (1985). 'The impact of export crop production on human nutrition', in: M. Biswas and P. Pinstrup-Andersen (eds.), *Nutrition and development.* Oxford, Oxford University Press, p. 43-59

Piperno, D.R., A.J. Ranere, I. Holst and P. Hansell (2000). 'Starch grains reveal early root crop horticulture in the Panamanian tropical forest', in: *Nature* 407, p. 894-897

Plan van Aanpak en Convenant De Venen. Nota voor Statencommissie (1998), SCGW 98-137, verg. 13-11-1998, agendapunt 10

Pollock, S. (2001). *Ancient Mesopotamia.* Cambridge, Cambridge University Press

Pomeranz, K. (2000). *The Great Divergence. Europe, China, and the Making of the Modern World Economy.* Princeton, NJ, Princeton University Press

Ponsich, M. (1974-79) *Implantation rurale sur le Bas-Guadalquivir,* I (1974) et II (1979). Madrid, Laboratoire d'archéologie de la Casa de Velasquez

Ponting, C. (1991). *A green history of the world.* London, Penguin Books

Popov P. (1925). *Balance of Cereals Production and Consumption (1840-1924). The Agriculture on the road of its recovering.* Moscow (in Russian)

Popper, K.R. (1957). *The Poverty of Historicism.* London, Routledge & Kegan Paul

Population of Russia in XX century, vol. 1 (1900-1939) (2000). Moscow (in Russian)

Porter, R.(1997). *The Greatest Benefit to Mankind. A Medical History of Humanity from Antiquity to the Present.* London, Harper Collins

Potter, T.W. (1979). *The Changing Landscape of South Etruria.* London, Paul Elek

Pounds N.J.J. (1973). *An historical geography of Europe 450 B.C.-1330.* Cambridge vol. I-III

Prentice, C., and T. Webb (1998). 'BIOME 6000: reconstructing global mid-Holocene vegetation paterns from palaeoecological records', in: *Journal of Biogeography* 25, p. 997-1005

Prigogine, I. (1980). *From being to becoming: Time and complexity in the physical sciences.* San Francisco, W.H. Freemand and Company

Prigonine, I., and E. Stengers (1984). *Order out of Chaos: Man's New Dialogue with Nature.* New York, Bantam Books

Pringle, H. (1998). 'The slow birth of agriculture', in: *Science* 282, 1446

Provost, M. (1982). 'L'Homme et les fluctuations climatiques en Gaule dans la deuxième moitié du IIᵉ siècle après J.-C.', in: *Revue Archéologique,* 1

Pyne, S.J. (1991). *Burning Bush. A Fire History of Australia.* New York, Henry Holt and Company

Pyne, S.J. (2001). *Fire. A Brief History.* Seattle, University of Washington Press

Quilley, S. *GM versus Organic: Civilising Processes, 'Great Transformations' and Path-dependency in Contemporary Regulatory Debates over Food and Farming.* University College Dublin, Sociology Department. Forthcoming

Raben, R. (1996). *Batavia and Colombo: The ethnic and spatial order of two colonial cities 1600-1800* [PhD thesis, Rijksuniversiteit Leiden]

Ramankutty, N., and J. Foley (1999). 'Estimating historical changes in global land cover: Croplands from 1700 to 1992', in: *Global Biogeochemical Cycles* 13 (4), p. 997-1027

Raychaudhri, T. (1984), in: D. Kumar and T. Raychaudhuri, *The Cambridge Economic History of India*, Volume II c. 1750-c. 1970. Cambridge

Read, D.W. (1998). 'Kinship based demographic simulation of societal processes', in: *Journal of Artificial Societies and Social Simulation* 1 (1)

Reader, J. (1988). *Man on earth*. New York, Perennial Library

Reale, O., and J. Shukla (2000). 'Modeling the effects of vegetation on Mediterranean climate during the Roman Classical Period Part II: Model simulation', in: *Global and Planetary Change* 25, p. 185-214

Redman, C.L. (1999). *Human impact on ancient environments*. Tucson, University of Arizona

Reid, A. (1983). 'Introduction', in: *idem* (ed.) *Slavery, bondage and dependency in Southeast Asia*, p. 1-43. St. Lucia, University of Queensland Press

Reid, A. (1987). 'Low population growth and its causes in pre-colonial Southeast Asia', in: N.G. Owen (ed.), *Death and disease in Southeast Asia*, p. 33-47. St. Lucia, University of Queensland Press

Reid, A. (1988-93). *Southeast Asia in the age of commerce, 1450-1680*. New Haven, Yale University Press [2 vols.]

Reid, A. (1990). 'The seventeenth-century crisis in Southeast Asia', *Modern Asian Studies* 24, p. 639-59

Reid, A. (1997). 'Inside out; the colonial displacement of Sumatra's population', in: Boomgaard, P., F. Colombijn and D. Henley (eds.) (1997)

Renberg, I., M.-L. Branvall, R. Bindler and O. Emteryd (2000). 'Atmospheric Lead Pollution History during Four Millennia (2000 BC to 2000 AD) in Sweden', in: *Ambio* 29 (3), p. 150-156

Renfrew, C. (1972). *The Emergence of Civilization*. London, Methuen

Renfrew, C. (1973). *Before civilization: the radiocarbon revolution and prehistoric Europe*. London, Penguin Books

Renfrew, C., and J. Cherry (eds.) (1985). *Peer polity interaction and socio-political change*. Cambridge, Cambridge University Press

Report of the Imperial Russian Geographical Society for 1905 (1907). C.-Petersburg (in Russian)

Rice, D.S. and P.M. Rice (1984). 'Collapse intact. Postclassical archaeology of the Peten Maya', in: *Archaeology* 37, p. 46-51

Rice, D.S. (1996). 'Paleolimnological Analysis in Central Petén, Guatemala', in: S.L. Fedick (ed.) (1996), *The Managed Mosaic: Ancient Maya Agricultural and Resource Use*. Salt Lake City, University of Utah Press

Rickleffs, M.C. (1986). 'Some statistical evidence on Javanese social, economic and demographic history in the later seventeenth and eighteenth centuries', in: *Modern Asian Studies* 20, p. 1-32

Ridley A. (1971). *Living in cities*. London, Heinemann

Riebsame, W.E. (1990). 'The United States Great Plains', in: Turner et al. (eds.) 1990, p. 561-575

Riesman, D. (1961). *The Lonely Crowd. Studies in the Changing American Character*. New Haven, Yale University Press [2nd ed.]

Ritchie, J.C., C.H. Eyles and C.V. Haynes (1985). 'Sediment and pollen evidence for an early to Mid-Holocene humid phase in the eastern Sahara', in: *Nature* 314, p. 352-254

Robequain, C. (1946). *Le Monde Malais: Péninsule malaise, Sumatra, Java, Bornéo, Célèbes, Bali et les Petites Iles de la Sonde, Moluques, Philippines*. Paris, Payot

Roberts, N. (1989). *The Holocene: An Environmental History*. Oxford, Blackwell Publishers

Robertson, C.C., and M.A. Klein (eds.) (1983). *Women and slavery in Africa*. Madison, The University of Wisconsin Press

Rodwell, W. (1975). *The small towns of Roman Britain*. Oxford, British Archaeological Reports

Rollefson, G., and I. Kohler-Rollefson (1992). 'Early Neolithic Exploitation Patterns in the Levant: Cultural Impact on the Environment', *Population and Environment: A Journal of Interdisciplinary Studies* 13 (4), p. 243-254

Romanova, E. (1997). *Landscapes of Europe*. Moscow, Moscow State University (in Russian)

Rose, H., and S. Rose (eds.) (2000). *Alas, Poor Darwin. Arguments Against Evolutionary Psychology*. New York, Random House

Rosen, R. (1985). *Anticipatory systems: Philosophical, Mathematical and Methodlogical Foundations*. New York, Pergamon Press

Rothenberg, T. (ed.) (1969). *Technicians of the Sacred*. Anchor Books, New York

Rothschild, E. (2001). *Economic Sentiments. Adam Smith, Condorcet, and the Enlightenment*. Cambridge, MA, Harvard University Press

Rotmans, J., and B. de Vries (eds.) (1997). *Perspectives on global futures: the TARGETS approach*. Cambridge, Cambridge University Press

Rougé, J. (1969). *Les Institutions romaines*. Paris, Arman Colin

Roymans, N. (1990). *Tribal Societies in Northern Gaul: an anthropological perspective*. Amsterdam, University of Amsterdam Press, IPP [CINGVLA XII]

Rudgley, R. (1998). *Lost civilizations of the Stone Age*. London, Arrow Books Ltd.

'Ruimte maken, ruimte delen'. *Vijfde nota over de Ruimtelijke Ordening 2000/2020* (2001). Den Haag, Ministerie van Volkshuisvesting,Ruimtelijke Ordening en Milieubeheer

Runnels, C.N. (1995). 'Environmental Degradation in Ancient Greece', *Scientific American* (March), p. 72-75

Ryan, W., and W. Pitman (1998). *Noah's flood: The new scientific discoveries about the event that changed history*. London, Simon & Schuster

Sahlins, M. (1972). *Stone Age Economics*. London, Tavistock Publications, Chicago, Aldine

Samarkin, V.V. (1976). *Historical geography of the Western Europe in the Middle Ages*. Moscow (in Russian)

Serebryany, L.R. (1980). *The Netherlands; traditions and modernity*. Moscow (in Russian)

Sanders, L., D. Pumain, H. Mathian, F. Guérin-Pace and S. Bura (1997). 'SIMPOP: a multi-agents system for the study of urbanism', in: *Environment and Planning* 24, p. 287-305

Sandweiss, D., K. Maasch and D. Anderson (1999). 'Transitions in the Mid-Holocene', in: *Science* 283 (22 january), p. 499-500

Sankaran, A.V. (1999). 'Saraswati: the ancient river lost in the desert', in: *Current Science* 77 (8), p. 1054-1060

Santley, R.S., T.W. Killion and M.T. Lycett (1986). 'On the Maya collapse', in: *Journal of Anthropological Research* 42, p. 123-159

Sauer, C. (1981). *Selected Essays 1963-1975*. Berkeley, Turtle Island Foundation

Schapiro, M. (1988). 'Judicial selection and the design of clumsy institutions', in: *Southern California Law Rev.* 61, p. 1555-1569

Schefold, R. (1988). *Lia: Das große Ritual auf den Mentawai-Inseln (Indonesien)*. Berlin, Dietrich Reimer

Schneider, S.H. (1976). *The Genesis Strategy. Climate and Global Survival*. New York, Plenum Press

Schoenbrun, D.L. (1993). 'We are what we eat: ancient agriculture between the Great Lakes', in: *Journal of African History* 34, p. 1-31

Scholz, U. (1984). 'Ist die Agrarproduktion der Tropen ökologisch benachteiligt? Überlegungen am Beispiel der dauerfeuchten Tropen Asiens', in: *Geographische Rundschau* 36, p. 360-66

Scholz, U. (1988). *Agrargeographie von Sumatra: Eine Analyse der räumlichen Differenzierung der landwirtschaftlichen Produktion*. Giessen: Selbstverlag des Geographischen Instituts der Justus Liebig-Universität Giessen. [Giessener Geographische Schriften 63]

Schumacher, E. F. (1977). *A Guide for the Perplexed*. London, Jonathan Cape Ltd.

Schumpeter, J.A. (1950). *Capitalism, socialism and democracy*. Harper and Row, New York

Schwartzberg, J. (1992). *A historical atlas of South Asia*. Oxford University Press, New York/Oxford [second impression; first impression 1978, University of Chicago]

Shnirelman V.A. (1989). *Beginning of the productive economy*. Moscow (in Russian)

Scott, W.H. (1994). *Barangay: Sixteenth-century Philippine culture and society*. Quezon City, Ateneo de Manila University Press

Seavoy, R.E. (1986). *Famine in peasant societies*. New York, Greenwood Press [Contributions in Economics and Economic History 66]

Segerstråle, U. (2000). *Defenders of the Truth: The Battle for Science in the Sociobiology Debate and Beyond*. Oxford, Oxford University Press

Shepherd, J.R. (1995). *Marriage and mandatory abortion among the 17th-century Siraya*. Arlington, Virginia, American Anthropological Association [American Ethnological Society Monograph Series 6]

Sieferle, R.P. (1997). *Rückblick auf die Natur. Eine Geschichte des Menschen und seiner Umwelt*. München, Luchterhand

Sieferle, R.P. (2001). *The Subterranean Forest. Energy Systems and the Industrial Revolution*. Cambridge, The White Horse Press

Simmons, I. G. (1989). *Changing the Face of the Earth: Culture, Environment, History*. Oxford, Blackwell Publishers

Simon, H.A. (1969). *The Sciences of the Artificial*. Cambridge, Mass., The MIT Press

Sisam, C. and K. (eds.) (1970). *The Oxford Book of Medieval English Verse*. Oxford, Clarendon Press

Slicher van Bath, B.H. van (1963). *Agrarian History of Western Europe, 1500-1850*. London, XXX

Smil, V. (1993). *Global Ecology: Environmental Change and Social Flexibility*. London, Routledge

Smil, V. (1997). *Cycles of Life: Civilization and the Biosphere*. New York, Scientific American Library

Smith, A., (1776/1976). *An inquiry into the nature and causes of the wealth of nations* (R.H. Campbell and A.S. Skinner, eds.). Oxford, Oxford University Press

Smith, E.D. (2001). 'Low Level Food Production', in: *J. Archaeol. Res.* 9, p. 1-43

Sonnabend, H. (eds.) (1999). *Mensch und Landschaft in der Antike: Lexikon der Historischen Geographie*. Stuttgart-Weimar, Verlag J.B. Metzler

Stahl, P.W. (1999). 'Structural density of domesticated South American camelid skeletal elements and the archaeological investigation of prehistoric Andean Ch'arki', in: *Journal of Archaeological Science* 26, p. 1347-1368

Street-Perrot, A.F. and Perrot, R.A. (1988). 'Holocene vegetation, lake levels and climate of Africa', in: Wright, H.E., Kutzbach, J.E., Thomson Webb III, Ruddiman, W.F., Street-Perrot, F.A. and Bartlein, P.J. (eds.), *Global climates since the last glacial maximum*, University of Minnesota Press

Street-Perrot, A.F., Holmes, J.F., Waller, M., Allen, M.J., Barber, N.G.H., Fothergill, P.A., Herkness, D.D., Ivanovich, M., Kroon, D., and Perrot, R.A. (2000). 'Drought and dust deposition in the West African Sahel: a 5500-year record from Kajemarum Oasis, northeastern Nigeria', in: *The Holocene* 10, p. 293-302

Sutton, J.E.G. (1993). 'The antecedents of the Interlacustrine Kingdoms', in: *Journal of Africa History* 24, p. 33-64

Swabe, J. (1999). *Animals, Disease and Human Society: Human-Animal Relations and the Rise of Veterinary Medicine*. London, Routledge

Tainter, J.A. (1988). *The Collapse of Complex Societies*. Cambridge, Cambridge University Press

Taylor, D., and R. Marchant (1995). 'Human-impact in south-west Uganda: long term records from the Rukiga Highlands, Kigezi', in: *Azania* 30, p. 283-295

Terra, G.J.A. (1958). 'Farm systems in South-East Asia', in: *Netherlands Journal of Agricultural Science* 6, p. 157-82

Thirgood, J.V. (1981). *Man and the Mediterranean Forest: A History of Resource Depletion*. Academic Press, New York

Thompson, M., R. Ellis and A. Wildawsky (1989). *Cultural theory*. Boulder, Westview Press

Thompson, L.G., E. Mosely-Thompson, M.E. Davis, P.E. Lin, K.A. Henderson, B. Cole-Dai, J.F. Bolzan and K. Liu (1995). 'Late glacial stage and Holocene tropical ice core records from Huascarán, Peru', in: *Science* 269, p. 46-50

Tiffen, M., M. Mortimore and F. Gichuki (1994). *More people, less erosion: Environmental recovery in Kenya*. Chichester, John Wiley

Tilly, C. (1984). *Big Structures, Large Processes, Huge Comparisons*. New York, Russell Sage Foundation

Togola, T. (2000). 'Memories, Abstractions, and Conceptualization of Ecological Crisis in the Mande World', in: McIntosh, R., J. Tainter and S. Keech McIntosh (ed.) (2000b)

Totman, C. (1989). *The Green Archipelago: Forestry in Pre-Industrial Japan*. Berkeley, University of California Press

Toynbee, A. (1972). *A Study of History*. New edition, revised and abridged by the author and Jane Caplan. Oxford, Oxford University Press

Toynbee, A. (1976). *Mankind and Mother Earth: A narrative history of the world*. Oxford, Oxford University Press

Turnbill, C. (1961). *The Forest People*. Academic Press, New York

Turner, B.L., W.C. Clark, R.W. Kates, J.F. Richards, J.T. Mathews and W.B. Meyer (eds.) (1990). *The Earth as transformed by human action: Global and regional changes in the biosphere over the past 300 years*. Cambridge, Cambridge University Press

Uhlig, H. (ed.) (1984). *Spontaneous and planned settlement in Southeast Asia: forest clearing and recent pioneer colonization in the ASEAN countries and two case-studies on Thailand*. Hamburg, Institute of Asian Affairs [Giessener Geographische Schriften 58]

United Nations (2001). *Human Development Report 2001: Making New Technologies Work for Human Development*. New York, Oxford University Press

Vandermeer, C. (1967). 'Population patterns on the island of Cebu, The Philippines: 1500 to 1900', in: *Annals of the Association of American Geographers* 57, p. 315-37

Vernadsky, V.G. (2001). *The Kievan Rus*. (in Russian)

Vert, N. (1995). *The History of the Soviet Union*. Moscow (in Russian)

Vilensky, E.L. (1980). *Liquidation of unemployment and agrarian overpopulation in Central Asia and Kazakhstan (1917-1932)*. Alma-Aty (in Russian)

Vincens, A., D. Schwartz, J. Bertaux, H. Elenga and C. Namur (1998). 'Late Holocene climatic changes in West Equatorial Africa inferred from pollen from Lake Sinnda, Southern Congo', in: *Quaternary Research* 50, p. 34-45

Vincens, A., D. Schwartz, H. Elenga, I. Ferrera, A. Alexandre, J. Bertaux, A. Mariotti, L. Martin, J.D. Meunier, N. Nguetsop, M. Servant, S. Servant-Vildary and D. Wirrman (1999). 'Forest response to climate changes in Atlantic Equatorial Africa during the last 4000 years BP and inheritance on the modern landscapes', in: *Journal of Biogeography* 26, p. 879-885

Visaria, L., and P. Visaria (1984). 'Population (1757-1947)', in: D. Kumar and T. Raychaudhuri, *The Cambridge Economic History of India*, Volume II

Volkstelling 1930, 1933-36 (8 vols). Batavia, Departement van Economische Zaken

Vrba, E.S., a.o. (1995). *Paleoclimate and Evolution with Emphasis on Human Origins*. New Haven, Yale University Press

Vries, B. de (1996). 'Contouren van een duurzame toekomst', in: R. Weiler en D. H. Gimeno, *Ontwikkeling Duurzaamheid*, p. 31-73. Brussel, VUBPress (in Dutch)

Vries, J. de (1983). *European urbanization 1500-1800*. Methuen and Co. Ltd., London

Vroon, P. (1989). *Tranen van de krokodil*. Ambo, Baarn (in Dutch)

Waerden, B.L. van der (1954). *Science Awakening*. Groningen, Noordhoff

Wagar, W.W. (1992). *The Next Three Futures. Paradigms of Things to Come*. London, Adamantine Press

Walker, D., and G. Singh (1993). 'Earliest palynological records of human impact on the world's vegetation', in: F.M. Chambers, *Climate Change and Human Impact on the Landscape*. London, Chapman & Hall

Wallerstein, I. (1974). *The Modern World System. Vol. 1.Capitalist Agriculture and the Origins of the European World-Economy in the Sixteenth Century*. New York, Academic Press

Warren, J.F. (1998) *The Sulu Zone: The world capitalist economy and the historical imagination*. Amsterdam, VU University Press [Comparative Asian Studies 20]

Waters, M.R., and J.C. Ravesloot (2001). 'Landscape Change and the Cultural Evolution of the Hohokam along the Middle Gila River and other River Valleys of South-central Arizona', in: *American Antiquity* 66, p. 285-299

Weber, M. (1922/1958). *The Protestant ethic and the spirit of capitalism*. New York, Scribner's

Weischet, W. and C.N. Caviedes (1993). *The Persisting Ecological Constraints of Tropical Agriculture*. Longman Scientific & Technical, New York

Weisz, H., M. Fischer-Kolawski, C.M. Grünbühel, H. Haberl, F. Krausmann and V. Winiwarter (2001). 'Global Environmental Change and Historical Transitions', in: *Innovation* 14, p. 117-42

Wendorf, F., A.E. Close, R. Schild, K. Wasylikowa, R.A. Housley, J.R. Harlan and H. Krolik (1992). 'Saharan exploitation of plants from 8,000 yr. B.P.', in: *Nature* 359, p. 721-724

Werkgroep Natuur in het kader van het Stimuleringsproject Kerngebied De Venen (1994). 'Natuur in De Venen. Rapport van de Werkgroep Natuur in het kader van het Stimuleringsproject Kerngebied De Venen', in: H. van Arkel (ed.), Prov. Utrecht Dienst Ruimte en Groen

Wesson, R.G. (1967). *The Imperial Order*. Berkeley, University of California Press

Westbroek, P. (1991). *Life as a Geological Force. Dynamics of the Earth*. New York, W.W. Norton and Company

Westbroek, P., M.J. Collins, J.H.F. Jansen and L.M. Talbot (1993). 'World Archaeology and Global Change: Did our Ancestors Ignite the Ice Age?', in: *Biomolecular Archaeology* 25, p. 122-33

White, B. (1973). 'Demand for labour and population growth in colonial Java', in: *Human Ecology* 1, p. 217-36

Whitmore, T., B. Turner, D. Johnson, R. Kates and T. Gottschang (eds.) (1990). 'Long-Term Population Change', in: Turner, B. L., W.C. Clark, R.W. Kates, J.F. Richards, J.T. Mathews and W.B. Meyer (eds.) (1990)

Wiggermann, F.A.M. (2000). 'Agriculture in the Northern Balikh Valley: The Case of Middle Assyrian Tell Sabi Abyad', in: R.M.Jas, *Rainfall and Agriculture in Northern Mesopotamia*, p. 171-231. Istanbul

Wilkinson, R. (1973). *Poverty and progress: an ecological model of economic development*. London, Methuen & Co.

Willcox, G. (1999). 'Charcoal analysis and Holocene vegetation history in southern Syria', in: *Quaternary Science Reviews* 18, p. 711-716

Willems, W.J.H. (1986). *Romans and Batavians: A regional study on the Dutch Eastern River Area*. Amersfoort, Rijksdienst voor het Oudheidkundig Bodemonderzoek

Williamson, O. (1975). *Markets and hierarchies, analysis and antitrust implications: a study in the economics of internal organization*. Free Press, New York

Wilson, E.O. (2002). *The Future of Life*. New York, Alfred A. Knopf

Wirtz, K.W., and C. Lemmen (2002). *A Global Dynamic Model for the Neolithic Transition*. Climatic Change (in press)

Wittfogel, K.A. (1957). *Oriental Despotism: A Comparative Study of Total Power*. New Haven, Yale University Press

Wolf, E.R. (1982). *Europe and the People Without History*. Berkeley, University of California Press

Wood, M. (1999). *Legacy: A Search for the Origins of Civilization*. London, BBC Worldwide Ltd.

World Watch Institute (2001). *State of the World 2001. A Worldwatch Institute Report on Progress Toward a Sustainable Society*. New York, W.W. Norton & Company

Woude, A. van der, A. Hayami and J. de Vries (eds.) (1990). *Urbanization in History: A Process of Dynamic Interactions*. Oxford, Clarendon Press

Wright, R. (2000). *Nonzero. The Logic of Human Destiny*. New York, Pantheon Books

Wylie, E.M. (1993). *Economic change and disease in Malaya c. 1820-1920: a study in human ecology*. Griffith University, PhD thesis

Yasuda, Y., and V. Shinde (2001). *Monsoon and civilization*. 2nd International Workshop of the Asian Lake Drilling Programme, Pune, Roli Books

Yates, R. (1990). 'War, Food Shortages, and Relief Measures in Early China', in: L. Newman, *Hunger in history: Food Shortage, Poverty, and Deprivation*, p. 147-177. London, Basil Blackwell

Yergin, D. (1991). *The Prize: The Epic Quest for Oil, Money and Power*. New York, Simon and Schuster

Yesner, D.R. (1980). 'Maritime hunter-gatherers: ecology and prehistory', *Current Anthropology* 21, p. 727-750

Zhang, H.C., Y.Z. Ma, B. Wünnemann and H.-J. Pachur (2000). 'A Holocene climatic record from arid northwestern China', in: *Palaeogeography, Palaeoclimatology, Palaeoecology* 162, p. 389-401

Zuo Dakang, and Z.P. (1990). 'The Huang-Huai-Hai Plain', in: Turner, B.L., W.C. Clark, R.W. Kates, J.F. Richards, J.T. Mathews and W.B. Meyer (eds.) (1990)

Zvelebil, M. (1996). 'The agricultural frontier and the transition to farming in the circum-Baltic region', in: Harris, D. (ed.) (1996)

About the authors

Nikolai M. Dronin is a senior researcher of Chair of World Physical Geography and Environment of the faculty of Geography of the Moscow State University, Russia. He received his diploma (1979) in Geography and his Ph.D. (1999) in Geography from the Moscow State University. His long-term research interest is a history of geography and his current research interest is a history of environmental policy of the USSR.

Johan Goudsblom is emeritus professor of Sociology at the University of Amsterdam. His publications in English include *Dutch Society* (1967), *Sociology in the Balance* (1977), *Nihilism and Culture* (1980), *Fire and Civilization* (1992) and *The Course of Human History* (with Eric Jones and Stephen Mennell (1996).

Jodi de Greef has a background in physics and chemistry and long-term experience in environmental systems modelling.

Sander van der Leeuw is an archaeologist and historian by training. After teaching appointments at Leiden, Amsterdam and Cambridge (UK), he presently holds the Chair of the History and Archaeology of Techniques at the Sorbonne in Paris. His main research interests are in archaeological and complex systems theory and man-land relationships and modelling. He has been involved in several research projects financed by the European Union, amongst others as coordinator of the ARCHAEOMEDES project on understanding and modelling the natural and anthropogenic causes of desertification, land degradation and land abandonment.

Robert Marchant has a background in biology and is presently working as a researcher at the Institute for Biodiversity and Ecosystem Dynamics of the University van Amsterdam. He is actively involved in the BIOME 6000 project with a special research interest in South American and African palaeo-vegetation dynamics.

Aromar Revi has a background in technology, management, finance and law and is currently the Director of TARU, New Delhi. He is a consultant and researcher with extensive interdisciplinary experience in the development, public policy, technology and sustainability areas with special reference to South Asia.

Michael Thompson is a social anthropologist. He is director of the Musgrave Institute, London, an adjunct professor in the Department of Comparative Politics at the University of Bergen, Norway, and a senior researcher at the Rokkan Centre, also at the University of Bergen. His current interest is in the democratisation of processes in areas (such as risk management, environment and development in the Himalaya, technology, and climate change) that have tended to be treated as merely technical.

Bert de Vries is senior researcher at the International Department of the Environmental Forecasting Bureau of the Dutch National Institute of Public Health and the Environment (RIVM) in Bilthoven, the Netherlands. He has a background in physics and chemistry and has over 20 year educational and research experience in energy- and environment-related issues. His main research interests are at present in energy and climate change and sustainable development strategies.

Peter Westbroek is emeritus professor in Geophysiology of Leiden University and has a background in Earth System Science and biogeochemistry. He wrote the book *Life as a Geological Force* and occupied in 1996-7 the Chaire Européenne of the Collège de France.

Kai Wirtz is mathematical modeller at the Institute for Chemistry and Biology of the Marine Environment, University of Oldenburg. His research fields comprise microbiology, marine ecosystems and tree physiology.